The Christian Democratic Parties
of Western Europe

THE ROYAL INSTITUTE OF INTERNATIONAL AFFAIRS is an unofficial body which promotes the scientific study of international questions and does not express opinions of its own. The opinions expressed in this publication are the responsibility of the author.

The Institute and its Research Committee are grateful for the comments and suggestions made by Professor Jean Blondel and Mr George Bull, who were asked to review the manuscript of this book.

The Christian Democratic Parties of Western Europe

R. E. M. IRVING
University of Edinburgh

The Royal Institute of International Affairs
George Allen & Unwin

First published in 1979

The Royal Institute of International Affairs
Chatham House, 10 St James's Square, London
SW1Y 4LE

George Allen & Unwin (Publishers) Ltd
Ruskin House, 40 Museum Street, London WC1A 1LU

© Royal Institute of International Affairs, 1979

British Library Cataloguing in Publication Data

Irving, Ronald Eckford Mill
    The Christian Democratic parties of Western
    Europe.
    1. Center parties – European Economic Community
    countries
    I. Title II. Royal Institute of International Affairs
    329′.02′094   JN94.A979   78–41082

ISBN 0–04–329028–0

Typeset in 10 on 11 point Plantin by Trade Linotype
and printed in Great Britain
by Billing and Sons Limited, Guildford, London and Worcester

To my wife

Preface

Christian Democracy has been a major political force in Western Europe since the Second World War. But, unlike Socialism and Communism, it has attracted the attention of relatively few scholars. When M. P. Fogarty wrote *Christian Democracy in Western Europe, 1820–1953* (1957), he emphasised the need for more studies of Christian Democratic political parties (his own book being concerned primarily with the social aspects of Christian Democracy). Since then a number of monographs have appeared,[1] but the literature (especially in English) has remained sparse, with, for example, no detailed studies of the important Christian Democratic movements in Italy, Belgium and the Netherlands, or of Christian Democracy at the level of the European Community. When, therefore, I was asked by the Royal Institute of International Affairs to write a book about 'Christian Democracy as a political phenomenon in the European Community', it struck me as being a particularly worthwhile subject, not least in the light of the United Kingdom's membership of the European Community and the likelihood that links will develop between the Christian Democrats and the Conservatives.

The theme of this book is slightly narrower than its title suggests, for I have stuck to my remit and concentrated on the Christian Democratic parties of the countries of the European Community. However, it should not be forgotten that there are also important Christian Democratic parties in Austria and Switzerland, increasingly important Christian Democratic movements in Spain and Portugal, and small Christian Democratic parties in Norway, Denmark and Sweden. Some reference has been made to these parties in the chapter on European integration, but no attempt has been made to analyse them in detail. My original intention was to write this book as comparatively as possible, but the further I pursued my research, the more I realised that direct comparisons between, for example, the Italian and German Christian Democratic parties would be of limited value owing to the very different political, social and economic climates in which these parties have evolved. Nevertheless, I have tried to make transnational comparisons wherever this has seemed appropriate, and Chapters 1, 2 and 8, as well as the Introduction and Conclusion, are directly comparative.

I am indebted to many people and organisations for making this book possible. At the most mundane level, I could not have carried out the necessary research without the funds provided by the Royal Institute of International Affairs and the Wolfson Foundation (through its European research fund organised by the British Academy). I am indebted to many people in Western Europe, particularly to various officials in the Christian Democratic parties and librarians. In particular I would like to thank the following: Dr Hildegard

[1]For example, A. J. Heidenheimer, *Adenauer and the CDU*; R. E. M. Irving, *Christian Democracy in France*; and Geoffrey Pridham, *Christian Democracy in Western Germany*. For a full list of books, see Bibliography, pp. 290–326.

Schlüter and the staff of the CDU *Bundesgeschäftsstelle* in Bonn; Dr Florian Harlander and the staff of the CSU *Landesgeschäftsstelle* in Munich; Dr Gianfranco Berti and various DC officials both at the party headquarters in Rome and at the party archives in EUR; Mr Frank Swaelen, National Secretary of the Belgian CVP–PSC; Mr D. Corporaal, Secretary of the Dutch ARP; Mr J. L. Janssen van Raay, Secretary of the Dutch CHU; Mr Rudolf van Glansbeek, Assistant Secretary of the Dutch KVP; Dr Karl Josef Hahn, Assistant Secretary General of the European Union of Christian Democrats and Director of the Centre International Démocrate Chrétien in Rome; Dr Josef Müller, head of the Christian Democratic Information Centre in Brussels; Dr Giampaolo Bettamio, Secretary General of the Christian Democratic Group in the European Parliament; and the librarians of the German Bundestag and Forschungsinstitut der Deutschen Gesellschaft für Auswärtige Politik in Bonn; of the Ministry of Foreign Affairs and the Istituto Sturzo in Rome; of the Fondation Nationale des Sciences Politiques in Paris (especially the Centre de Documentation); and of the Royal Institute of International Affairs, London (especially the Press Cuttings Library). I am also very grateful to the following for having read my draft chapters: Professor Gianfranco Poggi (the Italian chapter), Dr Geoffrey Pridham (the German chapter), Dr Marc Maresceau (the Belgian and Dutch chapters), and Mr Michael Steed (the chapter on European integration). They all made valuable suggestions, which I have tried to incorporate into the final manuscript. Any errors which remain are, of course, my responsibility.

Finally, I am indebted to Carol O'Brien, who edited the typescript with great perspicacity; to Sheila Gordon, who carried out the thankless task of proof-reading with meticulous care; to Peter McIntyre, who drew up the Index; to Joan Ludwick and Jean Tucker, who typed the manuscript; and to my wife and children, who have cheerfully tolerated many 'absentee' evenings and weekends during the last few years.

Department of Politics,
University of Edinburgh,
September 1978.

Contents

List of Abbreviations

ACI	–	Azione Cattolica Italiana
ACJF	–	Association Catholique de la Jeunesse Française
ACLI	–	Associazione Cristiana di Lavoratori Italiani
ACV	–	Algemeen Christelijk Vakverbond van België
ACW	–	Algemeen Christelijk Werkersverbond
AP	–	*L'Anneé Politique*
APSR	–	*American Political Science Review*
ARP	–	Anti-Revolutionaire Partij
Atti e Documenti		
DC	–	*Atti e Documenti della Democrazia Christiana*
Atti Parl.		
Camera	–	*Atti Parlamentari (Camera dei Deputati)*
Atti Parl.		
Senato	–	*Atti Parlamentari (Senato della Repubblica)*
BGS	–	Bundesgeschäftsstelle
BDA	–	Bundesvereinigung des deutschen Arbeitgeberverbände
BDI	–	Bundesverband der deutschen Industrie
BHE	–	Block der Heimatvertriebenen und Entrechteten
BP	–	Bayernpartei
BVP	–	Bayerische Volkspartei
CD	–	Centre Démocrate
CDA	–	Christen Democratisch Appel
CDP	–	Centre Démocratie et Progrès
CDS	–	Centre des Démocrates Sociaux
CDU	–	Christlich Demokratische Union
CEPESS	–	Centre d'Etudes Politiques, Economiques et Sociales
CFDT	–	Confédération Française Démocratique du Travail
CFTC	–	Confédération Française des Travailleurs Chrétiens
CGD	–	Christlicher Gewerkschaftsbund Deutschlands
CGIL	–	Confederazione Generale Italiana del Lavoro
CGT	–	Confédération Générale du Travail
CHU	–	Christelijk-Historische Unie
CISL	–	Confederazione Italiana di Sindicati Liberi
CNI (P)	–	Centre National des Indépendants (et Paysans)
CNPF	–	Conseil National du Patronat Français
Coldiretti	–	Coltivatori Diretti
Corriere	–	*Corriere della Sera*
CRISP	–	Centre de Recherche et d'Information Socio-Politiques
CSC	–	Confédération des Syndicats Chrétiens
CSU	–	Christlich-Soziale Union
CVP	–	Christelijk Volkspartij
DC	–	Democrazia Cristiana
DDP	–	Deutsche Demokratische Partei
DGB	–	Deutscher Gewerkschaftsbund
DNVP	–	Deutschnationale Volkspartei
DP	–	Deutsche Partei

DVP	–	Deutsche Volkspartei
ECSC	–	European Coal and Steel Community
EDC	–	European Defence Community
EEC	–	European Economic Community
ENI	–	Ente Nazionale Idrocarburi
EPP	–	European People's Party
EUCD	–	European Union of Christian Democrats
FAZ	–	*Frankfurter Allgemeine Zeitung*
FDF	–	Front Démocratique des Francophones
FDP	–	Freie Demokratische Partei
FEB	–	Fédération des Entreprises Belges
FGTB	–	Fédération Générale des Travailleurs Belges
Gazz. Uff.	–	*Gazzetta Ufficiale della Repubblica Italiana*
GB	–	Gesamtdeutscher Block
GB–BHE	–	Gesamtdeutscher Block–Block der Heimatvertriebenen und Entrechteten
ICPSR	–	International Consortium for Political Science Research
IFOP	–	Institut Français de l'Opinion Publique
INFAS	–	Institut für angewandte Sozialwissenschaft
IPOVO	–	Instituut voor Politieke Vorming
IPSA	–	International Political Science Association
IRI	–	Istituto per la Ricostruzione Industriale
ISTAT	–	Istituto Centrale di Statistica
JAC	–	Jeunesse Agricole Chrétienne
JCMS	–	*Journal of Common Market Studies*
JO (AN)	–	*Journal Officiel* (Débats de l'Assemblée Nationale)
JO (CR)	–	*Journal Officiel* (Débats du Conseil de la République)
JO (Sénat)	–	*Journal Officiel* (Débats du Sénat)
JOC	–	Jeunesse Ouvrière Chrétienne
JR	–	Jeune République
JU	–	Junge Union
MOC	–	Mouvement Ouvrier Chrétien
Monde	–	*Le Monde*
MRP	–	Mouvement Républicain Populaire
MSI	–	Movimento Sociale Italiano
Mulino	–	*Il Mulino*
NATO	–	North Atlantic Treaty Organisation
NPD	–	Nationaldemokratische Partei Deutschlands
NSDAP	–	Nationalsozialistische Deutsche Arbeiterpartei
Parlament	–	*Das Parlament*
Parl. Aff.	–	*Parliamentary Affairs*
PCF	–	Parti Communiste Français
PCI	–	Partito Comunista Italiano
PCS	–	Parti Chrétien Social
PDM	–	Progrès et Démocratie Moderne
PDP	–	Parti Démocrate Populaire
PEP	–	Political and Economic Planning
PLI	–	Partito Liberale Italiano
PPI	–	Partito Popolare Italiano
PR	–	Parti Républicain
PRI	–	Partito Repubblicano Italiano
PSC	–	Parti Social Chrétien

PSDI	–	Partito Socialista Democratico Italiano
PSI	–	Partito Socialista Italiano
PVDA	–	Partij van de Arbeid
RCDS	–	Ring Christlich-Demokratischer Studenten
RDP	–	*Revue du Droit Public et de la Science Politique*
RFSP	–	*Revue Française de Science Politique*
RI	–	Républicains Indépendants
RISP	–	*Rivista Italiano di Scienza Politica*
RKSP	–	Roomsch-Katholieke Staatspartij
RPF	–	Rassemblement du Peuple Français
RPR	–	Rassemblement pour la République
RW	–	Rassemblement Wallon
SFIO	–	Section Française de l'Internationale Ouvrière
SOFRES	–	Société Française d'Enquêtes par Sondages
SPD	–	Sozialdemokratische Partei Deutschlands
SPES	–	Servizio Propaganda e Studi
Spettatore Internazionale	–	*Lo Spettatore Internazionale*
Stampa	–	*La Stampa*
SVP	–	Südtiroler Volkspartei
SZ	–	*Süddeutsche Zeitung*
UDB	–	Union Démocratique Belge
UDF	–	Union pour la Démocratie Française
UDR	–	Union des Démocrates pour la République
UNR	–	Union pour la Nouvelle République
WAV	–	Wirtschaftliche Aufbauvereinigung
VDB	–	Verhandlungen des Deutschen Bundestages
Zeit	–	*Die Zeit*

Introduction

One of the most important developments in postwar Europe has been the emergence of Christian Democracy as a major political force. In West Germany the Christian Democrats were in power from 1949–69, and, with the exception of the years 1972–6, have always formed the largest group in the Bundestag. The Italian Christian Democrats have won a plurality of the votes cast at every postwar general election, formed the basis of every government, and held the premiership without a break since late 1945. In Belgium the Social Christians have also won a plurality of votes at every election since 1945, and been in office during the whole postwar period, with the exception of the years 1945–7 and 1954–8. In Luxembourg the Social Christians have consistently been the largest parliamentary party, and were in power without a break until 1974 (indeed, they had been in office since 1919). In the Netherlands the three confessional parties (united as Christian Democratic Appeal since 1976) have constituted the fulcrum of the party system, and the Catholic People's Party has participated in every government since the war. In France the Christian Democrats played a key role as a centre party throughout the Fourth Republic (1946–58), and, after surviving a series of vicissitudes in the Fifth Republic, still constituted a small, but significant, party within the governing coalition in the late 1970s.

At the level of the European Community, the Christian Democrats formed the largest group in the European Parliament (and its predecessor, the Common Assembly of the European Coal and Steel Community) without a break until 1975, when, on the arrival of the British Labour delegation at Strasbourg, the Socialists became the largest group. In addition the Christian Democrats have set up a transnational European party, the European People's Party, which was founded in 1976. Finally, the Christian Democrats have a well-organised group in the European Parliament and have held the presidency of that body (or of its precursor) for twenty of the twenty-six years of its existence (up to 1978); the Christian Democratic president elected in 1977 owed his success to Conservative and Liberal votes, perhaps a portent of future political developments if the European Parliament becomes a more important body after direct elections.

Thus, five of the nine Community countries have large Christian Democratic political parties (Italy, West Germany, Belgium, the Netherlands and Luxembourg), whilst France has a strategically significant Christian Democratic party, and there are also potentially important transnational Christian Democratic links at the European level. Between one-third and two-fifths of the electorates of the above five countries voted for the Christian Democrats at the general elections of the late 1970s, (36 per cent of all votes cast; if France is included the figure is 28 per cent). Denmark also has a small Christian Democratic party (the Christian People's Party, which won just under 4 per cent of the votes cast at the 1977 general election). In addition, the Irish Fine Gael (30 per cent of votes cast at the 1977 general election) belongs to the Christian Democratic group in the European Parliament and to the European People's Party (EPP), the transnational Christian Democratic Party of the European Community.[1]

Christian Democracy then, constitutes a powerful electoral and political force in Western Europe, and the purpose of this book is to examine its nature and assess its importance. Why did Christian Democracy emerge so dramatically after the Second World War? And, perhaps more important in the context of this book, why did it revive in the 1970s after declining considerably in the 1960s under the combined influence, *inter alia*, of secularisation, rural depopulation, and a widespread reaction against non-ideological, pragmatic, centrist parties? What is the significance of this revival, both internally in the politics of the Western European countries, and transnationally at the level of the European Community? How far is it appropriate to speak of a coherent Christian Democratic movement? Do the members of the European People's Party, for example, have sufficient in common to constitute an effective transnational political force? Or have they become so absorbed into the distinctive politics of their national systems that the EPP is little more than a political figleaf? What are the chances of genuine links, as opposed to superficial liaison, developing between Christian Democrats and Conservatives in the European Community? Precise answers to all these questions cannot be given, but it is clearly important – not least in the context of the United Kingdom's membership of the European Community – that an attempt should be made to gain some insight into one of the major political movements of Western Europe.

It is not easy to define Christian Democracy. There are considerable variations between the Christian Democratic parties of Western Europe. Broadly speaking the German Christian Democrats have many similarities with the British Conservatives, whereas the Belgian and Italian Christian Democratic parties are more left-oriented; the Dutch come somewhere between the two positions, with recent developments suggesting a 'German' rather than an 'Italian' orientation. But, despite these differences, which owe much to different historical, cultural and social traditions, there are a number of common characteristics and common principles which together constitute the distinctive political phenomenon of Christian Democracy. Of course, to some extent, Christian Democracy is no more than a manifestation of the eternal search for a middle way between liberalism and collectivism, between capitalism and communism – with a bias in the case of Christian Democracy in favour of capitalism and liberalism. But the middle way of Christian Democracy is based on certain distinctive principles, even if these principles do not amount to anything as precise as an ideology or *Weltanschauung*. The three basic principles, or underlying themes, of Christian Democracy are contained in the words 'Christian principles' (in the sense of a broad commitment to basic human rights, particularly those of the individual); 'democracy' (in the sense of a clearcut commitment to liberal democracy); and 'integration' (in the dual sense of a commitment to class reconciliation through the concept of the broad-

[1] For details, see below, Chapter 8.

based *Volkspartei* and to transnational reconciliation, manifested especially through the strong Christian Democratic commitment to European integration). These are, of course, relatively vague concepts, but, despite the wide interpretation to which they are open, they are, as the chapter on Christian Democratic theory shows, central to Christian Democratic political programmes and also, albeit with aberrations, to Christian Democratic political practice.

As well as devoting a chapter to Christian Democratic theory, it seemed to me to be important to comment briefly on the precursors of Christian Democracy – both individuals and parties, for the postwar Christian Democratic parties inherited some of the ideas of the former and most of the electoral base of the latter. Prior to the war there were a number of important Catholic parties – notably the German *Zentrum* and Italian *Partito Popolare* (both of which, of course, succumbed to fascism), the Belgian and Dutch Catholic Parties, and, less important, the French *Parti Démocrate Populaire*. But these were essentially 'confessional' parties, i.e. their main objective was to defend the interests of Catholics, rather than to appeal to the electorate as a whole, which, as we shall see, has been one of the main objectives of the postwar Christian Democratic parties.

The reasons why Christian Democracy emerged with such speed and power immediately after the war are relatively well known. The extreme Right was discredited by nazism and fascism, and the extreme Left came increasingly to be associated with the barbarities of Stalinism. The traditional conservative and bourgeois parties were also discredited, partly because of their *attentiste* attitude towards nazism, fascism and Pétainism, but also on account of their association with *laisser-faire* economics and traditional capitalism. The Christian Democrats, in contrast, could not be blamed for the political, social and economic bankruptcy of the interwar years. They had a respectable record of resistance to fascism and Pétainism. They had founded political *movements*, not *parties* (another discredited word), and they promised a new style of politics, based on participation, reconciliation, co-operation and traditional moral values. This vague but comforting programme, based to some extent on old values but envisaging a new and better future, appealed to many European electors; in particular to those who had had a surfeit of 'absolutist' political ideology, but who at the same time had no desire to return to pre-fascist political, economic and social systems. Christian Democracy was thus ideally suited to filling the postwar political vacuum, and the Christian Democratic parties received a further boost as the Cold War reached its bitterest in the late 1940s, because they were regarded as the main bulwark against communism.

After the death of Stalin, however, communism became less threatening, and in many countries Conservatives,[1] who had taken shelter under the Christian Democratic umbrella, moved back to their old political families (in France,

[1] I shall use the word conservative with a small 'c' when referring to social and economic attitudes, and with a large 'C' when referring to political parties or political groups of the Right, even though very few Continental European parties use the adjective 'Conservative' in their titles as it is virtually a synonym for 'reactionary'.

they had done so in 1947, when many Christian Democrats left the MRP to join De Gaulle's *Rassemblement du Peuple Français*). At the same time the Socialist parties gradually adopted a more centrist, less doctrinaire political approach, and as they began to appeal directly to liberally-minded Catholic voters in the 1960s and 1970s, there was evidence that the progressive wings of the Christian Democratic parties were being seriously undermined. In addition, growing secularisation and 'deconfessionalisation' at all levels of society constituted a further threat to the Christian Democratic parties, whose main – although by no means only – electoral strength lay in those parts of Europe where the Church (especially the Catholic Church) was still influential. As secularisation developed – and the Second Vatican Council acted as a catalyst to this development, albeit unintentionally – the traditional supporting organisations of Christian Democracy either declined in influence (this was especially true of Catholic Action) or loosened their links with the Christian Democratic parties (as did, for example, the Catholic trade unions and working men's associations). Finally, there were many young voters in the late 1960s and early 1970s, who expressed a desire for more 'ideological' politics, i.e. they wanted parties to state their objectives clearly, and when in office to implement them. They considered the Christian Democratic parties to be staid, pragmatic, compromised and compromising.

There was in consequence quite a strong electoral reaction against the Christian Democrats in the late 1960s and early 1970s: the German Christian Democratic Union was ousted from power by the Socialist–Liberal coalition in 1969, and the Social Democrats polled more votes than the Christian Democrats for the first time in 1972; the Belgian Social Christians lost a third of their electorate between 1958 and 1971 (dropping from 46 per cent to 30 per cent of the votes cast in that period); the Dutch Christian Democrats suffered a comparable decline (from 49 per cent in 1963 to 31 per cent in 1972); meanwhile, in Italy the gap between the Communists and Christian Democrats was steadily narrowing, although approximately two out of every five Italians continued to vote for the Christian Democratic party (at the regional elections of 1975 the Communists, with 33·4 per cent, came to within two points of the Christian Democrats, and at the 1976 general election, with 34·4 per cent, to within four points).

However, from the mid-1970s there was distinct evidence of a revival of Christian Democracy. Not only did the Italian Christian Democrats hold their own at the general election of 1976, but the German Christian Democrats polled 48·6 per cent of the votes cast in November of that year, their highest percentage since 1957, when they won an absolute majority. At the Belgian general election of 1977 the Social Christians polled 36 per cent (a gain of almost four points), and in the same year the Dutch Christian Democratic Appeal, with just under 32 per cent polled slightly better than the three confessional parties had polled when standing separately in 1972.

This revival of Christian Democracy has been due partly to particular social and economic factors, such as relatively high inflation and unemployment, which have helped to make the pragmatic Christian Democrats look less unattractive. But the revival has also owed much to the way in which the

Christian Democratic parties have adapted themselves to changed circumstances. As we shall see, the German Christian Democrats have reorganised themselves; the Dutch have fused their three parties; the Belgians have made a determined effort to solve the community/linguistic problem; and the Italians have made some attempt to reform their party, as well as to work out new governmental alliances. These factors have helped to compensate for the erosion of the traditional Catholic, rural and female electorate, which for long formed the basis of Christian Democratic strength and stability.

Religiosity, in the sense of a voter's general attitude to Christian values (whether or not he practises his religion), still remains a relatively important voting determinant in Western Europe; hence, the Christian Democratic parties continue to cultivate the practising Christian electorate (both Catholic and Protestant), amongst whom they still poll most strongly. But Christian Democracy is much more than a politico-religious movement. It also appeals widely to middle-class voters who do not practise their religion, to the increasingly important tertiary sector employees of the 'new' middle class, to the self-employed (both rural and urban), and to many industrial workers, particularly those with Catholic connections. In the context of the working-class Christian Democratic electorate, it should be stressed that Christian Democratic parties are not just Conservative parties. They nearly all have important 'Social Christian' wings, whose origins go back to the social teaching of the Catholic Church of the late nineteenth century (notably *Rerum Novarum* (1891) and the other encyclicals of Leo XIII). Despite the 'deconfessionalisation' of Catholic interest groups the Italian and Belgian Christian Democrats still have important informal links with the large Catholic trade union confederations in their respective countries.

Christian Democracy, then, is not a synonym for Conservatism, even though Christian Democracy is conservative in its respect for the individual, defence of the rights of property, aversion to communism, and general dislike of excessive state interventionism. But Christian Democrats reject the tenets of nineteenth-century liberalism: they accept the necessity for the state to protect the weak in society and to guide the economy, and they favour *concertation*, i.e. consultation between government, industry, the trade unions and other interest groups. Christian Democracy is essentially a political movement of the Centre, in the sense that it appeals above all to moderate pragmatists of all classes, who hope that conflicts may be resolved by compromise, reconciliation and synthesis. Even the German Christian Democratic movement, which is probably the most conservative in the European Community, has a strong base in the political centre and an important working-class wing. Of course, not all political, social and economic conflicts can be resolved by compromise. Nevertheless, an essential part of the political attraction of the Christian Democratic parties is that they, like many voters, do not see political issues in black-and-white terms. Indeed, the strength of Christian Democratic parties lies to a large extent in their being broad-based, non-ideological, catch-all parties. Their chief weakness perhaps lies in the imprecision of their political ideas, although, as will become apparent, the individual parties are all confronted with a number of other problems and dilemmas. It is, however, particularly difficult for centre parties to subscribe to clearcut political views, and this difficulty is particularly acute for Christian Democrats when they are in opposition: the German Christian Democrats, for example, have had some difficulty in showing the electorate how exactly their programme differs from that of moderate Social Democracy. However, this ideological problem perhaps matters less in Western Europe than in Britain, because all Continental Western European countries except France have electoral systems based on proportional representation, and such systems inevitably encourage compromises, coalitions and political pragmatism, i.e. the very qualities which are the essence of Christian Democracy.

I

The Origins of Christian Democracy: Italy, Germany and France

The Christian Democratic movement of the twentieth century can only be understood in the light of its nineteenth-century origins. Christian Democracy was essentially the response of Catholics to two revolutions, the French and the industrial. The former was mainly a political revolution, emphasising as it did that all men should have the right to participate in shaping the destiny of their state and society. Although such a view had been held by Protestants, notably by some of the Puritan sects, it was a revolutionary concept in Catholic Europe, and it was a concept which the Papacy refused to accept almost throughout the nineteenth century. Not all Catholics, however, accepted the Papal view, and amongst their number were to be found several of the precursors of Christian Democracy. The French Revolution was also a secular phenomenon, in so far as the revolutionaries rejected the idea of established, state-supported Churches; the individual, of course, could believe what he wanted. In nineteenth-century Europe the Liberals, the political and intellectual heirs of the Enlightenment and the Revolution, went a stage further and tried to secularise society by eliminating religious education in schools. This movement stimulated the political organisation of Catholics, and although it did not necessarily make democrats of them, it encouraged them to defend what they saw as their social rights by political means. Finally, there were Catholics who held that something must be done to alleviate the economic and social misery which had accompanied industrialisation and urbanisation. Amongst these 'Social Catholics', who often came round to the view that poverty and deprivation could be alleviated only by political action, were to be found many other precursors of Christian Democracy. In short, Christian Democracy developed as a political response to the French Revolution, a socio-political response to militant secularism, and an economic response to the industrial revolution. It was a response which developed at different times and in slightly different ways in Italy, Germany, France, Austria, Switzerland, Belgium and the Netherlands, but the underlying reasons for – as well as the outward manifestations of – the response were similar. In this chapter we shall look at the important 'cases' of Italy, Germany and France.[1]

Italy

> Let us approach the working man who is escaping us. Let us go into the
> workshops and the factories. . . . Let us sanctify democracy, with which the
> future lies. . . . The Christian transformation of society will be brought about
> with the support of the people, under the Church's guidance, against all
> forms of Liberalism.[2]

Italian Christian Democracy has a dual origin. In the first place, as the
above statement, by the Milanese journalist-priest David Albertario, suggests,
it developed as a reaction to anti-clerical liberalism. In the second place, it was
the Catholic response to atheistic socialism, which from the turn of the century
was rapidly increasing its appeal amongst the Italian working classes.

The Catholic political movement in Italy developed in a curious limbo,
in that after the unification of Italy Catholics were, so to speak, 'in the world
but not of it': as Italians they were citizens of the Kingdom of Italy, but as
Catholics they were instructed to turn a blind eye to the existence of that
kingdom. This strange schizophrenic situation in which practising Catholics
found themselves was a consequence of the means by which Italy was united,
for the Pope was deprived of the Papal States in 1862 and of Rome itself in
1870. The Pope's response to these developments was clearcut and simple:
he himself would have no dealings with the Italian state, and his flock was
instructed to boycott the liberal-democratic parliamentary system – the
encyclical *non expedit* of 1867 forbade Catholics to participate in elections.
The 'Roman Question', the problem of Church-State relations in general and
of the temporal possessions of the Papacy in particular, constituted the
dominant backdrop to the stage on which the Catholic social and political
movements gradually emerged between the unification of Italy and the First
World War.[3]

The year 1919 saw the final lifting of the ban on Catholics voting (*non
expedit* being withdrawn in that year) and the founding of a mass political
party of Catholic inspiration, the *Partito Popolare*. But it was not until 1929
that the Papacy finally made its peace with the Italian state by means of the
Lateran Pacts, by which the Fascist regime recognised the Vatican City as an
independent sovereign state and granted the Church certain rights and privileges in Italian society, notably with regard to marriage and education, in
return for the Church's agreement to avoid political involvement. In practice,
however, the Church continued to exert a degree of political, as well as social,
influence over Catholics by means of the various organisations of Catholic
Action, which were allowed to continue their 'independent' existence under
Mussolini.

This brief excursion into the history of Church-State relations in Italy has
been necessary, because it goes some way to explaining both the tentative
nature of Catholic involvement in Italian politics before 1914 and the political
inexperience and diffidence of the new Christian Democratic party, the
Partito Popolare, after the war.

The origins, as well as the contradictions, of Italian Christian Democracy can be traced back to the various Catholic social and political movements of the period 1874–1914. The most important of these in the last quarter of the nineteenth century was the Catholic Congress movement, the *Opera dei Congressi*.[4] The original aim of the papal-inspired and controlled Congress movement was quite simply to demand the full restoration of the Church's property taken over by the state on unification. But the *Opera* were also much involved in charitable and educational work, and this led militant Catholics to the verge of politics proper, as it became increasingly obvious that the social and economic problems of Italian workers and peasants could only be solved by political means. Leo XIII's encyclical *Rerum Novarum* (1891) gave the green light to the development of a number of socio-political organisations such as peasants' friendly societies and industrial workers' trade unions (the so-called 'white unions'), but in theory direct political involvement remained forbidden to Catholics. However, even before the turn of the century the devout Catholic social theorist and economics professor, Giuseppe Toniolo, was propounding clearly political views.[5]

The Turin Programme, drawn up by Toniolo and endorsed by the Young Christian Democrats at their 1899 congress, for example, called for a proportional electoral system, for administrative decentralisation, and for a state social security system. Toniolo never attacked the established views of the Church directly, but in effect he accepted the political evolution of Italy in the second half of the nineteenth century, whilst proposing a number of important amendments to the political and social system. He is perhaps best remembered for his advocacy of socio-professional 'corporations', which he hoped would supersede Liberalism and pre-empt socialism by eliminating some of the basic conflicts in society. But, in contrast to the later state-controlled corporations developed embryonically under fascism, Toniolo's corporations were to have functioned under the auspices of the Church. Impractical and imperfectly developed though many of Toniolo's ideas were, they provided an important part of the ideological framework within which Italian Christian Democracy developed. But perhaps Toniolo's greatest achievement was that he made it respectable for Italian Catholics to talk seriously and openly about political problems for the first time since unification.

Between 1900 and 1914 the Catholic political movement made rather uncertain progress in Italy.[6] The phrase 'Christian Democracy' was commonly used to describe the progressive wing of the Catholic political and social movements, and was endorsed by Leo XIII in the encyclical *graves de communi* in 1901. But when it became apparent that there were almost as many Christian Democrats as Catholic Conservatives in the *Opera dei Congressi*, and that some of them were coming under the influence of the increasingly radical Romolo Murri,[7] Pius X (1903–14) dissolved the *Opera* in 1904 and reformed them under the auspices of Catholic Action (previously only one of the five sections of the *Opera*). Pius also emphasised in his 1905 encyclical *fermo proposito* that *non expedit* still applied, and in 1909 he excommunicated Romolo Murri who had attacked the Church as a reactionary organisation. However, in other ways Pius X continued the *apertura politica* begun by Leo

XIII. One of Murri's disciples, Don Luigi Sturzo, was appointed Secretary General of Catholic Action (although, unlike Murri, Sturzo always remained strictly obedient to the Pope).[8] Moreover, in practice, *non expedit* was gradually being abandoned: at the 1904 general election Pius X let it be known that he would turn a blind eye to Catholics voting in 'critical' areas, where they could prevent the election of Socialists; this permission was broadened in 1909; and finally extended throughout the country by the Gentiloni Pacts of 1913, a series of theoretically secret agreements whereby Catholics could vote for Liberals who in turn agreed to respect Catholic views (i.e. moderate their anti-clericalism). As a result of these agreements thirty-five Catholic candidates and about two hundred Liberals sympathetic to the Catholics were returned to parliament.

Thus by 1914 a considerable Catholic political movement, underpinned by the development of Catholic banks, co-operatives and 'white' unions (both agricultural and industrial), had come into being in Italy in spite of the unresolved 'Roman Question'. It is of course important to stress that it was not a united movement. Already the different *tendenze* so characteristic of Italian Christian Democracy throughout the twentieth century were apparent. Even before 1914 there were, for example, 'autonomists', who emphasised that the emerging Catholic political movement, whilst taking its inspiration from the Church, should avoid undue dependence on the Vatican: their early leaders were Romolo Murri, Luigi Sturzo, Giuseppe Donati, later the editor of the Christian Democratic newspaper *Il Popolo*, and Giovanni Gronchi, a young trade union leader from Tuscany. The other wing consisted of 'integralists', men whose main objective was to work in close union with the Papacy. On the whole the 'integralists' were conservatives such as Counts Paganuzzi and Grosoli, whose main objective was to defeat socialism rather than liberalism, although they were openly critical of the latter for its anti-clericalism. The most important of the moderate Catholic leaders in the prewar period was the Milan lawyer, Filippo Meda, who was first elected to parliament in 1909 and later became a prominent cabinet minister during the war. Indeed, up to 1914 the Catholic political movement was predominantly 'moderate', approximately three-quarters of the Catholic members of parliament being followers of Meda.[9] Nevertheless, there was already a leaven of more progressive and autonomous Catholics – they were already known as 'Christian Democrats' (*Democristiani*) – and the upheavals of the war were to strengthen the progressive wing further, for many Catholics, not least in the agricultural regions, emerged from the war with a strong desire to see radical social changes. These rural Catholics were to be the main electoral reservoir for Italy's first mass Christian Democratic party, the *Partito Popolare* of 1919–26.

The *Partito Popolare Italiano* (PPI)

The *Partito Popolare Italiano* was launched in January 1919 by Don Luigi Sturzo with the full approval of Pope Benedict XV. Quickly establishing itself as a mass party, it polled well over a million votes (over 20 per cent of those cast) at the 'normal' elections of 1919 and 1921. Even at the 'abnormal' election of 1924, fought under the Acerbo Law which gave two-thirds of the seats to the national list which gained over a quarter of the votes (in practice, the Fascist list), the PPI still polled over 600,000 votes (9 per cent of those cast), although by this stage it had been more or less abandoned by the Vatican and the Catholic Right.[10]

The PPI was essentially a rural Catholic party, being particularly strong in the Catholic Veneto (over 35 per cent of votes cast) and in the agricultural districts of Lombardy (over 25 per cent of votes cast in this region), but it was also widely supported by the practising Catholic urban lower middle classes throughout Italy, notably in the Marches and Lazio, where it polled over 25 per cent and in Piedmont, Liguria, Tuscany, Umbria, Campania and Calabria, in all of which regions it polled between 15–24 per cent.[11] Its electoral appeal was limited in the south, where the peasants, still influenced by their landlords, tended to vote for the various right-wing parties. Nor did the PPI receive much support from the industrial working classes, who mostly voted Socialist or Communist.

Italian General Elections

	1919		1921		1924	
	%	Seats	%	Seats	%	Seats
Socialists and Communists	34·3	168	29·3	139	14·6	80
Popolari	20·5	100	20·0	107	9·0	39
Republicans	0·9	13	1·9	7	1·8	8
Liberals and other constitutional Democrats	44·3	248	47·1	274	7·2	25
Fascist List	—	—	6·9	35	64·9	375

The PPI had a clear, if brief, twelve-point electoral programme. Although theoretically independent of the Church (*aconfessionale*) the PPI emphasised its Catholic nature by stressing the importance of the family as a social unit, by demanding the right of Catholics to educate their children in Church schools, and by upholding the right of the Church to exercise its independence. However, it should be noted that the party did not specifically raise the 'Roman Question', which it regarded as having been by-passed by events. Indeed, the PPI's failure to stress the temporal claims of the Church and to demand a solution to the problem of Church-State relations was one of the major reasons for the Vatican's eventual abandonment of the *Popolari* in favour of the Fascists.

The PPI was a well-structured party with local sections, provincial committees, and a powerful central organisation, namely the National Council (thirty-five members) and the Directorate (seven members) under the political Secretary. The Directorate was elected by the National Council, which in turn was elected by the National Congress which met annually. But although well organised the PPI was always divided between the 'clerical moderates', i.e. the heirs of the prewar Catholic conservatives, and the 'Christian Democrats', i.e. the heirs of the prewar Catholic progressives. The party had a small trade union wing led by Achille Grandi, a revolutionary peasant wing led by Guido

Miglioli, and an extremely conservative wing led by Stefano Cavazzoni. Luigi Sturzo, whose own preference was for a social-reforming Christian Democratic party, had to weld these disparate elements into a coherent political force. In the circumstances, this was far from easy, for the PPI immediately found itself confronted by a major political dilemma, which was in turn a direct consequence of the party's awkward size. For the PPI was, paradoxically, both too large and too small. It could not be ignored, because both in 1919 and in 1921 it won over 20 per cent of the seats in parliament, compared with approximately 35 per cent for the left-wing parties and 45 per cent for the right-wing parties (the Liberals and their allies, and from 1921 the small but vocal group of Fascists). The Socialists refused to have anything to do with the 'clerical' *Popolari*, who were thus forced either to co-operate with the Liberals (which many had no wish to do, having entered politics in order to bring to an end the era of Giolitti), or to go into opposition and leave Italy with a weak government at a time of economic and social crisis.

Against the wishes of its left wing the PPI participated in the Liberal-led governments of Nitti and Giolitti in 1920–1, but after Giolitti's attempt to reduce the number of *Popolari* and Socialists by means of an early general election in 1921, the PPI refused to support any further governments led by Giolitti. The party did, however, support the more centrist government of Bonomi in 1921–2, but that government came under increasing pressure from the Fascists who had entered parliament in 1921, and was eventually brought down by the Liberals and Fascists. The PPI then agreed reluctantly to support the short-lived governments of Giolitti's 'lieutenant', Luigi Facta, in 1922, but by now Italian democracy was beginning to totter, and after the 'March on Rome' (25 October 1922) Victor Emmanuel appointed Mussolini prime minister. Again the *Popolari* were in a dilemma. Should they support a Fascist-led government in the hope of 'constitutionalising' it? Or leave that government to its own devices in the hope that it would collapse through lack of parliamentary support? The PPI opted for the former course. But at its fourth, and penultimate, National Congress at Turin in April 1923 the party displayed its uncertainty about this decision. Miglioli and the left wing wanted to have nothing further to do with Mussolini's government; the centre, led by Sturzo and De Gasperi, wanted to support the government, but with firm conditions, the chief of which were that the country's proportional representation system should not be changed and that Fascist violence should be halted. Meanwhile, the party's right wing advocated outright support for Mussolini's government, and several left the party at this time to join other conservative Catholics in launching the National Union as a pro-Fascist movement. Soon after the Congress Mussolini showed what he thought of the PPI's conditions by dismissing his four *Popolari* ministers, and then under pressure from the Vatican, Catholic Conservatives and Fascists, Sturzo resigned the secretaryship of the PPI (July 1923).

Deprived of its conservative wing, and without a full-time Secretary, the PPI fought an honourable, but hopeless, campaign in the face of Fascist violence at the spring 1924 election, and after the murder of Matteotti in June 1924 the *Popolari* joined the other opponents of Mussolini in the vain and probably ill-judged 'retreat to the Aventine', setting up their own assembly and boycott-ing the parliament elected under the Acerbo Law. In January 1925 Mussolini finally accepted full responsibility for the Matteotti murder, and during the next eighteen months the Fascist dictatorship was gradually established, with the 'Aventine' parties being dissolved at the end of 1926.

Why did Italy's first Christian Democratic party collapse so rapidly after such a successful start? And how far was its failure responsible for the success of Fascism?

There were perhaps three major reasons for the failure of the *Partito Popolare*. In the first place, Sturzo's concept of an independent (*aconfessionale*) Catholic party was undoubtedly premature. Italian Catholics, it is true, had become increasingly aware of their political and social potential during the first quarter of the twentieth century. But, accustomed as they were to papal guidance and control, they found it difficult to commit themselves unreservedly to the type of party advocated by Sturzo.[12] Even forty years later many Italian Catholics found the 'liberal' wine offered by Pope John XXIII too heady for their palates. It was not surprising then that, when in the 1920s Pius XI reversed Benedict XV's policy and abandoned the *Popolari* in favour of the Fascists, most Catholics followed him. Secondly, the PPI was unable to work out a satisfactory relationship with the other constitutional parties. Caught between the Scylla of Socialism and the Charybdis of Fascism, the PPI succeeded only in acting negatively, or at best hesitantly, until it was too late. Too large and too responsible to avoid political commitment, but too small to be able to exert decisive influence, the PPI floundered in the centre. The oppor-tunities to form effective coalitions with the Liberals and Democrats of the Centre-Right or the moderate Socialists of the Left were then all missed, though the blame for this failure must be attributed as much to the PPI's potential allies as to the PPI itself, for the Liberals always treated the *Popolari* with disdain, whilst the Socialists refused to consider an alliance with them until after the murder of Matteotti, by which time it was almost certainly too late anyway. Thirdly – and this factor was not surprising in view of the type of party Sturzo was trying to create and the widely differing political views in the Catholic world – the PPI was, as already stressed, a deeply divided political force: indeed, Richard Webster scarcely exaggerated when he wrote that the PPI remained to the end 'an aspiration rather than a great political force'.[13]

In Sturzo's view, Liberalism was bankrupt, but Socialism was sterile. What was needed was a society in which Christian principles and ideals predomin-ated, but Sturzo believed that such a society could best be achieved in a free and democratic environment in which Catholic arguments would win the day on their merits. Thus, he wanted the PPI to be democratic in its structure and objectives, and in so far as possible independent of the organised Church, although inspired by Catholic social teaching and in the last resort obedient to the Pope. Although Sturzo was himself a Catholic of the Left, and as such firmly opposed to propping up bourgeois liberalism, he also wanted the PPI to develop as an inter-class party which would bring together peasants and landlords, industrial workers and factory owners, into one political formation. Admirable though this objective may have been in theory – and it was

certainly wholly consonant with Catholic social teaching and Christian Democratic theory – in practice it did nothing to help to bring about a united,
politically powerful PPI. Indeed, from the start it was apparent that the PPI
had inherited most of the divisions of the prewar Catholic political movement.
From the time of its first congress at Bologna in 1919 there were quite
substantial differences of opinion within the party. In the opinion of Salvemini,
the majority of *Popolari* could be categorised as genuine reformers.[14] Men such
as Luigi Sturzo, Alcide De Gasperi, who presided at the congress, Giuseppe
Donati, the future editor of the party newspaper *Il Popolo*, Luigi Ferrari, a
former president of the Catholic University Federation, Guido Miglioli, the
leader of the peasants and sharecroppers of Cremona, and Giovanni Gronchi,
the Tuscan trade union leader, were all determined to bring to an end the
Liberal State, characterised in their view by the cynical electioneering and
political manipulations of Giolitti. But they were equally determined to prevent
a Marxist revolution. Certainly, they wanted a political and social revolution,
but they wanted it to be presided over in a non-violent manner by their own
new mass party, which would implement the social teaching of the Church
without being directly dependent on it. Even these leaders of the Left-Centre
were themselves divided. Miglioli wanted to carry through a social revolution,
principally the redistribution of land, in coalition with the Socialists, but
Sturzo, who was also a strong advocate of land reform, accepted the judgement of Benedict XV (a judgement endorsed even more decisively by Pius
XI) that no alliance should be formed with the anti-clerical Socialists. The
Left-Centre also included men whose relations had been clouded during the
war: Donati, who had supported intervention, Miglioli, who had not ceased
to condemn it in his journal *L'Azione*, and De Gasperi and Sturzo, who, like
Benedict XV, were inclined to neutralism, though in practice supported the
government's policy.

The Right of the party had a number of common characteristics, but was
also divided. Broadly speaking, the heirs of the Clerico-Moderate tradition,
led by Filippo Meda (although he was in fact one of their most moderate
figures) and Fathers Gemelli and Olgiati favoured the development of close
links between the PPI, Catholic Action and the Vatican. In addition, they had
all been in favour of intervention in the war, though none went along with the
hysterical nationalism of D'Annunzio. But men such as Stefano Cavazzoni, the
leading Lombard conservative, and Count Giovanni Grosoli, head of the so-
called 'Catholic Trust' group of newspapers, had argued that by supporting
Salandra and interventionism they would help to drive the 'pacifist' Giolitti
to the political sidelines and at the same time parry the Socialist threat. Thus,
they hoped, the Catholic political movement would take over from the Liberals
and preempt the Socialists.[15] But although the heirs of the Clerico-Moderates
had no love for the Liberals, they had a good deal less for the Socialists, and
they labelled those *Popolari*, who, like Miglioli, advocated an alliance with the
Socialists, 'Red Catholics'. Thus, it was not surprising that when the moderate
Catholics had to choose between the extreme right, i.e. the Fascists, and the
Socialists in 1923–4, they, like Pius XI and Cardinal Gasparri, the papal
Secretary, with whom they had close links, had little hesitation in choosing the

former. Not all conservatives in the PPI joined the Clerico-Fascist group, which fought the 1924 election in alliance with the Fascists: amongst the exceptions were Antonio Segni of Sardinia, a future Christian Democratic prime minister and President of the Republic, and Attilio Piccioni, a Piedmontese who was also destined to play a prominent role in the postwar Christian Democratic party. But by the time of its Turin congress (1923) it was apparent that the majority of the PPI's right wing was wholly in favour of Mussolini's 'reconstruction': men such as Livio Tovini of Brescia, Carlo Santucci, the Roman banker, Giovanni Grosoli, the press lord, and Filippo Crispolti, a close confidant of the Pope and Cardinal Gasparri.[16]

It is conceivable, but by no means certain, that the PPI would have been a more effective party if it had been led with more authority. Certainly, Sturzo had his limitations as a leader, although he also had many merits: he had had considerable experience in the Catholic political movement, having been the leader of its progressive wing since the eclipse of Murri in 1909; he had been active in local administration in Sicily since the 1890s; he was a devout Catholic, and had the determination of a man who is convinced of the righteousness of his cause. But he had some of the defects of his merits: he was no Lamennais or Murri, and when the Pope turned against him, he obediently resigned the secretaryship of the PPI and emigrated to France. Above all, he had one major disadvantage as the leader of a political party: as a priest, he was debarred from taking a seat in parliament. The PPI therefore lacked an authoritative leader at the centre of the political stage, for Filippo Media, the party's acknowledged parliamentary leader, had lost the taste for political battle by the postwar period: on three occasions between 1919–22 he refused to try to form a government when requested to do so by Victor Emmanuel III. It was indeed unfortunate for the PPI that its most powerful personality was outside parliament, whilst its parliamentary leader was a spent political force. There were, of course, up-and-coming leaders, notably Alcide De Gasperi, Antonio Segni, and Giovanni Gronchi, but none of these men had sufficient political reputation or experience to give to the PPI the sort of incisive leadership it needed in the difficult postwar years. However, even if Sturzo had been a member of parliament and in a position to direct the PPI with more authority, it is by no means certain that he would have been able to make such a diverse party into a more effective political force.

The final crisis for Italian democracy occurred between the murder of Matteotti in June 1924 and Mussolini's acceptance of responsibility for what the Fascists had done in January 1925, followed by the steps which brought about full dictatorship within the following eighteen months. By the time of the final crisis the PPI was already considerably weaker than it had been from 1919–22: it had been deprived of the leadership of Sturzo as well as of the support of Catholic Action and of many priests, and it had been abandoned by its right wing, the Clerico-Fascists, who had fought the spring 1924 election in alliance with Mussolini. Nevertheless, the six months between the murder of Matteotti and the Fascist takeover were a period of which the *Popolari* could be proud, for they provided *the* major resistance to Fascism at this time, and they did so whilst under constant attack from the Fascists and Clerico-Fascists and, hardest to bear, from the Vatican itself. For on 8 September 1924 the Pope condemned any collaboration between Catholics and Socialists at the very time when De Gasperi was trying to piece together an anti-Fascist alliance of *Popolari,* Democratic Centrists and moderate Socialists (the followers of Filippo Turati).[17] The Socialists were divided into three groups at this stage, so the type of anti-Fascist alliance proposed by De Gasperi would have been unlikely to have had sufficient strength and cohesion to save Italian democracy. Nevertheless, public opinion had turned against the Fascists after the Matteotti murder, and the Pope's outright condemnation of Catholic-Socialist collaboration at this time was of considerable importance in preparing the way for Mussolini's final 'coup'. Certainly it was a body blow to the PPI. Pius XI had made it clear that he was determined to direct Italian Catholics *politically* as well as spiritually. He was quite prepared to sacrifice the PPI and the independent Catholic trade unions, by now with over a million members, for the sake of a settlement of the 'Roman Question' with Mussolini who, in spite of his past, could certainly no longer be accused of having any sympathy for Socialism. Sturzo's concept of an independent Christian Democratic party was thus finally shown to be premature and unrealistic.

Sturzo was, of course, further handicapped by the relative political immaturity of Italian Catholics in the 1920s. The Catholic political movement had really only come into being with Toniolo's 'Christian Democracy' in the 1890s, and by the First World War only a tiny minority of Catholics had participated actively in politics. The Gentiloni Pacts and the gradual abandonment of *non expedit* opened the way for future participation, but all too suddenly, in the wake of a bloody war, Italian Catholic politicians found themselves catapulted onto the centre of the political stage. The *Popolari* were in addition divided both by the extent to which they wanted reforms and by the nature of their relationship with the Vatican. They knew they wanted to replace Liberalism with something better, but they were not sure what that 'something' was. And when their only potential political bedfellows appeared to be Socialists or Fascists, they were uncertain which way to turn. Both were objectionable, but whereas the majority of party militants found the Fascists more objectionable, an important group of party notables and nearly all the leaders of the Church considered the Socialists to be the worse of the two evils. And so a divided *Partito Popolare,* in company with other equally divided and irresolute constitutional parties, failed to prevent the final Fascist takeover. But the *Popolari* did perhaps hand down one important lesson to their post-war successors – the lesson that it was essential to maintain overall party unity, however great the internal political differences within the Christian Democratic party might be. In addition, they had shown that Catholics could be good democrats.

Germany

Christian Democracy is essentially a postwar phenomenon in Germany, for although the important Centre Party (*Zentrum*) of Bismarckian, Wilhelmine and Weimar Germany was a Christian – or at least confessional – party, it was never wholly committed to the tenets of liberal democracy. As one of its most distinguished scholars has pointed out, the *Zentrum used* the democratic system to uphold and defend the interests of Catholics without ever *committing* itself unreservedly to that system.[18] True, the Centre Party spent much of the nineteenth century trying to uphold civil rights, but it saw these – most notably in the *Kulturkampf* – essentially as Catholic rights. True, it played a key governmental and parliamentary role throughout the Weimar Republic, but, with a few notable exceptions, Catholic politicians regretted the passing of the monarchy and the demise of the structured, quasi-authoritarian social and political system of pre–1914 Germany.

However, although one cannot properly speak of a Christian Democratic party in Germany before 1945, there was certainly an important Catholic political party and Catholic political movement. Moreover, as this party and movement were absorbed into – indeed formed the core of – the postwar German Christian Democratic Party (CDU–CSU), it is important to comment briefly on the development of German political Catholicism and particularly on the characteristics and objectives of the *Zentrum*.

The first point that must be made is that the majority of Germans were converted to Protestantism during the Reformation. In spite of the Counter-Reformation and the spirited resistance of the Austrian Habsburgs, the Bavarian Wittelsbachs and the Society of Jesus, less than a third of Germans were Catholics after the wars of religion and the Treaty of Westphalia (1648), which enunciated the famous principle *cuius regio, eius religio.*

Nevertheless, in spite of their minority position, German Catholics strove in the eighteenth century to distance themselves from Rome. Owing to the fact that Germany was divided into about 350 states, which on the whole did not try to interfere with each other's affairs, the various Catholic princes, whether lay or ecclesiastical, did not feel the need to support each other or to look to Rome to defend their interests, and they were strongly encouraged in this 'independent Catholic' attitude by Joseph II of Austria (1741–90), one of the leading figures of the Age of Enlightenment. The zenith of this 'independent' Catholic attitude was reached in 1786, when the German bishops, meeting at Bad Ems, published a document calling for virtually total independence from papal control.

Thirty years later German Catholics found themselves in very different circumstances, and this major change in their position profoundly affected the development of political Catholicism throughout the nineteenth century. Napoleon had deprived the Church of its temporal possessions, abolished the Holy Roman Empire, and reduced 'Germany' from 350 to 39 states. In addition Prussia acquired vast new territories on both sides of the Rhine (notably Westphalia and the Palatinate) by the Treaty of Vienna, with the result that the rather enlightened Catholics of the Rhineland (to some extent influenced by French and Belgian 'liberal' ideas) found themselves subjects of the authoritarian Protestant Hohenzollerns. Prussia being a state without natural geographical boundaries or religious homogeneity (after 1815 one third of Prussians were Catholics), the Hohenzollerns and the Junker ruling class were as determined as ever to maintain their authority by means of a strong army and centralised bureaucracy. One aspect of this policy was to

'Protestantise the Catholics', if not by a policy of religious conversion, at least by seeing that the *Preussische Landrecht* of 1784, the law which ensured, *inter alia*, strict control of the Church by the state, was meticulously observed. As a result Catholics felt on the defensive, and not only in Prussia, for the other major states such as Württemberg (mainly Protestant, but with an important Catholic minority) and Baden (mainly Catholic, but ruled by Protestants) also tended to treat Catholics as 'outsiders'. Above all, however, it was Prussia which treated its Rhineland provinces almost as colonial possessions: often, for example, the sole Protestant in a Westphalian village would be appointed mayor, whilst it was almost impossible for Catholics to enter the Prussian civil service.

After 1815, then, German Catholics, in complete contrast to thirty years before, began to look to each other, and above all to Rome, in their weakness, and this 'siege mentality' of German Catholics was to persist throughout the nineteenth century. It was, of course, a natural response to the conditions in which they found themselves, but it was also somewhat counter-productive, in that it only provoked the Protestants and nationalists to regard the Catholic community as a 'state within the state', a community whose main loyalty lay outside the Fatherland. Taking advantage of this attitude of distrust towards the Catholics, Bismarck was later to embark on his infamous *Kulturkampf*.

Persecution of Catholics, such as the arrest of the Archbishop of Cologne in 1837 for not implementing the Prussian government's law on mixed marriages (by which male children of such marriages had to be baptised and brought up as Protestants), led Rhineland Catholics to co-operate with Liberals in defending civil rights against the prerogatives of the absolutist state. By the 1840s there was some evidence that this tacit alliance was beginning to bear fruit. In any case the accession of Frederick William IV to the throne of Prussia in place of the reactionary Frederick William III in 1840 created a more relaxed atmosphere. In 1841 Frederick William IV rescinded the government's decree on mixed marriages, created a special Catholic department within the Ministry of Education, and gave permission to the provincial Rhineland Diet to meet. At the Diet of 1841 (consisting of fifty-two Catholics and twenty-eight Protestants) Catholic conservatives and Protestant liberals united to demand liberty of the press, whilst the Catholics also demanded administrative parity between the two confessions. The same alliance reappeared in the Frankfurt Parliament of 1848, when Catholics and Liberals both favoured the extension of civil rights and the creation of a constitutional monarchy. Equally they were united in their opposition to anything that smacked of a proletarian revolution. However, one of the weaknesses of the Catholic–Liberal alliance – indeed one of the reasons for the collapse of the 1848 'revolution' – was that the Catholics and Liberals were uneasy allies. The Catholics frankly preferred a strong monarchical system, provided their own religious demands (principally the right to run their Church and schools without state interference) were guaranteed.[19] They also differed from the Liberals in their attitude to Catholic Austria which they wanted to see merged into Germany, whereas the Liberals, like the Prussian government, did not. Moreover, the Catholic associations, which sprang up throughout Germany in the

1840s and 1850s, emphasised their apolitical nature, whilst the bishops' conferences of the 1850s took a very conservative line, stressing their commitment to a strong state and criticising modernist and liberal developments. Even Bishop Ketteler, regarded by many as the precursor of German Christian Democracy (or at least of social Catholicism), roundly condemned both Liberalism and Marxism, whilst at the same time advocating greater social involvement by Catholics. But he envisaged this social involvement taking place in the context of an (ill-defined) return to mediaeval charity and corporatism.

The twenty-three years between the 1848 revolution and the foundation of the Bismarckian Reich in 1871 were paradoxically a period both of consolidation and of decline in the evolution of German political Catholicism. A *Katholische Fraktion* (Catholic parliamentary group) was formed in the Prussian Diet in November 1852 to defend Catholic interests, and succeeded in getting the Raumer decrees (niggling anti-Catholic legislation such as the prohibition of Catholics attending courses at the German College in Rome) abrogated. And in 1858 a group of lay Catholics, led by the Reichensperger brothers and Mallingkrodt, persuaded the parliamentary group in the Prussian Diet to change its name to *Zentrums Fraktion/Katholische Fraktion* (Osterath, Rohden and the bishops insisted on retaining the adjective *Katholische*). But in general there was a lull in the development of political Catholicism. In the first place the Prussian constitution of 1849 enshrined many of the religious liberties written into the abortive Frankfurt Constitution of 1848, so Catholics had less to complain about (especially after the abrogation of the Raumer decrees), although in practice they were still largely excluded from the Prussian bureaucracy and army. Secondly, the Catholics were divided in their attitude to Bismarck, the majority voting against increased military credits in 1863, whilst a significant minority voted for them. Thirdly, the Catholics took the 'wrong' side in Austro-Prussian War of 1866: as before, they would have preferred a loose confederation including Austria (*'gross Deutschland'*) to a North German Confederation dominated by Prussia. Finally, their pro-papal attitude during the years when Italy was being united in the face of strong Vatican opposition did nothing to endear them to German nationalists and Liberals. As a result the Catholics did badly at the polls in the 1860s: after the 1863 elections to the Prussian Diet there were only twenty-six Catholic deputies (mainly conservatives from the east), and after those of 1867 only fifteen. It looked as if the embryo Catholic Centre Party might wither away. But this was to count without Bismarck, who, contrary to his intentions, boosted both the *Zentrum* and the Social Democratic Party during the last twenty years of his chancellorship.

The Kulturkampf and the consolidation of the Zentrum
The *Kulturkampf* began in 1870, a year before Germany was united as the Prussian government's response to the doctrine of Papal Infallibility (July 1870). The Prussian government at once declared its support for the *Altkatholiken* ('Old Catholics'), those who rejected the new dogma. But it was only after the setting up of the German Reich in 1871 that the *Kulturkampf*

began in earnest, so called after Rudolf Virchow in an 1873 election address described the struggle against the Catholic Church as a 'struggle for culture' (*Kampf für die Kultur*).

Conscious of the weakness of the newly-created Reich (threatened externally by Catholic Austria and France, and internally by its relatively weak federal structure), Bismarck was determined to forge a greater degree of German unity and strength. To him, as to the Protestant Conservatives and anti-clerical Liberals, it seemed intolerable that the Catholics should form a 'state within the state' and owe their ultimate loyalty to a 'foreign power'. The Prussians – and to a lesser degree the other states within the German Empire, including strangely enough Bavaria, which was still much influenced by 'Josephist' ideas – thus began to implement the old policy of 'Protestantising the Catholics'. In July 1871 the Catholic section of the Prussian *Kultusministerium* was suppressed, and in March 1872 the Prussian *Landtag* passed a law placing the supervision of all schools in the hands of the state and forbidding members of religious orders to teach in schools. In July 1872 a law was passed by the Reichstag banning the Jesuits from German territory, and in 1873, 1874 and 1875 various 'May Laws' were passed which subordinated all Church life (appointment of priests and bishops, instruction of clergy, and so forth) to state regulation.

The Catholics decided on passive resistance and continued to act as though the 'May Laws' had not been passed. The result was that by 1876 nine Prussian sees were vacant, 1400 parishes were without lawfully appointed priests, and an untold number of Catholic priests and laymen had been fined or imprisoned for breaking the law. Moreover, the *Zentrum* (officially constituted as a political party in 1870) had increased its representation in the Reichstag from fifty-seven deputies in 1871 to ninety-one in 1873 and ninety-three in 1877. At the same time a large Catholic press had come into being – the *Kölnische Volkszeitung, Schlesische Volkszeitung* and *Germania* (official organ of the *Zentrum*) all dating from this period. In addition a Catholic leader who was as obstinate as Bismarck, namely Ludwig Windthorst, the former Hanoverian Minister of Justice, had emerged as a formidable champion of Catholic rights, and made it quite clear that his co-religionists were not going to be browbeaten by the Prussian Government, and that Bismarck would after all have to 'go to Canossa'.

By the late 1870s Bismarck had in any case decided that such a 'journey' (although he never admitted it openly) would be in his own best interests. Leo XIII had succeeded the ultra-conservative Pius IX in 1878, and the new Pope at once made it clear that he would show 'understanding' towards Germany if some concessions were made over the *Kulturkampf*. In addition Bismarck began to realise that the rising threat of Socialism was much greater than that posed by the Catholics. Indeed, throughout the *Kulturkampf* the Catholics had behaved in a wholly responsible and conservative manner, paying their taxes and refusing any resort to physical violence. Moreover, the Liberals (or at least the progressive Liberals) were beginning to talk in terms of parliamentary reforms, whereas the Catholics and Conservatives could be relied upon to support the Bismarckian governmental system, provided the Chancellor acted within the bounds of the 1871 Constitution. For these reasons then Bismarck discreetly called off the *Kulturkampf* in the early 1880s, and by 1887 all the anti-Catholic legislation (except for the banning of the Jesuits, who remained *personae non gratae* until 1917) had been repealed.

From 1881–1918 all German governments were based on an alliance of Conservatives, right-wing National Liberals and the Catholic Centre. At the 1881 Reichstag Elections the *Zentrum* emerged as the biggest single party (it had 104 seats to 98 for the National Liberals), and it held this position throughout most of the period up to 1914. The party also provided the President of the Reichstag from 1895–1906, and although there were no *Zentrum* ministers before the First World War, the Catholics had come full circle since the *Kulturkampf*. Their basic political line was to support the government whenever possible, i.e. unless it seemed to be acting unconstitutionally or threatening civil liberties. Thus, the majority of Centre deputies voted against the anti-Socialist law of 1878, not because they had any love for the Socialists but because this type of legislation was seen as a threat to the civil liberties they had always defended. Again, in 1886 the party voted against a seven-year military budget (the Catholics would have been prepared to accept three), because this was seen as a breach of the Constitution; moreover, the *Zentrum* voted as it did despite papal advice to vote for Bismarck. In 1893 the *Zentrum* also voted against increased military credits, and in 1905 the young Matthias Erzberger protested with a small group of Centre deputies against the violent colonisation of South-West Africa.

In general, however, the *Zentrum* from 1881–1914, and particularly in the Wilhelmine period (1890–1914), was a government party *par excellence*. Its social wing, led by Ketteler and Franz Hitze, had been tamed by the sickness, accident and old age insurance schemes introduced by Bismarck's laws of 1883, 1884 and 1889. And the vast majority of the party – much influenced by conservative Catholic prelates, nobles and industrialists – became increasingly complacent during the Indian summer of William II's reign. Even if 'the little Hanoverian', as Windthorst was known, had lived beyond 1891, it is extremely doubtful whether the evolution of the *Zentrum* would have been different. Windthorst was in his element in a period of persecution, but was at heart a conservative pragmatist. A lawyer by training, he was above all a believer in the legalistic concept of the *Rechtstaat*, but he was also a devout monarchist, and it is unlikely that he would have wanted to replace the authoritarian governmental system established by Bismarck with a parliamentary one, unless of course there had been another direct attack on civil liberties.

The Catholics seemed, as it were, worn out by the great struggle of the *Kulturkampf*, and, sensitive as they undoubtedly were about adverse comments on their patriotism, they became almost as nationalistic as the Conservative supporters of the government after the turn of the century. Indeed, the Catholics were so affected by *Staatsfrömmigkeit* – a mystical respect for the State – that they refused to look critically at the Wilhelmine governmental system. Men such as Ernst Lieber, Windthorst's successor, and Matthias Erzberger, one of the party's young leaders, seem to have wanted to orientate the party towards a strong commitment to parliamentary democracy, and Jules Bachem, in a famous article, called upon the party to break out of its confessional ghetto ('Wir müssen aus dem Turm heraus').[20] But these were voices crying in the wilderness. In the thirty years up to 1914 most of the *Zentrum* party leaders did nothing to face up to the problems posed by the governmental system or by its own narrow confessionalism. Doubtless in this, as in other matters, the leaders did no more than reflect the complacent conservatism of the vast majority of their electors, who remained as loyal as ever.

The Zentrum during the First World War and under Weimar
Germany's Catholic politicians seem to have been as taken aback as those of other parties by the outbreak of war in 1914. Foreign policy had for so long been the concern only of the Emperor and the diplomatic bureaucracy that the war came as a considerable surprise to most politicians and the *Zentrum* deputies joined those of all the other parties in voting the necessary military credits and proclaiming the conflict as a just, defensive war. And despite the 'peace resolution' of 19 July 1917, sponsored by Erzberger and proposing peace without annexations, the majority of *Zentrum* politicians followed such men as Peter Spahn and Adolf Gröber in supporting the war effort to the end. Just as the war came as a shock, so the collapse of Germany, and especially the November 1918 revolution, caught the *Zentrum* unprepared; but in accordance with its usual practice of accepting the *de facto* political regime, the *Zentrum* soon endorsed the Weimar Republic, albeit with less enthusiasm than it had endorsed Wilhelmine Germany or supported the war.

Throughout the Weimar Republic (1919–33) the *Zentrum* formed the fulcrum of the parliamentary majority; it participated in every government; it provided the Republic with four of its Chancellors, who together held office for over half of the Republic's fourteen years;[21] and its electoral support remained remarkably constant, about one fifth of the deputies being members of the *Zentrum* or *Bayerische Volkspartei* (BVP) throughout.[22] Yet the essential point to note is that the Catholic Centre was divided and unsure of itself throughout Germany's first experiment in parliamentary democracy. Like the German people as a whole, the Catholics were badly prepared for the sudden arrival of political responsibility. Many Catholics continued to hanker after the monarchy.[23] Franz von Papen, a *Zentrum* politician although no longer *persona grata* in the party by the early 1930s, played – perhaps unwittingly – a crucial role in destroying the parliamentary system between 1930–3. Even in 1925, when still an accepted member of the *Zentrum* and the largest shareholder in the party's newspaper *Germania*, von Papen campaigned for Hindenburg against the *Zentrum* candidate, Wilhelm Marx, in the presidential elections. Papen was joined in his campaign by the BVP, whose million votes made the difference between Hindenburg and Marx. In the last years of Weimar Fritz Schaeffer was to lead the BVP into a firmly anti-Nazi stance, but by then it was too late – the Bavarian Catholics had already done vital damage by constantly voting against the *Zentrum* in the years 1919–23 and by ensuring that a fundamentally anti-Republican soldier occupied the chief office in the land from 1925.

Up to 1925 the main coalition partners were Catholics, Social Democrats and progressive Liberals. But the Catholics were by no means united in their support for these 'Black-Red' coalition governments. In his first speech to the Constituent Assembly in February 1919 the *Zentrum* leader Adolf Gröber said that his party frankly regretted the November revolution: it would have preferred the imperial system to have been replaced by a constitutional monarchy like that of Great Britain or Belgium, but as the choice now lay between a 'democratic republic' and 'revolutionary chaos', the *Zentrum* would support the former.[24] Not only did the *Zentrum* endorse the Republic reluctantly, it also had grave doubts about the alliance with the Socialists. A few Catholics went over to the right-wing nationalists (the *Deutsch-Nationale Volkspartei*, DNVP), whilst others, such as the Catholic trade union leader Adam Stegerwald, had considerable doubts about working with the SPD. Although a trade unionist, Stegerwald had a vision of a conservative, Catholic, corporatist state, and wanted to keep his distance from the atheistic Socialists.[25] Men such as Matthias Erzberger (murdered by nationalists in 1921 – they had never forgiven him for the 'peace resolution' of 1917), and Joseph Wirth, who correctly and courageously stated in the Reichstag after the murder of Walther Rathenau in 1922 that 'The enemy is to the Right', were the exceptions to the rule, in that they were *Zentrum* leaders who were wholly committed to democracy and the Republic. For most members of the party the main victory was won – and perhaps was won too easily – in 1919 when the Weimar Constitution enshrined all the religious liberties for which Windthorst and Lieber had striven before the war. But although Weimar had given the Catholics what they wanted in *religious* terms, they remained only dilettante supporters of Weimar as a *political* system.

The *Zentrum's* steady drift towards the Right became fully apparent in 1928, when in a triangular contest for the party leadership the conservative priest Kaas was elected chairman with 160 votes to 95 for the progressive Joos and 40 for the trade-unionist Stegerwald. Moreover, since 1925 the *Zentrum* had been participating in coalitions which included right-wing Liberals and Nationalists. Thus, even before the economic crash the *Zentrum* had moved in the direction which Wirth had warned against in 1922.

The party, it is true, supported the Republic's last SPD Chancellor, Hermann Müller, in 1929–30, but it then agreed with the progressive Liberals that a cut in unemployment benefit must be made. Müller thus fell, and was replaced by Heinrich Brüning, an honourable but rather indecisive *Zentrum* leader, who encouraged Hindenburg to use presidential decrees (Article 48) to implement a deflationary policy after he (Brüning) had failed to win the election he had rather unnecessarily called in 1930, the fatal election which increased Nazi representation to 107 (compared with fourteen in 1928). By encouraging Hindenburg to rule by presidential decree, Brüning undoubtedly hammered a nail into the Republic's coffin. And when Brüning was dismissed in May 1932 (Hindenburg refused to accept a reduction in the agricultural subsidies being paid to the eastern provinces) and replaced by Franz von Papen, an even more important nail was hammered in. For although von Papen was still a member of the *Zentrum*, he was determined to carry out a conservative revolution with or without the wishes of the Reichstag, and his own party refused to support him. It was von Papen who on 20 July 1932 evicted the SPD-*Zentrum* coalition government in Prussia by presidential decree, and appointed himself *Reichskommisar* for Prussia, thus gaining control of the machinery of government of three-fifths of Germany and preparing the way for Goering's takeover of Prussia. Yet von Papen and Hindenburg were not ready to overthrow the constitution by force, so a general election was called in July 1932. This did nothing to resolve the crisis, the result being as follows: Nazis 230; Nationalists 37; Centre (including BVP) 97; SPD 133; Communists 89; others 22. The parties which were opposed in principle to the Republic (i.e. Nazis, Communists and Nationalists) thus had over half the seats (356 out of 608). But, with Hindenburg still unwilling to consider Corporal Hitler for the chancellorship, von Papen remained Chancellor, although he had the support of only a tiny minority of the members of the Reichstag.

The November 1932 general election reduced the Nazi representation by thirty-four, but did nothing to resolve the deadlock. Hindenburg, under the influence of General Schleicher and a camarilla of intriguers, agreed to dismiss von Papen in December 1932, but a month later von Papen got his revenge on Schleicher when he persuaded Hindenburg to replace Schleicher with Hitler, von Papen having assured the President that the Austrian corporal would be firmly controlled by himself and the Nationalists in his cabinet. Thus, thanks to the Catholic conservative von Papen, Hitler finally became Chancellor on 30 January 1933. Within seven weeks the Reichstag had been burnt down and the Enabling Act (23 March 1933) had been passed – this Act effectively suspended the constitution and gave the Cabinet power to legislate on its own authority. No *Zentrum* deputy joined the ninety-five Social Democrats who stood alone in voting against the Enabling Act . . . . Within four months Germany was a one-party state.

From this brief survey of the evolution of German political and social Catholicism up to 1933 it is clear that there was no such thing as Christian Democracy in Germany before the Second World War – that is in the sense of a substantial political movement committed to Christian and democratic principles. Indeed, it was only the experience of the Third Reich that finally converted Centre Party voters into democrats. The *Zentrum* of Windthorst had certainly supported legalism and constitutionalism, and had defended basic civil and religious liberties. But neither in Windthorst's time nor in the later Wilhelmine period did the *Zentrum* wage a campaign in favour of responsible parliamentary government. Even the social Catholic movement – from Ketteler to Stegerwald by way of Hitze – was essentially conservative and paternalistic, even at times mediaevally romanticist in its corporatist proposals. Under Weimar the *Zentrum* had a few leaders such as Wirth who were genuinely committed to liberal democracy. But, as the party moved to the Right in the late 1920s, it did no more than bring itself into line with the views of a conservative hierarchy and electorate. Political authoritarianism and social conservatism were much closer to Catholic ideals than democratic responsibility and libertarianism. Indeed, there is no doubt that certain aspects of National

Socialism appealed to Catholics – not only its clearcut anti-communism, but also its emphasis on a strong state, national greatness, and the replacement of *laisser faire* capitalism by corporatism. In *Mein Kampf* Hitler had written of the value of 'positive Christianity', and within six months of coming to power the first *Concordat* between the whole of Germany and the Papacy had been signed. Eventually of course it became apparent that nazism and Christianity were rival religions, and that the former was out to destroy the latter. But even after the encyclical *Mit brennender Sorge* (1937), which openly condemned the Nazis for breaking the Concordat as well as for their anti-semitism, most Catholics remained quite content in the Third Reich. A few priests were imprisoned for criticising euthanasia and Bishop Galen of Munster cour-ageously attacked some aspects of Nazi policy from 1941 onwards, but the vast majority of bishops and priests continued to pray for the Reich and the Führer until the end. It was only after the war was over that the evils of nazism were fully exposed, and it was only in the shock of this revelation that the majority of Catholics committed themselves for the first time to the democratic system and to reconciliation with their Protestant brethren.

France

Some of the most important Christian Democratic precursors were Frenchmen, notably Lamennais, Lacordaire, de Mun, Harmel and Sangnier, and France had two quasi-Christian Democratic parties, the *Parti Démocrate Populaire* and the *Jeune République*, before the Second World War.[26] Yet the develop-ment of Christian Democracy in France was slow and uneven. French Catholics were less united politically than those of Italy and Germany and no major Catholic democratic party such as the *Partito Popolare* or *Zentrum* emerged in France until after 1945. Even then the *Mouvement Républicain Populaire* (MRP) failed to attract the high degree of support from practising Catholics accorded to its counterparts in Germany and Italy.

The main reason for the slow and stunted growth of Christian Democracy in France was the bitterness of the conflict between Catholics and Republicans, which had its origins in the Great Revolution of 1789. Before the Second World War French Catholicism was generally equated with conservatism, often of the most reactionary kind. At the same time most Catholics never forgave the Republic for depriving the Church of its property in 1790 or for converting the Church into little more than a department of state by means of the Civil Constitution of the Clergy (1792). It is true that one of Napoleon's first acts was to try to breach the gap between Church and state. The Concordat of 1801, which remained in operation until the separation of Church and state in 1905, restored the pre-1789 *status quo*, in that the Church was re-estab-lished, but this gain was offset by the Organic Articles, which gave the govern-ment greater control over ecclesiastical appointments than had been the case before the Revolution. Moreover, when Napoleon crowned himself Emperor in the presence of the Pope in 1804, it was clear who was Master and who Servant.

The return of the Bourbons in 1814, accompanied by priests and nobles, seemed to show on whose side the Church was fighting, and it was not surprising that when Napoleon escaped from Elba he was greeted with cries of 'Long live the Emperor! Down with the clericals!' The Papacy was seen as the enemy of the Revolution, the Republic and the Empire, against 'liberty, equality and fraternity'; Marianne must go to Canossa and confess her Republican sins. In general the Catholics accepted this *Diktat,* whilst anti-clericals rejected it, and until the First World War the gulf between the two sides seemed to be wide and unbridgeable. At the turn of the century the anti-clerical supporters of Waldeck-Rousseau and Combes were no more conspicuous for their moderation than the anti-republican members of *Action Française.* The *union sacrée* of 1914, it is true, provided a temporary truce in the Catholic-Republican quarrel, but *Action Française* was as active after the war as before, and although Maurras's movement was condemned by the Papacy in 1926, the majority of its anti-Republican, anti-semitic members continued to be right-wing Catholics. Indeed, it was not until after the Second World War, in which many left-wing Catholics played a prominent role in the Resistance in spite of the Hierarchy's support for Vichy, that Catholics were fully accepted as good Republicans.

The kernel of the Catholic-Republican quarrel was *le problème scolaire,* which remained the 'Maginot line between the Left and Right'[27] until after the Second World War. And as this quarrel was so bitter and had such a divisive effect both politically and socially, it is important to comment further on it, not least because *le problème scolaire* was the reef on which so many of the embryonic Christian Democratic pilot schemes foundered.

Prior to the Revolution of 1789 education had been the prerogative of the Church, but as the Church was very closely linked with the state, education was in practice a public service entrusted to the Church. Under Napoleon the state officially took control of education with the establishment of *l'Université,* although the Concordat of 1801 permitted the clergy to teach in state schools. This relatively satisfactory situation continued after the Restoration, but a law of 1828 forbidding Jesuits to teach in state schools put the Catholics on the defensive, and they began to demand full recognition for their own 'free' schools. The Catholics were helped by the general decline of anti-clericalism and the revival in the fortunes of the Catholic Church in France in the 1830s and 1840s.[28] It was significant, for example, that during the 1848 Revolution churches were not attacked and destroyed as they had been in 1789 and 1830, and were to be again in 1871. But no sooner had the Catholic revival got under way than the Church embarked on the issue of 'free schools', which as Tocqueville remarked in 1850 was a 'huge blunder', for instead of 'restricting themselves to . . . their elementary rights, they [the clericals] revealed their intention of dominating and even controlling all forms of education.'[29]

The Catholic campaign was successful, in that the Falloux Law of 1850 allowed the establishment of Catholic secondary schools, so that by the end of the Second Empire (1870) there were more children in Church than in state secondary schools.[30] Moreover, the trend towards Catholic education continued in the early years of the Third Republic, whose first Chamber of Deputies was clerical and monarchical. An 1875 law, for example, permitted the establishment of Catholic universities. However, the Left won the 1876 general election, and the new Chamber was not only Republican but also distinctly anti-clerical.[31] It was not long before the prescience of Tocqueville's remarks of 1850 became apparent. It had indeed been a 'blunder' on the part of the Catholics to push their case too hard when in the ascendant. They were soon to reap a whirlwind from the seeds they had sown. For after the failure of the Right, the Republicans proceeded, in Brogan's phrase, 'to take over the Republic'.[32] An important part of their policy was to eliminate the anti-Republican influence of the Church. As they saw it, the Republic would be safe from counter-revolution only when all clerical influence had been eliminated from education.

In 1880 the Jesuits were expelled, and other religious orders were forbidden to teach without licence. In 1882 free state elementary education was introduced and religious instruction in schools abolished (although Thursday was made a holiday so that parents could arrange for extra-curricular religious instruction if they wished). At the same time the two great lay *Ecoles Normales* were established at Saint-Cloud and Fontenay-les-Roses to train men and women to go out to the provincial *écoles normales* to instruct the nation's elementary school teachers. *Lycées* for girls were also established at this time, and by the late 1880s there were more children at state than at Catholic 'free schools'.

After these *laïc* laws, for which Jules Ferry and Camille See were largely responsible, there was a lull in *la guerre scolaire* until after the turn of the century. Then a series of laws associated with the names of Waldeck-Rousseau and Emile Combes curtailed the rights of Catholics further; in particular members of religious orders were forbidden to teach in schools. Finally, in 1905 the battle between the Republicans and Catholics reached its climax with the separation of Church and state.[33] The disestablishment of the Church was regarded at the time by most Catholics as a disaster, but in fact it opened the way to reconciliation. Now that the quarrelling couple had been legally separated, they could begin to think in terms of peaceful coexistence, if not yet of harmony. The First World War, and even more the Second, helped to take the bitterness out of the Catholic-Republican quarrel by showing that Catholics could also be loyal Frenchmen. But *le problème scolaire* continued, albeit intermittently, to bedevil French political life until the 1960s. As long ago as 1919 the Astier Law had made state subsidies available to 'free' technical schools, and state grants were also given to Catholic youth organisations from the 1920s. The Poinso-Chapuis Decree of 1948, empowering family associations to underwrite the education of deprived children at Catholic schools, and the Barangé Law of 1951, granting subsidies to children at Catholic schools, were further steps towards a compromise solution. Finally, the Debré Law of 1959, resulting in the payment of Catholic teachers by the state (provided the schools in which they taught were recognised as efficient by the state), was the last in a long line of laws which more or less resolved *la guerre scolaire*.

In 1970 François Goguel was prepared to go so far as to say to the author that 'le problème scolaire est mort'. Despite the validity of this observation, it is important to emphasise the fundamental historical differences between Catholics and Republicans which affected French politics – and not least the development of Christian Democracy – from the Great Revolution to the Fifth Republic. The two sides were quarrelling not about political means but about ends. The Boulangists, the followers of Charles Maurras, and the Vichyites wanted, not merely to change the Republic, but to overthrow it. In trying to achieve their ends both sides ruled out compromise; hence the deep hatred between Dreyfusards and anti-Dreyfusards, Popular Front and *Action Française*, Clericals and Republicans. Under the Fourth Republic the quarrelling was to be less bitter, partly owing to the arrival on the political scene of the Christian Democratic MRP, but the presence of the MRP did not result in the complete disappearance of those fundamental politico-religious differences which had for so long divided the French nation.

Lamennais, Lacordaire and the precursors of Christian Democracy
Most of those who have written about the origins of Christian Democracy in France have tried to distinguish between 'Social Catholicism' and 'Christian Democracy'.[34] The ideas of Lamennais, Lacordaire, Ozanam, de Mun, Harmel and La Tour du Pin are said to have been essentially 'social', in that these men were trying above all to find social rather than political solutions to the problems created by industrialisation and economic liberalism. With the exception of Lacordaire they were not particularly interested in political democracy, preferring to adapt old-style paternalism and charity to modern economic and social circumstances. It was not until men such as Sangnier recognised at the turn of the century that deep-rooted economic and social change could only be achieved by political means that 'Christian Democracy' – a democratic political movement with clearcut social objectives – emerged in France. The distinction made between 'Social Catholicism' and 'Christian Democracy' in the scholarly work of J. B. Duroselle and H. Rollet seems to me too rigid. Many of the confused political ideas of Lamennais and Lacordaire, for example, clearly foreshadow the basic tenets of what later came to be known as Christian Democracy.

Lamennais has justifiably been described as a 'visionary genius'.[35] This headstrong Breton priest, who was forced to leave the Church in 1834 on account of his unorthodox views, 'foresaw with uncanny precision the collapse of temporal power, the declaration of Papal Infallibility, the separation of Church and State, the triumph of democracy and its ultimate reconciliation with the Church'.[36] Above all Lamennais advocated that the Papacy should espouse the cause of the people, and ally itself with the masses rather than with monarchs, nobles and established governments. It was this proposal which attracted Lacordaire, although, unlike Lamennais, he did not become a convinced Republican until the Revolution of 1848. However, it was with a view to forging a new alliance between the Church and the ordinary people that Lacordaire, Lamennais and a young nobleman, Charles de Montalembert, founded *L'Avenir* in 1830. This publication, which came out erratically for only a year, can justifiably be described as the first Christian Democratic journal. Many of the ideas put forward in *L'Avenir* were taken up again seventy years later by the Christian Democrats of the *Sillon*. *L'Avenir* advocated the separation of Church and state, which was to be accepted by the Sillonists, although not at first by the vast majority of Catholics; it advocated universal suffrage and a free press; and it proposed the development of intermediary bodies such as trade unions, another proposal which was revived at the turn of the century and fulfilled in 1919 with the establishment of the *Confédération Française de Travailleurs Chrétiens* (CFTC).

Lacordaire hoped that the Pope would support the ideas of *L'Avenir*, but, after his visit to Rome in 1831, Pope Gregory XVI condemned his views in the encyclical *Mirari Vos* (1832), which rejected the separation of Church and state, any alliance with 'liberal revolutionaries', and freedom of opinion. This looked like the failure of a movement which had hopes of opening up a new path for the Church in France, giving it a chance to come to terms with the political Revolution of 1789 and to some extent with the industrial revolution as well. Lacordaire, however, continued, albeit discreetly, to propagate his views, even after he became a Dominican in 1839, which led to his spending much of his time in the 1840s in a monastery near Grenoble. In 1848 he came out of his 'retirement' to welcome the Republic, and founded a daily newspaper, *L'Ere Nouvelle*, which was to all intents and purposes a new *L'Avenir*. Lacordaire used phrases such as 'Christian socialism' and 'Christian economy', and made it clear that he hoped the Revolution of 1848 would succeed where those of 1789 and 1830 had failed, namely in the realm of economic and social reforms. Lacordaire became a deputy in the Assembly elected in April 1848, but was deeply disappointed by the mob's invasion of the Assembly on 15 May, and resigned his seat a few days later. The closing of the national workshop and the bloody suppression of the workers symbolised the economic and social failure of the 1848 Revolution. Once again the changes had been political only. With his hope of Church and People united under the banner of social and economic reform frustrated, Lacordaire retired to Grenoble.

The Church's response to the 1848 Revolution was quite different from Lacordaire's. In the face of social revolution the Papacy and Hierarchy closed ranks and sided with the forces of reaction and conservatism. Even Montalembert, Lacordaire's friend of *L'Avenir* days, wrote: 'My choice is made. I am for authority against revolt, for conservatism against destruction, for society against socialism.'[37] Pius IX's *Syllabus Errorum* (1864), condemning 'progress, liberalism and modern civilisation',[38] symbolised the overall triumph of reaction in the mid-nineteenth-century Catholic Church. In these circumstances the Social Catholic, indeed Christian Democratic, ideals of Lacordaire could not be fulfilled. Lacordaire did not achieve his aim of reconciling Church and People, but he stands out as one of the outstanding precursors of Christian Democracy, and his bold progressive liberalism contrasts clearly with the negative, reactionary attitudes of the Church until the arrival of Leo XIII at the Holy See in 1878.

The *Ralliement*, the *Cercles* and the *Sillon*

Leo XIII (1878–1903) abandoned the purely negative attitude of the *Syllabus Errorum*. Adopting a Thomist attitude he tried to reconcile faith with reason. In a series of encyclicals – *Immortale Dei* (1885), *Libertas* (1888), *Rerum*

Novarum (1891), and *Au Milieu des Sollicitudes* (1891) – he continued to condemn materialism, socialism and secularism, but emphasised that the Church must face up to the challenges presented by economic and social liberalism. He argued that Catholics should exert pressure on governments to pass legislation to alleviate social and economic oppression, and that workers should form associations to defend their interests. In *Au Milieu des Sollicitudes*, addressed specifically to the French, he declared that all established governments were legitimate: Catholics should therefore rally to the Republic without making any concessions to doctrinaire anti-clericals. He made it clear that he wanted Catholics to co-operate with moderate Republicans in a broadly based, non-confessional political formation.

Leo XIII's successor Pius X (1903–14) was bitterly opposed to the separation of Church and state (1905) and condemned Sangnier's attempt to convert the *Sillon* into a Christian Democratic political party in 1910. Nevertheless, like Leo XIII, Pius X accepted the existence of the French Republic; and the new climate of opinion created by Leo, and reluctantly endorsed by his successor, made it possible for Catholics to adapt themselves to democracy and the Republic. There was a revival of Social Catholicism in the *Oeuvre des Cercles* organised by Albert de Mun and René de La Tour du Pin as well as in the *Cercles d'Etudes* of Léon Harmel. Both these *Cercles'* movements advocated the setting up of 'mixed' trade unions (bringing together employers and workers), family associations, and various social reforms, such as laws regulating the employment of young people, statutory holidays on Sundays, and accident, sickness and unemployment insurance schemes.[39]

The growing social concern of Catholics in the 1890s was accompanied by the development of political Catholicism both in the moderate *Ralliement* of de Mun and in the more progressive *Sillon* of Sangnier.

Albert de Mun had started his political life as a Catholic Royalist, but he rallied to the Republic at the time of *Au Milieu des Sollicitudes*, and in 1893 he formed a parliamentary group of thirty-five *Ralliement* deputies, i.e. Catholic deputies who accepted the Republic. Most of de Mun's supporters were Conservatives, but like Bismarck and Disraeli they advocated a limited amount of social legislation as a means to undermine Socialism. De Mun's *Ralliement* group was virtually destroyed by the Dreyfus Affair, but in 1901 de Mun and Jacques Piou formed *Action Libérale Populaire* (ALP), a loose parliamentary group of Catholics, whose twin objectives were to defend the interests of the Church – the ALP was strongly opposed to the separation of Church and state in 1905 – and to defeat revolutionary socialism by a programme of social reforms. The ALP reached a maximum of eighty deputies shortly before 1914, but in the face of criticism by both the *patronat* and the Hierarchy the ALP made little impact in the Chamber.[40]

Albert de Mun cannot be described as a Christian Democrat. He and his friends of the ALP were sincere Republicans but paternalistic conservatives. Nevertheless, it would be wrong to omit their contribution, albeit unintentional, to the emergence of Christian Democracy in France. The *Ralliement* and ALP accustomed Catholics to accepting the Republic and facing up to the need for governmental action to solve social problems. Indeed, perhaps de Mun's greatest achievement – in company with other *Cercles* leaders like Harmel – was to awaken the social conscience of Catholics in the light of Leo XIII's various encyclicals.

Prior to the First World War the political and social atmosphere in France was far from conducive to the emergence of a Christian Democratic movement. The anti-clericalism of the Left, the anti-Republicanism of the Right, and the bitterness aroused both by the Dreyfus Affair and by the separation of Church and state, ensured that the reservoir of progressive, democratic Catholics, i.e. of potential Christian Democrats, remained small. However, despite the unfavourable political and social climate, and despite the negative reaction of Pius X and of the Hierarchy to democratic, republican Catholicism, the seeds sown by the various Catholic 'social' and 'political' movements from Lacordaire to de Mun brought forth some fruit before 1914. Certainly Marc Sangnier's *Sillon*, and its successor the *Jeune République*, came close to meriting the epithet 'Christian Democratic'.

Marc Sangnier, founder of the *Sillon, grand bourgeois, Polytechnicien*, devout Catholic and life-long Republican, first entered 'politics' in the 1890s, when he began organising meetings of middle– and working–class Catholic youths to discuss the practical implications of the encyclical *Rerum Novarum* (1891). The movement soon spread, and *'Cercles d'Etudes'* and *'Instituts Populaires'* were established in country towns as well as in the larger cities with the object of encouraging Catholics both to become 'républicains démocrates sans équivoque' and to implement the social teaching of the Church.

Sangnier had sufficient means to buy a review, *Le Sillon* ('The Furrow'), in 1897,[41] and in *Le Sillon*, and later in the weekly *L'Eveil Démocratique* (1905–10), Sangnier and his friends propagated their pro-Republican, social-reforming (albeit paternalistic) views. They also won the support of Emmanuel Desgrées du Lou, a former naval officer who founded the Rennes daily, *Ouest-Eclair*, in 1899 and therein preached reconciliation between Catholics and Republicans. By 1914 *Ouest-Eclair*, predecessor of the famous *Ouest-France*, had the largest circulation of any provincial newspaper and probably played a greater role in spreading Christian Democratic ideas than any of the publications more closely associated with Sangnier.

French Christian Democrats were to look back on the *Sillon* period as a Golden Age, but it is doubtful whether 'les beaux temps du Sillon' were as idyllic as was later claimed, for, afflicted as the *Sillon* was by internal dissensions – Sangnier was a very autocratic personality – the movement seems to have been disintegrating even before it was formally condemned by the Pope in 1910. But despite the atmosphere in the France of Dreyfus and Combes, the flame lit by the *Sillon* was not extinguished by Pius X's decision of 1910. It was kept alight, if only just, by the *Jeune République*, which was founded in 1912 by Sangnier to further the ideas of the banned *Sillon*, and was revived after the First World War. There were never more than four *Jeune République* deputies, but they formed the left wing of the Christian Democratic movement, giving their full support, for example, to the Popular Front in 1936–8.

Before 1914, then, Christian Democracy hardly got off the ground in France, but some progress was made towards encouraging Catholics to accept the Republic, face up to their social responsibilities, and participate, albeit tentatively, in the democratic process.

The Parti Démocrate Populaire (PDP)

Marc Sangnier and a handful of other former Sillonists were elected to the Chamber in 1919, and Sangnier seems to have considered forming a *Jeune République* parliamentary group, but, unable to muster sufficient support, he dropped the idea.[42] However, although no specifically Christian Democratic parliamentary group came into being until 1924, two important Christian Democratic organisations were active in the country. These were the *Fédérations des Républicains Démocrates* of Finistère and Paris. The former had been founded in 1912 by Paul Simon, who was first elected to the Chamber in that year. In 1919 he was again elected in Brest, and in 1924 four other Breton Christian Democrats were elected, and all joined the new PDP group in the Chamber. The Paris Federation, formed in June 1919, brought together Catholics of 'political' (i.e. *Sillon*) and 'social' (i.e. *Cercles, Semaines Sociales* and *Action Catholique de la Jeunesse Française*, ACJF) backgrounds: men such as Robert Cornilleau, founder of the Christian Democratic newspaper, *Le Petit Démocrate*, Jean Lerolle of ACJF, and Georges Thibout, the first president of the Federation. Apart from the important Finistère and Paris Federations there were local Christian Democratic groups in Limoges, led by the Catholic trade unionist Maurice Guérin; in Rouen, led by another trade unionist, Etienne Touré; in Clermont, led by the former Sillonist Eugène Laudouze; and in Le Havre, led by Louis Siefridt, later an MRP deputy.

The logical next step was to set up a national Christian Democratic political party. This finally occurred in 1924 as a result of a proposal made by Gaston Tessier, the first secretary-general of the newly founded *Confédération Française des Travailleurs Chrétiens* (CFTC, founded 1919). In August 1922 Tessier had proposed that the disparate Christian Democratic groups should unite to defend themselves against the attacks of *Action Française*, and in January 1924 various men of Catholic Action (i.e. ACJF and other such groups), trade union, and political backgrounds held a conference in Paris, at which it was decided to set up a Christian Democratic political party. However, this party was not finally established until after the general election of May 1924, at which most Christian Democratic candidates, standing under a variety of political labels, did rather badly. Nevertheless, Sangnier and Simon managed to muster a sufficient number of sympathetic deputies to form a parliamentary group of fourteen (the minimum for such a group being thirteen), and at the same time the *Parti Démocrate Populaire* was formally founded as a national party. The parliamentary group, known as the *Groupe des Démocrates Populaires*, was joined by one more deputy in 1927 to give it a total of fifteen; between 1928–32 it had nineteen members; from 1932–6 it had sixteen; and from 1936–40 it had twelve.

The PDP never had a precise programme, but the press was informed of its principles on the day after its foundation. These were:

1. Full support for the Republic and for political liberties, i.e. freedom of conscience, freedom of education, freedom of the press and freedom of association;
2. Determination to realise a genuine democracy by reforming economic and social conditions and by sincere co-operation between employers and workers;
3. Promotion of civic and moral education through respect for religious convictions;
4. Implementation of a foreign policy which not only takes account of French national interests but also of all means of international co-operation.[43]

These principles were rather vague, but certain ideas characteristic of French Christian Democratic thinking run through them: the idea, for example, that democracy is not just political but also social and economic, the emphasis on international co-operation, and the emphasis on morals and religion.

From the beginning there was evidence of the regional tendency of Christian Democracy in France. Labelled a 'clerical' party by its opponents, the PDP made almost no impact outside the traditionally Catholic and conservative *départements*. The PDP reached its peak in 1928 with the return of nineteen deputies, fifteen of whom came from the Catholic west (Brittany and Normandy) and north-east (Alsace and Lorraine). One deputy was elected in Seine and one in Loiret (a department lying sixty miles south of Paris), whilst the other two came from Haute-Loire in the Massif Central and from Tarn in the south-west. In the Chamber the PDP was a rather cautious conservative party, with one or two exceptions: the party supported the extension of family allowances to all social categories in 1930 (Jean Lerolle of the PDP was the bill's *rapporteur*), and the PDP was as outspoken in its support for Briand's 'reconciliation' policy in the late 1920s and early 1930s as it was in its condemnation of fascism in the late 1930s.

Possibly the PDP's most important achievement was socio-political rather than directly political, in that the party gave its full support to the growth of Catholic Action organisations in the interwar years, organisations such as the *Association Catholique de la Jeunesse Française* (ACJF), *Jeunesse Agricole Chrétienne* (JAC), *Jeunesse Ouvrière Chrétienne* (JOC), and *Jeunesse Etudiante Chrétienne* (JEC), in which many MRP leaders had their first experience of Christian Democratic political and social action.[44] The PDP also played an important role in propagating Christian Democratic ideas, not only through *Le Petit Démocrate* (the PDP newspaper) and *L'Aube* (sympathetic to both the PDP and *Jeune République*),[45] but also through its press bureau, which distributed releases to such papers as *Ouest-Eclair, L'Etoile le la Vendée, L'Alsacien* and *L'Echo du Mulhouse*.

In sum the PDP was a Christian Democratic party, clearly committed to liberal democracy and to the achievement of a more just, 'Christian' society. But its influence was relatively small. Despite improving relations between Catholics and Republicans, no party which could be labelled clerical had much hope of electoral success outside traditionally Catholic areas. Moreover, as a Centre party, the PDP was adversely affected by *scrutin d'arrondissement à deux tours*, which encouraged electoral alliances and polarisation between Right and Left. The PDP, like its successor the MRP, favoured proportional representation for the simple reason that Christian Democrats abhorred electoral alliances with the anti-Republican Right almost as much as with the anti-clerical Left. However, although Georges Bidault justifiably likened the PDP to 'grain being crushed between two mill-stones',[46] it is unlikely that a different electoral system would have radically changed the fortunes of the PDP. Although the phrase 'Catholic Republican' was no longer a contradiction in terms by the interwar years, the number of people who were prepared to stand up and be labelled as such was still very limited. It took the traumatic experiences of Vichy and the Resistance to produce a significant Christian Democratic breakthrough in France.

These short case studies of the origins of Christian Democracy (or perhaps one should say proto-Christian Democracy) in Italy, Germany and France show that it was extremely difficult for Catholics to be committed liberal democrats before 1914. They could be good social workers, but not good democrats. The authoritarian structure of the Church, its resentment at the loss of its temporal possessions, its hankering after the *ancien régime*, and its resultant uneasy relationship with Republican France and Liberal Italy, all militated against its accepting the basic *political* tenet of Christian Democracy, namely that Catholics should involve themselves fully in all aspects of the democratic process. It is true that Leo XIII began to accept that the political and economic evolution of Europe since the French and Industrial Revolutions could not be reversed by papal pronouncements. In his important encyclicals of the 1890s he also accepted that the Church must face up to the realities of nineteenth-century economic and social life rather than continue to dream about a world that had passed away. But Leo's ideas were to some extent reversed by his successor Pius X, and in any case it inevitably took time for them to filter through to the faithful. It was thus not surprising that when Catholics were given the green light to participate in the democratic process after 1918 they did so rather tentatively (as in the case of the *Partito Popolare Italiano*) or without a fundamental commitment to the republican version of parliamentary democracy (as in the case of the *Zentrum*) or without being fully accepted as reliable democrats (as in the case of the *Parti Démocrate Populaire*). Moreover, when the Papacy indicated a clear preference for the authoritarian Right to the atheistic Left, it did no more than reflect the views of the vast majority of Catholic electors. Another European war was required before Catholics were finally convinced that it was only by political means that they could safeguard the social rights to which in principle they were committed.

2

Christian Democratic Theory and Practice

Experience has in fact shown that to draft a detailed party programme, to proclaim it to the people, and to remain tenaciously
attached to it through the precipitous changes of events . . . pays
less well than to create a nucleus of strength, and to set out with
this to win power, adapting one's programme from hour to hour
without fear of being reproached for inconsistency.[1]

The above quotation suggests that Christian Democrats are more interested in
power than in ideology. And it is easy to contend that the history of Christian
Democracy in Western Europe since the Second World War confirms such a
view. Indeed, it has been argued that Christian Democratic ideas cover such a
wide spectrum, both philosophically and politically, that there is no such thing
as Christian Democratic doctrine or ideology.[2] On the other hand, much has
also been published arguing that Christian Democratic ideology is a perfectly
valid phenomenon.[3] Of course, it is true that politicians calling themselves
Christian Democrats have pursued a wide variety of policies ranging from
decisive State interventionism by the French MRP in the post-Liberation period
to *laisser-faire* economics by the German CDU in the heyday of the
Wirtschaftswunder ('economic miracle'). Clearly it is legitimate to ask what
possible links there could be between traditional conservative economists like
Ludwig Erhard, Mario Scelba or Robert Schuman and progressive trade
unionists like Maurice Guérin, Carlo Donat-Cattin and Hans Katzer, or
between the conservative followers of Franz-Josef Strauss and the left-wing
correnti in the Italian DC.
   The answer lies in doctrine. For, although Christian Democrats have never
claimed to have an all-embracing ideology, or *Weltanschauung*, they are
committed to certain common ideas and principles which amount to a solid
corpus of Christian Democratic theory. Of course, every continuing social
or political organisation must have some sort of ideology or doctrine, in the
sense that its members and supporters must have some idea both of their
ultimate objectives and of the means they intend to use to achieve these
objectives. In the case of the Christian Democrats the means and the objectives may at times appear rather imprecise, but the same comment could be
made with equal validity of Social Democrats, Liberals or Conservatives: yet
each in their own way would claim to base their political commitment on cer-

tain goals; or at the very least they are determined to prevent others from achieving *their* goals. Christian Democratic political and social theory may not be as precise as that of Marxists, but it is nevertheless based on a number of important principles.

Political ideology should be analysed on at least three levels: at the highest level there is the question of ultimate values and long-term objectives; next there is the question of strategy and of medium-term policy; finally, there is the problem of day-to-day tactics and of the extent to which compromises should be made in particular committees or over specific pieces of legislation. All three are, of course, to some extent interlinked; hence my decision to entitle this Chapter 'Christian Democratic Theory and Practice', for it seems unreasonable to divorce the one from the other. To analyse Christian Democratic programmes and manifestos in a vacuum would be of limited value. On the other hand, to attempt to illustrate every aspect of Christian Democratic theory with case-studies would result in a disproportionately long chapter. So, by way of compromise, one or two case-studies will be made, but the chapter's main emphasis will be on theory.

The Italian Prime Minister, Alcide De Gasperi, once stated that 'Christian principles' were the fundamental political guideline for Christian Democrats,[4] and the French Christian Democratic philosopher, Etienne Borne, wrote that 'personalism' and 'pluralism' constitute the essence of Christian Democratic ideology.[5] These concepts and epithets may be vague, but they provide a useful basis from which to begin to analyse Christian Democratic theory.

Taking the sum total of Christian religious and moral principles as their starting point, Christian Democrats have made some attempt to reconcile liberal democracy and industrial society with traditional Christian teaching; to achieve class reconciliation rather than class conflict; and to find a middle way between liberalism and collectivism. An important watershed, at least for Catholics, was the papal encyclical *Rerum Novarum* (1891), which accepted, albeit conditionally, the French and industrial revolutions, on the grounds that both had prepared the way for *potentially* more humane, and therefore more Christian, societies: the French Revolution had emphasised individual human rights and the brotherhood of man, whilst the industrial revolution, by creating unheard-of material wealth, held out the possibility that man could be freed from the economic shackles which had hitherto prevented him from developing his full potential as a human being. But, Christian Democrats argued, both revolutions had gone astray, for the French Revolution had led in due course to a system of parliamentary democracy in which only an articulate and moneyed élite, the bourgeoisie, could play an effective part, whilst the industrial revolution had given freedom to a tiny minority of entrepreneurs (members of the same class), but what amounted to slavery to the vast majority of ordinary people. Thus Christian Democrats came to reject nineteenth-century liberalism on the grounds that, whilst liberalism may have spawned a form of political democracy, it failed to create social and economic democracy. At the same time Christian Democrats accept the liberal emphasis on the importance of the individual, although with some modifications: they lay great stress on human rights and on the value of individual initiative, but they reject liberal economic concepts such as the 'survival of the fittest' or 'social Darwinism'. Instead they advocate 'personalism', Emmanuel Mounier's modified, or perhaps one should say 'Christianised', version of individualism. It is difficult to define 'personalism' precisely, but the term was first used and the concept first developed by Mounier in the French progressive Catholic journal, *Esprit*, in the 1930s.[6] Mounier had considerable influence not only in his own country but in Catholic circles throughout Western Europe, and the term 'personalism' (or 'Christian personalism') constantly crops up in postwar literature by Christian Democrats or about Christian Democratic theory.[7] The essence of personalism is its strong emphasis on the importance of the development of *all* dimensions of human personality, social as well as individual and spiritual as well as material. Personalism differs from liberalism in two important respects: first, in its emphasis on the spiritual side of life – in practice, however, personalists are often very critical of the formal structures and conservative tendencies of the organised Church; and secondly, in its contention that the individual can only reach fulfilment within the 'natural social structures' of society, such as the family, the community or the place of work. And because these 'natural social structures' are so important for the individual and can only function effectively under the benevolent tutelage of the state, Christian Democrats advocate a degree of state interventionism which would be quite unacceptable to *laisser-faire* liberals.

Having rejected traditional liberalism, however, Christian Democrats show scant interest in the Marxist response to liberalism: indeed, they anathematise collectivism even more than liberalism. They regard Marxist communism as a straightforward denial of Christ's teaching about the infinite value of each human being. Thus, even if Christian Democrats express some sympathy for the Marxist concept of social justice and are prepared to go along with certain aspects of Marxist redistributive theory, they totally reject the notion that the collectivity can ever be more important than the individual. However, it must be emphasised that Christian Democrats, particularly those of the Left, do not reject *all* aspects of Marxism any more than they reject *all* aspects of liberalism. Etienne Borne, for example, once wrote that liberalism, Marxism and positivism were each in their own way anathema to Christian Democrats, but that Christian Democrats could not but admire the liberal emphasis on the individual, the Marxist emphasis on justice and the positivist emphasis on pluralism.[8] All three political theories, however, had gone astray in their more extreme versions. Comte, for example, in developing his theory of positivism, had pushed the concept of pluralism to the point where society was so hierarchical that it was almost fascist. And Marxism in practice meant not government by the majority but dictatorship by a self-perpetuating oligarchy: Marxism, therefore, merely replaced a number of petty tyrants with one over-riding tyrant, and the individual was worse off than ever before.[9]

The Christian Democratic answer was a 'middle way' between liberalism and Marxism, or, as their theorists put it, a 'combination of freedom and justice'. It is important to emphasise the word 'combination', because justice without freedom, or vice versa, was liable to result in tyranny:

The originality of our doctrine lies in the fact that we hold on to both ends of the rope at the same time. Justice and freedom must be pursued in tandem and with equal vigour. Freedom without justice is artificial, deceptive and hypocritical; it can be used to justify the mechanism of the free market and the servitude of the proletariat. Such freedom is, in fact, the antithesis of freedom. Likewise, justice without freedom leads to tyranny and to the totalitarianism of Soviet communism or Fascist corporatism.[10]

Borne went on to argue that Christian Democratic definitions of freedom and justice were wider than those used by the liberals and Marxists respectively. For liberals, freedom meant freedom to act within the limits of the law; but for Christian Democrats, freedom from want, fear and poverty was as important as freedom to do what was legally permissible. For Marxists and Socialists, justice meant 'from each according to his capacities to each according to his needs', but the Christian Democratic definition of justice was a fuller one which took account of the fact that Marxist redistributive theory could easily lead to injustice to individuals. Christian Democrats claim that the destruction of one human being, much less a social class, can never be anything but injustice:

Thus we believe in a more comprehensive definition of justice based on the absolute respect which a man owes to his fellow human beings. This makes it impossible for him to treat them as pawns or as means to an end, even if it is a question of the well-being and survival of the majority.[11]

Christian Democratic theory is thus extremely individualistic in a 'Christian personalist' sense, not in a nineteenth-century liberal sense. Man as an individual is always regarded as more important than society as a whole, but it is necessary for the state to provide a combination of freedom and justice, so that man can develop his full potential both spiritually and materially. However, this potential can only flourish in the context of appropriate 'social structures'; hence the strong Christian Democratic emphasis on pluralism.[12]

Of course, in the real world of politics, freedom and justice, no less than pluralism and centralisation, are often difficult to reconcile. Christian Democrats unashamedly like to emphasise the dualism of their doctrine, and to claim that they are aiming to achieve a political and social synthesis.[13] Their opponents, often with good cause, criticise them as trimmers and hypocrites. Certainly, the Christian Democratic tendency to borrow from the theories of others leads in practice to a weak ideology, or at least to an ideology which can easily be labelled as 'weak' and 'vague' by its opponents. Thus, whilst the Communist or Fascist militant (like the Jesuit or Puritan before him) can, or could, derive great strength from his single-minded commitment to an all-embracing ideology, the Christian Democrat, by trying constantly to reconcile, synthesise and arbitrate, frequently exposes himself to simultaneous crossfire from his political opponents of Right and Left. Christian Democrats have claimed that their aim is to 'transform enemies into partners';[14] they have described themselves as 'of the Centre, but orientated to the Left';[15] they have been prepared to co-operate in government with Liberals and with Socialists, as well as with Communists (in France and Italy from the Liberation to 1947), and even, albeit briefly, with neo-Fascists (in Italy in 1960).

In addition, Christian Democrats constantly expose themselves to the criticism that they are often very conservative in their attitudes – and it should be remembered that the adjective 'conservative' is much more pejorative on the Continent of Europe than it is in Britain. To this charge, Christian Democrats counter that change is not necessarily for the better, and that many traditions, particularly those associated with Christianity and Western civilisation, are of lasting value; moreover, Christian Democrats argue that reforms should only be carried out by constitutional means, and never as a result of revolutionary violence.[16] In other words, Christian Democrats do not object to being labelled 'conservative' if the epithet is taken to mean that they respect tradition and reject violent revolutionary change; but they react strongly to the imputation that they belong to the traditional European Right, whether in its authoritarian or in its clerico-conservative manifestations.

It is, of course, possible to argue that Christian Democratic theory is a sham, or at least that it amounts to little more than the political theory of progressive Conservatism or moderate Socialism, a general commitment to social justice, tolerance, pluralism, internationalism and the mixed economy. It is certainly true that Christian Democrats *are* committed to such values and objectives, but if Christian Democratic theory and practice are examined in detail in one or two key areas, it becomes apparent that Christian Democracy is clearly distinguishable from Social Democracy or moderate Conservatism. Apart from their views on personalism and pluralism, which have already been briefly discussed, Christian Democrats also have distinctive views about, *inter alia*, natural law, European integration, the nature of political parties and movements, and social policy (particularly family and educational policies). Rather than attempting to analyse the above policies individually, Christian Democratic theory will be examined in the context of two themes, which I have labelled 'Christian values and human rights' and 'democratic pluralism'. And in order to assess the extent to which Christian Democratic practice measures up to theory, appropriate case-studies will be introduced.

Christian Values and Human Rights

An examination of the literature on Christian Democratic parties and Christian Democratic theory makes it clear that 'Christian values' in the broad sense of 'the values of Western Christendom' are of fundamental importance to Christian Democrats.[17] Of course, Christian Democrats realise that they are living in a world where politics is essentially a secular activity: hence, their refusal to use the adjective 'Catholic' in the titles of their parties (the only postwar exception being the Dutch Catholic People's Party, now a constituent part of Christian Democratic Appeal);[18] hence, too, their desire to avoid a clerical or 'confessional' image and their commitment to the separation of Church and State (with the partial exception of the Italian DC).[19]

The inspiration for the Christian Democrats' 'Christian principles' comes from three main sources: the confessional, mainly Catholic, parties of prewar

Europe, which were the forerunners of the Christian Democratic parties; the social teaching of the Catholic Church, notably that to be found in *Rerum Novarum* (1891), *Quadragesimo Anno* (1931) and *Pacem in Terris* (1963); and the reaction against the inhumanity and paganism of Nazism and Fascism.

There is no need to elaborate further on the first of these sources.[20] As regards the encyclicals, the most important from the point of view of contemporary Christian Democracy is *Pacem in Terris*. Indeed, by its very nature, *Pacem in Terris* contains an interesting parallel with Christian Democracy, because the first part of the encyclical is addressed to 'all men of good will' and embodies the general 'Christian principles' to which Christian Democrats adhere, whilst the second part is specifically addressed to the 'faithful' and embodies more precise instructions (e.g. over divorce, birth control and abortion), which are relevant to practising Catholics (including, of course, Catholic Christian Democrats), but not to people who merely sympathise with Christian and Western political values in broad terms. In its general part *Pacem in Terris* emphasises that 'the basis of any well-ordered and healthy society' is respect for the individual, who is entitled to a number of 'universal, inviolable and inalienable rights'. The rights which are then enumerated are comparable to those which are to be found in one form or another in all the programmes of the Christian Democratic parties[21] – that each individual has not only a 'right to life', but 'a right to the necessary means to lead a decent life'; a right to 'freedom in his personal search for truth, freedom of expression, freedom of artistic creation, freedom to receive objective information, freedom of association, and freedom to express his religion in public or private according to his conscience'.[22] In addition, *Pacem in Terris* emphasises each man's right to work, to own private property, to take an active part in public life, and to emigrate and immigrate at will. Of course, many of these values can be regarded as little more than those of European humanism, but Christian Democrats would argue that humanism owes more of *its* values to the European Christian-cultural tradition than vice versa; indeed, that humanism is no more than a 'godless' offshoot of the main tree-trunk of Christian and Western values.[23]

Whatever the pros and cons of such arguments, there can be no doubt about the Christian Democratic parties' broad commitment to 'Christian principles'. All the parties under consideration in this book except for the French Christian Democrats emphasise their commitment to 'Christian principles' in their manifestos. The Dutch Christian Democrats are particularly outspoken: 'The three parties (of Christian Democratic Appeal) will pursue policies based on the inspiration of Scripture . . . they will strive for a society in which Biblical principles carry more weight than at present, in which the value of each individual will be given greater emphasis, and in which men can live in greater freedom and responsibility.'[24] The Biblical references are, of course, due to the Calvinists, who are more interested in bringing their Christian principles into politics than present-day Dutch Catholics.[25] Both the German parties also lay considerable emphasis on their commitment to Christian principles: the CDU's Berlin Programme of 1971 opens with the words 'The Christian Democratic Union of Germany bases its policies on the principles of

Christian responsibility';[26] and the CSU claims to be a political movement (*politische Aktionsgemeinschaft*) whose policies are based on 'Christian principles'.[27] In the German case there was, of course, a strong feeling of revulsion against nazism in the early postwar period, and a determination that Catholics and Protestants should come together to build a society based on the Christian values scorned by Hitler. Thus the Christian Democratic programme of Neheim-Hüsten (March 1946) specifically condemned nazism for putting the state and party before the individual, and called for

a return to the fundamentals of the Christian culture of the West, the essence of which is a high view of the dignity of the person and the value of each individual human being . . . the Christian outlook must again replace the materialistic outlook, and the principles of Christian ethics must replace the principles of materialism. Christian principles must be the determining factor in the rebuilding of the State and in fixing the limits of its power, in the rights and duties of individuals, in economic and social life, in our culture, and in our relationship with other nations.[28]

Such lofty principles may seem to contrast sharply with the materialism associated with the Christian Democratic era in West Germany (1949–69). But, as we shall see, German Christian Democrats have been staunch defenders of human rights and of Western Christian values: in particular, they have striven to emphasise the concept of the *Rechtstaat* and the rule of law, to bridge the gap between the two Christian 'confessions', to develop their parties as inter-class *Volksparteien*, and to promote the 'brotherhood of man' through their support for European integration.[29]

The preamble of the Italian Christian Democratic programme of 1946 emphasises the DC's commitment 'to uphold the Christian traditions of our people', and the main part of the programme goes on to say that the *Democrazia Cristiana* is a party 'of Christian inspiration' which is committed to the principles of liberal democracy.[30] It is clear that in practice the DC has acted in a very 'secular' manner. If, for example, the activities of the Christian Democrats in local and national politics are examined, it is obvious that they are as embroiled as any other Italian politicians in the whole system of bribery, corruption, patronage and *clientelismo*.[31] Nevertheless, it should always be borne in mind that the Italian Christian Democrats have had to live and work in a political culture which is quite different from that north of the Alps and which has centuries of tradition behind it. Indeed, for all its failings, the DC has one important achievement to its credit, namely that it has played a key part in 'integrating Italian Catholics and Conservatives into the liberal democratic tradition for the first time'.[32]

Belgium and the Netherlands, unlike Germany and Italy, have a long tradition of parliamentary democracy. Nevertheless, after the Second World War the Christian Democratic parties of both countries laid considerable emphasis on their determination to build liberal democracy on the basis of Christian values. The Belgian case is particularly interesting, for both the Walloon PSC and the Flemish CVP, whilst pointedly emphasising their non-confessional character, have regarded their commitment to Christian values as a means by which the two Belgian communities can, as it were, rise above their particularism by committing themselves to the higher values of European Christendom.[33]

It is now time to examine the Christian Democratic commitment to human rights in a little more detail. Man, as has already been emphasised, is at the centre of the Christian Democratic universe: as Etienne Borne wrote, 'the first act of our faith is the freedom of man, a freedom which is constantly threatened and constantly evolving.'[34] Another French Christian Democratic writer, Etienne Gilson, developed this point by emphasising that 'the role of the State is to contribute to the full development of all members of society . . . one aspect of which is to guarantee the natural rights of each individual.'[35] For all the failings of Christian Democrats to live up to the lofty Christian ideals outlined in their manifestos, in one area at least they can claim to have made a notable contribution to a more just society, namely in their determination to include human rights (or 'natural law', as Christian Democrats often label them) in the various constitutions they helped to draft after the Second World War, and by their advocacy of constitutional courts to enforce these rights. The cases of Italy, Germany and France illustrate the limitations, as well as the achievements, of the Christian Democrats in this field.

Mario Einaudi justifiably wrote that 'the most conclusive and the fairest initial test of the seriousness with which the [Italian] Christian Democratic Party looked upon its ideal programme is to consider the document for which the Party bears a great responsibility' (i.e. the Constitution).[36] The DC comes rather well out of this test, for the Italian Constitution, like the German Basic Law, includes a comprehensive bill of human rights. Perhaps the most important article is the second one: 'The Republic recognises and guarantees the inviolable rights of man, whether as an individual or in the social groups through which his personality develops, and requires the fulfilment of the unavoidable duties of political, economic and social solidarity.' The general provisions outlined in this article are made more precise by those which follow granting traditional human rights such as freedom of expression and freedom of association. But even more important in the context of Christian Democratic theory are those articles which go beyond the privileges and immunities outlined in documents such as the American Bill of Rights and the French Declaration of the Rights of Man. Article 4, for example, guarantees the right to work, and Article 32 states that 'The Republic protects the health of the individual as his fundamental right and as an interest of the collectivity, and guarantees free medical treatment to the poor.' Other articles direct the state to ensure that all citizens have a right to education, a right to social security, a right to form trade unions and a right to strike. Of course, it is not too difficult to find loopholes both in Italian theory and practice. Article 19 lays down that 'All have the right freely to profess their own religious faith in whatever form they choose, whether individual or associated, and to propagandise it and practise in private or in public, provided this does not involve rites contrary to public morality', but Article 7, by recognising the validity of the Lateran Treaties of 1929, enshrines the Catholic Church as the Established Church of the Italian State, with all the advantages accruing from this special status. Moreover, Article 21 casts some doubt on the extent of free expression, for the police have wide powers to search and seize newspapers and other literature. These powers are open to abuse, and have been abused, as in the case of a large-scale raid on the offices of the respected *Corriere della Sera* in May 1972. The only apparent reason for the raid was that the *Corriere* had had the audacity to criticise certain police methods.

In other areas, too, one may well be sceptical about the Italian bill of rights. What does freedom of expression mean in a country where radicals like the anarchist Valpreda could be held in prison for three years without trial? What does a guaranteed right to impartial education mean in a country where nearly all primary schools are run by the Church and therefore biased in a certain direction whether they intend to be or not? What does a guaranteed right to work mean in a country where unemployment, especially in the south, has been endemic since the war despite all the efforts of the Development Fund for the South (the *Cassa per il Mezzogiorno*)? What do guarantees about health mean in a country which probably has the worst hospitals in Europe (although ironically it also has a higher percentage of doctors than any other European country)? The Christian Democrats can, of course, counter that economic conditions (at least in the north) are better than they have ever been, that Italy's overall growth rate since the war has been very impressive (over 5 per cent per annum between 1955–70), and that the *Cassa per il Mezzogiorno,* whilst it may not have solved the southern problem, has at least contributed to a considerable transformation of the south, on the whole for the better.[37] And whatever the practical failings of the Italian Constitution, at least the Christian Democrats did not shun the difficult task of drawing up a bill of *economic* and *social* rights as well as of more traditional political rights. Moreover, despite the Italian political and social crisis of the late 1960s and 1970s, public opinion polls indicate that only a tiny percentage of Italian voters (well under 10 per cent) want to return (for the sake of 'order and efficiency') to a political system in which the rule of law no longer applies.[38]

The German Christian Democrats were also determined to enshrine basic human rights in their constitution, and in this they were fully supported by the Social Democrats who had suffered even more under nazism. But in keeping with the moderate conservatism of the Parliamentary Council, which drew up the Basic Law of the Federal Republic, much less attention was paid to economic and social rights than to traditional political rights. (Although the Christian Democrats and Socialists were equally represented on the Parliamentary Council, the smaller parties on it were mainly conservative, and this helped Adenauer to shape the constitution in a conservative direction.[39]) But whilst the German Constitution is more 'traditional' than the Italian in the sense that the fundamental rights (*Grundrechte*) which it guarantees are mainly political, it must be emphasised that these rights have been taken very seriously in Germany. Theoretically, the first nineteen Articles of the Basic Law are inviolable, although in practice, of course, the whole concept of the *Rechtstaat*, i.e. a State based on the rule of law, depends on the overall political and social climate. Article 1, like so many others in the first nineteen, indicates the Germans' desire to make a clean break with their totalitarian past: 'The dignity of man is inviolable. To respect and protect it is the duty of all State authority.' Article 3 guarantees equality before the law irrespective of 'sex, parentage, race, language, homeland and origin, and religious and political opinions.' Article 4 guarantees, amongst other things, the right to conscientious objection, (although in 1956 it was laid down that conscientious objectors must do some civilian task in lieu of military service). Other articles guarantee freedom of the press and of speech (Article 5); the right of association, including the right to form trade unions (Articles 8 and 9); the inviolability of the home (Article 13); and the right to political asylum for foreigners (Article 16).

As with the Italian Constitution, it is not difficult to pick holes both in the Basic Law and in the way it has operated. If one examines the Basic Law in the light of Christian Democratic political theory as expounded by progressive Christian Democrats like Jakob Kaiser and Karl Arnold in programmes such as those drawn up in Berlin in June 1945, at Neheim-Hüsten in March 1946 and at Ahlen in February 1947, one is struck by the fact that the Basic Law says almost nothing about economic and social rights. Article 6 includes a vague reference to social policy ('Every mother is entitled to the care and protection of the community'); Article 15 permits nationalisation ('Land, natural resources and the means of production may, for the purpose of socialisation (*Vergesellschaftung*), be transferred into public ownership or other forms of publicly controlled economy by a law which shall regulate the nature and extent of compensation'); and the second section of the Basic Law begins with the words 'the Federal Republic of Germany is a democratic and social federal State.' But, unlike the Italian Constitution, the Basic Law makes no reference to the right to work or the right to strike, nor (apart from Article 6) are there any specific references to the state's obligations in the field of social welfare, theoretically a Christian Democratic priority.

In practice, too, the Basic Law has fallen short of its objectives. Article 3, for example, refers to the equality of the sexes, but in the 1970s there was still a considerable gap between the incomes of men and women doing similar jobs in West Germany. There were also various examples of racial discrimination with regard to foreign workers (*Gastarbeiter*) in the 1960s. In addition, the notorious raid on the offices of the *Spiegel* in 1962 would appear to have been in direct contravention of Article 5 guaranteeing freedom of the press. Moreover, although Article 7 lays down that 'no teacher shall be forced against his will to give religious instruction', the fact remains that any teacher trying to take advantage of this provision in parts of the country where Catholic influence over education is still strong would simply fail to get the job for which he had applied. Finally, the whole operation of the *Berufsverbot* ('professional debarment') in the 1970s, i.e. job-screening to check the political views of state employees down to the lowest levels, would appear to infringe Article 5 of the Basic Law guaranteeing freedom of expression and opinion. Moreover, the *Berufsverbot* has been applied with particular severity in *Länder* run by the Christian Democrats.[40]

To return to the Basic Law, it was not surprising that the Germans, strongly influenced by bitter memories of the Nazi period, were more concerned with political than with economic and social rights. But in so far as the latter were to a large extent omitted from the Basic Law, it is reasonable to contend that the German Constitution does less than the Italian to enshrine those fundamental principles which were supposed to be the core of Christian Democratic doctrine. However, what actually happens in a country is clearly more important than what the constitution lays down. And here the Germans score highly (with the exception of the *Berufsverbot*), for the Federal Constitutional Court (*Bundesverfassungsgericht*) has taken its task of watching over individual human rights more seriously than its Italian counterpart.[41] It should perhaps be emphasised at this point that Christian Democrats in all countries have been firm advocates of constitutional courts, because they regard constitutional law as a form of 'natural law', and in particular they believe that those fundamental human rights which are written into most constitutions are superior to any other laws.[42]

Although the Italian Constitution decreed the setting up of a Constitutional Court, it did not in fact come into existence until 1956, but since then it has done much useful work in getting rid of Fascist legislation in fields where this legislation conflicted with the human rights guaranteed by the 1948 Constitution. The German Federal Constitutional Court has never hesitated in its championship of *Grundrechte*. In 1956 it took a controversial decision to ban the Communist Party on the grounds that its aims were in conflict with the democratic objectives and basic human rights enshrined in the Basic Law. But, more important, there have been numerous examples of its defending the rights of the individual.[43] One such case occurred in 1969, when the Court directed that if Parliament did not promulgate legislation to ensure that illegitimate children enjoyed the same rights as legitimate (as guaranteed in Article 6 of the Basic Law), the lower courts were to ignore the current legislation in so far as it conflicted with the Basic Law. Within three months the Bundestag and Bundesrat passed a law to ensure that there could be no further legal prejudice against illegitimate children.

In France the Christian Democrats were rather less successful in obtaining constitutional guarantees in the field of human rights. In 1946 the MRP proposed that a Declaration of Human Rights be an integral part of the Constitution. The Christian Democrats argued that, in order to protect the individual against the potentially overweening power of the state, it was essential that human rights should be constitutionally guaranteed, but, in accordance with Christian Democratic theory, they also wanted the rights of trade unions, professional bodies and similar social groups to be written into the Constitution.[44] In addition, the rights of the family should be guaranteed, including the right of the head of the family to choose his child's education and have it paid for by the state, whether he went to a religious or a lay school. But in the political circumstances of the immediate postwar period, it was inevitable that the Christian Democrats did not obtain their 'ideal' Constitution. Even after the rejection of the first constitutional draft on Christian Democratic, Conservative and Radical advice in the referendum of May 1946[45] and the MRP's increased poll in June (27 per cent of votes cast), the Christian Democrats were always in a minority on the constitutional committee on the issue of human rights. Instead of an exhaustive Declaration of Human Rights, the Constitution of the Fourth Republic included only a short preamble on the subject, and although economic and social rights were briefly mentioned, those of the so-called 'natural social groups' (trade unions, etc.) were not, nor did the MRP succeed in getting the inclusion of free education for children at Catholic schools despite a very close vote of 274–272 on 28 August 1946. One of the Christian Democratic leaders, Paul Coste-Floret, described the 1946 preamble as 'one step forward' from the 1789 Declaration of the Rights of Man, but he certainly exaggerated when he said that it marked 'the achievement of political, economic and social democracy in France'.[46]

By the time the constitution of the Fifth Republic was drawn up (in the summer of 1958), the influence of the French Christian Democrats had declined considerably. Only three of the thirty-nine members of the constitutional committee were Christian Democrats. So it was not surprising that the preamble of the Constitution of the Fifth Republic did little to reflect their views on human rights, proclaiming only 'the French people's attachment to the Rights of Man . . . as defined by the Declaration of 1789 and complemented by the preamble of the Constitution of 1946'. Nor has the Constitutional Council of the Fifth Republic (*Conseil Constitutionnel*), originally envisaged by the Christian Democrats as a supreme constitutional court, developed powers comparable to those of its German and Italian counterparts, although in practice, of course, the weakness of the Constitutional Council has been relatively unimportant in a country which has a well-established system of administrative courts (the *Conseil d'Etat* and *Tribunaux Administratifs*) with a high reputation for defending the rights of individuals.

The record, then, of Western European Christian Democrats in the field of human rights and of the Christian values that underpin these rights, has been a creditable one. In practice, of course, there have been shortcomings over the years, and, from the point of view of Christian Democratic theory, lacunae certainly exist in the constitutional theory and practice of France, Germany and Italy, notably over economic and social rights. Nevertheless, it should always be remembered that the rule of law applies more widely in Western Europe of the 1970s than it did in that of the 1930s, and the Christian Democrats can justifiably claim to have contributed significantly towards this situation by their staunch defence of human rights and Christian values in politics.

Democratic Pluralism

As part of their commitment to freedom Christian Democrats are strong advocates of pluralism, both 'horizontal' and 'vertical':[47] 'horizontal' in the sense that they champion parallel and competing institutions in social and economic life – the right, for example, of Christian trade unions to exist side by side with Socialist unions, of free schools to compete with those run by the state, and of private industry to compete with nationalised industry; and 'vertical' pluralism in the sense that Christian Democrats are committed, at least in theory, to the maximum degree of political, economic and social democracy, which means they claim that decisions should be taken, and information given, at the lowest possible level, whether it be nation, region, village, factory or family. In addition, they argue that in the modern world many decisions can only be taken at the international level: hence, for example, their strong commitment to European integration.[48] The principle behind this commitment to democratic pluralism is well expressed in the encyclical *Quadragesimo Anno*: 'It is an injustice, a grave evil, and a disturbance of right order for a larger and higher organisation to arrogate to itself functions which can be performed efficiently by smaller and lower bodies. . . . Of its very nature the true aim of all social activity should be to help individual members of the social body, but never to destroy them.'[49]

The Christian Democratic doctrine of pluralism, then, is a by-product of their commitment to the individual. But just as the individual can only hope to develop his full potential within the context of 'natural social structures', such as the family, trade union or local government unit, so these structures can only fulfil their role on behalf of the individual if there is a sufficient number of them, and if they are actively encouraged and properly organised. Christian Democrats advocate a system of checks and balances both within society and within the formal structures of the state, because, as befits those who profess to take the Gospel as their starting point, they believe that man is 'born in sin', and has to be protected from his own folly: hence their emphasis on legally guaranteed human rights and a form of 'natural law' which is superior to man-made law – the most obvious example being the 'inviolable' first nineteen articles of the German Basic Law. However, in the view of Christian Democrats, constitutional guarantees are not of themselves sufficient. Positive action must also be taken to improve the political and social climate in which men live. The state has a duty towards the individual in such matters as health, education and employment; hence, for example, the Christian Democratic commitment to social welfare, even in countries like West Germany where the Christian Democrats are relatively conservative. But Christian Democrats are suspicious of the over-powerful, centralised state of the twentieth century, and fear that the liberal democratic model may develop the faults of its collectivist counterpart, unless the 'natural social structures' are strong and the institutions of the state carefully balanced. Christian Democrats, then, believe that man, for all his failings, is capable of aspiring to a higher destiny as a responsible, rational being. They see him as a delicate plant, which is liable to wither when left unprotected – as in the nineteenth-century liberal state, but which is equally in danger of wilting under the excessive cosseting of the over-centralised twentieth-century state. It is therefore essential, they argue, to create political and social structures in which this delicate, but potentially resilient, plant can flourish.

Christian Democrats are not strong proponents of liberal democracy or of a pluralistic society out of any *a priori* conviction that liberal democracy is an ideal political model, or that well-organised interest groups have some god-given value. On the contrary, some form of benevolent despotism or Platonic republic might well have been the Christian ideal. But European Christians have come to realise through their experience of authoritarian politics in the twentieth century that liberal democracy and a pluralistic society are more likely to produce a climate in which men can develop as responsible individuals than any other political or social system so far devised. Christian Democrats, however, have always been critical of the nineteenth-century model of liberal democracy, a system in which only a tiny number of territorial representatives could play an active part in politics. Rather they have tended to advocate a particular variant of their own, a model in which not only traditional parliamentarians representing territorial constituencies, but also representatives of the 'natural social groups' – family organisations, trade unions and interest groups generally – could play a part. They have been far from successful in achieving their ideal, and have undergone some criticism as 'corporatists' for pronouncing such views, but they have never abandoned them completely.[50]

The Christian Democrats also have a distinctive view of political parties, which they prefer to see as no more than the most important part of a broad political and social movement. Indeed, they often prefer the word 'union', 'movement' or even 'appeal' (as in the case of the Dutch 'Christian Democratic Appeal') to 'party' with its traditional, and in some countries totalitarian, overtones. Christian Democratic movements or parties, whether national or transnational, do not claim to have the unified ideology of mass movements of the Left, but they claim to be much more than 'Anglo-Saxon' loose-associational electoral organisations. This view of the party as part of a wider political movement is connected with the Christian Democratic view of man. For the ideal Christian Democratic citizen is an educated, responsible person, fully involved in the life of his family, his community and his state (and ultimately of the international community). But having claimed this, the Christian Democrat is at once faced with some awkward questions. How is it possible for a man to be *engagé* in the widest possible sense in a mass industrial society? And what does political involvement really mean in a liberal democracy in which the average citizen can only vote in national elections every four or five years, and in local elections of one sort or another perhaps every two or three years?

The Christian Democratic answer is that industrial society and liberal democracy must be adapted to suit the needs of man, and not vice versa. Given the fact that direct democracy of the type advocated by Rousseau is both impractical (at least in a large state) and open to abuse by totalitarians of the Right and Left through plebiscites, Christian Democrats argue that traditional oligarchic political parties must be transformed into modern political movements, through which the militant can engage himself actively and regularly in politics; and, of course, the 'natural social structures', such as trade unions, family associations and regional bodies, must be given full rein to play their part in this new-style democracy, because they are the vehicle through which the individual can develop his full personality.

The Christian Democratic doctrine of pluralism covers so many aspects of life that a whole book could be written about it. It would, for example, be possible to examine in detail Christian Democratic family policy and educational policy. Family policy is certainly high on the list of Christian Democratic priorities, the family being seen as 'the cornerstone of the structure of society',[51] and Christian Democrats have played a considerable part in ensuring that family allowances are adequate throughout the countries of the European Community. Educational policy is also important to Christian Democrats, but the battle for equal subsidies for free schools was largely fought and won in (or before) the 1950s. Moreover, like family policy, Christian Democratic schools policy has been analysed in depth elsewhere.[52] So here we shall examine Christian Democratic theory and practice in relation to three other aspects of democratic pluralism; namely, industrial relations; constitutional theory and practice; and devolution. The first two will be analysed with particular reference to West Germany and France, and the third with particular reference to Italy.

With regard to industrial relations, Christian Democrats start from the premise that social justice and economic efficiency demand that employees should be fully conversant with the aims and objectives of their company, and that ideally they should play a part in its decision-making process. But precisely what part has remained a matter for debate. Roughly speaking the trade union wings of the Christian Democratic parties have adopted a maximalist position over industrial co-determination, whilst the moderate and conservative wings have been rather sceptical about its practical implementation. In the immediate postwar period the maximalists held sway, but since the 1950s the moderates and conservatives have tended to become more influential. We shall look in some detail at the attempts to move towards industrial co-determination in France and Germany, but it should be noted that Christian Democratic parties also played a key part in obtaining comparable legislation in other European countries, notably Austria (in 1947), Belgium (in 1948) and the Netherlands (in 1950).

In December 1944 a leader-writer in the French Christian Democratic newspaper *L'Aube* wrote that:

> One of today's major social needs is to bring the workers out of the isolated proletarian situation into which they were driven by nineteenth century capitalism . . . and to re-establish them as fully responsible members of their firms, instead of continuing to regard them as interchangeable elements in the impersonal system of production.[53]

The author went on to argue that the solution was not straightforward workers' control as advocated by the Communists and some Socialists, because that would undermine the capitalist system, which, for all its failings, had given 'incomparable material prosperity to the Western world'. Instead, Christian Democrats should aim 'to establish within all firms institutions through which the workers can control their own social interests and receive full information about the situation of their firm'.[54] The German Christian Democrats demanded much the same thing in their Ahlen Programme of 1947:

In firms which are too large for the relationship between worker and
employer to remain on a personal basis, the workers should be guaranteed a
share in control over the basic issues of economic planning and social
policy.[55]

It should be noted that in both cases the Christian Democrats demanded a
'share in control' rather than full control, and that there was no suggestion
that capitalism itself should be abolished.

In France the first step towards giving workers a greater say in the
running of industry was taken in 1945–6 with the setting up of works' councils
(*comités d'entreprise*). The *comités* were (in theory) established in all firms
employing fifty or more wage-earners. The *comité* consisted of the head of the
firm, together with representatives of the workers in firms with up to 500
employees, and representatives of both management and workers in firms
of over 500. The candidates were selected by the most representative trade
unions, and all employees aged eighteen and over could vote, provided they
had worked in the firm for at least six months. Candidates had to be at least
twenty-one years of age, and were elected on a two-ballot system (over 50 per
cent of votes were required at the first ballot; a simple plurality sufficed at
the second).[56] The *comité* had to be consulted about all matters concerned with
the management ('gestion') and general financial policy of the firm. It also
had the right to discuss working conditions with the management, and was
responsible for social affairs within the firm (recreation facilities, etc.). It
could not, however, put forward pay claims.

The Christian Democrats were enthusiastic supporters of the new scheme.
Marcel Poimboeuf, one of the party's trade union deputies, saw works'
councils as 'the beginning of genuine collaboration between the various
elements responsible for production, which for too long have been at loggerheads with one another'.[57] Other Christian Democratic trade unionists such
as Maurice Guérin spoke in the same vein. Enthusiasm for the works' councils
was, however, of no particular value in itself, for most companies simply paid
little or no attention to the *comité d'entreprise* legislation. As early as May
1946 *Le Figaro*'s labour correspondent commented:

> The tool is there . . . the question is, how will it be used ? . . . The *comités
> d'entreprise* are an act of faith. A radical change in habits is required; one
> can only hope for fair dealing from the management and loyal co-operation
> from the workers. Up till now, at least in France, these conditions have
> rarely been met. There is a tradition of excessive secrecy on the side of the
> *patronat*, and of distrust on the part of the workers.[58]

These words could equally well have been written twenty-five years later. But,
in the euphoria of the Liberation period, French Christian Democrats (and
not only French) were inclined to be naïvely over-optimistic about the
possibility of changing ingrained habits by legislation.

Paul Bacon, another Christian Democratic trade unionist, demanded the
proper implementation of the 1945–6 legislation at the 1947 MRP party
congress, and the Christian Democratic newspaper *L'Aube* called for 'a

workers' offensive to persuade the *patronat* to fulfil its obligations with regard to the *comités d'entreprise*'.[59] Bacon also proposed the establishment of a new type of industrial company, the *Société de Travail et d'Epargne*, in which the board would consist of one third workers, one third managers and one third share-holders. All three groups would be elected by their respective constituents, and the company's profits would be distributed in such a way that at least 50 per cent went to the workers. The establishment of such companies, Bacon maintained with some hyperbole, would constitute 'a revolution . . . workers would be liberated economically and spiritually.'[60]

However, these far-reaching proposals for co-determination and profit-sharing came to nothing. As the French economy began to expand in the 1950s they were quietly forgotten, although Bacon himself made another plea for *Sociétés de Travail et d'Epargne* at the 1957 Christian Democratic congress. However, by the mid-1960s it was apparent that many workers were dissatisfied in spite of relatively high wages; indeed, large numbers seem to have felt as alienated as ever from the capitalist system. Progressive Gaullists like Gilbert Grandval were determined to see that employers stopped flouting the *comité d'entreprise* law, and other Gaullist left-wingers such as Louis Vallon and René Capitant started talking again about 'associating capital and labour'.[61] Like the Christian Democrats, some Gaullists had toyed with this idea at the Liberation period.

In 1966 Grandval, who was Pompidou's Minister of Labour, tried to tighten up the *comité d'entreprise* legislation. The main reason for his decision to act was that an inquiry by his own Ministry had shown that *comités d'entreprise* existed in less than 50 per cent of firms employing over 500 workers, and in under 10 per cent of firms employing between fifty and 500, although by law all firms with over fifty workers should have had a *comité*. In some parts of France, notably the north-east, *comités* were almost non-existent. Georges Delfosse, a Christian Democratic labour expert, estimated that no more than 3,000 of the 10,000 *comités* in existence in 1966 were fulfilling their legal obligations.[62] Consequently the Grandval Law of June 1966 laid down that all firms with over fifty employees must report the fact to the Ministry of Labour, which could send an inspector at any time to see that the firm had a properly constituted *comité d'entreprise*; moreover, those elected to the *comité* were to be allowed to attend its meetings for up to twenty hours per month during working time without loss of pay (the 1945–6 legislation had not been clear on this point); finally, the management was to report to the *comité* every three months about the firm's investment situation, number of employees and future plans. The first and third points were less important than they appeared to be, as there were too few inspectors to check upon the 25,000 odd firms which were supposed to have *comités*, and companies could still keep 'confidential information' to themselves (a sore point with the unions). The Christian Democrats welcomed the law as a step in the right direction, although Georges Delfosse told *Témoignage Chrétien* (a newspaper which is representative of left-wing Catholic opinion) that the law was 'a victory for the *patronat*', because it did not go far enough in recognising the role of trade unions in firms.[63]

One of the causes of the Events of May–June 1968 was the high-handed action of Gaullist technocrats, who, like the *patronat*, seemed uninterested in the views of the working class.[64] A new social security package, increasing workers' contributions and decreasing their benefits, was pushed through by decree in October 1967 without any consultation with the trade unions. This technocratic high-handedness produced considerable trade union annoyance, and it was significant that the *Confédération Française Démocratique du Travail* (CFDT), which reacted more positively to the Events of 1968 than the other trade union confederations, showed itself to be as interested in demanding proper recognition for trade unions and *comités d'entreprise* as in wage rises *per se* during the negotiations which led to the end of the general strike. Thus the CFDT, which is the heir to the Catholic/Christian Democratic trade union confederation (the CFTC),[65] repeated a demand made many times over the years by Christian Democratic labour leaders such as Bacon and Delfosse. And in December 1968 they gained some of their ends with Maurice Schumann's trade union law, which fully recognised the right of trade unions to operate within firms, and laid down that henceforth works' councillors could do their business in the firm's time, and that firms were to provide *comités d'entreprise* with an office in each factory. Although the Schumann Law applied only to firms with at least fifty employees (so excluding 3,000,000 workers), it was welcomed by all three major trade union confederations, who realised that the full recognition of trade union rights was one *quid pro quo* for better industrial relations. And yet so long as the majority of French workers belong to the Communist-controlled *Confédération Générale du Travail* (CGT), it is unlikely that there will be any meaningful progress towards co-determination, because the CGT is not really interested in class reconciliation and 'collaboration' with capitalists. The present industrial structure in France certainly remains a far cry from the new type of industrial partnership between shareholders, management and workers envisaged by the more progressive Christian Democrats.

West Germany, Belgium and the Netherlands all have social climates and systems of industrial relations which come somewhat closer to the Christian Democratic ideal than those of France, although in no case has the long-term objective of total partnership between capital and labour been achieved.[66] Here we shall examine the case of West Germany.

Workers' participation in the Federal Republic takes two forms, that which is embodied in the works council (*Betriebsrat*) legislation of 1952 and 1972, and that which is embodied in the co-determination (*Mitbestimmung*) legislation of 1951, 1952 and 1976.[67] The German Christian Democrats have been united in their support for *Betriebsräte*, but much more divided in their attitude to *Mitbestimmung*. In general, they accept that workers should be kept as fully informed about their firm's activities as possible, and that they should have a chance to influence management decisions, but that in the last analysis management must manage, because only trained managers have the necessary expertise to take appropriate decisions. It follows that most German Christian Democrats have been sceptical about the extension of co-determination on the basis of complete parity between management and workers, but have had no doubt about the value of keeping employees well informed. Hence the Christian Democrats supported the works council legislation of 1952 and 1972, although at the time of the latter they were in opposition.

The 1952 works council law, complemented by the improvements made in 1972, was in direct line with Christian Democratic theory. Since May 1952 every West German firm employing five or more people has had to have a *Betriebsrat*, the equivalent of the French *comité d'entreprise*. Every three years the employer must provide time and facilities for the election of a works council. All employees over eighteen are eligible to vote, including (since 1972) foreign workers. The 1972 act also provides that both sexes should be proportionately represented on the *Betriebsrat*. The works council legislation does not recognise any formal connection between the works councils and the trade unions (unlike the situation in France since the 1968 Schumann Law), but works councils have the right to call in outside trade unionists in an advisory capacity, and in practice most works council members tend to be active trade unionists.[68] Works councils have the right to be consulted by management about all matters concerned with the welfare of the employees, for example working conditions, vocational training and holiday schedules. They must be consulted by the management about mergers and shutdowns, as well as about changes in the workforce, for example the employer must obtain the works council's consent to appoint and dismiss staff or to transfer or re-classify any of the firm's employees. In firms employing over a hundred persons, the works councils have even greater powers: in particular they must be given quarterly reports about the financial state and forward planning of the firm. In cases of dispute either the works council or the management can appeal to the industrial courts (*Arbeitsgerichte*). However, in the first instance the dispute must be referred by either side to the *Land* (state) government for mediation, and the *Land* Minister of Labour may in turn refer the case to a conciliation board comprising representatives of both sides, with an independent chairman. Under the provisions of the 1972 act the conciliation board's decisions are normally binding on both parties.

Whereas the Christian Democrats gave their full support to the important works council legislation of 1952 and 1972, their attitude to industrial co-determination, i.e. workers' participation in management, has been much more *nuancé*. The co-determination (*Mitbestimmung*) law of 1951 provided for co-management on a parity basis in all coal and steel companies with a payroll of over 1,000 employees (in 1975 there were fifty-seven such companies).[69] These companies are managed by two boards. The supervisory board (*Aufsichtsrat*) has eleven, fifteen or twenty-one members, depending on the size of the company. Half of the members of these supervisory boards are appointed by the shareholders and half by the employees. An extra member (the 'neutral man') is co-opted by joint agreement of the shareholders' and workers' representatives. He represents the public interest and has a casting vote in cases of deadlock. The *Aufsichtsrat* is responsible for general policy-making. The second board, the management executive committee (*Vorstand*), is responsible for the everyday running of the firm. This board consists of three members, the managing director, the production manager and the labour director. All three are equal partners, and the last-named cannot be appointed or dismissed without the approval of the workers' representatives on the supervisory board. The 1951 law, then, gave workers a legal right to co-management in the coal and steel industries. But not all Christian Democrats were happy about this development, particularly those on the conservative wing of the party. First of all, they did not like the way that Parliament had been 'intimidated' into passing the law by the threat of a general strike. But, as regards the law itself, they argued that the workers were over-represented; this conflicted with their belief that management must manage. In addition, the Christian Democrats were critical of the system where-by only two of the five workers' representatives had to be members of the firm concerned (and even they had to be approved by the appropriate trade union confederation); the remainder could be appointed from outside, and in practice were usually full-time trade union officials who came from the Socialist-dominated *Deutscher Gewerkschaftsbund* (DGB). This conflicted with the Christian Democratic idea that co-determination should mean co-operation between managers and workers *within* the firm.

In contrast, and in line with their theory, the Christian Democrats gave their full support to the 1952 co-determination law, which gave employees only one third representation on the supervisory boards of all companies with between 500 and 2,000 employees, and no exclusive right to appoint any individual member of the management board.

For a decade after the 1951 law the issue of *Mitbestimmung* lay dormant in German politics, but it was then revived by the DGB, which began to demand the extension of parity co-determination (the coal and steel model) throughout industry. So long as the conservative Ludwig Erhard was Chancellor (1963–6), the Christian Democrats showed little interest in the issue: indeed at his governmental declaration after the 1965 general election, Erhard specifically ruled out any extension of *Mitbestimmung*. But after the fall of Erhard and the setting up of the Grand Coalition of Christian Democrats and Social Democrats, which lasted from 1966–9, the CDU–CSU was forced to define its position. At first it was reluctant to do so, and as the SPD was at this time anxious to avoid a 'radical' image, the two parties agreed to set up a commission to examine industrial co-determination and make recommenda-tions in the light of its findings. The commission was appointed in 1968, the year in which the CDU at its Berlin Congress came out in favour of improv-ing the works council (*Betriebsrat*) legislation, but against any extension of *Mitbestimmung*. By the time the commission reported in 1970, the Christian Democrats were in opposition and there was a Social Democrat-Liberal Coalition in Bonn. However, both Government and Opposition parties had to define their attitude towards co-determination, which had by now developed into a politically contentious issue.

The commission reported favourably on the operation of co-determination, which, it was claimed, had not affected companies adversely, either in terms of efficiency or profitability. However, arguing that the main objective of companies should be to operate as efficient economic units, and that economic efficiency required effective decision-making, the report came out against a straightforward extension of parity co-determination, as demanded by the DGB and by a majority of SPD deputies. Instead, the report proposed supervisory boards with six shareholders' representatives, four workers and two outsiders, although on certain issues (closely connected with working conditions) it wanted the workers to have what would amount to a veto.[70]

The DGB welcomed the report half-heartedly, approving its endorsement of *Mitbestimmung*, but rejecting its recommendations in so far as they failed to endorse parity co-determination. The SPD was divided: the party leadership accepted the commission's proposals, although it did not support the special workers' veto in certain issues, but the party's trade unionists and the Young Socialists agreed with the DGB that the 'biased' form of co-determination proposed in the report was inadequate, and that they must continue to campaign for full parity. Meanwhile, the SPD's partners in government, the FDP (Liberal Party), accepted the report's recommendation that co-determination should be extended, but disagreed with the model proposed. Instead, the FDP, at its important congress in Freiburg in 1971 (at which a new programme was drawn up), proposed that the supervisory boards should consist of six representatives of the shareholders, two representatives of senior management, and four workers. Although in government with the Social Democrats, these proposals placed the Liberals not only to the left of the SPD on the issue of co-determination, but to the left of the moderate and progressive wings of the CDU.

Even before the report of 1970, the Christian Democrats were divided on the issue of co-determination. The left wing of the CDU, represented by the 100,000 or so members of the Social Committees (*Sozialausschüsse*), led by Hans Katzer and Norbert Blüm, had come out in favour of parity co-determination at their Offenburg conference in 1967.[71] The right wing, however, led by Franz-Josef Strauss, chairman of the Bavarian CSU, and Klaus Scheufelen, chairman of the Economic Council (the business 'wing' of the Christian Democratic movement), were against any extension of co-determination.[72] The war of words between the two sides was extremely bitter in the late 1960s, with Blüm pointedly emphasising that the CDU was a people's party (*Volkspartei*) and not a 'branch colony of the Economic Council'.[73] The party agreed to play down the issue at the 1969 general election and await the commission's report. But after 1970 the Christian Democrats had no option but to define their position.

At the CDU congress at Düsseldorf in January 1971 the majority of delegates supported a compromise based largely on the proposals of Professor Kurt Biedenkopf, one of the party's experts on co-determination.[74] Biedenkopf proposed a 'seven-five model', i.e. that supervisory boards should have seven shareholders' representatives to five workers' representatives; but he was against any special role for the workers' directors (as proposed in the 1970 report). This compromise could be no more than provisional, as it was rejected by the Social Committees, who complained that the congress had 'watered down' Biedenkopf's already weak proposals.[75]

After their defeat at the 1972 general election the Christian Democrats, with the important exception of the CSU, in effect moved to the left over

Mitbestimmung, for at their Hamburg congress in November 1973 they accepted the principle of equal representation for shareholders and employees on supervisory boards, with the important proviso that in cases of deadlock on the *Aufsichtsrat*, the *Vorstand* would have the right to act on its own initiative.[76]

Meanwhile, the government parties remained at loggerheads over the issue: indeed after the CDU Hamburg congress there was a wider degree of consensus between the CDU (with the exception of the CSU) and the SPD over *Mitbestimmung*, than between the SPD and FDP. In 1974 Werner Maihofer of the FDP tried to work out a compromise, but failed, and it was not until 1976 that final agreement was reached on a system which has more of the characteristics of a CDU–SPD compromise than of a SPD–FDP compromise.

In the coal and steel industries parity co-determination on the supervisory board continues as before. Likewise, for medium-sized firms (those with between 500 and 2,000 employees) the 1952 legislation continues to apply, i.e. such companies have two-thirds shareholders' and one-third workers' representatives on their supervisory boards. The new legislation applies to companies with over 2,000 employees not already covered by the coal and steel legislation, and affects about 650 middle-to-large firms, which together make up about 70 per cent of West German industry and employ over seven million workers. The 1976 law gives the employees parity with shareholders on the supervisory board.[77] However, on the assumption that senior management and shareholders are likely to have more in common than senior management and workers, the system is tilted in favour of the managers and shareholders, provided they can work in harmony. On a supervisory board with ten shareholders' representatives and ten employees' representatives, for example, one of the latter must be a senior executive. Both sides elect their own chairman and deputy chairman, and then by a two-thirds majority a joint chairman. However, if they fail to agree, the shareholders' chairman presides, with the workers' chairman as his deputy. The supervisory board then appoints the management board (*Vorstand*) by a two-thirds majority for the day-to-day running of the company. If such a majority cannot be found, the chairman can, after going through a complex mediation procedure, opt for a simple majority. However, experience in the coal and steel industries suggests that such problems rarely arise.

It is perhaps too early to pronounce judgement on the extended version of co-determination in West Germany. But, in the context of Christian Democratic theory, it can already be said that the system of industrial relations which operates in West Germany goes a considerable way towards the Christian Democratic objective of maximum information for workers, combined with a system of co-management weighted in favour of the shareholders and senior company executives. In France, on the other hand, the old traditions of nineteenth-century capitalism have died hard. Neither by law nor in practice are French *comités d'entreprise* as powerful as German *Betriebsräte*. The French *patronat* remains secretive, and the biggest trade union confederation, the Communist-controlled CGT, is opposed to co-determination, which is seen as a compromise with capitalism, whilst the Socialist-

Catholic CFDT is much less enamoured of co-determination than was the (mainly) Christian Democratic CFTC. Whether in the last analysis a system of total partnership between capital and labour – the Christian Democratic long-term objective – can ever be achieved is, of course, highly doubtful, because the two sides of industry inevitably have divergent interests over many issues. In practice, therefore, it is not surprising that Christian Democrats have opted for more down-to-earth schemes for improving industrial relations: notably better information for employees and some share in influencing company policy. But neither West Germany nor France has come near to achieving the Christian Democratic ideal of an economic and social democracy from which class conflicts have been eliminated. Nevertheless, in these countries and throughout Western Europe, Christian Democrats have made an important contribution to transforming the nineteenth-century model of capitalism into something much more humane.

It is now time to turn to two further aspects of 'democratic pluralism'. Just as Christian Democratic theorists have been profoundly critical of nineteenth-century economic liberalism, so they have also criticised the traditional models of liberal democracy: firstly, because these models allowed only a tiny number of territorial representatives to play an active part in politics; and secondly, because such models encouraged a growing centralisation of power at the level of the nation-state. In contrast, Christian Democratic theorists advocated an 'improved' type of liberal democracy, in which not only traditional parliamentarians, but also representatives of the 'natural social groups' could participate. In practice this led to the strong Christian Democratic commitment firstly to bicameralism, sometimes of a particular type in which the 'natural social groups' would have a part to play in the second chamber, and secondly to the devolution of powers to regional governments. Needless to say, the Christian Democrats have not always achieved their ideal. The French constitutional debates of 1945–6, however, provide an interesting example of the type of objectives the Christian Democrats had in mind.

In January 1946, Paul Coste-Floret, one of the MRP's leading constitutional lawyers, stated that the Christian Democrats were fundamentally opposed to *gouvernement d'assemblée*, i.e. to the concentration of virtually all political power in the National Assembly, as advocated by the Communists and Socialists. Instead the Christian Democrats favoured a 'mixed' system, in which a second chamber could play an important, if subordinate, role in the legislative process. The second chamber would be a 'house of second thoughts', ensuring that legislation was carefully drafted. It would have the power to delay in the form of a suspensive veto. But the second chamber's unique feature, distinguishing it from the old Senate of the Third Republic, would be that 'natural social groups' would be represented in it:

Are there not regional and local interests which must be defended? At the very moment when we are moving towards a tightening of community bonds, it would be illogical to give the country a purely individualistic representative system. The second chamber should represent these collective and community interests which are at present unrepresented.[78]

This proposal was supported by Maurice Guérin, a leading Christian Democratic trade unionist, who not surprisingly proposed that trade unions should also be represented in the second chamber. But, with the two large parties of the Left firmly opposed to such proposals, which in their view smacked of 'corporatism' and Vichy, the Christian Democrats did not achieve their new-style second chamber. However, it is interesting to note that schemes for an 'Economic Senate', representing social groups, regions and overseas territories, were put forward again fifteen years later by the Christian Democrats and the followers of Pierre Mendès-France. They had an even more ambitious scheme for combining the Senate and the Economic and Social Council; this new 'Economic Senate' would have had an important role in the legislative process and in planning the economy, whilst remaining subordinate to the National Assembly.[79] But neither in the Fourth nor in the Fifth Republic did such Christian Democratic proposals for representing 'natural social groups' come to anything.

In the political circumstances of the immediate postwar period it was perhaps inevitable that the French Christian Democrats failed to achieve their objective. The Communists and Socialists had an overall majority in the first Constituent Assembly (October 1945–May 1946), but their constitutional draft, essentially *gouvernement d'assemblée*, was rejected at the referendum of 5 May 1946 by a million votes. In the second Constituent Assembly (June–November 1946) the Communists and Socialists no longer had an overall majority and the Christian Democratic point of view gained some ground (in June 1946 the Christian Democrats reached their electoral zenith: 5·5 million votes, i.e. 27 per cent of those cast, resulting in the return of 169 deputies, 16 more than the Communists, the runners-up in the election). The concessions made to the Christian Democrats (after June 1946) with regard to the Presidency were quite substantial. In contrast to the original constitutional proposals it was now agreed that the President should be elected in secret by both Houses of Parliament; that he should preside over the Council of Ministers, the Committee of National Defence and the High Council of the Judiciary; and that he should appoint the prime minister without having first to consult the president of the National Assembly, (although the prime minister designate's programme still required the Assembly's approval). The MRP, in line with other European Christian Democrats, wanted a head of state with real, if limited, powers, and the party was very uneasy at the prospect of a virtually unbridled, unicameral legislature. Such an institution would be in total contrast with Christian Democratic theories about institutional checks and balances.

Twelve years later the French Christian Democrats at first welcomed the strengthening of the President's powers, which was one of the immediate consequences of the setting up of the Fifth Republic. Pierre Henri Teitgen, one of three Christian Democrats on the 1958 constitutional committee, told his party's National Committee:

The President has been given formidable powers, but he is neither the hierarchical superior to, nor the antagonist of, the Prime Minister. The

Prime Minister retains control of the policy of the government; he is responsible to Parliament; this is a genuine parliamentary régime.[80]

As it turned out, Teitgen was wrong. The Fifth Republic developed not into a parliamentary but into a presidential régime, and it is not surprising that the Christian Democrats were soon to be found criticising de Gaulle's authoritarian use of power in just the same way as they had criticised the excessive power vested in the National Assembly by the Left's proposed constitution of 1946.[81]

In West Germany, the Christian Democrats, particularly those of the South German *Länder* (states) grouped in the Ellwangen *Kreis,* strove hard to achieve considerable powers for the *Länder* and for the *Bundesrat,* the second chamber which represents the *Länder* through delegates sent by the *Land* governments in accordance with their political complexion. The Bavarians were not surprisingly the strongest supporters of decentralisation:

We are federalists from conviction and experience. We reject the centralised unitary state was much as sterile separatism. . . . The German federal state, for which we are striving, should arise from the voluntary union of the individual *Länder.*[82]

But all the Christian Democrats in the Parliamentary Council, which drew up the Basic Law (constitution) of the Federal Republic, favoured a decentralised system.[83] And this was in line with Christian Democratic theory about the desirability of taking decisions at the lowest possible level and balancing up one institution against another in a pluralistic liberal democracy. Of course, in Germany the Christian Democrats had the advantage of preaching to the converted, for even if some of the *Länder* were artificial creations and the Social Democrats favoured a more centralised state, there was a long tradition of federalism, or at least of regional identity, on which to build.

Italy, on the other hand, where in some regions there was also a strong sense of identity, provides an interesting example of the type of conflict which can arise between Christian Democratic theory and practice in the field of institutional pluralism. Almost all the Christian Democrats in the Italian Constituent Assembly were in favour of devolving powers to the regions. True, a distinction must be made between the out-and-out federalists, heirs to the traditions of Luigi Sturzo, who as long ago as 1919 had been demanding 'administrative decentralisation, local autonomy and the construction of the regions',[84] and the northern Christian Democrats, who wanted to clip the wings of the old Napoleonic state without risking the establishment of a confederation which might weaken Italy politically and economically. But the whole Christian Democratic party seemed to be convinced that some measure of devolution was necessary, both as a safeguard against any possible abuse of an over-centralised state by some future Mussolini, and in order that the 'natural social groups' should have a chance to voice their opinions. In the view of Attilio Piccioni, the DC Secretary, such groups could hardly be represented at the national level, whilst the provinces were too small for the adequate representation of any but the smallest of interest groups.[85] The obvious answer was to follow up the proposals of Luigi Sturzo and institute regional governments.

Given the composition of the Constituent Assembly, it was not surprising that a compromise form of regional government resulted from the debates of 1946–8, for the Liberals and Monarchists (i.e. Conservatives) were as firmly against devolution as they had been ever since the unification of Italy, and the Communists and Socialists (especially the latter) maintained that the working-class movement would be split if too much power were devolved to the regions. The form of regional government adopted by the Constituent Assembly has thus been appropriately described as 'a sort of half-way house between outright federalism and outright centralism'.[86] In particular Articles 115 and 117 of the Constitution appeared to conflict with each other. The former declared that the regions were 'autonomous bodies having their own powers and functions'; they were to be responsible for public health, public works, agriculture and forestry, public transport, the water supply and regional planning. However, Article 117 immediately limited the extent of this regional jurisdiction by laying down that 'such legislation may not contrast with the national interest'; if it did the central government could overrule the region.

The situation was complicated further by the setting up of two types of region. Article 116 granted a special form of autonomy to Sicily, Val d'Aosta, Trentino-Alto Adige, Friulia-Venezia Giulia and Sardinia. These regions were granted more wide-reaching powers than the others.[87] They were also given them much sooner. It looked as if these regions, all of which had had separatist movements over the years, were being given special privileges in order to keep them loyal to the Italian State. By 1948 all the regions of special status except Friulia-Venezia Giulia (which had to wait until 1964) had their own governments. The remaining fourteen regions (fifteen after the decision to separate Molise from Abruzzi in 1963) were Piedmont, Lombardy, Veneto, Liguria, Emilia-Romagna, Tuscany, Umbria, Marche, Lazio, Abruzzi-Molise, Campania, Apulia, Basilicata and Calabria. They had to wait until 1970 before regional governments were at last set up.

The regional institutions consist of an elected Regional Council, which in turn elects a President and a Government (*giunta*). Every law passed by the Regional Council must, however, be approved by the Commissioner appointed by the central government; he is in effect a super-prefect. If the Commissioner does not approve a law (and he must make a decision within thirty days), he can return it to the Regional Council. If the latter passes the law again – this time it must be by an absolute majority of its members – the central government may submit it to the Constitutional Court (if it disputes its legality) or to Parliament (if the conflict is political). In the latter case Parliament can dissolve the Regional Council if it decides that the Council has 'performed an act contrary to the Constitution', after which a regional election must be held within three months. The original constitutional provisions were later supplemented by various laws concerned with voting rights, eligibility of candidates, electoral laws (proportional representation in all cases), and the thorny problem of financial 'autonomy'. Regional governments are permitted to collect certain taxes, but these amount to no more than about one seventh of their required income; the rest comes from central government grants. The final jurisdictional boundaries between the central and regional governments in financial matters (as in a great many other areas) have still not been finally worked out, but it is clear that the central government has not loosened its grip on the purse-strings.[88]

One may well ask why the constitutional provisions for the setting up of the regions were not implemented until 1970 (twenty-two years after the promulgation of the Constitution), especially when every post-war Italian Government has been dominated by the DC, the party which professed itself to be strongly in favour of regional devolution. The Italian Christian Democrats can usually find good reasons for inaction. Regional devolution (or the lack of it) makes for no exception. In the immediate postwar years it was argued that the country's weak economy demanded strong central government. Then, as the Cold War developed, another argument was put forward, namely that Italy could not risk the possibility – remote though it was – that Communist-controlled regions such as Tuscany and Emilia might attempt to secede and join the Soviet Union, an action which would have provoked civil war. But there can be little doubt that the most important reason for inaction in the 1950s was simply that the DC was dominated almost to the end of the decade by its more conservative elements, those very elements in Italian society who have opted for the *status quo* (whatever it was at any given time) from unification to the present day. With the 'opening to the Left' in the 1960s regionalism became once more a live issue. Fanfani, Rumor and Moro all expressed their interest in regionalism at various times, but it was the last-named above all who fought for its implementation. Moro eventually succeeded after what was probably the longest parliamentary battle in Italian history: it took 213 votes in the Chamber, 825 in the Senate and 600 speeches before the regions (i.e. those without special status) finally came into being in 1970.

But what exactly has been achieved? There are now twenty regions (five of special status), all with their own elected Councils and Governments. But many questions remain unanswered. The precise jurisdictions of the central and regional governments have not been delineated. The creation of another layer of government increases the danger of bureaucratic proliferation at a time when Italy already suffers from an over-staffed, inefficient civil service. It is also likely to worsen the serious problem of corruption, euphemistically sheltering under the names of *sottogoverno* and *clientelismo*. Signor Guidicci, the Socialist economist, has suggested that the regions, which should have been set up with the European Community in mind, are already too small to be viable administrative units. Other critics have pointed out the considerable economic disparities between the regions. Lombardy, for example, with one-seventh of Italy's population, produces almost one-third of the country's Gross Domestic Product, whilst the combined contribution to GDP of Abruzzi, Molise, Campania and Basilicata is about one-third of Lombardy's. At the same time the limited financial powers granted to the regions make it unlikely that a healthy spirit of local autonomy will develop; and no government, regional or national, can retain much self-respect if it has to rely on financial handouts. And yet, according to Christian Democratic theory, the most important reason for devolution is to allow democracy to flourish at the grass-roots level. Finally, in contrast to Christian Democratic theory, there is no evidence that family associations, consumers' organisations, trade union branches or other 'natural social groups' have gained anything out of regional devolution. At the regional, as at the national, level the chief beneficiaries of the present Italian system have been the professional politicians and the bureaucrats. Indeed, the Christian Democratic theory about institutional pluralism has fallen far short of fulfilment in Italy.

Conclusion

In the course of this Chapter I hope to have shown that, whilst there are a number of important political and social principles underpinning Christian Democratic theory, these do not amount to a sufficiently precise corpus of doctrine for it to be appropriate to refer to Christian Democratic ideology. Indeed, part of the appeal of Christian Democracy undoubtedly lies in its pragmatism, but it is not the unalloyed pragmatism ('we know best how to run the government, full stop') of American Republicans and Democrats or even of British Conservatives. Christian Democracy is essentially a *European* phenomenon, not an American or British phenomenon, and as such it is a product of its environment – a more 'ideological' environment than that of the United States or the United Kingdom.[89] Professor Joseph Rovan, the distinguished historian of Christian Democracy, has argued that the 'Christian' emphasis has declined in recent years, but that it is a mistake to view Christian Democrats simply as Conservatives, even though there is a considerable degree of convergence between German Christian Democracy and British Conservatism.[90] Indeed, as the huge volume on Christian Democratic party programmes published by the Konrad Adenauer Stiftung[91] and the considerable number of Christian Democratic theoretical journals testify,[92] Christian Democratic politicians, academics and journalists are still concerned to relate theory to practice. Moreover, as has been shown in this Chapter, Christian Democrats have tried to apply their principles to their politics in such matters as human rights, industrial co-determination, constitutional separation of powers and devolution. And, as will become apparent in the Chapters which follow, Christian Democrats have other principled commitments, such as their strong support for European integration and the Atlantic Alliance, based on their desire to safeguard liberal democracy, and their commitment to social market economies, based on their desire to reconcile economic liberty with social justice.

It must by now be apparent that it is inappropriate to refer to Christian Democratic ideology, if by ideology one means a coherent view of politics based on a precise programme and objectives. However, there can be no doubt that both in theory and practice there are a number of political and philosophical principles which distinguish Christian Democracy from Socialism and Conservatism, even from the more moderate versions of these political philosophies. Like Conservatives, Christian Democrats stress the importance of the individual, but with a somewhat different emphasis, for Christian Democrats strive with equal vigour both to encourage individual initiative and to protect the weak in society. Like Social Democrats, Christian Democrats stress the importance of human rights, but again with a somewhat different emphasis, in that they see human rights primarily in terms of Christian values. Like both Social Democrats and Conservatives, Christian Democrats are committed to liberal democracy and to social pluralism, but their particular emphasis on the role of the 'natural social structures' distinguishes them from either of their rivals.

At the end of the day Christian Democratic theory may look rather like a rag-bag, garnered from the political and social theories of others. Moreover, some Christian Democratic objectives, such as the long-term goal of total partnership between capital and labour, or the hope that eventually there will be a large majority of politically active, socially responsible citizens, appear utopian to say the least. And in practice the Christian Democrats have often failed to live up to the ideals outlined in their early manifestos, or to implement the type of economic and social democracy to which they are theoretically committed. But on the positive side it cannot be denied that Christian Democrats have consistently stressed the importance of individual human rights; have striven to build 'capitalism with a human face', and in the process have helped to bring about better industrial relations and a more humane society; and, perhaps most important of all, have played a key part in bringing European Conservatives to accept the tenets of liberal democracy.

3
Christian Democracy in Italy

Christian Democracy in Italy cannot be defined: it is simply an established fact. (Jacques Nobécourt, *L'Italie à vif*, p. 63.)

Nobécourt's comment touches upon the unique nature of the Italian Christian Democratic Party (*Democrazia Cristiana*, DC), which is regularly supported by two-fifths of the electorate and has been in power ever since the war, either as the dominant coalition partner, the normal situation, or on its own, forming *monocolore* governments.[1]

The DC is not so much a party as a coalition of factions, or, to use the less pejorative Italian term, *correnti* (currents). It is difficult to categorise the DC in the usual terms of political science. Although the DC has a large membership – approximately one and three-quarter million members in the late 1970s – it is not what Duverger would describe as a 'mass' party, because it does not have a unified, common ideology.[2] It does, however, have what Geiger would describe as a 'mentality', based on anti-fascism, anti-communism and a Catholic view of life.[3] It has some of the characteristics of an 'electoral' party, but owing to its close identification with the Catholic sub-culture it would be wrong to categorise the DC as a catch-all voters' party of the Anglo-Saxon type. Equally, in spite of the DC's important links with the Catholic Church, it would be a mistake to classify it as a straightforward 'confessional' party, i.e. a party whose main function is simply to try to protect the interests of Catholics and to implement the policies of the Vatican. The DC does have some of the characteristics of the British Conservative Party or the German CDU–CSU. It is, for example, *par excellence* a party of government, led by pragmatists who have an insatiable appetite for power, and it is supported by moderate conservatives from all classes. Yet the DC differs considerably from these Northern European parties in its organisational structure and political philosophy. Indeed, the DC must be seen as a uniquely Italian phenomenon – a coalition of mini-parties run by an oligarchy of factional leaders.

The DC has been compared to a ship whose crew is in a permanent state of mutiny, except that at election times the crew sink their differences, man their guns, and fire off a succession of broadsides at their enemies to port and starboard. These salvoes consist mainly of anti-Communist and anti-Fascist slogans, and it may seem surprising that such a negative approach to politics has been so successful. But then the Italians are renowned for their cynical and negative attitude to politics.[4] Moreover, when one bears in mind that the Italian Communist Party (PCI) is the biggest in the non-Communist world and that memories of the Mussolini period (not to mention the postwar violence of the neo-Fascists) remain vivid, perhaps it is not so surprising. In addition, at elections the DC has the advantage of receiving powerful support from the Bishops' Conference, from most of Italy's 25,000 priests and from the Civic Committees of Catholic Action. And this support, when allied with the electorate's continuing uncertainty about the long-term objectives of the PCI, has been sufficient to ensure that the DC has always won a relative majority of the votes cast at national elections despite the incompetence and corruption of individual Christian Democrats and the *immobilismo* characteristic of the 'DC régime'.[5] Moreover, in recent years the DC has – as Giovanni Sartori forecast it would[6] – mopped up more and more lay votes on the Right and in the Centre as the PCI has steadily strengthened its position as *the* party of the Left. Another extremely important reason for the continued resilience of the DC is that it has succeeded in building itself into the Italian social structure by means of political patronage: all over the country are people who owe their jobs, their pensions, their new village hall or local highway to Christian Democratic patronage.[7]

DC Membership and Organisation

The DC is well implanted in the country, with a very large membership. At the time of the 1976 general election it claimed to have 1·9 million members. Even allowing for some inflation of numbers it probably does have between 1·5 and 1·7 million members, about 4·5 per cent of Italy's adult population. This figure has been fairly constant since the mid 1960s, up to which point the DC had grown from 600,000 members in 1946 (2·2 per cent of the adult population) to 1·4 million in 1962 (4·3 per cent of the adult population).[8] Since then the growth in numbers has merely kept pace with the growth in the population of Italy (54·1 million at the national census of 1971). The increase in membership between 1946–62 took place almost entirely in the south and the islands, whose local leaders however often claimed inflated membership figures in order to increase the bargaining strength of their faction at National Congresses.[9] Southern fiefs such as that established by the Gava brothers in Naples were particularly prone to use such tactics, whilst other leaders such as Aldo Moro in Apulia and Emilio Colombo in Basilicata could rely on a combination of patronage and southern deference to secure and strengthen their local positions.[10] Other areas where there has been evidence of inflated membership figures include Latium (Giulio Andreotti's fief), Avellino (Fiorentino Sullo's), and Cagliari and Nuoro (Antonio Segni's).[11]

The DC claims to be an 'inter-class' party. In terms of its electorate it does reflect the present Italian social structure quite accurately, but in terms of party membership, and even more of leadership, the reflection is less precise. Approximately 45 per cent of DC voters are wage-earners; about 36 per cent are self-employed, the vast majority being shop-keepers and small-scale farmers and businessmen; about 15 per cent receive monthly salaries – they are mainly executive grade civil servants and schoolteachers; just over 3 per cent are students and full-time practitioners of religion; and 1·6 per cent are large-scale entrepreneurs and professional people.[12] These figures approximate closely to those of the nation as a whole, and confirm that the DC is a true *Volkspartei* in terms of its electorate. It is also very much the party of the Catholic sub-culture. Despite the decline of organised religion and Church attendance in Italy, recent surveys indicate that 'religion is of prime importance in the political divisions of Italy'.[13] This is not to say that church-goers and DC voters are synonymous, but rather that those people who view the Church in a generally favourable light – whether or not they practise their religion – are more likely to vote for the DC than for any other party.[14] The DC is strongest in the 'white' or Catholic areas of Italy, notably the Veneto and parts of Lombardy, but since the 1950s it has increased its membership considerably in the south and the islands, and now it can claim to be a national party in terms of geographical spread except that it remains relatively weak in the anti-clerical regions of central Italy.

About one quarter of DC members are wage-earners, proportionately much less than the DC working-class electorate and than the PCI membership (50 per cent wage-earners), but significant nevertheless. Another 25 per cent are self-employed farmers, shop-keepers and small businessmen, whilst almost 25 per cent are housewives. Of the DC's 1·7 million members less than 5 per cent are 'activists', using this term very loosely to cover those who attend two or more party meetings a year. At elections, however, the 60,000 odd DC activists play a key part in distributing propaganda and encouraging the electors to turn out and vote. But the most important activists are the 13,600 section leaders and the 800 full-time provincial officials and 300 national officials. The higher echelons within the party, i.e. the provincial and national officials, are not exactly reflective of the diverse membership of the DC as a whole, since about 80 per cent of these senior officials are of middle-class background, with teachers predominating in the north and lawyers in the south. Besides the DC's social diversity, one of its great sources of strength is that it has a powerful hold on local government at all levels, as well as in all parts of the country except the 'red belt' of central Italy. Even after the regional elections of 1975, when the Communists and Socialists made serious inroads into the DC's urban vote, the DC claimed to have 360 of Italy's 1,000 regional councillors, 990 of its 2,760 provincial councillors and approximately half of its 144,000 local (communal) councillors.[15] Even allowing for the probable inflation of these figures, at least at the communal level where many candidates do not stand under party labels, the DC is clearly in a strong position to control local patronage, particularly in its areas of greatest strength, the north-east and the south.

Compared with other European Christian Democratic parties the DC is undoubtedly a well-organised party. This may seem surprising in view of the fact that the DC has been in power ever since the war, because in general governing parties, particularly those which lack a precise ideology, have a tendency to ignore their organisation in the country so long as they are in power in the capital. Since Fanfani's secretaryship (1954–9), however, the DC has always paid close attention to its nationwide organisation. In the first place the DC has been kept up to the mark by its chief rival, the Communist Party, which is a highly organised, structured and disciplined party.[16] Indeed, as various scholars have noted, the formal structure of the DC has many similarities with those of the PCI and PSI.[17] Secondly, the Italian electorate is 'politically under-socialised', i.e. there is a relatively low level of political knowledge and awareness in Italy. This means that it is particularly important for parties to be well-organised in order to mobilise their voters at elections. Thirdly, in a country where clientelism and patronage are still essential characteristics of the political culture, no party can afford to ignore its grass-roots organisation. Finally, although the DC has been in power since the war, it has – at least since 1953 – been only the 'party of relative majority', restricted to about 40 per cent of the electorate and a similar proportion of seats in Parliament; in other words the DC, unlike for example the CDU–CSU under Adenauer, has never been able to lapse into complacency about its electoral strength.

When the founders of the DC set about organising their party between 1943 and 1945, it was natural that they should look back to the *Partito Popolare* – Alcide De Gasperi, the DC's leading figure, had been the *Partito Popolare's* last Secretary – and the present-day structure of the DC is not surprisingly quite closely modelled on that of the *Partito Popolare*. Like its Christian Democratic precursor, the DC has local sections, provincial councils, a national council and secretariat, and national congresses. In addition the DC has a regional organisation, based on regional councils, but in spite of the regional reform of 1970 (instituting fifteen new regions in addition to the five set up soon after the war) the regional councils have not supplanted the provincial councils in importance, and the latter continue to play a significant political role, particularly in the run-up period before national elections. At each level of the party organisation functional responsibility is divided between an assembly or congress, an executive committee or directorate, and a secretariat.

In 1976 there were about 13,600 local sections. Their officials are unpaid, and they are mostly active only at elections, when they are helped by the Civic Committees of Catholic Action. Between 1954–9, during his first period as party Secretary, Fanfani tried to create local units below the level of the section, i.e. units comparable to the 50,000 odd Communist party cells. His aim was to make the DC less dependent on the Civic Committees and parish priests at elections, but the attempt foundered and was abandoned after the 1958 general election. The ninety-three provincial councils are the second most important rung within the DC structure. They are headed by executives of from seven to ten members and a provincial secretary. The executives are elected by the provincial assemblies. The councils vary in size from fifty-one members in provinces of over two million to thirty in provinces of under one million, but the key provincial figures are the seven or eight permanent, paid officials, including of course the secretary. One of their most important duties is to select candidates for elections, and although their choice is subject to ratification by the National Council, there have been very few cases where the provincial choices have not been ratified. The most important duty of the provincial assemblies is to select delegates for the National Congress. This is done, as are all elections in the party, by proportional representation, and this ensures that the factional strength of the party in the country as a whole is fairly accurately reflected in the membership of the National Congress.

The national level of the party consists of six structures: the National Congress, the National Council, the Executive Bureau (*direzione*), the Secretariat and the parliamentary groups, one each for the Chamber and the Senate.[18] According to the party statutes, the National Congress is the most important of these organs: it decides upon the general policy of the party and elects the National Council. However, as the Congress normally meets only every second year – and occasionally the gap is longer[19] – the real power lies with the more permanent organs, notably with the *direzione* and Secretariat. However, the National Congress is important in that it elects the National Council in such a way that the Council is representative of the various *correnti* in the party. The system of election (the 'highest average' system of proportional representation) slightly favours the larger *correnti*, and in 1973 an attempt was made to reduce the influence of the smaller *correnti* further, largely with a view to improving the party's public image. It was decided that no *corrente* with less than 10 per cent of the delegates at the Congress would be able to elect members of the National Council to represent its particular point of view. However, this '10 per cent rule' has to a large extent remained a dead letter as groups at the Congress come together to elect members of the Council, who, once elected, often form *correnti* with far fewer than 10 per cent of the members of the Council. Nevertheless, there has been some rationalisation since 1973. The National Council elected on 25 March 1976, for example, had 120 members elected by the National Congress. Although there were nine quite important *correnti* on the Council, as well as one or two tiny groups and non-aligned individuals, the main division was between the sixty-two who supported Benigno Zaccagnini and the fifty-four who supported Arnaldo Forlani (Fanfani's protégé). As a result of this fairly straightforward division of support – a division repeated in large measure amongst the seventy *ex officio* members of the National Council – the reformist Zaccagnini was confirmed in his position as party Secretary. The National Council varies in size from about 170–190 members. In 1976 it had 188 members. In addition to the sixty parliamentarians and sixty non-parliamentarians elected by the National Congress, there were twenty regional representatives, five representatives of the national movements, i.e. the women's, youth's, business, sporting and veterans' associations, twenty-four *ex officio* parliamentarians (twelve each from the Senate and Chamber), six mayors of important towns, and the rest were ex-prime ministers and party secretaries. In addition to the voting members of the National Council, organisations which function nationally in activities inspired by 'Social Christian principles' have a right to be consulted by the National Council. Such organisations include the Catholic-inspired trade union confederation, *Confederazione Italiana Sindacati Lavoratori* (CISL), the farmers' organisation, *Coltivatori Diretti*, and the various branches of Catholic Action.

The party statutes define the National Council as the organ which is sub-ordinated to the National Congress and, within the policy guidelines fixed by the Congress, as the main decision-making body in the party. The National Council guides and controls the activity of the party in all fields. Although the debates of the National Council are well covered in the national press, and it has an important influence in developing the party's broad political strategy, as well as, quite frequently, resolving, prolonging or delaying governmental crises, the key power within the DC inevitably lies elsewhere. No body as large and unwieldy as the National Council, meeting on average once every three months, could possibly run a political party, and the party statutes recognise this by delegating much of the National Council's power to the executive bureau (*direzione*) and secretariat.

The *direzione* is defined in the party statutes as the body which 'enacts the policies of the party in accordance with the directions promulgated by the National Council'. The *direzione* normally has about thirty-five members, of whom twenty-seven are elected by the National Council and seven or eight are members by virtue of past or present services in senior positions in the party or government. Cabinet ministers are normally invited to attend meetings of the *direzione* if the subject under discussion is of particular concern to them. However, they do not have full voting rights. The *direzione* meets frequently – on average once a fortnight – and has a significant influence on DC policy-making, but its most important role occurs at times of governmental crisis. At such times it is the responsibility of the *direzione*, with the agreement of the leaders of the two parliamentary groups, to work out the DC's position with a view to resolving the crisis. The National Council, however, must be convened within thirty days of the resolution of the crisis to confirm the decision taken by the *direzione* and leaders of the parliamentary groups.

As regards the day-to-day running of the DC, the key decision-making body is the Secretariat. This body consists of a political Secretary, an administrative Secretary, their vice-secretaries, and the directors of the party's national organisation, its publicity and press section (SPES), its local government organisation and its planning section. This small team is, as it were, the inner cabinet of the DC, and the influence of the political Secretary, especially when he is a powerful figure such as Fanfani, can hardly be over-estimated. The President of the Republic may be the man who selects a prime minister designate, but the man who most frequently makes and unmakes the prime minister is the DC political Secretary. According to the party statutes 'The political Secretary . . . represents the party, takes heed of the policy decisions made by the *direzione*, maintains contact with the government, with the parliamentary groups and with the other political and social movements, and promotes and co-ordinates the political policy and organisational activities of the party.' Despite this wide-ranging brief a political Secretary is only as powerful as he is strong in the party as a whole. Between 1954–9, when Fanfani's *Iniziativa Democratica* current was clearly the dominant one in the party, Fanfani could act as political Secretary in an almost autocratic way. Between 1973–5, when he was again Secretary, he was much more constrained by his declining influence within the party. And his successor, Zaccagnini, as already mentioned, had only a small majority on the National Council committed to his reformist strategy. He was thus inevitably constrained by the need to take account of those *correnti* who had doubts about his strategy.[20]

The DC: Electoral Record and Political Strategy

Before going on to analyse the particular problems faced by Italy's Christian Democrats in the late 1970s it is appropriate to comment briefly on the DC's past electoral record and governmental performance in order to set its present-day problems and strategy in perspective.

The DC has been the dominant party in Italian politics since the war, but apart from the years 1948–53, when it had an absolute majority of seats in Parliament (131 out of 237 in the Senate and 305 out of 574 in the Chamber), it has been only the 'party of relative majority', constrained by the need to form coalitions, which it has been able to dominate but not to control. Founded in 1943, the DC made its first significant breakthrough when Alcide De Gasperi succeeded Ferruccio Parri as prime minister of the provisional government in December 1945. This step was symbolically very important, because for the first time since the founding of the Italian state a practising Catholic had become prime minister. This Catholic success was followed by the DC's poll of 35 per cent at the Constituent Assembly election of June 1946. The Christian Democrats polled less than the combined Left's 40 per cent (21 per cent for the Communists; 19 per cent for the Socialists), but De Gasperi remained prime minister of the tripartite government consisting of the three major parties, which together received three-quarters of the votes cast.[21] The Right, discredited by its association with Mussolini, had been routed, and, as in France, most conservative voters took shelter under the umbrella of Christian Democracy, but in contrast to France, where the Gaullist *Rassemblement du Peuple Français* (RPF) soon made inroads into the conservative electorate, the Italian conservatives rallied even more decisively to the Christian Democrats as the rift between East and West widened in 1946–7, and at the general election of 1948 the DC polled almost half the votes cast and gained an absolute majority of seats in Chamber.

The DC owed its success in 1948 to a number of factors, of which two were particularly important and were not to be repeated with the same intensity at future elections. First, the Cold War was at its height: the Prague coup occurred two months before polling day in April 1948, and at the same time the Americans used all the pressure they could, verbally and financially, to ensure a DC victory. Secondly, conservatives of many shades, some still compromised by their connections with fascism, others deeply concerned about the communist threat, were 'scared' into voting for the DC. Additional factors favouring a Christian Democratic victory were that the working-class movement, in contrast to 1946, was divided. In January 1947 the Socialist Party had split into a reformist wing led by Giuseppe Saragat and a Marxist wing led by Pietro Nenni, the former favouring a break with the Communists and the latter, with memories of the working-class split of 1921, determined to continue in alliance with the Communist party, which in May 1947 had been forced out of the coalition government to which it had belonged since April

1944. The divisions in the working-class movement, Cold War tensions, the attitude of the Italian Right, and pressure from the United States, were thus key factors in creating an atmosphere favourable to the DC. Finally, the Vatican, determined to make amends for its rather half-hearted opposition to fascism, threw its weight one hundred per cent behind the Christian Democrats. Pius XII was almost pathologically anti-communist, and Italy's 25,000 priests, fully supported by Luigi Gedda's Civic Committees, exerted all their influence to polarise the battle between God and the Devil, between Christian Democrats and Marxists, at a time when communism appeared as a straightforward monolithic rival to Catholicism.

Having gained an absolute majority in Parliament, however, De Gasperi did not attempt to form a *monocolore* Christian Democratic government, as the Vatican wished. Instead he invited Social Democrats, Republicans and Liberals to join his government (the *quadripartito* Centre-Right formula which was to last until the late 1950s). This important decision was conditioned by De Gasperi's determination to keep his distance from the Vatican, to avoid dividing Italy into Catholic and Marxist blocs, and to enable the government to carry through the social and economic reforms to which the DC had committed itself at its early congresses. De Gasperi wanted his government to be 'of the centre, but moving to the left'.[22] He was relatively successful in achieving governmental unity as long as he kept to the centre, notably in overcoming the postwar economic difficulties mainly by encouraging free enterprise. But as soon as he attempted to 'move to the left', for example to carry through substantial land reforms and to tackle the problems of the south through the *Cassa per il Mezzogiorno* (the Southern Development Fund, set up in 1950), he ran into difficulties. His land reform programme was opposed not only by the forty odd right-wing deputies (Monarchists and members of the *Uomo Qualunque* party), but also by Liberals and conservative Christian Democrats. Meanwhile, the left-wing *correnti* in the DC, led by Giovanni Gronchi and Giuseppe Dossetti, were becoming increasingly critical of De Gasperi's 'compromises' with economic liberalism and his apparent unwillingness to implement far-reaching social reforms.

Italian Christian Democrats, like their French counterparts, were to look back nostalgically to the heady five years or so after the war when their party was strong in Parliament, well led, and, at least superficially, united. But in fact Christian Democracy in both countries, France even more than Italy, flattered only to deceive: perhaps inevitably, for Christian Democrats, like European federalists, seemed most capable of united action when under external pressure. Such pressure existed during the postwar reconstruction period and at the height of the Cold War. But even then there were signs of factionalism within the DC. Gronchi was opposed to NATO, whilst Dossetti's followers wanted absolute priority to be given to radical social reforms. In contrast those on the right of the party were wholly committed to NATO, but feared that radical reform measures, particularly in the south, would alienate the southern landowners, whose political support the DC was anxious to retain. De Gasperi had to reconcile the two sides. He was able to do so partly on account of his qualities as a manager of men and partly owing to the respect he was accorded as a former leader of the *Popolari* and founder of the DC. He was, however, perhaps fortunate in the year of his death (1954), shortly after the return of those 'more normal times' (Stalin had died in 1953) which were bound to expose the DC to some of the pressures arising from its own contradictions as a broad-based, inter-class party. Indeed even before the 1953 general election it was apparent that the DC was likely to lose votes to the reviving Right in the south. There had been clear evidence of such a revival at the municipal and provincial elections of 1951 and 1952, and at the same time the *quadripartito* formula was beginning to break down, with the Liberals leaving the government in 1950 and the Social Democrats in 1951. (Both parties, however, continued to support De Gasperi on most issues in the Chamber.)

In these circumstances De Gasperi and his colleagues unwisely decided to tamper with the electoral law, in order to give the Centre parties a bonus of seats if in alliance they received over 50 per cent of the votes cast. The aim of the new electoral law was to ensure that the democratic parties of the Centre could carry through their governmental programme without undue harassment from the extreme Left and extreme Right. But the new law smacked of Mussolini's Acerbo Law of 1923, by which a party getting over one quarter of the votes got two-thirds of the seats in the Chamber, and was at once labelled by the Communists as the *legge truffa* (swindle law). The Centre parties together polled 49·85 per cent of the votes cast at the 1953 general election (just 57,000 short of the necessary majority), but the DC lost 2 million votes, falling back to 40 per cent from its 1948 high-water mark of 48·5 per cent. The Liberals, Republicans and Social Democrats lost proportionately even more than the Christian Democrats, whilst the Communists and Socialists gained almost one and a half million votes. But, from the DC's point of view, the big disappointment was the revival of the extreme Right, especially in the south, where severe inroads were made into the DC's 1948 electorate (the combined Monarchist and neo-Fascist vote went up from 5 per cent to 14 per cent, the Monarchists returning forty deputies and the MSI twenty-nine). The Christian Democratic electoral spell was thus rudely broken in 1953, and ever since the DC has been constrained by its inability to poll more than two-fifths of the votes at general elections. The 1953 set-back was due in part to the *legge truffa*, which suggested that the DC was determined to stay in power at almost any price (a continuing characteristic of the party twenty years later), and in part to its relative failure to implement the economic and social reforms promised at the Liberation,[23] but above all it was an ironic consequence of De Gasperi's success in re-establishing normal conditions between 1948–53. Now that law and order had been restored and economic reconstruction was well under way the extreme Right was no longer worried by the threat of a Marxist take-over, and their adherents promptly abandoned the Christian Democrats whom they had supported in 1948 only as the strongest bulwark against 'Marxism'.

The upshot of the 1953 general election was that the *quadripartito* parties (Christian Democrats, Social Democrats, Republicans and Liberals) were reduced from a total of 352 out of 574 seats in the Chamber to 300 out of

590. Moreover, the Social Democrats, who had fared particularly badly at the election, became very wary about co-operating in coalitions which included the Liberals. Indeed, from 1953 to the present day one of the DC's perennial problems has been whether to seek alliance with the parties of the Centre-Left or with those of the Centre-Right, for in contrast to the De Gasperi period the left flank and the right flank of the democratic centre have become steadily less willing to co-operate in government together.

Broadly speaking the decade 1953–62 saw the DC moving very hesitantly to the Left and the main Socialist party (PSI) moving rather less hesitantly towards the Centre, as Nenni gradually disengaged his party from its alliance with the Communists. It was a decade of political manoeuvring rather than of political achievement. The *quadripartito* coalition of De Gasperi lacked sufficient parliamentary strength to be a viable long-term prospect. Pius XII and the DC right-wing factions would have happily seen the Monarchists and/or neo-Fascists brought into the governmental arena, but the majority of Christian Democrats showed that they would prefer to move to the left when they elected Amintore Fanfani, Dossetti's successor as leader of the main social-reforming current in the DC, as party Secretary at the 1954 Congress in Naples. However, a move to the left made no political sense, at least in terms of parliamentary arithmetic, so long as the Socialists remained allied with the Communists, which they did until their gradual separation between 1956–62.

The result of the parliamentary deadlock, which persisted throughout much of the period 1953–62, was governmental and political *immobilismo*. It is true that the Italian economy prospered in the 1950s, especially between 1957–60; that the nagging problem of Trieste was solved in 1954; and that the Treaty of Rome was signed in 1957. But domestic reforms were conspicuous by their absence, and the long-term consequences of the *immobilismo* of this period were still apparent in Italy of the 1970s, for example in education, housing and the health services.[24]

There were two *monocolore* Christian Democratic governments during the 1953–8 legislature (Giuseppi Pella's from June 1953–February 1954, and Adone Zoli's from May 1957–June 1958), but for most of the period the rather tired *quadripartito* formula was followed, albeit with little enthusiasm. Mario Scelba's 1954–5 government consisted of Christian Democrats, Social Democrats and Liberals, supported by the Republicans. However, after the election to the presidency of the left-wing Christian Democrat, Giovanni Gronchi, in 1955 (an election which incidentally brought to the fore the extent of DC factionalism),[25] Antonio Segni became prime minister of a government similar in complexion and support to that of Scelba, but slightly more oriented to the left in accordance with Segni's political predilections.

The 1958 general election produced results similar to those of 1953, but the election was politically important, because the Christian Democrats and Socialists both advanced by two percentage points (gaining ten and nine seats respectively), whilst the Communists stagnated for the only time since the war. The leading politicians in the Christian Democratic and Socialist parties not unnaturally concluded that the electorate approved the DC's leftish orientation and the PSI's tentative moves away from the Communist party. The reorientation of the DC had been going on since the Naples Congress of 1954, at which Fanfani's left-inclined *Iniziativa Democratica* emerged as the strongest current in the party,[26] and that of the PSI since the revelations about Stalin's Russia made at the Twentieth Congress of the Communist Party of the Soviet Union in 1956. Indeed, shortly after that Congress Pietro Nenni, Secretary of the Socialist party, had met the Social Democrat leader, Giuseppe Saragat, at Pralognan to discuss the possibility of a reconciliation between the two Socialist parties after ten years of separation; and the local election results of 1956, followed by the national results of 1958, encouraged Nenni to continue the move towards the Centre (or at least away from the extreme Left), a move which had been openly discussed and tentatively approved at the Socialist party congress in Venice in 1957.

The DC's 'opening to the left' (*apertura alla sinistra*) began to take concrete shape when President Gronchi invited Fanfani to form a government after the 1958 election. The energetic, but also somewhat enigmatic, Fanfani had been the architect of the DC moves towards the left since 1954, but he had acquired powerful enemies in the process, not only amongst the industrialists of *Confindustria*, hitherto a strong supporter of the DC, and the conservative members of the Vatican, but, more important, within the right-wing factions of the DC, those *correnti* which were most susceptible to pressure from the Church and industry. As a result Fanfani's first government lasted for only six months (July 1958–January 1959), being overthrown as a result of a DC right-wing revolt. Deeply disappointed Fanfani resigned the DC secretaryship as well as the premiership and retired to his Chair in Economic History at Rome University. He was succeeded as party Secretary by Aldo Moro, who was as convinced as Fanfani about the need for the opening to the left, but who was more circumspect in his approach to it;[27] and as prime minister by Antonio Segni, who, although a member of the reforming wing of the DC, presided over a *monocolore* DC government supported by the Right (Liberals, Monarchists, and usually MSI) until February 1960. By now the pattern of one step to the left by the DC, followed by a step, or at least half a step, back to the centre was becoming established. Segni's government may be seen as half a step back from that of Fanfani, but that of his successor, Fernando Tambroni, whose government of April–July 1960 was fully supported by the neo-Fascists, must be seen as a full step back to the right. However, the Tambroni interlude turned out to be a case of *reculer pour mieux sauter*, because the anti-Fascist riots, which broke up the MSI congress in Genoa in July 1960, not only destroyed the Tambroni government, but also cleared the ground for Aldo Moro to resume the opening to the left.

This opening, of course, depended not only on the DC but also on the Socialist party, and not least on its leader Pietro Nenni, who by now was personally in favour of moving into the governmental arena in order to obtain some of the reforms demanded by the Socialists, but who had at the same time to go very cautiously in order to avoid splitting his party. One sign that the gap between the Christian Democrats and Socialists was narrowing occurred in July 1960, when, after the Genoa riots, President Gronchi persuaded Fanfani to return to active politics and form a new government; now, for the first time since the Socialist split of 1947, the Nenni Socialists abstained rather than voting against a new DC government. Fanfani's second government received the biggest parliamentary majority since De Gasperi's 1948 government, and although it was a DC *monocolore* government, it had the full parliamentary support of the Liberals, Republicans and Social Democrats, and was regarded benevolently by the Socialists.

Despite the Socialists retreating somewhat from the political centre by their decision not to fight against the Communists at the local elections of November 1960, the first Centre-Left municipal councils, consisting of Christian Democrats, Republicans, Social Democrats and Socialists, were formed early in 1961 in Milan, Genoa and Florence. The Fanfani–Moro strategy of working towards a new governmental formula based on Christian Democratic–Socialist co-operation was clearly on the verge of bearing fruit at the national level. Moreover, events outside the DC were helping to prepare the way for such an outcome. For in November 1958 Pius XII had died and been succeeded by the much more open-minded John XXIII, whose liberal views were beginning to percolate throughout the Vatican by 1960. In addition the American administration of President Kennedy looked favourably on the idea of co-operation between Catholics and Socialists. In these circumstances Aldo Moro threw down a specific challenge to the Socialists at the DC Congress at Naples in January 1962, when he invited Nenni's party to support a government with a social-reforming programme.[28] The Socialists accepted the challenge, and Fanfani was able to form the first Centre-Left government in February 1962. Although the Socialists did not participate in this DC–PRI–PSDI government, they promised it their 'external support.'[29] The Socialists had, of course, laid down conditions for their support: notably more precise and far-reaching economic planning by the central government; nationalisation of electricity; educational reforms; and the implementation of the regional government provisions of the 1948 Constitution. The Christian Democrats accepted these conditions, and the real problem seemed to be whether Fanfani could introduce a sufficient number of reforms before the 1963 general election to convince the Socialists of the DC's good faith. In fact Fanfani's government of 1962–3 was reasonably successful in fulfilling its part of the bargain, given the short time available before the election: electricity was nationalised, economic planning made more formal, compulsory school attendance raised to fourteen, and stiffer taxes on speculation introduced; even one more region, Friuli-Venezia-Giulia, was created, although this still left Italy with only six regional governments, a far cry from the twenty envisaged in the 1948 Constitution. But, as it turned out, the real problem was not the reform programme, nor the extent of Fanfani's good faith in implementing it, but the attitude of the electorate, for, to the surprise of most political observers, the Christian Democrats lost three-quarters of a million votes and sixteen seats at the general election of April 1963, their percentage of the vote going down from 42·4 to 38·7, whilst the Communists gained over a million votes and twenty-six seats, their percentage of the vote going up from 22·7 to 25·3. The PSI and PSDI vote was virtually unchanged, although Nenni's party gained three seats (giving it a total of eighty-seven) and Saragat's gained ten seats (giving it a total of thirty-three).[30]

What went wrong for the Christian Democrats in 1963? Fifteen years later it is clear that the 1963 election result was a body-blow, or at the very least a severe set-back, for the embryo Centre-Left experiment. It did not destroy it, but it seriously undermined the morale and political credibility of its chief protagonists (Fanfani, Moro and Nenni) before the first fully-fledged Centre-Left government was formed in December 1963. And even before the Centre-Left formula began to operate, the same right-wing DC *correnti* and industrialists, who had attacked the *apertura alla sinistra* in the late 1950s and early 1960s, continued to try to put the brake on every attempt to consolidate the Centre-Left 'alliance' by opposing its reform programme. The result was that the Centre-Left experiment more or less ground to a halt by the mid 1960s, thus preparing the way for the political, economic and social crisis of the late 1960s and early 1970s.[31] In 1963 the Christian Democrats lost votes not only to their Right (many industrialists went over to the Liberals who gained twenty-five seats by increasing their percentage of the vote from 3·5 to 7·0), but, more disappointingly from the DC's point of view, to the Left. The main reasons for these losses were the more relaxed international atmosphere, the new attitude of the Papacy under John XXIII, and the rapid growth of the Italian economy since 1957. After the end of the Berlin crisis of 1958–61 and the Cuba crisis of 1962, Kennedy and Khruschev had embarked on a course of international relaxation and détente. Communism was no longer regarded as the bugbear it had been at previous elections. At the same time John XXIII appealed to 'all men of goodwill', whatever their political views, to co-operate to solve the world's social problems, and a fortnight before polling day in 1963 the Pope received Khruschev's son-in-law, the editor of *Izvestia*, at the Vatican. It must have seemed to a small number of left-wing Catholics, and a considerable number of Catholic wives of Communist or Socialist husbands, that it was now acceptable for them to vote for a left-wing party. Another important reason for DC losses in 1963 was pinpointed by Mariano Rumor, the party Secretary, at the national Congress at Rome in 1964;[32] this was the progressive breaking-up of traditional Italian social structures, which was a consequence of the economic miracle of 1957–62 and the mass migration of southern peasants to northern industrial towns, where, no longer subject to the influence of priests, they easily fell prey to Communist propaganda. The irony of the situation lay in the fact that the migration from the south greatly increased the need for a social-reforming government to carry out the reforms required to cope with the growing social problems in the northern cities, and yet the reduced Christian Democratic vote and increased Communist vote in 1963 decreased the chances of such reforms being implemented, because the election result was a considerable set-back for the protagonists of reform within the main governmental party, the DC. It was indeed ironical that the Christian Democrats' first real attempt to carry out a reform programme foundered, at least in part, as a result of growing Italian prosperity.

The Centre-Left Experiment

Although Fanfani appeared to have been rebuffed by the electorate in 1963, the political preferences of the majority of Christian Democrats and Socialists nevertheless suggested that the time was ripe for an attempt to form a Centre-Left government. Consequently President Segni (who had succeeded Gronchi in 1962) called upon Aldo Moro, one of the chief architects of the *apertura alla sinistra*, but a less abrasive man than Fanfani, to form a government. Moro was at first unsuccessful, as the Socialists refused to make any specific commitments until after their October 1963 Congress, and so Giovanni Leone, a middle-of-the-road Christian Democrat, formed a caretaker government for six months. Finally, in December 1963 Moro was able to form the first fully-fledged Centre-Left government, consisting of Christian Democrats, Social Democrats, Republicans and, for the first time, Socialists, because at their October Congress 57 per cent of the Socialist delegates had voted for full participation in a Centre-Left government led by the Christian Democrats. The Socialists had laid down important conditions, notably the co-ordination of economic planning under a Five Year Plan, tax reforms, and full implementation of the 1948 Constitution, notably the establishment of regional governments and the reform of the penal code to remove Fascist legislation still in force. Moro's government of December 1963–June 1968 consisted at first of sixteen Christian Democrats, six Socialists, three Social Democrats and one Republican. Pietro Nenni became Foreign Minister and deputy prime minister.

It was unfortunate that the Centre-Left experiment began in rather inauspicious circumstances. In the first place, the economy was beginning to run into difficulties after the boom of 1957–62. Secondly, twenty-five left-wing Socialists abandoned Nenni in January 1964, setting up the *Partito Socialista Italiano di Unità Proletaria* (PSIUP) under Tullio Vecchietti and Lelio Basso. Thirdly, the new Pope, Paul VI (elected in June 1963) was much less favourably disposed towards the Centre-Left experiment than his predecessor, John XXIII, had been. But, above all, it was the worsening economic situation which cramped the new government, for Italy ran into a balance of payments deficit in 1963, and there was also a run on private capital (much of it going to Switzerland). Consequently the new government, which was committed to economic expansion and social reforms, had to begin its term in office by imposing a credit squeeze, notably through the restriction of hire purchase facilities and by increasing purchase tax and fuel tax.

The Moro government almost foundered in June 1964 over increased subsidies to Catholic schools, and was further weakened by the wrangling which occurred in the autumn of 1964 over the election of the Social Democrat Giuseppe Saragat to the presidency (Segni had had to resign after only two and a half years in office owing to a stroke). The Christian Democrats had at first put up Giovanni Leone as their candidate, then some had supported Fanfani and others (of the left-wing *correnti*) Giulio Pastore, but finally after twenty-one ballots Saragat was elected. The political significance of the presidential election was twofold. It deflected the Centre-Left government from its work, and at the same time it showed up all too clearly the differences between the coalition parties and within the Christian Democratic Party. It was hardly surprising that by 1965 both the Socialists and the left-wing Christian Democrats were becoming increasingly restive at the government's inactivity at home and refusal to condemn American intervention in Vietnam abroad. Finally, in January 1966 the first Moro Centre-Left government fell when DC integralists[33] voted against a 'secular' measure to establish state nursery-schools for three- to six-year-olds. However, as all four coalition parties wanted to avoid a premature general election, Moro was persuaded to relaunch the Centre-Left coalition in February, and this government lasted until the general election of 1968.

Few steps, however, were taken to implement the reform programme outlined in December 1963. For one thing the Socialists and Social Democrats were embroiled throughout the later part of 1965 and all of 1966 in achieving a spurious unity. (The united Socialist-Social Democratic *Partito Socialista Unificato* lasted only from October 1966–9.)[34] For another the Christian Democrats were so divided by factional quarrels that it was difficult for them to give an effective lead to the government.[35] Apart from the five-year National Economic Plan (1966–70), passed by Parliament in 1967, and a promise of regional reform by 1970, the Centre-Left coalition had little to show in the way of positive achievement after five years in power. Nothing of importance had been accomplished in the field of educational reform, the reorganisation of the country's medical services, or urban planning. Above all, nothing had been done to reform the outmoded, over-manned, inefficient bureaucracy; and no root-and-branch reforms could be expected without a thorough overhaul of the very body (or bodies) which would have to implement the reforms. Hence, the first five years of Centre-Left government left most voters feeling that the politicians were getting increasingly out of touch with the everyday problems of life in Italy.

The 1968 general election did nothing to resolve Italy's complex political, social and economic problems, for although the Christian Democrats improved their position slightly (gaining six seats to 266), and the Republicans gained three seats (giving them nine), the combined Socialists party lost 6 per cent of the votes (compared with their joint percentage of 1963) and over thirty seats. The Communists gained 1·6 per cent and eleven seats (giving them 177), but the chief blow to the Centre-Left was that the Independent Proletarian Socialists (PSIUP) won twenty-three seats by polling 4·5 per cent of the votes cast.

Italy now entered a period of crisis under a series of lame-duck (mainly) Centre-Left governments. The crisis has been analysed in some depth elsewhere,[36] and here it will suffice to emphasise that it was extremely complex. Economically Italy was particularly badly hit by the industrial recession of 1969–71. Politically the Centre-Left was undermined (DC factionalism had reached its zenith, and the Socialists and Social Democrats had split again after only two and a half years of tenuous unity). Socially the country's problems were becoming ever more daunting, notably in education, health and housing, whilst the politicians appeared to be concerned only with *partitocrazia*, i.e. party political squabbling and in-fighting. Evidence that trade-unionists and students were becoming totally frustrated with the prevailing *immobilismo* was indicated by the direct action of workers and students in the 'Hot Autumn' of 1969, as well as by the extra-parliamentary demand for a referendum on divorce.[37] The only reform of any substance introduced during the 1968–72 legislature was the setting up of fifteen new regional governments (the first regional elections being held in 1970),[38] but instead of uniting the Centre-Left the regional reform virtually broke up the national coalition, because the decision by the Socialists to join the Communists in the regional governments of Tuscany and Umbria was a serious blow to the relations between the Socialists and the strongly anti-Communist Social Democrats.

To complete the unhappy picture, the presidential election of December 1971 (like its predecessor in 1965) brutally exposed the fragility of the Centre-Left coalition. The main contenders were Fanfani, the original candidate of the DC, but he was distrusted by the Left as an over-zealous Catholic and as a potential 'Gaullist' president; De Martino, the official Socialist candidate, who was supported by the Communists; and Aldo Moro, the leader of the Centre-Left governments of 1963–8, but now somewhat isolated within his own party, being regarded as rather too friendly towards the 'Marxists'. The key struggle took place amongst the Christian Democrats, between Fanfani supported by the right-wing *correnti* and Moro by the Left. If Moro had been elected, it would have been seen as a victory for the Socialists and Communists, who were more than anxious to vote for him; if Fanfani had been elected, it would have symbolised the end of the Centre-Left experiment with which Fanfani had become disenchanted, and it would perhaps have ushered in a period of stronger, semi-presidential government. In the event a compromise candidate was chosen – at the twenty-third ballot. A harmless Christian Democrat of the Centre, Giovanni Leone, was elected, but he owed his election to neo-Fascist votes, and his victory was thus regarded as a blow to the future prospects of the Centre-Left.

The presidential election ushered in a period of great political uncertainty during the early months of 1972. The endless days of balloting had strikingly revealed the factional divisions within the DC. The Socialists seemed to be moving away from the Christian Democrats and towards the Communists again. All the lay parties wanted to avoid the impending referendum on divorce. No government could be formed with the support of a majority in Parliament. Eventually, after much intrigue, a caretaker *monocolore* DC government was formed under Giulio Andreotti, a former Defence Minister regarded then as a man of the Centre-Right, and President Leone dissolved Parliament prematurely for the first time in the history of the Italian Republic as the only way to break the political deadlock.

After almost a decade of abortive Centre-Left government it was not surprising that the leading party of government, the DC, entered the election campaign more divided than ever.[39] However, as in previous elections the DC closed ranks in the face of its enemies to the left and right (the Communists and neo-Fascists), and emerged unscathed with a gain of one seat (267 instead of

266) and with two voters in five still prefering the DC to any alternative. The DC campaign was essentially 'negative', the party's main slogan being: 'No to Communism. No to Fascism. Forward to the Centre with the DC.' Indeed, anti-communism, which had been played down somewhat in 1963 and 1968, found a new lease of life in DC propaganda in 1972. One of the most widely-displayed DC posters showed a group of people cowering near a Red Army tank, under which were the words: 'No thank you. I prefer *my* way of democracy.' In 1972 the DC probably laid more emphasis on anti-communism than on anti-fascism – indeed the DC slogan 'Avanti al Centro' (rather than 'Centro-Sinistra') was itself evidence of the party's disillusionment with the Centre-Left experiment and of its reorientation towards the right. Nevertheless, Giulio Andreotti, the prime minister, and Arnaldo Forlani, the DC political Secretary, had no hesitation in rejecting the suggestion that the neo-Fascists might be permitted to enter a Centre-Right coalition after the election.[40] And at DC headquarters it was emphasised that the DC had tried working with the MSI in 1960 under Tambroni: it had proved a disaster, and the DC had no intention of repeating its mistake.[41]

The 'negative' campaign of 1972 proved a success, in that the Christian Democrats held their ground in spite of their prolonged failure to govern Italy effectively, and in spite of the fact that the party had lost votes to the MSI, especially in the south, at the regional and provincial elections of 1970 and 1971. Indeed, the election showed once again the remarkable stability, even conservatism, of the Italian electorate, for the Christian Democratic, Communist and (combined) Socialist vote was almost unchanged in percentage terms since 1968. But the election did nothing to clarify the political situation. The voters had failed to indicate whether they wanted a continuation of the Centre-Left experiment, or a return to the De Gasperi Centre-Right formula. There appeared to be two possible governmental majorities. Arithmetically the Centre-Left seemed to make more sense, for the Christian Democrats, Socialists, Social Democrats and Republicans now had 375 deputies out of 630 (six more than in the previous Chamber), whilst the Centre-Right (Christian Democrats, Liberals, Republicans and Social Democrats) only had 334 (four fewer than in the previous Chamber). But the DC leadership, notably Andreotti and Fanfani, had campaigned hard for a move to the right, and the Socialists had campaigned for 'more advanced equilibria', a strange phrase by which they appeared to mean some sort of governmental, or at least supporting, role for the Communists. In these circumstances President Leone called upon Giulio Andreotti to form a government, which, in view of Andreotti's preferences at that time, turned out to be a Centre-Right government.

The Centre-Left experiment lasted for only a year before the decision was taken to revert to a Centre-Right coalition of the type which had governed Italy for the previous decade. The experiment of 1972–3 failed partly because the business community was soon disillusioned by the inability of the Liberal Treasury Minister, Giovanni Malagodi, to control inflation, partly because the coalition was numerically weak in the Chamber – it only required the small Republican party to withdraw its support in May 1973 to produce its overthrow, but above all because the left-wing DC *correnti*, led by Moro, were opposed to the Andreotti government from the start, and did not hesitate to vote against it, putting it in a minority on several occasions before it finally fell. Indeed, if the Republicans were instrumental in bringing about the downfall of Andreotti, it was the DC left-wing *correnti* who really destroyed it. Moreover, by one of these strange, yet typical, ironies of Italian politics the man who played the key part in preparing the way for a renewal of the Centre-Left was none other than Amintore Fanfani, the *éminence grise* of the DC who only eighteen months previously had been campaigning for a Centre-Right government. Fanfani had concluded that the DC was in danger of losing a considerable part of its public support unless it succeeded in presenting itself as a more united party, genuinely interested in carrying out a number of much-needed reforms. He therefore persuaded the various *correnti* leaders to unite behind a programme of reforms at the DC National Congress in June 1973. This programme could be carried through only with Socialist support, so Fanfani reverted to his earlier position as a protagonist of the Centre-Left. At the same time he agreed to take on the important post of party Secretary; reconciled himself publicly with his old rival Moro; and persuaded Mariano Rumor, leader of the party's biggest faction, to accept President Leone's commission to form a government. In July 1973, the second version of the Centre-Left experiment began under Rumor (his new government included sixteen Christian Democrats, six Socialists, four Social Democrats and two Republicans).

As with the first Centre-Left experiment of almost exactly a decade before, the government at once found itself faced with formidable problems: the cholera outbreak of August 1973 in Naples, which highlighted the shortcomings in the nation's medical services; the 200,000 children on part-time schooling by 1975; the continuation of (mainly) neo-Fascist violence; and above all the severe inflation which was fuelled by the quadrupling of oil prices after the Arab-Israeli War in October 1973. Nevertheless, it appeared to many observers that the second version of the Centre-Left experiment had a slightly better chance of succeeding than the first (provided it could control inflation with some degree of success). In the mid 1970s, unlike the early 1960s, the Christian Democrats and the Socialists were reasonably united in their commitment to the Centre-Left. The Church's hostility to Catholics co-operating with Socialists had also declined considerably. Above all, perhaps, the ruling politicians in the two main coalition parties (the DC and PSI) realised that this might be their last chance to show that the Centre-Left formula could work. The neo-Fascists were meanwhile trying to exploit the situation for their own ends, whilst the Communists – although still distrusted by many – continued to emphasise their commitment to liberal democracy and their desire to enter the government arena. The second Centre-Left experiment therefore looked distinctly fragile from the start, and it eventually foundered over the divorce issue in 1974 and broke up in the aftermath of the 1975 regional elections, the final blow coming in January 1976 when the Socialists refused to give any further support to Moro's DC–PRI minority coalition.[42]

Before discussing the 1976 general election, which occurred a year early as a result of the collapse of the Centre-Left, and which led directly to the 'opening' to the Communists, it is important to emphasise that the DC entered the last quarter of the twentieth century faced with a number of acutely difficult problems. While in electoral terms the party appeared to be as resilient as ever, recovering its 1975 regional losses at the 1976 general election, the party was faced with at least four serious dilemmas. First, how was the DC to present itself as a united force as long as it continued to straddle the political spectrum from the moderate Right to the far Left? This dilemma centred on the problem of factionalism within the party. Secondly, how was the DC to fulfil its commitment to reform Italy's economic and social structures whilst remaining enmeshed in the *sottogoverno* (the sub-governmental patronage system)? This problem centred on the key issue of bureaucratic reform. Thirdly, what were the DC's relations with the Church to be? On the one hand, the party continued to need the support of the Church at elections and continued to benefit from its identification with the Catholic sub-culture. On the other hand, it could not afford to be too closely associated with organised Catholicism at a time when Italian society was becoming increasingly 'de-confessionalised'. This dilemma presented itself in an acute form at the 1974 divorce referendum and continued to dog the party over the issue of abortion in the period leading up to the 1976 general election. Fourthly, and perhaps most crucial of all, what attitude should the Christian Democrats adopt towards the Communists? The PCI claimed to be a democratic, constitutional party, and in 1973 had committed itself to the 'historic compromise', i.e. to an alliance with the 'progressive forces' in the DC and PSI with a view to reforming and modernising the Italian economy and Italian society. The majority of Christian Democrats was also committed to the 'modernisation' of Italy, but the Centre-Left had failed to achieve this objective. Could the DC, however, risk a governmental alliance with the PCI without undermining its own power position (based on entrenchment in the political and social structure of 'unreformed' Italy), and without destroying its *raison d'être*, (based in large measure on anti-Communism)?

The Problem of Factionalism

Political parties are inevitably coalitions to a greater or lesser extent, but the phenomenon of organised intra-party factionalism is peculiarly Italian, and even within Italy it is particularly (although not exclusively) a characteristic of the Christian Democratic and Socialist parties. As far as the DC is concerned, there are usually at least half a dozen formally structured, continuing factions or currents (*correnti*). According to Article 91 of the party statutes no such formal *correnti* are allowed to operate within the party, but since the mid 1950s this rule has been a dead letter. To some extent, of course, factionalism is both harmless and inevitable. It can be argued that the various *correnti* are evidence of the democratic nature of the DC – a party which allows free internal debate about the options open to it; also that an inter-class party, whose socio-economic base ranges from southern peasants to northern businessmen by way of housewives, bureaucrats and white-collar workers, inevitably contains people of widely differing political views. But the problem was that in the 1960s and early 1970s, as factionalism became more rife, the DC became more sclerotic: one faction pulled in one direction whilst another pulled in a different direction, and as a result they tended to neutralise each other with unfortunate consequences for the political image and governmental effectiveness of the party. Of course, the harmful effect of factionalism should not be exaggerated, because the DC always closes ranks at elections, and the party has for long had a broad consensus in favour of a left-of-centre strategy.[43] Nevertheless, all the Italian governments which fell in the Centre-Left period from 1962–76, did so either because one of the DC's partners, for example the Socialists or Republicans, withdrew their support, or because a DC *corrente* withdrew its support, and not because governments, were defeated in votes of censure. Thus factionalism contributed significantly both to governmental *immobilismo* and to the DC's disunited, undisciplined image. And, as the Communist Party's challenge became more threatening in the middle and late 1970s, it became increasingly important for the DC to put its house in order. Complete unanimity of views could, of course, not be expected. Nor would this have been desirable: after all the DC's great rival, the PCI, allows different views to be expressed in *L'Unità*. But constant public quarrelling and back-stabbing was, to say the least, inappropriate in a party which claimed to have a moral right to govern Italy.

The problem of factionalism has a long history in the DC, but until the 1960s arguments over political strategy usually stopped well short of the bitter polemicism which characterised the years of the 'opening to the left' and of the Centre-Left governments. One of the most important divisions in the DC goes back to its foundation and is too imprecise to be labelled a factional difference. This is the important, albeit *nuancé*, difference between integralists and autonomists. The former were (and are) themselves divided into conservative integralists like Luigi Gedda, a leading figure in Catholic Action, who wanted the DC to be a wholly 'confessional' party acting as the political arm of the Catholic Church, and progressive integralists like Giorgio La Pira and Giovanni Dossetti, who wanted to implement 'integrally' the social teaching of the Gospels and papal encyclicals, and thus mould Italy into a genuinely Christian polity. Conservative and progressive integralists tend to be wholly united on such moral questions as divorce and abortion, but over the years have had very different views about political strategy. The former have, for example, been strongly anti-Communist both in domestic and foreign affairs, whereas the latter were in favour of co-operating with the Socialists, and in recent years have advocated bringing the Communists into the 'area of government' in order to achieve a more socially just, or 'Christian', society.

The autonomists within the DC, unlike the integralists, want to keep *the* Vatican at arm's length. They have always taken the line that the DC is the party of Catholics but not a Catholic party pure and simple. As a *national* political party, inspired by Catholic principles, the DC should, they claim, be able to rely on the support of the Church, but it should not be subject to Vatican orders, because the interests of Italy and the interests of the Papacy are not necessarily identical. Religious principles should be applied in politics, but politics and religion should be regarded as separate activities. Hence, the DC should preserve its 'autonomy' from the Church. This was the strongly held view of the DC's leader in the decade after the war, Alcide De Gasperi. His successor as leading autonomist was Amintore Fanfani, although – and this shows the danger of trying to categorise DC politicians too precisely – Fanfani was often to be found expressing integralist views, especially with regard to moral issues. In the 1970s Aldo Moro was the most prominent autonomist, although he too maintained close contacts with the Vatican (Paul VI had for long been a personal friend of Moro's). The autonomists have, in fact, held a clear majority in the DC since 1952, when De Gasperi, despite strong pressure from Pius XII and Luigi Gedda, refused to form a right-wing alliance with the neo-Fascists in Rome. However, the differences between autonomists and integralists still periodically come to a head over moral and social issues: or at least ostensibly they do – in fact such issues are often used as a cover for political differences.[44]

Apart from the difference between 'autonomists' and 'integralists', which is a trans-factional phenomenon, there has always been a major ideological division within the DC between the Left and the Right. Although De Gasperi did his best to paper over the substantial differences between the two, he was not wholly successful in spite of his great skill as a manager of men and his prestige as a former *Popolare* and opponent of fascism. The two great left-wing *correnti* in the decade after the war were those led by Giovanni Gronchi (based on the review *Politica Sociale*) and by Giuseppe Dossetti (based on the review *Cronache Sociali*). Their successors today are the left-Catholic *Base* and the trade-unionist *Forze Nuove*. Now, as then, these 'social Christian' *correnti* of principle constitute a minority within the party, but a significant minority nevertheless (usually between 20–30 per cent at National Congresses) and, more important, a vocal and determined minority.

The two early left-wing *correnti, Politica Sociale* and *Cronache Sociali*, had many similarities, but, like their successors, a number of differences. Giovanni Gronchi's *corrente, Politica Sociale*, consisted mainly of old *Popolari*, friends of Gronchi's since the early 1920s when he had been a leading figure on the trade-union wing of the *Partito Popolare*. Gronchi had about thirty followers throughout the 1948–53 parliament, and their ideas were expressed in the reviews *Politica Sociale*, founded in 1946, and *La Libertà*, founded in 1948 by Gronchi's close friend Luigi Somma. Gronchi's *corrente* was the first DC faction to be formally constituted, holding a special congress at Pesaro in November 1948. At that congress Gronchi claimed that the DC had already become an oligarchic party, run by no more than twenty people who had developed close links with the conservative leaders of agriculture and industry.[45] He went on to criticise the 'centrist tendencies' of De Gasperi, and to demand the full implementation of the social and economic provisions of the Constitution. Later *Politica Sociale* was to be critical of the Atlantic Alliance.[46] Not surprisingly Gronchi's current came under fire from the *direzione* of the DC, both for existing at all (in contravention of the party statutes) and for its open criticisms of the government.[47] However, the strength of the Left was shown at the 1949 National Congress in Venice when Gronchi's faction joined Dossetti's to win 35 per cent of the seats on the National Council. Thereafter *Politica Sociale* was to some extent 'absorbed' by the larger Dossettian group which could count on the support of about sixty deputies. And in the early 1950s most followers of Gronchi joined the *Base* faction, founded in 1953, or went over to Fanfani's much larger left-of-centre current, *Iniziativa Democratica*, which won control of the party at the 1954 Congress in Naples. Gronchi himself, after being president of the Chamber, was elected President of Italy in 1955, an office which he held until 1962.

Meanwhile, in the De Gasperi era the most important left-wing *corrente* was Dossetti's *Cronache Sociali*. In some ways this was surprising, for Giuseppe Dossetti, who left politics in 1951 to found a religious community, was much less of a practical man of politics than Gronchi. However, he was by all accounts a man of great moral influence, almost a saint in politics. He attracted into his circle many of the most distinguished men of the post-*Popolari* generation, notably Amintore Fanfani, Aldo Moro and Mariano Rumor, all future DC Secretaries and prime ministers. Giorgio La Pira, the left-Catholic and somewhat maverick mayor of Florence, was also an important member of the Dossetti group. Many different ideas were expressed in *Cronache Sociali*, but the review's underlying philosophy could be described as 'Christian Socialism'. Dossetti would have liked to have seen a continuation of tripartism, i.e. the Christian Democratic–Socialist–Communist alliance of 1944–7, but his proposal to this effect was decisively defeated at the 1949 Congress, and two years later *Cronache Sociali* ceased publication when Dossetti left politics. Nevertheless, the kernel of the Dossetti programme remained important within the DC, namely the desire to make the DC into a social-reforming party; to implement the Constitution fully; to emphasise the importance of economic planning as a means of changing the old 'Liberal' state with its outdated economic and social structures; and finally to try to give Italy some independence *vis-à-vis* the blocs in foreign policy.[48]

So long as De Gasperi was at the helm (his last premiership ended in 1953, and he died in 1954) the DC remained reasonably united. Although he himself was a strong believer in neo-liberal economics and the free market economy, which the followers of Dossetti rejected, De Gasperi skilfully retained the support of men like Fanfani and Moro by making concessions to the *Dossettiani* over housing policy, agricultural reforms, and most notably by agreeing to the establishment of the Southern Development Fund, the *Cassa per il Mezzogiorno*, in 1950. He also constantly emphasised to the DC delegates at national congresses the importance of maintaining a united front, and unlike some of his successors he was listened to.[49] Moreover, he was helped both by external factors, notably the particularly bitter state of the Cold War until the death of Stalin, and by internal factors, notably the constant pressure brought to bear on the DC-led governments by the PCI–PSI 'Popular Front'. The real turning point as regards DC unity occurred in 1953, when Stalin died and the DC lost its absolute majority in Parliament. The *quadripartito* centrist formula was soon called into question, and, as it lost support, the internal divisions within the DC became increasingly apparent.

From 1954–9 the main DC *corrente* was Fanfani's *Iniziativa Democratica*, but its very success led to an internal party reaction on the Right and the Left, and in 1959 *Iniziativa Democratica* itself split up, ushering in a decade of increasing internecine feuding within the DC.

The review *Iniziativa Democratica* started to appear in 1952 after Dossetti's *Cronache Sociali* ceased publication. The new Fanfanian current consisted of two streams: former *Dossettiani* such as Moro, Zaccagnini, Gui and Fanfani himself, and former members of the left wing of De Gasperi's centrist group such as Rumor and Taviani. Fanfani was the leader of *Iniziativa Democratica*, but Moro was sympathetic to the current's objectives. (The two men, incidentally, were never on the best of terms despite their general agreement on political strategy at this stage.) At the 1952 Congress *Iniziativa Democratica* won almost a third of the seats on the National Council; in 1953–4 Fanfani made a series of tours throughout Italy to win support for his *corrente*, emphasising that the 1953 electoral set-back had been due to lack of party organisation and lack of clearcut progressive policies, and that it was essential to put both these matters right before the 1958 general election; and at the Naples Congress in 1954 *Iniziativa Democratica* won over half the votes and Fanfani was elected political Secretary. Fanfani then set about 'colonising' the DC's national organs with his own men and trying to build up the party in the country. But he was largely unsuccessful in achieving the latter. Meanwhile his proconsular style of politics was counter-productive, in that he provoked into being an organised right-wing *corrente*, *Primavera*, and gave new impulse to the left-wing *Base*.[50] Although Fanfani belonged to the progressive wing of the DC and wanted to detach the Socialists from the Communists and move towards a Centre-Left government, he had no time for those who criticised his policies or his timing. Thus he came into serious conflict with the *Base*, although its members advocated a similar strategy to his own. At the 1956 National Congress at Trent, for example, the *Base* proposed that the Socialists be asked to join the government. Fanfani regarded the proposal as premature and criticised the *Base* leaders, Marcora of Milan, Capuani of Novara, Marchetti of Verese and Galloni of Rome, for their undisciplined 'pressurisation' of the party leadership.[51] Fanfani further annoyed the *Base* by suspending three of its members from the DC for attending the Helsinki peace conference (sponsored by the Communists) in 1956 and by expelling Signor Marchetti, editor of the *Base's* journal, *Prospettive*, for criticising the party's leadership.

The other main current of the Left, the trade unionist *Forze Sociali*, which had from eight to twelve seats on the DC National Council throughout the 1950s, was less of a thorn in Fanfani's side. *Forze Sociali* approved the opening to the left in principle, but Giulio Pastore, the Secretary of CISL and leader of *Forze Sociali*, tended to act as a brake on Fanfani because he was worried that an over-friendly attitude towards the parties of the Left might weaken the cohesion of CISL and of the Catholic working class generally. On the other hand, the younger members of *Forze Sociali*, notably Carlo Donat-Cattin and Livio Labor, the leader of ACLI, wanted to see the government implementing as many social and economic reforms as possible in order to attract the Socialists to work with the Christian Democrats.[52]

In the De Gasperi era there had been no organised right-wing current. Men such as the liberal economists, Gordini and Falck, and the ex-Monarchist, Reggio d'Aci, were known as the *Vespisti* on account of their association with the conservative review *La Vespa*, but the *Vespisti* formed the right wing of De Gasperi's centrist current and did not constitute a separate faction. However, in 1954 Giulio Andreotti, whose power-base lay in traditionally right-wing Rome and Lazio, established *Primavera* as a specifically right-of-centre current to challenge Fanfani's leftward strategy. His main supporters were Scelba, Lucifredi and Bettiol. Only two *Primavera* candidates were elected to the National Council in 1954 and seven in 1956, but the current was strongly supported by businessmen and was more influential in Parliament than at the National Congress or in the National Council, and its members did all they could to retard the progress of the *apertura alla sinistra*, claiming that if the Socialists were brought into the government the DC would lose many middle-class voters to the Right (this did in fact happen at the general election of 1963 when the Liberals gained twenty-five seats), and that by 'endorsing' the Socialists the DC would unwittingly help to make the Communists more respectable.

Although *Iniziativa Democratica* was the predominant current from 1954–9, Fanfani's victory within the party was really Pyrrhic. The *apertura alla sinistra*, it is true, was eventually completed (in 1963), but part of the price paid was the disintegration of *Iniziativa Democratica*. Already in 1955, when Giovanni Gronchi was elected President with the support of the DC left-wing *correnti* in preference to Fanfani's candidate, Senator Merzagora, it was clear that Fanfani was by no means the undisputed leader of the DC in Parliament, even if he still had the support of the majority of the party in the country. And in January 1959 Fanfani was forced to resign from the premiership – he also resigned voluntarily from the party secretaryship – owing to opposition from the Centre-Right in the DC who had withdrawn their support from him. Fanfani fell partly because he was distrusted as an 'authoritarian', partly on account of his 'neutralist' foreign policy,[53] but above all because he had tried to go too far to the left too quickly: the centre of the DC was simply not ready in 1959 to make any further advances towards the Socialists. And the *Dorotei* current was the direct consequence of Fanfani's misjudgement. The *Dorotei* – so-called because they held their first meeting at the Convent of St Dorothée prior to the National Council meeting of March 1959 – consisted of the 'moderate' majority of *Iniziativa Democratica*, men such as Moro, Rumor, Colombo, Taviani and Piccoli. These were the leaders who were to dominate the DC in the 1960s. Fundamentally they were reformers and supporters of the Centre-Left, but they were determined to go at their own pace, and that pace was such that the epithet 'Dorotei' was in time to become almost a synonym for 'trimmer'. And as the *Dorotei* became increasingly associated with the *immobilismo* of the 1960s, so the Centre-Left experiment and the whole DC régime was increasingly called into question.

The break-up of *Iniziativa Democratica* was indeed of fundamental importance in the development of the DC. If Fanfani had succeeded in achieving for himself and his current the sort of authority De Gasperi and the centrists had previously wielded, it is possible that the Centre-Left experiment might have been more successful and that the DC might have remained more united. As it was, the DC entered the 1960s divided into two main left-wing *correnti* (the *Base* and the *Forze Sociali*, sometimes called *Rinnovamento* or *Forze Nuove*); two main centre-left currents (the *Dorotei* and the *Fanfaniani*, the latter sometimes known as *Nuove Cronache* on account of their review); and the centre-right group (at first called *Primavera*, but increasingly known as *Centrismo Popolare* or *Forze Libere*). As always, the boundaries between one *corrente* and another were far from clear-cut, but roughly speaking the Left could usually count on holding about 20 per cent of the seats on the National Council, the *Dorotei* 50–55 per cent, the *Fanfaniani* 10–15 per cent, and the Right about 10 per cent. There was always, however, a particularly high degree of fluidity between the Centre and Centre-Right.

An examination of the balance of forces within the DC during the first decade of Centre-Left governments (1963–72) provides an excellent case-study of the debilitating effect of factionalism in the DC. However, when making this examination it is important to take careful note of the balance of forces within the DC parliamentary groups as well as at Congresses and within the National Council, for the DC parliamentary groups were throughout this period more conservative than the party as a whole. At the Naples Congress in 1962, for example, 80 per cent of the delegates supported Moro in favour of the *apertura alla sinistra* (the *Dorotei*, *Fanfaniani*, *Base* and *Rinnovamento*), and yet in March of that year Signor Scalfaro, the candidate of the conservative *Centrismo Popolare* current, polled 99 votes against 140 for the Centre-Left candidate Zaccagnini at the election for the president of the DC group in the Chamber. Then in July 1962 forty-six members of the same group voted against the nationalisation of electricity, which was regarded by the Socialists as the *quid pro quo* for their entering the government. Again, in December 1963 thirty-four DC deputies, led by Scelba and Pella, the leaders of *Centrismo Popolare*, abstained in the vote of confidence on the first Centre-Left government led by Moro.[54] The members of *Centrismo Popolare* and the more conservative *Dorotei* claimed they were not against the Centre-Left *per se*, but that it was up to the PSI to demonstrate its good faith by breaking all contacts with the PCI in local government and in the trade unions. They also wanted the PSI to commit itself in advance not to form any alliances with the PCI in the new regional governments which were to be established as part of the Centre-Left package.[55] And although the majority of the *Dorotei* did not go quite as far as this, they tended to oppose the implementation of any reforms until Italy had overcome its balance of payments problem by traditional monetarist and economic policies. (The Italian balance of payments went into deficit in 1961 for the first time for several years, and throughout the 1960s continued to show an annual deficit.)

Meanwhile, the Left *correnti* mounted an attack on the *Dorotei* leaders for their moderation and immobilism. At the 1964 Congress in Naples, for example, Donat-Cattin accused the DC leadership of pusillanimity in the face of Italy's growing economic and social problems: 'it has done no more than adapt itself to the present power structure, which consciously or unconsciously it refuses to change . . . whilst not always appearing to do so, it acts as a brake on the development of a more democratic and just society.'[56] And at the 1967 Congress in Milan Donat-Cattin demanded effective economic planning and the implementation of regionalisation as gauges of the government's commitment to a reform programme.[57] Or again Galloni called upon the DC 'to cease being a party which is simply interested in holding on to the reins of government . . . and become the vehicle through which popular and progressive Catholic forces can participate in the life of the nation'.[58] Carrying this idea a stage further Dario Mengozzi of the trade-union current told the DC National Council in July 1968: 'it is essential that the parties of the Centre-Left make a decisive move to the Left. . . . Such a move presupposes a new majority. No new line will be credible if supported only by the present political forces which have shown themselves to be incapable of breaking out of the present deadlock.'[59] Mengozzi did not propose that the PCI be brought into government, but he suggested that some degree of 'normalisation of relations' with the PCI, the main party of opposition, was a necessary precondition to a genuine reform programme. Already, almost a decade before the DC–PCI 'tactical compromise',[60] the more progressive elements in the DC were hinting at some form of co-operation with the PCI. And there were others outside Parliament who began to call for what the *Corriere della Sera* christened the 'Repubblica Conciliare', i.e. some form of Catholic-Communist co-operation, as the only means to break the deadlock and *immobilismo* characteristic of the Centre-Left period. John XXIII's *Pacem in Terris* (1963), addressed to 'all men of goodwill' and calling for greater social justice throughout the world, encouraged moves in this direction. A leading Jesuit, Giuseppe de Rosa, proposed discussions between the DC and PCI, a proposal supported by De Mita of the *Base* and Pastore of *Rinnovamento*. And in 1964 a left-wing Catholic, Mario Gozzini, edited a book with five articles by Communists and five by Catholics entitled *Il Dialogo alla Prova*. Then in 1969 the Catholic trade unionists of the *Confederazione Italiana di Sindacati Liberi* (CISL) established contacts with the Communist *Confederazione Generale Italiana del Lavoro* (CGIL) during the social unrest and strikes of the 'Hot Autumn', and Livio Labor led the majority of the *Associazione Cristiana di Lavoratori Italiani* (ACLI), which had for long had close links with Catholic Action and the DC, to a position of independence to the Left of both. Meanwhile, the various extra-parliamentary *Gruppi di impegno politico* were all talking in terms of a 'Conciliar Republic' as the only solution to Italy's problems.

The effect of such proposals and criticisms was twofold: it both strengthened the determination of the Centre-Right to resist any further moves to the Left (between 1964–6 the *Centrismo Popolare* current integrated itself into the *Dorotei*), and it increased the doubts of the left-inclined *Dorotei*, notably the followers of Moro, as to whether the Centre-Left governments would ever be able to carry through the fundamental social and economic reforms to which in principle they were committed.

By the mid 1960s the leaders of the DC realised that the party's factional quarrels were destroying its ability to govern, and at the 1964 Congress the party Secretary, Mariano Rumor, appealed to all the *correnti* to draw together so that the party could present a more united front.[61] He proposed that the DC should appoint four deputy-secretaries, representing the main *correnti*, in an attempt to neutralise the disastrous effect of factional quarrelling. And in February 1965 four deputy-secretaries were elected by the National Council – Forlani representing the *Fanfaniani*, Galloni (the Left), Piccoli (the *Dorotei*) and Scalfaro (the Centre-Right) – but this arrangement amounted to little more than a non-aggression pact, and in 1966 it broke down. The Left *correnti* argued that they were being dominated by the *Dorotei* moderates, and that the only way to exert pressure for reforms was from outside the national party structure; they therefore withdrew Galloni from his position as deputy-secretary.[62] The Right then followed suit, setting up *Forze Libere* as an 'autonomous' conservative faction.

Under pressure from the Socialists and the DC left-wing *correnti* to carry out reforms, possibly with Communist support, and under pressure from the Right to implement no new reforms and to have no truck with the PCI, the *Dorotei* finally cracked, and with them all hope that the Centre-Left could provide an effective answer to Italy's problems. The personal followers of Taviani were the first to break from the *Dorotei* current (in 1967); Moro's friends, who had moved too rapidly and too far Left for the *Dorotei* moderates, were in effect abandoned by their colleagues in 1968; and in 1969 the *Dorotei* rump split into a Colombo-Andreotti faction and a Rumor-Piccoli faction, the former being slightly more conservative than the latter. Meanwhile, the controversial, mercurial Fanfani had moved to the right, although he was the original architect of the opening to the left.

When Taviani formed his own group at the Florence Congress in 1967 he claimed that he was only putting up a special 'Congress list', not forming a new current. But in reality he was breaking from the *Dorotei*, for his so-called 'Congress list', which resulted in fourteen of his friends being elected to the National Council, continued to exist as an independent current after the Congress. Taviani claimed that his objective was to draw the various *correnti* together and produce a less heterogeneous party image. He criticised both the extreme-left and extreme-right *correnti*, affirming his own commitment to the Centre-Left.[63] But it was far from clear why he thought that his decision to take an independent line would produce a more united party. In fact, he simply encouraged more splintering in the centre. The most likely explanation for his decision to 'go it alone' was that he hoped to strengthen his position *vis-à-vis* the other DC leaders by forming his own power base. [4] Taviani had been a leading figure in the DC since the early days. At one time close to Dossetti, he had been party Secretary, Minister of Defence (for five years), Minister of the Treasury (for three years) and Minister of the Interior (for six years). He had a powerful geographical base in Liguria and contacts with the leaders of many of the most important interest groups. The current he established was a typical 'personal' current rather than a current of 'principle'.[65]

In contrast the current set up by Moro in November 1968 was essentially a current of 'principle'. There had been a slight movement to the left at the 1968 general election,[66] and the *Base* leaders at once called for a more left-wing government.[87] Moro sympathised with this call, and joined the *Base* and *Rinnovamento* in opposing the election of the centrist Piccoli as party Secretary in place of Rumor at the National Congress of January 1969. Like Taviani, Moro claimed that he was not setting up a new current, but only taking account of the realities of the political situation. He called for a 'strategia dell' attenzione', by which he meant a more 'attentive', active, reformist style of Centre-Left government. This included a less critical attitude towards the Communist party. Moro always stated that there could be no question of the PCI participating in government, but the Centre-Left governments should be 'less insensitive' to the proposals put forward by the opposition.[68] Moro's new attitude – always couched in the vague jargon characteristic of Italian party politics – undoubtedly marked a real change in the DC's attitude to the PCI. Here was a major leader in effect admitting that the Centre-Left had failed, and that sooner or later some sort of agreement with the PCI might have to be considered. In the short term Moro provoked the more centrist *Dorotei* to form their own currents; and his 'leftist' line further soured his relations with Fanfani who was still firmly against any dealings with the PCI. In 1969 the *Dorotei* rump thus disintegrated into Rumor-Piccoli and Colombo-Andreotti factions, the former remaining theoretically committed to the Centre-Left but opposed to Moro's flirtations with the Marxists, the latter inclining towards the revival of the *quadripartito* Centre-Right formula (i.e. a DC–PLI–PRI–PSDI coalition).

By the time of the 1971 party Congress the DC had reached a nadir in terms of factionalism. No fewer than nine *correnti* were represented on the National Council elected in October of that year, and none held more than 20 per cent of the seats. Going from left to right the *correnti* were as follows (with their leaders in brackets): *Nuove Sinistra* (Sullo), 1·7 per cent; *Base* (De Mita), 11 per cent; *Forze Nuove* (Donat-Cattin) 7 per cent; *Morotei* (Moro), 13·4 per cent; *Tavianei* (Taviani), 10·5 per cent; *Nuove Cronache* (Fanfani, Forlani), 17·4 per cent; *Impegno Democratico* (Andreotti, Colombo), 15 per cent; *Iniziativa Popolare* (Rumor, Piccoli), 20 per cent; and *Forze Libere* (Scelba, Scalfaro), 4 per cent. All these mutations and divisions within the DC, particularly those which had occurred in the centre and centre-left of the party, whilst in no way diminishing the DC's passion for office-holding, seriously reduced its capacity to govern, with or without allies.

The DC and the Bureaucracy
Under increasing electoral pressure from the PCI in the 1970s there were signs that the DC might overcome the worst of its factional problems.[69] But something which was (and is) much more difficult for the DC to resolve – and which has important implications for the future of the Italian governmental system, indeed for liberal democracy in Italy – is the party's ambivalent relationship with the bureaucracy. The basic problem is what two distinguished sociologists have described as Italy's 'dualism',[70] the fact that Italy, which has many of the characteristics of a modern industrial state, is run by a cumbersome and inefficient bureaucracy, appropriately described by Sabino Acquaviva as 'the worst sort of Levantine administration . . . . [It] reflects the underdevelopment and traditional closed culture of the south.'[71] The DC's northern

technocratic wing would like to see the bureaucracy reformed, because they realise that the social and economic frustration, which produced the 'Hot Autumn' of 1969 and helped to breed the civil disorder of the 1970s, can only be ameliorated by greatly improved state services. Men such as Remo Gaspari, Minister for Reform of the Publication Administration in the early 1970s, and Ciriaco de Mita, Minister with special responsibility for the South in the late 1970s, have argued that the *sine qua non* for a better educational system, more efficient hospitals, the reduction of urban slums and an attack on environmental abuses, is a state apparatus which can translate legislative enactments into concrete achievements.[72] During the 1976 general election *Il Giornale*, a newspaper owned by Indro Montanelli, who constantly campaigns for higher standards in public life, published the names of forty DC candidates considered to be both honest and firmly anti-Communist. Thirty-eight of these candidates were elected, and one of their leaders, Massimo de Carolis, later stated: 'We are bent on replacing the patronage-based electoral machinery of the party with one based on persuasion through the mass media.'[73] However, the DC is confronted with a major dilemma, for the party has a vested interest in *not* carrying through a major reform of the bureaucracy owing to its involvement in the *sottogoverno* (sub-governmental structure) and in the whole system of patronage. Moreover, as the DC's traditional support groups have either declined in influence in the 1960s and 1970s (for example Catholic Action and the *Coldiretti* (direct cultivators)), or have distanced themselves somewhat from the party (for example the employers of *Confindustria*, the trade-unionists of the *Confederazione Italiana Sindacati Lavoratori* (CISL), and the members of the *Associazione Cristiana di Lavoratori Italiani* (ACLI)), it has seemed to many Christian Democrats that it is even more important for the DC to retain its control over patronage.

Joseph LaPalombara, in his classic study of interest groups in Italian politics, distinguished between *clientela* and *parentela* pressure groups.[74] The *clientela* type of relationship between government and interest groups is common in many countries, being based on a government department's acceptance of a particular interest group as the most representative spokesman for a particular sector. *Confindustria* (the Italian industrialists' confederation), for example, had such a relationship with the Ministry of Industry and Commerce and also with the Interministerial Committee for Economic Planning. It is correct to say 'had' rather than 'has', because, whilst *Confindustria* from 1946–55 worked closely with the DC, its relationship with the party became much more strained during the 'opening to the left' in the late 1950s and early 1960s. Indeed, Alighiero De Micheli, *Confindustria*'s president at that time, organised a pressure group, *Confintesa*, to support parliamentary candidates who were favourable to private enterprise, whatever their party, and at the 1963 general election *Confindustria* openly supported the Liberals (effectively Conservatives). After the 'Hot Autumn' of 1969 *Confindustria* under Renato Lombardi (president 1970–4) moderated its attitude towards the unions and government, and Lombardi's successors, Gianni Agnelli and Guido Carli, continued this line in the middle and late 1970s. The relationship between the DC and *Confindustria* has thus been closer in the 1970s than in the 1960s, but *Confindustria* has never regained the favoured *clientela* relationship it had with the DC in the De Gasperi era. Perhaps partly in compensation, the Christian Democrats have striven, with some success, to increase their influence – both in terms of patronage and through investment control – over the great parastatal corporations, notably the Institute for Industrial Reconstruction, IRI (which employs 450,000) and the National Hydrocarbons Board, ENI (which employs 80,000).[75] In addition, they have retained their tight control over RAI, the national broadcasting corporation.

The *clientela* type relationship which the DC had (and to a lesser extent has) with *Confindustria*, and increasingly has with the parastatal corporations, is based on expertise and precise contacts. But equally important for the Christian Democrats is the looser, more complex, and peculiarly Italian *parentela* relationship, which is based on 'cross-fertilisation' and infiltration, with the *parentela* type interest groups trying to place their supporters in the dominant political party (i.e. the DC), whilst at the same time the DC tries to fill the bureaucracy and sub-governmental structures with its supporters, many of whom also belong to these *parentela* groups. This *parentela* relationship, encouraged both by the DC and by certain interest groups, was characteristic of the DC's connections with Catholic Action and the *Coldiretti*, and to a lesser extent with CISL and ACLI, until the 1960s. It constituted one of the main elements of the so-called 'DC régime', although of course it also encouraged *immobilismo*, both Catholic Action and the *Coldiretti* being essentially conservative pressure groups.

The 1960s and 1970s, however, saw a dramatic decline in the strength of these *parentela* groups. In 1956, for example, there were 1,655,000 members of Catholic Action (950,000 adults and 705,000 juniors). But, under the influence of secularisation and the Second Vatican Council, Catholic Action began to collapse in the late 1960s, and by 1976 the total membership was 535,000 (395,000 adults and 140,000 juniors, a drop of 60 per cent in adult membership and 80 per cent in junior membership since 1956).[76] Although the Civic Committees of Catholic Action still play a relatively important role in elections, Catholic Action has lost much of its power and influence as a social and political force.[77] The same is true of the *Coltivatori Diretti* (or *Coldiretti*, 'direct cultivators') owing to the rural exodus of the late 1950s and the 1960s. In 1951 42·2 per cent of Italy's active population was employed in agriculture (of these 24·2 per cent were self-employed farmers, mainly *Coldiretti*); by 1971 17·3 per cent were employed in agriculture (of these 12·3 per cent were self-employed farmers).[78] The main exodus of self-employed farmers occurred between 1961–71, and it has continued unabated in the 1970s.[79] The Christian Democratic-run *Coldiretti*, who control the *Federconsorzi* (quasi-public bodies which provide farmers with credit, storage facilities, etc.) still have over a million members, about nine-tenths of all the direct cultivators, but they no longer have the political influence they had in their heyday under Paolo Bonomi, when they could on occasion make and unmake governments.[80]

Other props of the Christian Democratic régime, the ACLI and CISL, have either declined or taken their distance from the DC. ACLI, the Christian

Association of Italian Workers, has done both. Originally set up in 1944 as the Catholic workers' element within the united trade union movement, ACLI was (and is) not exactly a trade union confederation, being essentially a charitable and social organisation. When the Catholics broke from the Communist-dominated CGIL in 1948 and set up their own confederation, CISL, most of the latter's leading figures came from ACLI, but ACLI was throughout the 1950s much more closely associated with the Hierarchy and with the DC than was CISL. ACLI had a membership of about 700,000 throughout the 1950s, and it was said that it could deliver up to two million votes for the DC.[81] However, in the light of the Second Vatican Council and the 'Hot Autumn' of 1969 ACLI embarked on a radical course under Livio Labor. It ended its 'collateral relationship' with the DC, and announced that it would no longer automatically support DC candidates.[82] Under Labor's chosen successor, Emilio Gabaglio (Secretary-General, 1969–72), ACLI continued the process of deconfessionalisation, and the Church retaliated by cutting off its subsidy to ACLI. Meanwhile, Labor founded a left-wing Catholic party, the *Movimento Politico dei Lavoratori* (MPL) to fight the 1972 general election. The MPL, however, failed completely at the election, winning only 130,000 votes.[83] After 1972, under a new Secretary-General, Marino Carboni, ACLI returned to more friendly relations with the DC and with the Hierarchy, but the old intimate relationship with the DC had been destroyed and in the process ACLI had lost almost half its membership (there were fewer than 400,000 members by 1976).

CISL emerged from the labour troubles of the late 1960s unscathed (in 1976 it still claimed to have 2·4 million members, the same figure as in 1966).[84] CISL's relationship with the DC has always been more *nuancé* than that of ACLI (certainly this was true of the 1950s and most of the 1960s). Nevertheless, the support of CISL has always been important to the DC. According to a 1968 sample, 25 per cent of DC members belonged to CISL, and most CISL members vote for the DC.[85] It is significant too that, although CISL has important links with the left-wing *correnti* in the DC, it remains a rather conservative confederation owing to its strong representation amongst office workers in the public sector.[86] In addition, after the breakdown of the attempt to reunite the Communist-dominated CGIL and CISL in 1971–2, CISL moved back into a more friendly relationship with the DC, and supported the Christian Democrats much more decisively at the 1976 general election than at that of 1972.[87]

To summarise at this stage, then, the DC has seen its *clientela* relationship with *Confindustria* considerably weakened, although to some extent this has been counterbalanced by its increased 'colonisation' of the parastatal corporations. The DC's *parentela* relationship with Catholic Action, the *Coldiretti* and the trade unions has also been undermined, although it has not been completely destroyed in spite of secularisation, the rural exodus, and the growing 'independence' of ACLI and CISL. However, the weakening of the DC's supporting organisations undoubtedly created a vacuum, and it is this vacuum which the DC has striven to fill with new 'friends', largely consisting of *parassitari* from the *ceti medi* (parasites from the middle-class groups).[88]

A further word must be said here about the Italian bureaucracy and the *sottogoverno*. As the following table shows the steady growth of the bureaucracy is not a recent development, but there has been a massive expansion since the Second World War.

Number of Administrators, Private and Public, 1881–1962

	Population		Administrators (private)		Administrators (public)	
	No.	%	No.	%	No.	%
1881–2	28,951,000	100	452,000	100	98,000	100
1911–12	36,900,000	127	693,000	153	263,000	268
1961–2	50,600,000	174	2,734,000	604	1,340,000	1,362

At the time of the 1971 census the population of Italy was 54·2 million, almost double what it was in 1881. But between 1881–1971 the number of state employees had grown by an estimated 1,500 per cent. Of course, as governments have become increasingly involved in economic planning and social welfare, bureaucratic expansionism has affected all modern industrial nations. Nevertheless, the Italian bureaucratic expansion has been particularly serious for at least three reasons. First, in absolute terms, the increase has been fairly dramatic (in 1951 9·09 per cent of the active population were employed in the tertiary sector; by 1971 the figure was 15·9 per cent),[89] and more seriously it was becoming doubtful whether the Italian economy, despite the efficiency of northern industry, could continue to pay for this army of bureaucrats: in other words, the productive and unproductive elements in Italian society were getting dangerously out of balance.[90] Secondly, in comparative terms, Italy has a remarkably large number of civil servants: 30 per cent of all employees in the tertiary sector are civil servants, compared with 18·9 per cent in West Germany, 14·0 per cent in Belgium and 12·9 per cent in France.[91] Thirdly, and most serious, is what may be termed the 'southern factor'. This is not simply a matter of numbers, although it is true that the south provides Italy with approximately 80 per cent of its civil servants, whilst the north, with 46 per cent of the population, supplies only 15 per cent. Above all it is a question of attitude and psychology.[92] The southerners introduced their slow-moving, clientelist, semi-corrupt habits into the whole of the bureaucracy. Again, this is not a recent development – it goes away back to the 1880s, when the state's major ministries were moved from Turin to Rome. But in the postwar period it has accelerated with the state's increasing involvement in economic planning and restructuring (notably through the *Cassa per il Mezzogiorno*),[93] and in the social services generally. There is evidence that civil servants often only work for as little as 20 per cent of the time they should (their normal working day in Rome is in any case only from 8.00 a.m.–2.00 p.m.), that favours can be purchased by the famous *bustarella* (money-laden envelope), that entry into various civil service departments depends as much on who one knows as on what one knows in spite of written examinations for administrative and executive class entries.[94] Moreover, it is doubtful whether regional reform and administrative deconcentration have done much to solve the bureaucratic problem.[95]

One of its aspects is of course the *sottogoverno*, the sub-governmental structure which has grown rapidly in the postwar period with the full connivance of the DC. Indeed, in the 1960s the DC encouraged the growth of this substructure, which has no legal or institutional basis, to counter the declining direct influence of its *clientela* and *parentela* support groups.[96] It is very difficult to analyse the *sottogoverno* with precision, but a useful description of it has been given by Peter Nichols of *The Times*, an acute observer of Italian politics:

> It is the 'network' of interests cultivated and to some extent created by the Christian Democrats; it is the means by which favours are dispensed, how jobs are obtained in the apparatus of the State or any of its near relatives, directing an opera-house, a licence to run a tobacconist's shop, keeping the parish priests happy by granting small requests, bending the knee in exaggerated servility towards the local bishop, a job in the state radio and television corporation, presiding over the local tourist office. It is the way the ordinary citizen can be equipped to deal with the official administration, because a letter recommending him to an official may well solve his problem: in return for which, of course, he will vote for the party which helped him. The *sottogoverno* is post-war Italy's greatest contribution to the art of keeping a country running when government in the accepted sense of the term is lacking.[97]

It may be true that the *sottogoverno* has kept Italy 'running', but it is also true that it is a system which produces stagnation and frustration. The partial breakdown of Italy's hospital services and postal system in the 1970s, for example, was a direct consequence of this way of 'running' the country. The *sottogoverno*, and with it the DC, have not surprisingly come under increasing criticism in the 1970s. It has been estimated that there are almost 60,000 *enti pubblici* (public boards and agencies), of which perhaps as many as 16,000 are purely parasitical bodies, whose only merit is that they provide jobs in a country which suffers from chronic unemployment and underemployment.[98] These *enti pubblici* are largely colonised by Christian Democrats or people who feel under an obligation to support the DC[99] – those whom Ardigo has labelled the middle-class parasites.[100]

In the course of the 1960s the traditional Catholic and Marxist subcultures of Italy began to crumble under the influence of international détente, the 'opening to the left', secularisation and the Second Vatican Council. As a result the DC régime began to lose its solidarity: in particular the DC's key supporting organisations, Catholic Action, the *Coldiretti* and ACLI, for one reason or another, lost much of their former influence. The DC's reaction to these political and social changes was twofold. On the one hand, the party pressed forward with the Centre-Left experiment, and later began to co-operate with the Communists,[101] all the while emphasising that it was determined to reform both itself and the governmental system, with a view to carrying through economic and social reforms. On the other hand, the DC did all it could to further its colonisation of the public service and its associated agencies, but

in so doing it allied itself with an army of *parassitari*. It was a real dilemma
for the Christian Democrats: they had *somehow* to deal with the decimation
of their traditional support groups, but by consolidating their hold on the
bureaucracy and *sottogoverno* they reduced their capacity to modernise Italy.

The DC and the Church

If party factionalism and relations with the bureaucracy were serious problems
for the Italian Christian Democrats in the 1960s and 1970s, another, and
equally intractable, problem was the relationship between the DC and the
Church. Arguably the most important single *political* step taken in Italy since
the collapse of fascism was the Vatican's decision to give its full support and
encouragement to the emergent DC. But, as we have seen, the DC never became
a confessional party pure and simple. De Gasperi was determined to co-operate
with the lay parties of the centre primarily in order to prevent the division of
Italy into 'clerical' and 'anti-clerical' blocs. And the whole phenomenon of the
apertura alla sinistra was further evidence that the DC wanted, if not to distance
itself from the Church, at least to assert its independence *vis-à-vis* the Vatican.
However, this was easier said than done, for the leaders of the DC knew very
well that the party depended heavily on the support of Catholic priests and
of the Civic Committees of Catholic Action at elections. And whilst it was true
that many of the DC's thirteen to fourteen million voters at the general elections of 1972 and 1976 were not practising Catholics, the party nevertheless
remained *the* party of Catholics, with its main bastions of strength in those
parts of the country where Catholicism was still a powerful force, the north-
east and large parts of the south. However, as Italy became increasingly
'secularised' in the 1960s and 1970s, it became even more important for the
DC to redefine its relationship with the Church. The DC could hardly afford
to bite the Catholic hand which fed it. Equally, if it wanted to tap the important
reservoir of anti-Communist lay voters, it could not afford to be labelled a
'clerical' party by its opponents. Rather it had to continue to develop as an
'independent' Catholic party and to mould itself in the image of its sister-
parties north of the Alps. This dilemma came to a head over the issue of
divorce, which culminated in the referendum of 1974. It is worth analysing
the referendum in some detail, both because it provides an excellent case-
study of the complex relationship between the DC and the Church and because
it marked an important stage in the political and social development of postwar
Italy. It was indeed a watershed both for the Centre-Left experiment and for
the DC. It more or less marked the end of the shaky alliance between the
Christian Democrats and Socialists, and, as far as the Christian Democrats
were concerned, it forced them to think out what sort of a party they wanted
the DC to be – essentially 'integralist' or essentially 'autonomous'. During the
referendum campaign the DC projected itself mainly as a confessional, integralist party. But paradoxically the long-term effect has been that the DC has
emerged with a more secular and autonomous image than it ever had before.[102]

To understand why it should have been necessary to hold a referendum on
divorce in a Western industrial country in the 1970s it is important to remember
that the Church had an unusually powerful grip over Italian 'civil' society, in

particular with regard to education and marriage, as a result of the Lateran Pacts, i.e. the Treaty and Concordat of 1929, which were written into the Italian Constitution in 1947. Article 7 of the Constitution laid down that 'The State and Catholic Church are, each in its own sphere, independent and sovereign. Their relations are regulated by the Lateran Pacts. Modifications of the Pacts, accepted by the two parties, do not require the procedure for constitutional amendments.' But from the beginning it was not clear what this meant. Most practising Catholics maintained that the Church's privileged position, including its sole right to annul marriages,[103] was therefore part of the Constitution. But many lay lawyers, and even some devout Catholics like the Christian Democrat Giuseppe Dossetti, argued that Article 7 did not constitutionalise the *contents* of the Pacts, but merely stated what was the *basis* of Church–State relations in Republican Italy. Article 29 certainly implied that marriages could be dissolved. However, no provision for divorce was written into the Civil Code, and there is no doubt that any attempt to provide for civil divorce in the late 1940s would have been defeated.[104]

By the 1960s, however, Italian society had become much more secular, and there were increasing demands that Italy, like its northern European neighbours, should have provisions for civil divorce.[105] After several years of lobbying by the extra-parliamentary League for Divorce, the upshot was the Divorce Law of 1970 (sometimes called the Fortuna Law after its Socialist sponsor, Loris Fortuna). The new law provided that a judge could grant divorce in certain circumstances: these included attempted murder of spouse or children, incest, incitement to prostitution, criminal insanity and prison sentences of over fifteen years. Divorces could also be granted in cases of non-consummation, and to Italians married to foreigners who had been granted divorces in other countries. But the most important ground for divorce was simply that the partners had been legally separated for five years – this was important because it was estimated that at least 30,000 Italians were in this situation. The Fortuna Law, then, did not make divorce an easy option. Its most important effect was to allow people who were already separated to marry those with whom they now lived and to make their children legitimate. It was, therefore, seen by its proponents as a humane and socially just law.

Although divorce would be regarded in most modern societies as a matter of individual conscience, in Italy it could not be kept out of the political arena, because Catholic integralists – in and outside the DC – collected almost 1·5 million signatures demanding a referendum to abrogate the divorce law (only 500,000 were required under Article 75 of the Constitution). Most of the DC leaders (like the Communists who knew that many of their voters were Catholics) would have preferred to have avoided the referendum, but, when confronted with it, could do nothing but support it. One of those who signed the petition was Arnaldo Forlani, the DC Secretary. Indeed, the whole issue of divorce brought the DC face to face with the problem of its relationship with the Church. However, it should be noted that there were major differences of opinion within the party over divorce, as indeed there were – although less publicly – in the Vatican and in the Hierarchy.

In line with precedents set by Pope John XXIII, Paul VI avoided *direct* involvement in what was fundamentally an *Italian* political and social issue, although privately he made it clear that he was opposed to divorce.[106] The Bishops Conference in February 1974 (with the exception of the 'liberal' Archbishop of Turin), however, called on all Catholics to vote against the 'social sore' of divorce.[107] Not all Catholics agreed with the bishops. Many Christian Democrats, including practising Catholics, considered that Italy should come into line with other industrial societies in having provisions for divorce. An opinion poll of January 1974 showed that 47 per cent of practising Catholics favoured the Divorce Law, whilst 45 per cent opposed it. Sixty-three per cent of all those interviewed were in favour of divorce, whilst 30 per cent were against – figures which were broadly comparable to the actual votes cast in the referendum in May (59·1 per cent for, 40·9 per cent against).[108]

It is impossible to be precise about numbers, but many Catholic priests, Catholic trade-unionists and leaders of left-wing Catholic groups were pre-pared not only to vote for the Divorce Law but to support it publicly. The most prominent individual 'rebel' was Dom Giovanni Battista Franzoni, abbot of the Church of St Paul's Outside the Walls, Rome, who spoke all over Italy in favour of retaining the law on the grounds that it was a civil divorce law and that Italy was a pluralist society. Dom Franzoni was careful to point out that for practising Catholics the marriage bond remained indissoluble, but, despite his moderate approach to the whole question, he was suspended from the Benedictine order. Nevertheless, many Catholic priests attended rallies of the *Comitato dei Cattolici Democratici per il No*, whilst even in the strongly Catholic north-east the Cardinal Patriarch of Venice had to send letters to over twenty priests warning them not to participate in pro-divorce rallies.[109] Over the country as a whole, of course, the vast majority of priests, however uneasily, followed the exhortations of their bishops and condemned the Divorce Law. The Pope, however, maintained his silence throughout the campaign despite speculation that he would make a last-minute pronouncement against divorce.[110] Doubtless one reason for his silence was that opinion polls consistently indicated that the supporters of divorce would win.

Like the Catholic Church, the DC was faced with a considerable dilemma over the issue of divorce. Although many Christian Democrats supported the Divorce Law, no DC leader came out openly in favour of divorce during the campaign. However, important *correnti* leaders such as Aldo Moro and Carlo Donat-Cattin maintained a studious silence. The DC was, in fact, in a very awkward position. After the failure of the Centre-Right experiment of January 1972–June 1973, the party had opted for another Centre-Left government at its Congress of June 1973. At the same time there were signs that the party had achieved greater unity after all the factional disputes of the 1960s. The number of *correnti* had been reduced from nine to six, and more significantly Fanfani and Moro had become reconciled to each other after several years of estrangement. Fanfani had been elected political Secretary at the June 1973 Congress, and he and Moro had agreed to give their full support to the Centre-Left government led by Mariano Rumor which was formed after the June Congress.[111] The DC Leadership had no wish to alienate its Centre-Left lay

partners, the Socialists, Social Democrats and Republicans, and yet, for fear
of upsetting its devout Catholic supporters both in and outside Parliament, it
could not risk supporting the amendment put forward by Senator Carrettoni
(PCI) in October 1973 which would have provided better terms for divorced
wives and children of broken marriages. Acceptance of the Carrettoni amendment would have required a change in the terms of the referendum, which
would then have been postponed, but it would also have entailed tacit DC
approval of divorce, which *could* have provoked a split within the party – a
price which no DC leader was prepared to pay. But the DC's uneasiness about
the referendum was shown by the fact that the party did not finally decide
that there was no way of avoiding it until January 1974. It was then that
Fanfani announced that the referendum would definitely take place, and that
the Christian Democrats would throw their full weight against the Divorce
Law.

There were a number of reasons why the DC, in spite of deep misgivings
within the party, decided it must go ahead with the divorce referendum. In the
first place it was constitutionally necessary to hold the referendum unless the
Divorce Law was repealed or amended by Parliament. The law could have
been repealed by a joint DC–neo-Fascist parliamentary vote, but the DC had no
wish to ally itself openly with the neo-Fascists, and if it had tried to do so,
there would almost certainly have been a revolt by the 'autonomists', who were
particularly strong in the party's left-wing *correnti*. Equally, any attempt merely
to modify the law would have aroused the opposition of the 'integralists' present in
all *correnti*. A second major calculation of the DC leadership was that if the party
did not lead the fight against divorce, there was a danger that it would be out-
flanked on its right by the neo-Fascists who would be able to project themselves as
the representatives and defenders of traditional Italian society. Thirdly, the DC
could not risk alienating its Catholic electorate, particularly the vast number of
ordinary party members who would have been shocked if the Christian
Democrats had 'betrayed' the Church by publicly accepting divorce. Fourthly,
in so far as individual DC members of parliament were concerned, it was
important to stand up and be counted in the anti-divorce lobby in order to
avoid any loss of preference votes at future elections. And preference votes
are important for ensuring that a candidate comes out near the top of the
party list, and can easily be forfeited if a candidate falls out with the Church
Hierarchy or the Civic Committees in his constituency.[112] Fifthly, the DC
leadership hoped that the campaign against divorce would continue the process of uniting the DC, whilst at the same time it would harm the PCI by
splitting the female vote, the assumption being that Communist wives would
vote differently from their husbands over an issue like divorce. Finally, there
may have been some truth in the theory that Fanfani hoped to increase his
own prestige by leading a (successful) campaign against divorce, so preparing
the way for some 'Gaullist' move in the direction of stronger institutions.
There was speculation in the press that Fanfani might have been calculating
along these lines, as indeed there had been at the time of the 1971 presidential
election. On both occasions commentators probably read too much into Fanfani's
statements and silences. Although Fanfani would undoubtedly have liked to

have seen the development of a stronger executive in Italy, he was far too shrewd a politician to imagine that this could be achieved by means of a referendum on divorce, whatever the outcome. Indeed it is clear that the main calculation of Fanfani and of the other DC leaders was that, whatever the risks of the referendum, the party would suffer more damage by endorsing an 'anti-clerical' law than by campaigning for its repeal.

The Communists, Socialists and small lay parties all emphasised that divorce was a basic civil right in any truly democratic state, and pointed to the 600 million Catholics living in countries where divorce was allowed who had never requested its abolition. They argued that the moderate use made of the Divorce Law since its introduction (only 81,000 divorces had been granted between 1971–3, many of them merely regularising pre-existing situations) was evidence of the social maturity of Italians and proof that divorce did not destroy the family. The Communists warned of the danger of what they called 'the clerico-Fascist menace', but were careful not to attack the DC leadership directly except in so far as it had 'yielded' to pressure from the right wing of the party. The Communists thus left the way open for a future 'dialogue' with the Christian Democrats.

The Christian Democrats were also well aware of the political implications of the referendum. They realised that if voters deserted the DC over divorce, they might do the same thing at elections generally; they objected to being bracketed with the neo-Fascist MSI; they were concerned that a lasting wedge was being driven between them and their former lay partners; above all, they realised that a victory for the pro-divorce lobby would be a victory for the Communists. Fanfani thus concentrated the DC's campaign on this last point, hoping thereby to cajole as many anti-Communists as possible into the anti-divorce lobby. He also tried to woo the female Communist vote away from the PCI, arguing that divorce was a bourgeois luxury which the working class neither wanted nor could afford, and he made considerable use of quotations purporting to show that both Marx and Togliatti had been against divorce. But although Fanfani played upon anti-Communist fears and prejudices, he was careful, like the PCI leaders, not to burn all bridges between the two parties. He repeatedly argued that the divorce issue should not be allowed to alienate the DC from its lay partners in the Centre-Left government, and even hinted that the DC's total opposition to the PCI over divorce should not be taken to imply that the DC was irrevocably opposed to Berlinguer's proposal for a 'historic compromise'.[113] In general, in fact, the DC leaders conducted a less bitter campaign against the Divorce Law than might have been expected. This was no doubt partly because they realised that they would have to continue to govern with the lay parties, whatever the result of the referendum, but principally because the DC was itself deeply divided about the divorce issue. The left-wing *correnti* in particular favoured the continuation of the Law: *Settegiorni*, the weekly newspaper of *Forze Nuove*, for example, warned Fanfani that liberty was at least as important an ideal of Christian Democracy as was the indissolubility of marriage,[114] and CISL, the Catholic trade union confederation, advised its members to vote as they wished.

The divorce referendum finally took place on 12 May 1974, and the Italian electorate voted decisively in favour of retaining the divorce law (19 million for, 13 million against in an 88 per cent turnout). No attempt will be made to analyse the results here, except in so far as they affected the Christian Democrats.[115] Two inter-related factors, however, seem to have determined the overall pattern of the vote: the political tradition of the different parts of the country and the degree of social change (of which the most important indicators were urbanisation and the level of economic development). The political tradition, as judged by the vote given to the 'lay' and 'clerical' parties in successive general elections since the war, seems to have determined the *overall* pattern of the results. Although the anti-divorce vote was consistently below that received by the DC and MSI combined at the 1972 general election, there was nevertheless a marked correlation between the two. There was even a high correlation between the vote for the retention of the monarchy in 1946 and the anti-divorce vote in 1974. Indeed, the 1946 referendum, as Giorgio Galli and others have argued, has been a very useful yardstick by which to judge the basic clerical/conservative – lay/radical pattern of voting in post-war Italy.[116] Clearly all three types of vote – for the monarchy, for parties such as the DC, and against divorce – are associated with certain religious and social attitudes. Thus, it was not surprising that there were high pro-divorce majorities in 'lay' regions such as Piedmont, Liguria and Emilia, and clearcut anti-divorce majorities in the Catholic Veneto and Trentino-Alto Adige and in the conservative southern regions of Molise, Campania, Apulia, Basilicata and Calabria.

If political tradition was the major determinant affecting the overall pattern of the vote, the degree of social change since the war also played an important part in the final outcome. As at the 1946 referendum and at subsequent general elections there was a basic division between north, centre and south, but in 1974 there was also a clearcut split between the urban and rural areas, a split which was not apparent in 1946 but which was developing in the 1960s. It was to be expected that those living in cities would have greater tolerance of divorce than those living in small towns and agricultural communities, for the former inevitably have more contact with the values of the affluent and permissive society than the latter. Thus, in virtually every province the chief city had a far higher pro-divorce vote than the surrounding countryside. The strongly Catholic province of Brescia, for example, had an anti-divorce majority of 54 per cent, but the city of Brescia had a 62 per cent pro-divorce vote. One of the most interesting factors was that the urban-rural split was also clearly discernible in the south. The southern urban population, with large 'sub-proletarian' groups and many people engaged in low-productivity service activities, might have been expected to have preserved traditional values. But this was not so. Of the thirty-two provinces of the south and islands, twenty voted against divorce, but twenty-two of the thirty-two provincial capitals voted for divorce. In his study of Naples, published shortly before the referendum, Percy Allum suggested that Naples was poised between 'traditional' and 'modern' social values.[117] The divorce referendum indicated that the balance had tipped in favour of 'modern' values, because 60 per cent of Neopolitans voted for divorce, whereas in 1946 80 per cent had voted against the abolition of the monarchy. Naples may not be wholly typical of the south, but the referendum made it clear that the changes which had taken place in the former were affecting the latter to a significant degree, and the implications for the politicians, not least for those of the DC, were considerable.

What then did the result of the referendum mean for the Christian Democrats? Clearly it was a watershed in several ways. The whole divorce issue, which had dragged on for almost ten years, culminating in the referendum, demonstrated yet again the ambiguous, problematical relationship between the DC and the Church. On the one hand, the result supported the view of scholars such as Burgalassi that Italy was becoming increasingly 'secularised', that Catholicism was no longer the social and political cement it had for so long appeared to be, and that in consequence the DC could no longer rely on the Church to deliver the Catholic vote.[118] Italian Catholics were now apparently determined to behave like their counterparts north of the Alps, i.e. to remain basically loyal to the political party closest to the Church, but no longer blindly to follow the orders of the Vatican as they had done in the decade after the war. And yet, on the other hand, it was apparent that the Church's political influence was still considerable – after all 40 per cent of the electorate had voted against divorce. The lesson for the DC seemed to be that the party could not risk breaking all its links with the Vatican, and yet in an increasingly secular society it could no longer afford to appear merely as the political arm of the Catholic Church. The left-wing Christian Democrat, Carlo Donat-Cattin, called the referendum 'a strategic error of historic proportions', yet neither he nor any other DC leader came out openly in favour of divorce during the campaign. In other words, the DC recognised that, whilst it might be true that religious obedience and traditional values no longer had as much appeal to the voters as in the past, nevertheless it was too early to write off the phenomenon of the 'Catholic sub-culture' as the basis of DC strength.

Moreover, when looked at in the context of the overall postwar development of relations between the DC and the Church, the referendum was clearly of fundamental importance. De Gasperi had tried to emphasise that the DC was not a confessional party pure and simple, but in practice he had had to rely heavily on the support of the Church. The *apertura alla sinistra*, on the other hand, clearly showed that the DC was determined to assert its independence of the Church, for it was carried through (at least in its early stages) in the teeth of opposition from the Vatican, Catholic Action and most of the bishops, including John XXIII when he was still Archbishop of Venice. However, both John XXIII as Pope and the Second Vatican Council emphasised the distinction between the temporal and spiritual activities of the Church.[119] And now the divorce referendum took this distinction a significant stage further. Although the DC leadership paradoxically acted in a more 'confessional' way than it had for a long time, behaving in a manner which was in effect a throw-back to former times, the Catholic electorate demonstrated that it was ready to move from political adolescence into adulthood: it wanted to remain basically loyal to its own political family but no longer blindly to obey Mother Church. This cleared the way for the DC seriously to consider the PCI's proposal for a 'historic compromise' between the progressive forces represented both in Italy's Catholic and anti-clerical sub-cultures. But it also marked the beginning of a difficult new phase for the DC. For the first time since 1948 people began to talk seriously of possible alternatives to the 'Christian Democratic régime'. The twin pillars of DC strength since the war had been religious obedience and control of patronage. The latter, as we have seen, was being increasingly called into question, and now the former, it appeared, could also no longer be relied upon.[120] The DC therefore entered the post-referendum era with its traditional power-base threatened, but with the possibility of developing as a more independent, less 'integralist', political force. In the light of this Berlinguer's proposed 'historic compromise' held out interesting possibilities, if also considerable dangers.

The Christian Democrats and the Communists: the general election of 1976 and the 'historic compromise'
The fourth major problem facing the DC in the 1970s was the challenge increasingly posed by the Communist Party (PCI). On the one hand, this challenge was electoral – the PCI vote had been moving steadily upwards since 1958 (22·7 per cent of the votes cast in that year's general election, 25·3 per cent in 1963, 26·9 per cent in 1968, 27·2 per cent in 1972, 32·0 per cent at the regional elections of 1975, and 34·4 per cent at the 1976 general election). On the other hand, and more threatening from the DC's point of view, was the PCI's claim that Italy could no longer be effectively governed without Communist participation in the government. This double challenge to the Christian Democrats came to a head at – and in the aftermath of – the 1976 general election.[121] This election occurred a year ahead of schedule, partly because of the economic crisis, partly because the Socialists refused to give any further support to the Christian Democrats and the Centre-Left experiment had finally been admitted to be dead, and partly because an early general election was the only way to avoid a referendum on abortion – a referendum which none of the major parties wanted after their experience of the divorce referendum in 1974.

Coming in the wake of the sweeping left-wing gains at the 1975 regional elections,[122] and with young people aged eighteen to twenty voting for the first time, the thirty-year-old 'DC régime' was beginning to look distinctly vulnerable. There was a widespread feeling that whoever 'won' the election, emergency measures would have to be taken soon afterwards to stave off the collapse of the economy, and such measures presupposed an agreement between the Christian Democrats and Communists to secure the necessary parliamentary and trade union approval. The political effects of the economic crisis were, therefore, twofold: it made the Communist Party more 'respectable' – the PCI openly agreed that improved state management of the economy and cuts in public expenditure were essential – and it guaranteed the benevolent neutrality of many northern managers and professional people towards the Communists; but it also increased the impetus for change within the DC, strengthening the northern, progressive, 'technocratic' wing of the party. The two processes were to some extent personified by the Agnelli brothers. Gianni Agnelli, the chairman of Fiat and immediate past president of the employers' federation, called for emergency government measures to be taken with Communist and trade union support: 'the main problem is the working out of an emergency plan in which the Communists absolutely must take part.'[123] His brother Umberto stood successfully as a Christian Democratic candidate for the Senate, one of many new DC parliamentarians to appear in 1976. Thus, although Italy's severe economic difficulties benefited the Communists, they also encouraged the renovation of the DC.

Stimulus for change within the DC also came from increasing evidence of corruption in the 'old' DC. In January 1976 it transpired that several oil companies, including Shell and BP, had handed over large sums of money to various Italian political parties, and notably to the DC, apparently in return for tax concessions. The oil companies excused themselves on the grounds that such dealings were all part of the normal business ethic in Italy, whilst the politicians claimed that there was nothing corrupt about political parties receiving 'gifts' from industry. Not everyone was reassured, and even less so when further allegations about corruption occurred in connection with the Lockheed aircraft company, which had apparently made extensive payments to individual politicians in order to 'encourage' the Italian government to buy military aircraft. These politicians were said to include at least one former Christian Democratic prime minister, called 'Antelope Cobbler' in the Lockheed documents. Rumours as to the identity of this mysterious figure were naturally rife. At one time the President of the Republic, Giovanni Leone, was the most favoured candidate, but in the weeks before the election opinion hardened in favour of Mariano Rumor, the then Foreign Minister, The weekly journal *Panorama* claimed to have proof that 'Antelope Cobbler' was Rumor, and the PCI promptly demanded Rumor's resignation – but Rumor strongly denied the accusation and *Panorama* could not produce its 'proof'. Meanwhile the DC newspaper *Il Popolo* thundered against 'false moralists' and 'hypocritical rumour-mongers', and the political journalists hastily turned their attentions to the former Social Democratic Defence Minister, Mario Tanassi.

Financial scandals are no novelty in Italy, and the above scandals and rumours of scandals certainly had their baroque side; but they had serious aspects as well. Like Italy's economic problems, they tended to discredit the old guard of the DC (the so-called 'capi storici'). At the same time they were a gift to the PCI, which presented itself in contrast to the DC as a high-minded, serious, reforming party untainted by corruption; but they also provided a considerable impetus to moves for reform within the DC.

Further stimulus to change within the DC – and encouragement to the PCI – came from increasing political violence. Numerous gangs of the extreme Left and extreme Right had been operating with relative impunity in the 1970s, and there had been much criticism of antiquated police methods and cumbersome judicial procedures. Early in 1976, for instance, there were several armed attacks on barracks, unexplained fires at factories and department stores, and innumerable kidnappings. During the election campaign the violence continued. Shots were fired at a neo-Fascist rally in Rome on 4 June, and on the following day the Barberini cinema was burnt down shortly before a neo-Fascist rally was due to be held there. In addition, a young Communist was killed at Sezze by neo-Fascists, and a neo-Fascist deputy, Sandro Saccucci, fled to London to avoid arrest. Then on 8 June the public prosecutor of Genoa, Francesco Coco, was assassinated outside his house, and the left-wing 'Red Brigades' claimed responsibility.

These events naturally created an atmosphere of tension. There were rumours of official connivance on the part of Italy's secret police forces (particularly of the Carabinieri's *Servizio Informazione Difesa*, which was alleged to be involved in some of the killings), and discussion about the 'real' instigators of political violence. In fact, there was very little hard evidence, but it was clear that Italy had a serious 'law and order' problem. And the *political* effects of the terrorism were important. The neo-Fascist *Movimento Sociale Italiano* (MSI) was discredited by its part, or alleged part, in the violence, and opinion polls indicated that many right-wing voters would opt for the DC rather than the MSI. On the other hand, the violence made the 'old' Christian Democratic élite appear at best incompetent, at worst involved. The advocates of reform within the DC were thus given an additional platform. At the same time the Communists' drive for respectability was strengthened. The PCI denounced violence – including left-wing violence – in no uncertain terms. Meanwhile, the apparent intractability of the 'law and order' problem encouraged voters to think that only an exceptional 'emergency' government, with new men and new policies, could cope with the situation. Thus the violence both stimulated moves for reform within the Christian Democratic party and enhanced the credibility of the Communists, whilst at the same time preparing the electorate for some form of DC–PCI co-operation.

The DC's pre-electoral Congress of March 1976 showed that there was a fine balance between what might be described as its 'reformist' and 'traditionalist' wings. The state of the DC *correnti* was even more complex than usual, but 52 per cent of the National Council delegates elected in March 1976 were supporters of Benigno Zaccagnini, the reformist party Secretary, whilst most of the others favoured Amintore Fanfani, the party Chairman and leader of the 'traditionalists' and 'integralists'. Roughly speaking Zaccagnini could count on the support of the trade union current, *Forze Nuove*, most of the members of the left-wing *Base*, and most of the followers of Moro, Rumor, Gullotti and Taviani. Fanfani could rely on the support of Piccoli and the rump of the old *Dorotei* current, on the followers of Forlani and Bisaglia, and even on some members of the *Base* (essentially those of integralist leanings). As always, the edges between the *correnti* were frayed. A man like Andreotti, one of the DC's shrewdest leaders and a minister without a break for thirty years, for example, had moved to the left since the failure of his 1972–3 Centre-Right government and was reputed to have close links both with the reformers and the integralists. He was wisely keeping his options open, and could not be 'categorised' as a member of any specific *corrente*.

In these circumstances the DC, not surprisingly, fought a double-pronged campaign. The traditionalists, led by Fanfani, appealed to the Right and Centre, emphasising the need to return to the 'traditional values of Christian Democracy', described by one reformist member of the party as 'a dish composed of visceral anti-Communism, with a little power, a little Church, and a dash of law and order'. One of the DC's most widely displayed posters bore a table of the results of the 1975 regional elections with the legend: 'Only 3 per cent more votes need to go left to make Italy Communist: is that what you really want?' Fanfani made a powerful appeal throughout the campaign to right-wing voters – including those whom he termed 'honest neo-Fascists' – not to waste their votes on the MSI: on 17 June in Naples, for example, he said that in the Soviet Union Communism had led to the imprisonment of hundreds of opponents of the régime; Communism in Italy would lead to the same thing, and the only way to prevent such a grim prospect was for all conservative democrats to rally to the DC, which alone constituted a genuine barrier to Communism.[124] On the same theme a DC poster asked: 'How much are you prepared to risk to find out whether Italian Communism is different from Communism?'

Meanwhile, the reformers' campaign was led by Zaccagnini, who had replaced Fanfani as Secretary after the DC set-back at the 1975 regional elections, and whose position had been confirmed, albeit narrowly, at the National Congress of March 1976.[125] The reformers' campaign was exemplified by a picture of the party Secretary with the caption: 'The new DC has already begun.' There was indeed some truth in this claim, for since taking over as Secretary in July 1975 Zaccagnini had succeeded in reorganising the party's youth movement; had set up a special cultural committee to repair the party's links with intellectuals, many of whom had been alienated by Fanfani's arrogance; had tightened up the links between the DC and the Catholic trade union confederation CISL – and this paid off when the CISL leaders supported the DC much more decisively in 1976 than they had in 1972; and had travelled throughout Italy sounding out grass-roots opinion in the party. In addition, a progressive Catholic movement, *Comunione e Liberazione*, had been established within the DC, and this movement fought a vigorous election campaign throughout the country, endorsing progressive candidates and advocating the renaissance of the party. Nevertheless, the process of renewal within the DC – indeed the *potential* for renewal – should not be exaggerated. At the time of the general election Zaccagnini's reformers held only a bare majority within the party. Moreover, the DC remained so deeply enmeshed in the sub-structure of the Italian governmental system (the *sottogoverno*) that it was difficult for the party to commit itself unequivocally to a policy of reforms: if it did so, it risked undermining its own power base. Thus, the DC fought the campaign on what amounted to two platforms: the one an anti-Communist platform of the traditional type; the other, an attempt to persuade the voters that the DC really was changing and could offer more effective government in the future. In these circumstances the DC's electoral programme was inevitably rather vague, but somewhat surprisingly it had many similarities with the Communist manifesto, emphasising, for example, the need for cuts in public expenditure, for bureaucratic reform, and for improvements in the social services.

The Christian Democrats' main rivals were, of course, the Communists. Indeed, the Communists appeared to be in a very strong position by 1976. Student militancy, which had given them so much trouble between 1968 and 1972, had virtually died out; workers' militancy was also much less evident, and had apparently been 'absorbed' into the official trade union structure; and the threat from the extreme Left, from groups like *Il Manifesto* or other extra-parliamentary movements, had been contained. At the regional elections of June 1975 – held in fifteen of the country's twenty regions – the Communists polled 32 per cent of the votes cast (compared with 27·1 per cent at the general election of 1972). They gained control of most of Italy's major cities – Turin, Milan, Florence, Genoa, even Naples. Party membership had risen to over 1·75 million, an increase of 14 per cent since 1971; and the party Secretary, Enrico Berlinguer, a Sardinian aristocrat, had established himself as unquestioned leader, achieving higher opinion poll ratings amongst the Italian electorate as a whole than any other politician. The Communists seemed to be pursuing the same sort of strategy as the German SPD had done in the 1960s: they constantly emphasised that the PCI was a respectable, almost conservative party, committed to sensible change by constitutional means. Unlike the DC, the PCI gave the appearance of almost complete unity. Whereas a few years previously commentators had observed two major *tendenze* in the PCI, namely those of Giorgio Amendola (reformism, 'Euro-communism') and Pietro Ingrao (traditionalism, loyalty to Moscow), by the mid 1970s the 'reformists', personified by Berlinguer and his closest collaborator, Giorgio Napolitano, had clearly emerged as the dominant force in the party. The PCI's long-term objective was the *Compromesso Storico* ('historic compromise'), launched by Berlinguer in 1973 and endorsed at the fourteenth Party Congress in March 1975. As defined at that Congress, the 'compromise' would entail 'an understanding, a political alliance, between Communists, Socialists, Christian Democrats and other anti-Fascist popular forces both of Catholic origin and of lay and democratic tradition, in order to give the government of the country a wider basis of consent, and the strength and authority needed to overcome the crisis and enable Italy to advance'. But for the 1976 election the Communists adopted a short-term objective, namely the achievement of a broadly-based national government of all 'constitutional and democratic parties' from the Liberal Party on the Right to the PCI on the Left. This broad-based government was to set about tackling the country's most pressing economic and social problems. In their election manifesto the Communists stated that there were no easy solutions to the problems of corruption, tax evasion, privilege and patronage. It was essential, however, for Italy to purge itself of its 'parasitic sector', i.e. the many obsolete *enti pubblici* which the DC had 'colonised' with its supporters and therefore refused to abolish.[126] But the Communists claimed that they would only carry out their reform programme – notably the introduction of a national health service, educational reforms to benefit the underprivileged, and the expansion of the public housing sector – by democratic and constitutional means. Hence the PCI's strong emphasis on the need for a 'historic compromise', for Berlinguer frequently argued that a left-wing 'Popular Front' government, supported perhaps by only 51 per cent of the electorate (comparable to Allende's in Chile), would lack the necessary political legitimacy to implement the root-and-branch reforms needed by Italy.

Indeed, the Communists went out of their way to appeal to 'moderate reformers' of all classes. In their manifesto they listed a series of rights and freedoms which they would protect, including freedom of speech, of association and of religion. In fact, they laid great emphasis on reforming the state so as to make it more capable of guaranteeing democratic liberties under the law. As for economic policy, they advocated cuts in public expenditure, and implied, without making any specific commitments, that the party would be able to 'control the unions' more effectively than the DC, and thus curb inflation. They were also opposed to any further nationalisation of industry: their aim was to make the present nationalised sector work more efficiently, not to bring more industry into public ownership. The Communists also expressed concern about lawlessness in Italy, and advocated increased powers for the police. At the same time they emphasised their confidence in Italy's 'patriotic conscript Army' and called for a strengthening of the Navy. In foreign affairs they endorsed Italy's membership of NATO on the grounds that they had no wish to endanger détente by upsetting the balance of power. In the long term, of course, they hoped that both NATO and the Warsaw Pact would 'wither away', but in the short term Berlinguer made it clear that NATO could help guarantee the PCI's autonomy *vis-à-vis* Moscow, implying that the Western Alliance might act as a kind of shield behind which the PCI could build a democratic version of socialism without interference from the USSR.[127] The Communists also supported Italy's membership of the EEC, stating that their objective was to democratise the Community's institutions as a first step towards the building of a socialist Western Europe.[128]

Overall, then, the Communists behaved much as one would expect Social Democrats to behave in Northern Europe. Of course, their critics justifiably pointed out that there was very little *internal* democracy in the PCI, and doubts were expressed by many Christian Democrats (and others) about the sincerity of the PCI's commitment to pluralism, liberal democracy and European integration. But it was clear that the Communists – in spite of their strong attacks on the DC during the campaign – were holding out an olive branch to the Christian Democrats and preparing the way for some sort of governmental compromise.[129]

The Consequences of the Election for the DC and PCI
The results of the election brought this compromise one stage nearer, for, although the PCI polled 34·4 per cent of the votes cast (compared with 27·1 per cent in 1972), it did not emerge as the biggest single party, and, to the surprise of many – including most opinion pollsters – the DC maintained its 1972 percentage of the vote (38·7 per cent). Clearly there was no sign of the DC collapsing or of its being left stranded by social change. Nearly three-quarters of the voters (10 per cent more than in 1972) cast their ballots either for the DC or for the PCI.

In one sense the electorate maintained its traditional conservatism, or at least stability. Indeed, fear of radical change clearly motivated the choice of many electors. Both the DC and PCI stood for order and stability, and 'won'; whilst the next most important party, the Socialist PSI, appeared to stand for radical change and its corollary, instability, and 'lost'. The neo-Fascist MSI, from its ghetto on the Right, also stood for a leap into the unknown, and lost heavily. A vote for the smaller parties of the Centre (the Liberals, Republicans and Social Democrats) could also be construed as a vote for the unknown, in that such votes, if cast in sufficient numbers, might lead to a Christian Democratic defeat at the hands of the Communists. In these circumstances lay voters of the Centre, preferring the devil they knew to the one they did not, voted for the DC with (as one Liberal voter put it) 'their eyes open, but their noses held'. Only on the far Left, where the Radicals and Democratic Proletarians won ten seats, was there a vote for 'adventurism', but ten seats out of 630 hardly constituted a threat to the Establishment.

The most significant development was, of course, the advance of the PCI. Its poll of 34·4 per cent was 7·3 per cent higher than in 1972 (and 2·4 per cent higher than at the regional elections of 1975). Two hundred and twenty-seven Communist deputies were returned to the Chamber, forty-eight more than in 1972, and the gap between the PCI and DC was cut from eighty-seven seats to thirty-six. The PCI increased its percentage of the vote in its traditional areas of strength: in the Milan-Turin-Genoa industrial triangle it polled almost 40 per cent (an average gain of 7·5 per cent compared with 1972, but only 1·5 per cent since 1975), and in the 'Red Belt' of central Italy it polled just over 50 per cent (an average gain of over 5 per cent since 1972, but less than 1 per cent since 1975). More significantly, the Communists out-distanced the Christian Democrats for the first time in the cities of Rome and Naples, advancing by 10 per cent to 36 per cent in both cases, whilst in the south as a whole important gains were registered compared with 1972: 5 per cent in the constituency of Bari-Foggia (to 32 per cent), 8 per cent in Catanzaro-Reggio Calabria (to 33 per cent), 6 per cent in Sicily (to 27 per cent) and 10 per cent in Sardinia (to 35 per cent). In all cases the gains were made at the expense of the smaller left-wing parties (especially the Socialists and Social Democrats) and also to some extent at the expense of the DC, although the Christian Democrats were able to recoup their losses by making inroads into the MSI vote.

From the PCI's point of view, the election produced an optimum result, although the party leaders could hardly say so publicly. With a total left-wing vote of under 50 per cent the Christian Democrats could not opt for opposition and leave Berlinguer to tackle the country's acute economic and social problems with a weak 'Popular Front' government. Berlinguer at once renewed his call for a national government of all parties (except the MSI), but significantly stated that the PCI was in no hurry to enter the government: it would wait for proposals from the Christian Democrats and Socialists. The Communists knew that they would have to be consulted as the new DC-led government (whether *monocolore* or Centre-Left) drew up plans to deal with the economic crisis, for without PCI and Communist trade union support no emergency plan would have any chance of success. Thus, whether actually in government or not, the PCI would have its hands on the levers of power. Moreover, if progress were made in tackling Italy's problems, the PCI would be able to claim that it was thanks to its responsible, constructive support of the government that the improvements had occurred. In these circumstances, Berlinguer could contend that the Christian Democrats ought to go one stage further and implement the full 'historic compromise' by allowing the Communists to enter the government. On the other hand, if things went badly for the government, the Communists would be able to blame the Christian Democrats and argue that the only solution was for the electorate to vote for the PCI in even greater numbers and put it into power as the major party. Either way, Berlinguer's strategy looked as if it was likely to succeed.

Whereas the 1976 election produced short-term disappointment but long-term satisfaction for the PCI, it produced immediate euphoria in the DC but did little to solve the party's long-term problems. The Christian Democrats were certainly justified in celebrating their electoral success. Like the British Conservative Party in 1970, the DC gained approximately 4 per cent more votes than most pollsters had predicted (even the reliable DOXA, which detected the late swing to the DC, gave the party only 36 per cent; other polls during the last fortnight predicted 32–4 per cent and one gave it only 28 per cent). But with 38·7 per cent of the votes cast and 263 deputies elected, the DC demonstrated once again its remarkable resilience. The party recouped its losses of 1975 (its poll at the regional elections having been only 35·5 per cent); it won approximately one-third of the 'young' vote (the eighteen- to twenty-five-year-olds, amongst whom it had been expected to poll badly); its new candidates, many of them supported by *Comunione e Liberazione*, did well in the big cities, and the party actually increased its percentage slightly in Genoa, Milan, Bologna, Florence, Rome and Naples; moreover, it held its own in the south despite the Communist gains mentioned above.

The question, however, remained, where was the DC to go from here? In particular, what attitude should it adopt towards the PCI? The main emphasis of the DC's campaign had been on anti-Communism, and approximately two-thirds of its new votes came from the Right and only one-third from the Left.[130] The DC could not therefore openly embrace the PCI. On the other hand, the DC had made much of what Zaccagnini called its 'inner renewal', and even Fanfani had not ruled out the possibility of some form of collaboration with the Communists. One-third of the DC's deputies (88 out of 253) were elected for the first time in 1976, and the majority of them were on the reformist wing of the party. Clearly the DC could not return to its former, rather aimless, musical-chairs style of government. At the same time it was difficult for the party to decide what strategy to adopt.

There was no longer a Centre-Right majority in the Chamber (as there had been in 1972). A revived Centre-Left government remained arithmetically possible, but politically almost inconceivable. In theory there was a majority for such a government (a total of 349 Christian Democrats, Socialists, Social Democrats and Republicans, compared with 371 in 1972). But the Socialists had fought the election on the basis that they would only go into government again with the Christian Democrats if the Communists were also allowed in. If the Socialists were to have gone back on their electoral commitment, their left wing (Lombardi and his followers) might have broken away to form a new party or at least some sort of close parliamentary alliance with the PCI.

Indeed, the major loser at the 1976 election was the Socialist party, for although it maintained its 1972 poll of 9·6 per cent, it fell back 2·4 per cent compared with 1975 (i.e. it lost one-fifth of its 1975 voters). The electorate clearly rejected the Socialist Party as the 'honest broker' of the Left. The party's electoral strategy had misfired. The Socialists had unintentionally created the impression of being subordinate to the Communists: they thus failed to secure the votes of those who wanted a left-wing government but remained suspicious of the Communists. The loss of votes by the small lay parties (Liberals, Social Democrats and Republicans taken together – the Republicans actually gained fractionally) further restricted the possibility for political manoeuvre on the part of both the Christian Democrats and Socialists.

Thus the DC found itself face to face with a suitor for whom it had no love, namely the PCI. It might be assumed that the DC's progressive *correnti* would be seriously interested in Berlinguer's proposal for a 'historic compromise' on the grounds that a DC–PCI government might be able to enact some constructive social and economic reforms. But such an assumption would be erroneous, because Christian Democrats of *all correnti* were afraid that to allow the Communists to enter the government would be to undermine both an essential aspect of the DC's *raison d'être* (anti-Communism) and possibly its power-base (control of the patronage system). Thus, progressive Christian Democrats were as opposed as conservatives to the *full* 'historic compromise'. Throughout the 1976 election campaign, for example, Zaccagnini, the party's reformist Secretary, emphasised his total opposition to any post-electoral deal which would allow the Communists to enter the government, and Carlo Donat-Cattin, the leader of the left-wing *Forze Nuove*, said, albeit with some exaggeration, but nevertheless expressing the DC's widespread apprehension about the 'historic compromise': 'The DC will automatically lose four-fifths of its support on the day the Christian Democrats come to an agreement with the Communists.'[131]

In the aftermath of the 1976 general election it looked as if Italy was set for a period of political deadlock. The Christian Democrats refused to let the Communists enter the government. The Communists could not, and, even if they could, would not form a 'Popular Front' government with the Socialists and other left-wing forces. The Socialists refused to enter a government without the Communists. It looked as if the only solution was a minority DC government incapable of taking any positive action. However, the political situation was not as deadlocked as it appeared at first sight, for there was still some momentum left in the 'convergence' of the DC and PCI.

In the first place, there had been a considerable renewal of the DC, and many of the new Christian Democratic members of parliament wanted to see decisive measures taken to deal with Italy's profound economic and social problems. Such measures presupposed some measure of co-operation with the Communists, and Umberto Agnelli, a newly elected DC Senator and director of Fiat, at once emphasised the necessity for *confronto* with the PCI, i.e. an ongoing process of consultation with the main opposition party. At the same time the Communist leaders seemed more determined than ever to prove that the

PCI was a respectable, social-reforming party. The Communists certainly had no wish to come to power on the collapse of the Italian economy and democracy. So Berlinguer soon went back on his initial refusal to consider anything short of a full and open 'historic compromise'. Within a few weeks of the election the Christian Democrats and Communists came to an amicable agreement that Fanfani (DC) should preside over the Senate, whilst Ingrao (PCI) should preside over the Chamber. In August 1976 the two parties accepted what can best be described as a 'tactical compromise', when the PCI agreed that a DC minority government, led by Giulio Andreotti, should embark on a limited reform programme whilst the Communists abstained. Then in June 1977 the Communists won the right to be consulted about the government's programme, and finally in March 1978, following a two-month governmental crisis, the Communists agreed to give their full support to a new Andreotti administration – for the first time the PCI had decided not merely to abstain but to vote for a DC-led cabinet. One of the architects of this agreement was Aldo Moro, the President of the Christian Democratic party, who was brutally murdered in May 1978 by terrorists of the extreme-left 'Red Brigades', who seemed determined to split the Christian Democratic–Communist alliance by provoking a right-wing backlash. Although the atrocity was counter-productive (from the point of view of the 'Red Brigades'), in that it resulted in massive demonstrations against extremism and in favour of the Italian democratic system (despite all its shortcomings), the long-term future of the DC–PCI 'tactical compromise' remained uncertain. It could lead to a further revival of a 'renewed' DC or to a further advance for the 'responsible' PCI. Indeed, opinion polls in 1977–8 suggested that it was leading to both, with 42–44 per cent of voters claiming they would vote for the DC and 35–36 per cent for the PCI.[132] It could draw the two parties closer together, leading in due course to a full 'historic compromise', with the entry of the Communists into a coalition government with the Christian Democrats, that might be the prelude to more effective government in Italy. Equally, however, it might encourage greater instability, with more acts of violence being perpetrated by frustrated political extremists.

Certainly, it seems unlikely that Italy will develop a two-party system of the Anglo-Saxon type, for the desire to avoid open conflicts, to reconcile interests, to reach mutually acceptable compromises, is an important aspect of Italian political culture. Even before the 1976 general election there was a quasi-truce between the DC and PCI based on personal contacts and agreements reached in parliamentary committees. Power has always been more fragmented in the Italian Parliament than in the British or German: party discipline is less rigid, the division between government and opposition is less clearcut, and most legislation is passed relatively discreetly in committees rather than at plenary sessions. To some extent, therefore, the parliamentary system *imposes* compromises.[133] Moreover, the magnitude of the economic and social problems facing Italy is such that no solution seems likely without some sort of agreement between the two major parties. The political situation, then, also points in the direction of compromise, if not necessarily of coalition.

Conclusion

The *Democrazia Cristiana* of the late 1970s is a very different party from the *Democrazia Cristiana* of the late 1940s. The Christian Democrats have become much less dependent on the Church in their policy-making and policy-implementation, although they continue to rely heavily on practising Catholics – both the clergy and Civic Committees – at elections. Moreover, when it comes to moral issues like divorce or abortion, the DC has to align itself behind the official Church, albeit reluctantly, and not always effectively, as the divorce referendum showed.

The DC is unlike most northern European political parties for a variety of reasons. It consists of half a dozen (or more) organised *correnti*, which spread right across the political spectrum from the extreme Right to the extreme Left. Yet even within the *correnti* there is considerable cross-fertilisation and fluidity: 'integralists' and 'autonomists', for example, are to be found vying with each other in all *correnti*, and it is not uncommon for a deputy to move from one current to another. The DC has another unusual characteristic, in that it is both a pragmatic, government-orientated electors' party, and at the same time a 'mass' party in terms of membership, and to some extent of 'mentality'. Above all, the DC is enmeshed in the fabric of the state to a unique degree, notably through its involvement in the sub-governmental structure, the *sottogoverno*, and through its pervasive and powerful influence in broadcasting, the nationalised industries, and in the many thousands of *enti pubblici*, both useful and useless, which constitute such an important part of the Italian governmental and bureaucratic system.

At various times over the years the DC has appeared to be in a state of disarray, but it would be very unwise to underestimate the party's resilience. The political influence of the Vatican may have declined, but the determination of Italy's Catholics to hold on to power has not. The Catholics are well aware that for the first seventy-five years of the history of the Italian state they were political 'outsiders', and now that they have come in from the cold under the umbrella of the DC, they are unlikely to surrender their leading and directing role without a determined rearguard action. At the same time the Christian Democrats have often demonstrated their pragmatism and adaptability. Men like Fanfani, Moro and Andreotti, for example, have frequently embodied these characteristics. This, of course, is another reason why the DC should never be underestimated: the party takes its factional quarrelling only so far, and then it closes ranks in the face of its political opponents. The DC leaders realise very well that, whilst the party must retain its multi-faceted image as a lay-clerical, conservative-progressive, middle-class-working-class conglomerate, the various *correnti*, which articulate these *tendenze*, cannot be allowed to destroy the overall cohesion of the party, for, if they are permitted to do so, the chief beneficiary will be the PCI.

However, as we have seen, the Christian Democrats – in spite of their continuing doubts about the Communists – have not adopted a wholly negative attitude towards the PCI. Indeed, one of the most important developments in Italy during the last thirty years has been the gradually changing attitude of the

DC towards all the left-wing parties, as the boundaries between the 'Catholic' and 'Marxist' sub-cultures have steadily been eroded. The socio-political situation of the late 1970s is a far cry from that of the zenith of the Cold War, when to vote Communist or Socialist was a 'sin' in the eyes of the Church and the DC. Since then the DC has undergone the trials and tribulations of the Centre-Left experiment, the secularisation of Italian society, the redefinition of its relationship with the Church (symbolised by the Second Vatican Council and the divorce referendum), and a period of acute factional infighting. It has survived all these crises, and now in the late 1970s the DC has embarked on a dual policy of internal party reform and détente *vis-à-vis* the PCI. It is still not clear whether the outcome will be a strengthened Christian Democratic party, perhaps capable of dominating Italian politics as it did in De Gasperi's time, or merely a new type of DC, which accepts that its best interest lies in co-operating with the other giant of Italian politics, whilst doing all it can to retain its distinctive identity.

Table 1

Italy: Chamber Election Results, 1946–76

	1946 28,005,000 89·1			1948 29,118,000 92·2			1953 30,280,000 93·8		
Electorate Turnout (%)	Votes (mn)	%	Seats	Votes (mn)	%	Seats	Votes (mn)	%	Seats
Communists (PCI)	4·4	18·9	104	{8·1	31·0	183}	6·1	22·6	143
Socialists (PSI)	4·8	20·7	115				3·4	12·7	75
Social Democrats (PSDI)	—	—	—	1·9	7·1	33	1·2	4·5	19
Republicans (PRI)	1·0	4·4	23	0·7	2·5	9	0·4	1·6	5
Christian Democrats (DC)	8·1	35·1	207	12·7	48·4	304	10·8	40·1	263
Liberals (PLI)	1·6	6·8	41	1·0	3·8	19	0·8	3·0	13
Monarchists (PDIUM)	0·6	2·8	16	0·7	2·8	14	1·9	6·9	40
Neo-Fascists (MSI)	1·2	5·3	30	0·5	2·0	6	1·6	5·8	29
Others	1·4	5·6	20	0·6	2·4	6	0·7	1·8	3
Total	22·9		556	26·2		574	27·0		590

	1958 32,447,000 93·8			1963 34,127,000 92·9			1968 35,500,000 92·7			1972 37,039,000 93·1			1976 40,850,000 90·0		
Electorate Turnout (%)	Votes (mn)	%	Seats	Votes (mn)	%	Seats	Votes (mn)	%	Seats	Votes (mn)	%	Seats	Votes (mn)	%	Seats
PCI	6·7	22·7	140	7·8	25·3	166	8·6	26·9	177	9·1	27·2	179	12·6	34·4	227
PSIUP*	—	—					1·4	4·5	23	0·6	1·9	0	0·5	1·5	6
PSI	4·2	14·2	84	4·3	13·8	87	{4·6	14·5	91}	3·2	9·6	61	3·5	9·6	57
PSDI	1·3	4·5	23	1·9	6·1	33				1·7	5·1	29	1·2	3·4	15
PRI	0·4	1·4	6	0·4	1·1	6	0·6	2·0	9	1·0	2·9	15	1·1	3·1	14
DC	12·5	42·3	273	11·8	38·3	260	12·4	39·1	266	12·9	38·8	267	14·2	38·7	263
PLI	1·0	3·5	14	2·1	7·0	39	1·8	5·8	31	1·3	3·9	20	0·5	1·3	5
PDIUM	1·4	4·8	25	0·5	1·7	8	0·4	1·3	6	{2·9	8·7	56}			
MSI	1·4	4·8	25	1·6	5·1	27	1·4	4·5	23				2·2	6·1	35
Others	0·7	1·8	6	0·4	1·6	4	0·7	1·4	3	0·8	1·5	3	1·1	2·1	8
Total	29·5		596	30·7		630	31·9		630	33·4		630	36·9		630

* Proletarian Socialists, founded 1964; Democratic Proletarians (DP) in 1976

Table 2

*Italy: Regional Elections, 1970 and 1975**

	1970 Votes (mn.)	1970 %	1975 Votes (mn.)	1975 %
Communists	7·6	27·8	11·3	32·0
Socialists	2·8	10·4	4·2	12·0
Social Democrats	1·9	6·9	1·9	5·6
Republicans	0·8	2·8	1·2	3·3
Christian Democrats	10·3	37·8	12·5	35·5
Liberals	1·3	4·7	0·9	2·5
Neo-Fascists	1·4	5·2	2·4	6·8

* Minor parties omitted

4
Christian Democracy in Germany

West Germany has two Christian Democratic parties, the Christian Democratic Union (*Christlich Demokratische Union*, CDU), which operates in all the *Länder* of the Federal Republic except Bavaria, and the Christian Social Union (*Christlich-Soziale Union*, CSU), which operates only in Bavaria. Since the foundation of the Federal Republic the two parties have formed one parliamentary group (*Fraktion*) in Bonn, although relations between the two 'sister' parties have often been rather strained, particularly during the period in opposition since 1969. As the parties are rather different in character and organisation, it is appropriate to discuss them separately whilst bearing in mind that they are both constituent parts of what may be termed the 'German Christian Democratic movement'. Indeed the two parties are now regularly referred to in the German press as the *Unionsparteien*, an appropriate epithet, because the CDU and CSU are broadly united in their objectives and for most of the time co-operate closely, but they are nevertheless separate parties. The CDU is a more centrist, more pluralistic, less Catholic and less conservative party than the CSU, but an examination of their programmes indicates the broad similarity of their objectives.[1]

Christian Democracy is essentially a postwar phenomenon in Germany, despite the existence of the prewar *Zentrum* and *Bayerische Volkspartei*, which should probably be categorised as 'Catholic-confessional' rather than 'Christian Democratic' parties.[2] And by any standards German Christian Democracy has been a highly successful political movement. The combined CDU–CSU vote has never dropped below 45 per cent except at the first general election in 1949, and at the 1957 election the Christian Democrats won an absolute majority of the votes cast (50·2 per cent), the only time this has been achieved by one party (or, to be more precise, two closely united parties) in a free election in German history. Moreover, with the exception of the 1972–6 Bundestag, the CDU–CSU has always formed the largest single parliamentary group.[3] But perhaps even more important than the electoral achievements of the West German Christian Democrats has been the role they have played in integrating conservatives into the liberal-democratic system. As the German political scientist, Professor Sontheimer, has put it, the CDU was 'the first German party to gather together a pluralist collection of social interests into one single political organisation'.[4] Certainly, it is vital to an understanding of the CDU to bear in mind that it covers a wide range of the political spectrum: even if the CDU is essentially a centre-right party, it also has a significant trade union wing.

The Christian Democrats, for good or ill, impregnated the political culture of the Federal Republic with their rather unexciting, non-ideological values. They created the Republic after their own image – dull, bourgeois, pragmatic, almost hysterically anti-Communist and excessively critical of political 'extremism', but at the same time staunchly committed to parliamentary democracy and human rights, to the achievement of some sort of synthesis between economic liberalism and social justice, to closer co-operation between the nations of Western Europe, and to the alliance of those nations with the United States. It can even be argued that the CDU–CSU made the SPD what it has become, namely a very pragmatic, centrist Social Democratic party, for the popularity of the Christian Democrats' economic and foreign policies made it necessary for the SPD to make the changes it made at Bad Godesberg in 1959, or risk being perennially in the political wilderness.

CDU – Early Development and Characteristics

In order to understand the nature of the CDU it is important to comment on the origins of the party, for the CDU was very much the child of the years 1945–9. It was a party, whose leaders were determined to make a clean break with the past. They were opposed to the revival of the *Zentrum*, realising that such a 'confessional' party would have no appeal to Protestants.[5] In their view, the failure of the two branches of the Christian Church to co-operate politically under Weimar was one of the factors which made it possible for Hitler to come to power. At the same time the new Christian Democrats wanted to found a political movement – they deliberately avoided the word 'party' because of its associations with *the* party (i.e. Hitler's NSDAP), choosing instead the word 'union', partly because of its appeal to Protestants. The founders of the Union – in line with other European Christian Democrats at that time – also hoped that the new 'party' would overcome (*überwinden* is the word frequently to be found in CDU documents of 1945–6)[6] the old class divisions, which had contributed, through the medium of narrow, class parties, to the fragility of the Weimar Republic. From the start the CDU had Catholic and Protestant, trade union and business, working-class and middle-class 'wings' and members. In addition, it was loosely structured, because the occupation authorities wanted democracy to 'grow' from the base upwards: only *Land* and zonal parties were licensed during the period of 'denazification'. The CDU thus developed as a confederal party in which the regional associations (*Landesverbände*) wielded considerable influence, and, for as long as the party continued to win elections under Adenauer, it remained little more than an 'association for [the election of] the Chancellor' (*Kanzlerverein*). The price for this failure to build up an effective party organisation was not paid until the late 1960s–early 1970s.[7]

The pluralistic nature of the CDU was apparent from its earliest days, the party developing spontaneously in a number of centres, of which the two most important were Berlin and the Rhineland. In addition, important initiatives were taken in north Germany, Hesse, Württemberg and in (what later became) the Rhineland-Palatinate.[8] The CDU was diverse not only geographically but also politically, socially, and in terms of the religious beliefs of its members.[9]

The rapidity with which political activity revived after the war is surprising. Within six weeks of the German surrender CDU branches had been founded in Berlin and Cologne – by coincidence both parties were founded on the same day, 17 June 1945, although the Berlin CDU did not make a final decision about its name until 26 June, and neither party held its first full public meeting until somewhat later (the Berlin CDU in the Schiffsbauerdamm Theatre on 22 July and the Rhineland CDU in the Kölpinghaus, Cologne, on 2 September). More important than the timing of these early meetings was the type of person who attended them. If Catholics predominated, there was also a significant number of Protestants who were founding members – and not only in north Germany. And if former *Zentrum* adherents and Catholic trade-unionists and journalists were the most prominent advocates of the new inter-class, inter-confessional party, there were also many former Liberals (i.e. members of the *Deutsche Demokratische Partei*, DDP, or *Deutsche Volkspartei*, DVP) and conservative Nationalists (i.e. member of the *Deutschnationale Volkspartei*, DNVP) who were prepared to let bygones be bygones and join a party which was committed to the application of 'Christian principles' in politics. Although the term 'Christian principles' is, of course, vague, there was undoubtedly a strong feeling that, after the barbarities of the Third Reich, some attempt must be made to return to the old values – truth, honesty, respect for the individual, and so on.[10] This feeling acted as a catalyst towards the Europe-wide religious revival of the immediate postwar years, and, in political terms, there can be little doubt that it helped the growth of all the European Christian Democratic parties, and not least of the one which was established in the country which had been responsible for the worst of the barbarities.

In Berlin the first initiative was taken by Andreas Hermes, a former *Zentrum* leader who was awaiting execution in the Moabit prison when the Russians released him and appointed him deputy mayor of Berlin. The two most important Catholic politicians who responded to Hermes' initiative were Heinrich Krone, secretary-general of the *Zentrum* before 1933 and later a close adviser of Adenauer and a notably successful chairman of the CDU parliamentary party; and Jakob Kaiser, a former leader of the Catholic trade union confederation and later a rival to Adenauer for the leadership of the CDU and a strong advocate of 'Christian Socialism' – he believed, in particular, that if the CDU maintained close links with Socialists and implemented left-wing policies, this would help to maintain contact with East Germany and ultimately prepare the way for reunification. Other *Zentrum* politicians, who played their part in founding the Berlin CDU, were Otto Lenz, later an FDP Minister, Hans Lukaschek from Silesia, and the Catholic journalist Emil Dovifat. But it was important that there were also Liberal founder-members, notably Ernst Lemmer, former leader of the Liberal trade union confederation, and three former *Deutsche Demokratische Partei* politicians, Ferdinand Friedensburg, Walther Schreiber and Otto Nuschke (the last-named was later prominent as a leader of the East German CDU). Finally, there was a group of conservative Nationalist founder members, former members of the DNVP, namely Bishop Otto Dibelius, Rudolf Pechel, Wilhelm Laverrenz and Otto-Heinrich von der Gablentz. In a very real sense the Berlin CDU could claim to be an organisation which transcended the traditional party and religious cleavages of Germany.

Such a judgement would be less accurate if applied to the early Rhineland CDU. Here it was inevitable that Catholics should predominate, given the confessional balance in the Rhineland, but the Rhineland CDU was definitely an inter-class party with a strong leavening of trade unionists, and it also had a sprinkling of founder-members from other parties, notably Robert Lehr and Friedrich Holzapfel, both former members of the DNVP and both Protestants. As mayor of Herford, Holzapfel was able to travel fairly freely, and he played an important role in liaising with the mainly Protestant CDU leaders in north Germany. Another Protestant who was prominent in the foundation of the Rhineland CDU was Gustav Heinemann, one of the leaders of the 'Confessing Church' which had resisted the Nazis with great courage – Heinemann later became an SPD deputy (having changed parties) and Justice Minister, and finally was President of the Federal Republic from 1969–74. In addition, the Protestant pastor Hans Encke gave his full support to the idea of a mixed Catholic–Protestant party at the foundation meeting of the Rhineland CDU.

Nevertheless, the leading figures in the Rhineland CDU in 1945–6 were Catholics. Moreover, they were mainly left-wing Catholics, which may seem surprising in view of the fact that the septuagenarian Konrad Adenauer, one of the CDU's more conservative figures, emerged in due course not only as leader of the Rhineland CDU but of the West German CDU.[11] Lambert Lensing, first chairman of the Bochum CDU, was a Catholic journalist who originally advocated the setting up of a Christian-Social 'Labour Party'. Karl Arnold, first chairman of the Düsseldorf CDU and former secretary of the Düsseldorf branch of the Catholic trade union confederation, was also by inclination a 'Christian Socialist'. And Leo Schwering, the key figure in the foundation of the Rhineland CDU, first chairman of the Cologne CDU (Adenauer was initially only a committee member) and a former *Zentrum* member of parliament, helped to draw up the *Kölner Leitsätze* (Cologne Programme) of 30 June 1945, which although primarily concerned to emphasise the Christian principles of the CDU, also emphasised the need for a planned economy.[12]

In northern Germany developments were somewhat different. In Schleswig-Holstein Hans Schlange-Schöningen, formerly leader of the DNVP in Pomerania and a cabinet minister in the Brüning government of 1930–2, was suspicious of the domination of the CDU by Catholic Rhinelanders. Although he favoured the establishment of a new inter-confessional party, he at first wanted to set up a separate Protestant CDU in north Germany. If he had succeeded, his party would presumably have been comparable to the 'independent CDU' of Bavaria, i.e. the CSU, but Schlange-Schöningen was prevailed upon by Theodor Steltzer, *Oberpräsident* of Schleswig-Holstein and a former member of the DNVP, to opt for full participation in the inter-confessional CDU at a meeting at Bad Godesberg between 14–16 December 1945, attended by Christian Democrats from all parts of Germany except Bavaria. The CDU had some difficulty in establishing itself in largely Protestant Lower Saxony, Hamburg and Bremen, but by early 1946 branches had been constituted in all three *Länder*.

In Hesse there was an interesting mixture between left-wing Catholic intellectuals, Catholic trade unionists, and people of a more conservative background – both Catholics and Protestants. The Catholic left-wingers, led by the journalists Walter Dirks and Karl-Heinz Knappstein, at first made all the running, drawing up their *Frankfurter Leitsätze* of September 1945, which demanded, *inter alia*, that the CDU should develop as a 'Christian Socialist' party, basing its programme on 'Sozialismus aus christlicher Verantwortung' ('Socialism based on a Christian sense of responsibility').[13] They were supported in their demands both by Catholics, such as Jakob Husch and Josef Arndgen, and by Protestants, such as Ludwig Jost and Hans Wilhelmini. In Wiesbaden, on the other hand, the more conservative elements predominated, notably the Catholic Heinrich von Brentano, later chairman of the CDU parliamentary group, Foreign Minister and close colleague of Adenauer, and the Protestant Erich Köhler, former member of the conservative DNVP and future president of the Frankfurt Economic Council. The chairman of the Hesse CDU was not surprisingly a compromise – but not a figurehead – candidate, Werner Hilpert, a former *Zentrum* politician and concentration camp prisoner who had been appointed Finance Minister in Hesse by the Americans.

Finally, in the French zone the CDU developed more slowly (the French were the most reluctant of the Western allies to license parties), but a comparable, pluralistic party gradually emerged. In Württemberg the majority of the early CDU leaders were rather cautious and conservative, notably Kurt-Georg Kiesinger, one-time member of the *Zentrum* and of the Nazi party and later Minister-President of Baden-Württemberg and Federal Chancellor, but there were also advocates of 'Christian Socialism' to be found amongst the founder-members, men such as Fridolin Heurich, the Catholic trade union leader from North Baden and close friend of Jakob Kaiser, and Wilhelm Simpfendörfer, a progressive Catholic who even after the 1949 general election wanted to see the formation of a grand coalition between the CDU and SPD. In the Rhineland-Palatinate (the *Land* was not formally constituted until the end of 1946) former *Zentrum* supporters predominated in the northern part, around Koblenz and Trier, and as some of them favoured the reconstitution of the *Zentrum*, the CDU had some difficulty in establishing itself, but by March 1946 there were CDU associations in the north and the south of the Rhineland-Palatinate, and in March 1947 they amalgamated to form a single *Land* association (*Landesverband*).

Thus, within eighteen months of the end of the war a completely new type of party had emerged, bringing together Catholics and Protestants, former members of the *Zentrum* and of the Liberal and Conservative parties, trade unionists and businessmen, in one political formation. But the CDU was still very loosely organised compared with the SPD, and it was by no means clear where it was going politically, and whether it was more committed to progressive or conservative principles. During the years 1947–9 the crucial decisions were taken about what sort of a party the CDU would be, in terms both of organisation and policy, and these decisions have affected the nature of the CDU to this day.

The man who welded the pluralistic *Land* associations of the CDU into a highly successful, vote-winning machine was Konrad Adenauer, a devious and scheming but politically skilful and statesmanlike Rhinelander, who had been mayor of Cologne from 1917–33 and a prominent member of the *Zentrum* (he stood for the chancellorship twice in the 1920s). Reappointed mayor of Cologne in 1945, Adenauer was dismissed for 'incompetence' by the British military authorities in October 1945, and although he was a founding member of the CDU in Cologne he was not even chairman of the local branch at the beginning of 1946. Within two years, however, he had won complete control of the CDU, and a year later he was elected first Chancellor of the Federal Republic after the 1949 general election. Yet it would be a mistake to conclude that Adenauer had some grand political design, or that he had a clear vision of exactly how the CDU should develop. An examination of the CDU records of those years shows the extent to which Adenauer played politics by ear.[14] At the same time he was fortunate in the way the political and economic situation developed, and he showed great skill in taking advantage of situations as they evolved. He also had a remarkable ability to persuade both the left and the right of the party that he was acting in their interests, when in reality he was very much more on the side of the latter than of the former. Adenauer's good fortune and ability to take advantage of changing situations are best illustrated by the way he gained control of the party's organisation, whilst his skill as a compromiser emerged in the course of the party's policy discussions in the years 1947–9.

Adenauer was fortunate in being located in the British zone. The fact that he was dismissed as mayor of Cologne also proved to be a great advantage, as he could devote himself full-time to the CDU.[15] Equally important for both Adenauer and the CDU was the decision by the British authorities to license political parties at the *Land* level as from January 1946 – over a year before the Americans and French began to grant such licences. This gave Adenauer and the Rhineland CDU a headstart in the struggle for power, a headstart which was increased when the Russians, also early starters with licences, lost their enthusiasm for all parties except the Communist-dominated Socialist Unity Party (SED). Andreas Hermes was dismissed from his post as chairman of the Berlin CDU in December 1945 and was flown to the British zone by the RAF. As an intelligent and moderate man, he might have become a serious rival to Adenauer for the party leadership, but Adenauer refused to allow Hermes to attend the January 1946 meeting at Herford, at which preparatory discussions about the constitution of a zonal committee took place. Adenauer contended that Hermes was not eligible to attend as a 'Berliner', although he was now resident in the British zone. This was also the famous meeting at which Adenauer, as the oldest politician present, 'took the chair', without being formally proposed or seconded. A month later Adenauer was formally elected chairman of the CDU zonal committee at its first full meeting at Neheim-Hüsten. Holzapfel was elected vice-chairman. Thus, with a mixture of luck and political 'skill', Adenauer had emerged as the leading CDU figure in the

West. Meanwhile, in the East the situation was worsening for the CDU. Jakob Kaiser had hoped that the CDU in Berlin would somehow transcend the political differences between the Social and Christian Democrats, and even between the Russians and the Western Allies, but the grandly-named CDU *Reichsgeschäftsstelle* was increasingly restricted in its activities by the Russians from March 1946 onwards, and, after endorsing the American proposals for Marshall Aid in July 1947, Kaiser was boycotted by the Russians and, in effect, put in the position where he had either to submit to them or to leave for the West. In November 1947 he took the latter course, but, although his trade union friends in the West helped him to build a substantial political base there, he was never in a position to challenge Adenauer's leadership effectively.

As the CDU continued to develop in 1947–8, Adenauer constantly demonstrated both his political skill and his ability to exploit favourable situations. In February 1947 the CDU set up an inter-*Land* 'working association' (*Arbeitsgemeinschaft*) – it was not a full inter-zonal council, as the Americans and French had still not licensed *Land* parties. At the first meeting at Bad Königstein, near Frankfurt, Adenauer and Holzapfel represented the British zone, Müller and Köhler the American, Altmaier and Steiner the French, and Kaiser, Lemmer and Hickmann Berlin. Against the wishes of Adenauer the 'association' decided to have a rotating chairman. After disagreements the Bavarian diplomat Friedrich von Baffron-Prittwitz was elected, but when he made it clear that he preferred the 'Christian Social' views of Kaiser to the more conservative views of Adenauer, the latter deliberately boycotted meetings of the 'working association', which was further weakened by the periodic refusal of the French authorities to allow the representatives from their zone to attend meetings. The secretariat of the 'working association', established in Frankfurt under Dörpinghaus, played an important part in helping CDU parties in the *Länder* to fight the various elections of 1947–8. It later played a similar role in the 1949 federal elections, finally moving to Bonn as the CDU's national secretariat in 1950. But as from June 1948, the newly-established Conference of CDU *Land* chairmen, presided over by Adenauer and without any Berlin representatives, became the key national co-ordinating committee of the CDU, and remained as such until the establishment of the CDU as a federal party at Goslar in October 1950, a year after the first federal elections. At the Goslar party conference Adenauer was elected chairman, and Kaiser and Holzapfel vice-chairmen.[16]

Adenauer successfully exploited the developing political and economic situation to the advantage of himself and his party in other ways. One such was the political opportunity offered by the Frankfurt Economic Council, another that offered by the Parliamentary Council which drew up the Basic Law, the constitution of the Federal Republic.

The Economic Council was, as Heidenheimer has emphasised, 'immensely important for the future of German politics'.[17] Not only did the Economic Council implement the crucial currency reform of 1948, it was, in effect, also the embryo government of the American–British 'bizone' (set up in 1947, joined by the French in 1948). The Economic Council came into existence in June 1948, and consisted of five directorates (later six), responsible for

Economics, Finance, Transport, Postal Services, Food and Agriculture, and (later) Labour. The directors of these five 'ministries' were quasi-cabinet ministers, and the Economic Council itself was a quasi-parliament (though ultimately responsible to the occupation authorities), consisting of representatives elected by the *Land* parliaments. There was also an 'upper chamber', the *Länderrat*, consisting of representatives of the *Land* governments. The Economic Council, as finally constituted, had forty CDU–CSU members, forty SPD, six Communists, six Liberals (FDP), four *Zentrum*, four German Party (DP) and four Economic Reconstruction Association (WAV). Neither Adenauer nor Schumacher was a member, but Schumacher insisted that the SPD would consider a coalition with the CDU only if his party was allowed to control the two vital ministries, Economics and Finance. The leader of the CDU–CSU group, Holzapfel, who originally wanted a coalition with the SPD,[18] felt bound to reject these conditions, which were made on the grounds that the SPD had won more votes *in toto* that the CDU–CSU in the eight *Land* elections which had taken place. Thus, the CDU found itself participating in a loose anti-Socialist alliance with the FDP, DP and WAV members, whilst the opposition usually consisted of the SPD, KPD and *Zentrum* members. This was exactly what Adenauer wanted, but it marked a defeat for Jakob Kaiser and Karl Arnold, the left-wing Christian Democrats who wanted to reconstruct the German economy and society in alliance with the Social Democrats. When in addition, and apparently against all the odds, the free market policies of Professor Erhard, the Director of Economic Affairs on the Frankfurt Council, began to show signs of succeeding in late 1948–early 1949, the writing was on the wall for those in the CDU who advocated a controlled economy and strict controls.[19] Circumstances had played into the hands of *der Alte* (as Adenauer was known), in that Schumacher had rejected the CDU's tentative advances with disdain, and Erhard, who was at that time not even a member of the CDU, had successfully pursued economic policies which dovetailed closely with Adenauer's own economic views.[20]

Adenauer was chairman of the Parliamentary Council, which drew up the Basic Law between September 1948–May 1949. The Council consisted of twenty-seven CDU–CSU, twenty-seven SPD, five FDP, two *Zentrum*, two German Party and two Communist representatives of the *Länder*. There is no need to go into the details here of the Council's deliberations.[21] Suffice it to say that Adenauer did not get things all his own way (he would, for example, have preferred a less powerful upper chamber, *Bundesrat*), but he did succeed in having Bonn, rather than Frankfurt, chosen as the federal capital, and, more important, he got a good deal of publicity through newspaper and radio interviews. Meanwhile, Schumacher, relying on the traditional discipline of the SPD, had not become a member of the Parliamentary Council, preferring to control and criticise from outside.

Finally, in doctrinal matters, Adenauer succeeded in manoeuvring the CDU from the distinctly leftish stance adopted in the Berlin, Cologne, Bad Godesberg and Frankfurt Programmes of 1945 to the centrist – and in economic matters frankly conservative – proposals outlined in the Düsseldorf Programme of 1949, on the basis of which the CDU fought that year's general election.[22]

In the immediate postwar period the 'Christian Socialist' ideas of Jakob Kaiser (Berlin), Karl Arnold (Düsseldorf) and Eugen Kogon (Frankfurt) had undoubtedly predominated in CDU thinking. The three basic demands of the 'Christian Socialists' were (i) national economic planning; (ii) nationalisation of the key industries; and (iii) co-determination between workers and management in the running of industry.[23] However, the Catholic Church soon made it clear that it was not prepared to go beyond the social teaching contained in the 1931 papal bull, *Quadragesimo Anno*, which had declared that 'Christian Socialism is a contradiction in itself. It is impossible to be simultaneously a good Catholic and a real Socialist.'[24] And Adenauer showed that he agreed by remarking in June 1946 that 'The word Socialism is scientifically and semantically worn out. . . . If we use it, we may win five people, but twenty will run away.'[25] Whatever one may think of Adenauer's political views, it was certainly psychologically sound to criticise a party (the SPD) which claimed to have a monopoly (or even partial monopoly) of the truth: *Weltanschauungen* were very much out of fashion in the immediate postwar period. Already by the time of the Neheim-Hüsten Programme of February 1946, in the preparation of which Adenauer played a key part, the CDU was watering down its hitherto clearcut commitment to economic *dirigisme* and nationalisation of industry.[26] Significantly, paragraph 7 of the Programme stated that 'The question of nationalisation of parts of the economy, which is being strongly pressed, is currently not practicable since the German economy is not free',[27] and from late 1947 it became even less practicable as British influence declined (the Labour Government favoured large-scale nationalisation) *vis-à-vis* American influence (for free enterprise) owing to Britain's increasing economic difficulties. Once again outside circumstances gave the CDU a significant nudge in the direction in which Adenauer was already taking it.

The Ahlen Programme of February 1947 is usually regarded as the highpoint of the CDU's commitment to 'Social Christian' policies. The Ahlen Programme was certainly blunt in its criticism of the 'capitalist system', which it saw as being incapable of dealing with the 'political and social needs of the German people', but the Programme was imprecise in its commitment to a controlled economy.[28] Whilst agreeing with the Socialists and Communists that large-scale capitalism had helped Hitler to come to power in the early 1930s, the Christian Democrats went on to condemn the state capitalism of the later Nazi period, i.e. the state control of big industry by Albert Speer from 1942 until the collapse of the Third Reich. Instead of either 'private capitalism' or 'state capitalism' the Ahlen Programme proposed a typically Christian Democratic 'middle way', namely *Gemeinwirtschaft* (semi-public ownership). *Gemeinwirtschaft* was defined as a mixed system of ownership in which public bodies (such as *Land* governments, local governments or trade unions) would hold a majority of shares, but no single such body would be allowed to hold more than 15 per cent of the shares in a given enterprise. Individuals would also be entitled to hold shares, but no single person would be able to hold more than 10 per cent. The Ahlen Programme, which was endorsed by Adenauer, but which was only applicable to the British zone, was thus left-wing in its condemnation of traditional capitalism and its commitment to social justice, but unlikely to offend 'bourgeois' entrepreneurs such as farmers, small business-men, tradesmen and so on. And by 1949 the CDU was even less likely to upset such voters, because the Düsseldorf Programme committed the party to the 'social market economy' – Erhard's blend of free enterprise and social justice. In addition the Düsseldorf Programme emphasised the CDU's commitment to parliamentary democracy; to federalism; to individual responsibility in society, for example the right to choose one's children's education; to the family; to small businesses and farming; and to co-operation between manage-ment and workers. There was something for everyone, apart perhaps for the 'ideologues' and the 'poor in society'.[29]

The CDU was thus set to become, if not a conservative party in the tradi-tional sense, at least the party of all those who were suspicious of 'socialism' and 'collectivism' in the broadest sense of these words. In terms of political experimentation, the CDU might have been a more interesting party if it had pursued a 'Christian Socialist' line, but in terms of short-term tactics (winning elections) and long-term strategy (making German's second experiment in democracy work), there can be little doubt that Adenauer and all those who agreed with his pragmatic approach – notably Andreas Hermes, Josef Müller, Bruno Dörpinghaus, Hans Schlange-Schöningen, Carl Schröter, Heinrich Krone and Heinrich von Brentano – were wise to keep the party's membership and electoral appeal as wide as possible. Thus *der Alte* played a key part in diluting the ideological commitment of the CDU, and ensuring that the party remained pluralistic and pragmatic. Adenauer had suffered under the Third Reich,[30] but he was quite prepared to accept former Nazis into the party, thus helping to prevent the rise of a significant extreme-right party. He was a Catholic, but he made sure that Protestants were well represented in the leading organs of the party. He was no lover of 'socialism', but he presided over a party with a strong trade union base, and he remained on excellent terms with Hans Böckler, the Socialist leader of the main trade union confederation (the *Deutsche Gewerkschaftsbund*, DGB).[31] It is impossible, of course, to say how far the times produced the man or vice-versa. In the case of the CDU there was clearly something of both. But Adenauer cannot be denied considerable credit for helping to mould the party which integrated the vast majority of German conservatives of all classes into the liberal democratic system for the first time.

CDU – Organisation

The CDU's organisation was also much influenced by the party's early develop-ment and by its electoral successes in the 1950s.[32] For as long as the party continued to move from one electoral victory to another there seemed to be no need to build up a strong organisation. In the 1950s the CDU provided the unusual spectacle of a party which was highly disciplined – at least in terms of parliamentary voting and loyalty to its leader[33] – but very weakly organised. The CDU was little more than a *Kanzlerwählerverein*, an electors' party whose only purpose seemed to be to win elections for Adenauer and then go into hibernation again for another four years. Whereas in 1947 there were about 650,000 CDU members, by 1954 there were only 215,000. The figure crept up again in the 1960s to an average annual membership of around 300,000, but

it was only in the 1970s that the CDU began to develop some of the characteristics of a mass membership party, and by 1977 the party had more members
than ever before in its history (660,000 in June 1977).[34]

The campaign to recruit new members was one aspect of the party's attempt
to modernise itself after being forced into opposition for the first time in
1969.[35] Another aspect was the streamlining, and to some extent democratising, of its organisation. But it was an uphill task, because little had been done
during the Adenauer era to prepare for the succession. As long as Adenauer
was politically active, neither Erhard nor the Christian Democratic party was
allowed to forget that Adenauer wanted no change, either in the policies he
had pursued or in the party he had created: and in effect the Adenauer era
lasted until 1967, the year of *der Alte*'s death, not just to 1963, the year in
which he finally surrendered the chancellorship to Erhard.[36] Yet, by the early
1960s many of the party's wiser leaders realised that the CDU needed a
stronger organisation, and that in addition it must allow its members – or at
least the members of the parliamentary party – to play a more significant
policy-making role.[37] If nothing were done, there seemed to be a real possibility
that such a pluralistic party as the CDU might fall apart when it found itself
without its quasi-divine leader. The CDU was, and is, a pragmatic, government-
oriented party like the British Conservative party, the type of party which can
get along perfectly well with little more than good leadership when in office,
but which, when in opposition, needs rather more than effective leadership –
although it needs that too – to provide a real challenge to the government of
the day. Above all it needs policies (and they entail an effective research
organisation), and it needs the means to propagate them (and that entails an
efficient organisation, both national and local). These were what the party
lacked at the end of the Adenauer era.

As we have seen, the CDU grew from the base upwards, only becoming a
federal party at its first national congress held at Goslar in Lower Saxony in
October 1950, a year after Adenauer had become Chancellor of the Federal
Republic (15 September 1949). When Adenauer was elected chairman of the
CDU at the first party congress, with Kaiser and Holzapfel as his deputy-
chairmen, he wanted a powerful national secretariat, headed by Kurt-Georg
Kiesinger of Baden-Württemberg, but, owing to the strongly federalist (or at
least anti-centralist) views of the *Land* associations (*Landesverbände*), he did
not get his way.[38] Instead of a powerful party secretary-general – modelled on
those of the French and Italian parties – a five-man committee was elected
by the congress, the *Fünfer-Ausschuss*, which was the direct heir of the
Fünfer-Ausschuss of the inter-zonal *Arbeitsgemeinschaft* originally set up in
1947.[39] The new *Fünfer-Ausschuss* gave Christian Democrats of different backgrounds a chance to express their views, balancing, as it did, the north
and south, Catholics and Protestants, and progressives and conservatives.
But it fell far short of the powerful party secretariat originally envisaged by
Adenauer.

In 1950 the CDU federal offices were moved from Frankfurt to Bonn, and in
1952 Bruno Heck was appointed federal business manager (*Bundesgeschäfts-
führer*) in order to prepare the party for the 1953 election.[40] However, having

failed to get his way over the party's national organisation, Adenauer proceeded to treat it as he had the inter-zonal *Arbeitsgemeinschaft*: he boycotted it – in his fourteen years as Chancellor he visited the party headquarters in the Nassestrasse only once.

Yet the CDU was not the weak, decentralised party one might imagine from a reading of the party statutes endorsed at Goslar.[41] Adenauer used the party conferences to obtain grass-roots support for his policies, but to a large extent he simply by-passed the federal committee (*Bundesausschuss*) and executive committee (*Bundesvorstand*) – frequently they were not summoned when they should have been. Moreover, the *Vorstand* was expanded to the point where it became ineffective as a decision-making body. Adenauer was a great believer in democracy, except insofar as his own party was concerned. Yet he retained the loyalty of the CDU for over a decade: it was not until his abortive presidential candidature (1959) that the first real criticisms of his leadership emerged. Adenauer mantained strong, centralised control over the CDU by stretching to the limit his general constitutional right to lead and direct national policy as Chancellor (article 65 of the Basic Law);[42] by running his cabinet in an autocratic manner – it is probably true to say that Hans Globke, the Chancellor's Secretary, was more powerful than any cabinet minister;[43] by his firm control over the parliamentary party (*Fraktion*) – both Heinrich von Brentano and Heinrich Krone, the *Fraktion* leaders throughout the period 1949–63, were absolutely devoted to Adenauer; by carrying out a Western-oriented foreign policy which united all Christian Democrats, thus providing the party with the ideological unity it lacked in domestic policy;[44] and, above all, by presiding over the 'economic miracle' and winning general elections.

In theory the supreme organ in the CDU is the party congress (*Parteitag*).[45] It decides on the policy of the party, and its decisions are binding on the *Fraktion* and on CDU-led governments, whether in Bonn or in the *Länder*. It also elects the important party executive committee (*Vorstand*). But in practice, of course, the congress, which sometimes only meets bi-annually, cannot seriously influence the policies actually pursued by the party. The *Parteitag* is, in fact, essentially a meeting of the party faithful. Occasionally the militants are asked to endorse an important programme, as at Berlin in 1968. But the main object of the congress is to bring together the local party leaders so that they can hear the national leaders in person – rather like conservative party conferences in any country. The *Land* associations (*Landesverbände*) were originally represented at national congresses in proportion to the number of CDU votes cast at the previous general election in their area,[46] but in 1956, at the Stuttgart congress, it was decided that in addition to the one delegate sent for every 100,000 CDU votes (this figure is now 75,000) a delegate should also be sent for every 1,000 party members. This decision was taken in order to increase party membership, but in the 1960s was not very effective in achieving its objective. Since the CDU went into opposition, however, party membership has increased greatly – but for other reasons.[47]

The other federal organs are the federal committee (*Bundesausschuss*, henceforth referred to as the *Ausschuss*), federal executive (*Bundesvorstand*, henceforth referred to as the *Vorstand*), praesidium (*Präsidium*) and secretariat.[48]

The *Ausschuss* is the main liaison organ between the CDU's central organisation and its organisation in the country. The countrywide organisation consists of eleven *Land* associations (*Landesverbände*), 392 'regional' associations (*Kreisverbände*) and approximately 16,500 'district' associations (*Ortsverbände*).[49] The *Kreisverbände* meet four times a year, and, in conjunction with the *Land* associations, elect up to ninety candidates to serve on the federal committee. Otherwise, the *Kreisverbände* are responsible mainly for distributing party material and for electioneering. They tend to be the preserve of local notables. The *Ortsverbände* operate at a lower level, bringing together one or more small local government districts: they can be very small – only seven members are required to form an *Ortsverband* – and they are important only at election times, although they are expected to send reports periodically to the *Kreisverbände*.

To return to the federal committee (*Ausschuss*), it consists of approximately 160 members: ninety elected by the *Landes* – and *Kreisverbände*, the sixty or so members of the federal executive committee (*Vorstand*), the head of the party's research committee (*Bundesfachausschuss*), and one representative each from the party's seven national support organisations (*Vereinigungen*), i.e. the *Junge Union* (young members), *Sozialausschüsse* (social committees – essentially the party's trade union wing), *Kommunalpolitische Vereinigung* (local government association), *Mittelstandvereinigung* (artisans and small businessmen's organisation), *Wirtschaftsvereinigung* (economic association), and *Union der Vertriebenen und Flüchtlinge* (refugees' association). In theory the federal *Ausschuss* is a very important body, being responsible for 'all the political and organisational tasks allocated to it by the federal party',[50] but in practice its influence is greatly reduced owing to its large size and, more important, the irregularity of its meetings; it has a statutory obligation to meet at least twice per annum, but in the Adenauer era it often did not meet at all (e.g. in the years 1958 and 1959), and even in the 1970s it rarely exceeds its minimum obligation of two meetings a year.

Considerably more important than the federal *Ausschuss* is the federal executive committee (*Vorstand*). It consists of the party chairman, five vice-chairmen, general secretary, treasurer, chairman and vice-chairman of the parliamentary group, the eleven *Land* chairmen and seven *Vereinigungen* chairmen, and the federal Chancellor and President if they are members of the CDU; in addition, up to fifteen 'especially deserving' party members are elected every two years to the *Vorstand* by the party congress. Altogether, then, the *Vorstand* has about sixty members. It meets on average every two months, and, according to article 34 of the party statutes, it is the most important leading and directing organ in the CDU, its main duty being to ensure that the decisions of the party congress and federal committee are implemented. But, as with the *Ausschuss*, it is too large a body to fulfil its role effectively, and the key controlling organs in the CDU are in fact the praesidium, aided by the party secretariat, and at times in recent years the parliamentary party (*Fraktion*).[51]

The praesidium is indeed the most important central organ, atlhough it makes its decisions in the light of the climate of opinion prevailing in the parliamentary party, and in the country as a whole as reflected in the views expressed in the *Vorstand* and *Ausschuss*. The praesidium consists of the seven or eight leading figures in the CDU: the party chairman and secretary, the five vice-chairmen and the treasurer, and the chairman of the parliamentary party. (In addition, the federal Chancellor and President are *ex officio* members if they belong to the CDU.) The praesidium is in practice responsible for the day-to-day running of the party, for policy decision making, and for supervising and organising election campaigns. Since its establishment the party secretariat has worked in close liaison with the praesidium.

As previously mentioned, Adenauer originally wanted a strong party secretariat, but having built up his own 'conventional' means of controlling the party, he was later opposed to the development of a national organisation which might challenge his policies or his authority.[52] However, he was unable to prevent the 1962 congress (at Dortmund) from appointing Josef-Hermann Dufhues as the party's first 'business chairman' (*geschäftsführende Vorsitzender*), or quasi-secretary-general.[53] The delegates realised that once *der Alte* had gone there was going to be a void at the centre, and that it was essential to develop an effective national organisation before it was too late. However, this first attempt to give the CDU a proper central administration was essentially a failure, partly owing to opposition from the party's local barons, partly owing to the poor health of Dufhues, but chiefly because the CDU's main attention and energy were concentrated for several years in the early and middle 1960s on the 'succession problem':[54] first on how to get rid of Adenauer, and secondly on how to make Erhard into a more effective politician. Since Erhard's political skill fell so far short of his economic appeal, it might be supposed that the CDU would have done something about its central organisation between 1963–6, the period of Erhard's Chancellorship. And in fact the party did come close to tackling the problem, but things went wrong at the last moment. When Adenauer announced that he intended renouncing the party chairmanship on his ninetieth birthday in 1966, it was hoped that Dufhues would take over and carry out a thorough overhaul of the central party machinery. At first he agreed to stand, but after a serious illness he had to withdraw his candidature. At this point Rainer Barzel, the ambitious and articulate leader of the parliamentary party, decided to put himself forward as a candidate, which in turn provoked Erhard to stand himself: he simply could not afford to allow any further erosion of his authority within the party. The upshot was that in March 1966 Erhard was elected party chairman and Adenauer honorary life chairman, with Barzel vice-chairman and leader of the parliamentary party.[55] All this meant that the reorganisation of the party was put off again. For, although Erhard and Adenauer were on very bad terms, politically and personally, they did have one thing in common: they preferred to win elections by 'Chancellor appeal' (the so-called *Kanzlereffekt*) than through a strong party organisation. Although Erhard's successor as Chancellor and CDU chairman, Kurt-Georg Kiesinger, also preferred to rely on 'Chancellor appeal', he was persuaded to appoint Bruno Heck, a fellow Swabian, as the party's first full-time secretary-general in 1967. Heck in fact remained in Kiesinger's CDU–SPD coalition government as the minister responsible for Family and Youth until October 1968, but he then resigned to devote himself wholly to his job as secretary-general of the CDU in preparation for the 1969 general election. He remained in this post until 1971 when he was replaced by Konrad Kraske, who was in turn succeeded by Kurt Biedenkopf in 1973.[56]

In spite of the fact that Kiesinger ran well ahead of Brandt in public opinion polls during 1969, the Christian Democrats lost the election and found themselves in opposition for the first time.[57] The much better organised CSU fared considerably better than the CDU, and it was finally admitted that the CDU could no longer afford to rely on the 'Chancellor effect' to win elections.[58] The party's younger and more progressive leaders, such as Gerhard Stoltenberg from Schleswig-Holstein and Helmut Kohl from Rhineland-Palatinate, joined conservatives such as Alfred Dregger from Hesse in calling for the building up of an effective party organisation.[59] Typical of such demands was that made by Jürgen Echternach in November 1969 at the *Junge Union* congress:

> The CDU must at last become a party which is capable of taking action. At present it appears predominantly as a disorganised, loosely united reservoir of heterogeneous associations and autonomous regional branches . . . the federal party and its associations must become the centre of political decision making in the CDU. . . . That means tightening up the organisation and modernising the party machine.[60]

The upshot of such appeals was that the party began to strengthen its organisation nationally and locally, and to go out of its way to recruit new members. This process was incomplete by the time of the 1972 general election, but by that of 1976 the CDU was a very much better organised party than it had been a decade, or even five years, previously.

In 1970 the *Landesverband* organisation was streamlined. Originally there had been sixteen *Land* associations, a legacy of the piecemeal development of the CDU in the late 1940s. In 1968 they had been reduced to thirteen by the amalgamation of the three Lower Saxon *Land* associations (Brunswick, Hanover and Oldenburg), and in 1970 the process was completed with the amalgamation of the four *Land* associations in Baden-Württemberg (North and South Baden, North Württemberg, and Württemberg-Hohenzollern). As a result (in 1977) the CDU has one *Land* association for each *Land*, except for the huge *Land* of North Rhine Westphalia (population 17·5 million) which has two (Rhineland and Westphalia). Moreover, in order to maximise inter-*Land* cohesion the *Land* chairmen now meet monthly – almost a revival of Adenauer's Conference of *Land* Chairmen of the late 1940s.

The CDU also acquired a large new modern building as its headquarters in Bonn, the Konrad Adenauer Building, situated within a few hundred yards of the Bundestag. At the same time the party began to make full use of modern publicity techniques and research methods under the leadership of men such as Rüdiger Göb, an organisation and publicity expert who was appointed business manager in 1970, and Kurt Biedenkopf, who was secretary-general from 1973 to 1977. Professor Biedenkopf, an expert on co-determination in industry and vice-chancellor of Bochum University at the age of thirty-eight, was typical of the articulate, ambitious group of young men who were attracted to work full-time for the CDU in the 1970s. The party also developed a highly efficient research organisation, which was at the disposal both of the central organisation and of the parliamentary party (*Fraktion*).

Indeed, one of the most important changes in the CDU in the 1970s was 'the enhanced position of the Bundestag *Fraktion* as a centre of decision making within the party'.[61] In the Adenauer era the *Fraktion* had been under the thumb of the Chancellor, its weakness being well illustrated by its inability to influence Adenauer in any way in 1959 when he was making up his mind whether or not to stand for the federal presidency: in the end he did not' stand, much to the annoyance of most members of the *Fraktion*, who had hoped, as it were, to put him on ice.[62] Rainer Barzel, chairman of the *Fraktion* 1964–73, was determined to give the elected Christian Democratic parliamentarians an enhanced role within the councils of the party. He brought younger men into the *Fraktion*'s committee, increasing its size to twenty-one, and encouraged research by parliamentarians. Many young CDU deputies were determined to avoid a repetition of the post-1969 electoral situation, when the CDU leadership had no plan to counter the formation of the SPD–FDP coalition, and when the parliamentary party had no chance to let its views be known.[63] When Helmut Kohl became CDU chairman in 1973 there was a change of emphasis, because Kohl (with the full support of Biedenkopf) concentrated on strengthening the party's central organisation. As a result, by the second half of the 1970s the CDU had both an efficient and reasonably influential *Fraktion* and a well-organised party headquarters.

CDU–CSU – *Electoral Record and Electoral Geography*[64]

The German Christian Democrats have gone through three phases in their electoral history: establishment and consolidation in the 1950s; a bitter-sweet period of success and failure in the 1960s; and consolidation and reorganisation in the 1970s.

In spite of the fact that the Christian Democrats outdistanced the Social Democrats at the first Federal election in 1949,[65] and emerged from it with Adenauer as Chancellor heading a coalition of CDU–CSU, FDP (Liberals) and DP (the Protestant, conservative, north German *Deutsche Partei*), the election was a set-back for the Christian Democrats, in that their percentage of the poll (31 per cent) was down on average by 6·7 per cent compared with the *Landtag* elections of 1946–7. The SPD vote, at 29·2 per cent, was also down by 5·8 per cent compared with these elections.

As far as the CDU–CSU was concerned, the main lesson to be learned from the 1949 election was that the Christian Democratic 'movement' had still not established itself very effectively in the nation's political consciousness. For a new party the CDU–CSU had done creditably, but the 1949 result suggested that rapid growth might equally well be followed by rapid decline. This was one of the reasons why Adenauer was anxious to include those 'bourgeois' (*bürgerlich*) parties such as the DP, FDP and later the Refugees, in his coalition.

His strategy was to keep on good terms with the small centre-right parties with a view to absorbing them in due course, and it was a strategy which paid handsome dividends.

The 1949 electoral setback was due largely to the more flexible party licensing policy adopted by the Western Allies after the 1946–7 *Landtag* elections. In Bavaria, for example, the CSU vote was 29·2 per cent in 1949, a drop of 23·1 per cent compared with the 1946 *Landtag* election, and this 'collapse' of the Christian Democratic vote was almost entirely due to the intervention of the particularist, conservative *Bayern Partei* (BP), licensed in February 1948. Likewise, in north Germany the roughly equivalent particularist, conservative – but Protestant – *Deutsche Partei* cut into the CDU vote in 1949 by winning 18 per cent of the poll in Bremen, 17·8 per cent in Lower Saxony, 13·1 per cent in Hamburg and 12·1 per cent in Schleswig-Holstein. Although founded in 1945 the DP had only been licensed in time to stand for the Bremen *Landtag* election of October 1947 (when it received only 3·9 per cent). Other right-wing votes were siphoned off by the *Deutsche Rechtspartei* (DRP), which won 8·1 per cent in Lower Saxony, although only 1·8 per cent overall (altogether the DRP won five seats), and by the Bavarian refugee party, the *Wirtschaftliche Aufbauvereinigung*, WAV (the Union of Economic Reconstruction), which, under its demagogic leader Alfred Loritz, won twelve seats after polling 14·4 per cent in Bavaria. Despite these setbacks for the Christian Democrats Adenauer was certainly justified in bidding for the chancellorship in 1949, because the election had largely been fought on economic issues, and 13·9 million votes had been cast for 'free enterprise' parties, whilst only 8·5 million had been cast for those which favoured a planned economy; moreover, the CDU–CSU had outdistanced its main rival by 400,000 votes (1·8 per cent) at an election in which both parties made it clear that their main objective was to win control of the Economics Ministry.

The 1949 election had indicated the possibilities open to small parties with definite ideological views or particular clienteles, and the *Landtag* elections of 1949–52 seemed to confirm the worst of the CDU–CSU's fears. For, with a rash of smaller parties appearing on the scene, the Christian Democratic vote at the *Landtag* elections of 1949–52 declined to an average of 25 per cent (compared with 37·7 per cent in 1946–7 and 31 per cent in 1949). The worst threat came from the refugees, who outside Bavaria had had no party specifically committed to representing their interests at the 1949 general election, but in January 1950 the *Bund der Heimatvertriebenen und Entrechteten*, BHE, ('Union of those expelled from their homelands and of the dispossessed') was founded in Schleswig-Holstein, and at the subsequent *Landtag* election (July 1950) the BHE won 23·4 per cent of the votes, pushing the CDU, with 19·7 per cent, into third place (the SPD won 27·5 per cent). The BHE participated in eight *Landtag* elections between 1950–2, its average poll being 12 per cent largely at the expense of the CDU and FDP, who also lost votes to the extreme right *Sozialistische Reichspartei* (SRP) which gained 7·7 per cent in Bremen and 11 per cent in Lower Saxony in 1951.

Altogether the electoral prospects for the Christian Democrats looked far from favourable in the period leading up to the 1953 general election. Yet the

CDU–CSU won 45·2 per cent of the votes cast in September 1953, and with 244 out of 487 seats it became the first party in German history to win an absolute majority in parliament. In 1957 the Christian Democrats were to achieve a higher percentage of the poll, but the 1953 election was undoubtedly of greater significance both for them and for the development of West German democracy than that of 1957.

Why were the Christian Democrats so unexpectedly successful in 1953? In the first place they made full use of their position as the governing party to put forward their case. Moreover, unlike the 1949 election campaign, that of 1953 concentrated on foreign policy at a time when the Cold War was at its chilliest, with the Red Army having just suppressed the East Berlin rising (17 June). Adenauer's decisively pro-Western, anti-Communist attitude seemed convincing to a large number of the voters. Likewise, the Christian Democrats could emphasise their success in stabilising prices since 1949: by 1953 Erhard's 'social market economy' had shown distinct signs that it was working. There seemed to be no case for opting for the SPD's planned economy (even although the SPD had qualified its enthusiasm for economic controls at the Dortmund congress of 1952), nor for taking a chance with the SPD foreign policy of reunification *before* rearmament and commitment to the Western Alliance.[66] In terms of the actual voting, the Christian Democrats gained votes both from their coalition partners (the FDP fell back to 9·5 per cent from 11·9 per cent, and the DP lost 0·8 per cent to poll 3·2 per cent) and from the small parties generally. Moreover, the refugees – in spite of the amalgamation of the BHE and WAV – did relatively badly. Having averaged almost 12 per cent in the *Landtag* elections of 1950–2, they won only 5·9 per cent (twenty-seven seats) in 1953 in spite of the fact that they had changed their name to GB–BHE with a view to widening their appeal (GB = *Gesamtdeutscher Block*, All-German Block). The party's leaders, Waldemar Kraft and Theodor Oberländer, tended to make contradictory statements on foreign policy: on the one hand, they were firmly committed to German reunification and the return of the lost territories; on the other, they wanted to support Adenauer's pro-Western, anti-Communist policy – but already by the early 1950s (as the SPD pointed out) there were possible contradictions between the two objectives. Above all perhaps the GB–BHE did relatively badly because the refugees were already becoming integrated into the economic life of West Germany.[67] Other factors which helped the Christian Democrats in 1953 were that the extreme right was seriously weakened by the banning of the *Sozialistische Reichspartei* (SRP) by the Federal Constitutional Court in 1952: indeed, although five extreme right parties stood in 1953, none won as much as 1 per cent. Secondly, the CSU inflicted a severe defeat on the Bavarian Party (CSU 47·8 per cent, a gain of 18·6 per cent compared with 1949, and BP 9·2 per cent, a loss of 11·7 per cent since 1949). Bavarian electors clearly decided that it was pointless to vote for the BP, whose campaign was directed chiefly against the SPD and whose declared object was to join a Christian Democratic-led coalition after the election. Finally, most *Zentrum* voters went over to the CDU. Whereas in 1949 the *Zentrum* had polled 8·9 per cent in North Rhine Westphalia (the only *Land* where it had a serious following), and in 1950 at the *Landtag* election it had still polled 7·5 per cent, in 1953 its vote dropped to 2·7 per cent, and the party returned three deputies to the Bundestag only because one of its leaders, Johannes Brockmann, was directly elected on a joint *Zentrum*–CDU ticket in Oberhausen.

The Christian Democrats could have formed a government on their own after the 1953 election, but Adenauer, requiring a two-thirds majority to alter the constitution so that the Federal Republic could rearm, invited the Liberals, German Party and Refugee Party to join his coalition (this gave Adenauer 328 votes out of 497). The Refugee leaders, Oberländer and Kraft, enjoying ministerial portfolios, soon mitigated their criticism of Adenauer's eastern policy – or rather lack of it in the eyes of the more extreme refugees, who still hoped to recover the lands beyond the Oder-Neisse as well as the Sudetenland from Czechoslovakia – and as a result the Refugee Party split in 1955, with eighteen deputies going into opposition, whilst Kraft, Oberländer and seven others joined the CDU. Once again the Christian Democrats' policy of 'integrating' others into their political family had paid off. To a lesser extent the same thing happened with the Liberals, for after the 'Young Turks' revolt of 1956, which resulted in the formation of an SPD–FDP coalition in North Rhine Westphalia in place of Karl Arnold's CDU–FDP coalition, the FDP parliamentary party split, with thirty-three deputies going into opposition and sixteen (including four ministers) remaining loyal to Adenauer.[68] The latter did not actually join the CDU, but formed their own *Freie Volkspartei*, FVP, which in January 1957 merged with the German Party. However, the fact that one third of the parliamentary Liberal party had remained loyal to Adenauer augured well for the Christian Democrats at the general election of 1957: some at least of the breakaway Liberals and their supporters in the country could be expected to vote for the Christian Democrats rather than for the German Party. The other promising development for the Christian Democrats was that at the *Landtag* elections of 1953–6 their vote was up on average by over 4 per cent compared with the 1949–53 *Landtag* elections. As the SPD vote had increased by a similar percentage, it seemed likely that the Federal Republic was moving from a multi-party system to one dominated by – if not wholly controlled by – the two major parties.[69]

As it turned out, the CDU–CSU emerged from the 1957 general election as *the* dominant party, with 50·2 per cent of the votes cast and well over half the seats (270 out of 497). This was the election at which the CDU–CSU slogan 'Keine Experimente' ('no experiments') predominated. The economy was booming and the Federal Republic had become a full member of the Western Alliance. The suppression of the Hungarian rising by the Red Army in October 1956 seemed to confirm the wisdom of Adenauer's decisively pro-Western stance and the unrealistic nature of the SPD's continuing opposition to rearmament. Thus the CDU won an absolute majority by retaining all its 1953 voters and attracting others from the minor parties. The Refugee Party had lost 1·3 per cent since 1953, and by gaining only 4.6 per cent nationally, with no candidates directly elected, it failed to win any seats. Most of its voters went over to the Christian Democrats. Likewise the German Party (joined by the breakaway Liberals in 1957) only gained 0·2 per cent more than in

1953: the DP obviously should have gained more if all its own voters of 1953, together with the Liberal 'renegades' of 1956, had voted for it. Again, most of the 'lost' votes went to the Christian Democrats. Moreover, the German Party, with only 2·8 per cent of the national vote, was only represented in the Bundestag thanks to the CDU, which had allowed the DP to win six directly elected seats by not standing against it: as a result the German Party became eligible for eleven proportional seats, giving it seventeen in all. However, the manner of the German Party's entry into the Bundestag in 1957 meant that it was little more than a satellite of the CDU–CSU (the party's slogan was 'Kanzlertreue mit Rechtsblick' – 'loyalty to the Chancellor, but with a conservative outlook'). In view of the continuing success of the Christian Democrats' 'absorption' policy, it was not surprising that in 1960 nine of the German Party's deputies decided to join the CDU.[70]

In spite of the CDU–CSU's very considerable success in 1957 it was clear that their victory owed a great deal to Adenauer personally and to the absorption of the smaller parties. Adenauer, however, was now eighty-one (and presumably not immortal, despite political gossip to the contrary), and there were not many small parties left to absorb. Moreover, in spite of its failure, the SPD had gained 3 per cent in polling 31·8 per cent. More threatening to the Christian Democrats were the series of Social Democratic decisions of 1957–60 – the Bad Godesberg Programme of 1959 was the chief symbol – by which the SPD brought itself more or less in line with the CDU–CSU over rearmament, European integration and the social market economy. Having opposed the CDU–CSU vociferously throughout the 1950s (at least over foreign and defence policy) the SPD adopted the Wehner strategy of 'non-opposition' in the 1960s, hoping thereby to show that the SPD was a respectable, trustworthy party, for which the more enlightened members of the middle class could safely vote. There was some opposition to this strategy in the SPD, but the leaders of the party realised that it was the only way to break out of the 30 per cent 'class ghetto', to which the party had been confined since the war.

By the time of the 1961 general election the Christian Democrats and Social Democrats were more or less in agreement on foreign policy, and to all intents and purposes on economic policy as well. Moreover, the SPD had chosen the young and energetic Willy Brandt, mayor of Berlin, to oppose the ailing Adenauer, whose autocratic manner and quarrels with Erhard and the Christian Democratic parliamentary party were being increasingly publicised. However, despite a 4·8 per cent loss, the Christian Democrats emerged from the election with 45·4 per cent of the votes cast, almost nine points ahead of the SPD (who won 36·2 per cent).

Meanwhile, the Liberals had polled 12·8 per cent, a 5·1 per cent gain. Clearly the electorate was becoming doubtful about the CDU–CSU and sceptical about Adenauer continuing as Chancellor. The FDP's considerable gain was largely due to the party's slogan: 'With the CDU, but without Adenauer'. Almost half of the FDP's new voters seem to have come from the CDU, and the remainder from the German Party – especially in Lower Saxony – the German Party had rashly amalgamated with the Refugee Party in 1961 after the DP's parliamentary party had split in 1960. The new *Gesamtdeutsche Partei* (DP–BHE) neither appealed to the small, but hitherto loyal, north German Protestant conservative electorate of the German Party nor to the 'special interest' electorate of the Refugees. Only 2·8 per cent voted for the GDP (the two separate parties had won 5·7 per cent in 1957), and of their 'lost' votes just over half went to the CDU and the rest to the FDP.

As far as the Christian Democrats were concerned, the 1961 election marked a more severe setback than was apparent at the time. True, the 'Keine Experimente' slogan had succeeded again,[71] and many centre-left voters had still not fully perceived the extent of the changes in the SPD. But the CDU–CSU's *real* loss in 1961 was greater than the *apparent* loss indicated by the party's 4·8 per cent decline in votes. In particular, opinion surveys showed that most of the SPD's new voters were former Christian Democrats.[72] Other Christian Democratic voters – annoyed by Adenauer's refusal to give way to Erhard – opted for the FDP. So the *real* Christian Democratic loss in 1961 was in the order of 7 per cent (approximately 4·6 per cent to the SPD and 2·5 per cent to the FDP), and this loss was concealed only by the CDU–CSU's continuing ability to attract votes from the declining small parties (in 1957 the latter had won 10·7 per cent of the votes cast, in 1961 they won only 5·7 per cent).

The years 1961–5 were a period of indecision for the Christian Democrats. They at last succeeded in persuading Adenauer to stand down in favour of Erhard (October 1963), one of the conditions for the return of the Liberals to the governing coalition, and public opinion polls indicated the popularity of Erhard. He was regarded as 'der Vater des Wirtschaftswunders' ('the father of the economic miracle'), and his political shortcomings did not become fully apparent until another three years had passed. Indeed, after *Landtag* election setbacks in 1962–3 and the bad publicity gained for the party both by the Spiegel Affair and by the 'Gaullist-Atlanticist' foreign policy quarrel, it was important for Erhard to rally the CDU–CSU before the 1965 election. This he successfully achieved at the Baden-Württemberg *Land* election of April 1964, which both he and Brandt decided to use as a trial of strength before the general election. Erhard undoubtedly won the 'battle of Baden-Württemberg', the CDU vote going up from 39·5 per cent (in 1960) to 46·2 per cent, whilst the SPD had to be satisfied with a 2 per cent gain (from 35·3 per cent to 37·3 per cent).

At the 1965 general election Erhard's capacity as a vote winner – at least in boom times for the economy – was borne out once again, for the Christian Democrats won 47·6 per cent of the votes cast, a gain of 2·4 per cent since 1961, and the Social Democrats 39·3 per cent, a gain of 3·1 per cent. Brandt was very disappointed by the SPD's failure to reach its minimum target of 40 per cent, and very nearly retired from politics. To some extent his disappointment was understandable: the Christian Democrats had been fighting an election without Adenauer for the first time; it was a 'relaxed' election from a foreign policy point of view – there were none of the tensions of 1949 (Berlin blockade), 1953 (East Berlin rising), 1957 (Hungary aftermath) and 1961 (the Berlin Wall) to benefit the governing party; moreover the Christian Democrats were divided over foreign policy right up to the time of the election, with the 'Gaullists' Adenauer, Strauss and von Guttenberg openly criticising the pro-

American, pro-détente policies of the 'Atlanticists' Schröder, Erhard and Majonica. As it turned out, foreign policy played a small part in the general election for the first time since 1949, and this proved to be an advantage to the somewhat divided Christian Democrats. However, the real winner was the 'father of the economic miracle', Erhard, who ran well ahead of Brandt in the popularity polls throughout the campaign.[73]

Nevertheless, the underlying trends in 1965 were worrying for the Christian Democrats. They regained some of the anti-Adenauer voters of 1961 who had gone over to the FDP (at 9·5 per cent the FDP was down 3·3 per cent compared with 1961), and they continued to mop up small party votes, particularly former German Party votes in Lower Saxony, Bremen and Schleswig-Holstein. But there were two clouds on the CDU–CSU horizon. One, although still relatively small, was the threat to the Christian Democrats' right flank posed by the success of the *National-demokratische Partei Deutschlands*, NPD: in winning 2 per cent of the votes cast the NPD took well over half of the total extreme right vote of 3·6 per cent. The second, with equally serious implications, was the small but significant incursion by the SPD into the Catholic working-class electorate of the Ruhr and Rhineland, hitherto loyal to the CDU. In the more relaxed atmosphere pertaining at the time of the Second Vatican Council the Catholic Bishops gave no specific electoral advice to their flock – for the first time at a postwar German general election.[74] Moreover, the SPD had been emphasising for several years that it was in no sense an anti-clerical party. Whatever the precise reasons for the Catholic industrial workers' switch of party in 1965, it is clear that 1965 marked a significant change in voting patterns. The average swing to the SPD in the mainly Catholic *Ruhrgebeit* was 6 per cent, and in Cologne the SPD won two direct seats for the first time. In the four Cologne constituencies the average swing from the CDU to the SPD was 8·3 per cent. With 47·1 per cent (a loss of 0·5 per cent since 1961) the CDU remained the strongest party in North Rhine Westphalia, but the SPD gained 5·3 per cent in polling 42·6 per cent, a gain decisively above its national average of 3·1 per cent. Again, in the largely Catholic industrial Saarland the SPD advanced significantly, by 6·3 per cent to 39·8 per cent. If these trends continued, the Christian Democratic parliamentary majority would soon be threatened, for, although the SPD had fallen well short of winning the election, the Social Democrats had broken decisively out of their '30 per cent ghetto' by their gains of 1961 and 1965.

After the 1965 election, as after that of 1961, the CDU–CSU gave the impression of being a divided party. Adenauer and President Lübke favoured a grand coalition with the SPD, but Erhard and the majority of the parliamentary party was opposed to this course of action, whilst recognising that there were arguments in favour of it, notably that it would provide a large measure of consensus for *Ostpolitik* (eastern policy), electoral reform, and the proposed emergency laws. The much publicised quarrel about who should succeed Adenauer as CDU chairman (Erhard or Barzel) did nothing to allay the public's suspicion that the CDU–CSU had lost its political touch, a suspicion which seemed to be confirmed by the signs that the country was entering a period of economic recession (from spring 1966 onwards). To make matters worse,

Erhard's reputation as an election winner was severely damaged by the North Rhine Westphalia *Land* election of July 1966, in which the SPD, despite Erhard's heavy involvement in the campaign, overtook the CDU for the first time (49·5 per cent [+ 6·2 per cent] for the SPD, 42·8 per cent [− 3·6 per cent] for the CDU). When in addition the CDU–CSU and FDP were unable to agree about how to deal with the budget deficit forecast for 1967, and the FDP left the coalition (in September), Erhard was in a very difficult position. He was strongly opposed to a grand coalition with the SPD, but the only alternative appeared to be an SPD–FDP coalition. However, after NPD successes at the Hesse and Bavaria *Landtag* elections of November 1966,[75] there seemed to be no reasonable alternative to a grand coalition, so Erhard gave way to Kurt-Georg Kiesinger, then Minister-President of Baden-Württenberg, and the grand coalition was finally formed with Kiesinger as Chancellor and Brandt as Vice-Chancellor in December 1966. Despite the fears of Erhard and a minority of the CDU–CSU parliamentary party that the grand coalition would turn out to be the Christian Democrats' wooden horse – the SPD after all had been demanding such a coalition since 1961 – things went well for the Christian Democrats throughout most of 1967–8. The SPD's left-wing supporters objected vociferously to the grand coalition whilst the CDU gained credit as the law-and-order party during the many left-wing student disturbances of 1967–8. This was borne out, for example, at the Baden-Württemberg *Landtag* election of April 1968, when the CDU lost 1·9 per cent in polling 44·1 per cent, but the SPD lost 8·2 per cent in polling 29·1 per cent. Meanwhile, the NPD (which had not stood previously) won 9·8 per cent, and the FDP gained a little to finish with 14·4 per cent.

In 1969, however, the political situation worsened slightly for the Christian Democrats, because from the time of the presidential election (March), when the SPD and FDP combined their votes to elect Gustav Heinemann, it was clear – although never openly stated, including during the election campaign – that the Social Democrats and Liberals were ready to do a deal and form a government. As the opinion polls throughout most of 1969 showed the CDU–CSU and SPD running level, the situation was rather ominous for the Christian Democrats. It was ominous for other reasons too. The CDU–CSU had always based its campaigns on four main factors: its possession of the chancellorship, its ability to manage the economy, its foreign policy, and its identification with state authority as *the* party of the Federal Republic. In 1969, however, although there was a CDU Chancellor – indeed the Christian Democrats based their campaign on the slogan 'Auf den Kanzler kommt es an' ('it all depends on the Chancellor') – the CDU–CSU could no longer claim to be the only party with 'state authority', i.e. the only party fit to govern: after all, the SPD had been participating in the government since 1966. Moreover, foreign policy was not a major issue in 1969 – it was clear that the SPD and FDP would try to press ahead more quickly with *Ostpolitik* than the CDU–CSU, but the Christian Democrats had started the 'opening of the East' under Schröder, and the majority of them was certainly not opposed to *Ostpolitik* in principle.[76] However, during the campaign they adopted a fairly nationalistic tone, principally because they were worried that the NPD might by-pass them on the right. Indeed, the NPD's strength was a considerable disadvantage to the Christian Democrats, in that it tended to draw them away from their traditional centre ground to a more conservative position. Finally, and perhaps this was the key factor in 1969, the CDU–CSU no longer had the 'economic wizard' on their side: on the contrary it was believed that Karl Schiller, the SPD Minister of Finance, had played the main part in pulling the country out of the 1966–7 recession. Erhard meanwhile had dropped back into obscurity.

The Christian Democrats emerged from the 1969 election as the largest party in the Bundestag. With 46·1 per cent of the votes cast they won 242 seats, whilst the SPD polled 42·7 per cent (224 seats) and the FDP 5·8 per cent (30 seats). Nevertheless, the SPD and FDP quickly decided to form a coalition, and the Christian Democrats found themselves in opposition for the first time in the history of the Federal Republic.[77]

The Christian Democrats had performed a useful service in containing the NPD on their right: the NPD failed to enter the Bundestag, falling only 0·7 per cent short of the 5 per cent hurdle. But the price paid was a noticeable shift to the right, especially by the Bavarian CSU. At the same time the Christian Democrats had done well to win over a considerable number of the one million voters who deserted the FDP. In the Federal Republic as a whole the Christian Democratic vote was up in only forty-two constituencies, but nineteen of these were FDP *Hochburgen* (places of strength): in particular conservative Liberals, those from the old National Liberal current, voted for the CDU–CSU in 1969, confirming a trend already apparent in 1965.

However, in contrast to these gains, the Christian Democrats lost votes directly to the SPD, especially in Catholic metropolitan areas (where the CDU vote declined on average by 4·8 per cent), in Catholic industrial areas (2·8 per cent decline), in confessionally mixed industrial areas (1·9 per cent decline), and in Catholic rural areas (1·8 per cent decline). Further losses were registered by the Christian Democrats in the Ruhr and Rhineland, confirming the trends of 1965, but even more worrying for the Christian Democrats were their losses amongst *Angestellte* (white-collar civil servants) and in the tertiary sector generally. There were definite signs that the CDU–CSU was becoming the party of the small towns and of rural Germany: twenty of the thirty-four constituency seats lost to the SPD were in cities of over 100,000 people, and in cities of over half a million the CDU–CSU lost ten of its twelve constituency seats. Finally, the 1969 general election showed that the CDU–CSU was tending to become a more regional party, with its main strength concentrated in the south, but with growing weakness in the north: the CDU lost ground in four of the five northern *Länder* (Lower Saxony was the only exception, and there the CDU gained essentially from the FDP); it fell back slightly in the Saarland and Bavaria, but these marginal losses were more than compensated for by gains in Hesse and Baden-Württemberg. There was no change in Rhineland-Palatinate.[78]

After the *Machtwechsel* (change of power) of 1969, then, the CDU–CSU was still *the* party of Catholics despite further signs of a decline of Catholic working-class loyalty to the party, but it had lost ground amongst the middle classes, particularly amongst the growing tertiary sector. The north-south split and the 'ruralisation' tendency were also causes for concern, for if the party fell too much under the influence of southern conservatives, it would lose its appeal as a broad-based *Volkspartei*, whilst it could not afford to become a more rural party at a time when the agricultural vote was steadily declining. The major questions for the CDU–CSU as it moved into opposition were, first whether it could hold its disparate elements together without the cementing effect of power, and secondly whether it could devise broadly appealing policies for the future. Indeed, by 1969 the SPD had become as much a *Volkspartei* as the CDU, and both parties were now vying for the vital floating votes of the moderate centre.

The Christian Democrats in Opposition

During the years 1969–72 the CDU–CSU was like a fish out of water. It found itself in opposition for the first time, and failed to adapt itself psychologically or organisationally to its new environment.[79] The Christian Democrats, who, with 46·1 per cent of the poll and 242 seats after the 1969 election, still formed the largest group in the Bundestag, seem to have been taken aback by the rapidity with which the SPD and FDP formed a coalition, and some of the party's leaders even saw the new coalition as a 'falsification' of the voters' wishes.[80] Moreover, as the SPD–FDP coalition's majority was never more than twelve, and in practice usually about half that number, there was from the beginning of the legislature a temptation to try to overthrow the government at the earliest possible opportunity. This 'principled opposition' led to the unprecedented attempt by the CDU leader, Rainer Barzel, in April 1972 to overthrow the government by means of a 'constructive vote of no-confidence', under which a Chancellor can be replaced if a majority of the members of the Bundestag both vote against him and nominate a successor at the same time (article 67 of the Basic Law). Barzel failed by two votes to unseat Brandt, but his use of article 67, together with his refusal to consider Brandt's offer of a truce until the election (not due till 1973), indicated that the CDU–CSU was determined to overthrow the government at almost any cost. The Christian Democrats in fact forced Brandt to call an election a year early by their uncompromising attitude,[81] and thus, as one astute commentator remarked, in effect committed suicide at the 1972 election.[82] They 'committed suicide' partly because they failed to think out any new policies during their first period in opposition, but principally because they – or at least a sufficient number of them – were unwilling to face up to the realities of the post-Cold War situation, for the intransigent opposition of a small, but determined group of Christian Democrats to Brandt's *Ostpolitik* was sufficient to bring about the deadlock which forced Brandt to induce the fall of his government in September 1972. Strictly speaking, the vote which produced the deadlock in the Bundestag occurred on 28 April 1972, when the SPD–FDP coalition failed to carry its budget by one vote. But the fundamental reason for the erosion of the government's majority was the CDU–CSU's attitude to the *Ostpolitik*.

The *Ostpolitik* was in fact begun by Gerhard Schröder, the CDU Foreign Minister from 1963–6, with the so-called 'policy of movement', or gradual abandonment of the 'Hallstein doctrine' and of the Federal Government's claim to be the sole legitimate spokesman for both halves of Germany.[83] The gradual 'opening to the East' continued under the grand coalition of December 1966–September 1969, and then proceeded rapidly under the SPD–FDP coalition of 1969–72. The immediate objective of the *Ostpolitik* was to improve relations with the Eastern bloc countries by promoting economic and cultural links with them. The long-term objectives were vague, but one hope was that growing détente might eventually prepare the way for the two Germanies to draw closer together, even conceivably one day to be reunited.

Between 1970–2 the West German government effectively renounced all claim to the German Eastern territories incorporated into the Soviet Union and Poland after the Second World War (Moscow and Warsaw Treaties of 1970), whilst the Basic Treaty (*Grundvertrag*) of November 1972 amounted to the recognition of the German Democratic Republic. As a *quid pro quo* the Russians made an important concession by recognising West Berlin's *de facto* links with the Federal Republic in the Berlin Agreement of September 1971. But the Russians made it clear that the Berlin Agreement would be implemented only if the Moscow and Warsaw Treaties were ratified by the Bundestag.

The political crisis and parliamentary deadlock of 1972 were occasioned then largely by the *Ostpolitik*, or, to be more precise, by the strong opposition of a minority of Christian Democrats to the Eastern Treaties. Amongst this minority was a small number of principled opponents with a long record as such, notably the CSU foreign policy expert Freiherr von und zu Guttenberg,[84] but there can be no doubt that for most of the CDU–CSU, including Rainer Barzel, the opposition to the *Ostpolitik* was tactical[85] (comparable in some ways to the British Labour party's change of attitude towards the European Community after the 1970 general election). This was clearly shown in May 1972 when only ten Christian Democrats voted against the ratification of the Treaties after the government had accepted a series of opposition supplementary declarations designed to protect the Federal Republic's ultimate position on territorial adjustments, but having no validity in terms of international law. The Christian Democrats' opposition to the *Ostpolitik* was effective in reducing Brandt's majority in the Bundestag to nil by encouraging Herbert Hupka, the SPD's refugee spokesman, and four members of the FDP to 'cross the floor of the house',[86] but it was politically inept in view of the growing public approval of Brandt's *Ostpolitik*.[87] In one sense the CSU tail wagged the CDU dog over *Ostpolitik*, but equally it is clear that the dog was prepared to go along with its tail: as long as there was a chance to overthrow the coalition through opposition to *Ostpolitik* the Christian Democrats were quite ready to fly in the face of public opinion. They were still not interested in playing the role of a constructive opposition.

The campaign for the 1972 general election began promisingly for the Christian Democrats. It was generally agreed that Karl Schiller, the SPD Minister of Economics, had played a key role in winning over middle-class voters to the SPD in 1969,[88] and it was hoped that his resignation from the SPD would bring them back to the CDU–CSU. In addition, one or two damaging revelations about the financial affairs of SPD and FDP deputies appeared at this time,[89] and finally the Black September murders at the Munich Olympic Games gave the impression that the law and order problem was worse than it really was. All these factors – together with the Catholic Church's open condemnation of the coalition's proposed abortion bill and its implicit support for the CDU–CSU – were expected to be an advantage to the Christian Democrats. But, as it turned out, they were not, for the election was largely won and lost on foreign policy and on the personalities of the Chancellor (Brandt) and the Chancellor-candidate (Barzel).

The Christian Democrats concentrated their campaign on inflation and law and order with the slogan 'We will build progress on the basis of stability', but with average industrial wages at DM 1,250 (£160) per month and unemployment at 0·8 per cent (200,000), it was difficult to accept Strauss's claim that the *Marktwirtschaft* (free market economy) was on the way to becoming a *Marxwirtschaft* (Marxist economy) and would end up as a *Murkswirtschaft* (bungled economy).[90] And Helmut Schmidt rejected the Christian Democrats' attempt to play on the electorate's fears about inflation with the riposte: '5 per cent inflation is better than 5 per cent unemployment'.[91] Nor was it easy to accuse the coalition of weakness on the law and order issue, when the toughly conservative Hans-Dietrich Genscher of the FDP was Minister of the Interior. In addition most members of the Baader-Meinhof gang were arrested in the autumn of 1972.

The CDU–CSU had always concentrated in the past on its tenure of the chancellorship. But in 1969 the coalition had this advantage, and the SPD, like the CDU before it, made the election as much of a plebiscite as possible, using the simple slogan: 'Willy Brandt must remain Chancellor'. In contrast Barzel ran far behind Brandt in the public's estimation.[92] So the CDU–CSU – like the SPD in 1969 – tried to emphasise its 'team leadership': the moderate Barzel, conservative Strauss, Protestant Schröder, and trade unionist Katzer. In fact, it was all too obvious that the team was far from united, the differences between Strauss and Katzer over social policy being an obvious case in point.[93] For a long time the Christian Democrats wisely kept quiet about *Ostpolitik* – with the exception of the CDU in Hesse and Schleswig-Holstein and the CSU in Bavaria. Barzel was certainly in a dilemma over this issue, for opinion polls showed that over 50 per cent of the electorate approved Brandt's policy (a rise of 10 per cent in 1972 alone), but in the last week before polling day Barzel gave way to Strauss and condemned the Basic Treaty with East Germany (initialled on 4 November), maintaining that it was unacceptable and would have to be renegotiated.[94] As the public opinion organisation *Infas* found that 73 per cent of those polled approved the Basic Treaty, the Christian Democratic condemnation of it was clearly a major tactical error.[95]

Opinion polls in the weeks leading up to the 1972 election indicated that the SPD–FDP coalition was likely to win. In the event the victory was bigger than expected. The final Allensbach poll, however, rightly predicted an SPD advance (since 1969) of three percentage points and CDU–CSU stagnation. The FDP upward trend was detected but underestimated, whilst the popularity of the minor parties was exaggerated.[96] In comparison with 1969 the SPD advanced by 3·2 per cent to 45·9 per cent of second votes (the proportional representation votes which decide the final composition of the Bundestag) and the FDP by 2·6 per cent to 8·4 per cent, whilst the CDU–CSU fell back by 1·3 per cent to 44·8 per cent. The extremist parties of the Right and Left all did very badly. The uncertain *Machtwechsel* of 1969 became a decisive reality in 1972, and for the first time in the history of the Federal Republic the CDU–CSU had fewer seats (225) than the SPD (230). Together with the FDP (41) the SPD had a majority of forty-six over the Christian Democrats, and Brandt was duly re-elected Chancellor of an SPD–FDP coalition by the Bundestag on 14 December 1972.

From the point of view of the Christian Democrats the 1972 election was a major setback in spite of the fact that they won almost 45 per cent of the votes cast. Unlike the Christian Democrats, the electorate had shown its willingness to face up to reality by supporting the *Ostpolitik*. Indeed, various post-election surveys indicated that the *Ostpolitik* was the crucial factor in the SPD–FDP's victory and the CDU–CSU's defeat.[97] For the first time an SPD leader – admittedly with the advantage of being Chancellor – had appealed more to the public than his CDU rival. However, in a sense both *Ostpolitik* and the inability of Barzel to project an attractive image of himself could be regarded as passing problems. More serious for the Christian Democrats was the fact that their parties had been showing signs of stagnation for over a decade. Having lost 4·9 per cent in 1961, the Christian Democrats gained 2·3 per cent in 1965, but then lost 1·5 per cent in 1969 and 1·3 per cent in 1972. It is true that in 1972 the Bavarian CSU increased its percentage of the poll by 0·7 to 55·1 per cent and the Hesse CDU its percentage by 1·9 to 40·3 per cent, and that the losses in Baden-Württemberg, Rhineland-Palatinate and Hamburg were all under 2 per cent. But *Infas* estimated that the CDU–CSU lost 1·7 million votes to the SPD in 1972,[98] and that it was only by mopping up the vast majority of the NPD's 1969 electorate that the CDU–CSU restricted its overall percentage loss to 1·3 per cent (the NPD fell back from 4·3 per cent in 1969 to 0·6 per cent in 1972).[99] The CDU–CSU lost twenty-five constituency seats (*Direktmandate*) to the SPD, giving the SPD a lead of 152 to 84 in *Direktmandate*. The CDU lost five constituency seats each in Schleswig-Holstein, Lower Saxony and North Rhine Westphalia, three each in Rhineland-Palatinate and Baden-Württemberg and one in the Saarland, whilst the CSU lost three in Bavaria.

Of particular concern to the Christian Democrats was the evidence of a further breakthrough (already apparent in 1965 and in 1969) by the SPD into three groups traditionally loyal to the CDU–CSU: Catholics, women and rural voters.[100] In 1972 the increasing tendency for these groups to vote for the SPD was decisively confirmed. For the first time the Catholic Saarland cast a majority of votes for the SPD, and in other *Länder* the SPD also gained victories in such traditionally Catholic-CDU constituencies as Aachen-Stadt and Aachen-Land (both in North Rhine Westphalia) and Osnabrück in Lower Saxony. Women, too, voted in increasing numbers for the SPD, having for long been more reluctant than men to do so: in the four Cologne constituencies, for instance, *Infas* calculated that 53·5 per cent of women voted for the SPD compared with only 39·8 per cent in 1965. Finally, rural voters, both Protestant and Catholic, cast more ballots for the SPD than ever before – *Infas* estimated a 6·4 per cent increase in the Protestant rural areas of Schleswig-Holstein and Lower Saxony, and 4·9 per cent in the Catholic rural areas of Bavaria. Perhaps of less concern to the Christian Democrats was the SPD's success in mobilising unskilled industrial workers (hitherto a group with a relatively high abstention rate) on its behalf in 1972. *Infas* calculated that 3·9 per cent more unskilled industrial workers voted for the SPD than in 1969, and in some Ruhr constituencies the percentage increase was a good deal higher than the national average of 3·9 per cent, for example, 7·2 per cent Duisburg and 7·5 per cent in Oberhausen. One promising sign for the CDU–CSU was that the SPD had become the largest party in the Bundestag largely by mobilising its traditional supporters rather than by making any further advance into the middle-class electorate.

The 1972 election produced further evidence of a split between north Germany, where Christian Democratic strength was waning, and south Germany, where, with the exception of the Saarland, this trend was much less apparent.[101] The CDU's decline in Schleswig-Holstein, described in one newspaper as a 'landslide',[102] was particularly serious. Schleswig-Holstein had at one time been a CDU stronghold. In 1957, for example, all the Schleswig-Holstein constituency seats were won by the CDU, but in 1972 the SPD won nine out of eleven, a gain of five from the CDU since 1969. The CDU shadow Finance Minister, Karl-Heinz Narjes, failed to win a constituency seat in Schleswig-Holstein, whilst Kai-Uwe von Hassel, the respected Bundestag Speaker and former Minister of Defence, only just retained his.[103]

The success of the conservative Christian Democrats, Franz-Josef Strauss in Bavaria (+ 0·7 per cent) and Alfred Dregger in Hesse (+ 1·9 per cent), against the national trend, seemed to point to the advantages of a more conservative strategy. But if the Christian Democrats had opted for such a strategy they would doubtless have lost more votes in the centre than they could possibly hope to have gained on the right. For after 1972 the 'reservoir' of extreme-right voters had almost run dry. It was clear that the relative success of the Christian Democrats in Bavaria and Hesse was due to their winning over the NPD voters of 1969 (in 1969 the NPD poll in Bavaria was 5·3 per cent, but in 1972 0·8 per cent; in Hesse it was 5·1 per cent and 0·5 per cent respectively). Indeed, *Infas* found that CDU–CSU losses in 1972 were minimal (− 0·1 per cent) in all areas where the NPD had polled well in 1969, whereas their losses averaged 3·1 per cent in areas where the NPD had polled badly. A survey in Rhineland-Palatinate confirmed these findings, for example in sparsely populated rural areas, where the NPD average poll in 1969 was 8·5 per cent, but only 1·2 per cent in 1972, CDU losses were restricted to 0·3 per cent; and in sparsely populated Catholic rural areas, where the NPD polled an average of 4·5 per cent in 1969, but only 0·7 per cent in 1972, CDU losses were 3·2 per cent.[104]

The CDU–CSU could not but be concerned at the SPD breakthrough in Protestant and Catholic rural areas, and equally by the increasing tendency for Catholic industrial workers to vote for the SPD.[105] But they could hardly argue that the answer was to become more conservative: on the contrary, it seemed all the more essential to pay close attention to the views of such men as Hans Katzer, the former Minister of Labour and leader of the CDU's labour wing (still approximately one-fifth of the CDU's deputies belonged to the labour wing after the 1972 election), and Norbert Blüm, the leader of the *Sozialausschüsse*. The Christian Democrats certainly could not abandon the social-reforming objectives of Katzer and Blüm in favour of the more conservative policies of Strauss and Dregger, and still claim to be a *Volkspartei*.

Another problem for the Christian Democrats in the 1970s was that several of their traditional sectors of strength were declining.[106] One such was the agricultural community. Owing to the number of part-time farmers in Germany (*Pendler*, those who work partly on the land and partly in industry: approximately 60 per cent of the agricultural work-force are *Pendler*), it is difficult to estimate precisely what proportion of the working population is engaged in agriculture, but by the late 1970s it was in the region of 5–6 per cent.[107] And even in 1972 a considerable number of *Pendler*, particularly in Schleswig-Holstein, voted for the SPD despite their rural roots and conservative traditions.

An additional problem for the CDU–CSU – especially apparent at the time of of 1972 election – was the decline of the Catholic Church's political influence. In 1972 the Catholic bishops encouraged the faithful to vote for the Christian Democrats on account of the proposed abortion bill, but their appeals were widely rejected, not least by women, who voted in larger numbers than ever before for the SPD. As Alfred Grosser commented: 'The biggest loser in this election is the Catholic Church.'[108]

Another bastion of CDU–CSU support – the refugee vote – was steadily disappearing by the 1970s. Whereas in 1961 21 per cent of the electorate were refugees, by 1972 the figure was under 10 per cent, and even that 10 per cent had lost much of its former nationalistic zeal, for over 50 per cent of the refugees said that they approved of the *Ostpolitik*.[109]

Finally, the 1972 election showed that the Christian Democrats had been unable to resolve their leadership problem. Rainer Barzel was widely recognised as a very able parliamentarian, but he failed to win the confidence of his party or of the public. His task was particularly difficult, of course, in the *Ostpolitik* phase, when all too often he looked like Strauss's puppet: during the election campaign Helmut Schmidt took full advantage of this by constantly emphasising that 'He who votes for Barzel, votes for Strauss.'[110] Barzel himself was a moderate, both in foreign and domestic policy, but he failed to give effective leadership to the maladjusted, disorientated Christian Democrats between 1971–3. In the latter year he was replaced as party chairman by Helmut Kohl, another moderate who was then Minister-President of Rhineland-Palatinate, and as leader of the parliamentary party by Karl Carstens, a rather conservative former senior civil servant and expert on foreign policy who had first been elected to the Bundestag in 1972. It was clearly important that these new leaders should succeed in giving the Christian Democrats a fresh image and renewed lease of life before the 1976 general election, and in large measure they succeeded. But their success was due as much to changes in the Federal Republic's economic and social situation as to their qualities of leadership.

The 1976 General Election: Christian Democratic Revival

The 1976 general election represented a major advance by the Christian

Democrats after two elections in the doldrums.[111] With 48·6 per cent of the votes cast, they were more successful than at any election in the history of the Federal Republic, except for 1957 when they polled 50·2 per cent. They advanced 3·7 per cent compared with 1972, the second biggest gain by a major opposition party since 1949 (the SPD gained 4·6 per cent in 1961). They returned to their accustomed position as the largest parliamentary group, with 243 seats out of 496 (the SPD won 214 and the FDP 39). But it was a bitter-sweet result for the Christian Democrats who failed to defeat Helmut Schmidt's Socialist-Liberal coalition, which retained a ten-seat advantage in the Bundestag. This *succès manqué* showed that the Christian Democrats had overcome some, but by no means all, of their problems. They had accepted the *Ostpolitik*, reorganised themselves and partially solved their leadership problem, but they failed to present a really distinctive image of themselves and their policies; moreover, it was apparent that the relationship between the two 'sister parties', the CDU and CSU, remained uneasy, and a satisfactory relationship was − and is − of crucial importance to the success of the German Christian Democratic movement.[112]

The considerable advance made by the Christian Democrats in 1976 surprised those outside observers who noted only that Schmidt had proved to be a tough and business-like Chancellor since taking over from Brandt in 1974, and that the German economy remained the most powerful and stable in Western Europe. Moreover, in 1976, there appeared to be no over-riding, or polarising, issue such as the *Machtwechsel* in 1969 or *Ostpolitik* in 1972. There were not even major differences between the declared policies of the three main parties. All three were committed to the social market economy, the Atlantic Alliance, Western European integration, and the pursuit of improved relations with Eastern Europe. Indeed, there seemed to be no reason for the electorate to be discontented with the government of the day.

Yet, in the eyes of the electorate, all was not well within the Federal Republic, and the Christian Democrats showed no compunction about exploiting the situation. Perhaps the word *Angst* (fear) is a little too strong to describe the uncertainty felt by a substantial part of the electorate about the Federal Republic's economic prospects and social situation, but there is no doubt that at the time of the 1976 election there was a widespread feeling of unease.[113] In addition − and almost inevitably − there was some degree of disillusionment with the results of the *Ostpolitik* and the progress of détente generally.[114]

Fundamentally the West German economy was very sound, but there was some anxiety about job prospects for the young. Unemployment was relatively high amongst school-leavers, and, with the labour force due to expand by 850,000 between 1976–85, it was estimated that a real growth in investment of 8 per cent per annum would be required to keep unemployment at under one million or 6 per cent (1976 figures).[115] And even 8 per cent might not suffice owing to the fact that Germany had become a very high wage economy. It followed that industrial investment would be likely to be channelled primarily into capital-intensive projects. Moreover, industrialists seemed reluctant to invest, partly on account of electoral uncertainty, but also for sound economic reasons, such as signs that some traditional markets were declining (German cars, for example, were losing ground to Japanese models in the United States).

More important than any *Angst* about the economy was the uncertainty about certain developments in society, particularly over law and order, job-screening and education. The Federal Republic is basically a well-disciplined, orderly and rather conservative country, so that the vast majority of people felt particularly uneasy about the rash (or so it seemed) of urban terrorism. The Baader-Meinhof urban guerrillas were the most notorious group. But there were other disturbing examples of urban violence. In 1975 Guenther von Drenkmann, President of the West Berlin Supreme Court, was murdered by left-wing terrorists. In the same year Peter Lorenz, the chairman of the CDU in West Berlin, was held hostage for a week and only released in exchange for some convicted terrorists. Such examples of urban violence met with little sympathy in West Germany, and the Socialist-Liberal government always took a tough line on terrorism.[116] Nevertheless, the *Angst* produced by these serious law and order problems tended to benefit the conservative Christian Democrats, because some of the statements made by SPD left-wingers and intellectuals such as Heinrich Böll suggested that the SPD still harboured people who were prepared to *understand*, if not to excuse, political extremism.

Another cause for concern in 1976 (and since) was the *Berufsverbot* ('professional debarment'). Again, this practice of job-screening tended to benefit the Christian Democrats and cause disillusionment amongst more liberally-minded Social Democrats. The controversy began in January 1972 when the Ministers-President of the *Länder* issued a reminder that under a long-established civil service law, applicable both at Federal and *Land* level, public servants were obliged to defend the constitution. A number of guidelines followed indicating that applicants for posts in the public services who engaged in activities hostile to the constitution should not be engaged. These guidelines were interpreted with different degrees of severity in different *Länder*, but between August 1972 and March 1976 496,000 applicants for civil service jobs (which, of course, include teachers in Germany) were investigated and 428 rejected. Probably only a handful of people were unjustly treated, whilst the others were extremists who were trying to undermine the Federal Republic's liberal-democratic régime. Germans are particularly sensitive about their history, and recall that Weimar collapsed partly as a result of the disloyalty of its own civil servants; nevertheless, the *Berufsverbot* was probably applied with unreasonable strictness in some *Länder*, and aroused protest not only from radical youth, but also from distinguished moderates such as Ralf Dahrendorf and Alfred Grosser who were uneasy about the use of such illiberal methods to defend liberty.[117]

The educational system was another cause of dissatisfaction. Some Socialist voters were disappointed that after seven years of Socialist-Liberal government there were still so few comprehensive schools (*Gesamtschule*), although these were favoured by the SPD–FDP coalition. Such voters, of course, ignored the fact that the federal government's influence over schools' policy has always been strictly limited, as education is constitutionally the responsibility of the *Länder*. In addition, many middle-class voters were critical of the increasing use of the *numerus clausus* in the universities, i.e. restrictions on entry to courses such as medicine; the *numerus clausus* was seen as an attack on the traditional freedom of students to choose the subject they wished to study. Another cause for concern was the likelihood that graduates would have increasing difficulty in finding jobs.[118] But perhaps the greatest *Angst* arose in connection with the teachers' training colleges, and in particular the fear that teachers were graduating who might try to 'indoctrinate' children with certain social values. In Germany such values have traditionally been the responsibility of the family, and not of the school. The only time when this was not so was during the Nazi period, so that any suggestion that teachers might once again be trying to indoctrinate children was bound to upset not only the middle classes, but traditionalists in all classes. The electorate's underlying fears about various aspects of education in 1976 could be usefully exploited by the Christian Democrats.[119]

Another disappointment – at least for less sophisticated voters – was the outcome of the *Ostpolitik*. The 1972 election had been fought on a wave of emotion following the ratification of the Eastern Treaties. But a measure of disillusionment had soon set in despite increased trade with the Comecon countries and more opportunities for West Germans to visit East Germany (in 1975 alone 3 million West Germans visited the East). However, the wall between East and West Germany remained, literally as well as metaphorically, an undeniable fact of life. Again, this was not the fault of the coalition in Bonn, but rather of the East German government (and their Soviet allies), who interpreted the Basic Treaty and Helsinki Agreement in a very restrictive manner. Nevertheless, it was relatively easy for the Christian Democrats to play upon the underlying disappointment over the degree of détente achieved after 1972, and to claim that the government had given away too much for too little.

Thus, although in 1976 West Germans were prosperous and Helmut Schmidt's Socialist-Liberal coalition was governing the country effectively in relatively difficult circumstances, there was a sufficient degree of unease about the Federal Republic's situation and prospects for a skilful opposition party to exploit the underlying *Angst* and to claim that a change of government would lead to greater economic and social stability.

The 1976 election campaign aroused considerable public interest (culminating in a 91 per cent turnout) and cost an estimated DM 200 million,[120] and yet there were few substantive policy differences between the two major parties.[121] Moreover, unlike 1972, the major interest groups largely stood aloof, although the trade unions were naturally closer to the SPD, and business to the CDU.[122] Nor were the citizens' action groups, *Wählerinitiativen*, nearly as active as four years previously. Indeed, it was almost a 'Pseudo-Wahlkampf', and the main debate about 'Freedom versus Socialism' took place in 'cloud-cuckoo land'.[123] Clearly a renewed SPD–FDP coalition would not open the door to creeping Communism, nor would a Christian Democratic government mark a step towards fascism or a return to the Cold War. Indeed, the main objective of all three parties was simply to persuade the voters that they, rather than their opponents, were more fit to govern. Thus, the voters were asked to choose between 'the better man' (Schmidt) and 'the man you can trust' (Kohl); between a 'well-tried governmental team' (Schmidt, Genscher, Apel and Friderichs) and a team of 'trustworthy and dynamic men' (Kohl, Strauss, Carstens, Dregger and Stoltenberg); between a party which believed in peace, freedom and the Federal Republic as a 'model country' (SPD), and one which believed in peace and security, but claimed that the Federal Republic was losing its freedom under the increasing weight of bureaucratic controls and state socialism (CDU).

The Christian Democrats started with the advantage that they were on the offensive, in contrast to 1972 when they were clearly fighting a rearguard action against Brandt's popular *Ostpolitik*. They had completed the reorganisation begun in 1969–72, and had doubled their membership to approximately 800,000 (650,000 CDU and 150,000 CSU). Their confidence had been boosted by a series of swings to them in the *Land* elections of 1974–6 (the average swing to the Christian Democrats between the 1972 general election and the 1974–6 *Land* elections had been 13·9 per cent). On past evidence they could not expect such swings to be repeated at a general election.[124] Nevertheless, the underlying trend seemed very satisfactory. Moreover, in Helmut Kohl they had a much more effective leader than Rainer Barzel. In the summer of 1976, for example, Kohl came within five points of Schmidt (35 per cent to 40 per cent) in public opinion polls on the competence of the two leaders. Even though the gap widened in favour of Schmidt in the immediate pre-electoral period, Kohl still succeeded in projecting an unusually favourable image of himself for an opposition leader.[125]

The SPD inevitably tried to exploit the differences between Kohl and Strauss, but these differences were less obvious than in 1972. Strauss still viewed the outcome of the *Ostpolitik* with more scepticism than Kohl, but both were agreed that there could be no going back on the treaties which had been signed and ratified. The CSU's slogan 'Freedom or Socialism' was slightly more blunt than the CDU's 'Freedom instead of Socialism', but the implication of both was similar. Both slogans were, of course, carefully thought-out irrelevancies, but effective for all that, as they played upon the electorate's doubts about the long-term objectives of the Social Democrats and their ability to manage the economy. The Christian Democrats could not, of course, explain how they were going to manage the economy or govern the country more effectively than the SPD–FDP coalition, but, as successful electioneering depends on psychology as much as on political realism, the Christian Democratic campaign was nicely attuned to the doubts of the floating voters as well as to those of the moderate Right and Centre.

The SPD predictably concentrated its campaign – as the CDU had done so long as it held the chancellorship – on the merits of the Chancellor. Schmidt strove to denigrate Strauss ('the real danger man') and Kohl ('the man who would like to be Chancellor under Strauss'), and to emphasise that there were real differences between the CDU and CSU – the latter was said to constitute a danger to peace owing to its intransigent attitude towards the Eastern bloc. Like Kohl and Strauss, Schmidt doubtless often exaggerated, but overall he probably waged a more successful personal campaign than Kohl, who never-

theless proved an unexpectedly competent challenger.[126] Schmidt was also wise
to change the main emphasis of the SPD campaign from 'Model Germany' to
'Vote for Peace' – the former slogan sounded unduly complacent, and left the
SPD open to criticism over issues such as unemployment.

The Liberals (FDP) fought their campaign on the slogan: 'Freedom, Progress, Performance' (the title of their election manifesto), emphasising above
all that theirs was a party of achievement and moderation. The Liberals
claimed that they had men of outstanding ability, notably their leader,
Genscher (Foreign Minister and Vice-Chancellor), Friderichs (Minister of
Economics) and Maihofer (Minister of the Interior), and that these men –
together with the whole parliamentary party – could be relied upon to keep
the SPD on a moderate course. Indeed, it is unlikely that the FDP would have
committed itself to continuing in government with the SPD at its Freiburg
Congress in May 1976 had it not been for the fact that Schmidt was very
much on the right wing of the SPD.[127]

Unlike 1972, the opinion polls suggested a close result, and this no doubt
helped to keep up interest in a 'campaign without issues'. The Allensbach
poll published in *Stern* on 30 September gave the coalition 49·7 per cent to the
CDU–CSU's 48·6 per cent, but, more important, it gave the coalition a four
point lead on the vital second, or party list, votes (51·1 per cent to 47·5 per
cent). However, Christian Democratic voters appeared to be more strongly
motivated, 89 per cent stating they would definitely vote, compared with 80
per cent of the coalition's supporters. Clearly a very close result could be
expected.

In the event the Christian Democrats won 48·6 per cent of the votes cast (a
gain of 3·7 per cent), the Social Democrats 42·6 per cent (a loss of 3·2 per
cent) and the Liberals 7·9 per cent (a loss of 0·5 per cent). This was a very
encouraging result for the CDU–CSU, for, although the party failed to unseat the
Socialist-Liberal coalition, it won twenty-nine seats more than the SPD,
including a gain of thirty-nine constituency seats (*Direktmandate*) from the
SPD (the CDU–CSU now had 135 *Direktmandate* to the SPD's 113). Above all
the 1976 election was significant for the Christian Democrats, because they
regained most of the Catholic working-class and female voters who had
deserted them in 1972, whilst at the same time they made important gains
amongst those whom they had to win over if the CDU–CSU was ever going to
win a majority, notably white-collar civil servants (*Angestellte*) and those
employed in the tertiary sector of the economy.[128]

In 1976 the CDU–CSU gained more ground in urban than in rural areas,
thus reversing the trend towards 'ruralisation' apparent in 1969 and 1972.[129]
Moreover, the Christian Democrats polled better in every *Land* except
Schleswig-Holstein than they had done in 1969. Indeed, they polled better
than in 1965 – their last successful election – in six out of the Federal
Republic's ten *Länder* (North Rhine Westphalia, Rhineland-Palatinate, Saarland, Hesse, Baden-Württemberg and Bavaria). The one major cloud on the
horizon was the increasing evidence of a north-south split, with the Christian
Democrats consolidating their position in the Catholic south, but polling a good
deal less successfully in the Protestant north. The Christian Democrats

advanced by 3·7 per cent overall, but in south Germany (Bavaria, Baden-Württemberg, Hesse, Rhineland-Palatinate and Saarland) their average gain was 4·3 per cent, compared with 3·0 per cent in north Germany (Lower Saxony, Schleswig-Holstein, Hamburg and Bremen) and 3·5 per cent in Middle Germany (North Rhine Westphalia).

Swing to the CDU–CSU by Länder

Bavaria	4·9%	South Germany	4·3%
Hesse	4·5%	Middle Germany	3·5%
Rhineland-Palatinate	4·0%	North Germany	3·0%
Baden-Württemberg	3·5%		
Saarland	2·8%	National average swing	3·7%
North Rhine Westphalia	3·5%		
Lower Saxony	3·0%		
Bremen	2·9%		
Hamburg	2·6%		
Schleswig-Holstein	2·1%		

Closely associated with the north-south cleavage was the CDU–CSU's inability to appeal to Protestant voters as successfully as to Catholics. In the forty constituencies with the highest proportion of Protestants the CDU–CSU polled an average of 42·8 per cent, almost six points below their national average, whereas in the forty constituencies with the highest proportion of Catholics they polled an average of 63 per cent, over fourteen points above their national average. In Protestant rural areas the Christian Democrats gained only 2·1 per cent, and although they gained 3·3 per cent in Protestant urban areas, this was still below their national average gain (3·7 per cent).

However, apart from the Protestant factor and the north-south cleavage, all the other indicators were favourable to the CDU–CSU at the 1976 election. In the first place young voters showed much greater confidence in the Christian Democrats than in 1972. Although a majority of those aged between eighteen and twenty-three still preferred the SPD (47 per cent), 35 per cent voted for the CDU–CSU, compared with only 27 per cent in 1972. The majority of those who voted for the first time in 1972 (twenty-four- to twenty-nine-year-olds in 1976) remained loyal to the SPD, but the CDU–CSU gained considerable ground amongst those aged between thirty and sixty, whilst retaining their advantage amongst the over-sixties.

Voting by Age Groups, 1976
(1972 figures in brackets)

Age	CDU–CSU	SPD	FDP
18–23	35% (27)	47% (63)	8% (8)
24–29	31% (31)	54% (58)	11% (10)
30–44	45% (36)	40% (54)	8% (10)
45–59	49% (38)	35% (55)	5% (6)
60+	46% (46)	39% (45)	7% (7)

Source: *Sozialwissenschaftliches Forschungsinstitut* analysis of 1972 and 1976 elections.

In addition the Christian Democrats regained their former appeal to the female electorate, with 56 per cent of all women voting for them in 1976 (in 1972 the figure had dropped to 50 per cent).[130] Equally important for the Christian Democrats was their significant advance amongst voters belonging to the tertiary sector (service industries), and amongst white-collar *Angestellte*. These are the two most rapidly growing sectors of the West German population, and they form an essential part of the 'middle majority', whose votes must be won if the CDU–CSU is to return to power.[131] Amongst tertiary sector employees the CDU–CSU made a gain of 4·8 per cent; this was followed by a gain of 4·3 per cent amongst those employed in productive industry, and a gain of 4·2 per cent amongst *Angestellte*. In all three categories the Christian Democratic gain was considerably above its national average of 3·7 per cent. The party did less well in constituencies with a high percentage of farmers (+ 3·2 per cent) or of self-employed people (+ 3·5 per cent), but this mattered less, as the CDU–CSU already had a firm hold on these sectors (just over 60 per cent of both categories voting for the CDU–CSU in 1976). Finally, it was very important for the Christian Democrats that they should regain some of the ground they had lost in the cities in 1969 and 1972, and in fact their average gain in mainly urban constituencies was 4·3 per cent, compared with 3·5 per cent in mainly rural constituencies. In some cities they did even better, notably in Munich (+ 8·2 per cent) and Frankfurt (+ 5·2 per cent), whilst in Cologne and the Ruhrgebiet they regained the votes of all the Catholic workers who had deserted them in 1972.

It has been appropriate to pay considerable attention to the electoral performance of the Christian Democrats, because both the CDU and CSU are, if not straightforward electoral parties of the North American type, at least essentially pragmatic, government-orientated parties, for whom electoral success is the *sine qua non*. And in the centrist 'consumer culture' of the Federal Republic the major political parties really have no alternative but to appeal to the widest possible spectrum of the electorate.[132] The SPD recognised this when it embarked on the implementation of Herbert Wehner's strategy of 'moderation and respectability' after the party's 'conversion to political cosmetics'[133] at Bad Godesberg in 1959. But just as the SPD was developing into a *Volkspartei* – i.e. in the 1960s – there were signs that the CDU–CSU was becoming more rural, regional, middle-class, and conservative. The 1976 election to some extent reversed this development. It is true that it confirmed that the CDU–CSU is *the* party of Catholics; that it is stronger in the south than the north; and that it polls better in the countryside and in small towns than in the larger conurbations. But the election also showed that it is a mistake to regard the CDU–CSU simply as a conservative force, although the two Christian Democratic parties clearly tend to straddle the right-centre rather than the left-centre of the political spectrum. The CDU, in particular, with its still significant working-class wing (represented above all by the *Sozialausschüsse*)[134] and its Protestant working-group (the *Evangelische Arbeitskreis*)[135] can still claim to be a pluralistic *Volkspartei*. The 1976 election marked a victory (at least in the short term)[136] for the reformist, moderate wing of the CDU–CSU, led by Helmut Kohl and his close associates, Kurt Biedenkopf and Richard von Weizsäcker. In the 1972–6 Bundestag the Christian Democrats had adopted a much more moderate bipartisan approach than between 1969–72, voting, for example, for tax reforms and for the compromise law on industrial co-determination (*Mitbestimmung*) in 1975.[137] But, as the internal party crisis of November–December 1976 showed (when the CSU came close to destroying its traditional parliamentary links with the CDU)[138], there was still a considerable degree of tension between the two wings of the Christian Democratic movement. Indeed, the relationship between the CDU and CSU is clearly of crucial importance for the movement's future prospects. Thus, before attempting to make a final judgement on the state of German Christian Democracy, it is essential to comment briefly on the CSU, the distinctive Bavarian party within the Christian Democratic movement.

The Bavarian Christian Social Union

The Bavarian Christian Democratic party (*Christlich-Soziale Union*, CSU) is a rather unusual, even paradoxical, party which requires to be analysed separately from the CDU. In Catholic, conservative Bavaria – the only *Land* in the Federal Republic to retain its old boundaries and identity in the post-war reconstruction of Germany – there exists a party which is certainly predominantly Catholic and conservative in its general ethos, but is clearly at the same time not a straightforward conservative electors' party in its structure. Indeed, the CSU has developed many of the structural characteristics of a mass party of the Left.[139] Moreover, although the CSU is the main embodiment of the right-conservative (*rechtskonservative*) tradition in the Federal Republic, it is not a German nationalist (*deutschnational*) party in the style of previous right-conservative parties such as the prewar *Deutschnationale Volkspartei* (DNVP) or the postwar *Sozialistische Reichspartei* (SRP) and *Nationaldemokratische Partei* (NPD). Alf Mintzel's complex analysis of the right-conservative, Bavarian-particularist and European-federalist strands which, *inter alia*, mark the political style of the CSU, seems much more convincing than Abraham Ashkenasi's rather simplistic categorisation of the CSU as a straightforward right-wing nationalist party.[140]

It is also important to emphasise that the CSU is not simply the Bavarian wing of the CDU. It is true that the CDU and CSU have formed a joint parliamentary group (*Fraktion*) since 1949 – although the *Fraktionsgemeinschaft* nearly broke up after the 1976 general election,[141] but the two parties have their own organisations, national congresses, party chairmen and political programmes. Until quite recently, however, even academics had a tendency to regard the CSU simply as a rather colourful, slightly eccentric branch of the CDU.[142] In fact, the CSU can only be understood as a peculiarly Bavarian phenomenon, a party which could have evolved only in the distinctive political culture of Bavaria, the *Land* which proudly proclaims itself as the *Freistaat Bayern*, which has a strong federalist tradition historically based on resistance to Prussian centralisation, and which has an equally strong Catholic and hierarchical – even authoritarian – streak going back to the Counter-Reformation.[143] Of course, there is a significant Protestant enclave in Bavaria – in the northern, Franconian part of the *Land* centred on Nürnberg – nevertheless Catholicism has had a much more important influence on the political culture of Bavaria – and on its hegemonic party the CSU – than Protestantism. However, there is some evidence that this situation may be changing – certainly the CSU has been successfully recruiting a higher proportion of Bavaria's 25 per cent of Protestants as party members in the 1970s than it did in the 1950s and 1960s.[144]

With its distinctly Bavarian characteristics the CSU is very much the heir of the *Bayerische Volkspartei* (BVP), the Catholic party which 'absorbed' the *Zentrum* political tradition in Bavaria during the Weimar Republic and insisted on maintaining its autonomy *vis-à-vis* the *Zentrum* despite the similarity of their confessional aims. Today the CSU, likewise, insists on emphasising its distinctiveness and autonomy: its membership differs from that of the CDU; it is a very different type of party structurally; it is more committed to economic liberalism, and has closer relations with the employers' organisation (*Bundesvereinigung des Deutschen Arbeitgeberverbände*, BDA) and less friendly relations with the main trade union confederation (*Deutscher Gewerkschaftsbund*, DGB) than the CDU; it has had open differences with its sister-party over co-determination in industry, over its attitude to the Atlantic Alliance and Europe (the Gaullist-Atlanticist dispute of the 1960s), and above all in relation to the development and implementation of *Ostpolitik*. And yet, despite all these differences, it seems unlikely that the CSU will break its working relationship with the CDU, or attempt to become a federal party.[145]

CSU – History, Electoral Record and Organisation
The CSU is today (1977) the dominant political force in Bavaria: it has controlled the *Land* government in Munich since the end of the war with one short break (1954–7); it won 62·1 per cent of the votes cast at the 1974 *Land* election (compared with 56·4 per cent in 1970); and at the general election of 1976 it won 60·0 per cent of the votes cast (compared with 54·4 per cent in 1969, and 55·1 per cent in 1972); fifty-three of Bavaria's eighty-eight members of the Bundestag are members of the CSU.[146] But the CSU has only achieved its hegemonic position in Bavarian politics comparatively recently. After initial successes in the late 1940s the party went through a difficult phase in the 1950s, and it was only after major organisational reforms that it established itself as *the* political force in Bavaria in the 1960s and 1970s. The party has been led with considerable dynamism by Franz-Josef Strauss since 1961, but probably the main reason for its increasing success in recent years has been its skilful adaptation of itself to the changing needs of Bavaria, which has gone through a major economic and social transformation since the war. Although still the most important agricultural *Land* in the Federal Republic, Bavaria is now primarily an industrial *Land* both in terms of the population employed in industry and in terms of the proportion of gross domestic product attributable to industry.[147]

The men primarily responsible for the foundation of the CSU – officially constituted in Würzburg in October 1945 – were Adam Stegerwald, a former Catholic trade union leader in Bavaria, and Dr Josef Müller, a Munich lawyer with wide contacts throughout Germany who had been imprisoned after the

July 1944 plot. Both men wanted to see the formation of a broad-based political party, committed to Christian principles, reconciliation between the two confessions, understanding between agriculture and industry, and respect for the rights of trade unions and other interest groups. They also wanted the new party to maintain close links with the other Christian Democratic parties then being established in the various occupation zones of Germany, and it was the intention of Josef Müller that the new party should be a broad-based democratic movement with a large membership bringing together the different social, ethnic and religious groups within Bavaria. Müller was strongly opposed to the CSU developing either as a Bavarian particularist party, a confessional party or a straightforward conservative party.[148] He failed in his objective for a variety of reasons. In the first place, the vastly experienced and respected Stegerwald, who had at one time been Minister-President of Prussia although a native of Würzburg, and who also had important connections in largely Protestant northern Bavaria, died suddenly in December 1945. In addition the American occupation authorities were averse to the development of anything that smacked of an over-disciplined mass party. Moreover, General Patton expressed a preference for Bavarian separatism, and the decision by the US military authorities to license the avowedly separatist *Bayernpartei* (BP) in February 1948[149] (the BP's objective was 'an autonomous Bavarian state within a German and European community') was a further blow to the Müller concept of a rather cosmopolitan – or at least non-nationalist – party. The most important reason, however, for the failure of Müller to establish a broad-based, inter-confessional *Volkspartei* was the opposition from within the CSU of Catholic conservatives, notably Fritz Schäffer, Michael Horlacher, Alois Schlögl, Dr Joseph Baumgartner (who in 1948 left the CSU to become a leading figure in the *Bayernpartei*), and, above all, Dr Alois Hundhammer.

Hundhammer was indeed the dominating personality in the CSU from 1946 until about 1953. He remained on the party executive until 1957. Although the moderate Müller was party chairman from 1945–9, and he was succeeded by the equally moderate Hans Ehard (chairman 1949–55), it was Hundhammer who set the tone. A former BVP leader and prisoner of the Nazis, Hundhammer was in many ways a cultivated man, but he was also a sternly devout Catholic moralist, who as Minister of Education between 1946–50 wielded what amounted to 'a moral dictatorship over Bavarian cultural and academic life, restoring corporal punishment in the schools, and exercising behind-the-scenes censorship over radio programmes'.[150] Hundhammer was perhaps as much the reflection of developments within the CSU as he was their instigator. Certainly by the late 1940s–early 1950s the CSU had become a narrowly confessional notables' party (*Honoratiorenpartei*) with a declining membership, and firmly implanted only in traditional, rural Catholic Bavaria – in Oberbayern, Niederbayern, Oberpfalz and Schwaben. By 1948 over 90 per cent of CSU members were Catholic (8 per cent Protestant), although the confessional balance in Bavaria was only three to one in favour of the Catholics. In the major cities – Munich, Nürnberg and Augsburg – the party's organisation was virtually non-existent, and almost 70 per cent of CSU members lived in the above-mentioned rural Catholic provinces. Meanwhile, in the three northern, largely Protestant Franconian provinces there were only 21,000 members. So the CSU had developed into a largely southern, largely rural, almost wholly Catholic party by the late 1940s. The hope of Stegerwald and Müller that the CSU would overcome the traditional Bavarian cleavages had not been fulfilled.[151]

The CSU reached its electoral nadir at the *Landtag* election of November 1950, when the party polled 27·4 per cent (compared with 52·3 per cent at the 1946 *Landtag* election). The key factor, as at the 1949 general election, was the intervention of the *Bayernpartei* (BP) which made important inroads into the CSU vote, particularly in the strongly Catholic and particularist parts of the *Land*. The BP reached its peak in 1949 with 20·9 per cent of the votes cast (the CSU won 29·2 per cent), but at the *Landtag* election of 1950 the BP still succeeded in polling 17·9 per cent (compared with the CSU's 27·4 per cent). At the *Landtag* election of 1954 the CSU did much better (38 per cent), and the BP rather worse (13·2 per cent). Nevertheless, the BP formed a rather unlikely coalition, the so-called *Viererkoalition* (four-party coalition), with the Social Democrats, Free Democrats and Refugee Party, and as a result the CSU was relegated to the opposition benches. This period in opposition proved a salutary experience for the CSU, which began to reorganise itself in earnest from 1955 onwards. This reorganisation process may conveniently be divided into two phases. Up to 1961, when Strauss succeeded Hanns Seidel as party chairman, progress was made towards broadening the appeal of the party and drawing up new policies, but owing to the resistance of local notables no real attempt was made to build up the party's organisation and membership. Then from 1961 onwards the real drive to transform the CSU into a 'modern mass membership party' ('Massen und Apparatpartei modernen Typs')[152] began, led by the new party chairman, Franz-Josef Strauss. The success of this operation may be seen in electoral terms. At every *Landtag* election since 1958 the CSU's vote has increased (45·6 per cent in 1958, 47·5 per cent in 1962, 48·1 per cent in 1966, 56·4 per cent in 1970, and 62·1 per cent in 1974), and at every general election since 1957 the party has won an absolute majority of the votes cast in Bavaria (57·2 per cent in 1957, 54·9 per cent in 1961, 55·6 per cent in 1965, 54·4 per cent in 1969, 55·1 per cent in 1972 and 60·0 per cent in 1976).

The success of the CSU in winning a hegemonic position in Bavaria in the last twenty years or so cannot be attributed solely to reorganisation. Capable leadership and skilful adaptation of the party's policies to meet the changing needs of modern Bavaria have been at least as important as party reorganisation. Nevertheless, there can be little doubt that the CSU's ability to play a leading and directing role in Bavarian politics, and to convey its appeal and propaganda to all sections of the *Land's* electorate, owes much to the party's powerful organisation and mass membership.

Between 1955–75 the CSU more than trebled its membership (from approximately 40,000 to over 130,000).[153] Its full-time staff, i.e. those employed at the party headquarters in Munich and in the ten regional (*Bezirksverband*) offices, increased from fourteen to over two hundred. By 1974 they were costing over 3 million DM per annum out of the CSU's income of 26·6 million DM.[154] The party introduced modern equipment into its headquarters in Lazarettstrasse,

Munich: all data, for example, about party membership is computerised. It made a major effort to improve its information services: in 1967, for example, Max Streibl, secretary-general from 1967–71 and one of the party's ablest young leaders, reorganised the organisational and information sections at the *Landesgeschäftsstelle* in Munich. In addition the CSU acquired control of two commercial organisations, through which it does much of its publishing and advertising, the *Bavaria Werbe und Wirtschaftsdienst* and the *Tulong Werbegesellschaft*. Meanwhile, it extended the sale of its weekly newspaper, the *Bayernkurier*, edited by Strauss, throughout the Federal Republic. Like the CDU and SPD, the CSU also has its own foundation for political education, the *Hanns-Seidel-Stiftung*, founded in 1967. The *Stiftung* has a magnificent country-house conference centre at Wildbad Kreuth, near the Tegernsee in the Bavarian Alps. The *Stiftung* is divided into three 'branches': the *Bildungswerk der Hanns-Seidel-Stiftung*, the *Akademie für Politik und Zeitgeschehen* and the *Institut für Internationale Begegnung und Zusammenarbeit*.

According to the statutes of the CSU, the party is organised at four levels. Firstly, there is the *Land* organisation, the *Landesverband*, which is in turn subdivided into four organs: the *Parteitag* (party conference), *Parteiausschuss* (party council), *Landesvorstand* (*Land* executive committee) and *Präsidium* (praesidium). Of these organs the most important are the party executive and the praesidium.[155]

The party conference, like all such bodies, particularly in conservative parties, is essentially an annual meeting of the party faithful. Up to 4,000 representatives of the local organisations attend the conference, and their chief role is to endorse party policies, applaud the leadership, and return home convinced of the rightness of their cause. The party council has just over one hundred members – approximately half being members of the party executive and the remainder being representatives of the local party organisations. The chief task of the party council is to draw up the party programme and to see that it is implemented in so far as this is possible. The party executive committee has approximately forty-five members, including the party chairman, the three vice-chairmen, two treasurers, secretary and business-manager, the presidents of the party group in the *Bundestag* and the party group in the Bavarian *Landtag*, and the president of the *Junge Union*. It also has a number of *ex officio* members, such as the Bavarian Minister-President (assuming he is a CSU member) and one Federal Government Minister (assuming there is a Christian Democratic government in Bonn)..The chief role of the party executive committee, which meets at least once a fortnight, is to draw up policy, run the party organisation throughout the *Land*, and see that its information services are operating as efficiently as possible. However, the key organisation at the *Land* level is the sixteen- to eighteen-man praesidium. Presided over by the party chairman (Franz-Josef Strauss since 1961) the praesidium consists of the three vice-chairmen, two treasurers, two *Land* secretaries, the general secretary and business-manager, and seven other members of the party executive. In addition the party chairman has the right to co-opt additional members, who have full voting rights. Meeting two or three times a week, and sometimes daily, the praesidium is the most important policy-making body in the CSU. It is responsible for day-to-day problems, such as the line the party will adopt in *Landtag*, and even to some extent in *Bundestag*, debates. It is responsible for the party's finances and for the overall running of the party headquarters in Munich (i.e. the general-secretariat and *Landesgeschäftsstelle* (business organisation), jointly known as the *Landesleitung* (*Land* central office)). The praesidium is also responsible for electoral strategy and for tactical changes during election campaigns.

In Bavaria as a whole there are three other levels of organisation referred to in the party statutes, but in addition there is the non-statutory, but very important, *Bundeswahlkreisorganisation* (the federal election constituency organisation). Bavaria is divided into seven regions (*Bezirke*), and each region, together with the three major cities – Munich, Nürnberg and Augsburg – has its own CSU *Landesverband*. Since the 1972 local government reform there have been seventy-one *Landkreise* (districts) [hitherto there were 143] and twenty-five *Kreisfreie Städte* (middle-sized towns, which have their own local governments – they are comparable in status to *Landkreise*) [hitherto there were seventy-one]. Each *Landkreis* and *Kreisfreie Stadt* has its own CSU *Kreisverband*. Finally, Bavaria has over 7,000 rural districts (*Orte*) and the CSU has almost 3,000 *Ortsverbände* covering almost all of the rural districts either singly or jointly. Thus, the party, in one form or another, 'saturates' the Bavarian political landscape.

The important *Bundeswahlkreisorganisation* springs to life at general elections, and in the opinion of Alf Mintzel this organisation, which came into being in the mid 1960s, has been of great value to the party.[156] It has allowed members at the *Ort* and *Kreis* level to concentrate on the dissemination of electoral propaganda, whilst it has greatly helped candidates at federal elections to organise their campaigns. The lower organisations within the CSU are directly controlled from above, but the *Bundeswahlkreisorganisation* has brought together ordinary party members and senior party officials from Munich, giving to the former the sense that they are participating in a national campaign and to the latter the chance both to listen to grass-roots opinion and to co-ordinate the campaign in a uniform, disciplined manner. Indeed, the CSU has been rather successful in acting both as an *Apparatpartei* (one in which the central party organisation plays the key role) and as a *Mitglieder-partei* (a members' party, active at the grass roots level), to such an extent that it has been remarked that, as a result of the organisational changes and membership drives of the 1960s and 1970s, 'the CSU's reservoir of political strength now comes from its mass membership and no longer from the party's local notables.'[157]

CSU – Strategy and Problems

For all its organisational strength and impressive electoral performance, the CSU is confronted with a number of difficult problems. These relate in the first place to party membership, which remains weak in certain areas and social categories in spite of the overall success of recent recruiting campaigns. Secondly, Bavaria has been going through a period of rapid economic and social change, and the CSU has had to try to balance the modern with the traditional, and to ensure that in its bid to appeal to new voters it has not lost touch with its old supporters. Thirdly, there is the problem of long-term strategy at the federal level, and especially of course of the CSU's relations with the CDU. The first two problems may be taken together, as changes in the economic and social structure of Bavaria and the CSU's need to achieve a more balanced membership, reflecting the *Land*'s social and confessional structure, are clearly interconnected.

The confessional balance in Bavaria has altered very little since the interwar years. Surprisingly the large influx of refugees after the war made little difference, and about 75 per cent of Bavarians are still Catholics and 25 per cent Protestants. The Catholics predominate in southern and south-western Bavaria, and the Protestants in the old area of Franconia (except for the province of Unterfranken which is 80 per cent Catholic). However, apart from the confessional balance, little else has remained unchanged in postwar Bavaria. In 1946 Bavaria was primarily an agricultural *Land*, with a high proportion of farmers, peasants, forestry workers, small shopkeepers, craftsmen and tradesmen. Of the working population 37·2 per cent were employed in agriculture and forestry and 17·1 per cent were self-employed shopkeepers, craftsmen and tradesmen (a total of 54·3 per cent); 14·2 per cent were employed by the state as *Angestellte* (white-collar public service employees, including teachers). The total number of blue-collar workers (*Arbeiter*), mainly employed in industry but also including public service employees such as dustmen, was 27·4 per cent. By 1975 the agricultural sector was down to 13·2 per cent (− 24 per cent) and the tradesmen-craftsmen sector was down to 11·9 per cent (− 6·2 per cent), whilst the *Arbeiter* sector was up to 44·1 per cent (+ 16·7 per cent) and the *Angestellte* category was up to 26·5 per cent (+ 12·3 per cent). In other words, Bavaria had become an industrial *Land*, although farming, shopkeeping and craft industries remained relatively important.[158]

Clearly if the CSU were to be the *Volkspartei* it claims to be, it would want to keep its membership more or less in line with Bavaria's socio-professional and confessional balance. As we have seen, the party failed to do this over the first ten years of its existence, and although the situation has improved recently, the CSU is still proportionately over-represented amongst Catholics, farmers and tradesmen, and under-represented amongst Protestants, industrial workers and state employees. If it fails to win greater support from the latter categories, it is in danger of falling into the same trap as its predecessor, the *Bayerische Volkspartei*, which claimed to be a '*Volkspartei*, drawing together all classes of Bavarians on Christian principles in politics', but in practice never succeeded in making any real impact outside the traditionally Catholic and rural parts of Bavaria. In its early years the CSU failed to make much impression outside these parts, i.e. outside the three provinces of Altbayern and the preponderantly Catholic Schwaben and Unterfranken. In the Protestant parts of northern Bavaria the CSU was regarded as little more than the successor of the BVP, whilst in south and south-west Bavaria it was regarded as insufficiently 'Bavarian': hence the success of the Bavarian Party in the late 1940s and early 1950s. It was only with considerable difficulty that Josef Müller, Hans Ehard and Hanns Seidel were able to preserve the unity of the party and maintain a moderate course.[159]

In spite of the CSU's defeat by the *Viererkoalition*[160] in 1954 it was clear that the party was going to survive as an important political force in Bavaria, but the party leadership – and notably Hanns Seidel and Franz-Josef Strauss – realised that the CSU must adapt both its membership and its policies if it were to become the dominant political party in Bavaria. There is some evidence that the party has succeeded in making these adaptations, but it is too early to make a final judgement. By 1975 the CSU's membership was proportionately less rural, less Catholic and less aged than ten years previously. Nevertheless, the proportion of working-class and urban members was still relatively low. Likewise, in its policies, at least within Bavaria, the CSU had become a less conservative party: it is wrong to see the CSU simply as the party of industrial free enterprise and agricultural conservatism.

As regards membership, in 1975 86·1 per cent of CSU members were Catholics and 13·9 per cent were Protestants (compared with 91·3 per cent and 8·7 per cent in 1964).[161] Nevertheless, as the overall figures for Bavaria are 74·3 per cent and 25·7 per cent respectively, there is still considerable room for improvement in the party's confessional balance. However, on the positive side the 1975 figures show that the largest provincial increase was in Protestant Oberfranken (+ 13·8 per cent), whilst the proportion of Protestants who are party members in largely Protestant Mittelfranken, Oberfranken and Nürnberg/Furth is almost in line with the confessional balance in these areas. In 1975 the CSU was still somewhat over-represented amongst the liberal professions and *Beamte* (13·3 per cent of CSU members, 7·3 per cent of the Bavarian population), amongst farmers (17·0 per cent and 13·2 per cent respectively) and amongst tradesmen and shopkeepers (16·8 per cent and 11·9 per cent respectively). The party was somewhat under-represented amongst *Angestellte* (20·6 per cent and 26·5 per cent respectively) and seriously underrepresented amongst industrial workers (14·9 per cent and 44·1 per cent respectively). Although approximately 40 per cent of Bavaria's industrial workers voted for the CSU at the general election of 1976, very few are willing to join the party. Likewise, although the membership of the *Christlich-Soziale Arbeitnehmerschaft* (CSA) increased from 6315 members in 1964 to 12,245 members in 1977, the CSA remains very weak. It is little more than a small electoral pressure group whose objective is to show that the CSU does have *some* working-class militants. On the other hand, one encouraging development for the party has been its increasing appeal to younger electors. Of the 60,895 so-called 'new members', i.e. those with less than five years' membership, in 1975 20 per cent were in the eighteen to twenty-nine age bracket and 44 per cent in the thirty to forty-four age bracket, i.e. 64 per cent of 'new members' were under forty-four years of age, whilst only 47·5 per cent of the party's total membership was under forty-four. Clearly the CSU has some distance to go before it can claim that it is a genuine *Volkspartei* in terms of membership. Nevertheless, it has become significantly less Catholic and more youthful in recent years.

As regards policy, it is a mistake to regard the CSU simply as the party of big business or as the political mouthpiece of a Bavarian farmers' union (*Bayerische Bauernverband*).[162] It is true that in its early days the CSU showed no interest in the 'Christian Socialism' of Jakob Kaiser, although it is just possible that it might have done if Adam Stegerwald had not died suddenly in December 1945. In its 1946 programme the CSU maintained that, whilst some degree of state planning was necessary, it was committed to the encouragement of free enterprise in industry and in agriculture,[163] and in the Frankfurt Economic Council the CSU representatives gave their full support to Erhard's 'social market economy' policy. In the period when Hundhammer was the dominant CSU personality the party undoubtedly projected an anti-trade union, as well as a severely moralistic, image of itself. But with the eviction of Hundhammer from the party councils in 1957, the CSU began to adopt a more conciliatory tone. Hanns Seidel, the party's secretary-general from 1955–61, like Adenauer, was on good terms both with trade union leaders and industrialists. Since 1957 the CSU has both encouraged industrial development in Bavaria and tried to preserve, as well as improve, traditional craft-industries and agriculture. By the 1970s industry accounted for two-thirds of Bavaria's GDP, the four leading sectors being machine-tools, electronics, vehicle-building and chemicals. But it would be wrong to imagine that the CSU is a non-interventionist party. Like other conservative parties, who have held power in Western European countries since the war, the CSU has tried to control and guide the economy, although the party's programmes do not suggest that it believes in such interventionism.[164] In effect the CSU has its economic cake and eats it. On the one hand Strauss has been an outspoken advocate of private ownership and large-scale industry, and as such is regarded favourably by the employers' organisation.[165] Moreover, many of Bavaria's leading industrialists belong to the CSU or to the influential economic committee (*Wirtschaftsbeirat der Union*), men such as Rudolf Boelkow, Claudius Dornier, Rolf Rodenstock, Wolfgang Pohle, Karl-Heinz Spilker and Siegfried Balke. But at the same time Strauss pays close attention to the interests of agriculture and small-scale industry, and on many occasions has advocated the development of a balanced economy in Bavaria. At the party council meeting of October 1966 he said that the days of 'Supraliberalisierung' and *laisser-faire* economics were over; they had had their part to play in the period of economic reconstruction, but it was now necessary to 'guide the economy'.[166] Hans Eisenmann, the Bavarian Minister of Agriculture, produced a plan in 1969 for the future structuring of Bavarian agriculture. The plan envisaged a long-term future for family farming, including state subsidies for the improvement of such farms. And in March 1976 Max Streibl, the minister responsible for development policy and the environment, emphasised the CSU's commitment to a socially-responsible, balanced development of the Bavarian economy.[167]

So, in terms of membership and policies, it is wrong to regard the CSU merely as a traditional conservative party. Apart from its weakness amongst industrial workers and Protestants its membership is a fair reflection of Bavarian society. And in practice the party has played an important role in guiding and developing the Bavarian economy. Indeed, the CSU's biggest problem lies not in Bavaria but in Germany.

From the end of the Adenauer era the CSU has been determined to use its influence throughout the Federal Republic, and not just in Bavaria, and here it has run into difficulties with its sister-party, the CDU. Clearly, if the Union parties are to succeed in governing the Republic effectively again, they must resolve these difficulties. As far as foreign policy is concerned, the prospects for an amicable CDU–CSU relationship seem to have improved. A few years ago – at the height of the *Ostpolitik* controversy – such an outcome seemed unlikely, but after the ratification of the Moscow and Warsaw Treaties in 1972 and the Basic Treaty with East Germany in 1973, and the failure of the CSU's attempt to get the last-named treaty declared unconstitutional, the *Ostpolitik* has become history, at least in terms of legal formalities. And it is now possible for the CDU and CSU to act as watchdogs on the long-term implementation of *Ostpolitik* without offending the West German electorate or appearing as excessively nationalistic parties.

The CDU–CSU differences over *Ostpolitik* have been analysed in depth elsewhere,[168] but in the context of the CSU it is important to stress that most of the party's opposition to *Ostpolitik* was *principled*. Whereas many CDU opponents of *Ostpolitik* came out against the Brandt-Scheel eastern policy simply because they were the opposition party of the day, the CSU's opposition went back to the early 1960s when Gerhard Schröder, the CDU Foreign Minister, began the 'policy of movement' and the gradual abandonment of the Hallstein doctrine (no relations with countries which recognised East Germany) and *Alleinvertretungsanspruch* (the doctrine that only the democratically elected West German government had the right to speak for Germany). The CSU regarded itself as the true heir of Adenauer in its rejection of the Federal Republic's recognition of the Oder-Neisse line and of the German Democratic Republic. It claimed that these recognitions amounted to the end of all hope for a reunited Germany – certainly in the foreseeable future. Alfons Goppel, the Bavarian Minister-President stated in November 1972 that 'If developments [of *Ostpolitik*] go any further, we shall have reunification from the other side.'[169] Strauss's newspaper, the *Bayern Kurier*, labelled Brandt quite simply as 'the sell-out Chancellor', and Freiherr von und zu Guttenberg constantly emphasised the idea of Bavaria as the bulwark of European civilisation and democracy against the steady advance of Asian, autocratic values and Russian communism.[170]

To non-Bavarians the arguments of Strauss and Guttenberg about 'Christian civilisation' and 'creeping Communism' often seemed strangely unrealistic, and at times even dangerously nationalistic in the old-style *deutschnational* sense, but the most astute observer of the CSU, Alf Mintzel, has convincingly argued both that the concept of Bavaria as the 'Christliches Bollwerk' of Europe is genuinely held by many CSU members and that it is not a 'dangerous' concept in the old nationalistic sense.[171] Indeed, the corollary of the anti-Soviet, pro-Western arguments of Strauss and Guttenberg was not a commitment to some sort of 'roll-back' policy or the creation of a united Germany as a bulwark against Soviet expansionism so much as a strong emphasis on the need to unite Western Europe and to be constantly on guard against further communist encroachments into 'Christian' Europe. The ultimate hope of the CSU is that the 'Christian' parts of the 'Soviet Empire' will return to the fold of European civilisation, but not by means of armed force. This objective is evidently a very long-term one.

The CSU, of course, lost its battle over *Ostpolitik*, in that it failed to prevent the recognition of the *status quo* in Eastern Europe, but it has not lost the long-term battle to see that the corollary of *Ostpolitik* is the gradual improvement of relations with the Eastern bloc countries and the extension of human rights in these countries. By the late 1970s the CSU had moderated its language about *Ostpolitik* without abandoning its principled opposition to communist domination in Eastern Europe.

This more realistic approach to détente correlates closely with that of the CDU, which contends that improved relations with the East can only be pursued within the framework of the Eastern Treaties and the Helsinki Agreement, although this framework holds out little prospect for immediate or dramatic progress. This pragmatic, yet cynical, view of *Ostpolitik* and of détente probably reflects fairly accurately the views of the majority of West German electors in the late 1970s.

As regards domestic policy, the CSU is inclined to be its own worst enemy. The extremist language used at times by party leaders such as Franz-Josef Strauss and Richard Stücklen goes down well in Bavaria, but is not always appreciated north of the River Main. Anyone who has heard Strauss electioneering in Bavaria and speaking at academic gatherings will be aware of the CSU leader's chameleon qualities. Of course it is unfair to brand Strauss too harshly: all politicians adjust their language to suit their audiences. Nevertheless, the CSU often gives the impression that it is the 'Partei des Gross-kapitals',[172] and it is certainly true that the party's 'businessmen's group', the *Wirtschaftsbeirat der Union*, is much more influential than its labour wing, the *Christlich-Soziale Arbeitnehmerschaft*. Moreover, the CSU, and notably Richard Stücklen, fought a strong rearguard action against the extension of *Mitbestimmung* (co-determination) in industry between 1970–4, and had no compunction about criticising the compromise proposals put forward by the CDU's *Mitbestimmung* experts like Kurt Biedenkopf and Hans Katzer. And yet, as has been shown above, the CSU is not simply a *laisser-faire*, conservative party of the traditional type. In 1966 Strauss told the party executive committee that the CSU must avoid presenting itself as a conservative, rural party,[173] and in practice the CSU has played an important part in guiding and directing the Bavarian economy through its *Konjunkturpolitik* since the early 1960s. Reports on the future of the Bavarian economy, on agriculture, and on social policy were drawn up by the CSU in 1962 and 1963. Regular meetings between party leaders and leaders of the Bavarian branch of the DGB have been held since 1970, and similar meetings are also held with representatives of the white-collar public employees (*Angestellte*).[174]

Nevertheless, even if the CSU as a whole is less nationalistic and less conservative than its own spokesmen, as well as its critics, often imply, the party does have real difficulty in working in close harmony with the CDU. Ever since it became the dominant political force in Bavaria in the early 1960s, the CSU has been determined to play a federal role. Between 1963–5 Chancellor Erhard had as much trouble from the forty-nine members of the CSU as from the forty-nine Liberals in his coalition. By swinging the CSU behind Kiesinger in December 1966, Strauss ensured that the then Minister-President of Baden-Württemberg would be elected Chancellor in succession to Erhard. Strauss and his CSU 'Gaullists' made their opposition to Schroeder's 'Atlanticists', and to the first steps towards an opening to the East, very clear in the 1960s. And in the 1970s the CSU clashed with the CDU over *Ostpolitik* and *Mitbestimmung*. Moreover, many German electors north of the Main have doubts about Strauss – memories of the Spiegel Affair of 1962, when Strauss had to resign as Minister of Defence after lying to the Bundestag, die hard. All these factors, together with the differences in confessional balance, party membership, party support and policies, make it difficult for the CDU and CSU to work in harmony.

Yet it is unlikely that there will be a complete divorce. The nearest the two parties came to this was after the 1976 general election. In 1969 and in 1972 the CSU had threatened to end its joint parliamentary arrangement with the CDU if the latter did not take a tough line over *Ostpolitik* (after the 1972 general election the dispute was over the ratification of the Basic Treaty), but in the end did nothing. In November 1976, however, the CSU group, meeting at Wildbad Kreuth, voted to leave the CDU–CSU joint parliamentary party (*Fraktion*) in the Bundestag. The CSU deputies, led by Strauss, contended that Kohl should have conducted a more vigorous election campaign: after all, if the Christian Democrats in the rest of Germany had achieved anything like the 4·9 per cent swing achieved by the CSU, there would have been a CDU–CSU government in Bonn (in fact the average swing to the CDU in the other nine *Länder* was only 3·2 per cent). However, the possible risks of this step soon became apparent, and within three weeks the CSU had reversed its decision. This marked a short-term victory for Kohl over Strauss, for Kohl took an uncompromising stand towards the CSU: either the CDU–CSU alliance would continue, or the CDU would extend its organisation into Bavaria and campaign there at future elections. Opinion polls indicated that this would affect the CSU adversely, and the CSU deputies began to have doubts about their decision, doubts which were increased by CSU rank-and-file protests about the 'unilateral' break made by Strauss and the parliamentary group. As a result the two Christian Democratic parties decided to patch up their differences and continue the traditional *Fraktionsgemeinschaft*. The likelihood is that this arrangement will continue, and there will be two separate Christian Democratic parties in the country but one parliamentary group in Bonn. For all the evidence seems to support Mintzel's conclusion that the CSU has considerable weight in the Federal Republic only because it is *both* a powerful regional party *and* a close ally of the CDU in Bonn.[175] If the CSU were to attempt to 'go federal', it would have to tone down its Bavarian distinctiveness, and if it were to do that, it would in all probability lose votes in Bavaria. Indeed, in Mintzel's view, it is very likely that a new 'properly Bavarian' party, a successor to the Bavarian Party, would be set up and would soon make serious inroads into the CSU vote. If, moreover, the CSU were to form its own parliamentary group in no way linked to the CDU, it would no longer be to the advantage of powerful interest groups such as the BDI and BDA (employers) to count on the CSU as they do at present, and will doubtless continue to do, so long as the CSU remains closely linked to the CDU in Bonn. All the signs then are that the marriage of convenience between the CDU and CSU will continue, even if at times the relationship is somewhat strained.

Conclusion

The differences of opinion between the CDU and CSU certainly constitute the most obvious cleavage within the German Christian Democratic movement. But, as we have seen, the movement has other cleavages, which need to be bridged if Christian Democracy is to remain a significant political force in the Federal Republic. It is not easy to reconcile the views and interests of the Economic Council (*Wirtschaftsrat*) with those of the Social Committees (*Sozialausschüsse*), of former NPD voters with Catholic workers in the Ruhr, and of northern Protestants with southern Catholics. Under the impact of the NPD in the late 1960s and of the *Ostpolitik* in the early 1970s, the Christian Democrats, with one or two exceptions, had a tendency to abandon the middle ground of politics and project an essentially conservative image of themselves. The electoral defeat of 1972 encouraged a return to a more moderate, centrist approach, with Kohl and Biedenkopf exerting greater influence than Strauss and Dregger in the middle and late 1970s. But it was always a delicate balancing act: at any moment there was the risk that the Christian Democrats would lurch to the right for the sake of some short-term advantage. Yet, if they were to do so and lose again their Catholic working-class electorate (as they did temporarily in 1972), they would be unable either to win an absolute majority at a general election or to re-forge a parliamentary alliance with the Liberals. Like the SPD, the CDU–CSU has of necessity to maintain a strong foothold in the political centre of what is essentially a consumer-orientated and rather conservative and conformist society. Indeed, one of the major problems facing the CDU–CSU (as the 1976 election showed) has been how to draw up distinctively 'Christian Democratic' policies: when the SPD are in occupation of the middle ground under a man like Helmut Schmidt this is far from easy. But the Christian Democrats cannot afford (not even in Bavaria, as we have seen) to fall back on their most conservative supporters, i.e. practising Catholics and farmers, for both are declining groups within society. Indeed, another of the major problems facing the CDU–CSU is that German Christian Democracy is not as broad-based or socially integrative as that of Belgium or Italy.

To a large degree German Christian Democracy has become a conservative political force – hence the close links between the German Christian Democrats and the British Conservatives.[176] However, one important compensating factor for the CDU–CSU is that the West German electorate is possibly the most conservative in Western Europe. This should tend to be to the advantage of the CDU–CSU, especially now that the two parties have fully reorganised themselves, built up a considerable membership, and attracted able politicians into their ranks. Moreover, although the CDU and CSU are on the centre-right of the political spectrum, neither party is against the modern welfare state or some degree of macro-economic planning. They are certainly not against change *per se*, as were nineteenth-century conservative parties: rather they articulate a

Table 1
West German General Elections, 1949–76

	1949			1953			1957			1961			1965			1969			1972			1976		
	votes	%	seats	votes	%	seats	votes	%	seats	votes	%	seats	votes	%	seats	votes	%	seats	votes	%	seats	votes	%	seats
Electorate	31·2			33·2			35·4			37·4			38·5			38·6			40·6			41·6		
Turnout	78·5			86·2			88·2			87·7			86·8			86·7			91·2			90·7		
SPD	6·9	29·7	131	7·9	28·8	151	9·5	31·8	169	11·4	36·2	190	12·8	39·3	202	14·1	42·7	224	17·2	45·9	230	16·1	42·6	214
FDP	2·8	11·9	52	2·6	9·5	48	2·3	7·7	41	4·0	12·8	67	3·1	9·5	49	1·9	5·8	30	3·2	8·4	41	3·0	7·9	39
Extreme Left	1·4	5·7	15	0·6	2·2	—	—	—	—	0·6	1·9	—	0·4	1·3	—	0·2	0·6	—	0·1	0·3	—	0·1	0·3	—
Extreme Right	0·4	1·8	5	0·3	1·1	—	0·3	1·0	—	0·3	0·8	—	0·7	2·0	—	1·4	4·3	—	0·2	0·6	—	0·1	0·3	—
Total Deputies			402			487			497			499			496			496			496			496
CDU–CSU	7·4	31·0	139	12·4	45·2	243	15·0	50·2	270	14·3	45·4	242	15·5	47·6	245	15·2	46·1	242	16·8	44·8	225	18·4	48·6	243

N.B.
1. This table refers to 2nd votes, i.e., those which decide the final composition of the Bundestag.
2. The size of the electorate and the voting figures are in millions.
3. Minor parties, which were important in the early years of the Federal Republic (e.g., the Refugees), but which have not competed at recent elections, have been omitted. Hence the apparent discrepancy between party seats and total deputies up to 1957.
4. The Extreme Left have competed under a variety of names: KPD (*Kommunistische Partei Deutschlands*) in 1949 and 1953; DFU (*Deutsche Friedens Union*) in 1961 and 1965; ADF (*Aktion Demokratischer Fortschritt*) in 1969; DKP (*Deutsche Kommunistische Partei*) in 1972 and 1976. The Extreme Right competed as DRP (*Deutsche Reichspartei*) until 1961, and as NPD (*Nationaldemokratische Partei Deutschlands*) since 1965.

Burkean view of politics – they will carry out reforms, provided those who advocate them can make out a good case for their proposed changes; if they cannot, the Christian Democrats prefer to adhere to the traditional norms and structures within society and in the economy. No doubt this 'conservative' approach to politics contributes to the rather unexciting image of the CDU–CSU. But then that is part of the price which is paid for political pragmatism, and most Germans have had a surfeit of absolutist political solutions in the past. Thus, for all its problems and internal differences, the German Christian Democratic movement does reflect the views of a wide spectrum of opinion within the electorate, and so long as it continues to do this, it will remain a powerful force in German politics. Above all, it should not be forgotten that Christian Democracy has been *the* vehicle through which German conservatives have come to accept liberal democracy. In the light of Germany's past history this has been no mean achievement.

Table 2
West German Governments 1949–79

Chancellor	Parties in Government	Majority (max.)	Duration of Government
Adenauer (CDU)	CDU, CSU, FDP, DP	40	1949–53
Adenauer (CDU)	CDU, CSU, FDP, DP, GB–BHE	181	1953–7
Adenauer (CDU)	CDU, CSU, DP	77	1957–61
Adenauer (CDU)	CDU, CSU, FDP	119	1961–3
Erhard (CDU)	CDU, CSU, FDP	119	1963–5
Erhard (CDU)	CDU, CSU, FDP	92	1965–6
Kiesinger (CDU)	CDU, CSU, SPD	398	1966–9
Brandt (SPD)	SPD, FDP	12	1969–72
Brandt (SPD)	SPD, FDP	46	1972–4
Schmidt (SPD)	SPD, FDP	46	1974–6
Schmidt (SPD)	SPD, FDP	10	1976–

5
Christian Democracy in Belgium

In Belgium the phrase 'Christian Democracy' has a particular meaning: it refers to the working-class wing of *le monde catholique* – the Catholic trade unions, friendly societies, agricultural associations, and women's and youth groups, as well as more specifically to the progressive wing of the Social Christian Party. Nevertheless, the Social Christian Party is very much a 'Christian Democratic' party in the broader European sense of the term. It belongs to the European Union of Christian Democrats, and played a leading part in the foundation of the European People's Party, the Christian Democratic 'European Party' formed in 1976 with Leo Tindemans, the Belgian prime minister, as its first president.[1] And the Social Christian Party subscribes to the basic tenets of Christian Democratic political thinking.[2]

The Social Christian Party is strictly speaking two parties: the Dutch-speaking *Christelijke Volkspartij* (CVP) in Flanders and the French-speaking *Parti Social Chrétien* (PSC) in Wallonia. Both parties operate in Brussels. But although the two parties now have their own organisations, congresses and presidents, as well as separate party offices in the Belgian House of Representatives and Senate, they form a joint group in both houses of Parliament as far as representation on committees is concerned (like the CDU-CSU joint parliamentary group in West Germany), and they have a national headquarters in Brussels, a national secretariat, a national liaison committee (the praesidium) and a joint research organisation. A short time spent at the national headquarters of the two parties is sufficient to show how closely they work together: hence it is quite reasonable to refer to the CVP-PSC as a joint party, even though strictly speaking the Social Christians are divided into two autonomous parties.

Before analysing the Social Christian Party, it is important to comment briefly on the political atmosphere in which it functions, for in some ways the 'political culture' of Belgium is rather different from that of most other Western European states: certainly it is quite different from that of its large neighbours to the south and east, France and Germany, although it has a number of similarities to that of its northern neighbour, the Netherlands.

Political Background
From its foundation in 1830 the Belgian kingdom was a hybrid state, an amalgam of different ethnic and religious groups with disparate traditions. In the north there was Catholic, conservative, largely agricultural, Dutch-speaking Flanders, and in the south free-thinking, progressive, largely industrialised, French-speaking Wallonia. The capital was Brussels, situated in Flanders, and

(in the nineteenth century) populated largely by Flemings, although the ruling classes – as in Flanders itself – spoke French. Indeed, it was not until 1884 that the first Dutch speech was made in Parliament.

The Kingdom of the Belgians came into being because Belgian Catholics and Liberals came together in the 'Union of the Oppositions' in 1828 to rid themselves of the over-bearing rule of King William I, whose United Kingdom of the Netherlands had been created at the Congress of Vienna in 1815.[3] The tradition of Catholic-Liberal co-operation in the area which is now Belgium in fact goes back to pre-Napoleonic times, for the 'Statists' and 'Vonckists' of the 'United Belgian States' of 1788–90 were the direct precursors of the Catholic and Liberal 'rebels' of 1828: the 'Statists' wanted a confessional state, with Catholicism as the official religion, whilst the 'Vonckists' preferred a secular Belgium, in which Church and state would be separate but on friendly terms.[4]

King Leopold I, the first ruler of the new kingdom, did what he could to encourage 'unionism', and all the governments of the period 1830–46 were Catholic-Liberal coalitions.[5] 'Unionism', however, broke down towards the middle of the century, and there followed a period of Liberal dominance (from approximately 1846–84), and then of Catholic dominance (from 1884–1919). But neither Liberals nor Catholics tried to dominate each other in the French manner, with the one exception of the Liberal attempt to secularise education in the late 1870s, which was followed by the Catholic victory at the 1884 election. Many Liberals were also practising Catholics.[6] Indeed, this was one of the reasons why the Catholics were so slow to form their own party. And when the Catholics did have an absolute majority, as they did from 1884–1914, they bowed to Liberal and Socialist pressure to extend the franchise (1893) and to introduce proportional representation (1899). Both Catholics and Liberals were slow to introduce social legislation, but they were united in their tolerance of each other. They even found it quite easy to co-operate with the fledgling *Parti Ouvrier Belge*, the Socialist party founded in 1884, which strove mainly to achieve the extension of the franchise (finally achieving full male suffrage in 1919). The Socialists first entered the government in 1916, and participated again in crisis periods between the two World Wars, notably in the governments of 'national unity' of 1935–40, and in the London governments in exile from 1940–4. Since 1945 Belgium has been governed by various coalitions, mainly of the Social Christian-Socialist variety, but there have also been Socialist-Liberal, Socialist-Liberal-Communist, and Social Christian-Liberal coalitions, while in the late 1970s all three linguistic/regional parties also participated in government.[7] Postwar Belgium has thus been a country of coalitions, compromises, and *concertation* between government and interest groups. All the major political parties have contributed to – as well as been conditioned by – the tradition of moderation and compromise.

Belgium has also been notable for the stability of its voting habits, particularly in the twentieth century. In 1919 the three major parties – the Catholics, Socialists and Liberals – won 88 per cent of the votes cast; in 1961, 91 per cent; in 1971, 73 per cent – this was an all-time low, and marked the zenith of the regionalist/linguistic vote; and in 1977 the three-party vote rose again to 78 per cent. Until the mid 1960s there was also a high degree of party loyalty. In the interwar period the Catholics and Socialists regularly polled about 34–36 per cent each, with the Catholics a point or two ahead at all elections except at that of 1936 when they fell behind the Socialists owing to the Rexist incursion. In the postwar period, with the introduction of female suffrage, the Catholics have usually had about a ten point advantage over the Socialists (40 per cent for the former to 30 per cent for the latter on average). The Liberals (who are, of course, Liberals in the Continental sense, i.e. Conservatives in British terms), have trailed as the third party throughout the century, averaging about 15 per cent in the postwar period. Opinion polls also show that most Belgian voters remain loyal to *les Trois Grands* even when they are considering changing parties. Socialist and Social Christian voters, for example, would tend to cast a vote for each others' parties if they were to change rather than for the Liberals or regionalist parties.[8] However, the 1960s witnessed a sharp decline in electoral stability, and Belgian politics has never been quite the same since. At the 1965 general election the Flemish nationalist *Volksunie* party made a small but significant breakthrough with 6·7 per cent of the votes cast, and at the four subsequent elections its poll averaged about 10 per cent. Partly as a reaction to the success of the Flemish nationalist party, the Francophone *Rassemblement Wallon* (RW) in Wallonia and the *Front Démocratique des Francophones* (FDF) in Brussels were founded, and they also succeeded in winning between them an average of about 10 per cent of the votes cast in the decade 1965–75. The 1976 communal elections and the 1977 general elections both indicated that the regionalist/linguistic tide was on the ebb. Nevertheless, by their incursion on to the political stage, the regionalist parties acted as a catalyst for change both in the structure of the Belgian state and in the nature and organisation of the traditional political parties.

Although coalitions, compromises and *concertation* are key aspects of Belgian political culture, it would be wrong to assume that all has been sweetness and light in Belgian political history. It should be remembered, for example, that violent strikes occurred not only in the late nineteenth century, but as recently as 1960–1; that the question of Leopold III's return in 1950 sparked off great bitterness and brought the country to the verge of civil strife;[9] and that ugly scenes have often occurred between Flemings and Francophones over the community problem – in the course of 'l'affaire de Louvain', for example, when the French faculties at the famous Catholic University of Louvain were forced to transfer to Wallonia in the late 1960s.[10]

Moreover, despite the general preponderance of the forces in favour of moderation and compromise, there are three important cleavages which must be borne in mind when analysing the Belgian party system. Firstly, there is the Catholic/anti-clerical cleavage. Historically this centred on the schools issue. In Belgium, unlike France, the question was not *whether* 'free', i.e. Catholic, schools should be subsidised, but by how much. When the Socialist–Liberal coalition of 1954–8 cut the subsidy fractionally there was a powerful reaction from the 'Catholic world', resulting in the decisive Catholic electoral victory of 1958. After that victory the schools issue was really resolved with the Schools Pact of 1958, together with the Schools Law of 1973 which revised one or two anomalies of the Pact, such as the difficulty experienced by Catholic schools in getting grants for new buildings as opposed to getting grants to repair old ones.[11] Although the Schools Pact (and subsequent schools legislation) took the bitterness out of the clerical/anti-clerical quarrel, religiosity – in the broad sense of a person's attitude to the Christian (Catholic) religion – remained the most important single variable in electoral behaviour.[12] According to a 1967 survey, 42·9 per cent of Belgians were regularly practising Catholics (in 1972 the figure was 34·2 per cent); 93·6 per cent were baptised Catholics (1972, 90·2 per cent), and 86·1 per cent of marriages were consecrated in Church (1972, 82·3 per cent).[13] Despite the decline of church attendance in the 1970s, Belgium remained by international standards a very Catholic country, and not surprisingly this was reflected in the electorate's voting habits. Almost three-fifths of the Social Christian Party's voters at the 1971 and 1974 general elections were regularly practising Catholics. In contrast, 73 per cent of non-churchgoers and occasional practisers voted Socialist or Liberal (51 per cent for the former, 22 per cent for the latter). In other words, religiosity has remained a key factor in Belgian electoral politics despite the decline in the Church's influence.[14]

In analysing Belgian politics the class cleavage between capital and labour must also be borne in mind, but this cleavage too has tended to become less clearcut in the postwar period. It is true that the trade unions have presented an increasingly united front in the 1970s, with the Catholic *Confédération des Syndicats Chrétiens* (CSC) and the Socialist *Fédération Générale des Travailleurs Belges* (FGTB) acting in ever closer liaison, for example in their joint strikes against the Tindemans government's counter-inflationary measures in January 1977. But, at the same time, ever since the Resistance and the immediate postwar period there has been a strong emphasis on close co-operation (or *concertation*) between the 'social partners' (the phrase itself is significant, i.e. the major interest groups, including the employers' organisation, the *Fédération des Entreprises Belges* (FEB)) and the government of the day, whatever its political complexion. Moreover, the class cleavage has been further reduced by the fact that, for example, practising Catholics, of whatever social class, have a strong tendency to vote for the same party, namely the inter-class Social Christian Party.

Finally, there is the important linguistic cleavage between Dutch-speaking Flanders and French-speaking Wallonia. Although Flemings have always been in a majority in Belgium (and in the late 1970s outnumbered the Walloons by three to two), in the nineteenth century French was the language of government, administration and culture. Indeed, to this day one of the significant sub-cleavages of Belgian society lies between those educated middle-class Flemings who continue to speak the language of Flanders, Dutch, and those who prefer the main language of the capital, French. In Brussels itself second generation Flemings nearly all speak French, as much for social as for linguistic reasons.

French was at first the only official language of Belgium, but by 1914, as a result of pressure by Flemish 'nationalists', Dutch had been accepted as the normal language for education and administration in Flanders.[15] During the

First World War Flemish troops resented the fact that their officers spoke only French and often could not understand the language of their men. In 1917 this led to near-mutiny in the trenches with the protests of the 'Flemish Front Movement' (the *Vlaamsche Frontbeweging*) and the establishment of the 'Council of Flanders' (*Raad van Vlaanderen*) in occupied Belgium. These developments led after the war to the setting up of the *Frontpartij* as an exclusively Flemish, even anti-Belgian, party. The *Frontpartij* did badly at the 1932 general election and was replaced by the Flemish National Union (*Vlaamsch Nationaal Verbond* (VNV)), led by Staf de Clercq. Like its predecessor, the VNV was a small, but not insignificant, force in the Chamber, usually occupying fourth place after the three big national parties, and averaging about 5–8 per cent of the votes. In 1939 the VNV displaced the extreme right Rexist party as the fourth party in the Chamber (with seventeen seats out of 202), but after the war dissolved itself, as it had become very unpopular with most Flemings and with all Francophones owing to its collaboration with the Nazis.

In the late 1940s and early 1950s two attempts were made to form confessional Flemish nationalist parties, both without success, and it was not until 1954 that Flemish nationalism reappeared as a political force with Frans Van der Elst's avowedly non-confessional *Volksunie*. At the general elections of 1954 and 1958 the *Volksunie* won only 2 per cent of votes cast and one seat in the Chamber, but in 1961 it almost doubled its vote (to 3·6 per cent), winning five seats, and from 1968–77 it averaged 10 per cent (twenty seats). The *Volksunie* has not in fact broken much outside the electorate won by the VNV in the 1930s. Nevertheless, Flemish nationalism has had an important influence on the development of the traditional parties, and not least on the Social Christian Party, for the *Volksunie* appealed primarily to the CVP's Catholic electorate, and this in turn encouraged the CVP to emphasise its 'Flemishness' by breaking its formal links with the PSC in the late 1960s.[16] In addition the rise of the *Volksunie* did much to stimulate the regional debate, as well as to provoke the traditional parties into rethinking their attitude towards the unitary Belgian state.[17]

The same was true of the two parties on the other side of the community cleavage, the *Rassemblement Wallon* (RW) and the *Front Démocratique des Francophones* (FDF). Walloon nationalism does not have the long history or strong cultural emphasis of Flemish nationalism. Rather it has been the reaction of the Walloons to the declining economic importance of Wallonia compared with Flanders. With *per capita* incomes on average 17 per cent lower in Wallonia than in Flanders by the early 1970s, there was a feeling that Walloons must assert what economic muscle they had in order to obtain finance for industrial restructuring. Allied to this was the determination of French-speakers in Brussels to resist further Flemish pressure after the Flemish language law 'victory' of 1963, which divided Belgium into four linguistic regions: a Dutch-language region (Flanders), a French-language region (Wallonia), a German-language region (the cantons of the east, with a total population of only 50,000) and the bilingual region of Brussels. With Brussels three-quarters French speaking, but administratively and educationally bilingual, the French speakers felt sufficient resentment against the Flemings to set up the FDF to defend their interests. The FDF and RW are autonomous parties, although they liaise closely. They reached their peak in 1971 when the joint party won 13·0 per cent (fourteen RW and ten FDF), and did well again in 1974 with 11·0 per cent (thirteen RW and nine FDF), but slipped badly in 1977 when the RW lost half its votes and more than half its seats (2·8 per cent, five seats), partly as a result of a split late in 1976 when the conservative wing of the party, led by one of its founding members, Professor François Perin, joined the Walloon Liberals to form the *Parti de la Liberté et de la Réforme en Wallonie* (PRLW), presided over by Jean Rey, the former President of the EEC Commission.[18]

These linguistic and regional cleavages have had a considerable effect on the organisation and ideology of the traditional parties, which by the late 1970s had all split into two wings, including in practice the Socialist Party, which by tradition was the most unitary of the three major parties. The linguistic/regional problem indeed continues to be of fundamental importance in Belgian politics, and will be discussed further in the context of the problems facing the Social Christian Party.[19]

Political Catholicism in Belgium
The first organised political party in Belgium was the Liberal Party, which established a national organisation in 1846. The Catholics were slower to organise themselves, partly because in the mid-nineteenth century the Catholic bourgeoisie was divided into 'Catholic Liberals' (devout practitioners of their religion, but equally loyal to unionism and the liberal spirit of the Belgian Constitution of 1831) and 'Ultramontanes' (those Catholics who wanted to see Catholicism as the state religion of Belgium, and who contended that the Constitution was too liberal in its clauses on freedom of expression and belief, and therefore ought to be amended).[20] National political congresses of Catholics were held at Malines in 1863, 1864 and 1867, and at these it was apparent that Catholic Liberalism, personified by Edouard Ducpétiaux, was the predominant force within the movement. But it was not until the Liberals, in their one burst of anti-clericalism *à la française*, introduced a law threatening the independence of Catholic schools in 1879, that the Catholics really began to organise themselves politically, and then the impetus came from below, from the Catholic clergy and laymen who formed themselves into 'comités scolaires Catholiques' to ensure the election of deputies favourable to Catholic schools. These committees became the local branches of *le Parti Catholique*, which was founded in 1884 and remained the predominant force in Belgian politics until the Second World War.

Holding an absolute majority in the Chamber from 1884–1919, the Catholic Party was at first very much a bourgeois, conservative organisation, interested mainly in defending the interests of the Church, which in practice meant supporting the free (Catholic) schools. The party's leading conservative figure was Charles Woeste, for long president of the bourgeois *Fédération des Cercles et des Associations* (established in 1868). But gradually the party began to move away from its extreme conservatism, particularly with regard to the social problems of industrial Belgium. Auguste Beernaert, prime minister from 1886–94, was no liberal (in the progressive sense). However, under the influence of the Liberal-Catholic ideas of Ducpétiaux and the Social-Catholic ideas of De Jaer and the Daens brothers,[21] as well as of the papal encyclical *Rerum Novarum* (1891), Beernaert presided over a government which introduced legislation to prohibit the employment of women in the mining industry (1890), as well as to provide compensation for those involved in industrial accidents (also 1890). Then in 1896 a Factory Act, codifying earlier legislation about hours of work and safety standards, was passed, and under later Catholic ministries Sunday work was prohibited (except in essential services and industries) (1905), and the working day was limited to nine hours (1909).

The leaders of Catholic Belgium had been slow to introduce legislation to protect the weak in society – much slower than the leading politicians in Britain and Germany, and even France; nevertheless, the fact that action was finally taken was indicative of a change in the nature of, and power structure in, the Catholic Party. For between approximately 1890 and 1914 the working-class 'Christian Democratic' wing steadily increased its influence within the party, whilst that of the middle-class *Cercles* declined.

The phrase 'Christian Democracy' seems to have been used for the first time in Belgium in 1871, when Gustave De Jaer proposed the setting up of a 'Christian Democratic movement' as a counterweight to the various Socialist and Catholic workers' organisations which were at that time affiliated to the First International. De Jaer's proposals for reform, put forward in the review *L'Economie Chrétienne*, were, like those of Edouard Ducpétiaux, rather modest, such as restrictions on the use of child labour in factories and the prohibition of Sunday working. Nevertheless, the fact that a Catholic industrialist had proposed such reforms, and then set up a pressure group to work for them, was indicative of a change of attitude in the Catholic world, a change which in turn was even more apparent at the Catholic congresses held at Liège in 1886, 1887 and 1890. Whereas at the equivalent congresses at Malines in the 1860s Ducpétiaux's had been a lone voice crying for social reform, by the 1880s almost half the members of the Catholic congresses were advocates of social reform. It is true that many of the delegates agreed with Charles Woeste and Victor Jacobs that the way to deal with poverty was by private Christian charity, but the 'Christian Democrats', led by Arthur Verhaegen, were listened to with obvious sympathy.[22]

Verhaegen was indeed a leading figure in building up the Christian Democratic wing of the party. It was he who created the *Ligue Démocratique Belge* in 1891 out of the various Catholic working-class organisations, gradually forging it into a movement with as much influence in the party as the middle-class *Fédération des Cercles*. The aims of the *Ligue Démocratique Belge* were modest enough: Verhaegen and his friends did not criticise the capitalist system as such, but demanded accident and sickness insurance for workers, old age pensions, a graded income tax, and a rest day on Sundays.[23] Verhaegen was supported in his work by the Bishops of Ghent and Liège, who saw the *Ligue Démocratique Belge* as a vehicle through which the social teaching of *Rerum Novarum* could be implemented.[24] Another important branch of the Catholic Party which developed at this time was the Flemish peasants' league, the *Boerenbond*, set up by Augustin Helleputte in 1890. With the introduction of universal male suffrage in 1893, tempered by plural voting for those with special financial and educational qualifications, both the *Ligue Démocratique Belge* and the *Boerenbond* flourished. In 1907 the first 'Christian Democratic' ministers were appointed, in the persons of Jules Renkin of the *Ligue* and Augustin Helleputte of the *Boerenbond*, and by 1914 the Catholic Party consisted of three fairly well balanced wings: the conservative *Fédération des Cercles*, the working-class *Ligue Démocratique Belge*, and the peasants' *Boerenbond* (which contained a mixture of 'Christian Democratic' and conservative tendencies). Thus, even by 1914 the Catholic Party had acquired many of the inter-class characteristics of its successor of a generation later, the Social Christian Party.

In the immediate post-First-World-War period the 'Christian Democratic' element within the Catholic Party amounted to about one third,[25] and, in alliance with the Socialists, the progressive Catholics played a key part in carrying through the important reforms of 1919–21: universal suffrage for men, together with the abolition of plural voting for the more privileged classes; the introduction of surtax, and of old age pensions for all aged over sixty-five, together with a maximum working week of forty-eight hours (i.e. an eight-hour day for six days). However, apart from the years 1919–21, the interwar period was not a particularly fruitful one for the Catholic Party. The Catholics usually outdistanced the Socialists by a small margin at general elections, but then allied themselves with the Liberals owing to their continuing suspicion of Marxism in the Labour Party, although as from 1932 (when Henri de Man's 'Plan du Travail' was accepted as the Labour Party's Programme) the Socialists were very much 'revisionists'. The Liberals, meanwhile, took a conservative stance on all matters, not least on how to deal with the depression, which hit a manufacturing-trading nation like Belgium particularly badly. Thus, the Catholics, having lost their prewar absolute majority in Parliament, were constrained by their conservative allies. But they were also constrained by their own divisions. The Catholic Party preceded the *standen* (i.e. the various socio-political organisations like the *Cercles* and the *Boerenbond*), but by the interwar years the *standen*, whose development has been outlined above, had become more important than the party itself. The Catholic Party – known as the *Union Catholique* between 1921–36, and the *Bloc Catholique* from 1936–40 – had become a *standenorganisatie*, i.e. it was a party which was almost wholly dependent on its four 'estates' or *standen*: the *Fédération des Cercles et des Associations*, which grouped together the party's middle– and upper middle–class supporters; the *Boerenbond*, the Flemish Catholic farmers' organisation, and its Walloon equivalent, the *Alliance Agricole* (founded 1931); the *Ligue Nationale des Travailleurs Chrétiens*, which had replaced the *Ligue Démocratique Belge* in 1919, bringing together all the Catholic working-class organisations such as the important trade union confederation, the *Confédération des Syndicats Chrétiens* (CSC), the Catholic co-operative, and friendly societies; and finally the *Fédération des Classes*

Moyennes (*Middenstandbond* in Flanders), which was set up in 1919 to defend the interests of the middle classes (in the Belgian sense of the word), i.e. shop-keepers, artisans and small entrepreneurs of all kinds. People could not join the *Union Catholique* directly, but only one of its *standen,* which tended to cancel each other out by constantly jockeying for position within the party.[26] After their electoral setback of 1936, when a significant number of Catholics, both conservative and progressive, defected to Léon Degrelle's Rexist party (it returned twenty-one members to the Chamber and twelve to the Senate), the Catholics held a special unity conference. This resulted in the winding-up of the *Union Catholique* and its replacement by the *Bloc Catholique Belge* in October 1936. The *Bloc* consisted of Flemish and Walloon wings, the *Katholieke Vlaamsche Volkspartij* (KVV) and the *Parti Catholique Social* (PCS). Whilst the new *Bloc* recognised the existence of the *standen,* and the KVV specifically allowed them to continue to be represented within its struc-ture, the PCS opted for individual membership with a view to reducing the influence of the socio-professional organisations.[27] The directorate of the joint party (the *Bloc*) consisted of an equal number of Flemings and Walloons, whilst the national presidency was to alternate between the KVV and PCS. The new organisation, which in some ways foreshadowed that of the postwar Social Christian Party, hardly had time to prove itself before the German invasion of 1940.

However, the years from 1884–1940 had clearly shown that the Catholic Party had a capacity to adapt itself to changing social and political circum-stances, and had done so in spite of long periods of subservience to the *standen.* Nevertheless, it was also clear that throughout its entire history up to 1940 the Catholic Party had been above all a confessional party whose *raison d'être* had been to defend the interests of Catholics rather than to concern itself with the 'commonweal' of the Belgian people as a whole. In the immediate postwar period all this was to change, with the emergence of a non-confessional, essentially progressive Catholic party.

The Social Christian Party

The Social Christian Party, which replaced the Catholic *Bloc* in 1945, was in a very real sense a new party. Consisting of a Flemish wing (the *Christelijke Volkspartij,* CVP) and a French-speaking wing (the *Parti Social Chrétien,* PSC), the Social Christian Party nevertheless had a unitary structure. It terminated its formal links with the Catholic Church; it organised itself on the basis of individual membership rather than on that of *standen,* although it did not abolish the *standen* – it had no prerogative to do so; and it proclaimed itself as an inter-class party, whose main objective was to achieve social and economic justice for all citizens in a united, democratic Belgium.[28] In due course the Social Christian Party was to abandon its unitary structure, and then to modify its views on the structure of the Belgian state itself. Neverthe-less, by the late 1970s there was evidence that the party had adjusted itself successfully to changing political circumstances. In addition, the Social Christians could justifiably claim to have played a key part in modernising and reforming Belgian society since the war.

Emergence and doctrinal position of the CVP–PSC

The Belgian Social Christian Party, like its sister Christian Democratic parties in Europe, owed much to the Resistance period, when despite – or perhaps because of – the ban on political activity considerable thought was given to future political and social structures.[29]

Three groups were particularly important in preparing the way for the setting up of the new party: the Aalst group, the Herbert group, and the Catholic workers' group. The first was essentially a conservative group led by Baron Romain Moyersoen, the former leader of the Catholic *Bloc* in the Senate. Moyersoen organised various wartime meetings in Aalst, and although former Catholic parliamentarians predominated at these meetings, 'Christian Democrats' from the trade unions and farmers' organisations also participated. In 1943 the Aalst group produced a draft programme for postwar political action, the *Strekkingen* ('Conclusions'). The *Strekkingen* were rather conservative in their recommendations about the organisation of the state, but were distinctly progressive in their commitment to social and economic reforms. In this the *Strekkingen* were rather like the draft programmes drawn up in clandestinity by other embryo Christian Democratic parties. Moyersoen and his friends emphasised *inter alia* the need for a new inter-class, non-confessional party, which would nevertheless be committed to Christian principles and human rights; they stressed the importance of the family – again this was typical of Christian Democratic thinking in all countries – and in this context they wanted to see as many families as possible owning their own homes, and the head of family, if aged over thirty, having an additional vote. They stressed the importance of national unity, and, in order to obtain a more stable governmental system, proposed strict rules about votes of censure. Their most important economic proposal was that workers should be able to participate in profit-sharing schemes in their firms.[30]

The second group, led by the industrialist Tony Herbert, was equally important, because it brought together not only established politicians but also young activists from the world of Catholic Action, many of whom were later to play a prominent role in Belgian politics.[31] Their views differed little from those of the Aalst group, except that they laid great emphasis on the cultural heritage both of Flanders and of Wallonia, and therefore by implication seemed more in favour of a less unitary state. Their only unusual proposal – dropped in subsequent Social Christian programmes – was that the monarch should have the right to initiate legislation.

The third group was in effect a clandestine Catholic workers' movement. Organised primarily on the basis of the *Algemeen Christelijk Werkersverbond* (ACW), the Flemish working-class Catholic Action organisation, this group kept in close touch with the other two through P. W. Segers and G. Van den Daele. The ACW group was closer to the Church than the others, and favoured the re-establishment of a confessional party after the war, although it wanted the new party to be based on individual, not *standen*, membership. Not surprisingly, the ACW programme of 1944 laid great emphasis on social policy.[32] It advocated a more progressive taxation system, greater educational opportunities for the working classes, better housing, adequate family allowances, votes for women, and generally a complete break from the economic and social conditions of the 1930s.

As soon as Belgium was liberated the leading figures from the above groups, together with Catholic exiles newly returned from London, met in Brussels and decided to form a new party with a detailed programme based on the proposals put forward in the various resistance programmes and manifestos. In December 1944 a draft programme was produced,[33] and in February 1945 the old Catholic *Bloc* dissolved itself. Then in August 1945 the founding congress of the Social Christian party took place in Brussels, with August De Schryver being elected as national president and P. W. Segers and Augustin Roberti as presidents respectively of the Flemish and Walloon wings. De Schryver in particular was an ideal choice: a man of great organisational ability and a devout Catholic from the 'Christian Democratic' wing of the party, he also had many close contacts with the other Belgian political parties since the days of the government in exile in London.

The founding congress set up a number of committees with the task of drawing up a programme for the new party. These committees were responsible for the various sections of the programme – on finance and the economy, agriculture, social affairs, trade union affairs, the middle classes, planning and foreign policy. Their work was co-ordinated by Robert Houben, later national president of the Social Christian Party, and with great speed they produced the *Kerstprogramma* of December 1945, a comprehensive manifesto of seventy pages with the sub-title 'Belgium must be rebuilt. Who will be the architect?'[34] The Christmas Programme of 1945 was a remarkable document, in the first place it was surprising that it was produced at all: hitherto the Catholics had never published a comprehensive programme – they had simply committed themselves in broad terms to defending the rights of the Catholic community and to implementing the social teaching of the Church. In the second place it was remarkable for its clear statement that the new party would not be a confessional party: here, in Catholic Belgium, the Social Christian Party stated more bluntly than any other emerging Christian Democratic party that it would eschew any specific links with the Church. Of course, in practice it has often behaved as if it had such links, in particular over the schools' issue up to 1958, but Social Christians always claim that they did not choose to act in a confessional manner over the schools issue, but were driven to do so by the anti-clericalism of the 1954–8 Socialist-Liberal coalition. In the immediate postwar period the Hierarchy also made it quite clear that they preferred the Social Christian Party to the *travailliste* (socialist-Catholic) *Union Démocratique Belge* (UDB). In addition, the Church and the Social Christian Party strove together to achieve the restoration of the monarchy (with one or two exceptions in the PSC).

Whilst denying the confessional nature of the Social Christian Party, the Christmas Programme laid great emphasis on Emmanuel Mounier's concept of 'Christian personalism', that is the idea that every person, whatever his status in society, should have the opportunity to develop his personality to the full in his home, school and job. Much that followed in the Christmas Programme stemmed from this commitment to 'personalism'. Thus, the

Social Christians stated that it was essential for the state to establish adequate social services and a nationwide medical scheme in order to eliminate the fear of unemployment and illness. They advocated careers' guidance, job training, and workers' participation in industry, so that people could develop their full personalities at work. They laid strong emphasis on family policy: without a good home and secure upbringing no individual could hope to fulfil his potential in society; hence it was essential to have adequate family allowances and good housing for all working people, and ideally all mothers should be able to stay at home to bring up their families. In addition, votes should be given to women, and an extra vote should be granted to the head of the family. Catholic schools should be subsidised in order to give parents the chance to choose their children's education.

In economic matters the Social Christian Party stated that it was 'anti-capitalist', but was nevertheless against the nationalisation of industry in principle, although in exceptional cases it might be necessary for the state to take over certain industries, or at least to give them short-term aid. However, the Social Christians claimed that in general they would prefer to encourage private initiative and private enterprise, both on the land and in industry. At the same time they favoured long-term national economic planning, although they considered that annual budgets would be necessary as well. The Social Christians laid great emphasis on the importance of the 'middle classes', i.e. the small businessmen, artisans, shopkeepers and smallholders, who were still reckoned to account for about one-third of the total population (if their families were included). A commitment to the 'middle classes' was, of course, sound electioneering, but it also fitted in with the Christian Democratic emphasis on personalism and pluralism within society. As regards the institutions of the state, the Social Christian Party was strongly in favour of the monarchy, and of a bi-cameral legislature. It condemned corporatism of any sort, opposing for example the representation of socio-economic groups in the Senate, whilst at the same time arguing that such groups should be able to play their part as advisory bodies. The Social Christians also wanted to see a French-style Council of State (*Conseil d'Etat*) established for the first time in Belgium to help the government to draft legislation more quickly and efficiently as well as to act as a constitutional check on the legislature and on the administration. Finally, in international affairs, the Social Christians advocated the renunciation of Belgian neutrality: instead the country should commit itself fully to the United Nations, as well as emphasising its desire to work closely with its neighbours, particularly Britain, France, Holland and the Scandinavian countries.[35]

Many of the objectives outlined in the Christmas Programme were in due course achieved, notably votes for women, equal treatment for Catholic and state schools, adequate family allowances and social services, workers' participation through *conseils d'entreprise*, economic planning, and the chance for interest groups to participate in an advisory capacity in the governmental system. A *Conseil d'Etat* was also set up, and finally Belgium began a new era in foreign policy with a firm commitment to the Atlantic Alliance and to European integration.

Organisation and structure of the CVP–PSC

Like other Christian Democratic parties the CVP–PSC has an official structure –
the party organisation proper; and an unofficial structure – what is sometimes
referred to in Belgium as *le monde catholique,* i.e. the Catholic trade unions,
agricultural organisations and Catholic Action groups.

As far as the official structure is concerned, the CVP and PSC are two
separate parties, which nevertheless work in very close liaison with each
other.[36] Since 1968 the two parties have always held separate national congresses, and since 1972, after the resignation of Robert Houben, the post of
national president has been 'vacant', although strictly speaking it has not been
abolished. The national congresses of the parties are normally held annually,
although sometimes the yearly congress is omitted by the CVP, whilst at other
times, particularly in election years, two congresses may be held, one of them
an extraordinary one to endorse the party manifesto. In addition, the PSC
also organises two or three 'mini-congresses' each year, the so-called *congrès
de réflexion* and *congrès de participation,* which, as their names imply, give
party members a chance to contribute to policy-making and to participate in
the 'movement' – it should be noted that Belgian Social Christians, like
Christian Democrats in other countries, often prefer to use the broader word
'movement' rather than 'party'. In theory the national congresses are the
supreme policy-making bodies in the two parties, but in practice the main
decisions are taken by the national organs, i.e. the national bureaux and
presidents, who work in close liaison with the CVP–PSC praesidium. In addition,
between the level of the national congress and the national headquarters each
party has a national council, the *hoofdbestuur* of the CVP and the *conseil
permanent* of the PSC. These bodies, consisting of approximately forty members each (including co-opted members), are elected by the national congresses,
meet every second month, and are responsible for the general oversight of
party policy. However, the key bodies are the national organs.

Each party has a national president, whose role is comparable to that of the
party secretary in French or Italian parties.[37] He presides over the bureau
(the *dagelijks bestuur* of the CVP and the *comité directeur* of the PSC), and
plays an important role in coalition bargaining and in day-to-day policy-
making. The bureaux are quite small bodies, with approximately twenty
members in each, depending on the number of co-opted members, and they
meet at least once a week. Whilst the national presidents and bureaux are the
most important policy-making organs in the two parties, the unofficial
praesidium is the key liaison body. Each week the praesidium meets – appropriately enough on the top floor of the CVP–PSC headquarters in the rue des
Deux-Eglises in Brussels – and works out the joint party line for parliamentary
debates and divisions, and for national policy generally. The praesidium
consists of the national presidents, the national secretary (the CVP–PSC still
has a national secretary), the leaders of the parliamentary parties, and appropriate ministers (depending on the subject under discussion). The prime
minister usually attends,[38] as does the head of the party's research organisation.[39] The praesidium has no binding authority, and the national presidents

report back to their respective bureaux to obtain endorsement (or rejection) of the praesidium's proposals. In the opinion of the national secretary, Frank Swaelen, the two parties endorse the line proposed by the praesidium in 98 per cent of cases, a figure put at 80 per cent by Charles-Ferdinand Nothomb, president of the PSC from 1972–6.[40] Whichever figure is accepted, it is clear that there is a high degree of co-operation between the two parties. One other national body which should be noted is the Agenda Committee. In the judgement of one distinguished commentator on Belgian politics, this body, which brings together representatives of the two parties and of *le monde catholique* approximately ten times per annum, has (or had) a mysterious and powerful role in policy-making.[41] However, in 1976 this judgement was refuted by Frank Swaelen, the CVP–PSC national secretary, who maintained that the Agenda Committee was quite important as a *liaison* organ, in that it allowed the national leaders to gauge grass-roots opinion in the movement, but that it was not comparable as a decision-making body to the praesidium or the party bureaux.[42] There seems no reason to reject the national secretary's judgement in this matter.

In general Belgian parties are rather weakly organised at the local level. The CVP and PSC are no exception. Neither is a 'mass' party in Duverger's terms,[43] nor are they merely 'electors' ' parties, but both are nearer to the latter than to the former, with the important exception that both have a distinctive electoral base in the form of the various organisations which constitute *le monde catholique*. Neither Social Christian party has a provincial organisation,[44] but both have constituency (*arrondissement*) and local (*commune*) organisations.[45] The local sections are important only at election times, particularly during communal elections when their elected committees draw up the party lists and negotiate alliances (often of a surprising kind) with other parties. As far as national politics is concerned, the federations (i.e. the party organisations at the *arrondissement* level) still play an important part in the selection of candidates. In each of Belgium's thirty *arrondissements* the local party draws up a model list of candidates. This list is submitted to national headquarters, which normally makes no changes or suggestions, although the national bureau might, for example, propose a better 'mix' on a list; it might, for example, suggest that more female candidates be included.[46] The list is then returned to the federations, who, hold '*polls préparatoires*', in effect primary elections to endorse, or alter, the lists. Every party member who attends a *poll préparatoire*, which, it should be noted, are becoming much less important except in rural areas, is given a model list with a blank list on the right. He can alter the list in any way he wants, and a vote is then taken on his proposals. In practice, the model list is usually endorsed by the few members who bother to turn up, but in areas like West Flanders, where the *standen* are still important, *standen* representatives make a point of attending the *polls* and making sure that an appropriately balanced list is endorsed (i.e. one on which their candidates are well placed).[47]

With the exception of Brussels where the CVP and PSC present separate lists (prior to 1974 they presented a common list),[48] the two parties do not compete with each other, the CVP sticking to the Dutch-speaking region of

Flanders and the PSC to the French-speaking region of Wallonia. The CVP has approximately 100,000 members to the PSC's 50,000, so that in so far as the CVP–PSC can still be considered a joint party it is clear that Flemings predominate within it. As a result of its predominance in Flanders ('*l'Etat CVP*', as its critics call it), the CVP is perhaps a more confident party than the PSC, which in contrast is always conscious of its minority position (trailing the Socialists) in Wallonia. The CVP is also more united and left-inclined or *travailliste* than the PSC, largely owing to the overwhelming strength of the Dutch-speaking trade union confederation, the *Algemeen Christelijk Vakverbond van België* (ACV), in Flanders. But the working-class wing of the PSC has at times been more radical than the 'Christian Democratic' wing of the CVP, so that clashes between the Walloon *Mouvement Ouvrier Chrétien* (MOC) and the rather bourgeois leadership of the PSC have not been infrequent, and on various occasions the MOC leaders have openly criticised the policy of the party leadership.[49] Thus it can fairly be said that the CVP is more homogeneous, 'Christian Democratic' (in the Belgian sense), and united than the PSC. However, since breaking with the CVP in 1972, followed by a special doctrinal congress in 1973, the PSC has become a more effective party, as indicated by its electoral successes in 1974 and 1977.

As regards dissemination of their political views, both Social Christian parties publish monthly magazines for their members, the CVP *Zeg* and the PSC *Action*. In theory there is no daily newspaper which is openly committed to the Social Christians, but in practice the rather conservative *De Standaard*, the popular *Het Volk* and the left-inclined *De Nieuwe Gids* support the CVP. There is no French-language newspaper which is as close to the PSC as these Flemish papers are to the CVP. Both parties have political education and training centres, the *Instituut voor Politieke Vorming* of the CVP and the *Centre de Perfectionnement des Cadres Politiques* of the PSC, and in Brussels they have a joint research centre, which is probably better organised and more competent than that attached to any other Belgian political party. This research centre, CEPESS (*Centre d'Etudes Politiques, Economiques et Sociales/ Centrum voor Economische, Politieke en Sociale Studies*) employs twenty full-time staff, does research work for parliamentarians of both parties, and publishes a regular bi-monthly series of documents and reports (*Documents Cepess/Cepess Documenten*) consisting of parallel articles in French and Dutch. A condensed version of the above is published quarterly (*Cahiers Cepess/Cepess Bladen*).

Although the *standen* are no longer recognised as constituent parts of the Social Christian parties, *le monde catholique*, i.e. the socio-professional milieu in which the parties function, still remains an important electoral base – or voting reservoir – for the two parties. The 'Catholic world' is, of course, centred on the Roman Catholic Church, although the links between the two are informal rather than organic. This is particularly true of the trade union and farmers' organisations, though less so of the main Catholic Action groups, which are much more closely linked to the organised Church.[50]

The *Confédération des Syndicats Chrétiens* (CSC), whose Flemish equivalent is the *Algemeen Christelijk Vakverbond van België* (ACV), has, according to article 3 of its statutes, no organic links with the CVP–PSC, but it normally supports Social Christian candidates who are members of the wider-based Catholic working-class movement, the *Mouvement Ouvrier Chrétien* (MOC), whose Flemish equivalent is the *Algemeen Christelijk Werkliedenverbond* (ACW). Founded in 1909, the CSC was always smaller than the Socialist trade union confederation (*Fédération Générale du Travail de Belgique*, FGTB), founded in 1898, until the post-1945 period. Indeed, even in 1945 there were only 343,000 Catholic trade unionists to 553,000 Socialists, but in 1955 the Catholics overtook the Socialists, and have ever since outdistanced them.[51] By the late 1970s the CSC had well over a million members to about 850,000 in the FGTB, and in Flanders the Catholic trade unionists outnumbered the Socialists by two to one. Approximately three-quarters of the CSC (ACV) members were Flemings. As stated, the CSC (ACV) has no direct links with the CVP–PSC, but the wider-based working-class movement, the MOC, regularly supports the Social Christians at elections, and the *informal* links between Catholic trade unionists and Social Christians are still important.[52] The consequence is that the former have considerable influence over the latter, and are perhaps more politically effective than the avowedly Socialist FGTB.[53] The Social Christians can also rely on considerable support from the *Alliance Nationale des Mutualités Chrétiennes* (Catholic friendly societies) and the *Fédération Nationale des Coopératives Chrétiens* (Catholic co-operative societies), as well as from Catholic Action groups such as the women's leagues (*Vie Féminine* and *Kristlijke Arbeidersvrouwen*) and young workers (*Jeunesse Ouvrière Chrétienne* and *Katholieke Arbeidersjeugd*). Finally, the Social Christians have close links with the powerful Flemish farmers' organisation, the 800,000-strong *Boerenbond* and its Walloon equivalent, the *Alliance Agricole Belge*, and with the *Nationaal Christelijk Middenstand Verbond*, the Flemish shopkeepers and artisans organisation (there is no equivalent to the *Middenstand Verbond* in Wallonia).

Overall, then, the Social Christians form a powerful, well-organised political force in Belgian politics. Although the two parties are now organisationally separate, their political strength remains considerable: indeed, that of the CVP is overwhelming in Flanders. In the judgement of Frank Swaelen, the separation of the two parties – after the teething troubles of the late 1960s and early 1970s – has been a positive advantage, for the CVP's political opponents in Flanders can no longer accuse it of being under French influence, whilst the PSC in Wallonia can no longer be said to be dominated by the CVP.[54] Thus the CVP and PSC of the late 1970s are well-organised parties, with a strong base in *le monde catholique*. Moreover, as we shall see, the Social Christians seem to have successfully parried the serious electoral challenge posed to them by the regionalist parties in the late 1960s and early 1970s.

Electoral performance and governmental role
The Social Christian parties have played a predominant role in Belgian politics since the Second World War. They polled over 40 per cent of the votes at every election from 1945–61; declined somewhat in the 1960s, reaching their nadir with 30 per cent in 1971; but in 1977 climbed back to almost 36 per

cent. Their highpoint was between 1950–4, when they held an absolute majority in both houses of Parliament, and even during their worst period, i.e. the decade 1965–75, when their hegemony was threatened by the regionalist parties, they remained the biggest single party – usually at least 5 per cent ahead of their nearest rivals, the Socialists (see table, p. 189). As a result of their electoral predominance the Social Christians have also been the major party of government. From March 1946–September 1977 they were in government all the time except for a year from March 1946–March 1947 and for four years from April 1954–June 1958 (see table, p. 190). In this period of thirty-one years six months the Social Christians spent twenty-seven years two months in office (approximately 50 per cent more than the Socialists and 100 per cent more than the Liberals). They held the office of prime minister twice as often and for over twice as long as the Socialists; nevertheless, their main partners in government were the Socialists (about half the time), followed by the Liberals (between a quarter and a fifth of the time), and from 1974 they also brought the regionalist parties into various coalitions (the Walloon RW from 1974–7, and the Brussels FDF and Flemish *Volksunie* after the 1977 general election). The Social Christians may be said to have passed through three major phases: a successful period from the end of the war to the early 1960s; a considerable setback in the mid 1960s; and a significant renaissance in the mid to late 1970s.

The CVP–PSC was initially very successful for a variety of reasons. Perhaps the two most important were that it inherited the Flemish nationalist (mainly Catholic) vote of the 1930s, because Flemish nationalism was discredited in the immediate postwar period owing to the collaboration of many VNV leaders with the Nazis. Secondly, the introduction of female suffrage, which applied as from the 1949 general election, undoubtedly helped the CVP–PSC, which, although theoretically 'deconfessionalised', was still recognised as *the* Catholic party. In addition, the party succeeded in projecting itself as a *Volkspartei*, a moderate party of the Centre interested in the aspirations of all electors, not just those who were devout Catholics: in this context the Christmas Programme of 1945 was particularly important, as was the party's support for the introduction of industrial democracy (the setting up of consultative *Conseils d'Entreprise* in all firms with over fifty employees in 1947), and for economic planning, introduced by the Spaak government of 1947–9. By successfully projecting itself both as a moderate-conservative and as a social-reforming party the CVP–PSC beat off the challenge posed immediately after the war by the *Union Démocratique Belge* (UDB). The UDB, a left-wing Catholic party – but avowedly non-confessional – had three posts in Van Acker's provisional government of August 1945–March 1946, and was considered to be a serious threat to the emerging CVP–PSC.[55] But when the CVF–PSC indicated the degree of its commitment to social and economic reforms in its Christmas Programme, and in addition the Cardinal Archbishop of Malines endorsed the CVP–PSC rather than the UDB, the vast majority of practising Catholics opted for the Social Christians at the general election of March 1946, at which the UDB polled less than 1 per cent in Flanders and just over 4 per cent in Wallonia.[56] Moreover, in 1949 the former UDB leaders advised their supporters to vote for the Social Christians on the grounds that the CVP–PSC had not after all turned out to be 'a resurrection of the old Catholic Party'; on the contrary, it had shown its 'firm commitment to political and economic democracy, and to social reconciliation'.[57]

Supported by practising Catholics of all classes, and by those holding progressive as well as conservative views, the CVP–PSC reached its electoral zenith in 1949 and 1950. At the general elections of these years the party polled 43·5 per cent and 47·6 per cent respectively, falling two short of an absolute majority in the House of Representatives in 1949 (105 out of 212) and gaining an absolute majority in 1950 (108 out of 212).[58] In 1950 the CVP–PSC vote was boosted by the country's polarisation over the monarchy issue. Both the CVP–PSC (in particular the Flemings) and the Catholic Church were wholly in favour of the return of Leopold III, who had remained in Belgium during the war, and, it was claimed by his supporters, had interceded successfully with the Germans on behalf of his people as well as undergoing their sufferings with them. The Socialists and Communists, led by Paul-Henri Spaak, suspected that the king had collaborated and were determined to get rid of him. Neither the referendum (57·6 per cent voted for the return of the king: 42 per cent in Wallonia and Brussels, 69 per cent in Flanders) nor the general election of June 1950 solved the problem, and when the king returned in July there was a campaign of civil disobedience, amounting almost to an insurrection in the working-class districts of Wallonia and Brussels. Spaak did nothing to calm the situation, and the Social Christian government, led by the Walloon Duvieusart, decided to give in and persuade Leopold to abdicate in favour of his son Baudouin, who succeeded to the throne in 1951.

As far as the Social Christians were concerned, the 'royal issue' was important for three reasons. As already mentioned, it produced an unusual degree of polarisation in Belgian politics, and this boosted the CVP–PSC vote somewhat artificially at the general election of June 1950. Secondly, the royal issue produced real tension within the joint party for the first time, foreshadowing the formal split eighteen years later. The CVP president, Baron van der Straeten-Waillet, resigned in protest at the government's 'weakness' in giving in to mobs in the streets after a majority of the electorate had voted for the king's return, and the hapless Duvieusart of the PSC was forced to resign as prime minister largely as a result of CVP pressure. Finally, the 'royal issue' brought to an end the fruitful Social Christian-Socialist co-operation of 1947–9, and the two parties did not form another joint government until 1961, since when Social Christian-Socialist governments have become the norm again.

The Social Christians fell back to 41·1 per cent in 1954 (compared with 47·6 per cent in 1950) partly because their vote had been artificially high in 1950 owing to the royal issue, partly because they had formed governments on their own throughout the 1950–4 legislature and the reaction against the government of the day inevitably hit them as *the* party of government. In addition, by 1954 the Socialists had completely accepted King Baudouin, who in turn had proved himself to be an exemplary, if somewhat retiring, constitutional monarch, and they also made gains at the expense of the Communists.[59] Thus, the Social Christians had to be content with a 'cure d'opposition' when the Socialists and Liberals decided to form a coalition. However, the Van Acker government of April 1954–June 1958 unwisely decided to tamper with the delicate problem of the schools. A majority of Belgian children (still 60 per cent in the late 1970s) have always gone to Catholic schools, and since 1884 it has been accepted that Catholic and state schools should be treated more or less equally. Indeed, all that the Loi Collard of 1955 introduced was an increased subsidy for the building of state schools, so that, in the government's view, parents could have real freedom of choice for their children, for in some parts of the country there were still no state schools.[60] However, the Loi was seen as an attack on the 'free schools', and a *Comité de Défense des Libertés Démocratiques* was set up with the full support of Théo Lefèvre, president of the CVP–PSC, to fight against this 'attack' on Catholic education. The upshot was another very high Social Christian vote (46·5 per cent at the 1958 general election), but at the cost of the CVP–PSC appearing, as over the monarchical issue, a 'confessional' party once again.[61] However, the outcome was an appropriate Belgian-style compromise, namely the Schools Pact of 1958 – really a return to the *status quo* rather than a Catholic 'victory' – which finally removed the schools issue from party politics.[62]

Ironically, the resolution of 'la guerre scolaire' harmed the Social Christians in the short term, for at the 1961 election they fell back to 41·4 per cent in the more relaxed atmosphere following the Pact, whilst the Liberals, who had dropped their traditional anti-clericalism, began to make some inroads into the Catholic middle-class electorate.[63] In 1965 the Liberals, reformed and reorganised by the vigorous Omer Vanaudenhove, made a dramatic electoral breakthrough (21·6 per cent, compared with 12·3 per cent in 1961 and 11·1 per cent in 1958). This breakthrough was made largely at the expense of the Social Christians, whose upper middle-class voters, attracted by the neo-liberal economic views of Vanaudenhove, and feeling more free to vote as they wished in the post-John XXIII Catholic world, went over in large numbers to the Liberal Party both in Flanders and Wallonia. In addition, in Flanders the *Volksunie* doubled its vote (6·7 per cent compared with 3·6 per cent in 1961), again largely at the expense of the CVP. Catholic priests, particularly in the rural areas of east and west Flanders, tended to encourage the electors to vote for the *Volksunie* for cultural reasons, but they would have been unlikely to have done this if the schools problem had still been a live issue, or if the Catholic world had retained its pre-1958 homogeneity. Finally, the traditional Belgian party system – like that of the Netherlands (although to a lesser extent)[64] – was beginning to break down under the influence of economic and social change. Younger voters were beginning to challenge the old system based on unquestioning loyalty to the *standen* and the traditional parties. In 1965 Marcel Grégoire, a former UDB minister, wrote a book criticising the traditional parties for their complacency, the vagueness of their policies, and their constant compromising.[65] Of course, it was easy to make such criticisms without recognising that the obverse – adversary politics – might have considerable disadvantages too. But, in any case, such criticisms appealed to young people in the 1960s, especially in Belgium and Holland, and helped to bring about a profound change in the attitude of the parties in both countries. Under a barrage of criticism from the linguistic/regionalist parties, as well as from the renovated Liberals, the Social Christian vote declined to 34·4 per cent in 1965 and 31·7 per cent in 1968,[66] reaching its lowest point, 30·0 per cent, in 1971.[67] As the veteran Social Christian prime minister, Gaston Eyskens, was wont to say in the late 1960s: 'la Belgique de Papa est morte'.

The Regional Problem and Elections in the 1970s

In the middle to late 1970s the Social Christian parties experienced a revival after reaching their all-time low at the 1971 general election. But this revival was to some extent tempered by the fact that the linguistic/regional problem was becoming increasingly complex.[68] It was difficult to form stable governments owing to conflicting views about the regional problem both between and within the parties. The general elections of 1971 and 1974 both occurred a year early owing to the regional problem, whilst at the 1977 election the two main issues were regionalism and economic policy.

The regional problem has affected all the Belgian political parties – and not least the Social Christians as the leading party of government – to such an extent that it is essential to comment further on it. As established under the Constitution of 1831 Belgium was a unitary state with three levels of government: the central institutions (very much the most important); the provinces; and the communes. The constitutional reforms of 1893 (plural voting) and 1921 (universal male suffrage) in no way affected the structure of the Belgian state. However, the so-called 'Third Revision of the Constitution' (i.e. the changes of 1967–71) – carried through in response to the rise of Flemish and Francophone nationalism in the 1960s – introduced profound changes to the governmental structure of the country for the first time. The key new articles were 3B, 3C, 59B and 107D. Article 3B stated that 'Belgium comprises four linguistic regions: the French-language region, the Dutch-language region, the bilingual region of Brussels-Capital, and the German-language region', and Article 3C that 'Belgium comprises three cultural communities: French, Dutch and German. Each community enjoys the powers vested in it by the Constitution or such legislation as shall be enacted in virtue thereof.' Article 59B laid down that 'There is a Cultural Council for the French cultural community, made up of the members of the French linguistic group of both Houses, and a Cultural Council for the Dutch cultural community, made up of the members of the Dutch linguistic community.' (Article 59C also established a Cultural Council for the 50,000 odd German speakers in the *cantons de l'Est*). These Cultural Councils were to be given responsibility for cultural and educational matters (except in so far as education was already catered for under article 17 of the Constitution and the Schools Pact of 1958).[69] Finally, article 107D stated that 'Belgium comprises three regions: the Walloon region, the Flemish region and the Brussels region', and went on to provide for the setting up of regional institutions 'composed of elected representatives' with 'the power to rule on such matters as Parliament shall determine'. These regional institutions, together with their precise powers, were to be established by a special parliamentary majority consisting of a majority of each linguistic group in both Houses and a two-thirds majority overall.

The above changes showed that the Belgian Parliament had recognised, like Eyskens, that 'la Belgique de Papa' was dead, and that some sort of a federal, or quasi-federal, state must be established if Belgium were to survive as one country. After steering through the constitutional changes of the late 1960s and early 1970s with great difficulty Gaston Eyskens, the Social Christian prime minister from June 1969–November 1972, decided to pause and obtain the approval of the electorate before attempting to implement them in detail. However, his strategem failed. For to the disappointment of the Social Christians and Socialists (partners in the Eyskens government), and in contrast to what the opinion polls had forecast, the linguistic parties increased their vote at the 1971 general election. The *Rassemblement Wallon– Front Démocratique des Francophones* alliance increased its poll from 5·9 per cent in 1968 to 13·0 per cent in 1971, with the RW returning fourteen deputies and the FDF ten. The Flemish *Volksunie* also increased its share of the poll slightly, winning 11·1 per cent of the votes cast, compared with 9·8 per cent in 1968 (twenty-one seats compared with twenty). The linguistic parties made their gains mainly at the expense of the Liberals (down to 15·1 per cent from 20·8 per cent), but partly at the expense of the Social Christians, who fell back 1·7 per cent to 30 per cent, their lowest ever poll. The election, of course, did nothing to resolve the crucial regional problem, because although the RW–FDF and *Volksunie* both wanted to introduce a federal system, they were at loggerheads as to how this should be done. In particular they were in total disagreement as to the future of Brussels, which was constitutionally bilingual, but 80 per cent French-speaking. The RW–FDF wanted to expand the nineteen communes of Brussels-Capital to include the French-speaking communes in the Flemish region, and at the same time to ensure that Brussels had full regional status (similar to that of Flanders and Wallonia), whilst the *Volksunie* was determined to keep the 'oilstain' from spreading, i.e. to keep Brussels within the nineteen communes to which it had been restricted by the 1963 Language Laws; instead they wanted the status of Brussels to be inferior to that of Flanders and Wallonia, so that there could be no question of French-speaking Wallonia and Brussels forming an anti-Flemish alliance in the proposed federal state.

In the circumstances it was not surprising that there was a prolonged government crisis after the 1971 general election. Eyskens tried at first to reconstitute a Social Christian-Socialist coalition, but the more 'nationalistic' members of the CVP (under *Volksunie* pressure) and the more 'nationalistic' members of the Socialist Party (under RW pressure) refused to consider such a coalition. The Socialist leader Edmond Leburton also failed to form a government. Finally, after the crisis had lasted almost three months, Eyskens succeeded in putting together a Social Christian-Socialist coalition after all, but it was a disunited and cumbersome government: under the revised Constitution there had to be an equal number of cabinet ministers from the Dutch and French-speaking communities, not to mention two Ministers of Education (Dutch- and French-speaking), two Ministers of Culture, two Ministers for Institutional Reform, as well as a number of parallel Secretaries of State. The Eyskens ministry finally fell in November 1972, not because of differences between the Social Christians and Socialists, but because the Flemish wing of the Social Christian party, led by its rather 'nationalistic' new president, Wilfried Martens, was determined to see the Constitution fully implemented (in the Flemish sense of the word, of course), and because he wanted to get rid of Eyskens (then aged sixty-seven) and other members of the old guard of the CVP–PSC.

The continuing crisis in the Belgian governmental system was shown by the difficulty experienced in forming a new cabinet. After two months Edmond Leburton, the Socialist leader, succeeded in forming what amounted to a caretaker government of Socialists, Social Christians and Liberals. A year later this government in turn fell, ostensibly over the collapse of a Belgian-Iranian oil refining deal, but in reality because the Leburton government, like its two predecessors, had been unable to come to any agreement on the regional problem.

The Social Christians entered the 1974 election campaign in slightly better shape than they had that of 1971. The two parties had settled down as separate units; both had vigorous young presidents – Martens (CVP) and Nothomb (PSC), both of whom were thirty-six years old when elected in 1972; both parties had rid themselves of some of their 'elder statesmen', such as Eyskens of the CVP and Harmel of the PSC, although that veteran expert in conciliation, Paul Vanden Boeynants, remained a prominent figure in the joint party; in addition, the PSC had held a successful special congress in 1973, at which it had tried to revamp its image, emphasising in particular its progressive nature.[70]

To the disappointment of the Bruxellois Vanden Boeynants, the CVP and PSC presented separate lists in the capital for the first time: the PSC insisted on this, piqued as it was by the CVP's refusal to consider any extension of the nineteen communes of Brussels into Flemish territory (even if it was Flemish' territory where the majority of the population spoke French). However, despite their divisions in Brussels and over the community problem in general, the two parties presented a joint programme in all matters except the community one, and both gained ground in 1974, the first election at which they had done so since 1958. Their vote was up by 2·3 per cent (at 32·3 per cent) compared with 1971, and they gained five seats (four in Flanders and one in Wallonia). Significantly there was a sign that the regionalist tide had been checked: the RW–FDF fell back by 2 per cent (to 11 per cent), losing two seats, whilst the *Volksunie* dropped back fractionally in percentage terms (to 10·2 per cent), although, owing to the vagaries of the electoral system, they gained one seat.

Above all, the Social Christian 'success' and the regionalist *recul* was seen as a victory for Leo Tindemans, the moderate and respected leader of the CVP, who had been deputy prime minister in the Leburton government. The CVP had fought the election with the slogan 'With this man things will change'.

Nevertheless, the fifty-two-year-old Tindemans had some difficulty in forming a coalition. His first choice was a Social Christian-Socialist coalition,
principally because he realised that no long-term solution to the community
problem could be worked out without the agreement of the principal parties
of Flanders and Wallonia respectively. But owing to differing views over
state intervention in the economy (the main issue at the time was the control
of international companies in Belgium), as well as over abortion, the negotiations between the Social Christians and Socialists broke down. Tindemans,
who was determined to tackle the regional problem, then approached the
Volksunie and RW–FDF, but owing to their intransigent, and totally opposed,
views on Brussels, he got nowhere with either party. Finally, at the end of
April he formed what was then regarded as a weak coalition with the Liberals.
But when he made it quite clear that he was going to try and find a solution
to the regional problem, the *Rassemblement Wallon* decided to join the
coalition (June 1974), preferring to try to influence it from within rather than
from without.

The 'weak' Tindemans coalition, in fact, succeeded in passing what
amounted to a provisional regional law in August 1974. The government
itself realised that this law only marked a 'half-way house' to regionalisation:
it was in any case only passed with a simple majority, being opposed by the
Socialists, FDF and *Volksunie*. Three Regional Councils were established in
Flanders, Wallonia and Brussels, consisting of the Senators of those regions,
except for Brussels where the Senators were joined by forty-two of the
eighty-four members of the Greater Brussels Council (the *Conseil
d'Agglomération de Bruxelles*). The Regional Councils were given consultative
powers over town planning, land development, tourism and housing. Embryo
Regional Executives (the three Ministerial Committees for Regional Affairs)
were also set up, consisting of the various national ministers and state secretaries responsible for regional affairs. The Executives were to act on the advice
of the Regional Councils. The Socialists and the two regionalist parties not
represented in Tindemans' government (the RW and FDF) voted against the
law on the grounds that the Regional Councils were non-elected bodies, and
that their powers were too vaguely outlined. Nevertheless, it was to the credit
of Tindemans that he had even attempted – in very difficult circumstances –
to implement the constitutional amendments of 1967–71. Moreover, the
communal elections of October 1976, when the Social Christians consolidated
their position in Flanders and the Socialists theirs in Wallonia, whilst the
regionalists lost ground everywhere except in Brussels, indicated that the
electorate appreciated Tindeman's dogged determination to find a compromise solution to the very complex regional problem. Further gains by the
Social Christians at the general election of April 1977 seemed to confirm this
impression.

The 1977 election occurred a year ahead of schedule, because the
Rassemblement Wallon withdrew its support in a number of budget votes in
March. The election was fought mainly on the regional issue and on the
economic situation (unemployment was running at 6·8 per cent). The result
was a victory for Tindemans, who won 134,000 preference votes – the highest

ever achieved by an individual at a Belgian election – and for the Social Christians who advanced by 3·7 per cent (to 35·9 per cent) compared with 1974. The CVP gained five seats in Flanders and one in Brussels, and the PSC two in Wallonia, giving the combined party eighty seats out of 212 in the Chamber (its previous total had been seventy-two). As the Socialist and Liberal votes were virtually unchanged, whilst the linguistic parties lost overall (the *Volksunie* lost two seats, the FDF gained one, and the RW lost eight of its thirteen seats), the electorate had clearly indicated that it wanted the traditional parties to resolve the country's regional and economic problems.

Tindemans at first proposed a grand coalition of Social Christians, Socialists and Liberals, but the Socialists objected to Liberal participation owing to the economic policy of the Liberal Party – the Socialists wanted more state intervention to tackle unemployment, the Liberals a reduction in government spending.

Tindemans then invited the *Volksunie* and FDF to join a coalition (the RW had already indicated that it would not join him under any circumstances), but he did so only after precise proposals about a solution to the community problem had been worked out. At the same time a package to deal with the country's high unemployment was agreed with the Socialists. Finally, six weeks after the election Tindemans was able to form a Social Christian, Socialist, *Volksunie* and FDF coalition. With 172 seats out of 212 in the Chamber, the Tindemans coalition had considerably more than the two-thirds majority required for the implementation of a regional solution. The *Pacte Communautaire* of 1977–8 (i.e. the Egmont Agreement of May 1977 and the Stuivenberg Agreement of February 1978) envisaged in the first place a national Parliament responsible for foreign affairs, defence, justice, fiscal policy and macro-economic policy.[71] But the powers of the Senate, except in constitutional and regional matters, were to be considerably reduced, leaving the House of Representatives as the main legislative organ. The Senate would become instead a *chambre de réflexion*, concentrating its attention on regional affairs. It would consist of the regional councillors from the country's three regions, and would be organised on the basis of Dutch and French-speaking groups, which would work on the double majority principle (i.e. a majority would be required in each group as well as in the Senate as a whole). Secondly, the old Cultural Councils would be reorganised as Community Councils with wider powers in the area of culture, education and health. Thirdly, elected Regional Councils – effectively regional parliaments – would be set up. They would have as many members as there were members of parliament in the particular region; they would elect their own executives (governments), and would have clearly defined powers in all matters concerning their region. They would be largely dependent on government grants, but would be able to raise loans, and eventually might be given fiscal powers. Fourthly, an Arbitration Court would be established to settle conflicts between the Regions, Community Councils and Parliament.[72] As regards Brussels – the key to a solution to Belgium's community problem – the *Pacte* envisaged no expansion of the present nineteen communes of Greater Brussels, but Brussels was to be given a regional status comparable to that of the other two regions, except that the Brussels Regional Executive would have only four members, compared with eight each for Flanders and Wallonia. In addition, French speakers living in a number of communes lying just outside Brussels (probably thirteen) would be able to take out fictitious addresses in Brussels, and thus have the right, *inter alia*, to vote there, hold French identity cards, and fill in their tax returns in French. This ingenious solution was a concession to the FDF, but a concession which seemed unlikely to upset the *Volksunie* now that Brussels was definitely to be kept within its *carcan* (iron-collar).

There is, of course, no certainty that these proposals will solve all of Belgium's linguistic and community problems, but it is remarkable that within ten years of the major constitutional revision of 1967–71 Belgium seems to be within sight of a reasonable solution. And if such a solution is found, it will owe much to Leo Tindemans and the Social Christians, who have made a determined effort to tackle a very complex problem.

Conclusion

In their approach to the community problem, the Social Christians have demonstrated once again their adaptability and pragmatism: indeed, these have been the two most important characteristics of Christian Democracy in Belgium since the Second World War. The Resistance and Liberation gave Belgian Catholics a chance to reduce the overweening influence of the *standen*, to end their subservience to the Church Hierarchy in political matters, and generally to loosen their ties with conservative forces. But in transforming the 'Catholic' party into a 'Christian Democratic' party, they did not destroy their close links with *le monde catholique*, i.e. Catholic Action and the Catholic trade unions and farmers' organisations. As a result the CVP–PSC developed as a very successful *Volkspartei* a party which could help to bridge the various cleavages in Belgian society by carrying out social and economic reforms whilst at the same time remaining on good terms with the country's traditional socio-economic groups. To some extent, of course, the CVP–PSC has been fortunate, in that the political culture of Belgium – notably the long tradition of unionism, pragmatism and finding a 'middle way' – provided an ideal climate in which Christian Democracy could flourish. The tradition of *concertation* already existed, but the Social Christians developed and encouraged it, both in government (in a variety of multi-party coalitions) and in their dealings with industry and the trade unions. The practice of *concertation* and compromise has occasionally broken down, for example over the issue of the monarchy in 1950, during 'la guerre scolaire' of 1954–8, and during the violent strikes of 1960–1 and 1965. But these were exceptions to the rule. In general, Belgium's traditional religious, economic and class barriers have been steadily eroded since the war, not least thanks to the middle-of-the-road policies pursued by the Social Christians. The one cleavage, which for a time seemed unbridgeable, was that which separated the Dutch- and French-speaking communities. In the late 1960s and early 1970s it looked as if the community problem might not only destroy the traditional parties (it did, in fact, lead to all three major parties splitting into Flemish and Walloon wings), but the unity of Belgium itself. However, once again the CVP–PSC

Table 1
Belgian General Elections 1946–77[1]

	1946		1949		1950		1954		1958		1961	
	%	Seats	%	Seats	%	Seats	%	Seats	%	Seats	%	Seats
PSC–CVP (Social Christians)	42·5	92	43·5	105	47·6	108	41·1	95	46·5	104	41·4	96
PSB–BSP (Socialists)	31·5	69	29·7	66	34·5	77	37·3	86	35·7	84	36·7	84
PLP–PVV (Liberals)	8·9	17	15·2	29	11·2	20	12·1	25	11·1	21	12·3	20
PCB (Communists)	12·6	23	7·4	12	4·7	7	3·6	4	1·9	2	3·1	5
Volksunie[2]	—	—	—	—	—	—	2·2	1	2·0	1	3·6	5

	1965		1968		1971		1974		1977	
	%	Seats	%	Seats	%	Seats	%	Seats	%	Seats
PSC–CVP (Social Christians)	34·4	77	31·7	69	30·0	67	32·3	72	35·9	80
PSB–BSP (Socialists)	28·2	64	27·9	59	27·3	61	26·7	59	26·4	62
PLP–PVV (Liberals)	21·6	48	20·8	47	15·1	34	15·2	30	15·6	33
PCB (Communists)	4·5	6	3·3	5	3·1	5	3·2	4	2·7	2
Volksunie[2]	6·7	12	9·8	20	11·1	21	10·2	22	10·0	20
Rassemblement Wallon[3]	2·5	3	5·9	7	13·0	14	11·0	13	7·1	5
Front Démocratique des Francophones[3]		1		5		10		9		10

1. There are 212 seats in the Belgian House of Representatives (202 from 1946–9). Voting is compulsory.
2. *Volksunie* is the Flemish nationalist party.
3. The *Rassemblement Wallon* (RW) is the Francophone party in Wallonia. Its equivalent in Brussels is the *Front Démocratique des Francophones* (FDF). These two parties work in close liaison with each other; hence their joint percentages in the table.

Table 2
Belgian Prime Ministers and Coalitions, 1945–77

Prime Minister	Dates in Office	Parties in Government
Van Acker (Soc.)[1]	Aug. 1945–March 1946	Soc., Lib., Comm.
Spaak (Soc.)	March 1946	Soc.
Van Acker (Soc.)	March 1946–Aug. 1946	Soc., Lib., Comm.
Huysmans (Soc.)	Aug. 1946–March 1947	Soc., Lib., Comm.
Spaak (Soc.)	March 1947–Aug. 1949	Soc., Soc. Christian
Eyskens (Soc. Christian)	Aug. 1949–June 1950	Soc. Christian, Lib.
Duvieusart (Soc. Christian)	June 1950–Aug. 1950	Soc. Christian
Pholien (Soc. Christian)	Aug. 1950–Jan. 1952	Soc. Christian
Van Houtte (Soc. Christian)	Jan. 1952–April 1954	Soc. Christian
Van Acker (Soc.)	April 1954–June 1958	Soc., Lib.
Eyskens (Soc. Christian)	June 1958–Nov. 1958	Soc. Christian
Eyskens (Soc. Christian)	Nov. 1958–Sept. 1960	Soc. Christian, Lib.
Eyskens (Soc. Christian)	Sept. 1960–April 1961	Soc. Christian, Lib.
Lefèvre (Soc. Christian)	April 1961–July 1965	Soc. Christian, Soc.
Harmel (Soc. Christian)	July 1965–March 1966	Soc. Christian, Soc.
Vanden Boeynants (Soc. Christian)	March 1966–June 1968	Soc. Christian, Lib.
Eyskens (Soc. Christian)	June 1969–Jan. 1972	Soc. Christian, Soc.
Eyskens (Soc. Christian)	Jan. 1972–Jan. 1973	Soc. Christian, Soc.
Leburton (Soc.)	Jan. 1973–April 1974	Soc., Soc. Christian, Lib.
Tindemans (Soc. Christian)	April 1974–June 1977	Soc. Christian, Lib., R.W.
Tindemans (Soc. Christian)	June 1977–Oct. 1978	Soc. Christian, Soc., FDF, *Volksunie*

1.   Provisional Government.

demonstrated its adaptability, pragmatism and determination, as it struggled forward towards an acceptable solution – a typically Belgian, and, it should be emphasised, typically Christian Democratic compromise solution. Thus, by the late 1970s the Social Christians appeared not only to have turned the electoral tide after several lean years, but also to have found an answer to the community problem – an answer which recognises that, whilst 'la Belgique de papa est morte', 'la Belgique unie' is not.

Luxembourg: postscript
The Grand Duchy of Luxembourg has a population of just over 350,000, of whom over 90 per cent are Catholics. The Grand Duchy's Christian Democratic party, the *Parti Chrétien Social* (PCS), has been the dominant party since the Second World War. Regularly polling approximately one-third of the votes cast, the PCS easily outdistanced both the Socialists and the Liberals (Conservatives), until in the mid 1960s the Socialists began to win almost as many votes as the Christian Democrats. At the 1974 general election the Socialists out-polled the Christian Democrats for the first time (29 per cent to 28 per cent) and formed a coalition with the Liberals who had moved

towards the centre of the political spectrum, having for long been regarded as a rather right-wing party. The Socialist-Liberal coalition formed by Gaston Thorn in 1974 meant that for the first time since the war (indeed since 1919) Luxembourg did not have a Christian Democratic Prime Minister and Christian Democratic-dominated government. Nevertheless, the PCS remained the largest single party in the Chamber of Deputies (having eighteen seats to the Socialists' seventeen) and a major force in Luxembourg politics. Between 1947–1974 Luxembourg had Christian Democratic/Liberal coalitions for fifteen years and Christian Democratic/Socialist coalitions for thirteen years. All the Prime Ministers during those years were Christian Democrats: Pierre Dupong from 1947–54; Joseph Bech, 1954–8; Pierre Frieden, 1958–9; and Pierre Werner, 1959–74.

Luxembourg: Elections to the Chamber of Deputies (seats by each party)

	1946	1948[1]	1951[1]	1954	1959	1964	1968	1974
Christian Social	25	22	21	26	21	22	21	18
Socialist	11	14	18	17	17	21	18	17
Liberal	9	9	8	6	11	6	11	14
Communist	5	5	4	3	3	5	6	5
Others[2]	1	1	1	—	—	2	—	5
Total	51	51	52	52	52	56	56	59

1. In 1948 and 1951 only half the seats were up for election.
2. Apart from an Independent returned in 1946, 1948 and 1951, the 'others' have been 2 extreme-right deputies returned in 1964 and 5 Social Democrats returned in 1974 (in 1971 the Socialist Party had split, when a minority of right-wing members left it to form the Social Democratic Party).

6
Christian Democracy in the Netherlands

Whereas in Belgium by the 1970s Christian Democracy had well-established roots in the form of the Social Christian Party (CVP–PSC), in the Netherlands Christian Democracy was a relatively new political phenomenon, at least in terms of there being a single Christian Democratic party or even a loose federation of religious parties. It is true that for long there had been confessional or religious political parties in the Netherlands – indeed they played a predominant role in the political system from 1917–67, and participated in the European Union of Christian Democrats.[1] Yet the war and Liberation did not transform the Dutch party system as it did that of Belgium – with one exception, namely that the Labour Party became a very much more moderate Social Democratic party under the leadership of Willem Drees than it had been before the war. The confessional parties – the Catholic People's Party (*Katholieke Volkspartij*, KVP), and the two Protestant parties, the Anti-Revolutionary Party (*Anti-Revolutionaire Partij*, ARP) and Christian Historical Union (*Christelijk-Historische Unie*, CHU) – at first remained much as they had been in the 1920s and 1930s, in that they continued to articulate the political views of their own 'pillar' within society, but did not really attempt to become broad-based, deconfessionalised *Volksparteien* like the Christian Democratic parties of Germany or Belgium. In a sense, of course, the KVP, ARP and CHU were already inter-class parties, because their support (especially that of the KVP and ARP) came from practising Catholics and Protestants of all social classes. Moreover, their political objective was not merely to defend the religious interests of their voters – the Schools Pact of 1917 saved the Netherlands from *une guerre scolaire à la française* – but rather to look after the general interests of their social 'pillar'. And it should be emphasised that the three main 'pillars' (*zuilen*) played – and continue to play – a major part in Dutch society, if decreasingly so in politics: there are still Catholic, Protestant and 'neutral' trade unions, employers associations, agricultural organisations, and clubs of all sorts – even radio and television programmes continue to be specifically sponsored and controlled by one or other of the 'pillars'.[2]

This 'pillarised' society continued to be very much the norm until the late 1960s. But it depended on discipline and cohesion within the 'pillars', and 'accommodation' at the top by the political leaders of these 'pillars', for without accommodation and compromise no governmental coalitions could be formed, as none of the three pillars could hope to win an absolute majority at an election, especially after the introduction of proportional representation in 1917. However, it should be noted that pillarisation *preceded* proportional representation: the electoral system reflected the politico-religious divisions of the Dutch nation – it did not create them.[3] The leaders of the pillars wielded considerable authority, and their followers did not question that authority, that is until the mid 1960s, when the postwar generation started to criticise the system. The new generation began to ask why it should accept without question the political wisdom of its elders, and as a result young militants demanded internal 'democratisation' within the parties, which had hitherto been run by co-opted cliques of notables. They also demanded that the parties should draw up programmes and make their ideological position clear *before* elections, so that the voters could choose the government at the ballot-box rather than the party leaders choosing it behind closed doors after the election.

The political and social ferment of the late 1960s and early 1970s shook the traditional Dutch party system in much the same way as the community problem partially undermined the political stability of Belgium. But in the Dutch case, and particularly in so far as the confessional parties were concerned, the repercussions were more far-reaching. In the context of this book, the key development of recent years has been the formation of a genuine Christian Democratic movement in the Netherlands for the first time, namely Christian Democratic Appeal (*Christen Democratisch Appel*, CDA), which was formally constituted in 1976 by the Catholic People's Party, the Anti-Revolutionary Party and the Christian Historical Union in time to fight the 1977 general election as a Christian Democratic 'federation' comparable to the Christian Democratic Union in West Germany or the Social Christian Party in Belgium. In order to understand why it took so long for a Christian Democratic 'federation' (it is still not correct to call it a party)[4] to be formed in the Netherlands – a country in which religious parties have played a predominant role in the political system for almost a century – it is necessary to comment briefly on the unique (and the word is not an exaggeration) nature of the Dutch political system. The confessional, or perhaps 'embryo Christian Democratic', parties, will then be analysed prior to an assessment of the importance of the newly formed Christian Democratic Appeal.

The Dutch Political System

For fifty years from 1917–1967 there was a remarkable degree of political and party stability in the Netherlands. Five parties dominated the system: on the Left the Socialists (known as the Labour Party, PVDA, since 1945) regularly polled about one quarter of the votes; in the Centre the three 'confessional' parties, i.e. the precursors of today's Christian Democrats, usually polled over 50 per cent – the Catholic Party 30 per cent plus, and the two Protestant parties (Anti-Revolutionaries and Christian Historicals) 15 per cent plus; and on the Right, the Liberals (i.e. Conservatives in British terms) polled about 10 per cent. Despite proportional representation, based in effect on one national constituency,[5] the various small parties which competed at elections made little or no impression.[6] In 1922 the six major parties (the five mentioned above plus the left-of-centre Radical-Democrat party) won ninety-four of the hundred seats in the Second Chamber (the Lower House of the Dutch Parliament); in 1937, despite the effects of the depression and the deteriorating international situation, they still won eighty-nine. And after the upheavals of the Second World War, the five successors of the above-mentioned parties still won eighty-eight out of the hundred seats (ten others went to the Communists) in 1946. Until 1967 the 'traditional five' continued to poll about 90 per cent of the votes and win about 90 per cent of the seats.[7]

The Netherlands carried through major economic and social reforms after the war, but the country continued to have one of the most conservative and stable electorates in Europe. Then quite suddenly in the mid 1960s the electorate's faith in the traditional parties began to decline – a rash of new parties made a psychologically important, if numerically quite small, impact on the party system, and by 1972 the 'traditional five' polled only 73 per cent, the confessional parties having been particularly badly hit by the electorate's new-found volatility.[8] In 1977 the traditional parties recovered some of their strength in polling 83·7 per cent, but the Dutch party system had been profoundly affected. The cliché sometimes used to describe these developments – 'from pillarisation to polarisation' – may have been rather simplistic, but it certainly contained an element of truth: there was distinct evidence of the development of 'tri-polarisation', centred on the Labour Party, the Christian Democrats and the Liberals. The main casualty of this polarisation, or move towards 'bloc' politics, was the Catholic People's Party, for long the largest single party in the Lower House (almost without a break from 1918–71), but the other 'confessional' parties were adversely affected too, because, as centre parties, their *raison d'être* depended to a large extent on the avoidance of ideological commitment: they had to leave their options open with a view to negotiating alliances either with the Labour Party or with the Liberals, but by behaving in this way they exposed themselves to criticism for their indecision and ideological 'weakness'.[9]

In historical terms, what is surprising is that the confessional parties did not have to face up to the challenge of the decade 1967–77 sooner. The reason for this is complex, but is connected with the political and social development of the Netherlands, as well as with the nature of the three parties in question. Some comment on the historical background is therefore essential at this juncture.

In no other Western Europe country was political, cultural and religious segmentation as marked as in the Netherlands in the seventeenth and eighteenth centuries. The Dutch Republic was a very loose confederation, in which various provinces, headed by their regents, had a remarkable degree of autonomy: they had their own legal and monetary systems, their own taxation, even their own naval forces (for example that of the city of Amsterdam). Holland, of course, as the richest and most powerful province, tended to play a predominant role in the confederation. But the Netherlands only began to develop a centralised state structure during the French occupation from 1795–1813, and more especially under King William I (1813–40). Moreover, despite the setting up of new central government machinery under William I, the old political, cultural and religious segmentation continued as before. The provinces were still run by the old families and traditional oligarchies, and within the provinces fairly strict demarcation continued between religious and social groups. The result was that when political parties began to develop in the late nineteenth century they were marked by – indeed controlled by – those segments of society whose views they articulated and represented. Thus, Dutch parties, and especially the confessional parties, which were 'super-imposed' on particularly well-disciplined social 'pillars', developed in a way which made adaptation to postwar (i.e. post-1945) conditions unusually difficult.

Whilst Christian Democratic parties were emerging as mass political move-ments in other parts of Europe, in the Netherlands they still seemed out of place: certainly, the leaders of the Calvinist and Catholic pillars were willing to 'accommodate' and co-operate, but neither they nor their followers were prepared to consider merging their political parties into an inter-confessional movement like the Catholic-Protestant German Christian Democratic Union. In any case, this seemed unnecessary to the Dutch confessional parties, which had co-operated quite closely and effectively for over fifty years without merging. Indeed, one of the main reasons for the late development of modern-style Christian Democracy in the Netherlands was that the Calvinists and Catholics – in spite of their very different religious views – had for long formed coalitions against the Liberals in order to achieve and maintain treat-ment for confessional schools equal to that provided for the state schools.[10] This equality was finally achieved in 1917. But, having won their battle over education, the 'confessionals' neither split nor drew closer together: they could dominate the political system without doing either, as long as the Netherlands remained a stable, though segmented, society, and provided the pillars remained loyal to their political élites.

Before discussing the pivotal role of the confessional parties between 1917–67, and how this role inhibited the development of a single Christian Democratic movement, a brief comment must be made on the three confes-sional parties.

The Protestant Parties

Like the *Parti Catholique* in Belgium, the first organised religious party in the Netherlands, the Protestant Anti-Revolutionary Party (*Anti-Revolutionaire Partij*, ARP), was formed in protest against Liberal schools legislation. In the Dutch case it was the schools law of 1878, which, whilst endorsing the constitutional principle that the state had a duty to provide free 'neutral education', laid down that those citizens who wished to send their children to specifically religious schools would have to pay for the privilege. Out of the schools' petition movement, founded in 1878 to protest against this legislation, the Anti-Revolutionary Party was born. It was the first Dutch political party to have a national organisation and national programme, the latter endorsed at a special congress held in April 1879. The party's full title was (and is) *Anti-Revolutionaire Partij, Evangelische Volkspartij*, and the second part is as important as the first, because the ARP has always emphasised its evangelical vocation and been an inter-class 'people's party'. Most of its supporters belong to the *Gereformeerde Kerk*, which is more fundamentally Calvinist than the largest Dutch Protestant Church, the *Nederlands Hervormde Kerk*. The party always received the majority of its support in the north, particularly in the strongly Protestant provinces of Friesland and Groningen, but it was also traditionally *the* party of the Protestant lower middle classes, the so-called 'Kleine Luyden' ('small people'), i.e. shopkeepers, artisans and smallholders. The party was 'Anti-Revolutionary', not because it was opposed to economic and social reforms, but because it was opposed to the humanist, anti-clerical doctrines of the French Revolution. The founder of the ARP was Guillaume Groen van Prinsterer, a strict Calvinist who believed that the Netherlands should be governed on Christian principles; and to this day the ARP expects its members of parliament to be prepared openly to profess their Christian faith.[11]

The ARP concentrated its early energies on schools policy. Groen van Prinsterer, an idealist rather than a practical man of politics, seems even to have hoped that all state schools might be run on strictly Protestant lines, but it soon became apparent that this objective had no chance of fulfilment, and the Anti-Revolutionaries began to co-operate with the Catholics (still not organised as a specific political party) to obtain fair subsidies for all schools run on religious principles, of whatever confession. Groen van Prinsterer's successor, Abraham Kuyper (1837–1920), was a gifted organiser and leader, as well as being a distinguished Protestant intellectual. It was Kuyper who built up the party's organisation, and by 1901 the confessional parties had a clear majority in the Second Chamber (Lower House of Parliament) with fifty-eight seats out of a hundred (there were thirty-five Liberals and seven Socialists after the 1901 election). Between 1888–91, 1901–5, and 1908–13 the Netherlands was governed by confessional coalitions, approximately half of whose members were Protestants and half Catholics.

However, after 1894 the Protestants were divided, for in that year A. F. de Savorinin Lohman (1827–1924), together with a small group of politically conservative friends – they were opposed to any further extension of the franchise – left the ARP, and in 1908 they (and their successors) set up the Christian Historical Union (*Christelijk-Historische Unie*, CHU). The two Protestant parties always co-operated closely, but the CHU was smaller, less organised, and more conservative. However, there has always been much 'cross fertilisation' between the two parties, and in 1977, for example, the President of the CHU was a member of the *Gereformeerde Kerk*, the more 'orthodox' – or fundamentalist – branch of the Protestant Church, whose members traditionally voted for the ARP.[12] By 1977 the CHU had approximately 30,000 members to 60,000 in the ARP.[13]

Hans Daalder's analysis of the two parties (made in 1955) is still worth quoting, although it is not wholly apposite to the situation in the late 1970s:

It is still extremely difficult to explain to foreigners what a world of difference lies between the adherents of these two parties. The Christian-Historicals insist more strongly on the positive Calvinist character of the State, but are opposed less strongly to 'pagan' elements and are thus potentially less isolationist; they will give the government of the day either active co-operation or the benefit of the doubt. The Anti-Revolutionaries, on the other hand, are more militant, more of a *parti de masse*, and more sternly against non-Calvinists, although they tend to insist less that the State should be positively Calvinist and to assert rather the doctrine of 'spheres of sovereignty'.[14]

Since Daalder made these comments both parties have changed somewhat under the impact of the major social changes in the 1960s. Their commitment to particular Calvinist positions, for example, has mellowed: the CHU of the 1970s is essentially a conservative political party with a broad commitment to 'Christian principles' in politics, but it no longer requires its members of parliament to 'profess' their Christian faith. The ARP, however, takes its Calvinism rather more seriously, not only in terms of its requirements that its members of parliament should be prepared to confess their faith and to implement 'Biblical principles' in politics, but also in its strong emphasis on social and economic justice. Indeed, the ARP went through a period of fairly radical ideological ferment and self-questioning in the 1960s, and emerged in the 1970s as a progressive, almost 'Social Christian' party (if that traditionally Catholic epithet is not inappropriate in describing such a strongly Protestant party as the ARP).

Amongst the postwar leaders of the ARP, and particularly among the young people of academic background from the Free (Calvinist) University of Amsterdam, there are many who hold progressive views on social and economic questions as well as on foreign policy. The ARP, therefore, finds it quite natural to co-operate in government with the Labour Party: in the first Joop den Uyl government, for example, from 1973–7 the ARP participated as a full member, whereas the more conservative CHU refused to join the coalition although in practice it supported it. Since 1969 a majority within the ARP has advocated closer co-operation between the three confessional parties, although some of the more orthodox Calvinists had doubts about the wisdom of fusing with the Catholics and the more open-minded Christian Historicals.[15] However, on 23 June, 1973 the ARP voted by a large majority in favour of the setting up of the Christian Democratic Appeal, i.e. for the eventual amalgamation of the three confessional parties. The Christian Historicals, after their electoral setback of 1972, also voted for fusion, although as the smaller, less organised of the two Protestant parties they also had some doubts about the wisdom of taking this step, fearing the preponderant influence of the Anti-Revolutionaries and Catholics in the new Christian Democratic organisation.[16]

The Anti-Revolutionary Party has had a remarkably consistent electoral record since the war, always polling 8–13 per cent of the votes cast at general elections and returning between ten and fifteen members of parliament.[17]

The Christian Historical Union, on the other hand, after a long period of electoral stability, was badly hit by 'deconfessionalisation' and the general decline of 'religious politics', its poll declining from 8·1 per cent in 1967 to 6·3 per cent in 1971, and then to 4·8 per cent in 1972. By the last date it had only seven deputies, compared with thirteen after the general elections of 1956 and 1963. Perhaps one of the main reasons for the continuing success of the ARP was that it remained a highly organised party compared with the CHU, which was little more than a loose electoral alliance. In 1977, for example, the ARP still had 850 local associations with over 60,000 members.[18] The next 'layer' of the party's organisation consists of the sixty-five provincial constituency associations, above which were the eighteen national constituency associations. All three of these 'local' bodies send delegates to the national congress, whose five hundred delegates meet twice a year to debate party policy, and elect (every two years) approximately half the members of the party's national council (in addition eighteen are elected by the national constituency associations and six others by the subsidiary organisations, e.g. the women's association and seamen's association). In addition the party has a small 'daily' executive committee (the *Dagelijks Bestuur*) of fifteen and a praesidium, consisting of the president, vice-president and two or three other senior members of the party. The executive committee and praesidium both play a key part at elections by endorsing or rejecting the party lists submitted by the eighteen constituency associations. Finally, the party secretariat is at the service of these national organisations, as also is the Kuyper Foundation which finances political research. Altogether, the ARP seems to be an impressively organised party.

In contrast, the Christian Historical Union – on the admission of its own Secretary – has a weak organisation.[19] It has a small national secretariat, but the party is essentially a 'union of electoral committees': the representatives of these committees meet at the constituency level in the run-up to national elections and select candidates for the party lists. This method of candidate selection, of course, means that the CHU has a right to claim that it is a more 'democratic' party than the ARP, but the CHU's lack of structure also ensures that it is very vulnerable to changes in the political weather.

The Catholic Party

By the 1970s Catholics and Protestants were roughly equal in numbers in the Netherlands,[20] but for a long time the Catholics had constituted a minority, and they were concentrated largely in the two southern provinces of Limburg and North-Brabant. From the Peace of Westphalia in 1648 until the French occupation of the Netherlands (1795–1813) Catholics were treated as second-class citizens, and they developed a *laager* mentality *vis-à-vis* the Protestants of Holland and the northern provinces. The southern provinces were in fact governed almost as colonies, retaining the legal status of occupied territories (*generaliteitslanden*) until the French occupation. The main reason for this discriminatory treatment was that the northern Protestants feared that the Catholics might try to join up with the Catholic provinces of the Spanish (later Austrian) Netherlands, present-day Belgium. However, after the establishment of the independent Kingdom of the Belgians in 1830, which entailed a rebuff to the Dutch (both Catholic and Protestant) by the Belgians (both Catholic and Liberal), such a fusion was clearly impractical. The Dutch Catholics, therefore, began to strive for full emancipation and equality within their own country. However, it took a considerable time before they developed an effective political organisation.

As a result of the constitutional amendments of 1840 Dutch Catholics acquired full political rights, but, as in Belgium, the Catholics at first decided to work in liaison with the Liberals. A small number of Catholics formed an independent party, but it failed disastrously at the 1848 election, when the vast majority of Catholics aligned themselves behind Thorbecke's Liberals, giving the Liberals an unprecedented electoral triumph. However, partly owing to Calvinist pressure, the Liberals in practice did little for the Catholics (except for restoring the episcopal hierarchy in 1853), and when the Liberals, in common with Liberals in other European countries, began to lay greater emphasis on state education in the 1850s and 1860s, the Catholics broke with them. In 1868 the first Catholic electoral association was formed with the express purpose of electing deputies to defend the rights of Catholic schools.[21] This was followed in 1870 with the setting up of the first genuinely political Catholic organisation, the '*Roomsch-Katholieke Kiesvereniging Noord-Brabant*', presided over by J. B. Van Son. The setting up of the North Brabant electoral organisation really marked the final break in political co-operation between the Catholics and the Liberals, and from the 1870s the Catholics began to work with an unexpected bedfellow, the Calvinist Anti-Revolutionary Party, over the issue of 'free schools'. This 'marriage of convenience' of the early 1870s developed into a close political liaison after the Liberal schools law of 1878 had cut the subsidy to the 'free schools'. In 1888 the religious parties won a decisive electoral victory, and then formed the first of a series of confessional party coalitions.[22] The schools problem was really solved in 1889 with the passage of a law enshrining the principle of equality between public and private education, and this law was formally endorsed in 1917.

Despite their arrival in government the Catholics did not organise themselves into a proper political party for almost another forty years. At first many Catholics believed they should participate only in social activities (in charitable organisations, for example), but not directly in politics. Moreover, they were very much divided between conservatives and progressives. In the 1880s and 1890s the former, led by Bahlmann, predominated: they were opposed to state intervention of any sort, and wanted to keep Catholic political involvement to a minimum after the schools victory of 1889. The progressives, led by Father Herman Schaepman (1844–1903), the first priest to be elected to the Second Chamber (in 1880), began to increase their influence after the publication of *Rerum Novarum* in 1891, and Schaepman was largely responsible for the first Catholic political programme, published in 1897.[23] Seven years later (in 1904) the Catholics established a nationwide electoral organisation, the *Algemeene Bond van Roomsch-Katholieke Kiesverenigingen in Nederland*. This loose confederation of electoral associations remained the main Catholic political structure until 1926. It was not possible to join the confederation directly, although its constituent parts, i.e. the electoral associations, recruited members. Moreover, the electoral associations retained complete freedom in their choice of candidates for the electoral lists. However, there was a rudimentary central organisation in the form of the national committee, consisting of five representatives of the electoral associations. And in Parliament the Catholic deputies had their own political group, the *Roomsch-Katholieke Kamerclub*.

Some progressive Catholics wanted to form a proper political party towards the end of the First World War, but the Hierarchy was still opposed to this and forbade the setting up of the proposed 'Social Catholic Party' in February 1918.[24] However, after the adoption of universal suffrage (1917 for men, 1922 for women) and proportional representation (1917), the pressures in favour of a national political party rapidly increased, and in 1926 the Roman Catholic State Party (*Roomsch-Katholieke Staatspartij*, RKSP) was founded.[25] Its organisation was based on that of the *Algemeene Bond van Roomsch-Katholieke Kiesverenigingen*, but there were two important differences between the old confederation of electoral associations and the new party. In the first place it was possible to become an individual member of the RKSP, and in the second place a national congress was introduced.[26] This national congress – known as the 'general assembly' (*Partijraad*) – was in fact more of a mini-parliament of the Catholic world than purely an RKSP congress. It consisted of representatives of the electoral associations, representatives of the various Catholic social organisations (women's groups, youth groups, trade unions, etc.), and all the Catholic members of the two houses of Parliament. This general assembly of approximately a hundred delegates met annually and elected a five-man bureau (modelled on that of the *Algemeene Bond*) for a four-year term. After 1934 the president of the party was elected by the general assembly on the proposal of the bureau. The RKSP's nationwide organisation was based on local sections with their own elected assemblies (from 1934), and constituency electoral associations (comparable to those of the *Algemeene Bond*). The constituency associations also elected their own assemblies, which continued to play the key role in the selection of parliamentary candidates in spite of the RKSP's more centralised organisation compared with that of the *Algemeene Bond*. The RKSP remained very much a confessional party, with its statutes emphasising that its main objective was to defend Catholic interests by political means.

The postwar successor of the RKSP was the Catholic People's Party (*Katholieke Volkspartij*, KVP), founded in December 1945, when the RKSP general assembly voted to change its organisation, nature and name. In particular the general assembly decided to strengthen the new party's central organisation, to play down its clerical connections, and generally to present itself as a more progressive party. Whilst in large measure it succeeded in its first and third objectives, in the second it failed, for *nolens volens* the KVP remained essentially a Catholic confessional party.[27] Its statutes proclaimed that it was no longer necessary to be a Catholic to join the KVP, and the party appealed to non-Catholics 'of all classes' to vote for it. But all the evidence indicates that it failed to break out of the Catholic 'ghetto'. All KVP members of parliament from 1946–77 were Catholics,[28] and it has been estimated that 98 per cent of the party's voters up to 1963 were Catholics.[29] Up to 1959 approximately 90 per cent of Catholics voted for the KVP,[30] but in the 1960s, as the influence of organised religion generally, and of the Catholic 'pillar' in particular, declined, Catholics began to vote for other parties in large numbers. However, so long as the Catholic 'pillar' remained loyal to the KVP, the party polled, extremely well. At every election from 1946–67 it outdistanced its nearest rival, the Labour Party (except for 1952 when both parties won thirty seats and 1956, when the Labour Party won fifty seats to the KVP's forty-nine).[31] But in the decade 1963–72 approximately half the Catholic electorate deserted the KVP (its vote declined from 31·9 per cent to 17·7 per cent in this period), the majority of deserters going over to the Labour Party, whilst some conservative Catholics opted for the Liberal Party (and a few for the ultra-conservative Roman Catholic Party of the Netherlands). Meanwhile, the most progressive Catholics of all tended to vote for the Radical Party, which was founded in 1968 and reached its electoral peak in 1972 when it polled almost 5 per cent of the votes cast. Indeed, the obverse of what the KVP originally hoped for had occurred: instead of non-Catholics opting for the KVP, Catholics had opted for other parties. In other words the KVP had failed to transform itself into a Christian Democratic party in the sense of a party which appealed to those who sympathised with 'Christian principles' in politics, but who were not themselves Catholics. The result of this failure was that the KVP became in the late 1960s the most enthusiastic proponent (of the three confessional parties) of the formation of a broad-based Christian Democratic party – the future Christian Democratic Appeal. Even by the early 1960s the KVP's failure to broaden its appeal was apparent. As Robert Bone commented in 1962:

> In December 1945, the then Roman Catholic State Party changed its name to the Catholic People's Party and went through the motions of turning itself into a Christian Democratic Party. But neither in terms of politics nor of electoral support has there been any noticeable difference between the pre- and post-war period, and the party has continued as the political spokesman of the Catholic 'camp' in the Netherlands.[32]

As regards its organisation, the KVP modelled itself on the RKSP, but the party's central organs were strengthened in comparison with those of the RKSP. As before the war, there were local sections at the commune level and eighteen constituency organisations (one for each constituency into which the Netherlands is divided),[33] and, as with the RKSP, the sections and constituency organisations had their own general assemblies which elected bureaux. Party membership reached 409,000 in 1948, and, after declining to 257,000 four years later, rose to a peak of 430,000 in 1955, a year after the Hierarchy had appealed to Catholics to maintain their solidarity and to avoid joining Socialist trade unions or voting for the Labour Party. But by 1960 membership had declined to 385,000, and thereafter the decline was dramatic: in 1965 there were only 218,000 members, whilst twelve years later there were no more than about 60,000.[34]

The KVP national general assembly was similar to that of the RKSP, but the party bureau was increased in size to nine (the RKSP's had had five members) and in 1955 to fifteen. Three developments strengthened the national organs' control over the party. Firstly, a new body called the electoral council was set up. Consisting of the party bureau, together with eighteen 'distinguished public figures' nominated by the bureau (in practice KVP ministers and leaders of the parliamentary party) and eighteen representatives of the Catholic electoral associations (one per constituency), the electoral council made the final decision about the KVP lists to be presented in each constituency at elections. In the prewar period this decision had been left to the electoral assocations, whereas in the postwar period the electoral associations could only present their proposed lists to the electoral council. Although, in practice, the electoral council made relatively few changes to the lists proposed to it, the fact that its decisions were binding greatly strengthened the party's central organisation.[35] Secondly, another new body was established, namely the national congress – not to be confused with the general assembly. Each year the congress, consisting of representatives of the sections and constituency associations, would meet six months before the general assembly (which normally convened in September) and put forward proposals to the central bureau. Whilst in theory this development might appear to have augmented the influence of the sections and constituency associations, in practice the bureau had time to 'mould' the congress's proposals before they were put to the general assembly, thus increasing the influence of the party's national organs over its local associations.[36] Thirdly, a central organisation for political training and research was established in August 1945, the *Centrum voor Staatkundige Vorming*. Although the *Centrum* sometimes drew up rather independent reports, and maintained contacts outside the KVP, e.g. with the Catholic working-group in the Labour Party, its main role was to train party workers and to act as the party's information centre. Like the other two organs discussed above, it undoubtedly helped to make the KVP a more centralised party than its predecessor, the RKSP. In addition, over thirty full-time officials were employed by the KVP at its national headquarters, compared with fewer than ten before the war.

Sociologically the KVP remained an inter-class party, although the majority of its support (just over 50 per cent according to a 1963 survey) came from the middle classes, followed by 21 per cent from farmers and small-scale entrepreneurs, 11 per cent from workers, 9 per cent from professional classes, senior civil servants and senior managers, whilst 8 per cent were without classification.[37] The party could also rely on the support of the main Catholic Action organisations, the *Federatie van Bonden van Gemeenteraadsleden in Nederland* (the federation of commune officials), the *Federatie van R.K. Vrouwenbonden* (the federation of women's organisations), and the *Jongeren-organisatie* (the young people's organisation). However, the party's young people's organisation, like the KVP itself, suffered a massive loss of membership in the 1960s and 1970s. In the immediate postwar period the *Jongeren-organisatie* claimed 100,000 members; by 1977 there were about one-tenth of that number. Finally, until the 1960s the KVP could rely on the support of most members of the Catholic trade union confederation (the NKV), whereas in the 1970s most NKV members preferred to vote Labour. Moreover, by 1977 the Socialist and Catholic trade union confederations appeared to be on the verge of amalgamating, providing evidence of the continuing decline of 'pillar-isation', a development which could only be unwelcome to traditionalists in the KVP.[38]

The Role of the Confessional Parties in Dutch Politics, 1917–77

From 1917 to 1959 the three confessional parties controlled a majority in the Second Chamber of the Dutch Parliament. With the exception of a fortnight in 1939 the Catholics were in government throughout that time, whilst the Christian Historicals only had a short break from 1946–8, and the Anti-Revolutionaries a slightly longer one from 1946–52.[39] But even in the days when they held an absolute majority the confessional parties usually preferred to widen the basis of their coalitions: certainly in the 1930s coalitions normally included the Liberals and Radical-Democrats (as well as the confessionals), whilst in the period from 1946–58 all governments were essentially 'Roman-Red', i.e. the main parties of government were the Catholic People's Party and the Labour Party. In 1959 the confessional parties lost their absolute majority in the Chamber (they held exactly half the seats with seventy-five). In 1963 they regained a bare majority (seventy-six), but after that year lost their hegemonic position (69 seats in 1967, 58 in 1971, 48 in 1972 and 49 in 1977). However, they continued to play a key pivotal role, sometimes governing with the Labour Party and sometimes with the Liberals. But the price for this 'fickleness' was a loss of identity, causing internal conflicts within all three confessional parties, and a reduction of electoral support. These factors, when combined with the catalytic effect of rapid social change, led to ever-increasing demands for the fusion of the confessional parties into a Christian Democratic, or centrist, bloc.

Although the confessional parties polled no worse in the 1930s than they had done in the 1920s, from 1933 they widened their coalition majority to include the Liberals and Radical Democrats (and finally in August 1939 the Socialists joined the coalition as well to form a 'government of national union' – the first time Socialists had entered a Dutch government). The interesting question is why the confessional parties decided to widen the coalition in 1933, when they actually had the support of a majority of the deputies in the Second Chamber. In 1918 Ruijs de Beerenbrouck, the first Catholic prime minister of the Netherlands, had formed a government with a similar majority, whereas in 1933 the Anti-Revolutionary leader, Hendrikus Colijn, formed a government which included Liberals and Radical Democrats as well as Catholics and Christian Historicals. The main reason for this change seems to have been that the confessional parties wanted a wider-based coalition to cope with the difficult economic and social problems of the depression years. In any case, what mattered was that an important new precedent had been set: the confessionals had shown that they were willing to form coalitions with other parties even when there was no need for them to do so. The wartime governments in exile in London further eroded the traditional differences between the parties, or at least between their élites, as did the Resistance. The result was that in the immediate postwar period the Catholics and Socialists were prepared to let bygones be bygones and govern together.

The postwar Labour Party, led by Willem Drees, was in fact a very moderate Social Democratic party. At the same time the Catholic People's Party adopted a more progressive posture than the prewar RKSP. So it was not surprising that in February 1946 the KVP proposed to the Labour Party that they should present a joint programme for reconstruction. The Socialists rejected the proposal, because they expected to outdistance the Catholics at the forthcoming general election. This expectation was not fulfilled, although the Socialists polled better than ever before, winning twenty-nine seats to the KVP's thirty-two. However, the significant point was that the Catholics should even have proposed a joint programme: in the prewar period such a proposal would have been inconceivable, as most Socialists were (wrongly) considered to be 'Marxist atheists' by the conservative leaders of the RKSP.

The 'Roman-Red' coalition lasted until 1958, but from 1948 other coalition partners were always included, although, as was the case with the confessional-based governments of the 1930s, other parties were not strictly speaking necessary from the point of view of forming a parliamentary majority. However, the KVP always preferred to include other parties to balance the influence of the Labour Party. From 1948–52 the Christian Historicals and Liberals participated in the first and second Drees governments, and from 1952–8 the Anti-Revolutionaries replaced the Liberals in the third, fourth and fifth Drees governments, whilst the Christian Historicals continued to participate in government.[40] In view of developments in other European countries in the immediate postwar period, it may seem surprising that no attempt was made to form a unified Christian Democratic party in the Netherlands at this time. There were at least three reasons why this did not happen. In the first place, it is important to remember that the southern Netherlands was liberated in August-September 1944, whilst the rest of the country remained under German occupation until the spring of 1945. Political activity therefore revived in the Catholic south six months before any such activity was possible in the north, and, with the encouragement of the Hierarchy,[41] the Catholics decided to form an exclusively Catholic party once again, even if in theory it was open to non-Catholics. By the spring of 1945 the Catholics were simply not interested in the concept of an inter-confessional political party. In the second place, Dutch society – despite all the social upheavals of the war – remained remarkably 'pillarised': there was no evidence at the early postwar elections that the voters wanted to see the development of more 'ideological' parties or of 'bloc' politics.[42] Thirdly, the Catholic People's Party was in a uniquely advantageous position so long as it commanded at least one-third of the seats in the Second Chamber, for no coalition could be formed without the KVP. True, a coalition could have been formed by the Catholics with the Labour Party alone, but then the portfolios would have to have been divided on a fifty-fifty basis with perhaps an extra cabinet post for the Catholics after the 1946 and 1948 elections. Clearly it was much better for the KVP to widen the basis of the coalition by bringing in the Protestant confessional parties, or perhaps the Liberals (as between 1948–52), and balance them against the Socialists. The KVP could thus play a powerful mediatorial role in Dutch politics whilst commanding the votes of only one third of the electorate.[43] And, for as long as the voting habits of the electorate did not change, the KVP naturally showed no interest in merging with the Protestant parties to form some sort of 'Christian Democratic Union'.

However, from 1958 Dutch party politics began to change. The rising generation of Labour Party activists began to question the continuation of centrist politics and wanted to re-emphasise the Labour Party's ideological position as a party of the Left. This was the main reason why Labour broke with the confessional parties in 1958, although technically the Labour Party ministers resigned over a matter of tax legislation. That the confessional parties should form the succeeding interim government under Beel (KVP) was only to be expected, but at the 1959 general election the confessional parties lost their overall majority – they now held seventy-five seats instead of seventy-seven (out of 150). They could either have attempted to have repeated their feat of 1918–22 and governed with a near-majority, or they could bring the Liberals into the coalition (the Labour Party was not interested in a further coalition with the confessional parties at this stage). As the Liberals had gained six seats in 1959 (up from thirteen to nineteen), a confessional-Liberal coalition seemed the obvious political response to the voters' wishes, and from 1959–65 there were three such coalitions led respectively by the Catholics De Quay (two governments) and Marijnen. After gaining a seat at the 1963 general election the confessional parties could have formed a government on their own, but they chose once again to govern with the Liberals until 1965, and then briefly (from April 1965-November 1966) there was a coalition of Catholics, Anti-Revolutionaries and the Labour Party, led by Cals of the KVP.

In 1967 the confessional parties began to pay the price for their apparent fickleness. The KVP lost eight seats, with its percentage of the poll falling from 31·9 per cent to 26·5 per cent, a dramatic setback by Dutch standards. Yet, in spite of the clear evidence of the electorate's dissatisfaction with the government, another confessional-Liberal coalition was formed under De Jong of the KVP, and likewise after a further setback in 1971 (when the KVP lost seven seats, the ARP and CHU two each, and the Liberals one) yet another confessional-Liberal coalition was formed under Biesheuvel of the ARP, although this time with the addition of the Democratic Socialist Party, DS '70, which had won eight seats. This five-party coalition again lost seats at the 1972 general election: the Liberals in fact gained six seats and the Anti-Revolutionaries one, but the Catholic People's Party lost eight (with only 17·7 per cent of the votes cast it had lost half its electorate in nine years); meanwhile the Christian Historicals lost three, whilst DS '70 lost two. Finally, after a five-month governmental crisis, a coalition consisting of Labour, Democrats '66, the Radical Party, the Anti-Revolutionary Party and the Catholic People's Party was formed. Although this coalition, which lasted from 1972–7, had ARP and KVP ministers, the situation was complicated further, because the ARP and KVP parliamentary parties only 'suffered' the government rather than supporting it outright, whilst the CHU remained in opposition.

Why had the 'politics of accommodation' broken down, and what were the consequences for the confessional parties? The breakdown of the traditional party system was caused by dissatisfaction amongst a significant minority of voters right across the political spectrum during the 1960s and early 1970s, and this dissatisfaction was manifested by the mushroom growth of a number of new parties.[44] Whereas in 1959 the new party vote was only 2·5 per cent, by 1971 it was 17·0 per cent, and in 1972 it was 16·4 per cent. Thus, although the traditional parties resisted the challenge rather well – indeed after initial setbacks the Labour and Liberal Parties strengthened their position in the face of it[45] – the 'new parties phenomenon' (as Daalder labelled it)[46] had a profound effect on the political system, and especially on the confessional parties which were worst affected by it.

The first successful new party was the Farmers' Party, a Poujadist-type protest party, which won three seats in 1963 and seven in 1967; it appealed to tax protesters both in the country and in the main cities (notably in Rotterdam, Amsterdam and The Hague). The left-wing Pacifist Socialist Party, which advocated the withdrawal of The Netherlands from the Atlantic Alliance, also made considerable inroads in 1963 and 1967 (four seats at each election). But the most important new party was Democrats '66, which advocated radical changes in Dutch politics by means of constitutional and electoral reforms: in particular it wanted the parties to go to the polls on the basis of precise programmes, and then to stick to their programmes after the election; in other words D '66 wanted the *people* to choose their government rather than the *parties* (who traditionally did so after the elections). The move towards ideological politics was also strongly emphasised within the Labour Party itself by the 'New Left', a movement which more or less controlled the party between 1967–70, and thus 'provoked' into being the breakaway right-wing Democratic Socialist Party (DS '70) in 1970. This was followed by DS '70's considerable success at the 1971 and 1972 general elections.

This ideological ferment affected the confessional parties at least as much as the left-wing parties. The younger militants within all three parties, the KVP, ARP and CHU, wanted their parties to move to the left, and in particular to commit themselves to a left-wing alliance based on a definite political programme before the elections. They were aiming, in fact, at a fundamental transformation of their parties: they wanted opinions on current political issues to determine party policy, not religious convictions or 'outdated' loyalties to socio-political 'pillars'. Not surprisingly the young militants failed in their objective for the simple reason that parties like the KVP, ARP and CHU could not take up a precise position on the Left (or Right) without destroying their *raison d'être* as fulcrum parties of the centre. A number of 'Christian Radicals' (as they called themselves) refused to accept their defeat, and founded their own political party, the *Politieke Partij Radicalen* (PPR), which won almost 5 per cent of the votes cast in 1972 and seven seats in the Second Chamber.

The secession of the Radicals, who were mainly left-wing Catholics, together with the more ideological stance adopted by both the Labour and Liberal Parties under the influence of D '66, D '70, *et al*, finally forced the confessional parties to 'polarise' themselves, i.e. to face up to the necessity of forming a centrist 'pole of attraction' as the only means to prevent further erosion of their electorate.

Christian Democratic Appeal

It is as yet too early to judge the long-term significance of the formation of the first integrated Dutch Christian Democratic 'federation',[47] Christian Democratic Appeal (*Christen Democratisch Appel*, CDA) in 1976. But electoral tables 2 and 3 below make it very clear why the new federation was formed.[48] All the traditional parties lost votes in the late 1960s and at the 1971 general election, but at the general elections of 1972 and 1977 the two main non-confessional parties, the Labour Party and the Liberal Party, after openly emphasising their ideological position as the leading parties of the Left and Right, made considerable gains. In contrast, two of the three confessional parties, the Catholic People's Party and the Christian Historical Union, which had been steadily losing votes since 1963, continued their downward trend in 1972, when the Catholics lost more votes to the Labour and Radical Parties, whilst the Christian Historicals shed votes to the Liberal Party. Indeed, the KVP and CHU had lost almost half their electorates in less than ten years. Not surprisingly these two parties – particularly the KVP – were the most enthusiastic proponents of the new Christian Democratic party.

The CDA's roots go back to 1967 when the Catholic People's Party, after suffering its first major electoral reversal in the postwar period, initiated discussions with the Anti-Revolutionaries and Christian Historicals with a view to closer co-operation, leading ultimately to amalgamation. At this time the KVP was particularly keen to orientate the proposed new Christian Democratic federation to the left, fearing that if it did not, it would lose more working-class Catholics to the Labour Party, and this stance was disliked both by the conservative CHU and by the ARP, which prided itself on being an inter-class party. However, after three KVP members of parliament broke away from the party to join the newly-founded Radical Party (PPR) in 1968, the KVP became more oriented to the centre again. The first tangible sign that the 'confessional three' meant business with regard to closer co-operation occurred in 1971 when the KVP, ARP and CHU – doubtless influenced by the 'progressive three' (Labour Party, Radicals and D '66) – presented a joint electoral programme.[49] This programme was couched in very general terms compared with that of the 'progressive three', and this factor, combined with the lowering of the voting age from twenty-three to twenty-one and the ending of compulsory voting, seems to have worked against the confessional parties, whose combined vote declined from 44·5 per cent in 1967 to 36·7 per cent in 1971. The KVP, having been particularly badly hit (their poll declined from 26·5 per cent to 21·9 per cent), was reluctant to join another centre-right government under Biesheuvel, but after some hesitation did so on the understanding that it was an interim cabinet (it had only seventy-four out of the 150 seats in the Second Chamber), and that new elections would be held to clarify the political situation within a short time.

The second Biesheuvel government in fact lasted for just over a year, and then an early general election was held in November 1972. But prior to that the KVP held an important congress (in November 1971), at which Senator De Zeeuw, a strong proponent of a coalition with the 'progressive three', was elected president of the party by a large majority. Nevertheless, despite De Zeeuw's majoritarian position within the party, the KVP entered the 1972 election campaign divided. Both De Zeeuw and Andriessen, the leader of the party in the Second Chamber, favoured closer links with the Anti-Revolutionaries and Christian Historicals, but, unlike De Zeeuw, Andriessen did not wish to commit the confessionals to an alliance with the Left *prior* to the election. Meanwhile, Piet de Jong, the KVP prime minister from 1967–71 (i.e. during one of the periods of centre-right government) advocated the continuation of the Biesheuvel five-party centre-right coalition, i.e. KVP + ARP + CHU + DS '70 + Liberal Party. With the Catholic Party divided, the Christian Historicals still orientated to the Right, and the Anti-Revolutionaries remaining loyal to Biesheuvel, although basically in favour of an opening to the Left, it was not surprising that the confessional parties presented a very incoherent image of themselves at the 1972 election, even though, as in 1971, they published a joint outline programme (they also had their own manifestos to add to the confusion!).

With the voting age reduced to eighteen in 1972, and the 'progressive three' campaigning on a fairly precise programme of social and economic reforms, 'Turning Point '72', it was not surprising that the combined confessional party vote declined by another 5 per cent (to 31·3 per cent). Nor was it surprising that within a few days of the 1972 election the leaders of all three confessional parties were calling for the formation of a Christian Democratic party. The Catholic People's Party feared further losses to its Left (the left-wing Catholics of the Radical Party had just won seven seats, compared with two in 1971) and to its Right, where the new Roman Catholic Party of the Netherlands (RKPN) polled over 67,000 votes (almost 1 per cent) to win a seat. The Christian Historical vote declined from 6·3 per cent to 4·8 per cent, and the party returned three fewer members of parliament (seven compared with ten). As most of their losses almost certainly went to the Liberal Party, which gained 4 per cent (for a total of 14·4 per cent) and six seats (giving the party twenty-two in all), the Christian Historicals became less averse to moving towards the political centre than previously. Only the Anti-Revolutionaries still had doubts. Although the ARP was in some ways the most centrist of the three confessional parties owing to its inter-class electoral base, and therefore might have been expected to have been strongly in favour of a new Christian Democratic formation, this was not so, for, as the most traditionally Calvinist party, it feared that some of its voters might object to an amalgamation with the Catholic KVP. Moreover, unlike the other two confessional parties, the ARP's percentage of the poll – and hence its parliamentary representation – had been virtually unaffected by the political turmoils of the late 1960s and early 1970s: indeed, in 1972 it gained 0·2 per cent (8·8 per cent compared with 8·6 per cent) and one seat (fourteen instead of thirteen).

Although the CHU, unlike the ARP and KVP, refused to participate in the centre-left government formed by Joop Den Uyl of the Labour Party in May 1973, and the ARP continued to have doubts about the proposed merger, the leaders of the three confessional parties met in October 1973 and agreed to set up Christian Democratic Appeal (CDA). As yet there was no question of merging the three parties. In fact the CDA began life only as a 'provisional federation',[50] which would have a trial run at the 1974 provincial elections. If all went well, the three parties would consider a more permanent liaison, or 'umbrella' organisation, in the future. At the provincial elections of March 1974 CDA candidates stood in only five of the eleven provinces, and the results were inconclusive, although mildly encouraging. The two governmental parties, the KVP and ARP, lost a little ground, whilst the CHU gained fractionally. Overall the CDA vote in the five provinces totalled 30·9 per cent, compared with 31·3 per cent in 1972. As the turnout was down somewhat compared with the general election (75 per cent compared with almost 83 per cent), precise comparisons could not be made. However, the confessional parties were encouraged by their success in halting the overall decline of their vote, and all three party conferences in 1974 voted in favour of further discussions with a view to merging together under the banner of CDA. In August 1975 1300 delegates from the three parties held a joint congress for the first time, and sixteen months later at a second joint congress they agreed to fight the 1976 general election under the single banner of CDA. They elected the KVP leader in the First Chamber, Professor Steenkamp, as the first chairman of the CDA, whilst Andreas Van Agt, Deputy prime minister and Minister of Justice, was elected CDA leader in the Second Chamber.[51]

Opinion polls soon indicated that the CDA was popular with the electorate, and it seemed likely that the Christian Democrats (as they now began to be labelled) would outdistance Den Uyl's Labour Party at the forthcoming general election. Doubtless encouraged by the opinion polls, the KVP and ARP brought down the government in March 1977, and Den Uyl submitted his government's resignation eight months sooner than constitutionally necessary. The occasion for the resignation of the six KVP and ARP ministers was a government bill designed *inter alia* to prevent speculation in land needed for public use. The confessional party ministers, led by Andreas Van Agt and Alfons van der Stee of the KVP, objected in particular to the view of the 'progressive parties' (i.e. Labour, D '66 and the Radicals) that (i) financial compensation should be based on the 'use value' of the land at the time of its sale rather than, as hitherto, on its market value, and (ii) that municipal authorities should be given the right of 'first refusal' in respect of land sales. Although the ARP was more inclined towards working out a compromise solution than the KVP, the confessional parties were united in voicing the fears of many Dutch farmers and smallholders that the government's anti-speculation proposals could signal the beginning of more state ownership of land.

The general election of May 1977 was encouraging, but inconclusive, for the CDA, the new 'federation' gaining one seat compared with 1972 (forty-nine to forty-eight) and 0·6 per cent (31·9 per cent compared with 31·3 per cent). The three parties retained their traditional organisations and fought the campaign through them. But all candidates stood under the CDA label. The party lists were drawn up by an electoral committee of the three parties chaired by Janssen van Raay of the CHU. The lists were worked out on the basis of votes cast at the 1972 election, current party membership figures, and the evidence of opinion polls.[52] There were apparently no major disagreements over the balancing-up of the lists, and the upshot was that after the election the single CDA parliamentary group in the Second Chamber was composed of twenty-six KVP, thirteen ARP and ten CHU members. Later in the year the party Secretaries of the ARP and CHU claimed to have been satisfied with the election result on the grounds that it was the first general election fought by the CDA, and the new party label was still unfamiliar to some voters; moreover, it was argued, the South Moluccan train hijack and siege (which occurred towards the end of the campaign) had tended to benefit the prime minister's party, i.e. Joop Den Uyl's Labour Party.[53] The KVP was less satisfied, principally because the CDA candidates did relatively less well in Catholic areas, with the Labour Party making further gains amongst Catholic working-class voters. The CDA's electoral programme, 'Niet bij brood alleen' ('Not by bread alone') was in fact mildly progressive, emphasising *inter alia* the 'federation's' commitment to improving the 'quality of life' (i.e. a social policy which paid more attention to the problems of the handicapped, mentally sick, young workers between sixteen and twenty, and foreign workers); a more effective regional and environmental policy; a virtual halt in the constant striving for economic growth (3·5 per cent should be seen as a maximum *per annum* over the next four years); a greater percentage of GNP should be allocated to developing countries; and finally, a determined effort should be made to deal with unemployment amongst the young.[54]

Conclusion

In spite of the relative success of the CDA at the general election of 1977, and the reasonable degree of ideological unity within the federation, it is unlikely that the three confessional parties will merge fully in the near future. The party Secretaries of the KVP and CHU talked about a full merger 'within two legislatures' (i.e. within eight years); the ARP Secretary was unwilling to commit himself to a precise time scale, but clearly thought that full amalgamation might take longer.[55] Nevertheless, it is significant that all three men were talking in terms of 'when', not 'if'. Clearly this in itself is a major development. Nevertheless, it should be remembered that all three confessional parties have long traditions and have retained their own organisations. Moreover, the CDA can still take no decisions without the approval of its constituent parties,[56] and by the end of 1978 the CDA did not have its own headquarters (its secretariat being still housed in the ARP's headquarters in Kuyperstraat in The Hague).

The Catholics remained the most enthusiastic advocates of a full and rapid merger (by the 1981 election, they hoped), but this was not surprising in view of the KVP's electoral losses between 1963–77, whilst the pending amalgamation of the Catholic and Socialist trade union confederations seemed likely to diminish the support of the Catholic working classes for the KVP further. The Catholics, in addition, were not worried about being 'dominated' by the Protestants in the CDA, still having over twice as many members of parliament as either of the Protestant groups and an overall majority *vis-à-vis* the Protestants in combination (twenty-six KVP to thirteen ARP and ten CHU). The Christian Historicals also expressed a strong interest in moving towards an integrated Christian Democratic party, but the CHU party Secretary emphasised the 'absolute necessity' of keeping a fair balance within the CDA, or else the CHU might be swamped by the two larger, more organised parties.[57] After the 1977 general election it was agreed that the bureau of the CDA parliamentary group would have three KVP members and two each from the ARP and CHU. Likewise, the leading positions in the group were appropriately balanced, with a KVP chairman and ARP and CHU vice-chairmen. The CHU Secretary considered that this 'balancing' should be institutionalised, not formally in the CDA Statutes, but by conventions ('gentlemen's agreements', as he put it).[58] However, such conventions could only be institutionalised as an accepted code of practice over a considerable period of time. The ARP Secretary voiced similiar fears.[59] In addition, he pointed out that the Anti-Revolutionaries had a particular ethos of their own: they wanted to emphasise their determination to apply 'Biblical principles' in politics and to prevent the CDA from developing merely as an amorphous centrist bloc. The ARP was also worried that if it merged itself too rapidly into the CDA, it might upset some of its traditional voters: a new 'orthodox' Protestant party (the RPF), for example, polled 53,000 votes at the 1977 general election, and thus came within a few thousand votes of returning a member of parliament. Certainly the fear that an attempt to progress too rapidly towards a fully integrated Christian Democratic party might destroy old loyalties was understandable, particularly for the ARP with its long tradition of voter loyalty.[60]

The CDA had other problems too. In 1977, for example, it had only 10,000 members, whereas the KVP, ARP and CHU had approximately 100,000 between them. There was also the problem of 'ideological mix' within the CDA. In the aftermath of the 1977 general election it was apparent that the ARP preferred a centre-left coalition with the Socialists, whilst the CHU were more favourable to a centre-right coalition with the Liberals. On balance the KVP preferred a centre-left coalition, but, having lost so many of their working-class voters to Labour and the Radicals in the 1970s, the Catholics were not averse to a centre-right coalition. In the autumn of 1977 it looked as if a Labour-CDA-D '66 coalition would emerge under Joop Den Uyl (it would have had 110 seats out of 150 in the Second Chamber), but owing to the KVP's refusal to consider any liberalisation of the abortion law the proposed centre-left coalition fell through. Finally, after an eight-month governmental crisis, Andreas van Agt (CDA-KVP), succeeded in forming a centre-right coalition with the Liberals in December 1977. Van Agt's coalition, with seventy-seven seats out of 150, was obviously not particularly strong in the Chamber. Moreover, it seemed ironic that Labour should have lost office after their biggest electoral gain since 1945. On the other hand, the Liberals had also gained significantly at the general election, whilst the Christian Democrats had advanced marginally.

Whatever the future of this particular government, there can be no doubt that the emergence of the CDA as the first inter-confessional 'federation' in Dutch politics is an important development. Of course, as we have seen, there is a long tradition of Catholic-Protestant co-operation in the Netherlands. But in the 1970s rapid socio-economic change has encouraged fusion to develop out of co-operation. All the signs are that the Dutch party system is evolving along the lines now characteristic of so many other Western European countries, i.e. a party system based on three major 'poles of attraction', with Socialists on the Left, Christian Democrats in the Centre, and Liberals on the Right. But, as this chapter has shown, the Dutch political tradition is a rather unsual one; socio-economic factors are certainly replacing 'pillarisation' as the main voting determinant, but the traditional 'pillars' remain influential in many areas of life, including politics. It is, therefore, probable that the Christian Democratic movement will develop – at least in the short term – as a union of parties rather than as a tightly-knit unitary party.

Table 1

The Netherlands – Election Results for Second Chamber (Lower House of Parliament) in Seats, 1918–37

	1918	1922	1925	1929	1933	1937
Catholics	30	32	30	30	28	31
Anti-Revolutionaries	13	16	13	12	14	17
Christian Historicals	7	11	11	11	10	8
Total Confessional Parties	50	59	54	53	52	56
Socialists	22	20	24	24	22	23
Radical Democrats	5	6	7	7	6	6
Liberals	15	10	9	8	7	4
Communists	2	2	1	2	4	3
National Socialists						4
Others	6	4	5	6	9	4
Total	100	100	100	100	100	100

Table 2
The Netherlands – Election Results for Second Chamber (Lower House of Parliament), 1946–77

	Percentage cast for parties									
	1946	1948	1952	1956	1959	1963	1967	1971	1972	1977
Catholic People's Party (Katholieke Volkspartij, KVP)	30·8	31·0	28·7	31·7	31·6	31·9	26·5	21·8	17·7	
Anti-Revolutionary Party (Anti-Revolutionaire Partij, ARP)	12·9	13·2	11·3	9·9	9·4	8·7	9·9	8·6	8·8	31·9
Christian Historical Union (Christelijk-Historische Unie, CHU)	7·8	9·2	8·9	8·4	8·1	8·6	8·1	6·3	4·8	
Total confessional party percentage (Christen Democratisch Appel, CDA, from 1977)	51·5	53·4	48·9	50·0	49·1	49·2	44·5	36·7	31·3	31·9
Labour Party (Partij van de Arbeid, PVDA)	28·3	25·6	29·0	32·7	30·3	28·0	23·5	24·6	27·4	33·8
Democrats '66 (Democraten '66, D '66)							4·5	6·8	4·2	5·4
Radical Party (Politieke Partij Radikalen, PPR)								1·8	4·8	1·7
Total 'progressive parties' percentage	28·3	25·6	29·0	32·7	30·3	28·0	28·0	32·2	36·4	40·9
Liberal Party (Volkspartij voor Vrijheid en Democratie, VVD)	6·4	8·0	8·8	8·8	12·2	10·3	10·7	10·4	14·4	18·0
Communist Party (Communistische Partij van Nederland, CPN)	10·6	7·7	6·2	4·7	2·4	2·8	3·6	3·9	4·5	1·7
Democratic Socialists '70 (Democratisch Socialisten '70, DS '70)								5·3	4·1	0·7
Pacifist Socialist Party (Pacifistisch Socialistische Partij, PSP)					1·8	3·0	2·9	1·4	1·5	0·9
Farmers Party (Boeren-Partij, BP)					0·5	2·1	4·8	1·1	1·9	0·9
Others	3·2	5·3	7·1	3·8	3·7	4·6	5·5	9·0	5·9	5·0
	100	100	100	100	100	100	100	100	100	100

Table 3

Number of Seats per Party in the Second Chamber, 1946–77 (No. of seats increased from 100 to 150 in 1956)

	1946	1948	1952	1956	1959	1963	1967	1971	1972	1977
Catholic People's Party (KVP)	32	32	30	49	49	50	42	35	27	—
Anti-Revolutionary Party (ARP)	13	13	12	15	14	13	15	13	14	—
Christian Historical Union (CHU)	8	9	9	13	12	13	12	10	7	—
Christian Democratic Appeal (CDA)	—	—	—	—	—	—	—	—	—	49
Total confessional/Christian Democratic seats	53	54	51	77	75	76	69	58	48	49
Labour Party (PVDA)	29	27	30	50	48	43	37	39	43	53
Democrats '66 (D '66)	—	—	—	—	—	—	7	11	6	8
Radicals (PPR)	—	—	—	—	—	—	—	2	7	3
Total 'progressive' seats	29	27	30	50	48	43	44	52	56	64
Liberal Party (VVD)	6	8	9	13	19	16	17	16	22	28
Communist Party (CPN)	10	8	6	7	3	4	5	6	7	2
Democratic Socialists '70 (DS '70)	—	—	—	—	—	—	—	8	6	1
Pacifist Socialist Party (PSP)	—	—	—	—	2	4	4	2	2	1
Farmers' Party (BP)	—	—	—	—	—	3	7	1	3	1
Others	2	3	4	3	3	4	4	7	6	4
Total Number of Seats	100	100	100	150	150	150	150	150	150	150

Table 4
The Percentage of Votes Cast for the Traditional Parties (Religious Parties,
Socialists and Liberals) and for the smaller parties, 1918–77

	% votes (traditional parties)	% votes (smaller parties)
1918	87·2	12·8
1922	87·8	12·2
1925	88·4	11·6
1929	89·1	10·9
1933	83·9	16·1
1937	84·6	15·4
1946	86·2	13·8
1948	87·0	13·0
1952	86·7	13·3
1956	91·5	8·5
1959	91·6	8·4
1963	87·5	12·5
1967	78·7	21·3
1971	71·7	28·3
1972	73·1	26·9
1977	83·7	16·3

Table 5
Dutch Governments, 1946–77

Prime Minister	Duration	Political Composition	Seats in Parliament	Days needed to form government
Beel (KVP)	1946–8	Catholics and Socialists	61	45
Drees (PVDA)	1948–51	Catholics, Socialists, Christian Historicals, Liberals	76	30
Drees (PVDA)	1951–2	Catholics, Socialists, Christian Historicals, Liberals	76	50
Drees (PVDA)	1952–5	Catholics, Socialists, Christian Historicals, Anti-Revolutionaries	81	69
Drees (PVDA)	1955–6	Catholics, Socialists, Christian Historicals, Anti-Revolutionaries	81	15
Drees (PVDA)	1956–8	Catholics, Socialists, Christian Historicals, Anti-Revolutionaries	85	121
Beel (KVP) (interim government)	1958–9	Catholics, Christian Historicals, Anti-Revolutionaries	51	12
De Quay (KVP)	1959–61	Catholics, Christian Historicals, Anti-Revolutionaries, Liberals	94	63
De Quay (KVP)	1961–3	Catholics, Christian Historicals, Anti-Revolutionaries, Liberals	94	11
Marijnen (KVP)	1963–5	Catholics, Christian Historicals, Anti-Revolutionaries, Liberals	92	70
Cals (KVP)	1965–6	Catholics, Socialists, Anti-Revolutionaries	106	46
Zijlstra (ARP) (interim)	1966–7	Catholics, Anti-Revolutionaries	63	39
De Jong (KVP)	1967–71	Catholics, Anti-Revolutionaries, Christian Historicals, Liberals	86	49
Biesheuvel (ARP)	1971–2	Catholics, Anti-Revolutionaries, Christian Historicals, Liberals, DS '70	82	69
Biesheuvel (ARP) (interim)	1972–3	Catholics, Anti-Revolutionaries, Christian Historicals, Liberals	74	23
Den Uyl (PVDA)	1973–7	Socialists, Catholics, Anti-Revolutionaries, D '66, Radicals	97	163

7
Christian Democracy in France

As an organised political force Christian Democracy is now much less important in France than in West Germany, Italy, Belgium or the Netherlands. But no book on Christian Democracy in Western Europe would be complete without some analysis of the French Christian Democrats. In the Fourth Republic (1946–58) Christian Democracy was of course a major political force, with the *Mouvement Républicain Populaire* (MRP) playing a key governmental role. Indeed the MRP was to the Fourth Republic what the Radicals had been to the Third, the fulcrum within the parliamentary system. The Christian Democrats participated in twenty-three of the twenty-seven governments from 1944–8, supported all but that of Mendès-France (June 1954–February 1955), provided three of the Fourth Republic's prime ministers (Schuman, Bidault and Pflimlin), and ran the Ministry of Foreign Affairs from 1944–54 in the persons of Schuman and Bidault.

Even today the Christian Democratic *tendance* is important in France, for the backbone of the parliamentary Centre-Right group (one of the four major groups in the National Assembly, the others being Communist, Socialist and Gaullist)[1] still consists of Christian Democrats (although they do not call themselves such), i.e. politicians who are the direct heirs of the MRP, affiliate to the Christian Democratic group in the European Parliament, and are active in the various transnational Christian Democratic organisations of Western Europe. Thus in a very real sense Christian Democracy is not dead in France, even if it is not the force it was in the Fourth Republic.[2]

Christian Democracy in the Fourth Republic: the Mouvement Républicain Populaire (MRP)

The MRP arrived spectacularly on the French political scene, for, whilst in 1936 only 3 per cent of the electorate voted for the two prewar Christian Democratic parties, the PDP and *Jeune République*, in 1945 and 1946 no less than 25 per cent voted for the MRP. To some extent the MRP suffered from its rapid growth, but, after the 1947 desertions to the Gaullist *Rassemblement du Peuple Français* (RPF), the MRP settled down to a position of considerable importance in the politics of the Fourth Republic. The Christian Democratic electorate of five million of 1946 was cut by half in 1951, but there was virtually no change at the 1956 general election. And although the MRP's parliamentary representation dropped from over 170 to under 100 (out of approximately 600), the Christian Democrats continued to form an important element in the various centrist coalitions of that period.

Edmond Michelet, one of the few MRP deputies to leave the party and join de Gaulle's RPF in 1947, stated at that time that the MRP was 'Catholic against its wishes and the child of the Resistance . . . the party draws both strength and weakness from its dual background.'[3] The MRP was certainly an essentially Catholic party in spite of its attempt to embrace non-Catholics, and it became a major force on the French political scene owing to the Resistance record of its early leaders and militants.

The Resistance paved the way for the emergence of Christian Democracy as a significant political force in France in two important ways. It showed that Catholics, or at least those of progressive tendency, could co-operate loyally with other Republicans, and it provided the MRP with an élite of leaders, something which the PDP had always lacked.[4] In June 1943 Georges Bidault was elected president of the *Conseil National de la Résistance* (CNR) after the capture and execution of Jean Moulin, and three of the fourteen members of Bidault's CNR were future MRP ministers: the President himself, François de Menthon and Pierre-Henri Teitgen. Meanwhile, Maurice Schumann, a former *Jeune République* militant and future MRP founder-member and first President, was making a name for himself as the London 'Voice of Free France' from 1940–4. Another asset to the new party was Robert Schuman, for although his Resistance record was not as distinguished as those of the men mentioned above, he did enough to receive pardon for his pro-Pétain vote of 1940 and was thus able to stand for parliament in 1945. As an orthodox financier Schuman was able to reassure those Conservatives who voted MRP *faute de mieux* in 1945–6. He was also immensely popular in the MRP as a devout Catholic, moderate man, and proponent of European reconciliation. He was successively Finance Minister, Prime Minister and Foreign Minister in the early years of the Fourth Republic.

The Resistance thus provided the MRP with prestige, enthusiastic militants and a party élite. But the MRP's Resistance record was not an unmixed blessing. Many Conservatives got on to the MRP bandwagon in 1945–6 merely because their own parties had been discredited by their Vichy connections: they voted for the Christian Democrats, not because they wanted a new France with greater social and economic justice, but because they wanted to clear their consciences or because they saw the MRP as the strongest bastion against Communism. They were *with*, but not *of*, the MRP. Like the Gaullists, who wrongly assumed that *le Parti de la Fidélité* (as the MRP was sometimes known) would play follow-my-leader to the General whatever the circumstances, many Conservatives left the MRP in 1947. It is true that the abandonment of the MRP by Conservatives and Gaullists resulted in a more united – if numerically weaker – party. However, it is certainly arguable that the artificial over-inflation of the Christian Democratic vote in the immediate postwar period did more harm than good to the MRP, because it resulted in the election of a large number of deputies who had no political experience, and it stretched the party's organisation to the limit.

The party's organisational structure proved to be a major disappointment. The original hope was that the MRP would develop, not as an electoral machine, but as a great *rassemblement* (or *mouvement*) of ordinary men and women, inspired by their political doctrine and humanitarian idealism to bring about a new and genuinely democratic republican régime. Aiming at political activism as much as electoral success, the Christian Democrats laid great emphasis on their grass-roots organisation. In the party Statutes of 1944 the departmental federations, together with the sections and specialised teams (*équipes de recherche*), were seen as the most important elements within the movement. There was to be a constant flow of ideas from the base to the summit and vice versa. The national congress, representing the *forces vives* of Christian Democracy (trade unions, women's and youth movements, etc.) as well as the federations, was to be the key policy-making body, with the national committee and executive committee being left to implement congress's decisions. In practice the federations and *forces vives* were under-represented on the national organs, constrained by the party leadership, limited by financial weakness, and debilitated by the members' apathy. All too quickly the great new movement succumbed to Robert Michels' 'oligarchic' tendencies and became what Duverger calls a 'caucus party', with the national leadership taking all the key decisions.[5]

Above all, perhaps, the militants lacked commitment. Some found that political activism in peacetime was much less exciting than clandestine Resistance had been; others were disillusioned by the Fourth Republic's apparent failure to implement a profound social and economic revolution; others were depressed by the combined effect of Gaullist and Communist attacks on the MRP. The result was that at congress after congress the militants were called upon to give more time and effort to the party. These appeals had little or no effect, even after the structural reforms of 1959 which were designed to increase militant influence on the national organs. But by then it was too late. This minor injection of new blood did nothing to revive the ailing patient.

The MRP had other weaknesses. After the war there was a considerable growth of Catholic Action, i.e. of the various Catholic lay organisations approved by the Hierarchy (young Catholic workers, peasants, students, and so forth), but, whilst the majority of the members of these organisations tended to support the MRP, by no means all did. In his detailed study of French Catholic Action Bosworth has shown that the Catholic vote was divided between the Christian Democrats, Gaullists and Conservatives, and whilst the majority of people influenced by, or active in, Catholic Action supported the MRP, French Catholic activists voted less decisively for their Christian Democratic party than those of Italy, Germany, Belgium and the Netherlands.[6]

Nor could the MRP count on unequivocal support from the Catholic trade unionists of the *Confédération Française des Travailleurs Chrétiens* (CFTC). Like all French trade union confederations, the CFTC maintained a nominal independence of all political parties. But in practice its relationship with the MRP was quite close in the immediate postwar period.[7] However, with the failure of *la révolution par la loi* and the MRP's movement to the Right over economic policy in the 1950s, the CFTC's links with the MRP became more tenuous. The CFTC's fears about close identification with the Church and Christian Democracy were shown by the growing influence within the union of the Reconstruction group, which favoured a complete break with the Hierarchy and the MRP. By the late 1950s Reconstruction was commanding 40 per cent of the mandates at CFTC conferences, and its final triumph came in 1964 when the CFTC voted by nine to one to 'deconfessionalise' itself completely and change its name to *Confédération Française Démocratique du Travail* (CFDT).[8] The Christian Democratic political movement could thus no longer count on any official backing from Catholic trade unionists.

Another difficulty from which the MRP suffered was the weakness of the party's press. The party's own daily *L'Aube* collapsed in 1951, its circulation having fallen from a quarter of a million to 45,000 between June 1946 and June 1951. The paper collapsed partly for technical reasons, such as escalating distribution costs; partly because of certain national tendencies, such as the general decline of party political newspapers, especially those based on Paris; but partly also because of mistakes on the part of the management, who tried to make *L'Aube* into a mass popular daily, so that, when it failed as such, it had no readership on which to fall back. (In contrast many of *L'Aube's* readers in the 1930s were intellectuals who subscribed to the paper in order to read Bidault's detailed analyses of foreign policies.)[9] The Christian Democrats also published a fortnightly for militants, *Forces Nouvelles*, but, as the official organ of the party leadership, it was full of deadly orthodoxy, and did nothing to encourage serious political debate within the MRP. The Christian Democrats received some indirect support from Catholic weeklies such as Georges Hourdin's *La Vie Catholique Illustrée*, which had a circulation of over half a million in the 1950s, but was more concerned with the affairs of Catholic Action than with those of Christian Democracy. Georges Suffert's *Témoignage Chrétien* was at one time representative of the progressive wing of the MRP, but in the 1950s it spent most of its time attacking the Christian Democrats for their colonial and economic policy. Perhaps more important for the MRP were three periodicals, *Terre Humaine*, *France-Forum* and *Esprit*. *Terre Humaine* (1951–7) and *France-Forum* (1957–), both with circulations of about 5,000, were not specifically committed to the MRP or its successors, but nearly all their contributors, including such distinguished writers as Etienne Borne, were Christian Democrats. *Esprit* was never a Christian Democratic journal, but with a circulation of 15,000, as *the* vehicle for the expression of Mounier's personalist philosophy, and as a review written mainly by progressive Catholics, it undoubtedly influenced (and influences) an important minority of Christian Democratic intellectuals and activists.

The MRP's biggest problem was that it was, *malgré soi*, a regional and a Catholic party. At the general election of November 1946 the MRP polled almost five million votes (26 per cent of those cast), figures which were broadly in line with those of October 1945 and June 1946 (elections for the two Constituent Assemblies). At the general election of June 1951 the party won just under two and a half million votes (12·5 per cent of those cast), and in January 1956 the Christian Democrats polled almost the same number of votes (11 per cent of those cast). In 1946 the MRP polled between 30 and 45 per cent of the votes in ten departments, of which six were in the Catholic west (Normandy and Brittany) and three in the Catholic north-east (Alsace and

Lorraine), whilst the odd one out was in Savoy.[10] In 1951 and 1956 the same pattern was repeated, except that in only one department (Mayenne) did the party poll over 35 per cent. But all the departments in which the Christian Democratic vote was between 20 and 30 per cent (a total of eleven) were in the west, north-east or Savoy, except for Basses-Pyrénées in the south-west.[11] In sum, as Goguel has shown, the Christian Democrats were strong only in traditional areas of Catholicism and conservatism.[12]

Nevertheless, whilst it is true that the MRP's main support came from departments which had been moderate-Conservative before the war and from areas with a sizeable Catholic bourgeoisie, the party also won a significant number (about 20 per cent) of working-class votes – doubtless mainly Catholics – in Alsace-Lorraine and in parts of the Nord, and in the country as a whole the MRP's working-class vote averaged out at about 15 per cent.[13] This was insufficient to satisfy the MRP's progressive leaders such as Robert Buron and André Monteil, but, although the MRP vote remained predominantly rural and conservative throughout the Fourth Republic, the Christian Democrats retained the loyalty of a small but important minority of wage-earners (the Communists with *c.* 34 per cent and Socialists with *c.* 22 per cent not surprisingly had a bigger working-class electorate than the MRP).

The major characteristic of the Christian Democratic electorate was, of course, that it was Catholic. An IFOP poll of 1952 showed that 54 per cent of regular Catholic churchgoers voted for the MRP, compared with 20 per cent for the Conservatives (Independents and Peasants), and 18 per cent for the Gaullists.[14] Of MRP voters 43 per cent claimed they were considerably influenced by the Church in their voting habits, compared with 26 per cent of Conservatives and 18 per cent of Gaullists.[15] Yet the MRP probably only obtained the votes of a minority of the practising Catholic electorate, certainly in the general elections of the 1950s. For, although in 1952 54 per cent of regular churchgoers claimed to vote MRP, it has been calculated that if this percentage had in fact voted for the MRP in 1951, the party would have obtained 15 per cent of the votes cast and not just 12 per cent.[16] It seems clear that it was male practising Catholics who let the Christian Democrats down, for 66 per cent of female practising Catholics claimed to have voted MRP in 1951. The MRP's problem was that it was insufficiently 'confessional' to obtain a really high percentage of Catholic votes (especially those of men), but too 'confessional' to win anything but Catholic support.

In conclusion, then, the MRP was a regional party, although it made a partial break-out from the prewar confines of the PDP; an essentially rural party, although it had a sizeable industrial working-class vote in parts of Alsace-Lorraine and the Nord; a mainly conservative party, although many party workers and a few leaders had no wish to be shackled by their conservative electorate; and a Catholic party, although it had no direct links with the Hierarchy, and its founders had striven hard to avoid a 'confessional' image. Like the German, Belgian and Italian Christian Democratic parties of the 1940s and 1950s, the MRP was stronger in some regions than in others, but the MRP's regional pockets were smaller than those of its sister-parties. Like the Belgian, Dutch and Italian Christian Democratic parties, the MRP's main reservoir of support consisted of practising Catholics, but France's practising Catholics (especially men) were just as likely to cast their ballots for the Conservatives or Gaullists as for the MRP. In these circumstances, it was perhaps not surprising that Christian Democracy in the Fourth Republic did not fulfil its early promise.

Nevertheless, the historical balance-sheet of the MRP was by no means wholly negative. The MRP was *the* vehicle by which Catholics were reconciled to the Republic. By their support for nationalisation, economic planning and the welfare state in the Liberation period, the Christian Democrats showed that Catholics could be as interested as Socialists in economic and social justice. And, like the Socialists, they were prepared to put the Republic before their party in the difficult years between 1947 and 1951 when liberal democracy seemed to be threatened by the extreme Right (Gaullists) and extreme Left (Communists). And, whilst like most other French politicians, the Christian Democrats underestimated the strength of postwar nationalism and so committed various blunders in Indochina, Morocco and Tunisia, they finally came round to accepting the need to grant independence to Algeria and Black Africa. Moreover, they played a notable part in encouraging Franco-German reconciliation and closer co-operation generally between all the countries of Western Europe.[17] However, as a minority party – although a key one – the MRP constantly had to compromise, and this did not help it to gain credit either with its militants or with the electorate at large. The Christian Democrats agreed with the Socialists on most aspects of social and European policy, but totally disagreed with them and with the Radicals over educational policy. On the other hand, the economic and agricultural policy of the Christian Democrats usually coincided with that of the Conservatives. There were thus different majorities in the National Assembly for different policies, and this led to governmental instability and the discrediting of the Fourth Republic. Not surprisingly, when the Republic finally fell in 1958, the MRP – as the great new party of the Fourth Republic – was saddled with a disproportionate amount of blame for its collapse.

Christian Democracy in the Fifth Republic

The Fifth Republic has witnessed the decline and fall of the MRP and the emasculation of the centre parties which played such an important role in the Third and Fourth Republics. The chief characteristics of the pre-1958 party system were pluralism, instability and fluctuating majorities. Throughout most of the period 1875–1958 the centre parties played a key role in the governments which emerged under this system, notably the Radicals in the Third Republic and the Christian Democrats in the Fourth Republic. Since the re-introduction of *scrutin d'arrondissement à deux tours* in 1958, and more especially since the change to a directly elected President (October 1962) and the realignment of political forces at the general election of November 1962, a new party system has emerged. It remains multi-party, but has become quadripartite rather than hexagonal, various mergers resulting in there being four (albeit fluid) main political groupings rather than six. At the same time the two poles of Right and Left have increasingly exerted their attraction on the electorate, even although the phenomenon of bipolarisation has been more apparent at presidential than at general elections. Finally, the electoral alliances of the Right and Left have become more disciplined, with the result that centre parties have been squeezed and eroded.

In the early years of the Fifth Republic the Christian Democrats found themselves on the horns of a dilemma. On the one hand, the Christian Democratic leaders and militants were totally opposed to Gaullist foreign policy, both in its anti-Atlanticist and anti-European manifestations, and at the same time they were critical of de Gaulle's habit of governing 'auto-cratically' and 'technocratically' without paying due attention to the views of Parliament. On the other hand, the MRP supported the General's Algerian policy, and the Christian Democratic electorate preferred Gaullism to any alternative whenever a clearcut choice had to be made. But if the MRP leaders had accepted Gaullism in deference to their electorate's views, they would have had to have abandoned quite genuine principles on which they differed from the Gaullists. In the Fifth Republic, then, the key problem for the Christian Democratic political stream has been how to assert its own 'personality' in the face of Gaullism (and other rival movements on the Centre and Right of the political spectrum); and no simple solution was found either in the 'Gaullist' phase of the Fifth Republic or after the General's departure from the political scene in 1969.

The year 1962 marked a watershed in the evolution not only of French Christian Democracy, but of the party system as a whole. From 1958–62 the old parties of the Fourth Republic gave General de Gaulle a more or less free hand to solve the Algerian problem. But the Evian Agreements of March 1962 ended this marriage of convenience. Thereafter the parties of the Fourth Republic wanted to return to a system of parliamentary government. De Gaulle was determined to allow no such thing.[18] In April 1962 he threw down his first challenge to the traditional parties by appointing Georges Pompidou prime minister in place of Debré (Debré had never been defeated in the National Assembly, and Pompidou was an 'outsider' who had never been elected to any office). Then at his press conference of 14 May de Gaulle made it clear that he had no intention of relinquishing the political power he had acquired during the Algerian phase of the Fifth Republic; and this assertion – together with his scornful remarks about European integration – provoked the resignation of Pompidou's five MRP ministers. A week later the national executive of the Independent (CNIP, i.e. Conservative) party called for the resignation of its five ministers – they refused, and this marked the first step towards the establishment of the Independent Republican Party (known since 1977 as the Republican Party), i.e. those Independents who followed Giscard d'Estaing in supporting de Gaulle at the referendum and general election of late 1962.

By the summer of 1962 relations between de Gaulle and the parties (with the exception, of course, of the Gaullist UNR and Giscard d'Estaing's followers) were distinctly sour, and when the General announced his intention of modifying the Constitution by unconstitutional means (i.e. of changing over to the direct election of the President by means of a referendum, by-passing Parliament's right to vote on constitutional amendments), he was in effect throwing down his final challenge to the parties. On 5 October 1962 Pompidou was defeated on a censure motion by the National Assembly, and five days later the parties of the Fourth Republic set up a *cartel des non* under Paul Reynaud. The *cartel* consisted of the Socialists (SFIO), Radicals, Christian Democrats (MRP) and Independents (CNIP), and it was supported by the Communists (PCF) and independent Socialists (PSU), but not by the people of France. For on 28 October 1962 de Gaulle won his referendum: 62 per cent of the electorate voted yes to the direct election of the President, and 38 per cent voted no. As 23 per cent of the voters abstained, in fact only a minority of the electorate (46 per cent) voted yes to de Gaulle's constitutional amendment. But from the point of view of the traditional parties the referendum marked a significant setback, and when, a month later, the Gaullists won 36 per cent of the votes cast at the general election (first ballot), the setback was transformed into a severe defeat. The total Left vote did not in fact change much (the PCF gained 2 per cent at 21 per cent, the Socialists lost 3 per cent at 12·5 per cent, and the Radicals were unchanged at 7·5 per cent); indeed, overall the Left improved its parliamentary position by making informal electoral pacts. But what was really important for the future development of the party system – and not least for the future of Christian Democracy – was what happened on the Centre and Right of the political spectrum, where the MRP lost one third and the CNIP half of its 1958 electorate. By abandoning their traditional parties in favour of the new parties of the Fifth Republic (i.e. the Gaullist and Giscardien parties), the voters of the Centre and Right transformed the French party system 'at a stroke'. *Le fait majoritaire* was born, and *Gaullisme charismatique* was transformed into *Gaullisme partisan et majoritaire*. From now on all parties had to take account of the fact that a majority party system, based on a coherent and reasonably well-disciplined moderate conservative coalition, had supplanted the fragmented party system of the Third and Fourth Republics.

It soon became apparent to the traditional parties of the Centre and Left that there were only two possible strategies open to them – assuming that they had no wish to remain in the political wilderness until the Greek Kalends, and given the fact that the Christian Democrats ruled out any alliance involving the Communists. In order to beat the Gaullist *majorité, les oppositions* would either have to form a disciplined coalition of the Centre or a disciplined coalition of the Left. Moreover, if either strategy succeeded, the other would be almost bound to fail for simple arithmetical reasons. A Centre grouping capable of winning a majority in the National Assembly would have to win the support not only of all the non-Communist parties, i.e. Socialists, Radicals, Christian Democrats and Independents, but also of a significant number of Gaullists. Likewise, an effective left-wing coalition would have to have the full support of the Communists, Socialists, and as many Radicals as possible, if it were to mount an effective challenge to the Gaullist *majorité*. And if it were to succeed in doing this, the opposition Centrists would be forced to join either the left-wing or the right-wing camp, or remain an ineffectual rump. This was precisely the dilemma facing the Christian Democrats in the mid 1960s.

As far as the first strategy was concerned, the crucial event was the failure of Gaston Defferre's attempt to form a 'large federation' of Socialists, Christian Democrats and Radicals to support his presidential candidature between December 1963 and June 1965. Defferre's presidential bid and abortive *Fédération Démocrate et Socialiste* have been analysed in some detail elsewhere.[19] Suffice to say here that Defferre failed primarily because neither of the two key parties, the SFIO and MRP, really wanted him to succeed. Although the Christian Democrats voted in favour of Defferre's *Fédération* at their congress in May 1965, they laid down various conditions – notably that the SFIO should wind itself up (as the MRP was prepared to do) and that the adjective 'Socialiste' should be omitted from the *Fédération*'s title – conditions which effectively ensured that the *Fédération* would be stillborn. Likewise at their congress in June 1965 the Socialists voted in favour of the proposed *Fédération*, provided the SFIO did not have to be merged into it (which was of course the whole idea of the *Fédération*: that ultimately it would become a joint party), and provided the *Fédération* came out in favour of integrating the private, i.e. Catholic, schools into the state system. This last point was a concession to the Socialist Secretary, Guy Mollet, who had insisted that some reference to *laïcité* should be written into the *Fédération*'s programme. Clearly the Catholic MRP could never accept the Socialist proposal that talks be opened with the Communists with a view to 'reintegrating the PCF into French political life', for one of the MRP's conditions was that the *Fédération* should have no dealings with the Communists. In these circumstances Defferre's proposed *Fédération* – essentially a merger of Christian Democrats and Social Democrats – almost inevitably collapsed. It availed Defferre nothing to have the support of the (then important) political Clubs, of the leaders of the CFTC, and of the journalists of the widely circulated *L'Express*, if the Christian Democrats and Socialists were not prepared to back him unreservedly. On 25 June 1965 Defferre drew his conclusions by withdrawing his presidential candidature.

The upshot of the Defferre failure was that the non-Communist Left opted for the second strategy, i.e. for an alliance with the Communists. François Mitterrand fought the 1965 and 1974 presidential elections as a Popular Front candidate.[20] The Communists and Socialists made electoral agreements to present only one left-wing candidate at the second ballot of the 1967, 1968, 1973 and 1978 general elections.[21] In 1973 and 1978 (though with different interpretations in 1978) they campaigned on the basis of the *Programme Commun de la Gauche*, signed in June 1972. Meanwhile the SFIO had wound itself up in 1969, and reformed itself as the Parti Socialiste (PS), which elected Mitterrand as its First Secretary in 1971.[22] This is not the place to discuss in detail the realignment of the French Left, nor the continuing friction between the two Popular Front parties. But in the context of the evolution of Christian Democracy in France it is important to emphasise that Mitterrand's strategy put the Christian Democrats in a difficult position. Squeezed between the big battalions of the Left and Right, the Christian Democrats could at best only hope to win a sufficient number of seats to hold the balance in the National Assembly. To remain in a political limbo, incapable of influencing government or opposition, held no particular attraction to centrist politicians whose *raison d'être* was to be in a position to influence decision-making, whilst any alliance with the Left was out of the question for the Christian Democrats so long as the Socialists remained allied to the Communists.

The years 1965–73 saw France's Christian Democratic politicians pursuing the strategy of building the political Centre into a force which could hold the balance in parliament. The key proponent of this strategy was the Christian Democratic leader, Jean Lecanuet.

Lecanuet first made his name at the presidential election in 1965, when he stood as a Centre candidate after the collapse of the Defferre initiative. At the first ballot Lecanuet polled 3·7 million votes (15 per cent of those cast). This was sufficient to put de Gaulle *en ballottage*, but significantly Lecanuet was unable to prevent bipolarisation between de Gaulle and Mitterrand at the second ballot. Nevertheless, on the strength of his presidential poll, Lecanuet decided to launch a new Christian Democratic-Centrist party, the *Centre Démocrate* (CD) in January 1966. Proclaiming that his party was opposed both to Gaullism and Communism, and that 'the French will gather in the Centre',[23] Lecanuet declared that his aim was to rally the Social Democratic wing of the SFIO, the moderate wing of the Radical Party, the Independents who were opposed to Giscard d'Estaing, and all of the old MRP. From the start, however, he ran into difficulties, both from within the CD and from its opponents to Left and Right. The trade union wing of the MRP condemned Lecanuet's new party at their conference in January 1966, and a number of MRP left-wingers, led by Robert Buron and Jean Mastias, resigned from the party on the grounds that the CD was a Centre-Right party; in October 1966 they launched *Objectif 1972* (later known as *Objectif Socialiste*), whose aim was 'another majority . . . under the banner of socialism'.[24] Gaullist Christian Democrats such as Maurice Schumann and Pierre Pflimlin refused to have anything to do with the CD. The Radicals (except for the erratic Maurice Faure and a few of his friends) and the Socialists (except for André Chandernagor) also boycotted Lecanuet's new party. To make matters worse, Giscard d'Estaing, who had been dismissed from the Finance Ministry in January 1966, decided to organise the Independent Republican group into a political party, and when he declared that his party would be 'liberal, centrist and European',[25] it was clear that he was out to capture the Lecanuet electorate of December 1965.

In these circumstances it was not surprising that at the general election of 1967 Lecanuet's *Centre Démocrate* won only 13·5 per cent of the votes cast at the first ballot, compared with over 40 per cent for the Popular Front parties and 38 per cent for the Gaullists. Thus, within eighteen months of its foundation the CD had suffered a major setback. The writing appeared to be on the wall for Lecanuet's centrist strategy. Moreover, the events of May–June 1968 and the subsequent general election made Lecanuet's strategy look even more doubtful, for the CD vote was cut back to 10·3 per cent and it was only by combining with the Independents that the Christian Democrats were able to form a parliamentary group in the National Assembly (*Progrès et Démocratie Moderne*, PDM), which had thirty-one members, one above the minimum for a group. The year 1969, however, gave a considerable, if artificial, boost to the hopes of the Christian Democrats, for at the presidential election which followed de Gaulle's resignation[26] the Christian Democratic President of the Senate, Alain Poher, polled 23 per cent of the votes cast at the first ballot (7·8 million). This apparently impressive total was not in fact particularly significant, because Pompidou easily outdistanced Poher on both the first (44 per cent to 23 per cent) and second (58 per cent to 42 per cent) ballots. Moreover, if any candidate of the Centre ever had a chance of being elected, it should have been Poher, who, as President of the Senate and acting President of France, found himself very much in the political limelight, with the Gaullists discomfited by the General's sudden demise (although they rallied quickly to Pompidou) and the Left in complete disarray after the events of 1968 (Duclos (PCF) and Defferre (Socialist) eliminated each other at the first ballot). Yet Poher's first ballot poll was only slightly larger than the combined MRP-Radical vote at the 1958 general election. If the trend towards bipolarisation was ending, and France was 'rallying in the Centre' as Lecanuet and Poher claimed, one would have expected Poher, as the representative of the whole political family of the Centre, to have polled much more strongly than the Christian Democrats and Radicals had done at the last election at which the Centre parties had done reasonably well (i.e. 1958).

Within a month of Pompidou's election to the presidency Lecanuet's hopes of reviving Christian Democracy as a balancing force suffered a severe blow when Jacques Duhamel, Joseph Fontanet and René Pleven, who had all supported Pompidou in the presidential election, accepted invitations to join Chaban-Delmas's government (June 1969). Duhamel then set up the *Centre Démocratie et Progrès* (CDP) as a pro-Gaullist Centre party, and fourteen members of the parliamentary group, *Progrés et Démocratic Moderne* (PDM), followed Duhamel into the *majorité*. The Christian Democratic political family was thus split into two, and remained so for the next five years, although the opposition and *majorité* Christian Democrats continued to sit in the same parliamentary group.

Once again it began to look as if it would be only a matter of time before Lecanuet's small Christian Democratic political party, the *Centre Démocrate*, would, *nolens volens*, join the *majorité*. And indeed this was what did eventually happen, but not until 1974. The chief reason for the delay was the formation of *Mouvement Réformateur* in 1971. Lecanuet and Servan-Schreiber hoped that this new political formation, based on the combined forces of the Christian Democrats and Radicals, would succeed in winning enough seats at the 1973 general election to hold the balance of power in the National Assembly.

The *Mouvement Réformateur* was set up at Saint-Germain-en Laye outside Paris in November 1971. Its four constituent parties were the *Centre Démocrate*, the Radical Party, the *Parti de la Démocratie Socialiste* (subsequently known as the *Mouvement Démocrate Socialiste de France*), and the *Centre Républicain*. The last three parties were of virtually no importance, although Max Lejeune of the MDSF was the first president of the *Réformateur* group in the National Assembly. The key political forces within the *Mouvement* were, then, Lecanuet's Christian Democrats and Servan-Schreiber's Radicals, and much depended on whether Servan-Schreiber could bring a united Radical party into the new *Mouvement*.

At first things looked quite promising for the *Mouvement*. The energetic Jean-Jacques Servan-Schreiber, who had been elected Secretary of the Radical Party in 1969 on the proposal of its President Maurice Faure, had reorganised the party in the country and been largely responsible for writing the new Radical Manifesto of February 1970. But even at this stage it was apparent that not all Radicals were happy about the party's new programme or its flamboyant Secretary. In particular criticisms were made of Servan-Schreiber's enthusiastic espousal of 'regional power', for there was a strong tradition of Jacobinism in the Radical Party, particularly over national education and defence. Other members of the party, notably the influential Félix Gaillard, expressed doubts about the Manifesto's proposal for limiting the rights of inheritance, as it was felt that this might frighten off the many small entrepreneurs who were Radical supporters. However, smarting under its electoral defeat of 1968 (when only thirteen Radicals were returned), the Radical Party was determined to put on a show of public unity, and the Manifesto was accepted unanimously in February 1970 in spite of the doubts which had been expressed.

The Radical Party's confidence was further boosted in June 1970 when Servan-Schreiber won a Nancy by-election (against the Gaullist Souchal). However, in July 1970 the party suffered a serious loss when the intelligent and respected Félix Gaillard was drowned in a sailing accident off Brittany. It is just conceivable that Gaillard might have had the authority to control Servan-Schreiber, whose energy was undoubted but whose judgement was suspect. The first serious evidence of Servan-Schreiber's bad judgement occurred in September 1970 when he decided to challenge the prime minister, Chaban-Delmas, in a by-election at Bordeaux (caused by the death of Chaban's *suppléant*). Bourgès-Maunoury argued that it was a mistake to stand against Chaban-Delmas, a former Radical who accepted many of the ideas contained in the Radical Manifesto, and Maurice Faure, the Radical President, criticised Servan-Schreiber for his 'demagoguery'. Moreover, when Chaban-Delmas was re-elected at the first ballot with 63 per cent of the votes cast, and Servan-Schreiber polled only 17 per cent (the same as the CD candidate in 1967), all the political commentators were agreed that Servan-Schreiber had made a considerable blunder: he had been imprudent to stand in the first place, and even more imprudent in the extreme language he had used to describe his opponents of both Right and Left.

The extent of the opposition to Servan-Schreiber's centrist strategy became increasingly apparent in the eighteen months after the Bordeaux by-election, and by the time of the March 1971 municipal elections the Radical Party was beginning to split. Although most Radicals formed alliances with Christian Democrats at these elections, a minority rejected Servan-Schreiber's strategy and set up 'comités radicaux de gauche', allying with the Socialists. Overall, the Radicals lost ground, and this led to further criticism of Servan-Schreiber.[27] In the light of the 1971 electoral setback Maurice Faure and Robert Fabre came to the conclusion that the Radicals could not afford to break with the Socialists. They refused to endorse the Radical Party's membership of the *Mouvement Réformateur* in 1971, accepted the Left's Common Programme in 1972, and set up the *Mouvement des Radicaux de Gauche* (MRG) as a separate party. Seven of the thirteen Radicals in the National Assembly joined the MRG, and a majority of local associations also affiliated to the breakaway party. And so it was that the Radicals entered the 1973 general election split into two parties.

In these circumstances it was not surprising that the *Mouvement Réformateur*, which had now become predominantly a Christian Democratic formation led by Lecanuet, did rather badly at the 1973 general election. The *Mouvement* polled just over 3 million votes at the first ballot (almost 13 per cent of the votes cast), and eventually thirty-one deputies joined the *Réformateur* group (of these twenty-one were Christian Democrats, i.e. *Centre Démocrate*, five were Radicals and five MDSF). But Lecanuet had failed in his strategy. The Christian Democrats, Radicals and MDSF had not succeeded in forging the *Mouvement Réformateur* into a united and powerful centrist party; they had not made the hoped-for electoral breakthrough, and they could not form a *groupe charnière* ('hinge group') in the National Assembly.[28]

It was now apparent that the French electorate preferred bipolarisation to any centrist or Christian Democratic alternative. Thereafter it was only a matter of time before Lecanuet's Christian Democrats and the mainstream Radicals joined the *majorité*. Clearly they had no political future in the no-man's land between the Left and the *majorité*. Pompidou's death in April 1974 provided the necessary occasion. For in putting himself forward as a candidate for the presidency, Giscard d'Estaing appealed directly to the opposition Christian Democrats and Radicals of the *Mouvement Réformateur* by claiming that he would bring about reform without revolution, that he would get rid of the *blocages* in French society, and that he would ensure that France played a leading role in the further political development of the European Community. Giscard's promises may have been vague, but Lecanuet jumped at the chance to get back into the mainstream of French politics, opting for Giscard before the first ballot,[29] and Servan-Schreiber followed suit before the second ballot. As Giscard only defeated Mitterrand by half a million votes (50·8 per cent of those cast to 49·2 per cent), his victory clearly depended in the last analysis on Christian Democratic and Radical votes. On 27 May 1974 Giscard invited the *Réformateurs* to join the government, counterbalancing this move to some extent by appointing the Gaullist Jacques Chirac as prime minister.

The Christian Democratic Political Tendency in France since 1974
After the presidential election of 1974 the hopes of the Centre – both the Christian Democratic *tendance* and the Independent Republican *tendance* – were running high. Giscard d'Estaing had talked about *une ouverture au centre, une nouvelle majorité*, even about the possibility of introducing an

element of proportionality into the electoral system. The notion of *une nouvelle majorité*, and in particular of the demise of *l'Etat UDR* (the Gaullist-dominated state), appealed strongly to the non-Gaullist members of the *majorité*. But three years later the political parties of the Centre-Right appeared to be back to square one, having been mauled by the Union of the Left and Gaullists (particularly the former) at the municipal elections of 1977. Even traditional strongholds such as Brest, Nantes, Rennes and Le Mans were lost to the Left, and, as Nöel-Jean Bergeroux remarked in *Le Monde*, 'The West is no longer Christian Democratic'.[30] However, French politics is always full of surprises, and no less than a year later – at the general election of March 1978 – a new Centre-Right formation, *Union pour la Démocratie Française*, UDF (consisting of the Independent Republicans [now called *Parti Républicain*, PR], Christian Democrats [*Centre des Démocrates Sociaux*, CDS] and Radicals) did surprisingly well, emerging as one of the four major groups in the National Assembly.[31] At the first ballot the UDF had polled 21·5 per cent of the votes cast, compared with 22·6 per cent for the Gaullists, 22·6 per cent for the Socialists, and 20·6 per cent for the Communists. Did this sudden revival of the Giscardian Centre suggest a new lease of life for *centrisme* after its severe setback in 1977? And how important was the Christian Democratic *tendance* within the *Union pour la Démocratie Française*?

As regards the UDF's success in 1978, this can largely be attributed to the President, who refused to be panicked into a 'confrontation' election (Left versus Right) by the Gaullist Jacques Chirac in 1976; who consistently backed Raymond Barre's austerity programme from 1976–8, and warned against the inflationary dangers of the Left's Common Programme; and who succeeded in transmitting his own increasing personal popularity to the UDF (Giscard's silhouette was to be seen on all the UDF posters at the 1978 election). But whether the electoral success of the UDF in 1978 presaged a long-term revival of the Centre was questionable. After all, during the ten years up to 1978 the politicians of the Centre had frequently talked about *regroupement*, but hitherto all their new formations had foundered. The *Centre Démocrate* had failed to develop into anything more than a rump MRP, and the *Mouvement Réformateur*, whilst a relatively successful parliamentary group, never succeeded in fusing the Christian Democratic and Radical political families in the country as a whole.[32] Moreover, the *Centre des Démocrates Sociaux* (CDS), which brought together the followers of Lecanuet (*Centre Démocrate*) and Duhamel (*Centre Démocratie et Progrès*) in 1976, really did no more than heal the split in the Christian Democratic movement which had occurred in 1969, when half the Christian Democrats rallied to the *majorité* and the remainder stayed in opposition.

The chief components of the *Union pour la Démocratie Française* were the Republicans (formerly Independent Republicans, in reality Conservatives) and the Christian Democrats, with the Radicals a poor third. All three constituent parties were committed to the Atlantic Alliance and European integration, and strongly opposed to Communism, but their main loyalty was to the President, although they differed in the extent to which they supported his reformist strategy. The Radicals and Christian Democrats, particularly the former, emphasised their role as *l'aile gauche de la majorité*, whereas the Republicans were much more conservative in their attitude to social change and economic reform. On the other hand, the Republicans and Christian Democrats were heirs to the Catholic political tradition, whereas the Radicals were heirs to the anti-clerical tradition.[33]

Given these differences within the UDF, the emergence of a moderate conservative party comparable to the Christian Democratic Union of Germany seemed improbable, although by no means impossible. Such a centre-right party, consisting of Christian Democrats and moderate Conservatives – but using neither term to describe itself – would be likely to materialise, in the judgement of *Le Monde*'s specialist on the Centre parties, *only* if France adopted (as the Christian Democrats have for years demanded) a system of proportional representation.[34] Even then such a centre-right party would be able to develop as a predominant force only if Gaullism were to decline significantly or if the Union of the Left were to disintegrate. The 1978 general election showed that Gaullism had shrunk somewhat as a political force, and that the Union of the Left was in difficulties; moreover, the mutual recriminations of the campaign continued in its aftermath, with the Socialist and Communist parties equally adamant that the other was responsible for the Left's defeat. However, despite the relatively favourable situation provided for the Centre-Right by the above circumstances, and despite Giscard's commitment to *décrispation* – by which he meant blurring the sharpness of the Left-Right conflict – there seemed to be no chance of a major revival of *centrisme* without proportional representation. And as the Gaullists were adamantly opposed to any version of this electoral system, the emergence of a strong party of the Centre or Centre-Right seemed unlikely.

One may conclude, then, that without a change in the electoral system and without a considerable reduction in the differences between the UDF's Conservative and Christian Democratic components, the UDF is unlikely to develop into a cohesive force straddling the Centre and Centre-Right of the political spectrum. It is even less likely to develop as a mainstream Christian Democratic party. However, for as long as *centrisme* remains an important political *tendance* in France – and there was still no evidence of its impending demise in the late 1970s – Christian Democracy seems likely to remain a small, but not insignificant, political current of the Centre and Centre-Right. And, whatever the present weaknesses of this current, it should not be forgotten that Christian Democracy was *the* vehicle through which French Catholics were finally reconciled to the Republic and to the tenets of liberal democracy.

Table 1
France: General Elections in the Fourth Republic[1]

	October 1945		June 1946		November 1946		June 1951		January 1956	
	%	Seats	%	Seats	%	Seats	%	Seats	%	Seats
Communists	26·2	161	25·9	153	28·2	183	26·9	101	25·9	150
Socialists	23·4	150	21·1	129	17·8	105	14·6	107	15·2	99
Radicals[2]	10·5	57	11·6	53	11·1	70	10·0	95	15·2	94
Christian Democrats	23·9	150	28·2	169	25·9	167	12·6	96	11·1	84
Conservatives[3]	15·6	64	12·8	67	12·9	71	14·1	108	15·3	97
Gaullists	—	—	—	—	3·0	—	21·6	120	3·9	22
Poujadists	—	—	—	—	—	—	—	—	13·2	50

1. Percentage refers to votes cast. Minor parties are omitted.
2. Includes *Union Démocratique et Socialiste de la Résistance* (UDSR).
3. Independents and Peasants.

Table 2

France: General Elections in the Fifth Republic[1]

	October 1958		November 1962		March 1967		June 1968		March 1973		March 1978	
	%	Seats	%	Seats	%	Seats	%	Seats	%	Seats	%	Seats
Communists	19·2	10	21·7	41	22·5	73	20·0	34	21·4	73	20·6	86
Socialists	15·7	44	12·6	66	19·0	116	16·5	57	20·8	101	22·6	114
Radicals (Left)	8·3	32	7·8	39								
Christian Democrats /Centrists/ Radicals (Right)	11·1	57	8·9	38	13·4	41	10·3	33	13·1	64[2]	21·5	139[3]
Conservatives	22·9	133	9·6	30								
Independent Republicans	—	—	4·4	35		44		64		55		
Gaullists	19·5	199	31·9	233	37·7	201	44·7	296	36·0	183	22·6	150

1. Percentage of votes cast refers to first ballot. Minor parties are omitted.
2. 30 Centrists supported the government from March 1973. After the election of Giscard d'Estaing to the Presidency in May 1974 the remaining Centrists joined the *Majorité.*
3. In 1978 the Centrists and Republicans (Giscardiens) fought under the banner *Union pour la Démocratie Française* (UDF). Of the 139 UDF deputies elected, 71 belonged to the *Parti Républicain* (PR), 35 to the *Centre des Démocrates Sociaux* (CDS) (mainstream Christian Democrats), and the rest to small centrist groups closely affiliated to the PR and CDS.

8

The Christian Democrats and European Integration

Christian Democrats have been untiring advocates of European integration. It is true that the European Community of the 1970s is a far cry from the federal Europe advocated by many Christian Democrats in the decade after the war. It is also true that De Gasperi and Schuman were very disappointed towards the end of their lives by the evidence of reviving nationalism, and that Adenauer, for so long a champion of European federalism, 'capitulated' in the early 1960s to de Gaulle, whose vision of Europe differed markedly from his own. But whatever their later failings and disappointments, the Christian Democrats – and most notably Schuman, Adenauer and De Gasperi – were amongst the most important architects of European unity in the 1940s and 1950s. Their successors have achieved less in more difficult political and economic circumstances, but have not denied their birthright as enthusiastic – or naïve (depending on one's point of view) – supporters of European integration.

This chapter will concentrate first on the Christian Democratic contribution to European integration, and secondly on the transnational links of the various Christian Democratic parties, including their tenuous, although increasingly important, links with the Conservatives.

The Christian Democratic Contribution to European Integration
The Christian Democratic contribution to European integration in the 1940s and 1950s was personified by Schuman, De Gasperi and Adenauer. All three men were Catholic moderates from Europe's frontier regions – they were catholic as well as Catholic, men who were imbued with a broad sense both of Europe's Christian and of its cultural heritage; all three had suffered from the excesses of European nationalism; all three were tough, pragmatic, rather conservative, politicians, but at the same time they had a vision of a united and democratic Europe, a Europe from which chauvinism, fascism and communism would be excluded; all three at various times headed the governments of their respective countries.[1]

Robert Schuman was born in 1886 in Luxembourg as an exile from Lorraine, which had been incorporated into the German Empire in 1871. Educated at various German universities, he nevertheless regarded himself primarily as a Frenchman and was active in French political life from 1919, when he was first elected to the Chamber of Deputies, until his death in 1963. Alcide De Gasperi was born in 1881 in south Tyrol which was then part of the Austro-Hungarian Empire. He became an Italian citizen as a result of the Treaty of Versailles, was one of the leaders of Luigi Sturzo's *Partito Popolare* in the 1920s, and, after being imprisoned by Mussolini from 1927–9, spent the rest of the Fascist period in the relative safety of the Vatican Library. After the war he soon became the leading figure in the new Christian Democratic party, the *Democrazia Cristiana* (DC). Konrad Adenauer (1876–1967) was never a citizen of any country but Germany, but he had the Rhinelander's cosmopolitan outlook: he once said 'I am a German and will remain a German, but I am also a European, and I have always felt like a European.'[2] He had been active in politics in the Weimar period, chiefly as mayor of Cologne (from 1917–33), but he had also stood for the chancellorship twice in the 1920s. When Hitler came to power he was dismissed from his post as mayor of Cologne, and spent the rest of the Nazi period (apart from two brief periods under arrest) in premature retirement. He re-emerged soon after the war as the leader of the newly founded Christian Democratic Union (CDU), first in the British zone and later throughout Western Germany.[3]

If the Christian Democratic leaders had had their way, a federal Europe might have been created in the late 1940s. De Gasperi told a meeting of foreign ministers in Paris in 1945 that he was 'the protagonist of a new federated Europe', for the creation of which Italy was prepared to make all necessary sacrifices;[4] Adenauer made a similar statement in a newspaper interview in 1949;[5] and Schuman told the 1947 MRP congress that it was 'essential to prepare a system of European federalism, based on respect for the diverse cultures of the European peoples'.[6] In these circumstances it was not surprising that the Christian Democrats were disappointed with the Council of Europe and OEEC, both traditional intergovernmental organisations with weak institutions. Schuman, for example, described the Council of Europe as 'the headlamp lighting the road to Europe, but it lacks the authority of a body which can take decisions',[7] whilst De Gasperi's Foreign Minister, Count Sforza, took the view that, whilst the Council of Europe might do useful work in a variety of fields, it could do little to bring about European unity.[8] The movement towards European integration then appeared to have reached deadlock by 1949–50, but two developments gave it a new impetus – the setting up of the Federal Republic of Germany in October 1949, which aroused French suspicions, and the outbreak of the Korean War in June 1950, which led the Americans to demand German rearmament to counterbalance the reduced US military commitment in Europe.

Even before the establishment of the Federal Republic Schuman had told *Le Monde*, 'Personally, I think there can be no solution to the problems of Europe without the progressive integration of the new Germany into Europe; it is in the interests of France to reflect on how this may be done, and, when the time comes, to act with dynamism.'[9] Shortly afterwards Adenauer said that he hoped for 'a new entente with France . . . perhaps it might begin with an Anglo-French-German customs union.'[10] The way was clearly open for Schuman's famous initiative of 9 May 1950. This was the proposal which led to the setting up of the European Coal and Steel Community (ECSC), the unique feature of which was the High Authority, a 'supranational' body of 'independent persons' chosen by member-governments but responsible to the Community. This body had wide powers to implement the Treaty; a Court was established to see that the Treaty was not infringed; and a Common Assembly – an embryo Parliament – was nominated by the national Parliaments to keep a check on the High Authority and, if need be, to dismiss it by a two-thirds majority. The importance of the Coal and Steel Community was that it marked a new phase in the movement towards European integration. Having failed to achieve a federal system, the 'Europeans' – with Christian Democrats in the vanguard – opted for a 'functional' approach, i.e. integration by 'functions' or 'sectors' (in this case coal and steel), leading, it was hoped, to increasing '*de facto* solidarity' and ultimately to a federal or confederal Western Europe.[11]

The next 'sector' to be attempted was the military one. Christian Democrats like Schuman were sceptical about the advisability of tackling such a sensitive area so soon, but, with the Americans determined on German rearmament and many Frenchmen strongly opposed to it, René Pleven, the French premier, tried to reach a compromise by proposing that the new German army units be integrated into a European Army. Although Schuman had misgivings about the practicality of the European Defence Community (EDC),[12] Adenauer, and especially De Gasperi, were enthusiastic supporters of it. Indeed De Gasperi played the leading role in linking the idea of a European Political Community (EPC) to that of EDC – a proposal which marked 'the high-point of Italy's influence on the European integration movement. For De Gasperi had thrown his great moral pressure behind the European federation, and had done so more decisively than any other European leader.'[13] But although the EDC Treaty was signed in May 1952, it was soon apparent that signing was not the same as ratifying. In Germany the Treaty was strongly criticised by the Social Democrats; in France by the Gaullists and Communists; and in Italy by the Communists, Socialists and neo-Fascists. Moreover, the Christian Democrats – the strongest supporters of EDC – suffered major setbacks at the French general election of June 1951 and the Italian general election of June 1953. In addition, the death of Stalin in July 1953 ushered in a period of more relaxed East-West relations, marked by the Korean Armistice (July 1953) and the Indochina peace treaty (July 1954). In these circumstances it was almost inevitable that such supranational propositions as EDC and EPC should fall by the board. The Christian Democratic dream of a dramatic leap forward towards an integrated Western Europe proved to be a chimera, and for De Gasperi it may even have been a mortal blow. Certainly some of his close friends were convinced that his sudden death in August 1954 was caused as much by acute disappointment at France's imminent rejection of EDC as by physical ill-health.[14]

Christian Democratic faith in the functional approach to integration was shaken but not broken by the collapse of EDC. The European *relance*, beginning with the Messina meeting of the foreign ministers of the six ECSC countries in 1955, continuing with the Spaak Committee Report, and ending with the Treaties of Rome, received widespread Christian Democratic support. Arguably the French MRP was a little slow to grasp the full significance of the *relance*,[15] but when it came to the ratification of the Treaties of Rome, the French Christian Democrats – like their German, Italian, and Benelux colleagues – voted unanimously for them. Indeed the only major criticism voiced by Christian Democrats was that the Treaties did not go far enough politically. Pierre-Henri Teitgen argued that the Commission and Parliament were too weak in relation to the Council of Ministers, '[the EEC] is like a heavy lorry with a two horse-power engine.'[16] Adenauer also thought that the institutions would have to be strengthened if the Community were to function effectively; he saw economic integration as a sort of second best, remarking that 'the stronger political form can be forged later.'[17] The Italians professed to be satisfied with the Treaties as they stood, not least because their delegation on the Spaak Committee, led by the Christian Democratic deputy Lodovico Benvenuti, had been particularly successful in getting Italy's objectives written into the Treaties, namely the setting up of the European Investment Bank, free movement of labour and common social policy. The new mood of optimism was expressed by Antonio Segni, Italy's Christian Democratic prime minister, at the signing of the Treaties in Rome on 25 March 1957: 'it is not without deep significance that the Treaties should be signed in Rome, in this city which . . . has been recognised as the cradle of that European civilisation which these Treaties aim to advance . . . [the Treaties] will help to make Europeans politically important in the world once again.'[18]

In spite of the optimism expressed at the time of the signing of the Rome Treaties (setting up Euratom as well as the EEC), the 1960s were to be a disappointing decade for the advocates of European integration. At the risk of generalising rather broadly, it can be said that the Christian Democrats now had three main objectives: to achieve the maximum degree of economic integration within the Community, hoping thereby to make progress towards a federal Europe by 'functional' means; to strengthen the Community's institutions, especially the Commission and European Parliament; and to enlarge the Community. Progress in all three areas was very limited in the 1960s. A common agricultural policy was forged during the decade, but the French and German parity changes of 1969 (as well as subsequently) upset the financial basis of the system. By 1967 the external barriers to trade had been dismantled, but the Community made very little progress in dismantling non-tariff barriers. And although Value Added Tax was adopted by the Six, common commercial, fiscal and economic policies were little more than blueprints by the 1970s in spite of the mini *relance* marked by the Hague Summit of 1969. The institutional machinery of the Community remained heavily weighted in favour of the Council of Ministers, and after the Luxembourg crisis of 1965 (provoked by de Gaulle) there was little to distinguish the Council from any other intergovernmental body: unanimous voting remained the order of the day on all key issues. Nevertheless, one important achievement was registered with the accession (to the Community) of Britain, Denmark and Eire in January 1973. However, the halcyon – or naïve – days of European 'federalism' were now far in the past, and Robert Schuman no doubt prophetically expressed the feelings of many European Christian Democrats when he said as long ago as 1957: 'We are no longer fanatical Europeans. Certainly we believe in Europe, but not as a simple, infallible panacea. . . . After ratification constant efforts will be needed to implement the Treaties [of Rome] and to carry through the processes of re-adaptation and harmonisation. The European Community will be a continuous creation, an immense task.'[19]

General de Gaulle perhaps contributed more than any other individual to the destruction of the (doubtless premature) hopes of the European federalists, but the ideals of Adenauer, De Gasperi and Schuman perished for other reasons as well. After the building of the Berlin Wall (1961) and Adenauer's resignation as Chancellor (1963), the unreality of Adenauer's hopes that East Germany would somehow 'collapse' when faced by a prosperous, united Western Europe, supported by the USA, became fully apparent. Erhard was less committed emotionally than Adenauer to European integration, and Gerhard Schröder, the German Foreign Minister, began the opening to the East (Ostpolitik) in the mid-1960s, so inevitably weakening – in the short term at least – Germany's interest in Western European integration. And despite Brandt's frequent protestations to the contrary, this process continued during the Grand Coalition of Christian Democrats and Social Democrats (1966–9), and into the 1970s under the Social Democrats and Liberals. There was no question, of course, of the Federal Republic abandoning the Atlantic Alliance or the European Community. It was simply a question of diplomatic 'energy': so much of the latter was expended, and no doubt rightly expended, on Ostpolitik in the late 1960s and early 1970s that less was available for Westpolitik. The German Christian Democrats claim that they would have remained more committed to European integration than the Social Democrats, and that they would have implemented Ostpolitik more slowly than Brandt, and given away less in the process.[20] But this is doubtful: it was after all a Christian Democrat who began the Ostpolitik (Schröder), and if the CDU–CSU had not been deprived of office in 1969, their Ostpolitik would probably have been similar in content – albeit perhaps slower in execution – to that of the SPD–FDP coalition. In any case, what was really important about Ostpolitik in its domestic context was that it showed that West Germany had come of age: the economic giant was now a political giant as well, and political giants are inevitably attracted by the 'independent' tenets of 'Gaullism'. There is no reason to think that these tenets would appeal any less to the Christian Democrats if they were in office. For as long as the Federal Republic remains the most powerful country in the Community, the Christian Democrats (like the Social Democrats and Liberals) will doubtless put their country's interests before those of the Community whenever contentious issues arise.

In Italy, too, enthusiasm for Community Europe amongst Christian Democrats has declined somewhat in recent years, partly because the Community has not been able to give Italy what it hoped for and partly because Italy, unlike Germany, became weaker in the 1970s. Beset with serious domestic problems, Italian governments inevitably had to concentrate on them rather than on foreign policy. Nevertheless, in spite of these difficulties, the DC's verbal commitment to European integration and the Atlantic Alliance has remained strong, even if its practical commitment has often been rather weak.[21]

In the initial postwar period (approximately from 1944 to 1948), when Italian governments had to concentrate on domestic reconstruction, the Christian Democrats expressed little interest in European integration. Indeed, De Gasperi became a European integrationist, or at least a Western European integrationist, almost *malgré soi*.[22] He, and the party which he led, were, in effect, *forced* to think out their position and to commit themselves to 'Little Europe' as a result of the development of the Cold War. Originally the Christian Democrats were what one might call 'pan-Europeans'. In so far as they had a vision of a federated Europe, it was of a Europe which would include as many countries as possible, and certainly all those with Catholic and liberal-democratic traditions (widely interpreted).[23] It soon became apparent that such a vision had no chance of fulfilment, and by 1947 Italy was forced to make a straight choice between East and West. Given its political traditions, its geographical situation, its economic dependence on the United States, and its religious affiliation, it was inevitable that Italy's Christian Democratic governments opted for the Atlantic Alliance and European integration. But it is important to emphasise that they did not so much 'choose' Europe as 'get chosen' by the United States to participate in the construction of 'Western Europe'. This is not to say that De Gasperi was not a man of considerable integrity, who genuinely preferred the liberal democratic values of the West to the totalitarianism of Soviet communism. But in assessing Italy's subsequent commitment to European integration and the Atlantic Alliance, it is important to bear in mind that Italian governments really had no choice in the years 1947–50.

Although some Christian Democrats, notably the small group of followers of Giovanni Gronchi, had doubts about the way in which European integration developed, the DC was fundamentally united in its commitment to the *objective* of a closely integrated Europe. In the early days the chief motives were political (a strong preference for liberal-democratic values) and religious (Pius XII's pathological aversion to communism was well known). It was natural, too, that in the halcyon early days of Christian Democracy the DC should want to emphasise its transnational links with the important Christian Democratic parties of France, Belgium, West Germany and the Netherlands. The Italian Christian Democrats, like those of the other Western European countries, also claimed that they were in favour of an integrated Europe for social and economic reasons, and although there is no reason to dispute this claim, there is little doubt that the social and economic motives were less important than the political. In commending the Schuman Plan of 1950, for example, Paolo Emilio Taviani, a close friend of De Gasperi's, emphasised that it was important to improve the standard of living of the citizens of Western Europe, but above all it was essential for the ECSC to become a reality in order that the member-states could provide 'a united front against the spread of Soviet totalitarianism'.[24] He went on to say that the best way to neutralise the German threat was to integrate the German economy with that of its neighbours, an argument used of course by many others besides Christian Democrats.

The DC's strong commitment to EDC, a military organisation, may at first sight seem surprising in view of the fact that there were a number of 'Christian internationalists' in the DC who were opposed to the development of military blocs. This strong commitment to EDC was, however, perfectly logical, given De Gasperi's determination to integrate Europe *politically*. For De Gasperi argued that if the six ECSC countries merged their armies the next logical step would be the setting up of an embryo federal government to control them. Hence it was De Gasperi who was responsible for Article 38 of the EDC Treaty which empowered the ECSC Assembly to prepare plans for a European Political Community (EPC). As for Italy, De Gasperi stated that it was 'ready to transfer wide powers to a European Community, provided that it is democratically organised and gives guarantees of life and development'.[25] And after he had signed the EDC Treaty in Paris in May 1952, he told Italian journalists that EDC would make possible 'the necessary evolution to a vaster and deeper political and economic community'.[26] This, of course, may well have been true; but it was precisely why EDC soon ran into difficulties, not only with the French Gaullists and Communists, who were strongly opposed to the development of a supranational Europe, but also with the German Social Democrats who still paid lip service to the priority of German re-unification over European integration. There can be little doubt about the sincerity of De Gasperi's commitment to a politically united Europe, but as a political realist he must have been aware that the EDC and EPC had little chance of being created in the more relaxed international atmosphere of 1953–4. *Le crime du 30 août*, as the French Christian Democrats labelled the rejection of EDC by the National Assembly,[27] can hardly have come as a great surprise to the Italian Christian Democrats. Nevertheless, it is right to emphasise that the DC contributed significantly, if not always successfully, to the first phase of European integration through its decisive support for the ECSC and EDC.

Although Italy's contribution to the second phase of European integration, i.e. the *relance* of 1955–7, was not as significant as her contribution to the first phase, it was nevertheless important. The *relance* was originally proposed by the Dutch Foreign Minister, Johan Willem Beyen, but Beyen's initiative was at once welcomed by the Italian government, and the initial discussions took place at Messina, the native city of the Italian Foreign Minister, Gaetano Martino. Admittedly Martino, who remained Foreign Minister throughout the negotiations leading to the Treaty of Rome, was a Liberal. But the Italian delegation at the Spaak Committee negotiations in Brussels from July 1955–April 1956 was led by a Christian Democratic deputy, Lodovico Benvenuti, and the DC national congress at Trent in 1956 called for 'the social, economic and political integration of Europe'.[28] If this phrase was rather vague, it is nevertheless clear that the Christian Democrats were demanding a much more encompassing form of integration than that which had been achieved under the ECSC. Moreover, their demand for wide-ranging social and economic integration was met in principle when the Italian proposals for a European Social Fund and European Investment Bank were written into the Treaty.[29]

In practice, however, the post-1958 development of the Community has been a frustrating experience for Italy. The most frequently reiterated Christian Democratic argument in favour of the Community has been that only through full integration in Europe could Italy solve its economic, social and regional problems.[30] But the basic Community mechanism has always been to help those who help themselves, and to a large degree Italy has been unable to take full advantage of its Community membership owing to its own bureaucratic failings.[31] In addition, the enlargement of the Community, for which the Christian Democrats campaigned consistently, proved a further disappointment. The DC had supported British entry for four reasons, all of which turned out to be at least partially invalid: first, they believed that Britain would break the Franco-German entente, and that this would benefit Italy because there would be a 'balancing-up' between the four main countries; secondly, they hoped that Britain would work with Italy to achieve a more effective Community regional policy; thirdly, they believed that Italy would benefit from the opening-up of the British market to Italian goods; and finally, they expected the British to press for a more democratic Community, with a more effective Parliament.[32]

The Italian Christian Democrats have also consistently advocated the strengthening and democratising of the Community's institutions. In the Fouchet Plan negotiations of 1961–2, for example, Fanfani opposed the original French plan which would have entailed the setting up of institutions parallel to those of the Community.[33] Likewise, in the Luxembourg crisis of 1965–6, Fanfani supported the Commission in its attempt to increase the financial powers of the European Parliament and Commission.[34] It must be added that at the same time he refused to accept the other half of the Commission's package, namely that the Common Agricultural Market should be completed within two years. De Gaulle was thus able to accuse Italy of having provoked the crisis. Italy, however, played a significant part in preventing the crisis from leading to the disintegration of the Community, for Emilio Colombo, the DC Minister of Agriculture, acted throughout the seven-month crisis as the intermediary between France and the Five.

In 1969 Italy again influenced an important development in the Community, when, together with the Benelux countries, it insisted that the European Parliament should have the power from 1975 to control that part of the Community's budget which is allocated to running the institutions. This only amounted to 3·6 per cent of the Community's total budget, but it was at least a step towards increasing the powers of the European Parliament; moreover, there is some evidence that the Germans would have been prepared to compromise with the French if the Italians, Dutch and Belgians had not stuck firmly to their original position.[35] Then in March 1970, at the Foreign Ministers' meeting which appointed the Davignon Committee to work out means for the closer co-ordination of Community foreign policy, Aldo Moro, the Italian Foreign Minister, not only supported the Davignon proposals, but also put forward a three-point plan for the gradual achievement of a European federal union.[36] And in 1975, during Tindemans' fact-finding tour on the political future of the Community, the Italian Christian Democrats again emphasised their support for a directly elected European Parliament.[37]

It is, of course, easy to criticise Italy, and *a fortiori* the DC as the leading party of government, for its failures in the Community, for example its refusal to renew its delegation to the European Parliament between 1958–69 or its failure to implement Value Added Tax on time. But, as the preceding paragraphs have shown, the Italian Christian Democrats have made a number of positive contributions to the development of the Community, and they have done so whilst facing daunting problems at home.

There is no need to analyse the French Christian Democrats' contribution to European integration here.[38] Suffice to say that throughout the Fourth Republic the MRP was *the* European party in France, and that its successors in the Fifth Republic have maintained that tradition. In May 1962 the four MRP ministers in Pompidou's government resigned after de Gaulle had made disparaging remarks about the Community. This was the last occasion on which the MRP as such held ministerial portfolios, but those who remained within the Christian Democratic tendency, notably Jean Lecanuet and Joseph Fontanet, have supported such developments as the enlargement of the Community and the decision to hold direct elections to the European Parliament. In the light of the French general election of 1978 it seemed likely that the influence of the pro-Europeans would increase rather than the reverse.[39]

As we have seen, there have been a number of reasons why Christian Democrats have been committed supporters of European integration: amongst the most important have been economic, social, cultural and religious factors. But the over-riding motive has been political, namely anti-communism. The importance of this motive explains both the early enthusiasm and the subsequent lassitude of the Christian Democratic commitment to integration. The Christian Democrats were determined to build a liberal-democratic Europe in the void left by fascism and exposed to communism. In the Cold War atmosphere of the late 1940s and early 1950s the Christian Democrats had no hesitation in opting for the Atlantic Alliance and what at that time seemed to be its essential corollary, a united Western Europe. Adenauer talked about 'the danger from the East'; European unification would not only reduce that danger, it would also mean that 'we can throw the weight of a united Europe into the balance in the negotiations about security and reunification.'[40] Adenauer probably no longer believed in the validity of this argument by the end of his chancellorship, but in the 1950s it undoubtedly conditioned his attitude to the Western Alliance and European integration. For the French MRP anti-communism, both external and internal, was also the major motive for the party's determined advocacy of European integration. Two examples (out of many) will suffice as indications of this. Alfred Coste-Floret told his constituents in 1956: 'We are defending peace by building a united Europe in the face of the Soviet danger.'[41] And Alain Poher told the 1955 MRP congress that a united Europe would develop into a prosperous Europe, from which poverty, 'the springboard of communism',[42] would be banished. Other important factors influencing the MRP were of course the desire to integrate West Germany into the new Europe, plus the fact that as the party declined in the 1950s 'Europe' became a surrogate for MRP's failures at home; the

Christian Democrats realised that they had little future in France, but that they might have better prospects in a united Europe. The Italian Christian Democrats shared French fears about Germany, and they also had a strong feeling that Italy, as the cradle of European Christendom and civilisation, should participate actively in the creation of Community Europe. But anti-communism was the main unifying force behind the DC's commitment to European integration; the party projected its domestic battle with the PCI on to the European stage, constantly emphasising its determination to defeat totalitarianism at both levels.[43]

By the 1960s, and especially the 1970s, the communist threat was much less obvious. Despite the Berlin Crisis of 1958–61 and the invasion of Czechoslovakia in 1968, it was clear that the Russian steam-roller was not going suddenly to advance into NATO territory: the Iron Curtain was there to stay, and the only practical policy seemed to be to try to improve relations with the Eastern bloc – hence the Ostpolitik and détente. As the Cold War tensions declined and the *status quo* was increasingly accepted by both sides, so enthusiasm for the building of a federal Europe waned. Moreover, the declining interest in integration was encouraged by the fact that the Communist parties of Western Europe – for so long the arch-enemies of the Atlantic Alliance and the Community – had come round to accepting the continued existence of both, particularly of the latter.[44] In these circumstances of international détente and domestic quasi-détente between the Communists and their opponents it was difficult to generate the necessary political will to integrate Europe further. Although Christian Democrats would probably deny it, it is clear that they – like other 'European' enthusiasts – have been motivated over the years more by fear of the Soviet Union and of Germany (in that order) than by ideals about the brotherhood of man or the values of liberal democracy. By the 1970s the chief motivating force was too weak to bring about the degree of European integration dreamed of by the Christian Democratic pioneers Schuman, De Gasperi and Adenauer. The achievement of a federal Europe remained, as Schuman perspicaciously remarked in 1957, an 'immense task'.[45]

Christian Democratic Transnational Liaison in Europe

The Christian Democrats, as we have seen, have played an important, if not always successful, role in promoting and implementing European integration since 1945. In large measure filling the political vacuum left by nazism in Germany, by fascism in Italy, and by Pétainism in France, Christian Democrats helped not only to reconstruct the economic and political systems of their own countries, but also to ensure that human rights and the values of liberal democracy were safeguarded at the European level against totalitarian threats. But, although the Christian Democrats were powerful advocates of close collaboration between the European nation-states, their own collaboration at a transnational level remained fairly rudimentary until the 1970s. Indeed, as long as the institutional development of the European Community was at a standstill – as it was throughout the Gaullist-dominated 1960s – there was no particular reason why the Christian Democrats (or politicians of other persuasions) should consider setting up a 'European Party' or drawing up a 'European Manifesto'. The Hague summit conference of EEC heads of government in 1969, however, with its emphasis on the enlargement and further development of the Community, marked the beginning of a new European *relance*, whilst the Paris summit of 1974, envisaging direct elections to the European Parliament in 1978 (subsequently postponed to 1979), acted as a further catalyst to transnational co-operation by the main political parties in the European Community.

In April 1976 the Christian Democrats set up a European-level political federation (umbrella party), the European People's Party (EPP).[46] The Christian Democrats perhaps had an advantage over the Socialists, Conservatives and Gaullists owing to their long and clearcut commitment to political integration, and over the Liberals, because the Liberal parties of Western Europe vary so widely in political complexion. Moreover, in spite of the *institutional* weakness of their transnational links, the Christian Democrats had a useful structure on which to build.

There was no Christian Democratic 'International' until after the Second World War, although the seeds for such an organisation were sown by Don Luigi Sturzo in the 1920s and nurtured in the 1930s and during the war.[47] As early as 1921 Sturzo had proposed a transnational Christian Democratic organisation, and as an exile in Paris (from 1924) he set up an International Secretariat of Information and Liaison and organised one or two congresses of Christian-Democratic-type parties. One such congress took place in December 1925 in Paris, and was attended by representatives from France, Italy, Germany, Poland and Lithuania; in subsequent years Dutch, Swiss, Austrian and Czech delegates also attended these congresses. Sturzo kept this European Christian Democratic framework in being during the war with his People and Freedom movement (so-called because of the review of that name), which was run from London; through this movement he maintained liaison between European Catholic resisters and Christian Democratic exiles in the United States and Britain. In 1945 Sturzo replaced the People and Freedom movement with the International Information Service of Christian Democracy, which he ran from Switzerland. Various meetings of Christian Democrats – including representatives from Poland, Czechoslovakia and Hungary – took place in 1946, and the outcome was the setting up in 1947 of the *Nouvelles Equipes Internationales*, the first transnational Christian Democratic organisation with a proper, if weak, structure.

The *Nouvelles Equipes Internationales* (NEI), so-named to avoid a 'confessional' image, which would have upset the French MRP and Belgian PSC, was founded at Chaudfontaine in Belgium. Christian Democratic parties as such could join the NEI (as was the case with, for example, the CDU and DC), or they could send representatives without actually joining (as was at first the case with the MRP), or they could join as a team (*équipe*), (as, for example, did the three Dutch parties); even countries without a Christian Democratic party could join (the British, for example, sent along a small 'team' of sympathisers).

The structure of the NEI was fairly elementary, the main organ being the

Political Bureau, which was the small permanent organising committee which emanated from the International Committee on which all the parties or *équipes* were represented. The NEI also had a small permanent secretariat, with its seat at first in Brussels, then in Paris and finally in Rome. At various periods the NEI published *Cahiers*, and set up study groups to examine such matters as East-West relations, social policy and cultural policy. But probably the NEI's most important achievement was to bring together European Christian Democratic politicians at its annual congresses. The NEI congresses received considerable publicity in the late 1940s and early 1950s, as many of those who attended them were prominent politicians in their own countries – men such as Alcide De Gasperi from Italy, Georges Bidault and Robert Schuman from France, Konrad Adenauer from Germany, Paul van Zeeland and Auguste de Schrijver from the Netherlands, and Théo Lefèvre from Belgium. Besides giving publicity to the Europe-wide Christian Democratic movement and promoting liaison between practising politicians, the NEI also encouraged young Christian Democrats to meet together; hence the setting up of the International Union of Young Christian Democrats in 1951. In addition the NEI maintained links with Eastern Europe (the exile Christian Democratic Union of Central Europe constituting one of its *équipes*), and prepared the way for the setting up of Christian Democratic parliamentary groups in the Consultative Assembly of the Council of Europe and in the Common Assembly of the European Coal and Steel Community in the 1950s. The NEI also encouraged worldwide Christian Democratic links, and was a founder-member of the World Union of Christian Democrats which was set up in 1961. Other founder-members of this body (which still holds bi-annual congresses) were the important South American Organización Democrática Cristiana de América (ODCA, founded in 1948), the International Union of Young Christian Democrats, and the Christian Democratic Union of Central Europe.

By the 1960s it was felt that closer liaison between the European Christian Democratic parties was desirable, especially with a view to reconciling the differences between, for example, the Benelux Christian Democrats and the 'Gaullist' wing of the CDU–CSU in their attitude towards France in particular, and with regard to the European Community in general. As a result of such pressures the rather loose NEI was replaced with the more tightly structured European Union of Christian Democrats (EUCD) in 1965. Like its predecessor, the EUCD has its headquarters in Rome, but it also has an important sub-office in Brussels. The EUCD includes Christian Democratic parties from non EEC countries (Austria, Switzerland, Spain, Portugal and Malta), as well as from seven of the nine EEC countries (Britain and Denmark being the exceptions). The supreme organ of the EUCD is the Political Bureau, whose presidents between 1965–78 have been Théo Lefèvre, Mariano Rumor and Kai-Uwe von Hassel. Besides the president, the members of the Political Bureau are the four vice-presidents, five representatives from each of the member-parties, the presidents of the Christian Democratic groups in the European Parliament, the Council of Europe and Western European Union, and the EUCD secretary-general and his two assistant secretaries-general. In addition, former Christian Democratic EEC commissioners and presidents of the Christian Democratic group in the European Parliament are *ex-officio* members of the Bureau. The five representatives of the individual parties are normally their president, secretary, foreign affairs spokesman and two parliamentarians. Consisting, as it does, of up to eighty members the Political Bureau is rather an unwieldy body, and owing to its international character inevitably cannot meet very often. Normally, in fact, it meets only three or four times a year, holds debates and issues a communiqué. Before such meetings a good deal of preparatory work is done by multinational working parties and by bilateral discussions. All parties within the EUCD formally have the same status, but owing to their size the German and Italian parties tend to play a predominant role in the proceedings of the Political Bureau.

In practice the key body in the EUCD is not the Political Bureau, but the permanent Secretariat. Directly responsible to the Political Bureau – although in practice really to the president – the Secretariat is responsible for liaison between the member-parties, for providing them with information, and for running the Christian Democratic Documentation Centre in Rome, which publishes *Cahiers* on specific subjects on which the Christian Democrats have carried out research. The Documentation Centre also publishes *Panorama Démocrate Chrétien*, which comes out four times a year, and includes American and African, as well as European, contributions. There is, in addition, a semi-permanent research committee, Pensée et Action, which works under the auspices of the EUCD: it brings together parliamentarians and experts from the Christian Democratic parties' national research centres and from the Christian Democratic parliamentary group in the European Parliament to study matters of mutual interest to the parties. The reports of Pensée et Action are published either as *Cahiers*, or in such Christian Democratic reviews as the German *Politische Meinung*, Italian *La Discussione* and Dutch *Politiek Perspectief*, often appearing simultaneously in all three.

In 1972 the EUCD took an important step towards the setting up of a European political party by establishing a Political Committee consisting of the EEC members of the European Union of Christian Democrats and the Bureau of the Christian Democratic group in the European Parliament. This body was entrusted with the dual task of intensifying liaison between the Christian Democratic parties of the European Community and preparing the way for a European Christian Democratic party with a structure and programme. The final outcome of this initiative – stimulated by the Paris summit's decision of 1974 in favour of direct elections to the European Parliament – was the establishment in 1976 of the European People's Party (EPP), or, to be more precise, 'Federation', for article 2 of the EPP's Statutes emphasises that 'The member-parties shall retain their name, their identity and their freedom of action within the framework of their national responsibilities.' So the EPP is more a federation of parties than a unified party.[48]

Before discussing the European People's Party in detail it is appropriate to say something about the Christian Democratic group in the European Parliament, not least because the EPP is in part the creation of the European Parliament group, or to be more precise the creation of its Bureau, which was a member of the Political Committee (together with representatives of the EUCD) which gave birth to the EPP.

In considering the role of the Christian Democratic group in the European Parliament, it is important to bear in mind that the powers of the European Parliament are limited: it is not a legislature, but a consultative assembly; it has no control over the Council of Ministers, the Community's key decision-making body; and it does not appoint the Commission, although it has the power to dismiss it by a two-thirds majority (a rather meaningless power, as the Commission and Parliament are usually in agreement, and in any case there is not much point in being able to dismiss a body if one has no power to replace it). Nevertheless, even if the powers of the European Parliament are limited, it is likely to become an increasingly important body after its members have been directly elected. Indeed, it will almost certainly become the main forum for the advocacy of greater political and economic integration. And, on past evidence, the Christian Democrats, both individually and as a parliamentary group, are likely to be amongst the leading proponents of further integration.

Groups were first formed in the Common Assembly of the Coal and Steel Community (the direct precursor of the European Parliament) in 1953.[49] At that time thirty-eight of the Assembly's seventy-seven members were Christian Democrats, and from 1953–8, when the Assembly was merged into the European Parliament, the Christian Democrats had between 47 and 50 per cent of the members, providing the Assembly with all its presidents except for Paul-Henri Spaak, the Belgian Socialist who was its first president.[50] In the first decade of the European Parliament's history, the percentage of Christian Democratic members never dropped below 45 per cent, and all the presidents except Gaetano Martino (Liberal, 1962–4) were Christian Democrats until 1971.[51] With the decline in the Christian Democratic vote throughout Western Europe in the late 1960s and early 1970s and the inclusion of Communists in the Italian delegation from 1969, the percentage of Christian Democrats in the European Parliament declined to below 40 per cent for the first time in 1969, and in 1973 (after enlargement, but before the British Labour Party took up its quota of seats) the Christian Democratic percentage dropped to 28 per cent. Finally, after the arrival of the British Labour delegation in September 1975, the percentage of Christian Democratic members dropped to 26 per cent, and for the first time the Christian Democratic group was not the largest in the European Parliament: the Socialist group now had sixty-eight members, the Christian Democrats fifty-one, the Liberals twenty-four, the Conservatives and Gaullists seventeen each, the Communists fifteen, and six members were independents. Between 1971–7 the Christian Democrats lost their accustomed presidency of the Parliament to two Socialists (Walter Behrendt and Georges Spenale) and a Liberal (Cornelius Berkhouwer), but in 1977 another Christian Democrat, Emilio Colombo, the former Italian Minister of the Treasury and prime minister, was elected president with the combined votes of the Christian Democrats, Conservatives and Liberals.[52]

Although the European Parliament lacks many of the powers of national legislatures, it has become a more active body in the 1970s, not least since the British Conservative group (especially under Peter Kirk, who died in 1977) tried to exploit its power to the full. As a result the parliamentary groups have become more active: the Christian Democratic group, for example, held eighty meetings in 1974–5 compared with sixty in 1972–3. By 1975–6 the European Parliament was examining about 350 documents a year, and all those which were politically important were examined by the groups. Indeed, an efficient member of the European Parliament could expect to work for up to 150 days a year on European business, a considerable task, especially for members who were also deputies in the lower house of their national parliaments. And the problems of being a European member of parliament were worsened by the geographical 'dislocation' of the European Parliament, which continued to hold its plenary sessions in Strasbourg or Luxembourg and most of its committee meetings in Brussels; meanwhile, its secretariat remained in Luxembourg. This 'dislocation' made it all the more important for the parliamentary groups to have an efficient secretariat.

As far as the Christian Democratic group is concerned, its three main 'institutions' are its presidency, Secretariat and Presidential Bureau. The Secretariat is the permanent liaison and information organisation, and its secretary-general has the important task of keeping the group's far-flung membership informed about the various draft proposals of the Commission. The Secretariat publishes a bi-monthly information sheet, *DC-Europe*, and helps with the publication of *Cahiers Européens*, a joint EUCD-parliamentary group research journal. The president of the group has a key role, for not only is he a member of the Presidential Bureau of the European Parliament (the body which organises the assembly's business), but he also decides when to call meetings of the group, chairs such sessions, has overall responsibility for the work of the various specialist sub-committees of the group, and supervises the group's secretariat. In addition, he is a member of the EUCD Political Bureau, and of the important Political Committee, the joint EUCD-parliamentary group body set up in 1972.[53] It is generally agreed that the Christian Democratic group was particularly well served by the French Senator, Alain Poher, between 1958–66, in that he both strengthened liaison within the group and promoted closer liaison with the EUCD.[54] It was under Poher, for example, that the joint EUCD-parliamentary group study committees on European integration, social policy and economic policy were established. His successors have been Joseph Illerhaus (German CDU, 1966–70), Hans-August Lücker (German CDU, 1970–5), Alfred Bertrand (Belgian PSC–CVP, 1975–7), and Egon Klepsch (German CDU, elected in 1977). Under Lücker an important step was taken in 1975 with the setting up of the group Presidential Bureau, a committee of three (including the president), which initiates, organises and controls the business of the parliamentary group.

Normally the Christian Democratic group meets in Brussels in the week prior to plenary sessions, but sometimes it meets instead in Luxembourg or Strasbourg immediately prior to the plenary sessions. At such meetings Commission proposals are examined and debated by the group, which then agrees on a spokesman for the full session. European Parliamentary groups are also allowed to meet for three-day sessions twice a year in one of the EEC countries to discuss Community matters, and the Christian Democrats have taken full advantage of this regulation, meeting, for example, in Stresa and Paris in 1961, in Kiel and Rome in 1969, and in Dublin and Trent in 1974. Discipline within the group is good, although there are no precise disciplinary regulations. If a member disagrees with the group line, he is expected to state his reasons publicly. But this rarely happens, and on 90 per cent of issues the group votes unanimously. Sometimes there have been differences of view between northerners and southerners over agricultural policy, or between (some) Germans and the Belgians or Dutch over the policies of Gaullist France, but generally the group is remarkably united. This, of course, might change if the European Parliament were to become more powerful, and national issues were really at stake. In the meantime Christian Democratic unity has been assured, partly because of the domination of the group by the large German and Italian delegations, partly because the Christian Democrats are more united than the other groups in their commitment to the development of a federal Europe and all that that entails, e.g. majority voting in the Council, increased budgetary powers for the Parliament, a more important role for the Commission, and the promotion of common regional, industrial, economic and fiscal policies. The Christian Democratic commitment to such goals is constantly emphasised in *CD Europe Bulletin*, and it also formed a substantial part of the European People's Party Manifesto of February 1978. Indeed, it was entirely appropriate that the 1976 Report on the future political development of the Community was drawn up under the chairmanship of a Christian Democrat, the Belgian Prime Minister Leo Tindemans.

Obviously, if the European Parliament becomes a more important institution within the Community, the extent of group cohesion and of transnational party liaison will be of crucial importance; hence the potential significance of the establishment of the European People's Party and of the tenuous, but growing, liaison between the Christian Democrats and Conservatives.

The European People's Party (EPP) was founded in April 1976, and elected Leo Tindemans as its first president in July of that year. Tindemans stated that 'The major task of our new party will be to breathe new life into the idea of European union; to fight to ensure that European unity is eventually achieved.'[55] The EPP is a federation of the Christian Democratic parties of the European Community, the member-parties having lost none of their autonomy as national parties.[56] Nevertheless, the EPP has a more definite structure than either of its predecessors, the NEI and EUCD (the latter of course has not been superseded by the EPP), and it has drawn up a reasonably precise electoral Manifesto for the 1979 European Parliament elections, committing the EPP *inter alia* to a federal Europe, more frequent majority voting in the Council of Ministers, and increased powers for the Commission and Parliament.[57] This Manifesto was approved at the first EPP congress in March 1978. In its Statutes the EPP lays down that its objective is 'to support the process of European integration and to co-operate in the transformation of Europe into a European Union with a view to achieving a Federal Union' (Article 3). Inevitably some parts of both the Statutes and the Manifesto are couched in rather vague terms – in a federation of twelve parties (now ten owing to the amalgamation of the three Dutch parties) from seven countries this is hardly surprising. Nevertheless, both documents are quite specific in their commitment to the construction of a federal Europe, a commitment which would certainly not be forthcoming from European Conservatives or Socialists at this stage in the development of the Community, but is fully shared by the Liberals.

Moreover, the EPP has endowed itself with a useful structure, even though it is clear that much will depend on how this structure is developed. The EPP has four organs: the Congress, Political Bureau, Executive Committee, and Presidency.

The congress is due to meet at least once every two years. Consisting of the EPP Political Bureau, the members of the Christian Democratic group in the European Parliament, delegates of the national parties, and representatives of the women's and young Christian Democrats' associations, the congress decides on the main policy guidelines of the EPP – 'in particular, it shall agree on the electoral programme' (Article 6). Secondly, there is the Political Bureau, which has just over sixty members (the EPP president and four vice-presidents, the treasurer, fifty national party representatives, two representatives of the associations, and the three members of Presidential Bureau of the Christian Democratic group in the European Parliament).[58] The Political Bureau meets at least three times a year, and is the body which 'implements political decisions on the basis of the guidelines and political programme laid down by the Congress' (Article 7, f). In addition, the Bureau has the important task of electing the president, vice-president and treasurer; appointing the secretary-general and assistant secretaries-general; considering applications for membership; liaising with the European Union of Christian Democrats; and organising election campaigns for the European Parliament.

As the Bureau is a fairly large body and meets only three times per year, in practice the key organs in the EPP are almost certain to be the Executive Committee of twenty and the president, assisted of course by the permanent secretariat. The Executive Committee is a streamlined version of the Political Bureau, its members being the president, vice-presidents, treasurer, the Bureau of the Christian Democratic group in the European Parliament, and one member each from the national parties. Finally, much will depend – as in the past in the EUCD – on the president, who has the important responsibility of representing the EPP 'both internally and externally', presiding over 'all the party's organs', and ensuring close liaison 'between the party and the group in the European Parliament and the European Union of Christian Democrats', and 'between the party and other democratic parties and their European groupings' (Article 9). In its first president, Leo Tindemans, the EPP certainly had an able politician and committed 'European'.

It is too early to make any precise judgements about the EPP. All that can be said at this stage is that it is significant that such a transnational federation has come into being. It is also too early to judge the importance of the tenuous links which have developed between the Christian Democrats and Conservatives. The future of these links, as of the EPP itself, is closely bound up with the future of the European Parliament, and in particular the extent to which that body develops as a 'motor' of integration. In the meantime, all that can be said is that it is important that a number of links do exist between the Christian Democrats and the Conservatives, and that certain political views are common to both 'groups'.

Some of the Christian Democratic and Conservative parties of Western Europe have in fact held joint congresses since 1967,[59] and some of their youth movements have been in contact with each other since 1951, meeting together in the Democrat Youth Community of Europe (the former Conservative and Christian Democratic Youth Community). But it was not until the Paris summit of 1974 decided in favour of direct elections to the European Parliament, and the British Labour delegation arrived in Strasbourg in 1975, that the Conservatives and Christian Democrats began to talk seriously about forming an anti-Socialist alliance. The final resolution of the Salzburg Congress of Christian Democrats and Conservatives in September 1975, for example, called for a common stand against 'Socialism in Europe', and for the setting up of what Helmut Kohl, the CDU leader, called a 'Dachorganisation' (an umbrella organisation) as the first step towards the establishment of an anti-Socialist *Volkspartei*.[60] It should be noted, however, that these annual congresses have a 'Conservative' rather than a 'Christian Democratic' flavour, in that whilst the rather conservative German, Austrian and Swiss Christian Democrats have been regular attenders, the Benelux parties have been irregular attenders, whilst the Italian DC has never sent representatives (though the DC's sister party, the tiny *Südtiroler Volkspartei* has). In contrast the Conservative parties of Britain, Sweden, Norway, Finland and Denmark have attended all the congresses, and both Peter Kirk (leader of the Conservative group in the European Parliament, 1973–7) and Christopher Soames (European commissioner, 1973–7) were constant advocates of a Centre-Right alliance in the European Parliament, although not of any sort of merger between the Conservative and Christian Democratic groups.[61]

At their Copenhagen congress in 1976 the Conservatives and those Christian Democrats present took a further step towards the achievement of Kohl's proposed umbrella organisation by approving the idea of a 'European Democratic Union' of anti-Socialist parties. The Copenhagen congress was attended by representatives of the Conservative parties of Britain, Sweden, Norway, Finland and Denmark, and of the Christian Democratic parties of Germany, Austria, Luxembourg, France, Switzerland and Portugal. Finally, in April 1978, the right-of-centre European Democratic Union was officially set up at Salzburg in Austria, with the British, Danish, Norwegian and Finnish Conservatives, French Gaullists, and German, Austrian and Portuguese Christian Democrats as founder-members.[62] As far as the European Community is concerned the chief significance of the establishment of the European Democratic Union is that it further strengthens the links between the British Conservatives and German Christian Democrats (the latter of course belong to the EPP as well). The two parties have in fact been in close liaison for a long time, regularly sending official representatives to each other's congresses, and their links in the European Parliament were further strengthened in 1977 when Egon Klepsch, chairman of the CDU *Junge Union* from 1963–9 (and thus a man with long-established contacts with the Young Conservatives), became president of the Christian Democratic group in the European Parliament in place of the Belgian trade-unionist Alfred Bertrand.[63]

As previously emphasised, the future relationship between the Christian Democrats and Conservatives will doubtless depend to a large extent on the institutional balance within the Community. If the European Parliament acquires significant power, it is probable that the Christian Democrats and Conservatives will sink their differences and form some sort of an anti-Socialist alliance. It is true that the Italian Christian Democrats refused to consider joining the European Democratic Union because of its anti-Socialist philosophy.[64] The Germans, in contrast, were keen to join the EDU precisely because it was overtly anti-Socialist.[65] The Belgian Christian Democrats – owing to the many coalitions they have formed with the Socialists, as well as their close links with the Catholic trade unions – remain suspicious of the British Conservatives, and these doubts apply, although decreasingly, to the Dutch Christian Democrats.[66] It is also true that the Conservatives are rather 'Gaullist' in their attitude to institutional developments in the Community, whilst the Christian Democrats are advocates of more 'supranationalism'. However, if the European Parliament develops on ideological party lines (and it is by no means certain that it will, for example north-south conflicts may become increasingly important after the second enlargement), the Christian Democrats are more likely to line up with the Conservatives than with the Socialists. The Christian Democratic parties of Germany, the Netherlands, France and Luxembourg, have developed into essentially centre-right rather than centre-left parties.[67] Moreover, the Flemish wing of the Belgian Christian Democratic movement, as well as several of the *correnti* in the Italian DC, are more inclined to the Right than the Left. The British Conservative Party is likewise essentially a moderate party of the Centre-Right. One-third of its voters are working class, even though it does not have a trade union wing comparable to that of the German, Belgian and Italian Christian Democratic parties. And in practice the British Conservative Party is less conservative in its economic and social policies than the Dutch, Belgian and Italian Liberal parties. In other words the Christian Democrats and Conservatives tend to straddle the Centre and Centre-Right of the political spectrum, even if a minority of Christian Democrats are well to the left of Centre and a minority of Conservatives are well to the right of Centre.

In conclusion, it should be stressed that whilst the Left-Right analysis of political parties is rather crude, it still has some value. Certainly, for example, the Christian Democrats, moderate Conservatives and moderate Liberals do not appear to be unnatural political bedfellows (their joint vote in favour of Colombo as president of the European Parliament might even suggest the opposite). And, as Frank Swaelen, the CVP secretary-general pointed out in 1976, it is more than likely that if and when the Christian Democrats start working with the Conservatives the former will find that the Conservatives are not 'conservative' in the continental sense, i.e. reactionary, and likewise the Conservatives will doubtless find that the Christian Democrats are not just members of a 'Black International' or impractical 'Eurofanatics'.[68]

Conclusion: Christian Democracy in Europe since the War

A few years ago the Christian Democratic parties of Western Europe appeared to be in serious difficulties. The influence of religion on politics seemed to be declining, and this had worked to the disadvantage of the 'confessional' parties, for the Christian Democratic parties had never quite succeeded in getting rid of their 'confessional' image in spite of considerable efforts (at least in Europe north of the Alps) to do so. In addition, the much-heralded 'waning of ideologies' of the early 1960s seemed to come to an end (or even to be reversed) at the end of the decade, when there was evidence of a reaction against materialism, the consumer society, and the politics of pragmatism and compromise. At the same time, the European Community, into which the early Christian Democrats had poured so much of their enthusiasm, appeared to have reached a situation of deadlock: this depressed the morale of the Christian Democrats further, and encouraged the young to look elsewhere for the fulfilment of their ideals. Sometimes they looked to the established parties of the Left, such as the German Social Democratic Party or the Dutch Labour Party, sometimes to traditional parties of the Left with a 'new' image, such as the French Socialist Party or the Italian Communist Party, sometimes to new left-wing parties such as the Italian Independent Proletarian Socialists or the Dutch Democrats '66. Other voters showed an increased interest in right-wing constitutional parties such as the Belgian and Dutch Liberal (i.e. Conservative) parties, or in extreme right-wing parties such as the German National Democratic Party and the Italian neo-Fascist party. Yet others preferred regional parties, such as the Belgian *Volksunie*, *Rassemblement Wallon* and *Front Démocratique des Francophones*, or minor 'principled' parties such as the Dutch splinter parties of the Left and Right (e.g. the Radical Party and DS '70) or the French Unified Socialist Party. In any case, there was a widespread decline of loyalty to the Christian Democratic parties, which were seen (especially by the young) as pragmatic, compromising and rather boring parties. This decline was clearly shown at elections.[1]

In West Germany, for example, the Christian Democrats suffered a second electoral defeat in a row in 1972, and for the first time in the history of the Federal Republic the CDU–CSU had fewer seats in the Bundestag than the SFD. In the Netherlands the 'confessional'/Christian Democratic vote declined from over 50 per cent in 1956 to 31 per cent in 1972. In Belgium the Social Christian share of the poll went down steadily from 46·5 per cent in 1958 to 30 per cent in 1971. In France the once powerful MRP – fulcrum of almost every government in the Fourth Republic – had dissolved itself in 1966, and its heir the *Centre Démocrate* won only 10 per cent of the vote in 1973 (by then the *Centre Démocrate* was a constituent part of the *Mouvement Réformateur*). Meanwhile, in Italy in the mid-1970s, the Christian Democrats seemed to be seriously threatened for the first time by the Communists:

[1] See Appendix, p. 261.

whereas at the 1972 general election the Communists, with 27·2 per cent of the vote, were still eleven points behind the Christian Democrats, by the regional elections of 1975 they had closed the gap to two points (33·4 per cent to 35·3 per cent). Even tiny Luxembourg opted for a Socialist-Liberal coalition in 1974, having had predominantly Christian Democratic governments without a break since 1919. Finally, in the European Community the Christian Democrats lost their accustomed position as the largest group in the European Parliament for the first time in 1975, being relegated to second place behind the Socialist group when the British Labour Party members took their seats at Strasbourg.

But it is said to be darkest just before the dawn, and by the late 1970s the situation – at least electorally – looked much more favourable for the Christian Democrats. In the light of the energy crisis of the mid-1970s, inflation, relatively high unemployment (especially amongst the young), and sporadic outbursts of urban terrorism, there was a revival of interest in the 'old' Christian Democratic values – pragmatism, class reconciliation, *concertation*, concern for the security of the individual, and even European integration (shown, for example, by the decision to hold direct elections to the European Parliament). Certainly Christian Democracy remained a major political force throughout most of the countries of Western Europe, and in the five countries of the European Community which have significant Christian Democratic parties (i.e. Italy, Germany, Belgium, the Netherlands and Luxembourg), the average Christian Democratic poll at general elections in the late 1970s was approximately 36 per cent.[2]

In difficult circumstances the Italian Christian Democrats held off the challenge of the Communists at the general election of 1976 (38·7 per cent for the DC to 34·4 per cent for the PCI). In the same year the West German Christian Democrats almost unseated the Socialist-Liberal coalition, winning 48·6 per cent of the votes cast, their highest poll since the *annus mirabilis* of 1957 when, under Adenauer, they won an absolute majority. At the Belgian general election of 1977 the Social Christians polled 35·9 per cent, continuing the upward trend apparent in 1974, and moving well away from their nadir of 1971 (30 per cent). In the same year the Dutch Christian Democratic Appeal, fighting its first general election, polled 31·9 per cent, slightly more than the three confessional parties had polled when fighting separately in 1972 (their total then was 31·3 per cent, their lowest poll since the war), and at the provincial elections of 1978 the Dutch Christian Democrats made further progress, moving ahead of the Labour Party. Finally, at the European Community level, the European People's Party, a 'federation' of the Community's Christian Democratic parties, was launched in 1976, and agreed upon a manifesto for the 1979 elections to the European Parliament at its first full congress in March 1978.

Overall, then, in electoral terms the Christian Democratic parties had recovered much of their former strength by the late 1970s. In addition, they constituted the chief component of the Italian, Belgian and Dutch govern-

[2] If France is included, the figure was 28 per cent. See Appendix, p. 261.

ments, whilst the Christian Democratic *tendance* formed a minor, but not unimportant, part of the French *majorité*. And in the European Parliament they could wield considerable influence, especially when allied with the Conservatives and Liberals (as in the election of the Italian Christian Democrat Emilio Colombo to the presidency of the Parliament in 1977).

However, the Christian Democratic parties of Western Europe were in no position to be complacent. Amongst the transnational problems facing them, one of the most important was the declining influence of organised religion, even though, as we have seen, 'religiosity' (a person's general attitude towards Christianity, whether or not that person practises his religion) remains a significant electoral variable. But Christian Democratic parties can no longer rely on the Papacy or the Hierarchy to 'direct' the Catholic electorate: when the German Hierarchy tried to do so over abortion in 1972, and when the Italian Church tried to do so over divorce in 1974, many Catholics simply ignored the views of their leaders, deciding that these moral issues should be left to the individual conscience.

Another transnational problem for the Christian Democrats has been the declining political influence of agriculture. For long the Christian Democrats were *the* party of the small farmers of Italy, Belgium, France and West Germany. The decline of the rural vote has, of course, been most dramatic in Italy, because Italy had such a high proportion of its work-force engaged in agriculture (still over 40 per cent in 1951, but well under 20 per cent by 1971). Moreover, the Christian Democratic response to the decimation of its rural base in Italy has been a dangerous one, for, by increasing its 'colonisation' of some of the most parasitic sectors of society, the DC has exposed itself to the risk that it may not be able to carry out reforms even if it wishes to do so. The problem has not been quite so serious in Germany and Belgium, where the *Bauernverband* and *Boerenbond* have nevertheless both declined in influence in the 1970s. However, the decline in the rural vote has meant that the Christian Democratic parties in both these countries, as well as in France, have had to take greater account of the aspirations of the urban electorate.

In this connection the Christian Democrats are faced with another difficult problem, for generally speaking the one-time confessional trade unions of Western Europe have distanced themselves from the Christian Democratic parties. The mainly Catholic *Confederazione Italiana di Sindacati Lavoratori* (CISL) and the Catholic-Socialist *Confédération Française Démocratique du Travail* (CFDT) do not even belong to the World Confederation of Labour (the mainly Catholic successor to the International Confederation of Christian Trade Unions). The *Nederlands Katholiek Vakverbond* (the Dutch Catholic trade union confederation) works much more closely with the Socialist *Nederlands Verbond van Vakvereinigingen* than with the Catholic People's Party, and since 1956 NKV members have been given complete freedom to vote as they wished; many have voted for the Labour or Radical (Left Catholic) parties: hence the dramatic decline in the Catholic People's Party vote from 31 per cent in the late 1950s to just over 17 per cent in 1972. Belgium is to some extent an exception to the rule, in that the Catholic trade union confederation (CSC–ACV) is bigger than the Socialist confederation; moreover, although the CSC–ACV has no formal links with the Social Christian party, its informal links remain important. Finally, in Germany the specifically Christian Democratic confederation, the *Christlicher Gewerkschaftsbund Deutschlands* (CGD) remains very small (200,000 members), compared with the *Deutscher Gewerkschaftsbund* (DGB) (seven million members), and although the CDU–CSU has retained the loyalty of Catholic workers (except in 1972), it remains important for it to strengthen its appeal to working-class Protestants and agnostics as well as to Catholics. True, many DGB members vote for the CDU–CSU despite the Socialist orientation of the DGB, whilst the Christian Democratic *Sozialausschüsse* (social committees) remain numerically quite powerful (over 100,000 members in 1976), even if politically they are less influential than the Christian Democratic business wing (the *Wirtschaftsrat*, economic council). But it is particularly important for the German Christian Democratic parties to retain a strong working-class electorate, because their objective is to win an *absolute* majority at elections. In contrast, the Christian Democratic parties of Belgium and the Netherlands are essentially Centre parties, whose main objective is to dominate coalitions of the right-centre or left-centre rather than to govern on their own.

Apart from their transnational problems, the individual parties are confronted to a greater or lesser degree with various dilemmas and problems. The Italian DC has since the early 1960s been broadly in favour of an 'opening to the Left', and since the mid-1970s the 'reformers' have held a small majority in the directing organs of the party. But now that the 'opening to the left' and 'reform' have become synonymous with co-operation with the Communist Party, for so long the main political enemy of the DC, it has become very difficult for the Christian Democrats to cross the Rubicon and agree to a full 'historic compromise'. The assassination in 1978 of Moro, one of the long-time advocates of some sort of a working-arrangement with the Communists, and one of the few men trusted by a majority in the DC and PCI, perhaps worsened the dilemma. Moreover, the dilemma is a very real one, for no political party – however committed to resolving its country's economic and social problems – wants to court political suicide, and if the Communist Party were to succeed in proving that it was no more than a Social Democratic party in wolf's clothing, the DC would lose an essential aspect of its *raison d'être* as *the* bastion of liberal democracy against a possible Communist takeover. The Italian DC, then, is a party of the Centre orientated to the Left (hence its unwillingness to join organisations such as the largely Conservative European Democratic Union). But owing to its involvement in the *sottogoverno* and in all aspects of the patronage system, the DC cannot hope to carry out reforms of a far-reaching nature without the help of a party which it sees as the Trojan horse of a Marxist irruption.

The chief weakness of the German CDU–CSU is that it is two parties, not one. In addition – and the problem is closely connected – the CDU–CSU has been unable to decide whether to opt for a coalition strategy or a majoritarian strategy on its own. Basically these problems come down to the difficult relationship between the CDU and CSU. The CDU is essentially a party of the centre-right, whereas to a large degree the CSU is rather more conservative, but above all the CSU is very much the embodiment of *Bavarian* social and political values. The CSU has retained Catholic-conservative views with regard to 'Marxism' (using that word, as the CSU does, very broadly), whether in relation to its attitude to Communist Eastern Europe, the *Berufsverbot*, the *Jusos* (young Social Democrats) or integrated schools in Bavaria. As a result of its distinctive attitudes the CSU, under its formidable leader Franz-Josef Strauss (who is the embodiment of, as much as the moulder of, these distinctive attitudes), has tried to steer the whole German Christian Democratic movement in a direction which is not necessarily in its own best interests (for example, the CSU's intransigent attitude to the Eastern Treaties and its abrasive comments on the FDP, and hence by implication its rejection of a coalition strategy). The CSU has been a highly successful electoral party (winning 60 per cent of the votes in Bavaria in 1976), which makes it all the more difficult for the leader of the CDU to know how to deal with it. The moderate Barzel was in one sense destroyed by Strauss, because against his own better judgement he came out against the *Ostpolitik*, and therefore lost the 1972 election and subsequently his chairmanship of the CDU. Helmut Kohl, an equally moderate man, who realises the importance of balancing up the various wings of the Christian Democratic movement, succeeded in persuading Strauss and the CSU to rescind their decision of November 1976 to break the CDU–CSU *Fraktionsgemeinschaft* (joint parliamentary group). But it would be a mistake to regard this success as a long-term 'victory' for Kohl. It was certainly a short-term victory, but the underlying tensions and dilemmas remain. The CDU cannot afford to abandon the middle ground of politics, but the CSU criticises the CDU for not being more aggressive and decisive, whilst ignoring the probability that such an approach would be counterproductive in every *Land* except Bavaria. The two parties then seem condemned to live together, but mutual incomprehension often appears to be at the heart of their relationship.

The Dutch Christian Democrats (formerly confessionals) have had to face up to the difficulties posed by the breakdown of 'pillarisation'. For fifty years from 1917–67 there had been a remarkable degree of party stability in the Netherlands, with the Left (Labour Párty since 1948) regularly polling about 25 per cent, the Centre (the three confessional parties) about 50 per cent, and the Right (Liberals) about 10 per cent. This stability suited the confessional parties well, as they could form a coalition on their own when they wanted, or choose to govern with the Right (the norm in the interwar period) or the Left (as they did from 1945–58). But the collapse of 'pillarisation' and of the 'politics of accommodation' in the 1960s and early 1970s meant that the confessional parties lost their traditional position as arbiters in the coalition-making process. As the Dutch party system began to polarise on the Left (Labour Party), Right (Liberal Party) and Centre (Christian Democrats), it became essential for the last-named to present a more coherent, united image of themselves. Hence, the gradual emergence of Christian Democratic Appeal in the 1970s, but, as we have seen, the three partners in the CDA are somewhat uneasy bedfellows: the Christian Historical Union is really the conservative wing of the CDA; the Catholic People's Party has lost so many of its working-class supporters that it is also essentially a centre-right party, but it does not want to lose any more of its working-class supporters, so tries (with limited success) to project an inter-class image; the Anti-Revolutionary Party, on the other hand, has retained a distinctive image as an inter-class party of practising Protestants. On the whole, the ARP is a more left-wing (or at least socially reforming) party than are the KVP and CHU. Despite these differences, the three Dutch confessional parties – like the CDU and CSU – seem to have no alternative but to co-operate with each other. The CDA, still a 'federation' rather than a party, has made a promising start, and this will doubtless encourage further moves to integration, but owing to the continuing importance of 'pillarisation' in many spheres of Dutch life (despite its decline at the level of national political parties), it is unlikely to be easy to achieve a successful balance between the different political, religious and social traditions embodied in the CDA.

The Belgian Social Christians seem to be faced with fewer problems than most of the other Western European Christian Democratic parties, in that they have to some extent succeeded in overcoming two of Belgium's traditional cleavages (religion and class), and seem to be well on the way to finding a solution to the third (the community problem). However, whilst the Social Christians have increased their influence in Flanders, they remain relatively weak in Wallonia, which is still essentially a Socialist fief. There is obviously some danger in this situation, because if the community/language problem were to flare up again, it might be harmful to the unity of Belgium if the Social Christians were to appear as *the* party of Flanders and the Socialists as *the* party of Wallonia. Hence, the importance of finding a satisfactory solution to the community problem, not only from the point of the unity of Belgium, but also from that of the Social Christian party: only in the aftermath of such a solution are the Social Christians likely to be able significantly to increase their appeal in Wallonia.

In France the heirs of the MRP, the various centrists of the *Centre des Démocrates Sociaux*, a constituent part of the Giscardien *Union pour la Démocratie Française*, have found themselves in a particularly difficult position owing to the trend towards bipolarisation which has been characteristic of the Fifth Republic (in large measure this has been a consequence of the two-ballot electoral system). The French 'Christian Democrats' are fundamentally opposed to the development of two rival blocs in the French party system, but, squeezed between the upper and nether millstones, they have had no choice but to opt for one side or the other. Being strongly opposed to the Socialist-Communist bloc, owing to their antipathy to the Communists, they opted for the 'Gaullist' side. However, within the *majorité* they are very much 'Giscardiens', i.e. they hope to orientate the *majorité* towards the centre or even centre-left, with a view to detaching the more moderate Socialists from their Communists allies. The evidence so far is that such a strategy has only a limited chance of succeeding: the 1978 general election indicated some movement towards the centre and a slight strengthening of the Christian Democratic current (CDS), but without proportional representation the re-emergence of a powerful centre grouping seems unlikely in France, and any hope of forming a 'Social Christian' party (consisting of Christian Democrats and moderate Socialists) seems even more remote.

Overall, then, the Christian Democrats are faced with many transnational and national problems in spite of their electoral revival in the late 1970s. But it should not be forgotten that their achievement has been considerable. By rejecting both nineteenth-century Liberalism and twentieth-century totalitarianism (communism as well as fascism), they have helped to create a new political 'milieu' based on a commitment to liberal democracy, class reconciliation, *concertation,* and integration (both domestically through the concept of the inter-class *Volkspartei* and transnationally through their commitment to European integration). By adopting this essentially non-ideological, pragmatic approach to politics – which, as we have seen, is not an approach without *principles* – the Christian Democrats have played a vital role in integrating German and Italian conservatives of all social classes into the liberal democratic political system. By 'deconfessionalising' the Catholic political parties of Belgium and Germany – and later of the Netherlands – they have played a key part in drawing Catholics out of their political ghetto. By showing that Catholics could be good republicans, they have helped to bridge a major cleavage in French society. By forming coalitions with Socialists on various occasions and in various countries – notably in Italy, Belgium, France and the Netherlands – Christian Democrats have shown that they are concerned about social justice. Equally, by not excluding Conservatives from governing coalitions – on various occasions in the same four countries – the Christian Democrats have helped to keep right-wing voters away from the extreme parties. Indeed, in Germany and Italy the Christian Democrats have sometimes been criticised for appealing too blatantly to neo-Nazis and neo-Fascists, but it has doubtless been preferable for such voters to be 'absorbed' by the Christian Democrats than to be ostracised.

The German CDU–CSU can in fact be categorised essentially as a Conservative party (albeit of the moderate variety), partly because it has absorbed various right-wing political currents, notably the Refugees, German Party and NPD, but also partly because there is no party of importance to its right: the German Liberal Party – unusually for a Continental Liberal party – stands at the centre of the political spectrum. However, none of the other major Christian Democratic parties of Western Europe – certainly not those of the European Community – can be categorised as Conservative parties. Rather they are Centre parties – essentially of the Centre-Left in Belgium and Italy, and of the Centre-Right in France and the Netherlands. It is true that they are all committed to certain 'conservative' principles, notably emphasis on individualism, the rights of property, and traditional social and moral values. But, as *Volksparteien*, they are also committed to social justice, co-operation between the 'natural social groups' (trade unions, employers, consumers' organisations, family groups and so forth) and regional integration (the development of a federal European Community). For these reasons Christian Democrats are unlikely to fuse with Conservatives at the European level, although on balance they are more likely to co-operate with Conservatives than with the more 'collectivist' parties of the Left.

Christian Democracy has, then, been a distinctive and important political force in most Western European countries since the Second World War, but how far it is appropriate to describe it as a 'movement' – in the sense of a coherently motivated, well-organised, transnational political force – remains an open question. As this book has shown, the typology of the Christian Democratic parties varies considerably. Those Christian Democratic parties which *absorbed* conservative parties – as has been the case in Germany and Austria – are now themselves essentially conservative parties. On the other hand, those Christian Democratic parties which still have to *compete* with conservative parties – as do the Italians with the MSI and PLI, the Belgians and Dutch with the Liberals, and the French with the *Gaullistes* and *Giscardiens* – are essentially centrist in orientation. The Christian Democratic 'pole of attraction' is, then, on the Right in some countries and in the Centre in others. As a result Christian Democracy remains a somewhat incoherent force at the level of the European Community. On a majority of issues, notably those to do with the economy, Christian Democrats are likely to be in basic agreement with Conservatives – at least in the sense of preventing the Socialists from implementing their more interventionist policies. On other issues, such as the development of a more politically integrated Western Europe, the Christian Democrats and Liberals have more in common. On matters concerned with social policy, on the other hand, some of the Christian Democrats – notably those of Belgium and Italy – are likely to align themselves with the Socialists. On yet others, for example those concerned with agriculture and regional policy, there may well be a north-south division within the Christian Democratic group.

Altogether then it would seem to be unwise to expect too much of Christian Democracy as a political force in the European Community – at least in the short term: there are powerful Christian Democatic parties in many of the Community countries, a rich and varied Christian Democratic tradition, but as yet no such thing as a unified, transnational European Christian Democratic movement.

Appendix

The Christian Democratic Parties of Western Europe[1]
(The dates and figures in this Table refer to the most recent general elections)

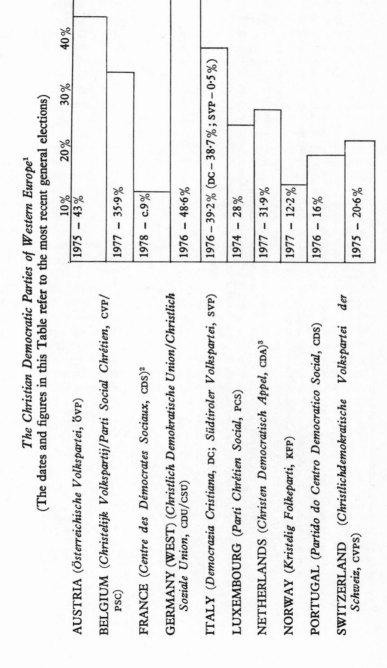

	10%	20%	30%	40%	50%
AUSTRIA (Österreichische Volkspartei, ÖVP)	1975 – 43%				
BELGIUM (Christelijk Volkspartij/Parti Social Chrétien, CVP/PSC)	1977 – 35·9%				
FRANCE (Centre des Démocrates Sociaux, CDS)[2]	1978 – c.9%				
GERMANY (WEST) (Christlich Demokratische Union/Christlich Soziale Union, CDU/CSU)	1976 – 48·6%				
ITALY (Democrazia Cristiana, DC; Südtiroler Volkspartei, SVP)	1976 – 39·2% (DC – 38·7%; SVP – 0·5%)				
LUXEMBOURG (Parti Chrétien Social, PCS)	1974 – 28%				
NETHERLANDS (Christen Democratisch Appel, CDA)[3]	1977 – 31·9%				
NORWAY (Kristelig Folkeparti, KFP)	1977 – 12·2%				
PORTUGAL (Partido do Centro Democratico Social, CDS)	1976 – 16%				
SWITZERLAND (Christlichdemokratische Volkspartei der Schweiz, CVPS)	1975 – 20·6%				

1   In addition to the above mainstream Christian Democratic parties, there are small Christian Democratic parties in Finland (*Suomen Kristillinen Liitto*; 4·5% at 1975 general election), Denmark (*Kristeligt Folkeparti*; 3·7% at 1977 general election) and Sweden (*Kristen Demokratisk Samling*, 1·4% at 1976 general election). In Spain there is a considerable, but unquantifiable, Christian Democratic political tendency. At the 1977 general election the *Federacion Democratica Cristiana* won 11 seats out of 350 and the Catalan *Democracia Cristiana* won 2 seats; in addition, however, a considerable number of 'Christian Democrats' stood as candidates of the umbrella centrist formation, *Union Centro Democratico* (UCD), which won 165 of the 350 seats in the Cortes – it is reckoned that up to one-third of UCD deputies are Christian Democrats of one sort or another. Finally, the Irish *Fine Gael* party (30% at 1977 general election) belongs to the Christian Democratic group in the European Parliament.

2   The CDS was a constituent part of the Giscardien *Union pour la Démocratie Française* (UDF) which won just under 22% of the votes cast at the first ballot at the 1978 general election. Rather less than half of the UDF voters probably belonged to the Christian Democratic stream (i.e, the former MRP/*Centre Démocrate*/*Réformateur tendance*).

3   CDA consists of the Catholic *Katholieke Volkspartij* (KVP), Protestant *Anti-Revolutionaire Partij* (ARP) and Protestant *Christelijk-Historische Unie* (CHU). They remain separate parties, but combine into one 'federation' for electoral purposes.

SOURCES: *Europa Year Book*, 1978, and Keesing's *Contemporary Archives*.

Notes

Books and articles are cited as briefly as possible throughout the Notes. For full references, consult Bibliography.

1
The Origins of Christian Democracy

1   For a brief analysis of the background to Belgian and Dutch Christian Democracy, see Chapters 5 and 6, pp. 165–72 and 193–202 below. For Austria, see A. Diamant, *Austrian Catholics and the First Republic*; and for Switzerland, G. Beuret, *Die Katholisch-soziale Bewegung in der Schweiz, 1848–1919* and E. Gruner, *Die Schweizerische Bundesversammlung, 1848–1920.*
2   David Albertario at the Catholic Congress at Bergamo, 1877. Cited in Fausto Fonzi, *I cattolici e la società italiana dopo l'unità*, pp. 65–6.
3   For detailed accounts of Church-State relations in the period 1870–1914, see G. Dalla Torre, *I cattolici e la vita pubblica italiana*; C. M. Buonaiuti, *Non Expedit: storia di una politica, 1866–1919*; G. Mollat, *La question romaine de Pie VI à Pie XI*; and G. De Rosa, *Il movimento cattolico in Italia dalla restaurazione all' età giolittiana.*
4   On this movement, see especially A. Gambasin, *Il movimento sociale nell'opera dei congressi, 1874–1904.*
5   For Toniolo's views (including the Turin Programme), see G. Toniolo, *Opera omnia.*
6   For a detailed account of this period, see G. De Rosa, *Il movimento cattolico*; and specifically for the development of Christian Democracy, see L. Bedeschi, *I pionieri della D.C.* and I. Giordani, *Pionieri della democrazia Cristiana.*
7   For Murri's views, see G. De Rosa, *Storia politica dell'azione cattolica in Italia*, vol. I, p. 200 and ff.
8   The best biography of Sturzo is by F. Piva and F. Malgeri, *Vita di Luigi Sturzo.*
9   Beniamino Palumbo, *Il movimento democratico cristiano in Italia*, p. 67.
10 The leading Italian historian of the *Partito Popolare* is Gabriele De Rosa: see especially his *Il Partito Popolare Italiano* and *Il movimento cattolico in Italia dalla restaurazione all' età giolittiana.* In English the most useful studies are J. N. Moloney, *The Emergence of Political Catholicism in Italy* and R. A. Webster, *Christian Democracy in Italy, 1860–1960.*
11 For details, see *Il Comportamento Elettorale in Italia*, published by Istituto 'Carlo Cattaneo', vol. I, pp. 21–41.
12 For Sturzo's views about the desirability of an *aconfessionale* party, see Don Sturzo, *I discorsi politici*, pp. 1–25. On Sturzo's early years, see A. Gaudenti, *Luigi Sturzo: il pensiero e le opere*, and for his life as a whole F. Piva and F. Malgeri, *Vita di Luigi Sturzo.*
13 R. A. Webster, *The Cross and the Fasces*, p. 102.
14 G. Salvemini, *Stato*, p. 119; see also, A. C. Jemolo, *Chiesa e stato in Italia negli ultimi cento anni*, p. 423.
15 For these arguments, see G. De Rosa, *L'Azione Cattolica*, vol. II, pp. 425–30.
16 See, for example, *Il Corriere d'Italia*, 3 April 1924, for the arguments of the right-wing *Popolari* and the Clerico-Fascists; and A. C. Jemolo, *Chiesa e stato in Italia*, pp. 605–8.
17 *Osservatore Romano*, 10 September 1924. For De Gasperi's proposed alliance, see G. De Rosa, *Il Partito Popolare*, p. 472.
18 J. Rovan, *Le catholicisme politique en Allemagne*, pp. 54 and 167.

19   See, for example, the opening address of Archbishop Geissel of Cologne at the Würzburg congress of German bishops in October 1848. This was incidentally the first bishops' congress since 1786 – in the years of 'absolutism' the Prussians refused to allow the bishops to meet.

20   J. Bachem, 'Wir müssen aus dem Turm heraus'.

21   These were: Constantin Fehrenbach, June 1920–May 1921; Joseph Wirth, May 1921–Nov. 1922; Wilhelm Marx, Nov. 1923–Jan. 1925 and May 1926–June 1928; and Heinrich Brüning, April 1930–May 1932.

22   The BVP separated from the *Zentrum* in 1919, but after 1923 usually voted with it.

23   See Emil Ritter, *Die katholisch-soziale Bewegung Deutschlands im 19 Jahrhundert.* p. 385.

24   K. Bachem, *Geschichte der deutschen Zentrumspartei*, vol. VIII, p. 258. Bachem's 8-volume history published between 1927 and 1932 is still the key work on the *Zentrum*.

25   E. Ritter, *Die katholisch-soziale Bewegung Deutschlands im 19 Jahrhundert*, p. 366.

26   For a detailed discussion of these parties and of the early development of Christian Democracy in France, see R. E. M. Irving, *Christian Democracy in France.*

27   G. Suffert, *Les catholiques et la gauche*, p. 71.

28   For French Catholicism in the nineteenth century, see P. Spencer, *The Politics of Belief in Nineteenth Century France.*

29   A. de Tocqueville, *Oeuvres et correspondances inédites*, vol. II, p. 121.

30   D. W. Brogan, *The Development of Modern France, 1870–1939*, p. 147.

31   A. Coutrot and F. Dreyfus, *Les forces religieuses dans la société française*, p. 18.

32   Brogan, *The Development of Modern France*, p. 149.

33   For a detailed discussion of the separation issue, see M. Larkin, *Church and State after the Dreyfus Affair.*

34   For example. J. B. Duroselle, *Les débuts du catholicisme social en France, 1822–70*, and H. Rollet, *L'action sociale des catholiques en France, 1871–1914* (2 vols.).

35   Spencer, *The Politics of Belief*, p. 39.

36   ibid., p. 39.

37   Cited in ibid., p. 134.

38   H. Bettenson, *Documents of the Christian Church*, p. 381.

39   For details, see Rollet, *L'action sociale des catholiques*, vol. I, pp. 338–89.

40   Some members of the ALP approved the *Sillon*, which was condemned by the Pope in 1910 (see below, pp. 25–6). As a result the ALP tended to get tarred with same brush as the *Sillon* when the latter was criticised by the Hierarchy. Cf. ibid., vol. II, pp. 52–9, especially pp. 57–9.

41   Each copy of *Le Sillon* carried a small picture of St Francis of Assissi ploughing a furrow. The name of the review was adopted by the movement in 1899.

42   J. Raymond-Laurent, *Le Parti Démocrate Populaire, 1924–44*, p. 38.

43   ibid., pp. 47–8.

44   For the important growth of Catholic Action in the interwar years, see W. Bosworth, *Catholicism and Crisis in Modern France.*

45   *L'Aube* was founded in 1932. For a full discussion of its role in the 1930s, see Françoise Mayeur, *L'Aube: étude d'un journal d'opinion, 1932–40.*

46   Quoted in Raymond-Laurent, *Le Parti Démocrate Populaire*, p. 97.

2
Christian Democratic Theory and Practice

1   S. Jacini, *Storia del Partito Popolare Italiano*, p. 24.

2   B. Georges, *Problèmes du catholicisme français*, p. 145.

3   See in particular A. Beckel, *Christliche Staatslehre*, 2 vols.: 1, *Grundlagen und Zeitfragen*; 2, *Dokumente*; J. C. Bennet, *Auch Christen sind Staatsbürger: Fragen aus der Praxis der Demokratie*; E. Borne, M. Byé, *et al.*, *Le MRP, Cet Inconnu*, an unpublished collection of articles on Christian Democratic doctrine (henceforth cited as *Cet Inconnu*); M. P. Fogarty, *Christian Democracy in Western Europe, 1820–1953*, pt. II; R. E. M. Irving, *Christian Democracy in France*, ch. II; Otto Kress (ed.), *Kirche, Staat und Katholiken: Dokumentation, 1803–1967*; R. Kothen, *La pensée et l'action sociale des catholiques, 1789–1944*; H. Maier, 'Politischer Katholizismus, sozialer Katholizismus, christliche Demokratie', in *Civitas*, 1962, Vol. I, pp. 9–27; J. N. Moody, *Church and Society: Catholic Social and Political Thought and Movements, 1789–1960*; and Werner Weidenfeld's introduction to *Synopse der Parteiprogramme der Christlich-Demokratischen Parteien Westeuropas.*
4   G. Gonella, *Il Programma della Democrazia Cristiana per la Nuova Costituzione*, pp. 28–9.
5   *Cet Inconnu*, pp. 26–35; for similar views, see writings of the Belgian Christian Democrat, R. Houben, especially *La politique méconnue*, pp. 85–104, 'Réflexions sur la doctrine politique chrétienne' and 'Les chrétiens devant la politique'.
6   For a detailed analysis of personalism, see E. Mounier, *Le personnalisme*; also R. Houben, *La politique méconnue*, pp. 103–6.
7   See, e.g., J. Hours, *La doctrine de la démocratie chrétienne*, and n. 3 above.
8   *Cet Inconnu*, p. 29.
9   ibid.
10   ibid., p. 32; see also R. Houben, *Démocratie Chrétienne*, pp. 1–6.
11   ibid., p. 34.
12   See below, pp. 40–56.
13   R. Houben, *Démocratie Chrétienne*, p. 3.
14   *Cet Inconnu*, p. 30; *Atti e Documenti della Democrazia Cristiana, 1943–67*, p. 9; and MRP Congress, Paris, 1947, report on 'La politique générale'.
15   A phrase used frequently by the Italian DC, French MRP and Belgian CVP–PSC. It may have been coined by De Gasperi, who seems to have been the first to use it.
16   The essence of this view was contained in the MRP slogan 'La révolution par la loi'.
17   See, for example, articles by B. Gebauer and W. Weidenfeld in *Synopse der Parteiprogramme der Christlich-Demokratischen Parteien Westeuropas*, and R. Houben, *La politique méconnue*, pp. 94–103.
18   See below, pp. 207–10.
19   See below, pp. 91–8.
20   See above, pp. 1–28.
21   See *Synopse der Parteiprogramme der Christlich-Demokratischen Parteien Westeuropas*, pp. 8–9.
22   *Pacem in Terris* extracts from R. Houben, *Le PSC Contesté*, pp. 66–7.
23   Interview with Etienne Borne, 1976.
24   Statutes of *Christen Democratisch Appel* (1976), ch. I.
25   This is accepted by Catholics as well as by Protestants; interviews with KVP, ARP and CHU leaders, July 1977.
26   *CDU Berlin Programme* (1971), preface.
27   *Grundsatzprogramm der CSU* (1976), preamble.
28   Cited in Leo Schwering, *Frühgeschichte der Christlich-Demokratischen Union*, p. 223.
29   See below, ch. 4 & 8.
30   *Il Programma della DC* (1946), ch. II.
31   See, for example, P. A. Allum, *Politics and Society in Post-war Naples*, and S. S. Acquaviva and M. Santuccio, *Social Structure in Italy: Crisis of a System*.
32   Interview with Prof. Serra, University of Florence, June 1976.
33   See *Statuts du PSC*, ch. I, and *Parti Social Chrétien* (Centre de Perfectionnement des Cadres Politiques, 1976), pp. 22–25; and *CVP Kerstprogramma*, 1945, ch. I.
34   *Cet Inconnu*, p. 32.

35   Article in *L'Aube*, the French Christian Democratic newspaper, 2 May 1948.
36   M. Einaudi and F. Goguel, *Christian Democracy in Italy and France*, p. 39.
37   See, for example, K. J. Allen and A. A. Stevenson, *An Introduction to the Italian Economy*.
38   See Martin Clark and R. E. M. Irving, 'The Italian Political Crisis and the General Election of May 1972', pp. 198–223, and the same authors, 'The Italian General Election of June 1976', pp. 8–31; also L. Graziano, 'La crise d'un régime libéral-démocratique: l'Italie', pp. 259–89.
39   A. J. Heidenheimer, *Adenauer and the CDU*, pp. 161–68.
40   See, for example, K. H. F. Dyson, 'Anti-communism in the Federal Republic of Germany: the case of the *Berufsverbot*', *Parliamentary Affairs*, Winter 1975, pp. 51–67, and below p. 143.
41   See W. Heyde, *The Administration of Justice in the Federal Republic of Germany* and G. Leibholz, 'The Federal Constitutional Court' in *Legal Essays: a tribute to Frede Casteberg*.
42   See M. Einaudi and F. Goguel, *Christian Democracy in Italy and France*, p. 49; see also, R. Houben, *La politique méconnue*, p. 32.
43   For examples, see book and article in n. 41 above.
44   See below, p. 51.
45   The Christian Democrats, Conservatives and Radicals opposed the first draft because it gave too much power to the Assembly ('convention government') and too little to the second chamber, the Council of the Republic.
46   *Journal Officiel* of the French National Assembly, 20 August 1946.
47   See, for example, M. P. Fogarty, *Christian Democracy in Western Europe, 1820– 1953*, and J. Lenoir, *Essai sur la démocratie chrétienne et ses fondements philosophiques*, ch. 2, pp. 41–100.
48   See below, ch. 8.
49   *Quadragesimo Anno*, 1931, CTS edition, p. 37.
50   See below, pp. 51–2.
51   Belgian cvp–psc Christmas Programme, 1945, section 3; see similar statements about the family in programmes of German, French, Dutch and Italian Christian Democrats in *Synopse der Parteiprogramme der Christlich-Demokratischen Parteien Westeuropas*, pp. 74–6.
52   See, for example, M. P. Fogarty, *Christian Democracy*, ch. 5.
53   *L'Aube*, 28 December 1944.
54   ibid.
55   For the Ahlen Programme, see K. Stollreither's excellent collection of documents and commentary on co-determination, *Mitbestimmung: Ideologie oder Partnerschaft?*, p. 115 (henceforth cited as Stollreither, *Mitbestimmung*).
56   After 1947 election was by proportional representation.
57   *Journal Officiel*, Assemblée Nationale, 12 December 1944.
58   *Le Figaro*, 15 May 1946.
59   *L'Aube*, 22 April 1949.
60   mrp National Congress, 1947.
61   The Vallon 'Amendment' of 1967–8 introduced a mild profit-sharing scheme in companies with over 100 employees. For details, see *Ordonnance* no. 67–694, 17 August 1967, and *Decret* no. 68–528, 30 May 1968.
62   *Forces Nouvelles*, 30 September 1966.
63   *Témoignage Chrétien*, 8 July 1965.
64   See, for example, D. B. Goldey, 'The events of May and the French general election of June 1968'.
65   The *Confédération Française des Travailleurs Chrétiens* (cftc), decided in 1964 to end its confessional links and to change its name to *Confédération Française Démocratique du Travail* (cfdt). 90 per cent of the delegates at the 1964 Congress voted for this change. 10 per cent decided to remain as before under the name of *La CFTC maintenue*.
66   For an interesting comparative study of France, Belgium, Luxembourg and the United Kingdom, see J. R. Carby Hall, *Worker Participation in Europe*.

67 For details of these laws see Stollreither, *Mitbestimmung*, p. 146 and ff.
68 At the first election after the new law of 1972 there was little change in this respect. 78 per cent of these elected were active trade unionists. Although foreign workers were enfranchised for the first time, fewer of them were enrolled as trade unionists. The figure of 78 per cent was comparable to previous figures. See G. Kloss, *West Germany: an Introduction*, p. 97.
69 The law also applies to a small number of other joint-stock companies (*Aktiengesellschaften*).
70 Stollreither, *Mitbestimmung*, p. 156 & ff.
71 See *Zur Diskussion gestellt*, 4 pp., pamphlet published by Sozialausschüsse in 1968.
72 See G. Pridham, *Christian Democracy in Western Germany*, pp. 179–80; and for conservatism of CSU, see below, pp. 149–60.
73 *Frankfurter Allgemeine Zeitung*, 25 July 1968.
74 For Düsseldorf debate and resolution, see *CDU Bundesparteitag*, 1971, p. 246 and ff; for Biedenkopf's views, see also his book *Mitbestimmung*.
75 See, for example, Hans Katzer's speech at Düsseldorf congress in *CDU Bundesparteitag*, 1971, pp. 265 and ff; also Norbert Blüm's *Reaktion oder Reform: wohin geht die CDU?*
76 *CDU Bundesparteitag*, 1973, pp. 512–14; see also 'Die Mitbestimmungsmodelle der CDU-CSU im Jahre 1973' in Stollreither, *Mitbestimmung*, pp. 234–44.
77 In the following proportions: firms with up to 10,000 employees, 6:6; with 10,000–20,000 employees, 8:8; with over 20,000 employees, 10:10.
78 Cited in Einaudi and Goguel, *Christian Democracy in Italy and France*, p. 134.
79 See, for example, J. E. S. Hayward, *Private Interests and Public Policy: the Experience of the French Economic and Social Council*, pp. 91–8.
80 *Le Monde*, 9 September 1958.
81 For details, see R. E. M. Irving, *Christian Democracy in France*, pp. 231–43.
82 *Die Dreissig Punkte der Union*, p. 7.
83 See J. F. Golay, *The Founding of the Federal Republic of Germany*, pp. 41–4.
84 Cited in E. Santarelli, *Dossier sulle regioni*, p. 52.
85 A. Piccioni, *Dal congresso di Roma al congresso di Napoli*, p. 14.
86 P. A. Allum and G. Amyot, 'Regionalism in Italy: old wine in new bottles', p. 56.
87 For full details, see Martin Clark, 'Italy: regionalism and bureaucratic reform', pp. 44–73, in J. Cornford (ed.), *The Failure of the State*.
88 ibid., p. 56.
89 There is, of course, an important Christian Democratic movement in South America, but here I am concerned to make the contrast between Anglo-Saxon parties and European Christian Democratic parties.
90 J. Rovan, unpublished paper on 'Christian Democracy and the Left in Europe', presented at Washington conference on 'Christian Democracy in Europe', November 1976.
91 *Synopse der Parteiprogramme der Christlich-Demokratischen Parteien Westeuropas*; see especially introduction by Werner Weidenfeld.
92 e.g., *Politische Meinung* and *Sonde* (both German), *Politiek Perspektief* (Dutch), *La Discussione* (Italian), *France-Forum* (French) and the various publications of CEPESS, the research department of the Belgian Social Christian Party.

3
Christian Democracy in Italy

1 See table, pp. 108–9.
2 M. Duverger, *Political Parties*, pp. 13, 211–14, and 240.
3 See T. J. Geiger, *On Social Order and Mass Society*.
4 See, for example, Edward Banfield, *The Moral Basis of a Backward Society*; Gabriel Almond and Sidney Verba, *The Civic Culture*; Giorgio Galli and Alfonso Prandi, *Patterns of Political Participation in Italy*.

5   For an analysis of the 1972 and 1976 Italian General Elections, see M. Clark and R. E. M. Irving, 'The Italian political crisis and the general election of May 1972', and the same authors' article, 'The Italian general election of June 1976: towards a "historic compromise"?'.

6   G. Sartori, 'European political parties: the case of polarized pluralism', in J. LaPalombara and M. Weiner, eds., *Political Parties and Political Development*.

7   See J. LaPalombara, *Interest Groups in Italian Politics* and the more recent study by S. S. Acquaviva and M. Santuccio, *Social Structure in Italy*; also below, pp. 85–91.

8   Galli and Prandi, *Patterns of Political Participation*, p. 110; Acquaviva and Santuccio, *Social Structure*, p. 183; and F. Cervellati Cantelli, *et al.*, *L'organizzazione partitica del PCI e della DC*, p. 390 and ff.

9   J. P. Chasseriaud, *Le parti démocrate chrétien en Italie*, p. 205; on importance of factions, see A. Zuckerman, *Political Clienteles in Power: Party Factions and Cabinet Coalitions in Italy*; also below, pp. 75–85.

10 ibid., p. 27; Galli and Prandi, *Patterns of Political Participation*, p. 120.

11 ibid., p. 132.

12 V. Galletti, 'La questione democristiana, la base sociali e i collegamenti di massa', pp. 28–9; see also Barnes-CISER survey data, 'Income and party preference', in R. Rose (ed.), *Electoral Behaviour*, p. 204.

13 See survey material and 'tree' analysis, S. H. Barnes 'Italy: religion and class in electoral behaviour', pp. 171–221, in Rose (ed.), *Electoral Behaviour*. For the declining importance of religion generally, see S. Burgalassi, *Il comportamento religioso degli italiani.*

14 As well as the Barnes-CISER survey evidence, see F. Cervellati Cantelli, *et al.*, in G. Poggi (ed.), *L'organizzazione partitica del PCI e della DC*, p. 430.

15 DC's own figures, June 1976.

16 For a comparison, see F. Cervellati Cantelli *et al.*, in *L'organizzazione partitica del PCI e della DC*, esp. pp. 319–473.

17 For example, M. Duverger, *Political Parties*, p. 43, and R. Zariski, 'Intra-party conflict in a dominant party: the experience of Italian Christian Democracy'.

18 For details, see *Statuto del Partito*, 1968.

19 For example, over three years between the third congress at Venice (1949) and the fourth at Rome (1952), and between the sixth at Trent (1956) and the seventh at Florence (1959). On the other hand, extraordinary congresses are always held shortly before general elections.

20 See below, pp. 100–1.

21 For election results since the war, see table 1 below, pp. 108–9.

22 See, for example, article in *Il Popolo*, 24 April 1949, and closing speech at Florence Congress 1951, 'Our unique feature as Christian Democrats is that we are a party of the Centre which is marching towards the Left, a party of stability but also of progressive economic and social ideas.'

23 See, for example, the wide-ranging reform programmes outlined in 1944 and 1946, *Atti e Documenti della Democrazia Cristiana, 1943–1967*, vol. 1, pp. 23–34 and 232–54. [Henceforth cited as *Atti e Documenti DC.*]

24 See below, pp. 72–5 and 99–103.

25 For a detailed discussion of the problem of DC factionalism, see below, pp. 75–85.

26 *Atti e Documenti DC*, p. 681.

27 See, for example, Moro's speech at DC national congress, Florence, October, 1959.

28 *Atti e Documenti DC*, Vol. 1, p. 1194 and ff.

29 This is quite a common formula in Italian politics. It means that a party votes for a government and its policies in Parliament, but does not have any ministers in the government.

30 For an analysis of the 1963 election, see P. A. Allum, 'The Italian Elections of 1963'.

31 For an analysis of the crisis, see M. Clark and R. E. M. Irving, 'The Italian Political Crisis and the General Election of May 1972'.

32 N. Gullotti (ed.), *Dieci Congressi, DC, 1946–67*, p. 392.

33 For a definition of 'integralism', see below, p. 77.
34 See Felice Rizzi, 'From Socialist unification to Socialist secession, 1966–69'.
35 See below, pp. 82–5.
36 See, for example, M. Clark and R. E. M. Irving, 'The Italian Political Crisis and the General Election of May 1972', to which the following paragraphs owe much.
37 See below, pp. 91–7.
38 For a detailed discussion of the regional reform, see M. Clark, 'Italy: Regionalism and Bureaucratic Reform', in Cornford (ed.), *The Failure of the State*, pp. 44–73; and above, pp. 53–6.
39 For the problem of factionalism in the DC, see below, pp. 75–85.
40 *Corriere della Sera*, 5 May 1972, for Andreotti's statement; Forlani's statement was made on TV on 3 May 1972.
41 Interviews with the author, May 1972.
42 For details, see below, p. 98.
43 See, for example, F. Cazzola, 'Partiti, correnti e voto di preferenza'.
44 Interview, Professor Gian Poggi, January 1978.
45 *Corriere della Sera*, 15 November 1948.
46 See below, p. 239.
47 *Atti e Documenti DC*, p. 406.
48 For the Dossettian programme, see Giuseppe Mammarella, *Italy after Fascism: a Political History, 1943–65*, p. 211.
49 See, for example, *Dieci Congressi, DC*, p. 129; and *Atti e Documenti DC*, 1949, p. 412, and 1951, p. 518.
50 For an analysis of the reaction to Fanfani's martinet style of leadership, see Spreafico and LaPalombara, *Elezioni e comportamento politico in Italia*, p. 158 and ff.
51 *Atti e Documenti DC*, pp. 730–70.
52 For the relationship between the DC, CISL and ACLI, see below, pp. 87–8.
53 See below, ch. 8.
54 *Atti e Documenti DC*, p. 1705.
55 ibid, p. 1642.
56 *Atti del IX Congresso della DC*, p. 226.
57 *Atti del X Congresso della DC*, p. 209.
58 G. Galloni, *Una politica per la Democrazia Christiana*, p. 40.
59 Mengozzi at DC National Council of 29–31 July 1961, in *La Sinistra DC di Forze Nuove di fronte ai probleme del paese*, p. 48.
60 See below, pp. 106–7.
61 *Atti del IX Congresso della DC*, p. 477; for similar pleas for unity, see M. Rumor, *La DC e i problemi della societa Italiana*, p. 56.
62 G. Galloni, *Una politica nuova per la Democrazia Cristiana*, p. 7.
63 *Dieci Congressi, DC*, p. 504.
64 See, e.g., E. Scalfari, *L'autumno della Repubblica*, p. 153.
65 See Alan Zuckerman, *Political Clienteles in Power*.
66 The parties to the left of the DC, i.e., PCI, PSIUP, PSU and PRI, won 47·9 per cent of the votes cast compared with 46·6 per cent in 1963.
67 See *Quaderni Politici*, no. 2, 1969, p. 8.
68 Moro's speech to the DC *direzione*, as reported in *Agenzia Progetto* (the organ of the Morotei), 21 February 1969.
69 See below, p. 100.
70 S. S. Acquaviva and M. Santuccio, *Social Structure in Italy*, p. 8 (and elsewhere).
71 ibid., p. 141.
72 *The Economist*, 'A survey of Italy', 1 April 1978. For the inefficiency of the social services, see G. Berlinguer and F. Terranova, *La strage degli innocenti*; for that of the prison services, A. Ricci and G. Salierno, *Il carcere in Italia*; for that of the educational system, T. Aymone, *Scuola dell 'obbligo e città operaia*.
73 *The Economist*, 1 April 1978.
74 J. LaPalombara, *Interest groups in Italian politics*, pp. 252–348.

75   Much has been written about ENI and IRI. For an up-to-date discussion in English, see J. Earle, *Italy in the 1970s*, pp. 115–24. For the relationship between the DC and these parastatal corporations, as well as with *Confindustria*, see J. LaPalombara, *Interest Groups in Italian Politics*; R. Zariski, *Italy: the Politics of Uneven Development*, ch. VI, and Acquaviva and Santuccio, *Social Structure in Italy*, ch. V.

76   For 1956 figures, see *Annuario della Azione Cattolica Italiana* (1956); the 1976 figures are based on research by Professor Italo Sandre and are reproduced in Acquaviva and Santuccio, *Social Structure in Italy*, pp. 176–7. By 1978 there was some evidence of a slight revival in Catholic Action, a membership of 600,000 being claimed in that year, *The Economist*, 1 April 1978.

77   This is the view of Gianfranco Poggi, interview 1978. In the 1940s and 1950s, in contrast, Catholic Action was much more important: see G. Poggi, *Catholic Action in Italy*; also T. Godechot, *Le parti démocrate chrétien en Italie*, especially p. 152.

78   For these figures, see ISTAT, XI Censimento, 1971, vol. 1, pp. 1 and 5.

79   Approximately 10 per cent of the 12 per cent drop (between 1951–71) occurred between 1961–71; estimate of G. Mottura and E. Pugliese, 'Agricoltura capitalistica e funzione dell'inchiesta'.

80   They were for example responsible for depriving Fanfani of the DC secretaryship at the 1959 Florence congress, and this led indirectly to the fall of Fanfani's first government.

81   J. Earle, *Italy in the 1970s*, p. 158.

82   *La Stampa*, 20 May 1969; and G. Picciotti, 'Le ACLI contro la DC'.

83   See M. Clark and R. E. M. Irving, 'The Italian political crisis and the general election of 1972'.

84   For 1966 figure, see G. Galli, *Il bipartitismo imperfetto*, p. 192; for 1976 figure, see Acquaviva and Santuccio, *Social Structure in Italy*, p. 212, n. 64.

85   P. H. Merkl, 'Partecipazione di sindacati e di partiti in Germania Occidentale e in Italia'.

86   G. Galli, *Il bipartitismo imperfetto*, p. 236; see also A. Cavazzani, *La DC dopo il primo ventennio*, p. 115.

87   See M. Clark and R. E. M. Irving, 'The Italian general election of June 1976'.

88   The word 'parasite' may seem rather strong to Anglo-Saxon ears, but is used freely by Italian social and political scientists, as well as by journalists, to describe the 'placemen' who are discussed in the following pages.

89   Acquaviva and Santuccio, *Social Structure in Italy*, p. 48.

90   See arguments of P. Sylos Labini in *Sindacati, inflazione, produttività* and in 'Sviluppo economico e classi sociali in Italia', in P. Farneti (ed.), *Il sistema politico italiano*.

91   *Consiglio Superiore dell'economia e del lavoro, VII Rapporto sulla situazione economica del paese*, 1973, p. 37 and ff.

92   F. De Marchi, *La burocrazia centrale in Italia*; see also De Marchi's 'Organizzazione e burocrazia'.

93   For the inefficiency of the *Cassa*, see Acquaviva and Santuccio, *Social Structure in Italy*, p. 146.

94   ibid., pp. 142–8, and p. 159.

95   See M. Clark, 'Italy: regionalism and bureaucratic reform', in J. Cornford (ed.), *The Failure of the State*, pp. 44–73.

96   See especially G. Tamburrano, *L'iceberg democristiano*.

97   P. Nichols, *Italia, Italia*, p. 116.

98   J. Earle, *Italy in the 1970s*, p. 70; see also Acquaviva and Santuccio, *Social Structure in Italy*, p. 60. Amongst the wholly parasitical *enti* are bodies such as the agency responsible for the 1906 Vesuvius eruption victims and the agency responsible for the 1908 Reggio Calabria earthquake victims.

99   See M. Caciagli, *Democrazia Cristiana e potere nel Mezzogiorno*. This book shows that parasitic *enti* are increasing, at least in the South.

100 A. Ardigo, 'Stratificazione sociale e potere politico in Italia', see also Ardigo's important book, *La stratificazione sociale.*
101 See below, pp. 103–7.
102 For a detailed analysis of the divorce referendum, see M. Clark, D. Hine and R. E. M. Irving, 'Divorce-Italian style'. I have borrowed freely from the parts of this article which concern the DC in this section.
103 Even under the Lateran Pacts the State could grant legal separations; but only the Church could grant annulments.
104 For the legal background and constitutional arguments, see A. Coletti, *Il Divorzio in Italia.*
105 For the decline of religious practice, see S. Burgalassi, *Comportamento Religiosa degli Italiani* and the same author's *I Italiani in Chiesa.* For the changing attitude of women to marriage, divorce and abortion, see A. Ardigò, *Emancipazione femminile e urbanesimo,* L. R. Sansone, *I fuorilegge del matrimonio* and P. Fortuna, L. Jorio and A. Pandini, *Rapporto sul divorzio in Italia.*
106 See *La Stampa,* 10 May 1974.
107 *Corriere della Sera,* 22 February 1974.
108 See below, p. 96.
109 *Corriere della Sera,* 1 May 1974.
110 *La Stampa,* 10 May 1974.
111 For details, see Muriel Grindrod, 'Italy: back to Centre-Left'.
112 See in particular G. Sartori, *Correnti, frazioni e fazioni nei partiti politici italiani,* ch. 4.
113 For example, in a speech at Florence on 9 May 1974, *Corriere della Sera,* 10 May 1974, though Fanfani completely rejected the idea of the Communists actually joining the government. For further discussion of the 'historic compromise', see below, pp. 98–105.
114 *Settegiorni,* 13 January 1974; 'Libertas' is of course the motto of the DC.
115 For a detailed analysis of the results, see M. Clark, D. Hine and R. E. M. Irving, 'Divorce-Italian style'.
116 V. Capecchi, *et al., Il comportamento elettorale in Italia,* p. 260 and pp. 388–9.
117 P. A. Allum, *Politics and Society in post-war Naples,* p. 72.
118 See in particular S. Burgalassi, *Italiani in Chiesa.*
119 See in particular Peter Nichols, *The Politics of the Vatican.*
120 See, for example, F. L. Cavazza and S. R. Graubard (eds.), *Il caso italiano.*
121 For a detailed discussion of the 1976 general election, see M. Clark and R. E. M. Irving, 'The Italian General Election of June 1976: towards a "historic compromise"?' I have drawn extensively from those parts of the article which deal with the DC in the course of the next few pages.
122 See below Table 2, p. 111.
123 Interview in *La Stampa,* 6 July 1976.
124 Speech made at rally attended by author, Naples, 17 June 1976.
125 See above, p. 100.
126 See above, pp. 85–91.
127 Interview with Berlinguer, *Corriere della Sera,* 15 June 1976.
128 See D. Sassoon, 'The Italian Communist Party's European strategy', and R. E. M. Irving, 'The European policy of the French and Italian Communists'.
129 For the electoral programmes of the other parties, see M. Clark and R. E. M. Irving, 'The Italian General Election of June 1976: towards a "historic compromise"?', pp. 20–5. Here I have concentrated chiefly on the DC and PCI, as this section is concerned primarily with the developing relationship between these two parties.
130 See G. Trovati, 'L'analisi del voto', *La Stampa,* 23 June 1976.
131 Interview in *The Economist,* 26 June 1976.
132 *The Economist,* 1 April 1978.
133 See, for example, P. A. Allum, *Italy – Republic without Government?,* pp. 128–37, especially p. 133.

4
Christian Democracy in Germany

1   See *Synopse der Parteiprogramme der Christlich-Demokratischen Parteien Westeuropas* (Politische Akademie Eichholz der Konrad-Adenauer-Stiftung e.V., 1971). Conrad Taler came to a similar conclusion after examining the 1969 electoral programmes of the two parties; see C. Taler, 'Über das Verhältnis der CSU zur CDU'.
2   See above, Chapter 1.
3   See tables at end of this chapter, pp. 162–3.
4   Kurt Sontheimer, *The Government and Politics of West Germany*, p. 85.
5   The *Zentrum* was refounded in 1945–6 by Rudolf Amelunxen. It was represented on the Frankfurt Economic Council (below, p. 118) and on the Parliamentary Council which drew up the Basic Law (below, p. 119). In the first Bundestag there were ten *Zentrum* deputies and in the second two. They joined the SPD in opposition to Adenauer, acting as a 'Christian conscience' on the Left. The *Zentrum* deputies were firmly in favour of a planned economy and the nationalisation of industry, but when Erhard's 'economic miracle' occurred they gradually lost what support they had amongst the Catholic working classes of the industrial Rhineland. Most of their deputies went over to the CDU, but Helene Wessel, after adhering to Gustav Heinemann's neutralist *Gesamtdeutsche Volkspartei* (GVP), joined the SPD in 1957 after the failure of the GVP. No *Zentrum* deputies were returned to the third, or subsequent, Bundestags. The most useful book on the *Zentrum*, and on political Catholicism generally in Germany, is Joseph Rovan, *Le Catholicisme Politique en Allemagne*.
6   See, e.g., H. G. Wieck, *Die Entstehung der CDU und die Wiedergründung des Zentrums im Jahre 1945*, p. 14 and ff.
7   See below, pp. 126–7.
8   And, of course, in Bavaria. For the development of the CSU, see below, pp. 148–61.
9   The most useful books on the origins and early history of the CDU are A. J. Heidenheimer, *Adenauer and the CDU: The rise of the leader and the integration of the party*; Leo Schwering, *Die Frühgeschichte der Christlich-Demokratischen Union*; Ernst Lemmer, *Manches war doch Anderes*; Konrad Adenauer, *Erinnerungen, 1945–53*; Hans-Joachim Netzer (ed.), *Adenauer und die Folgen*; Gerhard Schulz, 'Die CDU: Merkmale ihres Aufbaus; Paul Weymar, *Konrad Adenauer*; Terence Prittie, *Adenauer: A Study in Fortitude*; H. C. Wieck, *Die Entstehung der CDU und die Wiedergründung des Zentrums im Jahre 1945*. For other books and articles, see bibliography, pp. 304–12.
10   See, for example, the *Kölner Leitsätze* and *Leitsätze der Christlich-Demokratischen Partei in Rheinland und Westphalen*, in appendix of Leo Schwering, *Die Entstehung der CDU*, p. 32. Similar sentiments were expressed in the early programmes of the Berlin and Frankfurt branches of the CDU.
11   Adenauer, born in 1876, was in his seventieth year when the war ended.
12   See also below, pp. 116 and 120.
13   Cited in A. J. Heidenheimer, *Adenauer and the CDU*, p. 39. For details about the Hessen CDU group, see H. G. Wieck, *Christliche und Freie Demokraten in Hessen, Rheinland-Pfalz, Baden und Württemberg, 1945–46*.
14   See, for example, Annual Reports of Rhineland CDU (1946 and 1947), in Bundesgeschäftsstelle (BGS) der CDU; also BGS, *Dokumentation: die Geschichte der CDU* (1972), and Konrad-Adenauer-Stiftung (ed.), *Konrad Adenauer und die CDU der britischen Besatzungzone*.
15   However, he never quite forgave the British for the brusque manner of his dismissal; see Terence Prittie, *Adenauer: A Study in Fortitude*, pp. 106–10.
16   See below, pp. 121–7, for organisational developments.
17   A. J. Heidenheimer, *Adenauer and the CDU*, p. 133.

18 *Erster Parteitag der CDU der Britischen Zone, 14–15 August 1947* (Cologne, CDU *zonal secretariat*), p. 6.

19 The success of Erhard's policies is indicated by the figures: in June 1948 industrial production was at 54 per cent of the 1936 level; in February 1949 it was at 84 per cent, and before the end of the year it was over 100 per cent. Moreover, prices began to decline in 1949. Social security benefits, however, were very low at this stage of the economic recovery, so that, although Erhard's policies greatly benefited all those who were employed, they did relatively little to help the unemployed (between 1–2 million in 1949 and 1950), the refugees and the widows (of whom there were many – over 2 million German troops were killed in the war, and there were an estimated 1·2 million war widows in 1945).

20 See above, n. 19 and below, p. 121.

21 See G. Binder, *Deutschland seit 1945*, pp. 250–7.

22 See below, p. 127.

23 See, e.g., Otto-Heinrich von der Gablentz, *Über Marx Hinaus*.

24 Pope Pius XI, *Über die gesellschaftliche Ordnung*, p. 156.

25 Quoted, A. J. Heidenheimer, *Adenauer and the CDU*, p. 120.

26 For the Neheim-Hüsten Programme, see O. K. Flechtheim (ed.), *Dokumente zur parteipolitischen Entwicklung in Deutschland seit 1945*, vol. 2, pp. 50–3.

27 ibid.

28 ibid., pp. 53–8.

29 In its early stages the 'social market economy' worked in a notably un-social manner. In 1950, for example, the income of the poorer half of the population – widows, refugees, the sick and unskilled – was proportionately one third less than it had been in 1914; see Henry C. Wallich, *Main Springs of the German Economy*, pp. 74 and ff. In due course, as national wealth increased, the West German social security system became one of the best in Europe.

30 See Terence Prittie, *Adenauer: A Study in Fortitude*, pp. 77–101.

31 In a letter to Wilhelm Scharnagl in August 1945, Adenauer summed up his view in one sentence by stating that 'I am in favour of progressive social reform, but not of Socialism'; cited in H. G. Wieck, *Die Entstehung der CDU*, p. 73.

32 See below, pp. 127–31.

33 See, for example, Kaack, *Geschichte und Struktur des deutschen Parteiensystems*, pp. 199–240; and Heidenheimer, *Adenauer and the CDU*, pp. 178–229.

34 Figure provided by CDU Bundesgeschäftsstelle. It should be noted that the CDU's sister party, the CSU, developed a strong organisation and high membership over a decade earlier; below, pp. 150–4. For membership figures for earlier years, see appropriate *Politisches Jahrbuch der CDU–CSU*, published annually.

35 See G. Pridham, *Christian Democracy in Western Germany*, pp. 280–7.

36 This was true because Adenauer continued to use his influence as party chairman against Erhard and against changes in the CDU; see, for example, T. Prittie, *Adenauer: A Study in Fortitude*, pp. 285–316.

37 See Kaack, *Geschichte und Struktur des deutschen Parteiensystems*, p. 278 and ff.

38 Heidenheimer, *Adenauer and the CDU*, p. 199 and ff.

39 See above, p. 118.

40 Heck continued in this office until 1958 when he was replaced by Konrad Kraske, who held it until 1971.

41 The party statutes may be found in the *Jahrbücher der CDU–CSU*; also in O. K. Flechtheim (ed.), *Dokumente zur parteipolitischen Entwicklung in Deutschland*.

42 Article 65 lays down that 'The Federal Chancellor shall determine, and be responsible for, the general policy guidelines. Within the limits set by these guidelines, each Federal Minister shall conduct the affairs of his department autonomously and on his own responsibility. The Federal Government shall decide on differences of opinion between Federal Ministers. The Federal Chancellor shall conduct the affairs of the Federal Government in accordance with rules of procedure adopted by it and approved by the Federal President.'

43 F. R. Allemann, *Bonn ist nicht Weimar*, p. 345.

44 For the few disagreements which did occur between Adenauer and the parliamentary party, mainly over economic policy, see Jürgen Domes, *Mehrheitsfraktion und Bundesregierung*, for the degree of Adenauer's control over the party, see especially A. J. Heidenheimer, 'Der Starke Regierungschef und das Parteiensystem: der "Kanzler-Effekt" in der Bundesrepublik', and the same author's, 'Foreign policy and party discipline in the CDU'. On party discipline in the CDU-CSU, see *So haben sie abgestimmt: Register und Tabellen der namentlichen Abstimmungen im Bundestag*, published by the Bundestag information office after the end of each legislature.

45 Article 29 of *Statut der Christlich Demokratischen Union Deutschlands* (as revised in 1971).

46 Which might not necessarily coincide with a *Land*, as until 1970 some *Länder* had more than one *Landesverband*; see below, p. 126.

47 see below, p. 145.

48 *Statut der CDU*, articles 30–7.

49 A *Kreis* is a local government unit, roughly comparable to an English county; an *Ort* is a much smaller unit, roughly comparable to a parish. Figures provided by CDU Bundesgeschäftsstelle in 1977.

50 *Statut der CDU*, article 31b.

51 For the important role of the *Fraktion* since the Christian Democrats went into opposition, see Geoffrey Pridham, 'The CDU–CSU Opposition in West Germany 1969–72: a party in search of an organisation'; and below, p. 127.

52 On this subject, as well as on Erhard's and Kiesinger's lack of interest in developing the party's organisation, see R. Altmann, 'Die Wandlungen der Union'.

53 *Bundesparteitag der CDU*, June 1962, p. 312.

54 Kaack, *Geschichte und Struktur der deutschen Parteiensystems*, p. 482.

55 *Bundesparteitag der CDU*, March 1966, p. 193 and ff.

56 See below, p. 127.

57 On the change of power (*Machtwechsel*), see Wolfgang Dexheimer, *Koalitionsverhandlungen in Bonn, 1961–1965–1969: zur Willensbildung in Parteien und Fraktionen*; also *Comparative Politics*, July, 1970, a special number on the 1969 federal election.

58 See below, pp. 134–6.

59 See Georg Gölter and Elmar Pieroth (eds.), *Die Union in der Opposition: Analyse-Strategie-Programm*, esp. pp. 130–52.

60 Cited, Pridham, 'The CDU–CSU in opposition, 1969–72', p. 208.

61 ibid., p. 208.

62 A. J. Heidenheimer, *Adenauer and the CDU*, p. 223 and ff.

63 Interview with Wolfgang Dexheimer, personal assistant to Richard von Weizsäcker (since 1977), in 1975.

64 For the purposes of electoral results it is correct to add together the votes and seats of the CDU and CSU, because the two parties have always formed a joint parliamentary group (*Fraktion*), although even within that group the CSU *Landesgruppe* jealously guards its autonomy. Therefore, although it seemed to me appropriate to write a separate section on the Bavarian CSU (pp. 149–61), and my main concern in this section will be with the CDU, I will nevertheless make frequent reference to the CDU–CSU (or simply to the Christian Democrats) owing to the fact that the two parties are in a sense one for electoral purposes.

65 For full table of general election results, see p. 162.

66 On the SPD's foreign policy in the 1950s, see W. E. Paterson, *The SPD and European Integration*.

67 See Werner Kaltefleiter, *Wirtschaft und Politik*, p. 111.

68 See R. E. M. Irving, 'The German Liberals: changing image of the FDP'; and Gerhard Braunthal, 'The FDP in West German politics'.

69 Weiner called it a 'hegemonic party system' owing to CDU–CSU dominance in the 1950s; see 'The origin and development of political parties', in J. LaPalombara and M. Weiner (eds.), *Political Parties and Political Development*.

70   For a detailed analysis of the 1957 election, see Uwe Kitzinger, *German Electoral Politics: A Study of the 1957 Campaign.*
71   Though it was less in evidence than in 1957; see Bernhard Vogel and Peter Haungs, *Wahlkampf und Wählertradition*, p. 313.
72   See especially *Jahrbuch der öffentliche Meinung, 1958–64*, p. 303.
73   See table, below, n. 92.
74   See the useful electoral maps in F. G. Dreyfus, 'Les élections au cinquième Bundestag: étude de géographie électorale'.
75   In Hesse the NPD polled 7·9 per cent; in Bavaria 7·4 per cent.
76   See below, p. 137.
77   On the rapid formation of the new coalition, see W. Dexheimer, *Koalitionsverhandlungen in Bonn.*
78   For analysis of the 1969 election, see especially David P. Conradt, *The West German Party System: an Ecological Analysis of Social Structure and Voting Behaviour, 1961–69*; and *Comparative Politics*, July 1970.
79   See especially Dietrich Rollmann (ed.), *Die CDU in der Opposition, eine Selbstdarstellung*; Dierk-Eckhard Becker and Elmar Wiesendahl, *Ohne Programm nach Bonn: oder die Union als Kanzlerwahl-Verein*; Georg Gölter and Elmar Pieroth (eds.), *Die Union in der Opposition: Analyse-Strategie-Programm*; Klaus Otto Skibourski, *Zukunft mit der CDU? Fehler und Chancen der Opposition*; and G. Pridham, *Christian Democracy in Western Germany.*
80   Bruno Heck, the CDU Secretary-General, and Franz-Josef Strauss, the CSU chairman, both made remarks to this effect (see *Der Spiegel*, 20 October 1969, and *Die Zeit*, 17 April 1970); see Geoffrey Pridham, 'The CDU–CSU Opposition in West Germany 1969–72', p. 203. On the rapidity of the SPD–FDP coalition formation and the CDU–CSU's unpreparedness, see Wolfgang Dexheimer, *Koalitionsverhandlungen in Bonn.*
81   It is, in fact, extremely difficult for a Chancellor to call an early election. He must arrange to lose a vote of confidence in himself (article 68). He can then ask the President to dissolve the Bundestag after another twenty-one days have passed, and call an election within sixty days of the parliamentary defeat. But if the Bundestag can find another Chancellor, by using the 'constructive vote of no confidence' in the intervening twenty-one days period, no election can be called. By September 1972 Brandt really had no option but to implement article 68, which he did by means of asking his cabinet to abstain on a vote of confidence (22 September). By September his majority had been eroded to nothing, and the CDU–CSU had refused to consider what would have amounted to an all-party coalition. Barzel did not attempt to use article 67, having failed once with it; hence, the early election of November 1972, one year ahead of schedule. For full details, see R. E. M. Irving and W. E. Paterson, 'The West German parliamentary election of November 1972'. Parts of this article are produced, mainly in abridged or altered form, in the following pages.
82   Sebastian Haffner, 'CDU – was nun?', pp. 114–6, in O. K. Flechtheim (ed.), *Die Parteien der Bundesrupublik Deutschland.*
83   By the 'Hallstein doctrine' the Federal Republic refused to have any dealings with those countries which had diplomatic relations with East Germany. Much has been written on the *Ostpolitik*. In English, see in particular, K. Kaiser, *German Foreign Policy in Transition*; L. Whetten, *Germany's Ostpolitik*; W. F. Hahn, *Between Westpolitik and Ostpolitik: Changing West German Security Views*; R. B. Tilford (ed.), *The Ostpolitik and Political Change in Germany*; E. H. Albert, 'Bonn's Moscow Treaty and its implications'; A. Bromke and H. von Riekhoff, 'The West German Polish Treaty'; D. Mahncke, 'The Berlin Agreement'; and G. K. Roberts, 'The West German parties and Ostpolitik'.
84   See especially Karl Theodor Freiherr von und zu Guttenberg, *Im Interesse der Freiheit*, ed. Paul Pucher.
85   See Christian Hacke, *Die Ost– und Deutschland Politik der CDU–CSU: Wege und Irrwege der Opposition seit 1969*, esp. pp. 27–79.

86   In addition the coalition could not rely on the votes of Günther Müller, the
SPD right-winger from Munich, or from July 1972 of Karl Schiller, who resigned
from the Ministry of Economics and SPD in that month, later joining the CDU
(in October). Their opposition was essentially to the governments's economic
policy, and not to *Ostpolitik.*

87   See G. K. Roberts, 'The West German Parties and *Ostpolitik'.*

88   Perhaps as many as 5–7 per cent of the SPD's voters were Schiller-*Wähler*: see
Hans D. Klingemann and Franz Urban Pappi, 'The 1969 Bundestag Election in
the Federal Republic of Germany', in *Comparative Politics,* July 1970.

89   Two parliamentary State Secretaries, Wolfram Dorn (FDP) and Joachim Raffert
(SPD), were found to be in receipt of large 'consultancy fees' from *Quick,* an
anti-government weekly, and Karl Wienand, the parliamentary *Geschäftsführer*
of the SPD, was involved financially in the PAN International scandal.

90   *Die Zeit,* 3 November 1972.

91   *Die Zeit,* 20 October 1972.

92   The 'governmental bonus' of being in office is clearly illustrated by the following
table, based on a similar table in *Comparative Politics,* July 1970, p. 598,
together with information from *Die Zeit,* 24 November 1972.
Question: Whom would you prefer as Chancellor?

	Chancellor Candidates in Office	Percentage of Respondents in Favour	Chancellor Candidates not in Office	Percentage of Respondents in Favour
1961	Adenauer	22%	Brandt	21%
	(Erhard)	(28%)		
1965	Erhard	38%	Brandt	15%
1969	Kiesinger	40%	Brandt	21%
1972	Brandt	58%	Barzel	26%

93   *Frankfurter Allgemeine Zeitung,* 15 September 1972.

94   For example at a public meeting in Bad Godesberg on 15 November 1972
(attended by the author). See also Christian Hacke, *Die Ost– und Deutschland
Politik der CDU–CSU,* esp. pp. 69–79.

95   Only 9 per cent agreed with CDU–CSU criticisms of it; *Frankfurter Allgemeine
Zeitung,* 23 November 1972.

96   Allensbach Opinion Poll of 18 November 1972 (one day before the election):

		Actual Result
SPD	46·4	45·9
CDU–CSU	44·7	44·8
FDP	6·5	8·4
Others	2·4	1·0

97   For example, the Marplan survey of 20 November 1972. See also, W.
Kaltefleiter, *Die Bundestagswahl 1972* (CDU Archiv, 1973), p. 70.

98   For *Infas* figures contained in this paragraph, see *Die Zeit,* 24 November 1972
and *Süddeutsche Zeitung,* 21 November 1972. (*Infas*=Institut für angewandte
Sozialwissenschaft, one of West Germany's most important opinion polling
organisations.)

99   See below, p. 140, for further details of the CDU–CSU's 'absorption' of the
NPD electorate.

100   See in .particular Hans D. Klingemann and Franz Urban Pappi, 'The 1969
Bundestag Election in the Federal Republic of Germany'; also Max Kaase,
'Determinanten des Wahlverhaltens bei der Bundestagswahl 1969'; and R. E. M.
Irving and W. E. Paterson, 'The West German parliamentary election of
November 1972'.

101	*Land*	CDU–CSU	SPD	FDP
Schleswig-Holstein	−4·2	+5·1	+3·3
Bremen	−2·8	+6·1	+1·8
Saarland	−2·7	+8·0	+0·4
North Rhine Westphalia	−2·6	+3·6	+2·4
Lower Saxony	−2·4	+4·3	+2·8
Rhineland-Palatinate	−1·9	+4·8	+1·9
Baden-Württemberg	−0·9	+2·3	+2·7
Hamburg	−0·7	−0·1	+4·9
Bavaria	+0·7	+3·2	+2·0
Hesse	+1·9	+0·3	+3·4

102 *Süddeutsche Zeitung*, 21 November 1972.
103 In December 1972 von Hassel was succeeded as Speaker by Annemarie Renger of the SPD. By tradition the largest party in the Bundestag selects the Speaker. Hence in 1976 the Speaker's chair reverted to the CDU–CSU, when Karl Carstens of the CDU was elected.
104 *Der Spiegel*, 27 November 1972.
105 *Infas* calculated that whereas overall 81 per cent of the CDU–CSU's 1969 voters remained loyal to the party in 1972, the figure dropped to 72 per cent in industrial areas.
106 For a rather pessimistic view of the CDU–CSU's prospects in the light of these socio-economic changes, see Derek Urwin, 'Germany: continuity and change in electoral politics', in R. Rose (ed.), *Electoral Behaviour: A Comparative Handbook*, pp. 109–64. For a more optimistic analysis of the CDU–CSU's prospects, see research done by Klaus Liepelt and his colleagues at the Institut für angewandte Sozialwissenschaft, e.g., Ursula Feist, Manfred Güllner and Klaus Liepelt, 'Party membership patterns, electoral mobilisation and social change in West Germany', paper presented at International Political Science Association meeting, Edinburgh, August 1976.
107 It was approximately 10 per cent in 1965 and 7 per cent in 1972, *Financial Times*, 9 October 1972.
108 *Le Monde*, 25 November 1972.
109 WDR survey of March 1971 showed that 62 per cent of refugees approved the Moscow and Warsaw Treaties, and support for the Basic Treaty of 1972 amongst refugees was even higher.
110 For example, *Die Zeit*, 20 October 1972.
111 For a detailed analysis of the 1976 election, see R. E. M. Irving and W. E. Paterson, 'The West German general election of 1976'. I have made considerable use of those parts of this article which deal with the CDU–CSU in the next few pages. For table of election results, see p. 162.
112 On CDU–CSU relationship, see below, pp. 156–63.
113 See especially Ralf Dahrendorf, 'Themen, die keiner nennt', *Die Zeit*, 24 September 1976.
114 Helga Haftendorn, '*Ostpolitik* revisited'.
115 Federal Ministry of Economics report, *Süddeutsche Zeitung*, 8 September 1976.
116 Before the 1976 election Schmidt refused to bargain with the Stockholm terror gang, and since then a similar line was taken over the kidnapping of the German industrialists' leader Hanns-Martin Schleyer in 1977 (members of the 'Red Army Faction' finally claimed responsibility for 'executing' Schleyer).
117 *Die Zeit*, 24 September 1976.
118 *Süddeutsche Zeitung*, 26 July 1976.
119 See, for example, *CDU-CSU Wahlprogramm, 1976*, section on education.
120 Approximately £50 million, about ten times the cost of a British election. The exact amount spent by the parties is a matter of conjecture, but their income for 1974 was as follows: SPD, DM 95m; CDU, DM 88m; CSU, DM 26m; FDP, DM 19m. Approximately half of this income, i.e., about DM 100m, was 'officially' spent on

the 1976 election. In addition, another DM 100m was probably spent by individuals and local parties. There is no upper limit to expenditure at elections. Under the Political Parties Law, all parties obtaining at least 0·5 per cent of second votes are reimbursed by the state at the rate of DM 3·5 per vote. For estimated costs of the election, see *Süddeutsche Zeitung*, 30 September 1976, 'Election supplement'; also *Die Zeit*, 24 September 1976, p. 17.

121 See SPD programme, *Weiter arbeiten am Modell Deutschland: Regierungsprogramm 1976–80*; FDP programme, *Freiheit, Fortschritt, Leistung*; and CDU–CSU *Wahlprogramm 1976*.

122 See Wolfgang Hoffmann, 'Unternehmer und Gewerkschaften im Wahlkampf', *Die Zeit*, 1 October 1976.

123 Theo Sommer in *Die Zeit*, 1 October 1976.

124 See R. J. C. Preece, *Land Elections in the German Federal Republic*, and Heino Kaack, *Geschichte und Struktur des deutschen Parteiensystems* (sections on *Landtag* elections).

125 Question: Whom would you prefer as Chancellor?

	Chancellor candidates in office	% in favour	Chancellor candidates in opposition	% in favour
1961	Adenauer	22%	Brandt	21%
	(Erhard)	(28%)		
1965	Erhard	38%	Brandt	15%
1969	Kiesinger	40%	Brandt	21%
1972	Brandt	58%	Barzel	26%
1976	Schmidt	53%	Kohl	34%

Sources: *Comparative Politics*, July 1970, p. 598; *Die Zeit*, 24 November 1972; *Der Spiegel*, 27 September 1976.

126 See Nina Grunenberg, 'Kohl war gut, Schmidt besser', *Die Zeit*, 1 October 1976.

127 Interview with Genscher in *Frankfurter Allgemeine Zeitung*, 31 May 1976.

128 For the importance of these voters to both main parties, see Feist, Güllner and Liepelt, 'Party membership patterns, electoral mobilisation and social change', esp. pp. 6–7.

129 For the figures and statistics contained in the next three paragraphs, see analysis of the 1976 Election done by Professor Dieter Oberndorfer for the *Sozialwissenschaftliches Forschungsingstitut der Konrad Adenauer Stiftung*; also R. Wildenmann, 'Warum sie so gewählt haben', in *Die Zeit*, 8 October 1976.

130 The male-female ratio in the Federal Republic in 1976 was 46·6 : 53·4.

131 On the 'middle majority', see Feist, Güllner and Liepelt, 'Party membership patterns, electoral mobilisation and social change', pp. 8–12.

132 ibid.

133 P. G. J. Pulzer, 'The German party system in the 1960s', pp. 5 and 13.

134 See especially Ferdi Breidbach and Rüdiger May, *Das soziale Feigenblatt? Die Sozialausschüsse in der Union*; also Rolf Ebbighausen and Wilhelm Kaltenborn, 'Arbeiterinteressen in der CDU? Zur Rolle der Sozialausschüsse', in Dittberner and Ebbighausen (eds.), *Parteiensystem in der Legitimationskrise*, pp. 172–99. Approximately one-sixth of the CDU's deputies after the 1976 election belonged to the labour wing (forty deputies).

135 See Peter Egen, *Die Entstehung des Evangelischen Arbeitskreises der CDU–CSU* (PhD. Bonn, 1974).

136 See below, pp. 160–1.

137 Even in the 1969–72 Bundestag the CDU–CSU's opposition was largely confined to *Ostpolitik*. The Christian Democrats voted for over 90 per cent of domestic legislation in their so-called period of 'principled opposition': see Hans-Joachim Veen, *Die CDU–CSU Opposition im parlamentarischen Entscheidungsprozess*, p. 106.

138 See below, p. 160.
139 For classification of political parties, see M. Duverger, *Political Parties.*
140 Alf Mintzel is the most distinguished scholar of the CSU. See in particular his detailed study, *Die CSU Anatomie einer konservativen Partei;* also his 'Die CSU in Bayern', pp. 349–426, in J. Dittberner and R. Ebbighausen (eds.), *Parteiensystem in der Legitimationskrise,* and 'Strukturwandel und Rolle der CSU', pp. 116–28, in O. K. Flechtheim (ed.), *Die Parteien der Bundesrepublik Deutschland.* See also Günter Müchler's important study, *CDU–CSU: das schwierige Bündnis.* For other books and articles on CSU, see bibliography, pp. 304–12. For Ashkenasi's analysis, see his *Modern German Nationalism,* pp. 161–83.
141 See below, p. 160.
142 See, for example, Wolf-Dieter Narr, who sees the CSU as a 'Quasi-regionalorganisation' of the CDU, in *CDU–SPD: Programm und Praxis seit 1945,* p. 73 and ff.
143 See especially Hans-Dieter Bamberg, 'Zu konservativen, autoritären und restaurativen Strömungen im westdeutschen Katholismus'.
144 See below, p. 156.
145 See below, p. 160.
146 See table, p. 162. In addition to the fifty-three CSU deputies elected in 1976 in Bavaria, there were twenty-nine SDP and six FDP.
147 See especially Klaus Schreyer, *Bayern: ein Industriestaat.*
148 On the early development of the CSU, see Walter Berberich, *Die historische Entwicklung der CSU in Bayern bis zum Eintritt in die Bundesrepublik* (PhD. Würzburg, 1965); also J. Müller's fascinating autobiography, *Bis zur letzten Konsequenz.*
149 The BP had been constituted in November 1946, although it was not officially licensed till February 1948.
150 A. Grosser, *Germany in Our Time,* p. 241.
151 According to figures given to the author by the CSU there were 82,189 party members at the beginning of 1948. The *Bezirksverbände* figures were as follows: Oberbayern, 20,971; Niederbayern, 11,930; Oberpfalz, 13,037; Schwaben, 10,648; Oberfranken, 8,298; Mittelfranken, 3,815; Unterfranken, 9,097. In other words, over 56,000, i.e., 68.8 per cent of the CSU's 82,000 members were from the four rural *Bezirksverbände* of Altbayern (the first four on the list), whilst only just over 21,000 were from the three Franconian *Bezirksverbände.* The remaining 4,000 were from the cities, which had very low membership figures: Munich, 2,695; Nürnberg, 1,102; and Augsburg, 596.
152 The phraseology is Mintzel's, but the categorisation is adapted from Sigmund Neumann, *Die deutsche Parteien: Wesen und Wandel nach dem Kriege,* p. 101.
153 By June 1977 the CSU had 153,718 members.
154 There is no data available about CSU income in 1955, but the 1974 income of 26·6 million DM came from the following sources: members' dues, 3·08 million DM; deputies' contributions, 1·32 million DM; income from property, 0·17 million DM; income from commercial enterprises, 0·34 million DM; donations, 8·10 million DM; investment income, 2·28 million DM; public subsidy, 11·34 million DM. (Figures supplied by CSU.)
155 For much of the information which follows I am indebted to Herr Florian Harlander, the CSU *Geschäftsführer,* interview in March 1976 and correspondence in 1977.
156 Mintzel, in Dittberner and Ebbighausen (eds.), *Parteiensystem in der Legitimationskrise,* p. 365. By 1977 there was a *Bundeswahlkriesgeschäftsstelle* (headquarters) in forty-three of Bavaria's eighty-two constituences; information given by CSU *Landesgeschäftsstelle,* September 1977.
157 ibid., p. 365.
158 For above figures, see *Statistisches Jahrbuch für Bayern.* Neither the 1946 nor the 1975 figures add up to 100 per cent, as in both cases the small number (5–7 per cent) of self-employed professional people and senior civil servants (*Beamte*) have been omitted. See also Klaus Schreyer, *Bayern: ein Industriestaat;* and for

280 *The Christian Democratic Parties of Western Europe*

the development of agriculture, Hans Eisenmann, 'Zukunftsperspektiven der Landwirtschaft in Bayern', in Ernst Schmacke (ed.), *Bayern auf dem Weg in das Jahr 2000*, p. 118 and ff.

159 See Walter Berberich, *Die historische Entwicklung der CSU* (PhD. Würzburg, 1965).

160 This coalition consisted of the SPD, FDP, BP (Bavarian Party) and GB–BHE (Refugee Party). It lasted till 1957, the only three years the CSU have not been in office in Bavaria since 1947.

161 The figures used in this paragraph were provided by the CSU *Landesgeschäfts-stelle.*

162 See esp. Mintzel, in Dittberner and Ebbighausen (eds.), *Parteiensystem in der Legitimationskrise*, pp. 399–403.

163 *Dreissig Punkte der Union*, 1946, cited in Walter Berberich, *Die historische Entwicklung der CSU* (PhD. Würzburg, 1965), p. 182 and ff.

164 See, for example, *CSU Grundsatzprogramm*, 1968.

165 cf. BDA *Jahresbericht*, 1970. Also its slogan 'Die CPU braucht F. J. Strauss' directly echoes the CSU slogan 'Deutschland braucht Bayern'.

166 See *Protokoll der Sitzung der Landesvorstandschaft der CSU*, 7 October 1966.

167 Speech at Wildbad Kreuth made in presence of author, 20 March 1976. A similar theme was developed by Streibl at CSU *Parteitag*, 10 April 1970.

168 On *Ostpolitik*, with particular reference to CDU and CSU attitudes, see Christian Hacke, *Die Ost– und Deutschland Politik der CDU–CSU.*

169 Cited in Geoffrey Pridham, 'The *Ostpolitik* and the Opposition in West Germany', in R. Tilford (ed.), *The Ostpolitik and Political Change in Germany*, p. 50.

170 ibid.

171 A. Mintzel, in Dittberner and Ebbighausen (eds.), *Parteiensystem in der Legitimationskrise*, pp. 390–9. Also Paul Noack, 'Die CSU – nationalistisch oder was sonst?'; Detlef Stronk, 'Die Zukunft der CSU'; and for contrasting arguments, Abraham Ashkenasi, *Modern German Nationalism.*

172 For example, F. J. Strauss, 'Konzeption dient den Grossmachtzielen der Monopole', in *Die Wahrheit*, 24 September 1970; Karl Bredthauer, 'Zur Lage der CDU–CSU nach den Parteitagen in Saarbrücken und München'; and Klaus Dieter Herrmann, 'CSU – extremer Freind jeder selbständigen Arbeiter – und Gewerkschaftsbewegung in der BRD', p. 12.

173 *Protokoll der Sitzung des Landesvorstandschaft der CSU*, 13 May 1966, p. 77.

174 Interview with Herr Harlander, *Landesgeschäftsführer* of CSU, 18 March 1976.

175 A. Mintzel, 'Die CSU in Bayern', p. 354 and ff, in Dittberner and Ebbighausen (eds.), *Parteiensystem in der Legitimationskrise*; also Conrad Taler, 'Über das Verhältnis der CSU zur CDU', p. 338 and ff.

176 See below, pp. 251–2.

5
Christian Democracy in Belgium

1 See below, pp. 249–51.

2 See for example, *Synopse der Parteiprogramme der Christlich-Demokratische Parteien Westeuropas*, pp. 8–111, also *Les chantiers sont ouverts . . . quel sera l'architecte? Programme de Nöel 1945*, and the 1974 election programmes of the CVP and PSC, Documents-*CEPESS*, 1974, No. 4, pp. 11–114.

3 On the 'Union of the Oppositions', see especially F. van Kalken, *Histoire du Royaume des Pays-Bas et de la révolution belge de 1830*, p. 92 and ff.

4 H. Haag, *Les origines du catholicisme libéral en Belgique*, pp. 47–60.

5 On 'unionism' and the attitude of Leopold I, see H. Pirenne, *Histoire de Belgique*, vols. VI and VII.

6 See, for example, F. van Kalken, *La Belgique contemporaine; histoire de l'évolution politique de 1780 à 1949*, p. 34 and ff.

7 See table, p. 190.
8 See, for example, statistical data contained in Keith Hill, 'Belgium: political change in a segmented society', in R. Rose (ed.), *Electoral Behaviour: a Comparative Handbook*, pp. 76–7.
9 For an analysis of this controversy see R. Arango, *Leopold III and the Belgian Royal Question*.
10 For details, see André Philippart, 'The University in Belgian politics since the *contestation* of 1968'.
11 For details about the Schools Pact, see R. Senelle, *The Belgian Constitution*, commentary on article 17, pp. 39–46; also R. Houben and F. Ingham, *Le Pacte Scolaire*, and V. Mallinson, *Power and Politics in Belgian Education, 1815–1961*.
12 K. Hill, in R. Rose (ed.), *Electoral Behaviour*, p. 96.
13 See Centre de Recherche et d'Information Socio-Politiques (CRISP), *Cahier*, no. 664, 6 December 1974. 'L'évolution du "monde Catholique": le devenir de la pratique religieuse', p. 28.
14 Precise correlations between religious and voting habits cannot be made, but several interesting studies of the phenomenon have been made in Belgium. Besides two CRISP dossiers ('Structures et évolution du "monde catholique" en Belgique', February 1967, and 'L'évolution du "monde catholique" en Belgique depuis 1968: le devenir de la pratique religieuse', December 1974), see *Statistiques de base des Doyennes et Diocèses de la Province Ecclésiastique Belge* (Centre interdiocésain – Service des Statistiques religieuses, Brussels); Liliane Voye, *Sociologie du geste religieux*; E. Collard 'Commentaire de la carte de la pratique dominicale en Belgique'; R. Moles, 'La pratique dominicale en Belgique'; and Wilfried Dewachter (ed.), *Carte Politique de la Belgique*.
15 For the early history of Flemish nationalism, see M. Basse, *De Vlaamsche Beweging van 1905 tot 1930*, and S. Clough, *A History of the Flemish Movement in Belgium*; for postwar developments, see *Res Publica*, no. 2, 1968, special number on 'La question flamande'.
16 See below, pp. 176–9.
17 See below, pp. 183–8.
18 For election results, see table 1, p. 189; and below, pp. 179–87.
19 See below, pp. 183–8.
20 On the Catholic political movement in the nineteenth century, see H. Haag, *Les origines du catholicisme libéral en Belgique*; G. Guyot de Mishaegen, *Le Parti Catholique Belge*; and for the twentieth century as well (up to 1945), see A. Simon, *Le Parti Catholique Belge*; there is also a brief historical sketch in J. Beaufays, *Les Partis Catholiques en Belgique et aux Pays-Bas, 1918–1958*, pp. 53–71.
21 Ducpétiaux had carried out a survey of working-class conditions in Flanders in 1864 (E. Ducpétiaux, *Mémoire sur le Paupérisme dans les Flandres*), and in the 1870s both he and Gustave De Jaer frequently advocated factory legislation, particularly to limit the hours worked by children. Adolf and Pieter Daens, who were both strong social-reforming Catholics (the latter was a priest), also advocated the use of political pressure to achieve social reforms. However, they were too progressive for the Hierarchy, who condemned the 'Christene Volkspartij' they founded in 1893. The word 'Daensisme' is sometimes used in Belgium as a synonym for progressive (or social) Catholicism.
22 A. Simon, *Le Parti Catholique Belge*, p. 86 and ff.
23 *Het Volk*, the *Ligue Démocratique Belge* journal, 9 November 1890.
24 On the development of the 'Christian Democratic' wing of the Catholic party, see especially M. Vaussard, *Histoire de la Démocratie Chrétienne: France, Belgique, Italie*, p. 147 and ff.
25 ibid., p. 156.
26 A. Simon, *Le Parti Catholique Belge*, p. 115.
27 M. Van den Wijngaert, *Ontstaan en stichting van de CVP–PSC: de lange Weg naar het Kerstprogramma*, p. 11.
28 See in particular *PSC Programme de Noël, 1945*.

29   See M. Van den Wijngaert, *Ontstaan en stichting van de CVP–PSC*, pp. 13–22,
30   For details about the *Strekkingen*, see ibid., pp. 14–15.
31   Men such as Théo Lefèvre, A. De Clerck, R. Vandekerckhove and J. Duvieusart.
32   The programme was called *De nieuwe arbeidersstand in de maatschappij van morgen* ('The new working class in the society of tomorrow').
33   *Elementen van een programma voor nationale hernieuwing* ('Elements for a programme for national renewal'). It brought together the main points of the Aalst, Herbert and ACW programmes.
34   Also available in French at CEPESS, the Social Christian Party's research department, under the title, *Les chantiers sont ouverts . . . quel sera l'architecte? Programme de Noël 1945*.
35   For *Kerstprogramma* in full, see M. Van den Wijngaert, *Ontstaan en stichting van de CVP–CSC*, pp. 91–161; also available at CEPESS the documentation centre at the CVP–PSC party headquarters in Brussels.
36   I am indebted to Frank Swaelen, National Secretary of the CVP–PSC, for much of the information in this section, which comes from material and interviews given to the author in December 1976. On the organisation and structure of the parties, see especially 'L'évolution récente des structures du CVP–PSC', *Courrier Hebdomadaire*, no. 484, June 1970.
37   See 'L'élection des nouveaux présidents du CVP et du PSC, mars 1972', *Courrier Hebdomadaire*, no. 565, June 1972.
38   Assuming, of course, that he is a Social Christian, which he always has been since the war, with the exception of the years 1954–8 and 1973–4.
39   See below, p. 178.
40   Interviews with Swaelen and Nothomb, December 1976. Swaelen in addition pointed out that as national secretary he held no formal power; his role was entirely one of co-ordination and liaison.
41   See K. Hill, 'Belgium', ch. 3, p. 82, in S. Henig and J. Pinder (eds.), *European Political Parties*.
42   Interview with Swaelen, December 1976.
43   See M. Duverger, *Political Parties*, pp. 63–71.
44   Belgium is divided into nine provinces: Antwerp, Brabant, East Flanders, West Flanders, Hainaut, Liège, Limburg, Luxemburg and Namur.
45   Belgium is divided into thirty constituencies and (since the 1976 local government reorganisation) 596 communes (previously there were 2585).
46   As indeed the CVP did for the communal elections in October 1976; interview with Swaelen, December 1976.
47   Interview with Swaelen, December 1976.
48   Paul Vanden Boeynants, the PSC leader in Brussels and minister (and prime minister) in many postwar governments, was strongly opposed to the move, but in the end had to give in to PSC pressure in favour of separate lists.
49   For example at the time of the great strikes of 1960–1. On disagreements in general in the PSC, see Vincent Goffray, 'La démocratie chrétienne en Wallonie', and Max Bastin, 'La démocratie chrétienne politique en Belgique francophone'. The MOC is rather like the Italian ACLI (see p. 88), i.e., a Catholic working-class movement with close connections with Catholic Action. MOC is not a trade union, though many of its members are members of the CSC.
50   On Catholic Action in Belgium, see J. Arendt, *Action Catholique et Ordre Social*, B. Chlepner, *Cent Ans d'Histoire Sociale en Belgique*, and appropriate sections in M. P. Fogarty, *Christian Democracy in Western Europe, 1820–1953*.
51   Catholic trade unionists (with Socialists in brackets) rounded to nearest 1,000:

1910	49,000	(69,000)	1960	762,000	(717,000)
1930	213,000	(458,000)	1965	844,000	(750,000)
1945	343,000	(553,000)	1970	965,000	(817,000)
1955	654,000	(638,000)	1975	1,140,000	(845,000)

Figures from G. Spitaels, *Le Mouvement Syndicale en Belgique*, pp. 32 and 48; and *Rapport d'Activité de la CSC, 1972–75*, pp. 53–7.

52 Interview with Swaelen, December 1976.
53 See Guy Spitaels, *Le mouvement syndicale en Belgique*, p. 61.
54 Interview with Swaelen, December 1976.
55 See M. Vaussard, *Histoire de la Démocratic Chrétienne*, p. 175 and ff.
56 See J. Alexandre, 'Géographie politique de la Belgique' (1946).
57 *La Relève* (review of the Catholic Left), 18 June 1949.
58 For an analysis of the 1949 and 1950 elections, see J. Alexandre, 'Géographie politique de la Belgique' (1950); and R. De Smet, 'La géographie électorale en Belgique'; for 1950 alone, *Institut de Sociologie de Solvay*, 'Les élections du 4 juin 1950'.
59 For analysis of 1954 elections, see R. Evalenko, 'Les élections du 11 avril'; J. Gérard-Libois, 'Géographie électorale de la Belgique'; and O. Grégoire, 'Les élections du 11 avril 1954'.
60 On the Loi Collard, see P. De Visscher, 'Les principes constitutionnels en matière d'enseignement'.
61 For analysis of the 1958 election, see CEPESS, 'Elections législatives du juin 1958'; R. Evalenko, 'Regards sur la sociologie électorale belge'; and P. Vermeylen, 'Les élections du 1er juin et leurs enseignements'.
62 See 'Le Pacte Scolaire et son application', *Revue Politique*, no. 5–6, 1960.
63 For detailed analysis of the 1965 election, see E. Cammaerts, 'La campagne électorale de mai 1965'; also J. Daloze, 'La réorientation du PSC'.
64 See below, pp. 205–7.
65 M. Grégoire, *La Particratie*.
66 On the 1965 and 1968 elections, see J. De Meyer, 'Elections et partis en Belgique'; on the 1968 election, 'Les élections du 31 mars 1968', *Courrier Hebdomadaire*, no. 402, April 1968; and for postwar elections in general, W. Dewachter, 'General elections as a process of power achievement in the Belgian political system'.
67 On 1971 election, see 'Les élections législatives du 7 novembre 1971', *Courrier Hebdomadaire*, nos. 544–5, December 1971.
68 On the 1974 election, see 'Les élections législatives du 10 mars 1974', *Courrier Hebdomadaire*, no. 638, March 1974; and on the regional problem CRISP dossier, no. 6, 1973, 'Les institutions de la Belgique régionalisée'.
69 See R. Senelle, *The Belgian Constitution*, pp. 39–46.
70 For the new PSC programme of 1973, see *Le Parti Social Chrétien* (Centre de Perfectionnement des Cadres Politiques, Brussels, 1976), pp. 31–49.
71 For full details, see 'Annexe à la Déclaration gouvernementale du 7 juin 1977' *Annales Parlementaires*, Chambre de Représentants, 7 June 1977, and 'Annexe à la Déclaration gouvernementale du 28 février 1978; Complément au Pacte Communautaire du 24 mai 1977', *Annales Parlementaires*, Chambre de Représentants, 28 February 1978.
72 It should be noted that the court is an 'Arbitration' rather than a 'Constitutional' court. The phrase *Cour d'Arbitrage* was preferred owing to the 'legalistic' connotations of constitutional courts. In fact, six of the court's twelve members will be politicians, the other six being lawyers. The role of the court will be to see that the three tiers of government – Parliament, Community Councils and Regions – do not exceed their legislative competence in respectively passing *lois*, *décrets* and *ordonnances*.

6
Christian Democracy in the Netherlands

1 See below, pp. 245–6.
2 See especially A. Lijphart, *The Politics of Accommodation: Pluralism and Democracy in the Netherlands*, ch. 2 and 3.
3 Hans Daalder, 'Extreme proportional representation – the Dutch experience', in S. Finer (ed.), *Adversary Politics and Electoral Reform*, p. 235.

4   See below, pp. 207–10.
5   Strictly speaking the country is divided into eighteen constituencies, but in practice, owing to the system whereby parties can connect their lists across constituencies, the entire country is treated as one constituency. Seats are therefore allocated on the basis of the share of the national vote received by each party. At present only two-thirds of 1 per cent of the national vote (or about 60,000 votes) is required to entitle a party to a seat in the Second Chamber. For details about the system, see H. Daalder, 'Extreme proportional representation – the Dutch experience', in S. Finer (ed.), *Adversary Politics*, pp. 228–9.
6   See table 1, p. 212.
7   The number of seats in the Second Chamber (Lower House of Parliament) was raised to 150 in 1956. See table 3, p. 214.
8   See tables 1 and 2, pp. 212–13.
9   See Professor J. J. Vis 'Politics in Holland today', unpublished paper presented at University Association for Contemporary European Studies conference on the Benelux countries.
10 For example, Catholics and Calvinists rarely competed against each other in the pre–1917 single member constituencies; see J. Verhoef, 'Kiesstelsels: politieke Samenweking in Nederland, 1888–1917'.
11 Interview with D. Corporaal, Secretary of the ARP, July 1977. See also *ARP Statuten* (revised edition, 1971), article 2.
12 Interview with J. L. Janssen van Raay, Secretary of the CHU, July, 1977.
13 Information given at headquarters of ARP and CHU, July 1977.
14 H. Daalder, 'Parties and Politics in the Netherlands', p. 3, n. 3.
15 The ARP congress of November 1969 voted by a two-thirds majority in favour of 'exploratory talks' with the other two confessional parties. For more details about the steps towards amalgamation of the confessional parties, see below, pp. 207–10.
16 Interview with J. L. Janssen van Raay, Secretary of the CHU, July 1977; and see below, p. 208.
17 See tables 2 and 3, below, pp. 213–14.
18 I am indebted to D. Corporaal, Secretary of the ARP, for most of the information which follows in this paragraph.
19 Interview with J. L. Janssen van Raay, July 1977.
20 Approximately 40 per cent of Catholics to 37 per cent of Protestants; A. Lijphart, *The Politics of Accommodation*, p. 16.
21 See L. Rogier, *Katholieke Herleving*, p. 146 and ff.
22 For details, see P. Verschave, *La Hollande Politique*, p. 17 and ff.
23 For details, see J. Beaufays, *Les Partis Catholiques en Belgique et aux Pays-Bas, 1918–1958*, p. 375.
24 J. De Jong, *Politieke Organisatie in West Europa na 1800*, p. 355.
25 For details see J. P. Gribling, 'Uit de geschiedenis van de RKSP'.
26 The RKSP Statutes are published in full in Beaufays, *Les Partis Catholiques en Belgique et aux Pays-Bas*, pp. 744–55.
27 See Wilhelmus van Eekeren, 'The Catholic People's Party in the Netherlands', PhD, Georgetown University, 1956.
28 Information provided at KVP headquarters, July 1977.
29 W. J. J. Kusters, 'Stembusgedrag en maatschappijstructuur', p. 233.
30 Beaufays, *Les Partis Catholiques en Belgique et aux Pays-Bas*, p. 536.
31 See table 3, p. 214 below.
32 Robert C. Bone, 'The dynamics of Dutch politics', p. 37, n. 39.
33 See n. 5 above, for electoral system.
34 The official figure given to the author at KVP headquarters in July 1977 was 78,000, but this figure was almost certainly on the high side. Dr Bibo, head of the party's research institute, suggested that about 60,000 would be more realistic.
35 Beaufays, *Les Partis Catholiques en Belgique et aux Pays-Bas*, p. 553.
36 ibid., pp. 418–19.
37 ibid., p. 422.

38 In 1977 the Catholic NKV was still the second biggest trade union confederation, with about 30 per cent of trade unionists affiliated to it. The Socialist NVV had over 35 per cent, and the Protestant CNV under 20 per cent.
39 See tables 1–4 below, pp. 212–15.
40 See table 5, p. 216.
41 Beaufays, *Les Partis Catholiques en Belgique et aux Pays-Bas*, p. 382.
42 A. Lijphart, *The Politics of Accommodation*, pp. 16–58.
43 Bram de Swaan, 'Parties, policies and pivots: coalition politics in the Netherlands', especially p. 73.
44 *Percentage of Votes for New Parties, 1959–77*

	1959	1963	1967	1971	1972	1977
Pacifist Socialist	1·8	3·0	2·9	1·4	1·5	0·9
Peasant Party	0·7	2·1	4·7	1·3	1·9	0·8
Democrats '66	—	—	4·5	6·8	4·2	5.3
Radicals	—	—	1·7	1·8	4·8	1·7
Democratic Socialists '70	—	—	—	5·3	4·1	0·7
Conservative Catholics	—	—	—	0·4	0·9	0·4
Total	2·5	5·1	13·8	17·0	16·4	9·8

45 See tables 2, 3 and 4, below pp. 213–15.
46 H. Daalder, 'Extreme proportional representation – the Dutch experience', in S. Finer (ed.), *Adversary Politics*, p. 237.
47 The looser word 'federation', rather than party, was the preferred word of the CDA leaders in 1977; various interviews with CDA leaders by author.
48 See below, pp. 213–214.
49 *Joint Emergency Programme, 1971–75*. For details, see *Synopse der Parteiprogramme der Christlich-Demokratischen Parteien Westeuropas* (1971), p. 8 and ff.
50 The phrase used by Janssen van Raay, Secretary of the CHU, and a leading advocate of the CDA, in an interview with the author, July 1977.
51 For details about the background history leading up to the formation of the CDA, and the main speeches made at the Hague Congress of 1975 and 1976, see *Vernieuwing in Samenspraak*, published by the CDA, 1977.
52 Interview with Janssen van Raay, July 1977.
53 Interview with Corporaal and Janssen van Raay, July 1977.
54 For full details, see *Niet bij brood alleen: CDA Verkiezingsprogram 1977–81* (1977).
55 Interviews with KVP, CHU and ARP Secretaries, July 1977.
56 See *Statuten voor het CDA*, preamble, p. 1.
57 Interview with Janssen van Raay, July 1977.
58 ibid.
59 Interview with Corporaal, July 1977.
60 See tables 2 and 3, pp. 213–14.

7
Christian Democracy in France

1 See below, pp. 230–1.
2 For a full analysis of the movement in France from its origins to the demise of the MRP in 1966, see R. E. M. Irving, *Christian Democracy in France*.
3 Quoted in J. Fauvet, *De Thorez à de Gaulle: les forces politiques en France*, p. 168.
4 On the role of Catholics in the Resistance see especially H. Michel, *Histoire de la Résistance en France*, H. R. Kedward, *Resistance in Vichy France*, and H. Noguères, *Histoire de la Résistance en France, 1940–45*. On the PDP see above, pp. 26–8.
5 R. Michels, *Political Parties*, and M. Duverger, *Political Parties*, especially pp. 17–23.
6 W. Bosworth, *Catholicism and Crisis in Modern France*.

7   Interview with Paul Vignaux of the CFTC, January 1967. Thirty-one of MRP's 173 deputies elected in 1946 came directly from the CFTC, although they had to resign their trade union membership on election to parliament. Several ex-CFTC deputies played a prominent part in MRP: Paul Bacon and André Monteil both became ministers, whilst Francine Lefebvre, Maurice Guérin, Fernand Bouxom and Marcel Poimboeuf were prominent members of the National Assembly.

8   A small minority, who preferred to retain close links with the Church, continued as 'La CFTC maintenue'.

9   See Françoise Mayeur, *L'Aube: étude d'un journal d'opinion, 1932–40*.

10   See F. Goguel, *Géographie des élections françaises*, p. 109.

11   ibid., pp. 127 and 147.

12   ibid., pp. 123, 127, 145, 147 and 175. The only qualification which should be added is that not all the MRP votes in the west were in traditionally conservative areas, e.g., this would not be true of parts of Finistère, Côtes-du-Nord and Mayenne. Nevertheless, the generalisation about MRP's vote being essentially conservative is valid.

13   *Sondages*, 16 July 1946, and *Réalités*, May 1952.

14   *Réalités*, November 1952.

15   ibid. Goguel has also shown the striking similarity between areas of 'satisfactory religious practice' and Christian Democratic strength, *Elections*, p. 175.

16   Fogarty, *Christian Democracy in Western Europe*, p. 358; see also Rémond, *Forces religieuses et attitudes politiques*, p. 79.

17   On decolonisation, see R. E. M. Irving, *The first Indochina War*; on European integration, see below, pp. 234–43.

18   See C. de Gaulle, *Mémoires*, vol. II, p. 27.

19   See, for example, R. E. M. Irving, *Christian Democracy in France*, pp. 243–51.

20   For detailed discussion of these elections, see P. M. Williams, 'The French Presidential Election of 1965'; J. E. S. Hayward and V. Wright, '*Les deux France* and the French Presidential election of May 1974'.

21   For detailed discussion of these elections, see P. M. Williams and D. B. Goldey, 'The French general election of March 1967'; D. B. Goldey, 'The events of May and the French general election of June 1968'; J. E. S. Hayward and V. Wright, 'Presidential supremacy and the French general elections of March 1973'.

22   On the Socialists in the 1970s, see, *inter alia*, V. Wright and H. Machin, 'The French Socialist Party in 1973'; D. Bell, 'The *Parti Socialiste* in France'; and I. Campbell, 'The end of the Mitterrand experiment?'

23   *Le Monde*, 21 December 1965.

24   *Le Monde*, 19 October 1966.

25   *France Moderne* (the Independent Republican monthly), April 1966.

26   For a detailed analysis of the 1969 referendum and election, see J. E. S. Hayward, 'Presidential suicide by plebiscite: de Gaulle's exit', and D. B. Goldey, 'The French Presidential election of 1969'.

27   For a detailed analysis of the 1971 municipal elections, see J. E. S. Hayward and V. Wright, 'The 37,708 microcosms of an indivisible Republic'.

28   For an analysis of the 1973 election, see J. E. S. Hayward and V. Wright, 'Presidential supremacy and the French general elections of March 1973'.

29   Giscard put himself forward as a candidate on 8 April; Lecanuet went to see him on the morning of 10 April, and on the afternoon of the same day announced the CD's support for Giscard after this move had been ratified by the CD *Conseil Politique* by 157 to 84; *Le Monde*, 12 April 1974.

30   *Le Monde*, 25 March 1977. For an analysis of the municipal elections, see J. Hayward and V. Wright, 'Governing from the Centre: the 1977 French local elections', and D. Goldey and D. Bell, 'The French municipal election of March 1977'.

31   See table, p. 233. Other minor parties and groups also fought the 1978 election under the UDF's umbrella, e.g., the MDSF and a number of 'independent' (*majorité présidentielle*) candidates.

32 For a detailed discussion of the *Mouvement Réformateur*, see R. E. M. Irving, 'The centre parties in the Fifth French Republic', especially pp. 270–7.
33 On the whole religiosity is declining in its influence on voting habits, but practising Catholics are more likely to vote for the CDS and Republican Party than for any other. See *Etudes et Documents*, January 1978, 'Les choix politiques des catholiques', and *Le Monde Dossier*, 'Les élections législatives de mars 1978', pp. 58–9.
34 See various articles by N.-J. Bergeroux, e.g., *Le Monde*, 21 May 1976, 25 May 1976 and 25 March 1977; and in *Le Monde Dossier*, 'Les élections législatives de mars 1978', pp. 8–9.

8
The Christian Democrats and European Integration

1 Adenauer was Chancellor of West Germany from 1949–63; De Gasperi Prime Minister of Italy from 1945–53; Schuman Prime Minister of France in 1947–8 and Foreign Minister from 1948–52.
2 *Rede . . . Konrad Adenauer*, 24 March 1946, p. 3.
3 See above, Chapter 4, especially pp. 113–21.
4 P. Canali, *De Gasperi nella politica estera italiana*, p. 33.
5 *Le Monde*, 5 November 1949.
6 MRP National Congress Report, May 1947.
7 R. Schuman, *Pour faire l'Europe*, p. 133.
8 F. Roy Willis, *Italy Chooses Europe*, p. 27.
9 *Le Monde*, 14 August 1949.
10 *Le Monde*, 4 April 1950.
11 For a detailed analysis of ECSC, see William Diebold, *The Schuman Plan*.
12 For Schuman's doubts, see R. E. M. Irving, *Christian Democracy in France*, pp. 177–80.
13 F. Roy Willis, *Italy Chooses Europe*, p. 44; and see below, pp. 238–42.
14 M. Catti De Gasperi, *La nostra patria Europa*, p. 66.
15 See Edelgard Mahant, *The French and German Political Parties and the Common Market negotiations, 1955–57* (PhD. London, 1970), pp. 111–13
16 *Journal Officiel* (Assemblée Nationale), 15 January 1957.
17 VDB, 5 July 1957.
18 A. Segni, in Presidenza del Consiglio, *Comunità Economica Europea*, 1957, p. 99.
19 *Journal Officiel* (Assemblée Nationale), 9 July 1957.
20 See, for example, C. Hacke, *Die Ost– und Deutschland politik der CDU–CSU*, pp. 43–5, 51–3, 96–118.
21 See, for example, Primo Vannicelli, *Italy, NATO and the European Community*, pp. 22 and 28–30; also Cesare Merlini, 'Italy in the European Community and the Atlantic Alliance' and 'Italy in the European Community'. For a detailed discussion of the DC's European policy, see R. E. M. Irving, 'Italy's Christian Democrats and European Integration'. (The following pages owe much to that article.)
22 P. Canali, *De Gasperi nella politica estera italiana*, p. 33.
23 F. Roy Willis, *Italy Chooses Europe*, p. 9. An excellent book, with perhaps an inappropriate title (see the argument in the rest of this paragraph).
24 P. E. Taviani, *Il Piano Schuman*, p. 9.
25 *Le Monde*, 14 December 1951.
26 M. Catti De Gasperi, *La nostra patria Europa*, p. 61.
27 For a detailed discussion of the French rejection of EDC, see R. E. M. Irving, *Christian Democracy in France*, pp. 170–88.
28 DC – *Atti e Documenti*, vol. 1, pp. 846–7.
29 The Italian negotiators also succeeded in getting the original allocation of $50 million to the EIB raised to $1000 million.

30 See, for example, the debates on the Treaties of Rome in the Italian Chamber, *Atti Parlamentari Camera dei Deputati,* July 1957; see also Prime Minister Segni's speech after the signing of the Treaties, in Presidenza del Consiglio, *Comunità Economica Europea,* p. 99.

31 Italy has, for example, failed to profit fully from the funds available under the European Agricultural Guidance and Guarantee Fund (FEOGA); see articles on Italian agriculture by Bruno Musti de Gennaro in *Lo Spettatore Internazionale,* vol. VII, no. 3–4, July–Dec. 1972 and vol. IX, no. 3–4, July–Dec. 1974.

32 *Il Popolo,* 6 June 1968 and 4 May 1971.

33 For details, see R. E. M. Irving, 'Italy's Christian Democrats and European integration', p. 409.

34 *Il Popolo,* 22 July 1965.

35 *Spettatore Internazionale,* 1970, p. 272.

36 For details, see *Spettatore Internazionale,* 1970, p. 273.

37 *Le Monde,* 9 October 1975.

38 For a detailed analysis up to 1973, see R. E. M. Irving, *Christian Democracy in France,* pp. 159–98.

39 See above, pp. 229–31.

40 K. Adenauer, *Erinnerungen,* vol. III, pp. 27 and 30.

41 France, Assemblée Nationale, *Recueil des textes,* vol. I, p. 495.

42 MRP national congress, 1956; report on 'La politique extérieure'.

43 This thesis is convincingly argued by Primo Vannicelli in *Italy, NATO and the European Community: the interplay of foreign policy and domestic politics.*

44 See R. E. M. Irving, 'The European policy of the French and Italian Communists'.

45 See above, pp. 237–8.

46 The Christian Democrats were second in the field with a transnational European party, the Liberals having set up theirs in March 1976.

47 For most of the information in the following pages (on the various Christian Democratic organisations from the *Nouvelles Equipes Internationales* to the European People's Party), I am indebted to interviews and correspondence with K. J. Hahn, Assistant Secretary-General of the European Union of Christian Democrats in Rome, and with Josef Müller, head of the EUCD and Christian Democratic information centre in Brussels. K. J. Hahn, *Histoire, structure, action de la democratie chrétienne en Europe; La Démocratie Chrétienne dans le Monde* (Résolutions et déclarations des organisations internationales démocrates chrétiennes de 1947–53, published by Union Mondiale Démocrate Chrétienne, Rome, 1973); the *Statutes of the European People's Party;* and the *Manifesto of the European People's Party,* were also useful sources of information. Finally, I must thank Geoffrey Pridham for allowing me to read two draft chapters on transnational parties in the European Community, to be published in a forthcoming PSI book on European parties.

48 Article 1 of the party's Statutes states that 'The party is called European People's Party, Federation of Christian Democratic Parties of the European Community.'

49 On the ECSC Assembly, see P. J. G. Kapteyn, *L'Assemblée de la Communauté Européenne du Charbon et de l'Acier.*

50 On the party groups in the European Parliament, see G. van Oudenhove, *The Political Parties in the European Parliament* (up to 1961), and J. Fitzmaurice, *The Party Groups in the European Parliament* (up to 1973); also G. Pridham, 'Transnational party groups in the European Parliament'. Spaak's Christian Democratic successors as president of the Assembly were Alcide De Gasperi (May–August 1954; died in office), Giuseppe Pella (Nov. 1954–Nov. 1956), and Hans Furler (Nov. 1956–March 1958).

51 The Christian Democratic presidents were Robert Schuman (March 1958–May 1960), Hans Furler (May 1960–March 1962), Jean Duvieusart (March 1964–September 1965), Victor Leemans (September 1965–March 1966), Alain Poher (March 1966–March 1969), and Mario Scelba (March 1969–March 1971).

52 Colombo led on the first two ballots against the French Socialist Georges Spenale and the Irish Fianna Fail Michael Yeats, but failed to reach an absolute majority (100 out of 198). Spenale dropped out at the third ballot, and with the Communists abstaining and most Socialists switching to Yeats, Colombo was elected by the relative majority of 85–77 (all that was required on the third ballot).

53 The Political Committee not only did the groundwork for the setting up of the European People's Party, it also has an important role as the 'permanent liaison organisation between the parties and parliamentary groups at the national and European level', Article 1 of *Regulation setting up the Political Committee of the Christian Democratic Parties of the EEC*, 7 April 1972.

54 Interview with J. Müller in Brussels, December 1976.

55 *Financial Times*, 9 July 1976.

56 See Article 2 of EPP Statutes. The founding members were the Belgian CVP and PSC; the German CDU and CSU; the Dutch ARP, CHU and KVP; the Italian DC and SVP; the French CDS; the Luxembourg PCS; and the Irish Fine Gael. The Christian Democratic group in the European Parliament is also a member.

57 *European People's Party Manifesto*, 1978, 22 pp.

58 The fifty national party representatives are allocated as follows. Each of the seven countries represented in the EPP (i.e., all the Community countries except Britain and Denmark) has two members as of right, making fourteen in all. The remaining thirty-six seats are allocated proportionally as follows: Germany eleven, Italy eleven, Belgium four, Netherlands four, France, Ireland and Luxembourg two each; *Appendix to Rules of Procedure, EPP Statutes*.

59 See below, pp. 251–2.

60 *Frankfurter Allgemeine Zeitung*, 10 September 1975.

61 See, for example, *Daily Telegraph*, 18 October 1975.

62 Other parties which sent observers to Salzburg, but did not actually join the EDU, were the Italian SVP, French *Parti Républicain*, Greek New Democrats, Spanish Democratic Centre Union, Swedish People's Party, Swiss Christian People's Party and Maltese National Party; *The Economist*, 29 April 1978.

63 See *European Report*, June 1967, for details about Klepsch's political career.

64 See statement of DC secretary-general Zaccagnini to this effect in *Frankfurter Allgemeine Zeitung*, 21 February 1976.

65 See interview with CDU secretary-general Biedenkopf in *Le Monde*, 26 February 1976.

66 Interviews with Frank Swaelen, Belgian CVP, December 1976, and D. Corporaal, Dutch ARP, July 1977.

67 See Chapters 4, 6 and 7 above, and pp. 259–60 below.

68 Interview with Swaelen, December 1976.

Bibliography

This bibliography is divided into three parts:

I *General Literature*: this section includes literature on Christian Democratic theory and transnational organisations, as well as books and articles which, whilst not specifically concerned with Christian Democracy, contain important material on the subject.

II *The Origins of Christian Democracy*: this section is concerned with the origins of Christian Democracy, particularly with the precursor parties in Italy, Germany and France. It is divided into sections on these countries.

III *The Christian Democratic Parties of Western Europe since 1945*: this section is the main part of the bibliography and is subdivided into sections on Italy, Germany, Belgium, the Netherlands and France.

In consulting the bibliography it will normally be best to turn in the first instance to Section III under the appropriate sub-section, unless the reference is to prewar Christian Democracy or to some broad aspect of the Christian Democratic movement, in which case Sections I or II would be more appropriate: for example, a reference to the postwar foreign policy or political theory of the Italian Christian Democratic party will be found in Section III under 'Italy'. If, however, the reference is to Christian Democratic theory in general or to the Christian Democratic transnational organisations, Section I of the bibliography should be consulted. The primary sources referred to in Section III include memoirs and collections of speeches by Christian Democrats as well as specific party documentation.

PART I – GENERAL LITERATURE

Almond, G., 'The political ideas of Christian Democracy', *Journal of Politics*, November 1948.

Almond, G., and Verba, S., *The Civic Culture*, Princeton: Princeton University Press, 1963.

Beckel, A., *Christliche Staatslehre*, 2 vols., (1) *Grundlagen und Zeitfragen*; (2) *Dokumente*, Osnabrück: Fromm, 1961.

Bennett, J. C., *Christians and the State*, New York: Scribners, 1958.

Bernassola, A., ed., *Democrazia cristiana – realta internazionale*, Rome: Cinque Lune, 1968.

Bettenson, H., *Documents of the Christian Church*, London: Oxford University Press, 1943.

Beuret, G., *Die katholisch-soziale Bewegung in der Schweiz, 1848–1919*, Winterthur: Keller, 1959.

Blondel, J., *An Introduction to Comparative Government*, London: Weidenfeld and Nicolson, 1969.

Buchan, A., *Europe's Future, Europe's Choices: Models of Western Europe in the 1970s*, London: Chatto & Windus, 1969.

Carby Hall, J. R., *Worker Participation in Europe*, London: Croom Helm, 1977.

Christian Democratic Group, European Parliament,
CD - Europe (monthly).
Manifesto of the European People's Party, 1976.
Programme of the European People's Party, 1978.
Statutes of the European People's Party, 1976.
Report of the Activities of the Christian Democrat Group (annual).
Cornford, J., ed., *The Failure of the State*, London: Croom Helm, 1975.
Diamant, A., *Austrian Catholics and the First Republic*, Princeton: Princeton University Press, 1960.
Diebold, W., *The Schuman Plan*, New York: Praeger, 1959.
Dogan, M., and Rose, R., *European Politics: a Reader*, London: Macmillan, 1971.
Duverger, M., *Political Parties*, London: Methuen, 1954.
Einaudi, M., and Goguel, F., *Christian Democracy in Italy and France*, Notre Dame: Notre Dame University Press, 1952.
European Union of Christian Democrats, *L'avenir démocratique de l'Europe*, Brussels: EUCD, 1967.
Finer, S., ed., *Adversary Politics and Electoral Reform*, London: Wigram, 1975.
Fitzmaurice, J., *The Party Groups in the European Parliament*, Farnborough: Saxon House, 1975.
The European Parliament, Farnborough: Saxon House, 1978.
Fogarty, M. P., *Christian Democracy in Western Europe, 1820–1953*, London: Routledge & Kegan Paul, 1957.
Geiger, T. J., *On Social Order and Mass Society*, Chicago: University of Chicago Press, 1969.
Graubard, S., ed., *A New Europe?* Boston: Houghton Mifflin, 1964.
Gruner, E., *Die Schweizerische Bundesversammlung, 1848–1920*, 2 vols., Berne: Helvetia Politica, 1966.
Hahn, K. J., *Histoire, structure, action de la démocratie chrétienne en Europe*, Rome: Centre International DC de Documentation, 1975.
Henig, S., ed., *Political Parties in the European Community*, London: Allen & Unwin for PSI, 1979.
Henig, S., and Pinder, J., eds., *European Political Parties*, London: Allen & Unwin for PEP, 1969.
Holt, S., *Six European States*, London: Hamish Hamilton, 1970.
Houben, R., *La politique méconnue*, Brussels: CEPESS, 1963.
'Réflexions sur la doctrine politique chrétienne', *Revue Politique*, October 1951, pp. 5–40.
'Les Chrétiens devant la politique', *Revue Politique*, October 1953, pp. 481–507.
Hours, J., *La doctrine de la démocratie chrétienne*, Paris: Colin, 1952.
Hürten, H., ed., *Christliche Parteien in Europa*, Osnabrück: Fromm, 1964.
Irving, R. E. M., 'Italy's Christian Democrats and European integration', *International Affairs*, July 1976, pp. 400–16.
Kapteyn, P. J. G., *L'Assemblée de la Communauté Européene du Charbon et de l'Acier*, Leiden: Sijthoff, 1962.
Konrad-Adenauer-Stiftung, ed., *Synopse der Parteiprogramme der Christlich-Demokratischen Parteien Westeuropas*, Bonn, 1971.
Kothen, R., *La pensée et l'action sociale des catholiques, 1789–1944*, Louvain: Editions Universitaires, 1946.
Kress, O. E., ed., *Kirche, Staat und Katholiken: Dokumentation, 1803–1967*, Augsburg: Winfried-Werk, 1967.

LaPalombara, J., and Weiner, M., *Political Parties and Political Development*, Princeton: Princeton University Press, 1966.

Lenoir, J., *Essai sur la démocratie chrétienne et ses fondements philosophiques*, Monte Carlo: Regain, 1954.

Lijphart, A., *Politics in Europe*, Englewood Cliffs: Prentice-Hall, 1969.

Mahant, E., 'The French and German political parties and the Common Market negotiations, 1955–57', London: Ph.D. Thesis, 1970.

Maier, H., *Revolution and Church: the Early History of Christian Democracy, 1789–1901*, Notre Dame: Notre Dame University Press, 1969.

Maritain, J., *L'homme et l'Etat*, Paris: Presses Universitaires de France, 1953.

Mayne, R., *The Recovery of Europe*, London: Weidenfeld & Nicolson, 1970.

Merlini, C., 'Italy in the European Community and Atlantic Alliance', *The World Today*, April 1975, pp. 160–6.

Michels, R., *Political Parties*, New York: Collier, 1962.

Moody, J. N., ed., *Church and Society: Catholic Social and Political Thought and Movements, 1789–1960*, New York: Arts Inc., 1953.

Mounier, E., *Le personnalisme*, Paris: Presses Universitaires de France, 1949.

Neumann, S., ed., *Modern Political Parties: Approaches to Comparative Politics*, Chicago: University of Chicago Press, 1956.

Oudenhove, G. van, *The Political Parties in the European Parliament*, Leiden: Sijthoff, 1965.

Pflimlin, P., and Legrand-Lane, R., *L'Europe communautaire*, Paris: Plon, 1966.

Pridham, G., 'Transnational party groups in the European Parliament', JCMS, March 1975, pp. 266–9.

Rogger, T., and Weber, E., *The European Right*, London: Weidenfeld & Nicolson, 1965.

Rommen, H., *The State in Catholic Thought*, London: Herder, 1945.

Rose, R., ed., *Electoral Behaviour: a Comparative Handbook*, London: Collier Macmillan, 1974.

Rumor, M., *La Democrazia Cristiana nella politica internazionale*, Rome: Cinque Lune, 1966.

Schuman, R., *Pour faire l'Europe*, Paris: Nagel, 1963.

Sturzo, L., *Church and State*, 2 vols., Notre Dame: Notre Dame University Press, 1962.

Talmon, J. L., *The Origins of Totalitarian Democracy*, London: Secker & Warburg, 1952.

Tocqueville, A. de, *Oeuvres et correspondances inédites*, Paris: Levy, 1867.

Troeltsch, E., *The Social Teaching of the Christian Churches*, 2 vols., London: Allen & Unwin, 1931.

Union Mondiale Démocrate Chrétien, *La Démocratie Chrétienne dans le monde: résolutions et déclarations des organisations internationales démocrates chrétiennes de 1947 à 1973*, Rome: UMDC, 1974.

Vaussard, M., *Histoire de la Démocratie Chrétienne: France, Belgique, Italie*, Paris: Seuil, 1956.

Verkade, W., *Democratic Parties in the Low Countries and Germany*, Leiden: Universitaire Pers, 1965.

Villain, J., *L'enseignement social de l'Eglise*, 3 vols., Paris: Spes, 1954.

Willis, F. Roy., *France, Germany and the New Europe*, London: Oxford University Press, 1968.

PART II – THE ORIGINS OF CHRISTIAN DEMOCRACY
Italy
Ambrosoli, L., *Il primo movimento democratico cristiano in Italia, 1847–1904*, Rome: Cinque Lune, 1958.
Bedeschi, L., *I pionieri della DC, 1896–1906*, Milan: Saggiatore, 1966.
Romolo Murri, la Romagna e il modernismo, Parma: Guarda, 1966.
Dal movimento di Murri all'appello di Sturzo, Milan: Saggiatore, 1969.
Bertoli, B., *Le origini del movimento cattolico a Venezia*, Brescia: Morcelliana, 1965.
Binchy, D. A., *Church and State in Fascist Italy*, London: Oxford University Press/Royal Institute of International Affairs, 1941.
Braga, G., *Il Partito Popolare Italiano*, Rome: Cinque Lune, 1970.
Buonaiuti, C. M., *Non Expedit: storia di una politica, 1866–1919*, Milan, 1971.
Candeloro, G., *Il movimento cattolico in Italia*, Rome: Rinascita, 1955.
Cappelli, G., *La prima sinistra cattolica in Toscana, 1893–1904*, Rome: Cinque Lune, 1963.
Cervelli, I., *I cattolici dall 'unità alla fondazione del Partito Popolare*, Bologna: Il Mulino, 1969.
Clough, S. B., and Saladino, S., *A History of Modern Italy*, New York: Columbia University Press, 1968.
Croce, B., *Storia d'Italia dal 1870 al 1915*, Bari: Laterza, 1928.
Dalla Torre, G., *I cattolici e la vita pubblica italiana*, Rome, 1962.
De Rosa, G., *Filippo Meda e l'età liberale*, Florence: Saggiatore, 1959.
Il movimento cattolico in Italia dalla restaurazione all' età giolittiana, 2nd edn., Bari: Laterza, 1972.
Il Partito Popolare Italiano, 2nd edn., Bari: Laterza, 1972.
I conservatori nazionali: biografia di Carlo Santucci, Brescia: Morcelliana, 1962.
Storia del movimento cattolico in Italia, 2 vols., Bari: Laterza, 1966.
Storia politica dell'azione cattolica in Italia, 2 vols., Bari: Laterza, 1953.
Fonzi, F., *I cattolici e la società italiana dopo l'unità*, 2nd edn., Milan: Giuffre, 1965.
Gambasin, A., *Il movimento sociale nell'opera dei congressi, 1874–1904*, Rome: Università Gregoriana, 1958.
Gaudenti, A., *Luigi Sturzo: il pensiero e le opere*, Rome, 1945.
Giordani, I., *Pionieri della Democrazia Cristiana*, Rome, 1945.
Gualerzi, G., *La politica estera dei Popolari*, Rome: Cinque Lune, 1959.
Guasco, M., *Romolo Murri e il modernismo*, Rome: Cinque Lune, 1968.
Howard, E. P., *Il Partito Popolare Italiano*, Florence: La Nuova Italia, 1957.
Istituto Luigi Sturzo, ed., *Saggi sul Partito Popolare Italiano*, Rome, 1969.
Jacini, S., *Storia del Partito Popolare Italiano*, Milan: Garzanti, 1951.
Jemolo, A. C., *Chiesa e stato in Italia negli ultimi cento anni*, Turin: Einaudi, 1949.
Mack Smith, D., *Italy: a Modern History*, Ann Arbor: University of Michigan Press, 1967.
Malgeri, F., ed., *Gli atti dei congressi del PPI*, Brescia: Morcelliana, 1969.
Maranini, G., *Storia del potere in Italia, 1848–1967*, Florence: Vallecchi, 1968.
Mayeur, J. M., 'La démocratie chrétienne en Italie avant 1914', *Archives de sociologie des religions*, January 1962.

Mollat, G., *La question romaine de Pie IX à Pie XI*, Paris, 1932.
Moloney, J. N., *The Emergence of Political Catholicism in Italy: Partito Popolare, 1919–26*, London: Croom Helm, 1977.
Moro, A., *Luigi Sturzo*, Rome, 1959.
Murri, R., *Dalla democrazia cristiana al Partito Popolare Italiano*, Florence, 1920.
Carteggio, 2 vols., Rome: Edizioni di Storia e Letteratura, 1970.
Palumbo, B., *Il movimento democratico cristiano in Italia*, Rome: Cuor di Maria, 1950.
Piva, F., and Malgeri, F., *Vita di Luigi Sturzo*, Rome: Cinque Lune, 1972.
Rizzo, F., *Luigi Sturzo e la questione meridionale*, Rome: Cinque Lune, 1957.
Salvemini, G., *Stato e chiesa in Italia*, Milan: Garzanti, 1968.
Scoppola, P., *La chiesa e il fascismo*, Bari: Laterza, 1969.
Seton-Watson, C., *Italy from Liberalism to Fascism, 1870–1928*, London: Methuen, 1967.
Spadolini, G., *Giolitti e i cattolici, 1901–14*, Florence: Vallecchi, 1960.
ed., *Romolo Murri*, Rome: Cinque Lune, 1965.
Sturzo, L., *Church and State*, 2 vols., Notre Dame: Notre Dame University Press, 1962.
Il Partito Popolare Italiano, 3 vols., Bologna: Zanichelli, 1956.
Toniolo, G., *La Democrazia Cristiana*, Rome, 1900.
Opera omnia, 16 vols., Vatican City, 1947–53.
Valente, G., *Aspetti e momenti dell'azione sociale dei cattolici in Italia, 1892–1926*, Rome: Cinque Lune, 1968.
Vaussard, M., *Il pensiero politico e sociale di Luigi Sturzo*, Brescia: Morcelliana, 1966.
Vercesi, E., *Il movimento cattolico in Italia, 1870–1922*, Florence: La Voce, 1923.
Webster, R. A., *Christian Democracy in Italy, 1860–1960*, London: Hollis & Carter, 1961.
The Cross and the Fasces: Christian Democracy and Fascism in Italy, Stanford: Stanford University Press, 1960.

Germany

Bachem, J., 'Wir müssen aus dem Turm heraus', *Historische Politische Blätter*, 1906, p. 376 and ff.
Bachem, K., *Vorgeschichte, Geschichte und Politik der deutschen Zentrumspartei*, 9 vols., Aalen: Scientia Verlag, 1927–32.
Bergsträsser, L., *Studien zur Vorgeschichte der Zentrumspartei*, Tübingen, 1910.
ed., *Der politische Katholizismus: Dokumente seiner Entwicklung, 1815–70*, Munich, 1928.
Bracher, K. D., *Die Auflösing der Weimarer Republik*, Stuttgart: Ring, 1960.
Buchheim, K., *Die Weimarer Republik*, Munich: Kösel, 1960.
Ultramontanismus und Demokratie, Munich: Kösel, 1963.
Constabel, A., *Die Vorgeschichte des Kulturkampfes*, Berlin: Rütten & Loening, 1956.
Eschenburg, T., *Die improvisierte Demokratie: gesammelte Aufsätze zur Weimarer Republik*, Munich: Piper, 1963.
Eyck, E., *Geschichte der Weimarer Republik*, 2 vols., Stuttgart: Rentsch, 1954–6.
Heidemann, K., *Bismarcks Sozialpolitik und die Zentrumspartei, 1881–84*, Göttingen: Ph.D. thesis, 1930.
Holborn, H., *A History of Modern Germany, 1840–1945*, London: Eyre & Spottiswoode, 1969.
Hüsgen, E., *Ludwig Windthorst*, Cologne, 1911.

Kissling, J. B., *Geschichte des Kulturkampfes im Deutschen Reiche*, 3 vols., Freiburg, 1911–16.
Mann, H., *Der Beginn der Abkehr Bismarcks vom Kulturkampf, 1878–80*, Frankfurt: Ph.D. thesis, 1953.
Mommsen, W., *Deutsche Parteiprogramme*, Munich: Olzog, 1960.
Morsey, R., *Die deutsche Zentrumspartei*, Düsseldorf: Droste, 1966.
Neumann, S., *Die deutsche Parteien: Wesen und Wandel nach dem Kriege*, Berlin: Junker & Dunnhaupt, 1932.
Die Parteien der Weimarer Republik, 2nd edn., Stuttgart: Kohlhammer, 1970.
Ritter, E., *Die katholisch-soziale Bewegung Deutschlands im 19 Jahrhundert und der Volksverein*, Cologne: Bachem, 1954.
Rovan, J., *Le catholicisme politique en Allemagne*, Paris: Seuil, 1956.
Schauff, J., *Die deutsche Katholiken und die Zentrumspartei*, Cologne: Bachem, 1928.
Schmidt-Volkmar, E., *Der Kulturkampf in Deutschland, 1871–1890*, Göttingen: Musterschmidt, 1962.
Treue, W., *Die deutsche Parteien*, Wiesbaden: Steiner, 1962.
Windthorst, L., *Ausgewählte Reden, 1851–1891*, 3 vols., Osnabrück, 1901–2.

France
Anderson, R. D., *France, 1870–1914: Politics and Society*, London: Routledge & Kegan Paul, 1977.
Biton, L., *La démocratie chrétienne dans la politique française*, Paris: Giraudeau & Cie, 1953.
Bodley, J. E. C., *The Church in France*, London: Macmillan, 1906.
Borne, E., *De Marc Sangnier à Marc Coquelin*, Toulouse, 1953.
Bosworth, W., *Catholicism and Crisis in Modern France*, Princeton: Princeton University Press, 1962.
Brogan, D. W., *The Development of Modern France, 1870–1939*, London: Hamish Hamilton, 1940.
Caron, J., *Le Sillon et la démocratie chrétienne, 1894–1910*, Paris: Plon, 1966.
Cornilleau, R., *Souvenirs et témoignages*, Rennes, 1959.
Coutrot, A. and Dreyfus, F., *Les forces religieuses dans la société française*, Paris: Colin, 1965.
Crouzil, L., *Quarante ans de séparation, 1905–45*, Paris: Didier, 1946.
Dansette, A., *Histoire religieuse de la France contemporaine*, 2 vols., Paris: Flammarion, 1952.
Darbon, M., *Le conflit entre la droite et la gauche dans le catholicisme français, 1830–1953*, Toulouse, 1953.
Derro, A., *L'épiscopat français dans la mêlée de son temps, 1930–54*, Paris: Bonne Presse, 1955.
Duroselle, J. B., *Les débuts du catholicisme social en France, 1822–70*, Paris: Presses Universitaires de France, 1951.
Gay, F., *Pour un rassemblement des forces démocratiques d'inspiration chrétienne*, Paris: Bloud & Gay, 1935.
Goguel, F., *La politique des partis sous la IIIe République*, Paris: Seuil, 1946.
Irving, R. E. M., *Christian Democracy in France*, London: Allen & Unwin, 1973.
Kedward, H. R., *Resistance in Vichy France*, Oxford: Oxford University Press, 1978.
Larkin, M., *Church and State after the Dreyfus Affair*, London: Macmillan, 1974.

Lepointe, G., *Les rapports entre l'église et l'état en France*, Paris: Presses Universitaires de France, 1960.

Mayeur, F., *L'Aube: étude d'un journal d'opinion, 1932–40*, Paris: Colin, 1966.

Megrine, R., *La question scolaire en France*, Paris: Presses Universitaires de France, 1960.

Montagne, H. de la, *Histoire de la démocratie chrétienne de Lamennais à Georges Bidault*, Paris: Amiot-Dumont, 1948.

Montuclard, M., *Conscience religieuse et démocratie: la deuxième démocratie chrétienne en France, 1891–1902*, Paris: Seuil, 1965.

Pezet, E., *Chrétiens au service de la cité: de Léon XIII au Sillon et au MRP*, Paris: Nouvelles Editions Latines, 1965.

Raymond-Laurent, J., *Le Parti Démocrate Populaire, 1924–44*, Le Mans, 1966.

Rémond, R., *La droite en France de 1815 à nos jours*, Paris: Aubier, 1954.

Lamennais et la démocratie, Paris: Presses Universitaires de France, 1948.

Renard, G., *Pour connaître le Sillon*, Paris, 1966.

Rollet, H., *Sur le chantier social: l'action sociale des catholiques en France, 1870–1940*, Lyon, 1955.

L'action sociale des catholiques en France, 1871–1914, 2 vols, Paris: Boivin, 1947 (vol. 1) and 1958 (vol. 2).

Albert de Mun et le parti catholique, Paris: Boivin, 1949.

Sangnier, M., *L'esprit démocratique*, Paris, 1906.

Siegfried, A., *Tableau des partis en France*, Paris: Grasset, 1930.

Spencer, P., *The Politics of Belief in Nineteenth Century France*, London: Faber, 1954.

Suffert, G., *Les catholiques et la gauche*, Paris: Maspero, 1960.

Thibaudet, A., *Les idées politiques de la France*, Paris: Stock, 1932.

PART III – THE CHRISTIAN DEMOCRATIC PARTIES OF WESTERN EUROPE SINCE 1945

Italy
See also 'Origins of Christian Democracy', Italian section, above.

Primary sources Party documentation can be consulted at the DC archives, Piazza Luigi Sturzo, EUR, Rome, and at the Istituto Sturzo, Rome. The DC's *Servizio propaganda e studi* (SPES) also publishes much party material. In addition, primary material can be consulted at the National Library, Florence. Note in particular the following:

Atti del [number] Congresso della DC, Rome: SPES.

Atti e Documenti della Democrazia Cristiana, 1943–67, 2 vols., Rome: Cinque Lune, 1968.

Statuto del Partito (DC statutes), Rome: SPES, 1968.

Andreotti, G., *De Gasperi e la ricostruzione*, Rome: Cinque Lune, 1974.

Trento-Vienna-Roma: De Gasperi e il suo tempo, Milan: Mondadori, 1964.

Catti De Gasperi, M. R., *De Gasperi: Uomo solo*, Milan: Mondadori, 1964.

La nostra patria Europa: il pensiero europeistica di Alcide De Gasperi, Milan: Mondadori, 1969.

De Gasperi, A., *I Cattolici dall'opposizione al governo*, Bari: Laterza, 1955.

Discorsi parlamentari, 3 vols., Rome: Camera dei Deputati, 1973.

Discorsi politici, 2 vols., Rome: Cinque Lune, 1969.
Idee ricostruttive della Democrazia Cristiana, Rome, 1945.
Demofilo (De Gasperi, A., pseudonym), *Tradizione e ideologia della Democrazia Cristiana*, Rome, 1944.
Fanfani, A., *Anni difficili ma non sterili*, Bologna: Cappelli, 1958.
Da Napoli a Firenze, Milan: Garzanti, 1959.
Dopo Firenze, Milan: Garzanti, 1961.
Centro-Sinistra, Milan: Garzanti, 1962.
Forlani, A., *I Democratici Cristiani e la società nuova*, Rome: Cinque Lune, 1966.
Galloni, G., *Una politica per la Democrazia Cristiana*, Rome: Stampa Nova, 1966.
Gonella, G., *Il programma della Democrazia Cristiana per la nuova costituzione*, Rome: SPES, 1946.
Guiso, N., ed., *Idee sulla Democrazia Cristiana*, Rome: Cinque Lune, 1974.
Gullotti, N., ed., *Dieci Congressi DC, 1946–1967*, Rome: SPES, 1968.
La Pira, G., *Per una architettura cristiana del stato*, Florence: Fiorentina, 1954.
Lucini, G., 'Presuppositi ideologici della DC', *Idea*, June 1966, pp. 249–54.
Moro, A., *Il pensiero politico di Luigi Sturzo*, Naples: Edizioni Politica Popolare, 1959.
Per garantire e sviluppare la democrazia in Italia, Rome: SPES, 1961.
Pella, G., *Tre documenti della rinascita*, Rome: Cappelli, 1953.
Piccioni, A., *Dal congresso di Roma al congresso di Napoli*, Rome: SPES, 1947.
Piccoli, F., *Il futuro della DC nella società italiana*, Rome: Cinque Lune, 1969.
Rumor, M., *La Democrazia Cristiana e i problemi della società italiana*, Rome: Cinque Lune, 1966.
Traverso, C., ed., *I partiti politici: leggi e statuti*, Milan: Cisalpino, 1966.

Secondary sources The following newspapers and journals are useful sources of information on Christian Democracy: the independent dailies, *La Stampa*, *Corriere della Sera* and *Il Giorno*; the weeklies *L'Espresso* and *Il Mondo*; the reviews *Nord e Sud*, *Tempi Moderni*, *Il Mulino* (sympathetic to the DC though independent) and *Civiltà Cattolica* (Jesuit); and the academic reviews *Rassegna Italiana di Sociologia* and *Rivista Italiana di Scienza Politica*. The DC publishes its own daily newspaper, *Il Popolo*, and theoretical journal, *La Discussione*. Useful statistical information and results of opinion polls are published in the *Bollettino Doxa* and *Ricerçhe Demoscopiche*.

Books and articles

Acquaviva, S. S., and Guizzardi, G., *Religione e irreligione nell 'età post-industriale*, Rome: Ave, 1971.
La secolarizzazione, Bologna: Il Mulino, 1973.
Acquaviva, S. S., and Santuccio, M., *Social Structure in Italy: Crisis of a System*, London: Martin Robertson, 1976.
Adams, J. C., and Barile, P., *The Government of Republican Italy*, 3rd edn., Boston: Houghton Mifflin, 1972.
Adstans (P. Canali, pseudonym), *De Gasperi nella politica estera italiana, 1944–53*, Milan: Mondadori, 1953.
Alberoni, F., ed., *L'attivista di partito*, Bologna: Il Mulino, 1967.

Alberoni, F., and Baglioni, G., *L'integrazione dell 'immigrato nella società industriale*, Bologna: Il Mulino, 1965.

Allen, K. J., and Stevenson, A. A., *An Introduction to the Italian Economy*, London: Martin Robertson, 1976.

Allum, P. A., *Italy – Republic without Government?* London: Weidenfeld & Nicolson, 1973.

    Politics and Society in Post-war Naples, London: Cambridge University Press, 1973.

    'The Italian Election of 1963', *Political Studies*, 1965, pp. 324–45.

Allum, P. and Amyot, G., 'Regionalism in Italy: old wine in new bottles', *Parliamentary Affairs*, winter 1970–1, pp. 53–78.

Ardigò, A., *Emancipazione femminile e urbanesimo*, Brescia: Morcelliana, 1964.

    La stratificazione sociale, 2nd edn., Bologna: Patron, 1975.

    'Stratificazione sociale e potere politico in Italia', *Aggiornamenti sociali*, 1973, no. 4, pp. 321–32.

    'Evoluzione, crisi e prospettive della presenza politico-sociale dei cattolici in Italia', *Aggiornamenti sociali*, 1974, no. 6, pp. 29–64.

Aymone, T., *Scuola dell'obbligo e città operaia*, Bari: Laterza, 1972.

Banfield, E., *The Moral Basis of a Backward Society*, Glencoe: Free Press, 1958.

Barberis, C., *Da Giolitti a De Gasperi*, Bologna: Capelli, 1953.

Bassetti, P., Gorrieri, E., and Scoppola, P., *DC: tra rifondazione e secondo partito*, Milan: Contemporanea Edizioni, 1976.

Battaglia, A., *et al.*, *Dieci anni dopo (1945–1955)*, Bari: Laterza, 1955.

Berlinguer, G., and Terranova, F., *La strage degli innocenti*, Florence: Nuova Italia, 1972.

Berstein, S., and Milza, P., *L'Italie contemporaine: des nationalistes aux européens*, Paris: Colin, 1973.

Beyme, K. von, *Das politische System Italiens*, Stuttgart: Kohlhammer, 1970.

Bibes, G., *Le système politique italien*, Paris: Presses Universitaires de France, 1974.

Biblioteca di Storia Sociale, ed., *Il movimento cattolico e la società italiana in cento anni di storia*, Rome: Ediz. di Storia e Letteratura, 1976.

Binchy, D. A., *Church and State in Fascist Italy*, London: Oxford University Press/Royal Institute of International Affairs, 1941.

Bocardi, F., *Dossetti e la crisi dei cattolici italiani*, Florence: Parenti, 1956.

    'La DC e le sue correnti', *Problemi del socialismo*, March 1959.

Bocca, G., *Storia d'Italia nella guerra fascista*, Bari: Laterza, 1969.

Brunelli, L., *et al.*, *La presenza sociale del PCI e della DC*, Bologna: Il Mulino, 1968.

Brunetta, G., 'Le elezioni politiche dal 1946 al 1968 – retrospettiva statistica', *Aggiornamenti sociali*, 1972, no. 4, pp. 295–380.

Burgalassi, S., *Italiani in chiesa*, Brescia: Morcelliana, 1967.

    Il comportamento religioso degli italiani, Florence: Vallecchi, 1968.

Caciagli, M., *Democrazia Cristiana e potere nel Mezzogiorno*, Milan: Guareldi, 1978.

Canali, P., see Adstans.

Candeloro, G., *L'azione cattolica in Italia*, Rome: Cultura Sociale, 1951.

Capecchi, V., *et al.*, *Il comportamento elettorale in Italia*, Bologna: Il Mulino, 1968.

Capecchi, V., and Galli, G., 'Determinants of voting behaviour in Italy', in M. Dogan and S. Rokkan, *Quantative Ecological Analysis in the Social Sciences*, Cambridge, Mass.: MIT Press, 1969, pp. 235–83.

Car Boara, L., *Pluripartitismo e struttura democratica dello stato partitocratico,* Bologna: Forni, 1964.

Carbonaro, R., *Religione e politica: il caso italiano,* Rome: Coines, 1976.

Carocci, G., *Storia d'Italia dall'unità ad oggi,* Milan: Mondadori, 1974.

Carrillo, E. A., *Alcide De Gasperi: the Long Apprenticeship,* Notre Dame: University of Notre Dame Press, 1965.

Cavallari, A., *Il potere in Italia,* Milan: Mondadori, 1967.

Cavazza, F. L., and Graubard, S. R., eds., *Il caso italiano,* Milan: Garzanti, 1974.

Cavazzani, A., *La Democrazia Cristiana dopo il primo ventennio,* Rome: Marsilio, 1967.

Cazzola, F., 'Partiti, correnti e voto di preferenza', RISP, 1972, pp. 569–88.

Cervellati Cantelli, F., *et al.,* *L'organizzazione partitica del PCI e della DC,* Bologna: Il Mulino, 1968.

Chasseriaud, J. P., *Le parti démocrate chrétien en Italie,* Paris: Colin, 1965.

Clark, M., 'Italy: regionalism and bureaucratic reform', in J. Cornford, ed., *The Failure of the State,* London: Croom Helm, 1975, pp. 44–73.

Clark, M., and Irving, R. E. M., 'The Italian political crisis and the general election of May 1972', *Parliamentary Affairs,* summer 1972, pp. 198–223.
'The Italian general election of June 1976: towards a "historic compromise"?' *Parliamentary Affairs,* winter 1977, pp. 7–34.

Clark, M., Hine, D., and Irving, R. E. M., 'Divorce: Italian-style', *Parliamentary Affairs,* autumn 1974, pp. 333–58.

Coletti, A., *Il Divorzio in Italia,* Rome: Savelli, 1974.

Consiglio Superiore dell'Economia e del Lavoro, *VII Rapporto sulla situazione economica del paese,* Rome: Censis, 1973, p. 37 ff.

D'Amato, L., *Correnti di partito e partito di correnti,* Milan: Giuffrè, 1965.
'Il voto di preferenza in Italia', *Rassegna italiana di sociologia,* 1962, pp. 205–58.

D'Antonio, M., *Sviluppo e crisi del capitalismo italiano, 1951–72,* Bari: De Donato, 1973.

D'Ascenzi, G., *Coltivatori e religione,* Bologna: Edagricole, 1973.

De Marchi, F., *La burocrazia centrale in Italia,* Milan; Giuffrè, 1966.
'Organizzazione e burocrazia', *Questioni di sociologia,* 1966, pp. 361–419.

De Mita, E., 'Passato e presenze della Democrazia Cristiana', *Vita e Pensiero,* May 1966, pp. 428–61.

De Rosa, G., *I partiti politici in Italia,* Milan: Minerva Italica, 1973.

Di Renzo, G. J., *Personality, power and politics: a study of the Italian deputy and his parliamentary system,* Notre Dame: Notre Dame University Press, 1967.

Dogan, M., 'Le donne italiane tra Cattolicesimo e Marxismo', in A. Spreafico and J. LaPalombara, eds., *Elezioni e comportamento politico in Italia,* Milan: Comunità, 1963.

Dogan, M., and Petracca, O. M., *Partiti politici e struttura sociale in Italia,* Milan: Comunità, 1968.

Dore, G., *Il movimento laureati di Azione Cattolica,* Rome: Studium, 1960.

Duva, A., 'Dopo i dorotei', *Nord e Sud,* December 1969, pp. 7–18.
'La sinistra DC tra l'unità e la coerenza', *Nord e Sud,* January 1970, pp. 36–43.

Earle, J., *Italy in the 1970s,* London: David & Charles, 1975.

Edelman, M., 'Sources of popular support for the Italian Christian Democratic party in the post-war decade', *Midwest Journal of Political Science,* May 1958, pp. 143–59.

Einaudi, M., and Goguel, F., *Christian Democracy in Italy and France*, Notre Dame: Notre Dame University Press, 1952.

Falconi, C., *Gedda e l'azione cattolica*, Florence: Parenti, 1958.

Fanfani, A., *Giorgio La Pira: un profile*, Milan: Rusconi, 1978.

Farneti, P., *Sistema politico e società civile*, Turin: Giappicchelli, 1971.

ed., *Il sistema politico italiano*, Bologna: Il Mulino, 1973.

Finzi E., 'La democrazia italiana deve "inventare" il suo futuro', *Il Mulino*, July 1968, pp. 610–17.

Fortuna, P., Jorio, L., and Pandini, A., *Rapporto sul divorzio in Italia*, Rome: Savelli, 1970.

Forze Nuove, *La sinistra DC di Forze Nuove di fronte ai problemi del paese*, Rome: Forze Nuove, 1969.

Galano, G., 'La DC tra gollismo e nuova frontiera', *Nord e Sud*, January 1966, pp. 20–31.

Galati, V., *Storia della Democrazia Cristiana*, Rome: Cinque Lune, 1955.

Galletti, V., 'La questione democristiana, la base sociali e i collegamenti di massa', *Rinascita*, 1973, xx, pp. 28–9.

Galli, G., *I partiti politici in Italia, 1861–1973*, Turin: Giappicchelli, 1975.

Il bipartitismo imperfetto: Comunisti e Democristiani in Italia, Bologna: Il Mulino, 1966.

Il governo difficile: un analisi del sistema partitico italiano, Bologna: Il Mulino, 1972.

Storia della Democrazia Cristiana, Rome: Laterza, 1978.

'L' influenza dell 'organizzazione politica sul voto', *Rassegna italiana di sociologia*, 1972, pp. 149–69.

'Più difficile del previsto', *Il Mulino*, 1967, pp. 787–95.

Galli, G. and Facchi, P., *La sinistra democristiana*, Milan: Feltrinelli, 1962.

Galli, G. and Prandi, A., *Patterns of Political Participation in Italy*, New Haven: Yale University Press, 1970.

'The Catholic hierarchy and Christian Democracy in Italy', in eds. M. Dogan and R. Rose, *European Politics: a Reader*, London: Macmillan, 1971, pp. 353–9.

Ghini, C., *Le elezioni in Italia, 1946–68*, Milan: Calendario, 1968.

Giordani, I., *Alcide De Gasperi, il ricostruttore*, Rome: Cinque Lune, 1955.

Godechot, T., *Le parti démocrate chrétien en Italie*, Paris: Librairie Générale du Droit, 1964.

Gorresio, V., *et al., Stato e chiesa*, Bari: Laterza, 1957.

Graziano, L., 'La crise d'un régime libéral-démocratique: l'Italie', RFSP, April 1977, pp. 259–89.

Grindrod, M., *The Rebuilding of Italy*, London: Oxford University Press/ Royal Institute of International Affairs, 1955.

Italy, London: Ernest Benn, 1968.

'Italy: back to Centre-Left', *The World Today*, August 1973.

Guarino Cappello, S., and Sani, G., 'La DC come sistemo organizzativo', *Il Mulino*, March 1969, pp. 311–17.

Hahn, K. J., 'Le Congrès de la DC et la formation du nouveau gouvernement italien', *Panorama Démocrate Chrétien*, July 1969, pp. 9–14.

Horowitz, D., *The Italian Labor Movement*, Cambridge, Mass.: Harvard University Press, 1963.

Hughes, H. S., *The United States and Italy*, Cambridge, Mass.: Harvard University Press, 1965.

Irving, R. E. M., 'The European policy of the French and Italian Communists', *International Affairs*, July 1977, pp. 405–21.
Istituto Carlo Cattaneo, *Il comportamento elettorale in Italia* (see Capecchi above).
Jemolo, A. C., *Church and State in Italy*, Oxford: Blackwell, 1960.
Kogan, N., *The Politics of Italian Foreign Policy*, New York: Praeger, 1963.
   A Political History of Post-war Italy, New York: Praeger, 1966.
LaPalombara, J., *Interest Groups in Italian Politics*, Princeton: Princeton University Press 1964.
   'Italian political culture: fragmentation, isolation, alienation', in L. Pye and S. Verba, eds., *Political Culture and Political Development*, Princeton: Princeton University Press, 1965.
   'Parentela relationships in Italian government', in M. Dogan and R. Rose, eds., *European Politics: a Reader*, London: Macmillan, 1971, pp. 513–27.
La Roca, F., 'La DC nella fase integralista', *Nord e Sud*, May 1966, pp. 7–24.
Leoni, F., *Storia dei partiti politici italiani*, Naples: Guida, 1971.
Lombardini, G., *De Gasperi e i cattolici*, Milan: Comunità, 1962.
Lucini, G., 'Presuppositi ideologici della DC', *Idea*, June 1966, pp. 249–54.
Macchi, A., 'La DC verso il X Congresso', *Aggiornamenti sociali*, September 1967, pp. 417–20.
   'Democrazia Cristiana e Chiesa dopo il concilio', *Aggiornamenti sociali*, November 1967, pp. 497–504.
   'Il X Congresso della DC', *Aggiornamenti sociali*, January 1968, pp. 45–84.
   'Il XI Congresso della DC', *Aggiornamenti sociali*, September 1969, pp. 569–80.
Mack Smith, D., *Italy: A Modern History*, Ann Arbor, Mich.: University of Michigan Press, 1959.
Magri, F., *L'azione cattolica in Italia*, Milan: Facciola, 1953.
   Dal movimento sindacale cristiana al sindacalismo democratico, Milan: Facciola, 1957.
   La Democrazia Cristiana in Italia, 2 vols., Milan: Facciola, 1955.
Mammarella, G., *Italy after Fascism: a Political History, 1943–65*, Notre Dame: University of Notre Dame Press, 1966.
Maranini, G., *Storia del potere in Italia, 1848–1967*, Florence: Vallecchi, 1967.
Marazza, A., 'I cattolici e la Resistenza', in *Il movimento di liberazione in Italia*, July 1956.
Marradi, A., 'Analisi del referendum sul divorzio', RISP, 1974, pp. 589–644.
Merkl, P., 'Partecipazione di sindacati e di partiti in Germania Occidentale e in Italia', RISP, 1971, pp. 325–66.
Merlini, C., 'Italy in the European Community and the Atlantic Alliance', *World Today*, April 1975.
Meynaud, J., *Les partis politiques en Italie*, Paris: Presses Universitaires de France, 1965.
   Rapporto sulla classe dirigente italiana, Milan: Giuffrè, 1966.
Morandi, C., *I partiti politici nella storia d'Italia*, Florence: Le Monnier, 1965.
Mottura, G. and Pugliese, E., 'Agricoltura capitalistica e funzione dell'inchiesta', *Inchiesta*, 1971, no. 1, pp. 3–18.
Musti de Gennaro, B., 'Italian agriculture and international policy', *Spettatore Internazionale*, 1972, pp. 111–34, and 1974, pp. 223–47.
Nichols, P., *The Politics of the Vatican*, London: Pall Mall, 1968.
   Italia, Italia, London: Macmillan, 1973.
Nobécourt, J., *L'Italie à vif*, Paris: Seuil, 1970.

Orfei, R., 'Il doroteismo', *Relazioni sociali*, May 1967, pp. 512–20.

Ottone, P., *De Gasperi*, Milan: Della Volpe, 1968.

Parisi, A., 'Questione cattolica e referendum: l'inizio di una fine', *Il Mulino*, 1974, pp. 410–38.

Passigli, S., *Emigrazione e comportamento politico*, Bologna: Il Mulino, 1969.

Pedrazzi, L., 'Ne necessaria ne sufficiente', *Il Mulino*, 1967, pp. 319–26.

'La DC per la razionalizzazione della vita politica in Italia', *Il Mulino*, 1966, pp. 501–19.

'DC e gerarchia prima e dopo il 12 maggio', *Il Mulino*, 1974, pp. 439–52.

Picciotti, G., 'Le ACLI contro la DC', *Nord e Sud*, July 1969, pp. 24–34.

'Le ACLI in parcheggio', *Nord e Sud*, March 1971, pp. 19–28.

'Il secondo partito cattolico', *Nord e Sud*, October 1970, pp. 34–51.

'Un potere povero di idee', *Nord e Sud*, February 1971, pp. 7–11.

Pizzorno, A., 'Le classi sociali', in A. Pagani, ed., *Antologia di scienze sociali*, vol. I, Bologna: Il Mulino, 1959.

'I sindacati nel sistema politico italiano: aspetti storici', *Rivista trimestrale di diritto pubblico*, 1971, vol. 4, pp. 1510–59.

'Il sistema politico italiano', *Politica del diritto*, April 1971, pp. 197–209.

Poggi, G., *Catholic Action in Italy: the Sociology of a Sponsored Organization*, Stanford: Stanford University Press, 1967.

Il clero di reserva, Milan: Feltrinelli, 1963.

Le preferenze politiche degli italiani, Bologna: Il Mulino, 1968.

'The Church in Italian politics, 1945–50', in S. Woolf, ed., *The Rebirth of Italy*, London: Longman, 1972, pp. 135–55.

'Studio dell'ideologia nella sociologia dei partiti politici', *Rassegna italiana di sociologia*, 1961, pp. 205–20.

Posner, M. and Woolf, S., *Italian Public Enterprise*, London: Duckworth, 1967.

Possenti, P., *Storia della Democrazia Cristiana*, Rome: Silva e Ciarrapico, 1972.

Prandi, A., *Chiesa e politica*, Bologna: Il Mulino, 1968.

Preti, L., *Diritto elettorale politico*, Milan: Giuffrè, 1957.

Ricci, A., and Salierno, G., *Il carcere in Italia: inchiesta sui carcerati, i carcerieri e l'ideologia carceraria*, Turin: Einaudi, 1971.

Rizzi, F., 'From Socialist unification to Socialist secession, 1966–69', *Government and Opposition*, spring 1974, pp. 146–64.

Romano, S., *Histoire de l'Italie du Risorgimento à nos jours*, Paris: Seuil, 1977.

Rossi, E., *et al.*, *La federconsorzi*, Milan: Feltrinelli, 1963.

Rossini, G., *Il movimento cattolico nel periodo fascista*, Rome: Cinque Lune, 1966.

Rumor, M., 'La Democrazia Cristiana nella politica internazionale', *Civitas*, May 1967, pp. 3–17.

Sansone, L. R., *I fuorilegge del matrimonio*, Milan: Avanti! 1956.

Santarelli, E., *Dossier sulle regioni*, Bari: De Donato, 1970.

Sartori, G., ed., *Il parlamento italiano, 1946–63*, Naples: Edizioni Scientifiche Italiane, 1963.

Correnti, frazioni e fazioni nei partiti politici italiani, Bologna: Il Mulino, 1973.

'European political parties: the case of polarized pluralism', in J. LaPalombara and M. Weiner, eds., *Political Parties and Political Development*, Princeton: Princeton University Press, 1966, pp. 137–76.

Sassoon, D., 'The Italian Communist Party's European Strategy', *Political Quarterly*, June 1976, pp. 253–75.

Scalfari, E., *L'autunno della Repubblica: la mappa del potere in Italia*, Milan: Etas-Kompass, 1969.
Schepis, G., 'Analisi statistica dei risultati', in A. Spreafico and J. LaPalombara, eds., *Elezioni e comportamento politico in Italia*, Milan: Comunità, 1963, pp. 329–406.
Scoppola, P., *Coscienza religiosa e democrazia nell'Italia contemporanea*, Bologna: Il Mulino, 1966.
Sivini, G., ed., *Partiti e partecipazione politica in Italia*, Milan: Giuffrè, 1972.
Sivini, G., 'Gli iscritti alla DC e al PCI', *Rassegna italiana di sociologia*, 1967, pp. 429–70.
Spataro, G., *I democratici cristiani: dalla dittatura alla repubblica*, Milan: Mondadori, 1968.
Spettatore Internazionale, 'Italy in the European Community', 1968, pp. 358–68; and 1970, pp. 272–300.
Spinetti, G., *Parlamentarismo e burocrazia*, Bologna: Zanichelli, 1964.
Spreafico, A., and LaPalombara, J., eds., *Elezioni e comportamento politico in Italia*, Milan: Comunità, 1963.
Studi per il Ventesimo Anniversario dell'Assemblea Costituente, 6 vols., Florence: Vallecchi, 1969.
Sylos Labini, P., *Sindacati, inflazione, produttività*, Bari: Laterza, 1972.
'Sviluppo economico e classi sociali in Italia', in P. Farneti, ed., *Il sistema politico italiano*, Bologna: Il Mulino, 1973.
Tamburrano, G., *Storia e cronaca del centro-sinistra*, Milan: Feltrinelli, 1971.
L'iceberg democristiano, Milan: Sugarco, 1974.
Tarrow, S., *Peasant Communism in Southern Italy*, New Haven: Yale University Press, 1967.
Taviani, P. E., *Il Piano Schuman*, Rome: Apollon, 1954.
Tenti, E., *Les courants internes dans la démocratie chrétienne italienne*, Paris: dissertation, 1971.
Tupini, G., *I Democratici Cristiani: cronache di dieci anni, 1943–53*, Milan: Garzanti, 1954.
Turone, S., *Storia del sindacato in Italia, 1943–69*, Bari: Laterza,, 1976.
Vannicelli, P., *Italy, NATO and the European Community*, Cambridge, Mass.: Harvard University Press, 1974.
Vaussard, M., *Histoire de la démocratie chrétienne: France, Belgique, Italie*, Paris: Seuil, 1956.
Storia della Democrazia Cristiana, Bologna: Cappelli, 1969.
Vigorelli, G., *Gronchi*, Florence: Vallecchi, 1956.
Webster, R. A., *The Cross and the Fasces: Christian Democracy and Fascism in Italy*, Stanford: Stanford University Press, 1960.
Christian Democracy in Italy, 1860–1960, London: Hollis & Carter, 1961.
Willis, F. Roy, *Italy Chooses Europe*, London: Oxford University Press, 1961.
Zariski, R., *Italy: the Politics of Uneven Development*, Hinsdale, Ill.: Dryden Press, 1972.
'Partiti e fazioni', *Studi Politici*, 1961, pp. 383–403.
'Intra-party conflict in a dominant party: the experience of Italian Christian Democracy', *Journal of Politics*, 1965, pp. 3–34.
Zuckerman, A., *Political Clienteles in Power: Party Factions and Cabinet Coalitions in Italy*, London: Sage, 1975.

Germany
See also 'Origins of Christian Democracy', German section, above.

Primary sources Party documentation can be consulted at the headquarters of the CDU in Bonn (*Bundesgeschäftsstelle,* BGS) and the CSU in Munich (*Landesgeschäftsstelle,* LGS). Both have useful archives. The Bundestag Library also has much documentation on all the political parties. Note in particular the following:

BGS, *CDU Dokumentation* (party structure, programmes, etc., revised every few years).
   Dokumentation: die Geschichte der CDU (party history: revised every few years).
   Landesverbände annual reports (regional association reports useful for early history of CDU).
   Bundesparteitage der CDU (party conference reports from 1950).
   Politisches Jahrbuch der CDU/CSU (annual reports on party organisation, membership, etc. of both parties).
   Die dreissig Punkte der Union (party objectives).
   Statut der CDU (party statutes).
LGS, *CSU: Profil einer Partei* (history and programme).
   CSU: Satzung, Schiedsgerichtsordnung, Finanzstatut (statutes and organisation).

There is also useful primary material to be found in the following:

Behn, H., ed., *Die Regierungserklärungen der Bundesrepublik Deutschland,* Munich: Olzog, 1971.
Flechtheim, O. K., ed., *Die Parteien der Bundesrepublik Deutschland,* Hamburg: Hoffmann & Campe, 1973.
   ed., *Dokumente zur parteipolitischen Entwicklung in Deutschland seit 1945,* 9 vols., Berlin: Dokumenten, 1962–71.
Morsey, R., and Repgen, K., *Adenauer Studien,* 4 vols., Mainz: Matthias Grünewald, 1971–7.
Politische Akademie Eichholz der Konrad-Adenauer-Stiftung, ed., *Dokumente zur Christlichen Demokratie,* Bonn, 1969.
Presse und Informationsamt der Bundesregierung, *Jahresbericht der Bundesregierung.*
   Regierung Adenauer, 1949–63.

The following memoirs and collections of articles and speeches by Christian Democrats are also useful:

Adenauer, K., *Erinnerungen,* 4 vols., Stuttgart: Deutsche, 1965–9.
   Bundestagsreden, Bonn: AZ Studio, 1967.
Barzel, R., *Karl Arnold: Grundlegung christlich-demokratischer Politik in Deutschland: eine Dokumentation,* Bonn: Berto, 1960.
   Gesichtspunkte eines Deutschen, Düsseldorf: Econ, 1968.
Biedenkopf, K., *Fortschritt in Freiheit,* Munich: Piper, 1974.

Brentano, H. von, *Germany and Europe: Reflections on German Foreign Policy*, London: Deutsch, 1964.

Ehlers, H., *Um dem Vaterland zu dienen: Reden und Aufsätze*, Cologne: O. Schmidt, 1955.

Gedanken zur Zeit, Stuttgart: Kreuz, 1955.

Gerstenmaier, E., *Reden und Aufsätze*, Stuttgart: Evangelisches Verlagswerk, 1956.

Verschleuderung der christlichen Namens? Bonn: CDU, 1960.

Mayer-Vorfelder, G., and Zuber, H., eds., *Union Alternativ*, Stuttgart: Seewald, 1976.

Müller, J., *Bis zur letzten Konsequenz: ein Leben für Frieden und Freiheit*, Munich: Süddeutscher, 1975.

Seidel, H., *Weltanschauung und Politik: ein Beitrag zum Verständnis der CSU in Bayern*, Munich: Verlag Bayern-Kurier, 1961.

Strauss, F. J., *Der Auftrag*, Stuttgart: Seewald, 1974.

Bundestagsreden, Bonn: AZ, 1968.

Secondary sources The independent newspapers, *Die Zeit*, *Frankfurter Allgemeine Zeitung* and *Süddeutsche Zeitung*, are useful sources of information and comment on all political parties, as is the weekly *Der Spiegel*. *Bayern Kurier* is the main CSU paper, whilst *Di Welt* and the Springer press generally support the CDU. See also the following journals in particular: *Blätter für deutsche und internationale Politik, Civitas, Politische Meinung, Politische Studien, Politische Vierteljahresschrift, Sonde, Zeitschrift für Parlamentsfragen* and *Zur Politik und Zeitgeschichte*.

Books and articles

Albert, E. H., 'Bonn's Moscow treaty and its implications', *International Affairs*, April 1971, pp. 316–26.

Allemann, F. R., *Bonn ist nicht Weimar*, Cologne: Kiepenheuer & Wietsch 1957.

Altmann, R., 'CDU und Geist', *Civitas*, 1964, no. 6, pp. 6–7.

'Die Wandlungen der Union', *Politische Meinung*, 1970, no. 4, pp. 43–6.

Amelung, E., 'Die Union als Partei', *Civitas*, 1954, no. 5, pp. 68–70.

Aretin, K., 'Bürgerliche Mitte oder konservative Rechtspartei? Der Strukturhandel innerhalb der CDU', *Blätter für deutsche und internationale Politik*, 1967, no. 3, pp. 252–8.

Arnold, F., *Zur christlichen Lösung der sozialen Frage*, Stuttgart: Schwaben, 1949.

Ashkenasi, A., *Modern German Nationalism*, New York: Wiley, 1976.

Bamberg, H.–D., 'Zu konservativen, autoritären und restauritiven Strömungen im westdeutsche Katholizismus'. *Blätter für deutsche und internationale Politik*, March 1969, pp. 213–20.

Baring, A., *Aussenpolitik in Adenauers Kanzlerdemokratie*, Munich: Oldenbourg, 1969.

ed., *Sehr verehrter Herr Bundeskanzler! Heinrich von Brentano im Briefwechsel mit Konrad Adenauer, 1949–64*, Hamburg: Hoffmann & Campe, 1974.

Baukloh, F., 'Auf dem Wege nach rechts. Die CDU in der grossen Koalition', *Blätter für deutsche und internationale Politik*, 1967, no. 4, pp. 344–54.

Becker, D.–E., and Wiesendahl, E., *Ohne Programm nach Bonn: oder die Union als Kanzler-Verein*, Hamburg: Rowohlt, 1972.

Beger, B., 'Das schmale Fundament: der CDU fehlt die Mitglieder', *Politische Meinung*, 1960, no. 5, pp. 3–8.

Berberich, W., *Die historische Entwicklung der CSU in Bayern bis zum Eintritt in die Bundesrepublik*, Würzburg: Ph.D thesis, 1965.

Bertsch, H., *CDU/CSU demaskiert*, Berlin: Rütten & Loening, 1961.

Beyme, K. von, *Interessengruppen in der Demokratie*, Munich: Piper, 1974.

Biedenkopf, K., *Mitbestimmung*, Cologne: Bachem, 1972.

Bilstein, H., *Jungsozialisten – Junge Union – Jungdemokraten: die Nachwuchs-organisationen der Parteien in der Bundesrepublik*, Opladen: Leske, 1971.

Binder, G., *Deutschland seit 1945*, Stuttgart: Seewald, 1969.

Blankenburg, E., *Kirkliche Bindung und Wahlverhalten*, Olten: Walter, 1967.

Blüm, N., *Reaktion oder Reform: wohin geht die CDU?* Reinbek: Rowohlt, 1972.

Böhm, A., 'CDU-Reform: Grenzen und Ziele. Eine neue Etappe auf dem Wege zur modernen Volkspartei', *Politische Meinung*, 1959, no. 4, pp. 13–24.

Bracher, K. D., 'Die Kanzlerdemokratie', in ed., R. Löwenthal and H. P. Schwarz, *Die Zweite Republik*, 1975, pp. 179–201.

Braunthal, G., *The Federation of German Industry in Politics*, New York: Cornell University Press, 1965.

  'The FDP in West German politics', *Western Political Quarterly*, June 1960, pp. 332–48.

Bredthauer, K., 'Zur Lage der CDU/CSU nach den Parteitagen in Saarbrücken und München', *Blätter für deutsche und internationale Politik, 1971, p. 1118–25.*

Breidbach, F., and May, R., eds., *Das soziale Feigenblatt? Die Sozialausschüsse in der Union*, Düsseldorf: Econ, 1975.

Bromke, A., and Riekhoff, H. von, 'The West German Polish Treaty', *World Today*, March 1971.

Buchheim, K., *Geschichte der christlichen Parteien in Deutschland*, Munich: Kösel, 1953.

Burkett, T., *Parties and Elections in West Germany: the Search for Stability*, London: Hurst, 1975.

Comparative Politics, 'The West German Election of 1969', special no., July 1970, pp. 519–700.

Conradt, D. P., *The West German Party System: an Ecological Analysis of Social Structure and Voting Behaviour, 1961–69*, London: Sage, 1972.

  'Electoral law politics in West Germany', *Political Studies*, 1970, pp. 341–56.

Conze, W., *Jakob Kaiser: Politiker zwischen Ost und West, 1945–49*, Stuttgart: Kohlhammer, 1969.

Dahrendorf, R., *Society and Democracy in Germany*, London: Weidenfeld & Nicolson, 1968.

Deuerlein, E., *CDU/CSU, 1945–57*, Cologne: Bachem, 1960.

Dexheimer, W., *Koalitionsverhandlungen in Bonn, 1961–1965–1969: zur Willens-bildung in Parteien und Fraktionen*, Bonn: Eichholz, 1973.

  'Die CSU – Landesgruppe: ihre organisatorische Stellung in der CDU/CSU Fraktion', *Zeitschrift für Parlamentsfragen*, 1972, no. 3, pp. 307–13.

Dittberner, J., *Die Bundesparteitage der Christlich Demokratischen Union und der Sozialdemokratischen Partei Deutschlands von 1946 bis 1968. Eine Untersuchung der Funktionen von Parteitagen*, Augsburg: Blasaditsch, 1968.

Dittberner, J., and Ebbighausen, R., *Parteiensystem in der Legitimationskrise: Studien und Materialien zur Soziologie der Parteien in der Bundesrepublik Deutschland*, Opladen: Westdeutscher, 1973.

Domes, J., *Mehrheitsfraktion und Bundesregierung: Aspekte des Verhältnisses der Fraktion der CDU/CSU im zweiten und dritten Deutschen Bundestag zum Kabinett Adenauer*, Cologne: Westdeutscher, 1964.

Dreher, K., *Der Weg zum Kanzler: Adenauers Griff nach Macht*, Düsseldorf: Econ, 1972.

Dreyfus, F. G., 'Les élections au cinquième Bundestag: étude de géographie électorale', *RFSP*, April 1966, pp. 286–305.

Dyson, K. H. F., 'Anti-communism in the Federal Republic of Germany: the case of the *Berufsverbot*', *Parliamentary Affairs*, winter 1975, pp. 51–67.

Edinger, L. J., *Politics in Germany*, Boston: Little Brown, 1968.

Egen, P., *Die Entstehung des Evangelischen Arbeitskreis der CDU/CSU*, Bonn: Ph.D. thesis, 1974.

Eisenmann, H., 'Zukunftsperspektiven der Landwirtschaft in Bayern', in E. Schmacke, ed., *Bayern auf dem Weg in das Jahr 2000*, Düsseldorf: Droste, 1971.

Eisner, E., *Das europäische Konzept von Franz Josef Strauss: die gesamt-europäischen Ordnungsvorstellungen der CSU*, Meisenheim am Glan: Hain, 1975.

Ellwein, T., *Politische Verhaltenslehre*, Frankfurt: Europäische Verlagsanstalt, 1963.

Elschner, G., 'Zwanzig Jahre Christlich Demokratische Union: Reflexionen über Eigenart und Struktur', *Civitas*, 1965, no. 4, pp. 167–89.

Epstein, K., 'The Adenauer era in German history', in ed. S. Graubard, *A New Europe*, Boston: Houghton Mifflin, 1964.

Ermecke, G., *Christliche Politik: Utopie oder Aufgabe?* Cologne: Bachem, 1966.

Eyck, E., *Geschichte der Weimarer Republik*, 2 vols., Erlenbach-Zürich: Rentsch, 1974.

Faul, E., ed., *Wahlen und Wähler in Westdeutschland*, Villingen: Ring, 1960.

Feisst, U., Güllner, M., and Liepelt, K., 'Party membership patterns, electoral mobilisation, and social change in West Germany', *IPSA Report*, 1976.

Flechtheim, O. K., ed., *Die Parteien der Bundesrepublik Deutschland*, Hamburg: Hoffmann & Campe, 1973.

ed., *Dokumente zur parteipolitischen Entwicklung in Deutschland seit 1945*, 9 vols., Berlin: Dokumenten, 1962–71.

Foelz-Schroeter, M., *Föderalistische Politik und nationale Repräsentation, 1945–47*, Stuttgart: DVA, 1974.

Gablentz, O.-H. von der, *Über Marx hinaus*, Berlin: Wedding, 1946.

Gaus, G., 'Die Zukunft der Kanzlerpartei: Kiesinger, die CDU und die Grosse Koalition', *Der Monat*, 1967, no. 223.

Gillessen, G., 'Zu alt, zu klein, zu katholisch und zu ländlich. Messbares über die CDU', *FAZ*, 28 December 1965.

Golay, J. F., *The Founding of the Federal Republic of Germany*, Chicago: University of Chicago Press, 1958.

Gölter, G., and Pieroth, E., *Die Union in der Opposition*, Düsseldorf: Econ, 1970.

Grosser, A., *Germany in Our Time: a Political History of the Post-War Years*, London: Penguin, 1970.

Guttenberg, K. T., Freiherr von und zu, *Im Interesse der Freiheit*, Stuttgart: AZ Studio, 1970.

Günther, K., Der Kanzlerwechsel in der Bundesrepublik: Adenauer – Erhard – Kiesinger, Hanover: Verlag für Literatur und Zeitgeschehen, 1970.

Hacke, C., Die Ost und Deutschland Politik der CDU/CSU, Cologne: Wissenschaft und Politik, 1975.

Haftendorn, H., 'Ostpolitik revisited', World Today, June 1976.

Hahn, W. F., Between Westpolitik and Ostpolitik: Changing West German Security Views, London, Sage: 1975.

Hartenstein, W., and Liepelt, K., 'Party members and party votes in West Germany', in S. Rokkan, ed., Approaches to the Study of Political Participation, Bergen: Michelsen Institute, 1962.

Haseloff, W., Die politischen Parteien in der Bundesrepublik Deutschland, Frankfurt: Moritz Diesterweg, 1975.

Heidenheimer, A. J., Adenauer and the CDU: the rise of the leader and the integration of the party, The Hague: Nijhoff, 1960.

'Federalism and the party system: the case of West Germany', APSR, September 1958, pp. 809–28.

'Foreign policy and party discipline in the CDU', Parliamentary Affairs, winter 1959–60, pp. 70–84.

'German party finance', APSR, June 1957, pp. 369–85.

'La structure confessionnelle, sociale et régionale de la CDU', RFSP, 1957, pp. 626–45

'Der starke Regierungschef und das Parteiensystem: der "Kanzler-Effekt" in der Bundesrepublik', Politische Vierteljahresschrift, 1961, pp. 241–62.

Hennis, W., Grosse Koalition ohne Ende? Munich: Piper, 1968.

Herrmann, K. D., 'CSU – extremer Feind jeder selbständigen Arbeiter – und Gewerkschaftsbewegung in der BRD', Dokumenten der Zeit, 1971, p. 12 and ff.

Heyde, W., The Administration of Justice in the Federal Republic of Germany, Limburg: Vereinsdrückerei, 1971.

Hirsch-Weber, W., and Schutz, K., eds., Wähler und Gewählte: eine Untersuchung der Bundestagswahlen, 1953, Berlin: Vahlen, 1957.

Hornung, K., 'CDU vor der Bewährungsprobe: notwendige Entscheidungen für eine grosse konservative Volkspartei', Politische Welt, 1967, no. 3, pp. 2–6.

Irving, R. E. M., 'The German Liberals: changing image of the FDP', Parliamentary Affairs, winter 1969–70, pp. 45–54.

Irving, R. E. M., and Paterson, W. E., 'The West German parliamentary election of November 1972', Parliamentary Affairs, spring 1973, pp. 218–38.

'The West German general election of 1976', Parliamentary Affairs, spring 1977, pp. 209–25.

Jahn, H. E., ed., CDU und Mitbestimmung, Stuttgart: Seewald, 1969.

Johnson, N., Government in the Federal Republic of Germany: the Executive at Work, Oxford: Pergamon, 1973.

Kaack, H., Geschichte und Struktur des deutschen Parteiensystems, Opladen: Westdeutscher, 1971.

Kaase, M., 'Determinanten des Wahlverhaltens bei der Bundestagswahl 1969', Politische Vierteljahresschrift, 1970, pp. 46–110.

Kaiser, K., German Foreign Policy in Transition, London: Oxford University Press, 1968.

Kaltefleiter, W., Wirtschaft und Politik, Opladen: Westdeutscher, 1968.

Zwischen Konsens und Krise: eine Analyse der Bundestagswahl 1972, Bonn: Konrad-Adenauer-Stiftung, 1973.

'Konsens ohne Macht? Eine Analyse der Bundestagswahl von 19 September 1965,' *Verfassung und Verfassungswirklichkeit*, 1966, pp. 14–62.

Kirchheimer, O., 'The waning of oppositions in parliamentary regimes', *Social Research*, 1957, pp. 127–56.

Kitzinger, U., *German Electoral Politics: A Study of the 1957 Campaign*, Oxford: Clarendon Press, 1960.

Klingemann, H. D. and Urban Pappi, F., see *Comparative Politics*.

Kloss, G., *West Germany: an Introduction*, London: Macmillan, 1976.

Knorr, H., *Der Parlamentarische Entscheidungsprozess während der Grosse Koalition 1966 bis 1969*, Meisenheim am Glan: Hain, 1975.

Kohl, H., and Klein, H. A., 'Die Zukunft der CDU', *Politische Meinung*, May 1973, pp. 43–62.

Konrad-Adenauer-Stiftung, ed., *Christliche Demokraten der ersten Stunde*, Bonn, 1966.

Konrad Adenauer und die CDU der britischen Besatzungszone, 1946–49, Bonn, 1975.

Kosthorst, E., *Jakob Kaiser: Bundesminister für gesamtdeutsche Fragen*, Stuttgart: Kohlhammer, 1972.

Kraiker, G., *Politischer Katholizismus in der BRD: eine ideologiekritische Analyse*, Stuttgart: Kohlhammer, 1972.

Kühr, H., *Parteien und Wahlen in Stadt und Landkreis Düsseldorf*, Düsseldorf: Droste, 1974.

Leder, G., 'Politik für morgen. Die Unionsparteien sind zur Offensive verpflichtet', *Politische Meinung*, October 1965, pp. 17–26.

Leibholz, G., 'The Federal Constitutional Court in the constitutional system of the Federal Republic of Germany', in *Legal Essays: a Tribute to Frede Casteberg*, Copenhagen: Universitetsforlaget, 1963.

Lemmer, E., *Manches war doch Anderes*, Frankfurt: Scheffler, 1968.

Liepelt, K., 'Esquisse d'une typologie des électeurs allemands et autrichiens', *RFSP*, 1968, pp. 13–32.

Liepelt, K., and Mitscherlich, A., *Thesen zur Wähler-fluktuation*, Frankfurt: Europäische Verlagsanstalt, 1968.

Loewenberg, G., *Parliament in the German Political System*, Ithaca: Cornell University Press, 1966.

'The remaking of the German party system', in, ed., M. Dogan and R. Rose, *European Politics: a Reader*, London: Macmillan, 1971, pp. 259–80.

Löwenthal, R., and Schwarz, H. P., *Die zweite Republik: 25 Jahre Bundesrepublik Deutschland – eine Bilanz*, Stuttgart: Seewald, 1974.

Luda, M., 'Die CDU/CSU und ihr föderalistisches Programm', Cologne: Ph.D. dissertation, 1955.

Mahncke, D., 'The Berlin Agreement', *The World Today*, December 1971.

Maier, H., ed., *Deutscher Katholizismus nach 1945*, Munich: Kosel, 1964.

'Die Kirchen', in R. Löwenthal and H. P. Schwarz, eds., *Die zweite Republik*, Stuttgart: Seewald, 1974, pp. 494–515.

Majonica, E., *East-West Relations: a German View*, New York: Praeger, 1969.

Mayntz, R., *Parteigruppen in der Grossstadt: Untersuchungen in einem Berliner Kreisverband der CDU*, Cologne: Westdeutscher, 1959.

Merkl, P., *The Origins of the West German Republic*, London: Oxford University Press, 1963.

'Equilibrium, structures of interest and leadership: Adenauer's survival as Chancellor', *APSR*, 1962, pp. 634–50.

Meyn, H., *Die Deutsche Partei*, Düsseldorf: Droste, 1965.

310   *The Christian Democratic Parties of Western Europe*

Mintzel, A., *Die CSU: Anatomie einer Konservativen Partei*, Opladen: West-
deutscher, 1975.
  'Die CSU in Bayern: Phasen ihrer organisationspolitischen Entwicklung',
  Politische Vierteljahresschrift, October 1972, pp. 205–43.
  'Die CSU in Bayern', in J. Dittberner and R. Ebbighausen, eds., *Parteiensystem
  in der Legitimationskrise*, Opladen: Westdeutscher, 1973, pp. 349–426.
Molt, P., 'Die Christlich Demokratische Union Deutschlands: Anfänge,
  Programmatik, Entwicklung', in *Politische Bewegungen in Deutschland*,
  Bonn: Konrad-Adenauer-Stiftung, 1967.
Müchler, G., *CDU/CSU: das schwierige Bündnis*, Munich: Vögel, 1976.
  'Zum früheren Verhältnis von CDU und CSU', *Politische Studien*, 1972, pp.
  595–613.
Narr, W. D., *CDU–SPD: Programm und Praxis seit 1945*, Stuttgart: Kohl-
  hammer, 1966.
Netzer, H. J., ed., *Adenauer und die Folgen*, Munich: Beck, 1965.
Nipperdey, T., *Die Organisation der deutschen Parteien vor 1918*, Düsseldorf:
  Droste, 1961.
Noack, P., 'Die CSU-nationalistisch oder was sonst?', *Monat*, June 1970.
Nolte, E., *Die parlamentarische Opposition*, Munich: Piper, 1974.
Oberndorfer, D., *Die Bundestagswahl, 1976*, Bonn: Konrad-Adenauer-Stiftung,
  1977.
Olzog, G., 'Die christlichen Parteien in Deutschland', *Politische Studien*, 1964,
  pp. 406–15.
  Die politische Parteien, Munich: Olzog, 1964.
Paterson, W. E., *The SPD and European Integration*, Farnborough, Saxon House,
  1974.
Pius XI, Pope, *Über die gesellschaftliche Ordnung*, Freiburg, 1948.
Portisch, H., *Die deutsche Konfrontation: Gegenwart und Zukunft der beiden
  deutschen Parteien*, Munich: Molden, 1974.
Preece, R. J. C., *Land Elections in the German Federal Republic*, London:
  Longmans, 1968.
Pridham, G., *Christian Democracy in Western Germany*, London: Croom
  Helm, 1977.
  'Christian Democracy in Italy and West Germany: a comparative analysis', in
  M. Kolinsky and W. Paterson, eds., *Social and Political Movements in
  Western Europe*, London: Croom Helm, 1976, pp. 142–77.
  'The CDU/CSU Opposition in West Germany 1969–72: a party in search of an
  organisation', *Parliamentary Affairs*, Spring 1973, pp. 201–17.
  'A "nationalization" process? Federal politics and state elections in West
  Germany', *Government and Opposition*, autumn 1973, pp. 455–72.
  'The Ostpolitik and the Opposition in West Germany', in R. Tilford, ed., *The
  Ostpolitik and Political Change in Germany*, London: Saxon House, 1975,
  pp. 45–58.
Prittie, T., *Adenauer: A Study in Fortitude*, London: Stacey, 1972.
Pulzer, P. G. J., 'The German party system in the sixties', *Political Studies*,
  March 1971, pp. 1–17.
  'Responsible party government and stable coalition: the case of the German
  Federal Republic', *Political Studies*, June 1978, pp. 181–208.
Ritter, E., *Radowitz, Windthorst, Stegerwald: drei Vorläufer der CDU*, Frankfurt
  am Main: Warte, 1966.
Roberts, G. K., 'The West German parties and Ostpolitik', *Government and
  Opposition*, autumn 1972, pp. 434–49.

Rollmann, D., ed., *Die Zukunft der CDU: Christlich Demokratische Konzeption für die Zukunft*, Hamburg: Wegner, 1968.

Die CDU in der Opposition: eine Selbstdarstellung, Hamburg: Wegner, 1970.

Rose, R., and Urwin, D. W., 'Persistence and change in Western party systems since 1945', *Political Studies*, 1970, pp. 287–319.

'Social cohesion, political parties and strains in regimes', *Comparative Political Studies*, 1969, pp. 7–67.

Roth, R., *Parteiensystem und Aussenpolitik: Zur Bedeutung des Parteiensystems für den aussenpolitischen Entscheidungsprozess in der Bundesrepublik Deutschland*, Meisenheim am Glan: Hain, 1974.

Rovan, J., *Le Catholicisme Politique en Allemagne*, Paris: Seuil, 1956.

Rummel, A., *et al.*, *Die Grosse Koalition, 1966–69*, Freudenstadt: Lutzeyer, 1969.

Schardt, A., 'CDU und CSU', in *Christliche Parteien in Europa*, Osnabrück: Fromm, 1964, pp. 45–74.

Wohin steuert die CDU? Osnabrück: Fromm, 1961.

Schorr, H., *Adam Stegerwald*, Recklinghausen: Kommunal, 1966.

Scheuch, E., and Wildenmann, R., eds., *Zur Sociologie del Wahl*, Cologne: Westdeutscher, 1965.

Schreyer, K., *Bayern: ein Industriestaat*, Munich: Olzog, 1969.

Schulz, G., 'Die CDU: Merkmale ihres Aufbaus', in M. Lange, ed., *Parteien in der Bundesrepublick: Studien zur Entwicklung der deutschen Parteien bis zur Bundestagswahl 1953*, Stuttgart: Ring, 1955, pp. 3–156.

'Die Organisationstruktur der CDU', *Zeitschrift für Politik*, 1956, pp. 147–65.

Schwering, L., *Die Frühgeschichte und die Entstehung der Christlich-Demokratischen Union*, Recklinghausen: Kommunal, 1963.

Skibourski, K. O., *Zukunft mit der CDU? Fehler und Chancen der Opposition*, Düsseldorf: Econ, 1970.

Sontheimer, K., *The Government and Politics of West Germany*, London: Hutchinson, 1972.

Spotts, F., *The Churches and Politics in Germany*, Middleton: Wesleyan University Press, 1973.

Stollreither, K., *Mitbestimmung: Ideologie oder Partnerschaft?* Munich: Bayerische Landeszentrale für Politische Bildungsarbeit, 1975.

Storz, H., *Aussenpolitik als Gesellschaftspolitik: die aussenpolitische Konzeption der CDU mit besonderer Berücksichtigung der Zeit der Grossen Koalition, 1966–69*, Berlin: Ph.D. thesis, 1973.

Strobel, R., *Adenauer und der Weg Deutschlands*, Frankfurt: Bucher, 1965.

Stronk, D., 'Die Zukunft der CSU', *Sonde*, June 1969.

Taler, C., 'Über das Verhältnis der CSU zur CDU', *Neue Rundschau*, 1970, pp. 338–54.

Tilford, R., ed., *The Ostpolitik and Political Change in Germany*, Farnborough: Saxon House, 1975.

Treue, W., *Die deutschen Parteien*, Wiesbaden: Steiner, 1961.

Urwin, D. W., 'Germany: continuity and change in electoral politics', in R. Rose, ed., *Electoral Behaviour: a Comparative Handbook*, London: Collier Macmillan, 1974, pp. 109–64.

Varain, H. J., *Parteien und Verbände: eine Studie über ihren Aufbau, ihre Verflechtung und ihren Wirken in Schleswig-Holstein, 1945–58*, Cologne: Westdeutscher, 1964.

ed., *Interessenverbände in Deutschland*, Cologne: Kiepenheuer & Wietsch, 1973.

Veen, H. J., *Die CDU/CSU Opposition im parlamentarischen Entscheidungs-prozess. Zur Strategie und zum Einfluss der CDU/CSU Bundestagsfraktion in der Gesetzgebungsarbeit des 6 Deutschen Bundestages*, Munich: Vogel, 1973.

Vogel, B., and Haungs, P., *Wahlkampf und Wählertradition*, Cologne: Westdeutscher, 1965.

Von der Heydte, F., and Sacherl, K., *Soziologie der deutschen Parteien*, Munich: Isar, 1955.

Wallich, H. C., *Main Springs of the German Economy*, New Haven: Yale University Press, 1955.

Weber, W., and Jahnn, W., *Synopse zur Deutschlandpolitik 1941–73*, Göttingen: Schwartz, 1974.

Weizsäcker, R. von, *et al.*, *Protestantische Positionen in der deutschen Politik*, Frankfurt am Main: Otto Lembeck, 1972.

Weymar, P., *Konrad Adenauer*, London: Deutsch, 1957.

Whetten, L., *Germany's Ostpolitik*, London: Oxford University Press, 1971.

Wieck, H. G., *Die Entstehung der CDU und die Wiedergründung des Zentrums im Jahre 1945*, Düsseldorf: Droste, 1953.

  Christliche und Freie Demokraten in Hessen, Rheinland-Pfalz, Baden und Württemberg, 1945–46, Düsseldorf: Droste, 1958.

Wildenmann, R., 'CDU/CSU: Regierungspartei von morgen – oder was sonst?', in R. Löwenthal and H. P. Schwarz, eds., *Die Zweite Republik*, Stuttgart: Seewald, 1974, pp. 345–66.

Zahn, P. von, ed., *Profil der CDU*, Hamburg: Glöss, 1975.

Belgium

Primary sources The chief primary sources are to be found at the Centre d'Etudes Politiques, Economiques et Sociales (CEPESS), the research centre of the CVP–PSC located in the party headquarters in the rue des Deux-Eglises, Brussels. The following proved particularly useful:

(i) National Congress Reports;

(ii) National Statutes;

(iii) Electoral programmes: see especially *Les chantiers sont ouverts . . . quel sera l'architecte? Programme de Noël, 1945*; *Les Programmes Electoraux*, 1974; and *Le Parti Social Chrétien*, 1976 – all published by CEPESS;

(iv) *Bulletin d'Information* (Social Christian Party monthly);

(v) CEPESS *Documents* (Social Christian Party bi-monthly. See in particular *Belgique: le Parti Social Chrétien*, 1962; Robert Houben, *Le PSC contesté*, preface de Pierre Harmel, 1963; Robert Houben, *La Politique méconnue*, 1963; and regular post-electoral series, *Les programmes électoraux et la formation du gouvernement;*

(vi) CEPESS 'faits et documents' series, especially no. 1 of each year, reviewing previous year's political developments.

In addition, see Congress reports of *Confédération des Syndicats Chrétiens*, available at the confederation's headquarters in the rue de la Loi, Brussels. For the prewar period a number of documents relating to the *standen* can be consulted, e.g. those of the *Ligue Nationale des Travailleurs de Belgique,* the *Fédération des Associations et Cercles Catholiques et des Associations Ouvrières*, etc. (for details, see J. Beaufays, *Les Partis Catholiques en Belgique et aux Pays-Bas, 1918–58*, pp. 680, 685–6–7, and 691).

Secondary sources The chief secondary source consists of the many scholarly analyses, published under the auspices of the Centre de Recherche et d'Information Socio-Politiques (CRISP), rue du Congrès, Brussels. See in particular (i) *Série documentaire*, CRISP, and (ii) *Courrier Hebdomadaire*, CRISP. (For further details about CRISP series, see below under books and articles.)
The most useful newspapers and journals are:
De Standaard; Dossiers de l'action sociale catholique; Notes et documents de la Fédération des Associations des Cercles Catholiques; La Libre Belgique; La Revue nouvelle; La Relève; La Terre wallonne; Res Publica; Revue catholique des idées et des faits; Revue générale; Revue générale belge; Socialisme.

Books and articles

Alexandre, J., 'Géographie politique de la Belgique', *Revue Nouvelle*, March 1946, pp. 283–89, and August 1950, pp. 78–85.
Anon., 'Où va le PSC?' *Dossiers de l'Action Sociale Catholique*, January 1966, pp. 47–52.
'Perspectives sociales chrétiennes', *Revue Politique*, March 1958, pp. 365–410.
'La platforme électorale du PSC', *Revue Politique*, July 1958, pp. 345–50.
'Die christlichen Parteien in Europa', *Politische Studien*, no. 156, July 1964.
'Les positions fondamentales du PSC', *Revue Politique*, June 1960, pp. 301–10.
Le Bloc Catholique Belge, Brussels, 1937.
'Les conclusions du IXᵉ Congrès National du PSC', *Revue Politique*, December 1953, pp. 690–701.
'Les élections législatives du 1ᵉʳ juin 1950', *Cahiers de l'Institut de Sociologie*, no. 6, 1953.
'L'enseignement libre en Belgique', *Revue Nouvelle*, November 1967, pp. 369–408.
'Le pacte scolaire et son application', *Revue Politique*, 1960, no. 5.
La Participation Politique en Belgique, Société d'études politiques et sociales, Cahier no. 5, 1966.
Arango, R., *Leopold III and the Belgian Royal Question*, Baltimore: John Hopkins, 1963.
Arendt, J., *La Nature, l'Organisation et le Programme des Syndicats Ouvriers Chrétiens*, Brussels: Spes, 1926.
Le Mouvement Ouvrier, Brussels: Spes, 1928.
Action Catholique et Ordre Social, Louvain: Rex, 1934.
Aubert, R., 'L'église et l'état en Belgique au XIXᵉ siècle', *Res Publica*, 1968, special no. 2, pp. 9–31.
Bartier, J., 'Partis politiques et classes sociales en Belgique', *Res Publica*, 1968, no. 2, pp. 33–106.
Basse, M., *De Vlaamsche Beweging van 1905 tot 1930*, Ghent, 1933.
Bastin, M., 'La démocratie chrétienne politique en Belgique francophone', *Revue Nouvelle*, October 1970, pp. 281–94.

Baudhuin, F., *Belgique 1900–1960: Explication Economique de Notre Temps,* Louvain: Héverlé, 1961.

Beaufays, J., *Les Partis Catholiques en Belgique et aux Pays-Bas, 1918–1958,* Brussels: Bruylant, 1973.

'Tentative d'analyse sociologique du député catholique belge', *Courrier Hebdomadaire,* September 1972, pp. 1–27.

Beaufays, J., and Breny, H., 'La représentation proportionnelle dans les systèmes électoraux belges', *Annales de la faculté de droit de Liège,* 1971, pp. 529–59.

Bernard, S., 'Esquisse d'un plan d'étude du système politique de la Belgique', *Cahiers Economiques de Bruxelles,* 1966, pp. 133–42.

Bibliothèque de l'Institut Belge de Science Politique, *Les Elections Législatives Belges du 1er Juin 1958,* Brussels, 1959.

Boussart, E., 'Sur le parti catholique social', *La Terre Wallonne,* June 1936, pp. 203–13.

Cammaerts, E., 'La campagne électorale de mai 1965', *Res Publica,* 1966, pp. 5–183.

Centre de Recherche et d'Information Socio-Politiques (CRISP), 'L'arrondissement de Bruxelles: structures de la fédération sociale-chrétienne', *Courrier Hebdomadaire* (CH) no. 14, April 1954; 'Les structures catholiques belges: le MIC', *CH* no. 21, June 1956; 'Les projets de réorganisation du Parti Social Chrétien', *CH* no. 291, July 1965; 'Le "phenomène" FDF', *CH* no. 299, October 1965; 'Les problèmes d'organisation interne soumis au congrès du PSC des 18 et 19 décembre 1965', *CH* no. 312, February 1966; 'La politique régionale', *CH* nos. 317, 324, 327 & 329, April–July 1966; 'L'affaire de Louvain', *CH* no. 333, September 1966; 'La Volksunie', *CH* nos. 336 & 345, September and December 1966; 'Structures et évolution du "monde catholique" en Belgique', *CH* nos. 352–4, February 1967; 'Les élections du 31 mars 1968', *CH* no. 402, April 1968; 'Les trois grands partis belges et l'intégration européenne', *CH* no. 433, February 1969; 'L'évolution récente des structures du CVP–PSC', *CH* no. 484, June 1970; 'Le système politique belge: situation 1970', *CH* no. 500, November 1970; 'Le FDF–RW', *CH* nos. 516 & 517, April 1971; 'Le révision de la Constitution', *CH* no. 518, April 1971; 'L'église et l'état au XXe siècle', *CH* no. 542; 'Les élections législatives du 7 novembre 1971', *CH* nos. 544 & 545, December 1971; 'L'élection des nouveaux présidents du CVP et du PSC, mars 1972', *CH* no. 565, June 1972; 'Le rôle des dirigeants nationaux de parti dans la sélection des candidats parlementaires', *CH* no. 591, February 1973; 'L'évolution récente de la Volksunie', *CH* no. 604, May 1973; 'Les élections législatives du 10 mars 1974', *CH* no. 638, March 1974; 'L'évolution du "monde catholique" depuis 1968: le devenir de la pratique religieuse', *CH* no. 664, December 1974; 'La régionalisation: la loi du 1er aout 1974 et sa mise en œuvre', *CH* no. 665, December 1974; 'Le phénomène "Relève" ', *CH* nos. 701 & 702, November 1975.

Also the following CRISP dossiers: 'Qui décide en Belgique?', no. 2, 1969; 'Les institutions politiques de la Belgique régionalisée', no. 6, 1973; and 'Les partis politiques en Belgique', no. 7, 1975.

CEPESS, see above, primary sources(v).

Chavanne, J., 'La vie politique: propagandes électorales', *Revue Nouvelle,* March 1954, pp. 291–5.

Chlepner, B., *Cent Ans d'Histoire Sociale en Belgique,* Brussels: Institut Solvay, 1956.

Ciselet, G., *et al., Aspects du Régime Parlementaire Belge,* Brussels: Institut Belge de Science Politique, 1956.

Claeys, P. H., *Groupes de Pression en Belgique*, Brussels: CRISP, 1973.
Clough, S., *A History of the Flemish Movement in Belgium*, New York: R. R. Smith, 1930.
Collard, E., 'Commentaire de la carte de la pratique dominicale en Belgique', *Lumen Vitae*, 1952, pp. 644–52.
Coombes, D., and Norton Taylor, R., 'Renewal in Belgian politics: the elections of March 1968', *Parliamentary Affairs*, winter 1968–9, pp. 62–72.
Cornez, E., *Cent ans de législation sociale en Belgique*, Brussels: Editions Labor, 1948.
Courrier Hebdomadaire (CH) see above, under Centre de Recherche et d'Information Socio-Politiques (CRISP).
Daloze, J., 'La réorientation du PSC', *Revue Générale Belge*, January 1966, pp. 106–11.
De Bruyne, E., 'Le mouvement flamand et les tendances fédéralistes', *Revue Générale*, April 1937, pp. 451–72.
Debuyst, F., *La Fonction Parlementaire en Belgique*, Brussels: CRISP, 1967.
'Les Parlementaires belges', *Revue Nouvelle*, February 1968, pp. 130–44.
De Corte, M., 'La crise des partis politiques en Belgique', *Revue Nouvelle*, October 1945, pp. 321–36.
De Croo, H. and Seigneur, P., *Parlement et Gouvernement*, Brussels: Centre Universitaire de Droit Public, 1965.
Defourny, M., *Histoire Sociale de la Belgique*, Brussels: Spes, 1929.
De Greef, E., 'Naissance le l'UDB', *Revue Nouvelle*, February 1946, pp. 81–6.
De La Vallée, Poussin, E., 'La crise politique et l'avenir du Parti Catholique', *Revue Générale*, January 1937, pp. 4–21.
'Fortune et infortune du parti catholique', *Revue Générale*, July 1937, pp. 93–104.
'Après le congrès de la Fédération des Cercles', *Revue Générale*, October 1937, pp. 471–77.
'Les catholiques et les partis', *Revue Nouvelle*, January 1946, pp. 3–15.
'Partis politiques en Belgique', *Revue Politique*, September 1954, pp. 307–16.
Deleeck, H., 'Analyse sociologue des résultats électoraux en Belgique', *Dossiers de l'Action Sociale Catholique*, January 1958, pp. 19–26.
De Meyer, J., 'Elections et partis en Belgique', *Verfassung und Verfassungswirklichkeit*, 1969, no. 4, pp. 49–81.
De Moreau, E., *Histoire de l'Eglise en Belgique*, 2 vols., Brussels: Hayez, 1940.
Delruelle, N., Evalenko, R., and Fraeys, W., *Le comportement politique des électeurs belges*, Brussels: Université Libre de Bruxelles, 1970.
Deruelles, H., 'Le rôle des partis politiques dans les décisions relatives à la politique économique', *Cahiers Economiques de Bruxelles*, 1966, no. 29, pp. 77–84.
De Schryver, A., 'The Social Christian Party', *Annals of the American Academy of Political and Social Science*, September 1946, pp. 5–11.
'Le PSC devant les élections', *Revue Générale Belge*, May 1958, pp. 1–11.
De Smet, R., 'La géographie électorale en Belgique', *Revue Française de Science Politique*, 1952, pp. 87–95.
'Méthodes d'analyse et d'interprétation appliquées aux élections législatives belges', in ed. F. Goguel, *Nouvelles Etudes de Sociologie Electorale*, 1954, pp. 133–52.
De Visscher, P., 'Les principes constitutionnels en matière d'enseignement', *Revue Politique*, April 1955, pp. 101–15.

Dewachter, W., 'General elections as a process of power achievement in the Belgian political system', *Res Publica*, 1967, no. 3, pp. 369–412.

  ed., *Carte Politique de la Belgique*, Brussels: Editions Scientifiques Erasme, 1970.

Dobbelaere, K., *Sociologische analysevan de Katholiciteit*, Antwerp: Wetenschappelijke Uitgeverij, 1966.

Dubois, B., and Van Hiller, J., 'Quelques observations sur les rapports entre les élections communales et législatives', *Res Publica*, 1960, no. 1, pp. 67–73.

Du Bus de Warnaffe, C., 'La question scolaire vue sous deux angles', *Revue Générale Belge*, April 1949, pp. 875–84; 'Le problème scolaire', *Revue Politique*, July 1955, pp. 247–54.

Duchateau, V., 'Equivoques et contradictions du Parti Catholique', *La Terre Wallonie*, June 1936, pp. 143–56.

Ducpétiaux, E., *Mémoire sur le Paupérisme dans les Flandres*, Brussels: 1864.

D'Ydewalle, C., *Pierre Harmel à l'Heure Atlantique*, Brussels: De Meyer, 1971.

D'Ydewalle, H., 'L'école officielle', *Revue Nouvelle*, November 1968, pp. 369–406.

Eloy, E., 'Géographie religieuse de la Belgique', *Revue Générale Belge*, October 1954, pp. 2055–64.

Evalenko, R., 'Géographie électorale', *Socialisme*, January 1954, pp. 36–46.

  'Les élections du 11 avril', *Socialisme*, May 1954, pp. 263–9.

  'Sociologie électorale', *Socialisme*, September 1957, pp. 469–80.

  'Les élections du 1er juin', *Socialisme*, July 1958, pp. 343–54.

  'Les élections du 1er juin et leurs enseignements', *Socialisme*, September 1958, pp. 440–53.

  'Regards sur la sociologie électorale belge', *Revue de l'Université de Bruxelles*, September 1958, pp. 413–44.

Evalenko, R., De Smet, R., and Fraeys, W., *Atlas des Elections Belges, 1919–54*, 2 vols., Brussels: Institut Solvay, 1958.

  Atlas des Elections Belges, 1919–54: Supplément Comprenant les Résultats des Elections Législatives du 1er Juin 1958, Brussels: Institut Solvay, 1959.

Eylenbosch, G., *Cinquante Années d'Action Sociale et Politique Catholique, 1884–1934*, Ghent: Dubrulle, 1936.

Fosty, J., 'La vie politique: quelques réflexions sur le Congrès Extraordinaire du PSC', *Revue Nouvelle*, October 1950, pp. 298–302.

Fraeys, W., 'Les résultats des élections du 26 mars 1961', *Res Publica*, vol. 3, 1961.

  'Les résultats des élections législatives du 23 mai 1965', *Res Publica*, vol. 8, 1966.

Ganshoff van der Meersch, W., *Pouvoir de Fait et Règle 'de Droit dans le Fonctionnement des Institutions Politiques*, Brussels: Libre Encyclopédique, 1957.

Gérard-Libois, J., 'Géographie électorale de la Belgique: les résultats du 11 avril 1954', *Revue Nouvelle*, May 1954, pp. 508–14.

  'La vie politique: comment les Belges ont voté le 1er juin 1958', *Revue Nouvelle*, July 1958, pp. 51–8.

  'Conditionnement et tendances de la politique belge', *Revue Nouvelle*, May 1966, pp. 521–9.

Gerin, P., *Les Débuts de la Démocratie Chrétienne à Liège*, Brussels: La Pensée Catholique, 1959.

  Les courants de pensée et d'action sociale chez les catholiques de Wallonie, 1830–1914, Liège: Gothier, 1967.

Gilissen, J., *Le régime représentatif en Belgique depuis 1790*, Brussels: La Renaissance du Livre, 1958.

Goffray, V., 'La démocratie chrétienne en Wallonie', *Revue Nouvelle*, February 1966, pp. 113–39.

Gol, J., *Le monde de la presse en Belgique*, Brussels: CRISP, 1970.

Grégoire, M., *Le particratie*, Liège: Editions du Grand Liège, 1965.

Grégoire, O., 'Les élections du 11 avril 1954', *Dossiers de l'Action Sociale Catholique*, 1954, pp. 272–86.

Guyot de Mishaegen, G., *Le Parti Catholique Belge de 1830 à 1884*, Brussels: Larcier, 1946.

Haag, H., *Les origines du catholicisme libéral en Belgique, 1789–1839*, Louvain: Bibliothèque de l'Université, 1950.

Hallet, J., 'Le Parti Social Chrétien au pouvoir', *Dossiers de l'Action Sociale Catholique*, July 1958, pp. 485–7.

Hill, K., 'Belgium', in S. Henig and J. Pinder, eds., *European Political Parties*, London: Allen & Unwin for PEP, 1969, pp. 68–96.

'Belgium: political change in a segmented society', in R. Rose, ed., *Electoral Behaviour: a Comparative Handbook*, London: Collier Macmillan, 1974, pp. 29–107.

Hirson, N., *Paul Vanden Boeynants*, Brussels: Capitales, 1969.

Hislaire, J., *Gaston Eyskens*, Brussels: Editions Labor, 1971.

Höjer, C. H., *Le régime parlementaire belge de 1918 à 1940*, Brussels: CRISP, 1969.

Houben, R., *Le PSC contesté*, Brussels: CEPESS, 1963.

Houben, R., and Ingham, F., *Le Pacte Scolaire*, Brussels, 1960.

Houtart, F., and Lewin, R., *L'Etat et l'Eglise en Belgique*, Brussels: Editions du Cercle d'Education Populaire, 1967.

Houtart, F., and Mury, G., *Aspects religieux des sociétés industrielles*, Brussels: Mame, 1967.

Hoyois, G., *La jeunesse catholique et l'action politique*, Louvain: Rex, 1925.

'La situation morale et religieuse en Belgique d'expression française', *Lumen Vitae*, 1948, no. 2, pp. 224–46.

Hoyois, G., and Picard, L., *L'Association Catholique de la Jeunesse Belge: ses principes et son histoire*, Louvain: Rex, 1924.

Huggett, F., *Modern Belgium*, London: Pall Mall, 1969.

Huyse, L., Hilgers, W., and Henryon, C., *La participation politique en Belgique*, Louvain: Nauwelaerts, 1966.

Institut de Sociologie de Solvay, *Les élections législatives du 4 juin 1950*, Brussels, 1953.

Jacquemyns, G., *Régime parlementaire et système électoral en Belgique*, Brussels: Institut Universitaire, 1954.

Jaset, C., *Un siècle de l'Eglise Catholique de Belgique, 1830–1930*, 2 vols., Courtrai 1934.

Joye, P., and Lewin, R., *L'Eglise et le Mouvement Ouvrier en Belgique*, Brussels: Jacquemott, 1967.

Kerkhofs, J., and Vanhoutte, J., *De Kerk in Vlaanderen*, Tielt, 1962.

Kothen, R., *La Pensée et l'Action Sociale des Catholiques, 1789–1944*, Louvain, 1945.

Lamberty, M., 'La question flamande', *Res Publica*, 1968, special no. 2, pp. 143–55.

Laureys, J., 'Le statut social du Bloc Catholique belge', *Revue Générale*, November 1937, pp. 540–51.

Leclercq, J., *Les Catholiques et la Question Wallonne*, Liège: Documents Wallons, 1963.

Levie, J., *Michel Levie et le Mouvement Chrétien-Social de son Temps*, Louvain: Nauwelaerts, 1962.

Lorwin, V., 'Belgium: religion, class and language in national politics', in R. Dahl, ed., *Political Oppositions in Western Democracies*, pp. 147–87, New Haven: Yale University Press, 1966.

Luyckx, T., *Politieke geschiedenis van Belgie van 1789 tot heden*, Brussels: Elsevier, 1969.

Mallinson, V., *Power and Politics in Belgian Education, 1855–1961*, London: Heinemann, 1963.

Melot, A., *Le Parti Catholique en Belgique*, Louvain: Rex, 1934.

Meynaud, J., Ladrière, J., and Perin, F., *La Décision Politique en Belgique*, Paris: Colin, 1965.

Moles, R., 'La pratique dominicale en Belgique', *Nouvelle Revue Théologique*, April 1971, pp. 387–425.

Nossent, R., 'De la paix de Noël à la guerre scolaire', *Revue Politique*, February 1955, pp. 67–80.

Nuyens, Y., 'De selektie van kandidaten en de politieke partijen in Belgie', *Res Publica*, 1966, no. 2, pp. 233–54.

Oleffe, A., 'La position du Mouvement Ouvrier Chrétien devant des problèmes économiques', *Cahiers Economiques de Bruxelles*, July 1959, pp. 557–62.

Oppenheim, F., 'Belgium: party cleavages and compromise', in ed. Neumann, S., *Modern Political Parties*, pp. 155–68.

Perin, F., *La démocratie enrayée: essai sur le régime parlementaire belge de 1918 à 1958*, Brussels: Institut Belge de Science Politique, 1960.

Philippart, A., 'Analyse statistique de la stabilité ministérielle en Belgique de 1830 à 1961', *Res Publica*, 1962, pp. 275–96.

'The University in Belgian politics since the *contestation* of 1968', *Government and Opposition*, autumn 1972, pp. 450–63.

Pirenne, H., *Histoire de Belgique*, 7 vols., Brussels: La Renaissance du Livre, 1951 (1st edn 1929).

Rapport d'Activité de la CSC, 1972–75, Brussels: CSC, 1976.

Res Publica, 'La question flamande', special no., no. 2, 1968.

Revue Politique, 'Le Pacte Scolaire et son application', special no., no. 5, 1960.

Rezsohazy, R., *Histoire du mouvement mutualiste chrétien en Belgique*, Brussels: Erasme, 1957.

Origines et formation du catholicisme social en Belgique, Louvain: Nauwalaerts, 1958.

Riche, R., *Catholicisme et politique*, Brussels: La Pensée Catholique, 1938.

Scholl, S., ed., *150 ans du Mouvement Ouvrier Chrétien en Europe de l'Ouest de 1789 à 1939*, 3 vols., Brussels: De Arbeiderspers, 1963–6.

Senelle, R., *The Belgian Constitution*, Brussels: Ministry of Foreign Affairs, 1974.

Servais, P., 'Le sentiment national en Flandre et en Wallonie', *Recherches Sociologiques*, December 1970, pp. 123–44.

Simon, A., *L'Eglise Catholique et les débuts de la Belgique indépendante*, Wetteren: Scaldis, 1949.

La politique religieuse de Léopold I, Brussels: Goemaere, 1953.

Le Parti Catholique Belge, 1830–1945, Brussels: Notre Passé, 1958.

'L'influence de l'Eglise sur la vie politique dans l'entre-deux-guerres', *Res Publica*, 1962, pp. 387–401.

Skinkel, R., 'Le rôle du candidat dans la campagne électorale', *Res Publica*, 1966, pp. 128–32.
Spitaels, G., *Le mouvement syndicale en Belgique*, Brussels: Université de Bruxelles, 1974.
Statistiques de base des doyennes et diocèses de la province ecclésiastique de Belge, Brussels: Centre Interdiocesain de Statistiques.
Stengers, J., 'Belgium', in H. Rogger and E. Weber, eds., *The European Right*, London, Weidenfeld & Nicolson, 1965, pp. 128–67.
'Regards sur la sociologie électorale belge', *Revue de l'Université de Bruxelles*, January 1958, pp. 122–74.
Stengers, J., and Philippart, A., *Une expérience d'enquête électorale*, Brussels: Institut Universitaire d'Information Sociale et Politique, 1959.
Swaelen, F., 'De samenstellung der Kandidatenlijsten in de Vlaamse CVP', *Res Publica*, 1969, pp. 77–94.
Troclet, L., *Les partis politiques en Belgique*, Brussels: L'Eglantine, 1931.
Urbain, R., *La fonction et les services du premier ministre en Belgique*, Brussels: Libre Encyclopédique, 1958.
Urwin, D. W., 'Social cleavages and political parties in Belgium', *Political Studies*, 1970, pp. 320–40.
Van den Daele, G., 'De verkiezingen van 11 april 1954', *De Gids op maatschappelijk gebied*, 1954, pp. 637–67.
'De verkiezingen van 1 juni 1958', *De Gids op maatschappelijk gebied*, 1958, pp. 791–816.
Van den Wijngaert, *Ontstaan en stichting van de CVP/PSC: de lange Weg naar het Kerstprogramma*, Brussels: IPOVO, 1976.
Van Impe, H., *Le rôle de la majorité parlementaire dans la vie politique*, Brussels: Bruylant, 1966.
Le régime parlementaire en Belgique, Brussels: Bruylant, 1968.
Van Isacker, K., 'La querelle des catholiques libéraux et des ultramontains', *Revue Nouvelle*, 1966, pp. 250–7.
Van Kalken, F., *Entre deux guerres: esquisse de la vie politique en Belgique de 1918 à 1940*, Brussels: Office de Publicité, 1945.
Histoire du Royaume des Pays-Bas et de la révolution belge de 1830, Brussels: Office de Publicité, 1947.
La Belgique contemporaine: histoire de l'évolution politique de 1780 à 1949, Brussels: Office de Publicité, 1950.
Varzim, A., *Le Boerenbond belge*, Paris: Desclée de Brouwer, 1934.
Vaussard, M., *Histoire de la Démocratie Chrétienne: France, Belgique, Italie*, Paris: Seuil, 1956.
Verkade, W., *Democratic Parties in the Low Countries and Germany*, Leiden: Universitaire Pers, 1965.
Vermeylen, P., 'Les élections du 1er juin et leurs enseignements', *Socialisme*, September 1958, pp. 454–72.
Vidick, G., 'Les partis politiques belges: démocratie ou oligarchie?', *Res Publica*, 1967, pp. 353–68.
Voye, L., *Sociologie du geste religieux*, Brussels: Vie Ouvrière, 1973.
Weil, G., *The Benelux Nations: the Politics of Small-Country Democracies*, New York: Holt, Rinehart & Winston, 1970.
Wigny, P., *Comprendre la Belgique après la révision constitutionnelle*, Verviers: Gérard, 1974.

The Netherlands

Primary sources   The chief primary sources are to be found at the party headquarters of the Anti-Revolutionary Party, the Christian Historical Union
and the Catholic People's Party in The Hague. The Christian Democratic
Appeal shares offices with the Anti-Revolutionary Party in Kuyperstraat.
Note the following in particular:

   (i) National Congress Reports of all three parties, and since 1976 of the
       CDA;
  (ii) National Statutes of all three parties and of the CDA;
 (iii) Electoral programmes of all three parties to 1974, and from 1976 joint
       programme of CDA (*Niet bij brood alleen*);
  (iv) Various publications of the Catholic *Centrum voor Staatkundige
       Vorming* and of the Abraham Kuyper Stichting, the research centre of
       the Anti-Revolutionary Party.
   (v) Various documents published by CEPESS, the research centre of the
       Belgian Social Christians, are also of relevance to the Dutch Christian
       Democratic ('confessional') parties.

In addition, for trade unions see congress reports of the *Christelijk Nationaal
Vakverbond in Nederland* and Central Bureau voor de Statistiek annual
reports on 'Omvang der Vakbeweging', and for Catholic Action reports and
documents published by *Hollandische Katholische Aktion*. For documents
on the Roman Catholic State Party, see J. Beaufays, *Les Partis Catholiques
en Belgique et aux Pays-Bas*, 1918–58, p. 716.

Secondary sources   The most useful newspapers and journals are:
   Anti-Revolutionaire Staatkunde; *Bijdragen voor de Geschiedenis der Neder-
   landen*; *Katholiek Staatkundig Maandschrift*; *Socialisme en Democratie*;
   Tijdschrift voor Geschiedenis; *Streven*; *Sociologische Gids*; *Tijden Taak*.

Books and articles

Alberling, L., 'Analyse van de verkiezingen van 1946', *Katholiek Staatkundig
   Maandschrift*, March 1947, p. 30 & ff.
'La situation du parti populaire catholique aux Pays-Bas', *Revue Politique*,
   October 1951, pp. 83–97.
'La situation politique aux Pays-Bas', *Revue Politique*, February 1952, pp.
   49–58.
'Het verkiezingsprogram 1952 der KVP', *Katholiek Staatkundig Maandschrift*,
   May 1952, pp. 91–9.
'Na de verkiezingen van 1952', *Katholiek Staatkundig Maandschrift*, July 1952,
   pp. 133–41.
'La situation politique aux Pays-Bas', *Revue Politique*, October 1952, pp. 558–
   70.
'Partij-organisatorische vraagstukken', *Katholiek Staatkundig Maandschrift*,
   February 1953, pp. 347–52.

'La situation politique aux Pays-Bas', *Revue Politique*, December 1953, pp. 633–43.

'Le Mandement 1954 des évêques néerlandais et la situation des catholiques aux Pays-Bas', *Revue Politique*, November 1954, pp. 424–38.

'De verkiezingen van 1956', *Katholiek Staatkundig Maandschrift*, July 1956, pp. 173–85.

'Reacties op het Rapport: "Grondslag en Karakter van de KVP"', *Politiek*, February 1966, pp. 34–54.

'Nederland: De verkiezingen van de Provinciale Staten', *Politiek*, April 1966, pp. 33–43.

'Politieke eenheid der Katholieke Nederlands', *Documentatie ten behoeve van kadervorming*, pp. 74–9.

Andriessen, W. J., 'Maatschappij Politiek en Politieke Partijen', *Katholiek Staatkundig Maandschrift*, February 1952, pp. 409–18.

Anon., *Algemeene bond van Roomsch Katholieke Rijkskieskringorganisaties in Nederland*, 1919.

'Les catholiques hollandais pourront desormais adhérer aux syndicats socialistes', *Le Soir*, 10 September 1965, p. 3.

De Katholieke Volkspartij, Amsterdam, 1951.

'Katholieke werk gemeenschap: grondslagen van ons socialisme', *Socialisme en democratie*, October 1963, pp. 664–82.

Hergroepering der Partijen? (interviews with leading Dutch politicians), The Hague, 1974.

Baas, L., *Een R.K. visie op de verhouding kerk-wereld*, Driebergen: Kerk en Wereld, 1964.

Baehr, R. P., 'The Netherlands', in S. Henig and J. Pinder, eds., *European Political Parties*, London: Allen & Unwin for PEP, 1969, pp. 256–81.

Barents, J., 'La vie politique hollandaise depuis la Libération', *Revue Française de Science Politique*, July 1951, pp. 371–82.

Barents, J., and De Jong, J. J., *Partis Politiques et Classes Sociales aux Pays-Bas*, Paris: IPSA Report, 1955.

Beaufays, J., 'Le député catholique aux Pays-Bas: 1918–65', *Res Publica*, no. 2, 1971, pp. 275–84.

Beernink, H. K. J., *Geschiedenis, Organisatie en Beginsel van de CHU*, 's-Gravenhage: Bureau CHU, 1960.

Boas, H. J., *Religious Resistance in Holland*, London: Netherlands Government Information Bureau, 1945.

Bone, R. C., 'The dynamics of Dutch politics', *Journal of Politics*, 1962, pp. 23–49.

Bornewasser, E., 'Candidaatstelling en Fractie', *Katholiek Staatkundig Maandschrift*, October 1951, pp. 294–300.

Bornewasser, J., 'Schaepman en het isolement der Nederlandse Katholieken', *Katholiek Staatkundig Maandschrift*, September 1963, pp. 209–20.

Braure, M., *Histoire des Pays-Bas*, Paris: Presses Universitaires de France, 1951.

Bruins Slot, J. A. H. J. S., *Binnen en Buiten de Grenzen: Anti-Revolutionaire Partij-Stichting*, The Hague: ARP, 1960.

Kleine Partij in Grote Wered, Kampen: Kok, 1963.

Brummelkamp, A., *De ARP*, Baarn: Hollandia-drukkerij, 1918.

Cloudt, H. G., 'Les partis démocrates chrétiens hollandais face à la gauche qui se cherche', *Panorama Démocrate Chrétien*, November 1968, pp. 9–12.

Couwenberg, S. W., *Pleidooi voor een Christelijke Doorbraakgedachte*, The Hague: Pax, 1959.

Het Nederlandse Partijstelsel in Toekomstperspectief, The Hague: Pax, 1960.

Daalder, H., 'Nederland: het politieke Stelsel', in L. van der Land, ed., *Repertorium van de Sociale Wetenschappen: Politiek,* Amsterdam: Elsevier, 1958.

'The Netherlands', in K. Lindsay, ed., *European Assemblies,* London: Stevens, 1960.

Politiserung en Lijdelijkheid in de Nederlandse Politiek, The Hague, 1974.

'Parties and politics in the Netherlands', *Political Studies,* February 1955, pp. 1–16.

'The Netherlands: opposition in a segmented society', in R. Dahl, ed., *Political Oppositions in Western Democracies,* New Haven: Yale University Press, 1966, pp. 188–236.

'Extreme proportional representation – the Dutch experience', in S. Finer, ed., *Adversary Politics and Electoral Reform,* London: Wigram, 1975, pp. 223–48.

Daalder, H., and Rusk, J. G., 'Perceptions of party in the Dutch Parliament', in S. Patterson and J. Wahlke, eds., *Comparative Legislative Behaviour: Frontiers of Research,* New York: Wiley, 1972.

Daalder, H., Geertseema, W., and Millenaar, K., *Parlement en Politieke Besluitvorming in Nederland,* The Hague, 1975.

Daudt, H., 'Party systems and voters' influence in the Netherlands', in O. Stammer, ed., *Party Systems, Party Organisations and the Politics of the New Masses,* Berlin: Free University Press, 1968.

De Jong, J., *Politieke Organisatie in West Europa na 1800,* The Hague: Nijhoff, 1951.

Delfgaauw, G., *De Staatsleer van Hoedmaker: een Bijdrage tot de Kennis van de Christelijk – Historische Staatsopratting,* Kampen: Kok, 1963.

De Rooy, N., 'De Nederlandse politiek en de Katholieken in de afgelopen eeuw', *Katholiek Staatkundig Maandschrift,* May 1953, pp. 72–81.

Diepenhorst, I., *Christelijke Politiek,* Kampen: Kok, 1958.

Duynstee, F., *Het Heilige Huis: KVP Beleid in Discussie,* Rotterdam: De Maasbode, 1951.

De Kabinetsformaties, 1946–65, Deventer: Kluwer, 1966.

Eekeren, W. A. M. van, 'The Catholic People's Party in the Netherlands', Georgetown University, Ph.D. thesis, 1956.

Gaay Fortman, B., *Christen-Radicaal,* Kampen: Kok, 1967.

Geismann, G., *Politische Struktur und Regierungssystem in den Niederlanden,* Bonn: Athenäum, 1964.

Goudsblom, J., *Dutch Society,* New York: Random House, 1967.

Goudzwaard, B., *A Christian Political Option,* Toronto: Wedge, 1972.

Gribling, J. P., 'Uit de geschiedenis van de RKSP', *Politiek Perspectief,* November 1956, pp. 1–64.

Hillenaar, H., and Peters, H., *Les Catholiques hollandais,* Paris: Desclée, 1969.

Hoekstra, D. J., ed., *Partijvernieuwing in Politiek Nederland,* Alphen aan den Rijn: Samsom, 1968.

Homan, G. D., 'Catholic emancipation in the Netherlands', *Catholic Historical Review,* 1967, no. 2, pp. 201–11.

Hoogerwerf, A., *Verkenningen in de Politiek,* 2 vols., Alphen aan den Rijn: Samsom, 1971 and 1976.

'Attitudes politiques des électeurs néerlandais', *Annales de la Faculté de Droit de Liège,* 1968, no. 3, pp. 419–50.

Protestantisme en Progressiviteit, Meppel: J. A. Boom, 1969.

Kasteel, P., *Abraham Kuyper*, Kampen: Kok, 1938.

'Colijn en de Nederlandse politiek', *Streven*, February 1970, pp. 509–13.

Klompe, M., 'De KVP en de Buitenlandse Politiek', *Katholiek Staatkundig Maandschrift*, January 1952, pp. 379–85.

Kothen, R., *La vie catholique en Hollande*, Louvain: Warny, 1951.

Kruyt, J. P., 'Rooms Katholieken en Protestanten in Nederland', *Sociologisch Bulletin*, 1947, no. 1, pp. 3–29.

Kuipers, G., *Het Politieke Spel in Nederland*, Meppel: J. A. Boom, 1967.

Kusters, W. J. J., 'Stembusgedrag en maatschappijstructuur', *Sociologische Gids*, September 1963, p. 233 and ff.

Leih, H. G., *Kaart van Politieke Nederland*, Kampen: Kok, 1962.

Lijphart, A., *The Politics of Accommodation: Pluralism and Democracy in the Netherlands*, 2nd edn., Berkeley: University of California Press, 1975.

'Class voting and religious voting in the European democracies', Occasional Paper no. 8, Survey Research Centre, University of Strathclyde, 1971.

Lipschits, I., 'De organisatorische structuur der Nederlandse politieke partijen', *Acta Politica*, 1966–7, no. 2.

'De politieke partij en de selectie van candidaten', *Sociologische Gids*, September 1963, pp. 273–81.

Mast, A., *Les Pays du Bénélux*, Paris: Pichon & Durand-Auzias, 1960.

Mekkes, J. P. A., and Donner, A. M., *Antirevolutionaire Beleid: Gedachtenwisseling*, Franeker: Wever, 1954.

Mourits, H., *Une foi qui cherche: éclaircissements sur le catéchisme hollandais,* Paris: Fayard, 1969.

Oormes, J., 'Nederland: partij-politieke onduidelijkheid', *Streven*, April 1968, pp. 707–11.

Oud, P., *Honderd Jaren, 1840–1940*, Assen: Van Corcum & Gomp, 1954.

Prinsterer, G. Groen van, *Le Parti Anti-Révolutionnaire et Confessionel dans l'Eglise Réformée des Pays-Bas*, Amsterdam, 1860.

Puchinger, G., *Colijn*, Kampen: Kok, 1962.

Quaevlieg, A., 'Katholieke politieke organisatie een zaak van beginsel en van opportuniteit', *Katholiek Staatkundig Maandschrift*, March 1958, pp. 30–6; May 1958, pp. 89–98; and October 1958, pp. 261–74.

Rhijn, A. A. van, *De Protestants-Christen in der Partij van de Arbeid*, Amsterdam: De Arbeiderspers, 1956.

Robinson, A., *Dutch Organised Agriculture in International Politics, 1945–60*, The Hague: Nijhoff, 1961.

Rogier, L. J., *Katholieke Herleving: Geschiedenis van Katholiek Nederland sinds 1853*, The Hague: Pax, 1956.

Rogier, L. J., and De Rooy, N., *In Vrijheid Herboren: Katholiek Nederland, 1853–1953*, The Hague: Pax, 1953.

Romme, C., 'De politieke positie der Katholieken', *Katholiek Staatkundig Maandschrift*, April 1958, pp. 59–71.

Ruppert, M., *De Nederlandse Vakbeweging*, Haarlem: Volksuniversiteit, 1953.

Ruyers, G., 'Christendom en Socialisme: de verhouding van PVDA en KVP', *Socialisme en Democratie*, February 1956, pp. 10–14.

Savornin Lohman, A. F. de, *Bijdragen tot de Geschiedenis der Christelijk-Historische Unie*, The Hague, 1923.

Schillebeeckx, E., 'L'église catholique aux Pays-Bax', *Septentrion*, June 1972, pp. 25–39.

Schotten, L. W. G., Bornewasser, J., Schöffer, I., Manning, A., and Bosmans, J., *De Confessionelen: Ontstaan en Ontwikkeling van hun Politieke Partijen,* Utrecht: Ambo, 1969.

Stouthard, P. C., ed., *Dutch Election Studies, 1970–73*, 2 vols., Ann Arbor. ICPSR, 1976.

Swaan, B. de, 'Parties, policies and pivots: coalition politics in the Netherlands', *Delta*, autumn 1973, pp. 65–80.

Van Den Berg, J., *De Anatomie van Nederland*, Amsterdam: De Bezige Bij, 1967.

Van De Poel, J., 'La situation politique aux Pays-Bas', *La Revue Politique*, April 1955, pp. 143–53.

Van Praag, P., 'Quelques aspects et problèmes du mouvement syndical aux Pays-Bax', *Travail*, May 1960, pp. 646–63.

Van Raalte, E., *The Parliament of the Kingdom of the Netherlands*, London: Hansard Society, 1959.

Van Wely, J., *Schaepman*, Bussum: Paul Brand, 1954.

Verbrugh, A. J., *Politieke Richtlijnen en de Politieke Partijen in Nederland:* vol. II, *De Christelijke Partijen: KVP en SGP*; vol. III, *De Christelijke Partijen: ARP, CHU, GPV*, Rotterdam: Groenendijk, 1959–63.

Verhoef, J., 'Kiesstelsels: politieke Samenweking in Nederland, 1888–1917', *Acta Politica*, 1971, pp. 261–8.

Verkade, W., *Democratic Parties in the Low Countries and Germany*, Leiden: Universitaire Pers, 1965.

Verschave, P., *La Hollande Politique: un parti catholique en pays protestant*, Paris: Rousseau, 1910.

Versluis, W. G., *Beknopte Geschiedenis van de Katholieke Arbeidersbeweging in Nederland*, Utrecht: Dekker & Van de Vegt, 1949.

Verstraelen, J., *De Grauwe Revolutie: Inleidung tot de Geschiedenis van de Arbeidersbeweging*, Brussels: DAP Uitgaven, 1965.

Vis, J. J., 'Politics in Holland today', paper presented at University Association for Contemporary European Studies conference on Benelux at Hull, September 1977.

Waltmans, H., *De Nederlandse Politieke Partijen en de Nationale Gedachte*, Sittard: Alberts, 1962.

Weil, G., *The Benelux Nations: the Politics of Small-Country Democracies*, New York: Holt, Rinehart & Winston, 1970.

France

See also 'Origins of Christian Democracy', French section above.

A comprehensive bibliography is contained in R. E. M. Irving, *Christian Democracy in France*, London: Allen & Unwin, 1973. For a detailed list of MRP publications, see Jean Charlot, *Répertoire des publications des partis politiques français, 1944–67*, Paris: Colin, 1970. Source materials on the various French Christian Democratic parties can be found at the Fondation Nationale des Sciences Politiques, Paris, and there are archives on the MRP and its successors at 207, Boulevard St Germain, Paris. The following is a brief list of the main literature on French Christian Democracy, together with other books and articles referred to in Chapter 7.

Adam, G., *La C.F.T.C., 1940–58*, Paris: Colin, 1964.

Bell, B., 'The *Parti Socialiste* in France', JCMS, June 1975, pp. 419–31.

Bidault, G., *Resistance: the Political Autobiography of Georges Bidault*, London: Weidenfeld & Nicolson, 1967.

Biton, L., *La démocratie chrétienne dans la politique française*, Paris: Giraudeau & Cie, 1953.

Borne, E., *et al.*, *Le MRP: Cet Inconnu*, Paris: Editions Polyglottes, 1961.

Bosworth, W., *Catholicism and Crisis in Modern France*, Princeton: Princeton University Press, 1962.

Bur, J., *Laïcité et problème scolaire*, Paris: Bonne Press, 1959.

Buron, R., *Le plus beau des métiers*, Paris: Plon, 1963.

Campbell, I., 'The end of the Mitterrand experiment?' University of Warwick, Politics Paper no. 5, August 1975.

Cet Inconnu, see Borne.

Chelini, J., *La ville et l'église: premier bilan des enquêtes de sociologie religieuse urbaine*, Paris: Cerf., 1958.

Coutrot, A., and Dreyfus, F., *Les forces religieuses dans la société française*, Paris: Colin, 1965.

Dansette, A., *Histoire religieuse de la France contemporaine*, 2 vols., Paris: Flammarion, 1952.

Destin du catholicisme français, 1926–56, Paris: Flammarion, 1957.

De Gaulle, C., *Mémoires*, 5 vols., Paris: Plon, 1954–71.

Delmasure, A., *Les catholiques et la politique*, Paris: La Colombe, 1960.

Duquesne, J., *Les catholiques français sous l'occupation*, Paris: Grasset, 1966.

Einaudi, M., and Goguel, F., *Christian Democracy in Italy and France*, Notre Dame: Notre Dame University Press, 1952.

Fauvet, J., *De Thorez à de Gaulle: les forces politiques en France*, Paris: Le Monde, 1951.

Frears, J. R., *Political Parties and Elections in the French Fifth Republic*, London: Hurst, 1977.

Gay, F., *Les démocrates d'inspiration chrétienne à l'épreuve du pouvoir*, Paris: Bloud and Gay, 1950.

Georges, B., *Problèmes du catholicisme français*, Paris: Fayard, 1953.

La presse catholique, Paris: Fayard, 1957.

Goguel, F., *Géographie des élections françaises*, Paris: Colin, 1970.

Goldey, D. B., 'The events of May and the French general election of June 1968', *Parliamentary Affairs*, autumn 1968, pp. 307–37, and spring 1969, pp. 116–33.

'The French Presidential election of 1969', *Parliamentary Affairs*, autumn 1969, pp. 320–48.

Goldey, D. B., and Bell, D., 'The French municipal election of March 1977', *Parliamentary Affairs*, autumn 1977, pp. 408–26.

Hayward, J. E. S., *Private Interests and Public Policy: the Experience of the French Economic and Social Council*, London: Longmans, 1966.

'Presidential suicide by plebiscite: de Gaulle's exit', *Parliamentary Affairs*, autumn 1969, pp. 289–317.

Hayward, J. E. S., and Wright, V., 'The 37,708 microcosms of an indivisible Republic: the French local elections of March 1971', *Parliamentary Affairs*, autumn 1971, pp. 284–311.

'Presidential supremacy and the French general elections of March 1973', *Parliamentary Affairs*, summer 1973, pp. 274–306, and autumn 1973, pp. 372–402.

'*Les deux France* and the French Presidential election of May 1974', *Parliamentary Affairs*, summer 1974, pp. 208–36.

'Governing from the Centre: the 1977 French local elections', *Government and Opposition*, autumn 1977, pp. 433–54.

Irving, R. E. M., *The First Indochina War: French and American Policy in Vietnam, 1945–54*, London: Croom Helm, 1975.

Irving, R. E. M., *Christian Democracy in France*, London: Allen & Unwin, 1973.

'The MRP and French policy in Indochina, 1945–54', Oxford: D.Phil. thesis, 1968.

'The centre parties in the Fifth French Republic', *Parliamentary Affairs*, summer 1976, pp. 264–80.

Kedward, H. R., *Resistance in Vichy France: a Study of Ideas and Motivation in the Southern Zone, 1940–42*, London: Oxford University Press, 1978.

Latreille, A., and Siegfried, A., *Les forces religieuses et la vie politique*, Paris: Colin, 1951.

Lemieux, V., 'Le MRP dans le système politique français', Paris: dissertation, 1960.

Maritain, J., *Christianisme et démocratie*, Paris: Hartmann, 1953.

Mayeur, F., *L'Aube étude d'un journal d'opinion, 1932–40*, Paris: Colin, 1966.

Michel, H., *Histoire de la Résistance en France, 1940–44*, Paris: Presses Universitaires de France, 1963.

Michel, H., and Mirkine-Guetzevitch, B., *Les idées politiques et sociales de la Résistance*, Paris: Presses Universitaires de France, 1954.

Montagne, H. de la., *Histoire de la démocratie chrétienne de Lamennais à Georges Bidault*, Paris: Amiot-Dumont, 1948.

Noguères, H., *Histoire de la Résistance en France, 1940–45*, 4 vols., Paris: Laffont, 1967–76.

Pezet, E., *Chrétiens au service de la cité: de Léon XIII au Sillon et au MRP*, Paris: Nouvelles Editions Latines, 1965.

Rémond, R., *Forces religieuses et attitudes politiques dans la France contemporaine*, Paris: Colin. 1965.

Rochefort, R., *Robert Schuman*, Paris: Cerf., 1968.

Williams, P. M., *Crisis and Compromise: Politics in the Fourth Republic*, 3rd edn., London: Longmans, 1964.

'The French presidential election of 1965', *Parliamentary Affairs*, winter 1965–6, pp. 14–30.

Williams, P. M., and Goldey, D. B., 'The French general election of March 1967', *Parliamentary Affairs*, summer 1967, pp. 206–21.

Wright, V., and Machin, H., 'The French Socialist Party in 1973', *Government and Opposition*, spring 1974, pp. 123–45.

Index

Wherever possible initials only have been used in the Index. For their full meaning, see List of Abbreviations, pp. XIII–XV.